2012

Revenue Recognition

Guide

Scott Taub

.CCH

a Wolters Kluwer business

This publication is designed to provide accurate and authoritative information in regard to the subject matter covered. It is sold with the understanding that the publisher is not engaged in rendering legal, accounting, or other professional services. If legal advice or other professional assistance is required, the services of a competent professional person should be sought.

—From a *Declaration of Principles* jointly adopted by a Committee of the American Bar Association and a Committee of Publishers and Associations

ISBN: 978-0-8080-2650-1

Portions of this work were published in previous editions.

Printed in the United States of America

SUSTAINABLE FORESTRY INITIATIVE
Certified Sourcing
www.sfiprogram.org
SFI-01028

Revenue Recognition Guide

by Scott Taub

Highlights

Revenue Recognition Guide is a comprehensive reference manual covering key concepts and issues that arise in determining when and how to recognize revenue. It covers the litany of existing authoritative literature related to revenue recognition and clarifies those revenue recognition concepts that are vague. *Revenue Recognition Guide* also provides examples of key points, includes excerpts from the financial statements of public companies to illustrate key concepts and judgments, and looks ahead to the future of revenue recognition by examining the guidance that has been proposed to replace today's standards.

2012 Edition

This edition covers new revenue-related accounting standards, issued in response to specific revenue recognition problems or other prevalent accounting issues. It also includes cross-references to the FASB's new Accounting Standards Codification, which replaced the original pronouncements as the authoritative source of U.S. Generally Accepted Accounting Principles on July 1, 2009.

In addition, this edition includes a discussion of the October 2011 Exposure Draft that would replace and significantly change revenue recognition accounting standards.

Accounting Research Manager

Accounting Research Manager is the most comprehensive, up-to-date, and objective online database of financial reporting literature. It includes all authoritative and proposed accounting, auditing, and SEC literature, plus independent, expert-written interpretive guidance.

Our Weekly Summary e-mail newsletter highlights the key developments of the week, giving you the assurance that you have the most current information. It provides links to new FASB, AICPA, SEC, PCAOB, EITF, and IASB authoritative and proposal-stage literature, plus insightful guidance from financial reporting experts.

Our outstanding team of content experts takes pride in updating the system on a daily basis, so you stay as current as possible. You'll learn of newly released literature and deliberations of current financial reporting projects as soon as they occur! Plus, you benefit from their easy-to-understand technical translations.

With **Accounting Research Manager**, you maximize the efficiency of your research time, while enhancing your results. Learn more about our content, our experts and how you can request a FREE trial by visiting us at **http://www.accountingresearchmanager.com**.

CCH Learning Center

CCH's goal is to provide you with the clearest, most concise, and up-to-date accounting and auditing information to help further your professional development, as well as a convenient method to help you satisfy your continuing professional education requirements. The CCH Learning Center* offers a complete line of self-study courses covering complex and constantly evolving accounting and auditing issues. We are continually adding new courses to the library to help you stay current on all the latest developments. The CCH Learning Center courses are available 24 hours a day, seven days a week. You'll get immediate exam results and certification. To view our complete accounting and auditing course catalog, go to: **http://cch.learningcenter.com.**

11/11

---

* CCH is registered with the National Association of State Boards of Accountancy (NASBA) as a sponsor of continuing professional education on the National Registry of CPE Sponsors. State boards of accountancy have final authority on the acceptance of individual courses for CPE credit. Complaints regarding registered sponsors may be addressed to the National Registry of CPE Sponsors, 150 Fourth Avenue North, Nashville, TN 37219-2417. Telephone: 615-880-4200.

*CCH is registered with the National Association of State Boards of Accountancy as a Quality Assurance Service (QAS) sponsor of continuing professional education. Participating state boards of accountancy have final authority on the acceptance of individual courses for CPE credit. Complaints regarding QAS program sponsors may be addressed to NASBA, 150 Fourth Avenue North, Suite 700, Nashville, TN 37219-2417. Telephone: 615-880-4200.

Preface

Revenue recognition . . . The mere mention of the topic elicits thoughts of complex accounting and difficult judgments fraught with the potential for unfavorable high-profile financial statement restatements. Revenue is the top line in the income statement, and one of the most important indices of financial health to both preparers and users of financial statements. Reporting the correct amount of revenue on a timely basis is also one of the most difficult tasks in financial reporting.

Despite the importance of revenue recognition to the financial statements of virtually all companies, the accounting literature addressing revenue recognition is not as well-developed as the literature addressing many other areas of financial reporting. Although many accounting pronouncements directly or indirectly address revenue recognition, most of the guidance is extremely narrow in scope and addresses a particular issue or narrowly defined transaction. This lack of authoritative literature addressing certain issues and industries has resulted in the development of revenue recognition for some transactions on the basis of industry practice.

The lack of comprehensive guidance combined with the variety and complexity of revenue transactions has resulted in a large number of issues in revenue recognition, including many financial statement restatements and SEC enforcement cases. In fact, two reports issued by the SEC staff in 2003 illustrate that revenue recognition is an area prone to problems: (1) Report pursuant to Section 704 of the Sarbanes-Oxley Act of 2002 (Section 704 Report) and (2) Summary by the Division of Corporate Finance of Significant Issues Addressed in the Review of the Periodic Reports of the Fortune 500 Companies (Fortune 500 Report). The Section 704 Report showed that improper revenue recognition was the area where the SEC brought the greatest number of enforcement actions during the report period and the Fortune 500 Report found that accounting policy disclosures related to revenue recognition was an area frequently questioned by the SEC's Division of Corporate Finance. These reports confirmed the findings from several other studies conducted in recent years.

In response to the growing number of problems in the area of revenue recognition, the SEC staff issued Staff Accounting Bulletin No. 101 (SAB 101), *Revenue Recognition in Financial Statements*, in late 1999. SAB 101 summarized the existing revenue recognition guidance and the SEC staff's views on the application of that guidance. In addition to causing a number of companies to change their revenue recognition policies, SAB 101 also helped to focus the attention of nearly every public company, as well as analysts and other financial statement users, on revenue recognition.

While that attention has resulted in improvements in revenue recognition policies and disclosures, it has also served to prove that better accounting standards for revenue recognition are needed. The FASB and IASB have been involved for several years in an effort to create a comprehensive revenue recognition standard. While that project appears to be headed for completion in the not-too-distant future, we still have at least several years of working with the current literature.

This book addresses the key issues faced in revenue recognition, identifies the appropriate accounting literature, explains both the required accounting and the reasons for that guidance, and often illustrates the application through recourse to disclosures and excerpts from the financial statements of publicly traded companies. For issues not addressed in the accounting literature, this book suggests accounting treatments that are consistent with general revenue recognition concepts and principles. This book also highlights the problem areas noted in the Section 704 and the Fortune 500 Reports.

This edition of the *Revenue Recognition Guide* incorporates changes in accounting literature and interpretive developments through June 2011. Most significantly, it is updated to reflect the application of new guidance on the milestone method of revenue recognition and multiple-deliverable arrangements, as well as the application of the special requirements for recognition of revenue in software arrangements. It also includes a discussion of the proposed new comprehensive standard on revenue recognition, which the FASB hopes to issue in final form sometime in 2012.

Within the 13 chapters of the book, a number of Observations, Practice Pointers, and Practice Alerts highlight key consequences of the accounting guidance and identify issues to watch for when dealing with certain revenue transactions. SEC Registrant Alerts highlight issues that the SEC is particularly focused on, as well as additional guidance provided by the SEC beyond the guidance typically followed by non-public companies.

The book also includes a topical index as well as a cross-reference to the authoritative literature that indicates the chapters where specific pieces of authoritative literature are discussed. In addition, the text includes references to the paragraphs of the authoritative literature that address key points.

Abbreviations

The following abbreviations are used throughout the text to represent the various sources of authoritative literature discussed in this book:

AAG	AICPA Audit and Accounting Guide
AcSEC	AICPA Accounting Standards Executive Committee
AICPA	American Institute of Certified Public Accountants
APB	Accounting Principles Board Opinion
ARB	Accounting Research Bulletin
ASC	FASB Accounting Standards Codification
ASU	Accounting Standards Update
CIRP	SEC Current Issues and Rulemaking Projects
CON	FASB Statement of Financial Accounting Concepts
EITF	Emerging Issues Task Force
FAS	FASB Statement of Financial Accounting Standards

FASB	Financial Accounting Standards Board
FSP	FASB Staff Position
FTB	FASB Technical Bulletin
IAS	IASB International Accounting Standard
IASB	International Accounting Standards Board
IFRIC	International Financial Reporting Interpretations Committee
REG S-X	SEC Regulation S-X
SAB	SEC Staff Accounting Bulletin
SEC	Securities and Exchange Commission
SOP	AICPA Statement of Position
TPA	AICPA Technical Practice Aid

Acknowledgments

The author thanks all of the former members of the Professional Standards Group at Arthur Andersen for their guidance, counsel, and friendship. A better group of people will never be found. Most important, Scott thanks his wife, Lynn, for her endless patience during the writing of this book and her support of Scott in every one of his career decisions.

About the Authors

AUTHOR

Scott A. Taub is a Managing Director of Financial Reporting Advisors, LLC (FRA), which provides consulting services related to accounting and SEC reporting and litigation support services. FRA specializes in applying generally accepted accounting principles to complex business transactions and also provides litigation support and expert services. Mr. Taub is also a member of the IASB's IFRS Interpretations Committee, and previously served as a member of the FASB's Valuation Resource Group.

Prior to writing the first edition of this book in 2002, Mr. Taub was a partner in Arthur Andersen's Professional Standards Group (PSG), where he consulted on complex financial reporting matters, helped to establish and disseminate Andersen's policies regarding financial reporting matters, and represented the firm before various standards setters, including the FASB, SEC, AICPA, and IASB. Mr. Taub also authored interpretive guidance for Andersen on a wide variety of accounting and reporting issues.

From September 2002 through January 2007, Mr. Taub was a Deputy Chief Accountant at the Securities and Exchange Commission (SEC) and twice served as Acting Chief Accountant for a total of 14 months. He played a key role in the SEC's implementation of the accounting reforms under the landmark Sarbanes-Oxley Act and was responsible for the day-to-day operations of the Office of the Chief Accountant. Mr. Taub represented the SEC in many venues, including the FASB and IASB's advisory committees, and served as the SEC Observer to the FASB's Emerging Issues Task Force (EITF) and as Chair of the Accounting and Disclosure committee of the International Organization of Securities Commissions (IOSCO).

Mr. Taub is a frequent speaker, having addressed numerous audiences sponsored by a variety of organizations. He is a co-author of CCH's *Financial Instruments*, and writes a periodic column for *Compliance Week* on financial reporting developments. He is a licensed CPA in Michigan and Illinois.

CONTRIBUTING AUTHOR

Ashwinpaul (Tony) C. Sondhi is the Founder and president of A. C. Sondhi & Associates, LLC, a Financial Advisory Services firm located in New Jersey. He is currently a member of the Emerging Issues Task Force (EITF) of the Financial Accounting Standards Board (FASB), the EITF Agenda Committee and its 2008 Working Group on EITF 08-01. He is also a member of the Expert Advisory Panel on Fair Value of the International Accounting Standards Board (IASB). From 2001–2003, he was a member of the Accounting Standards Executive Committee (AcSEC) of the American Institute of Certified Public Accountants (AICPA) and the Planning Subcommittee of the AcSEC. He has also been a member of the Global Financial Reporting Advocacy Committee and Chairman of the Financial Accounting Policy Committee of the CFA Institute.

Mr. Sondhi served on the FASB Task Force on Accounting for Impairments of Long-lived Assets and on the Steering Committee for the Statement of Cash Flows of the International Accounting Standards Committee. Mr. Sondhi was also an advisor to the FASB on its project comparing U.S. and International Financial Reporting Standards.

Mr. Sondhi received his Ph.D. in Accounting and Economics/Management Science from New York University. He has taught at New York University, Columbia University, and Georgetown University. He has been a Visiting Professor at Stockholm University, Sweden, and Copenhagen Business School, Denmark. His research has been published in several accounting and finance journals.

In addition to co-authoring the 2006–2011 editions of CCH's *Revenue Recognition Guide*, Mr. Sondhi co-authored *The Analysis and Use of Financial Statements*, Third Edition, which is a recommended text for the Chartered Financial Analysts (CFA) program. Mr. Sondhi has also edited *Credit Analysis of Nontraditional Debt Securities*, co-authored *Impairments and Write-offs of Long-Lived Assets*, and co-edited *CFA Readings in Financial Statement Analysis*, and *Off-Balance Sheet Financing Techniques*.

Mr. Sondhi serves on the Board of Directors of an investment advisory services firm and one charitable foundation. He is also an advisor to several U.S. and foreign companies. His consulting activities include revenue recognition, valuation, and comparative analyses of financing and capital structure alternatives, creation and operation of finance, securitization, intellectual property, and investment subsidiaries, analyses of covenants, and the development of debt agreements. Mr. Sondhi has also served as an expert witness on many financial reporting issues.

Contents

CHAPTER 1
INTRODUCTION

CONTENTS

OVERVIEW

Revenue is one of the most important indicators of a successful business. It is a key statistic used in the assessment of a company's financial health. The source, amount, and timing of reported revenue is relevant to all parties interested in financial data: company management, regulators, auditors, and users of financial statements. However, the determination of when and how much revenue to recognize remains difficult for accountants and industry professionals. The principal objective of *Revenue Recognition Guide* is to help all parties become more efficient and effective users of the revenue recognition and reporting literature. The *Guide* will also help its users develop more comprehensive revenue recognition policies.

The *Guide* comprehensively addresses the most important revenue reporting issues. It describes the appropriate accounting for each issue and explains the reasons for that accounting. The *Guide* also provides practical examples and financial statement disclosures from public companies that illustrate the application of key concepts and judgments.

WHY A BOOK ON REVENUE RECOGNITION

Revenue Recognition Is Important to Financial Statement Users

Revenue-generating transactions are varied and can be extremely complicated. Because revenue reporting directly affects a company's results of operations and financial position, a thorough knowledge of the underlying concepts and practices is essential to the preparation and understanding of a company's financial statements.

The importance of revenue to the assessment of company performance has long been clear to the financial world. Revenue is the starting point for just about any forecast about a company's operations, and therefore users of financial statements are keenly interested in revenue recognition policies and trends. There is no other financial statement line item that has such a significant effect on company valuation as does revenue.

The Authoritative Literature Does Not Address All of the Issues

Despite the importance of revenue recognition to the financial statements of virtually all companies, the accounting literature on revenue recognition is neither comprehensive nor easy to apply. The revenue recognition guidance was originally published in over 200 separate documents by multiple standard-setters, including the Accounting Principles Board (APB), the Financial Accounting Standards Board (FASB), the Emerging Issues Task Force (EITF), and others. The introduction of the FASB Accounting Standards Codification™ (ASC) has significantly reduced the chances of being unable to identify relevant literature for a transaction, but other difficulties remain.

Most of the revenue recognition guidance is narrow in scope and only addresses specific issues or types of transactions. As a result, there is detailed guidance on some issues and little or no guidance on others. In addition, the development of revenue recognition guidance has occurred on an industry-by-industry basis, with the result that the models used by different industries are often inconsistent with one another.

Revenue Recognition Is a Leading Cause of Financial Reporting Errors

The lack of comprehensive guidance, combined with the variety and complexity of these transactions, has resulted in a large number of financial reporting errors. The staff of the Securities and Exchange Commission (SEC) issued two reports in early 2003 that highlighted revenue recognition as an area prone to problems: (1) Report Pursuant to Section 704 of the Sarbanes-Oxley Act of 2002 (Section 704 Report) and (2) Summary by the Division of Corporation Finance of Significant Issues Addressed in the Review of the Periodic Reports of the Fortune 500 Companies (Fortune 500 Report).

In developing the Section 704 Report, the SEC staff studied enforcement actions filed during the period July 31, 1997, through July 30, 2002. Improper revenue recognition was the area where the SEC brought the greatest number of enforcement actions during this period. The types of improprieties ranged from the improper timing of revenue recognition (e.g., improper recognition of revenue related to bill-and-hold sales and consignment sales) to fictitious revenue (e.g., falsification of sales documents, failure to consider side letter agreements) to improper valuation of revenue (e.g., failure to appropriately consider rights of return). Other revenue-related areas where the SEC brought a significant number of actions were nondisclosure of related party transactions and the accounting for nonmonetary and round-trip transactions.

The Fortune 500 Report resulted from the SEC's Division of Corporation Finance's (Corp Fin) review of all annual reports filed by Fortune 500 companies. This report provides insight into areas commonly questioned by Corp Fin during their reviews of annual reports. Revenue recognition accounting policy disclosures was an area frequently questioned by Corp Fin. In many cases, Corp Fin requested that companies significantly expand these disclosures. Industries where these requests were common included computer software, computer services, computer hardware, communications equipment, capital goods, semiconductor, electronic instruments and controls, energy, pharmaceutical, and retail. The revenue-related topics precipitating these requests included accounting for software, multiple-element (or multiple-deliverable) arrangements, rights of return, price protection features, requirements for installation of equipment, customer acceptance provisions, and various types of sales incentive programs.

In addition, several other studies have shown that revenue recognition issues cause more financial statement restatements than any other accounting topic. Several high-profile revenue restatements over the last few years have reinforced the focus of regulators and the investing public on revenue recognition policy and disclosure.

The Authoritative Literature Is Changing

Largely in response to these problems, the SEC issued Staff Accounting Bulletin No. 101 (SAB 101), *Revenue Recognition in Financial Statements*, in late 1999, which explained the SEC staff's views on the application of the existing revenue recognition guidance. As a result, some companies were required to change their revenue recognition policies. The most significant impact of SAB 101, whose updated guidance is included in SAB Topic 13, *Revenue Recognition*, of the Codification of Staff Accounting Bulletins, however, is that it focused the attention of most public companies on their revenue recognition policies and procedures. Even companies whose revenue recognition policies did not change as a result of the guidance in SAB Topic 13 have paid more attention to their revenue recognition policies and procedures since it was issued.

The FASB has made considerable progress on its project to provide comprehensive guidance on revenue recognition. This project will likely result in substantive changes to revenue reporting. See Chapter 13, "Future Expectations," for a discussion of this FASB project.

Tying the Literature Together

Because the revenue accounting literature is incomplete and was originally issued in many different pronouncements, it is often difficult to understand how it all fits together. This product makes it easier to identify the appropriate literature to follow (or analogize to) by: (a) addressing the issues in a topical manner, (b) providing references to the authoritative literature where appropriate, (c) providing guidance in areas that have not yet been addressed by standard-setters, and (d) providing explanations beyond those in the authoritative literature.

Seeing the Big Picture

The discussion above provides several good reasons why a product on revenue recognition is timely. This product addresses revenue recognition on a comprehensive basis, instead of issue-by-issue or transaction-by-transaction, making it easier to understand the fundamental principles and see common threads in the literature. Focusing on the fundamental principles can also reveal the underlying logic that sometimes generates seemingly inconsistent conclusions. For example, although the same principles may be used to account for two different revenue transactions, the facts and circumstances related to each transaction will determine how to apply these principles and ultimately account for the transactions.

HOW THIS PRODUCT IS ORGANIZED

Introduction and Framework of Revenue Recognition

After an introduction and brief survey of the authoritative accounting literature in Chapter 2, Chapter 3, "General Principles," provides a detailed explanation of the FASB's conceptual framework on revenue recognition and a discussion of the criteria for revenue recognition that commonly appear in the revenue recognition literature and how these conditions are consistent with the conceptual framework. In addition, guidance is provided on how to evaluate satisfaction of these conditions.

Applying the Literature to Specific Transactions

The framework discussed in Chapter 3, "General Principles," is enhanced in Chapters 4–8, which discuss application of the general principles and criteria to specific types of transactions and issues. Chapter 4, "Multiple-Deliverable Revenue Arrangements," addresses multiple-element transactions and explains when and how to account for separate deliverables. Chapters 5–7 discuss product, service, and intellectual property deliverables and explain how the general principles and criteria should be applied to these types of transactions. Chapter 8, "Miscellaneous Issues," addresses assorted issues that can affect revenue recognition in certain types of transactions. The discussion in these chapters is presented in the context of the conceptual framework.

Detailed Models in the Accounting Literature

Chapter 9, "Contract Accounting," and Chapter 10, "Software—A Complete Model," discuss two revenue recognition models that are comprehensively addressed in the accounting literature. Each model applies to a narrow group of transactions—accounting for certain long-term contracts (Chapter 9) and software revenue recognition (Chapter 10). Unlike the discussion of other issues in this product that is based, to a large extent, on analogy to common principles and concepts in revenue accounting, the guidance on contract accounting and software revenue recognition is taken directly from the accounting literature that was created to address these transactions. The recognition guidance in Chapters 5–8 generally does not apply to these transactions.

Financial Reporting

Chapter 11, "Presentation," and Chapter 12, "Disclosures," deal with issues that directly affect the financial statements. Chapter 11 focuses on an issue that is perhaps just as important as the timing of revenue recognition—the determination of what amounts should be reported on the revenue line of the financial statements as opposed to some other line. Chapter 12 discusses revenue recognition disclosures that are either required or desirable in the financial statements.

A Look Toward the Future

The product closes with a discussion of projects that have not yet been completed by the various accounting standard-setters, including the FASB's proposal that would replace all of the revenue recognition guidance currently in the ASC. Given the ever-changing nature of the accounting literature on revenue recognition and the broad implications that certain projects-in-progress will have on revenue recognition, readers should closely monitor these projects.

CHAPTER 2
A BRIEF SURVEY OF REVENUE-RELATED LITERATURE

CONTENTS

BACKGROUND

Revenue recognition receives more attention than any other accounting topic. Despite this, standard-setters have not developed comprehensive, internally-consistent, and broadly applicable accounting standards for revenue. Instead, revenue recognition has been addressed on a fragmented basis, with various pieces of literature that deal with a wide range of topic- or industry-specific issues. Given the multitude of ways that companies earn revenue, it is not surprising that separate standards have been developed for specific types of transactions. For example, selling real estate is very different than selling software and leasing a product is different than originating loans. Accordingly, divergent approaches have been developed to address revenue recognition in these and other situations.

PRACTICE ALERT: In response to the level of attention paid to revenue recognition and the state of the authoritative literature on the topic, the FASB has undertaken a project to comprehensively address this subject. The tentative conclusions reached by the FASB would change current practice. Chapter 13, "Future Expectations," discusses the status of this project, including the key decisions and the differences between these decisions and current practice. A final standard is expected in 2012, although adoption of the guidance would likely not be required until 2015 at the earliest.

OVERVIEW

This chapter provides an overview of the revenue recognition guidance in existence today. The literature has been classified into three categories: (1) literature that provides general guidance applicable to all (or most) revenue transactions, (2) literature that addresses specific transactions or types of revenue, and (3) literature that addresses specific issues in revenue recognition that may arise in various types of transactions.

Topics identified in this survey of literature that are too narrow or complex for a book intended to broadly address revenue recognition are not discussed in this publication. Readers should consult the "Cross-Reference to GAAP" at the end of this book for a complete listing of accounting literature discussed and the chapter(s) in which the discussion can be found. Guidance not listed in the cross-reference list is not covered in any detail in this book.

GENERALLY ACCEPTED ACCOUNTING PRINCIPLES

The body of literature that companies in the Unites States follow is commonly referred to as U.S. generally accepted accounting principles (GAAP). U.S. GAAP is made up of guidance originally published in many individual pronouncements by a number of different standard-setting bodies over eight decades. Needless to say, the results are sometimes uncoordinated or even contradictory. It is not unusual for standard-setters to have used differing logic in resolving various issues over time.

The FASB, recognizing this problem, undertook a project beginning in the early 1980s to create a Conceptual Framework for accounting standards. The purpose of the Conceptual Framework, which is documented in the FASB's Statements of Financial Accounting Concepts, is to describe the objectives and principles that should underlie accounting standards. In this book, references are often made to the Conceptual Framework to help explain the theory behind accounting standards. However, while the Conceptual Framework is very useful in understanding accounting standards, it is not part of authoritative U.S. GAAP. As such, it is not included in the FASB Accounting Standards Codification™ (ASC), which is discussed in more detail below.

Original Pronouncements

As noted above, U.S. GAAP was developed over a long period of time by several different bodies, each of which has promulgated its guidance in multiple types of documents. The result of this, after decades of work, was that U.S. GAAP was spread across over 2,000 pronouncements in at least a dozen different forms. The accounting standard-setters and the categories of documents they have produced include:

- AICPA Committee on Accounting Procedure:
  - Accounting Research Bulletins (ARB).
- Accounting Principles Board:
  - Accounting Principles Board Opinions (APB).

- AICPA Accounting Standards Executive Committee (AcSEC):
  - Accounting and Audit Guides (AAG);
  - AICPA Statements of Position (SOP);
  - AICPA Practice Bulletins (PB); and
  - Technical Practice Aids (TPA).
- Financial Accounting Standards Board:
  - Accounting Standards Updates (ASU);
  - Statements of Financial Accounting Standards (FAS);
  - FASB Interpretations (FIN);
  - FASB Technical Bulletins (FTB);
  - EITF Consensuses (EITF);
  - FASB Staff Positions (FSP); and
  - FASB Staff Implementation Guides.

The Accounting Standards Codification

Particularly when combined with the lack of consistency in the scope and style of the guidance, this array of guidance was often difficult to navigate. Historically, the U.S. GAAP hierarchy was in place to help those applying U.S. GAAP to determine which of the many different pronouncements should carry greater weight in assessing how to handle a particular accounting issue. The different types of pronouncements were categorized into Levels A through D to indicate their relative authority. In general, Level A documents were those that had gone through the most extensive public review and comment process, with each successive level indicating a reduced amount of public discussion and input. Although the GAAP hierarchy was often helpful in resolving inconsistencies among different pieces of literature, it did not help practitioners ensure that they were considering all of the relevant guidance.

In 2009, the ASC became the sole source of authoritative GAAP. The ASC uses a consistent structure that categorizes U.S. GAAP literature into 90 topics. The ASC incorporates all of the accounting standards that were previously listed in Levels A through D of the U.S. GAAP hierarchy.

The ASC is organized by topic, rather than by standard. Whereas previous pieces of GAAP were considered authoritative on their own, requiring practitioners to consult numerous types of documents, each with its own numbering sequence, changes to GAAP now update various sections of the ASC directly. As such, the ASC will always include the current authoritative guidance in full, eliminating the need to consult multiple sources to identify relevant guidance. Every update to the ASC is issued in the form of an Accounting Standards Update (ASU). ASU's are numbered sequentially by year of issuance (i.e., ASU 2010-1, 2010-2, etc.).

The ASC uses a numerical classification scheme with a four-level hierarchy—Topic-Subtopic-Section-Paragraph (referenced as XXX-YY-ZZ-PP). The topics reside in five main areas as follows:

1. General Principles (Topics 105-199). These topics relate to broad conceptual matters. Topics include Generally Accepted Accounting Principles.

2. Presentation (Topics 205–299). These topics relate only to presentation matters and do not address recognition, measurement, and derecognition matters. Topics include Income Statement, Balance Sheet, Earnings per Share, and so forth.

3. Financial Statement Accounts (Topics 305–700). The ASC organizes topics in a financial statement order, including Assets, Liabilities, Equity, Revenue, and Expenses. Topics include Receivables, Revenue Recognition, Inventory, and so forth.

4. Broad Transactions (Topics 805–899). These topics relate to multiple financial statement accounts and are generally transaction-oriented. Topics include Business Combinations, Derivatives, Nonmonetary Transactions, and so forth. Of particular relevance to this publication, Revenue Recognition is Topic 605.

5. Industries (Topics 905–999). These topics relate to accounting that is unique to an industry or type of activity. Topics include Airlines, Software, Real Estate, and so forth.

Subtopics represent subsets of a topic to which different guidance applies. For example, Products and Services are separate subtopics of the Revenue Recognition topic in the ASC. ASC sections represent the nature of the content in a subtopic, such as Recognition, Measurement, Disclosure, and so forth. The section numbers are the same for each subtopic as follows:

- XXX-YY-00 Status
- XXX-YY-05 Overview and Background
- XXX-YY-10 Objectives
- XXX-YY-15 Scope and Scope Exceptions
- XXX-YY-20 Topical Definitions—Glossary
- XXX-YY-25 Recognition
- XXX-YY-30 Initial Measurement
- XXX-YY-35 Subsequent Measurement
- XXX-YY-40 Derecognition
- XXX-YY-45 Other Presentation Matters
- XXX-YY-50 Disclosure
- XXX-YY-55 Implementation Guidance and Illustrations
- XXX-YY-60 Relationships
- XXX-YY-65 Transition and Open Effective Date Information
- XXX-YY-70 Links to Grandfathered Material

One of the benefits of the ASC is that all U.S. GAAP is now accessible in one place, reducing the chances that guidance relevant to an issue will be missed. In addition, access to the ASC is free at http://asc.fasb.org/home or through a link on the FASB's website (http://www.fasb.org). Further information about the structure and features of the ASC is also available on the FASB website.

SEC Guidance

Pursuant to U.S. law, the SEC has the authority and responsibility to prescribe accounting standards to be used by public companies. Virtually since its inception, the SEC has looked to private-sector bodies to set standards. It is because the SEC looks to the FASB that FASB standards are required to be applied by public companies. Nonetheless, it is the SEC that has the statutory responsibility and authority to prescribe the standards to be used by public companies. As such, rules, interpretations, and other guidance issued by the SEC must be applied by public companies in the financial statements they include in SEC filings. Much of the accounting-related guidance that the SEC has issued is included in Regulation S-X.

In addition to official releases by the SEC itself, the SEC staff periodically issues Staff Accounting Bulletins (SABs) that explain the staff's interpretations of existing accounting literature. Because SABs are not intended to contradict or supersede existing accounting literature, the guidance in a SAB should not contradict guidance in accounting standards issued by the FASB or other accounting standard-setters. Both releases of the SEC itself, as well as SABs, are included for convenience in the ASC. While it is expected that the ASC will be kept up-to-date with any changes in SEC guidance, the official version of this guidance will continue to be maintained by the SEC and its staff, and may be found at the SEC's website (http://www.sec.gov).

In December 1999, the SEC staff issued a significant SAB related to revenue recognition. This guidance, which has been updated several times since it was released, is codified by the SEC in SAB Topic 13, *Revenue Recognition*, and in the ASC in ASC 605-10-S99. The interaction of these SAB Topics with other authoritative literature is clearly described in SAB Topic 13A1. In summary, if other authoritative literature applies to the situation, it should be followed. If no other authoritative literature applies to the situation, the guidance in the SAB Topics should be followed in lieu of analogizing to other authoritative literature.

REVENUE RECOGNITION LITERATURE

As mentioned previously, revenue recognition guidance has been published in a great many standards. The balance of this section of this chapter lists those publications, grouped into topics or industries, and identifies where each publication's guidance now resides in the ASC. Documents are referenced using the defined abbreviation and their number, while ASC citations use the classification scheme and numbering system in the ASC.

Not all of the literature identified below is discussed further in this book. Refer to the U.S. GAAP cross-reference index at the end of the book to determine whether a particular piece of literature is discussed further.

In addition to the authoritative guidance in U.S. GAAP identified below, two of the FASB Concepts Statements provide overall context and guidance:

1. FASB Statement of Financial Accounting Concepts No. 5, *Recognition and Measurement in Financial Statements of Business Enterprises* (CON-5), provides broad recognition guidance.

2. FASB Statement of Financial Accounting Concepts No. 6, *Elements of Financial Statements* (CON-6), provides broad presentation guidance.

GENERAL REVENUE RECOGNITION GUIDANCE

General Guidance

Publication	ASC	ASC Topic
SAB Topic 13, *Revenue Recognition*	605-10-S99	Revenue Recognition

Product Sales

Publication	ASC	ASC Topic
FAS-48, *Revenue Recognition When Right of Return Exists*	605-15-25-1	Revenue Recognition
FAS-49, *Accounting for Product Financing Arrangements*	470-40	Debt
EITF 95-1, *Revenue Recognition on Sales with a Guaranteed Minimum Resale Value*	840-10-55-12	Leases
EITF 95-4, *Revenue Recognition on Equipment Sold and Subsequently Repurchased Subject to an Operating Lease*	605-15-25-5	Revenue Recognition
EITF 01-8, *Determining Whether an Arrangement Contains a Lease*	845-10-15	Nonmonetary Transactions
EITF 03-12, *Impact of FASB Interpretation No. 45 on Issue No. 95-1*	460-10-55-17	Guarantees

Service Transactions

Publication	ASC	ASC Topic
SAB Topic 13, *Revenue Recognition*	605-10-S99	Revenue Recognition
EITF 01-8, *Determining Whether an Arrangement Contains a Lease*	845-10-15	Nonmonetary Transactions
EITF D-96, *Accounting for Management Fees Based on a Formula*	605-20-S99-1	Revenue Recognition
ITC-Service, *FASB Invitation to Comment: Accounting for Certain Service Transactions*	N/A	N/A

Licenses of Intellectual Property Not Addressed Elsewhere

Publication	ASC	ASC Topic
SAB Topic 13, *Revenue Recognition*	605-10-S99	Revenue Recognition
EITF 07-1, *Accounting for Collaborative Arrangements*	808-10	Collaborative Arrangements

Multiple-Deliverable Arrangements

Publication	ASC	ASC Topic
ASU 2009-13, *Multiple-Deliverable Revenue Arrangements*	605-25	Revenue Recognition
SAB Topic 13, *Revenue Recognition*	605-10-S99	Revenue Recognition

Multiple-Deliverable Arrangements

Publication	ASC	ASC Topic
EITF 00-21, *Revenue Arrangements with Multiple Deliverables*	605-25	Revenue Recognition
EITF 01-8, *Determining Whether an Arrangement Contains a Lease*	840-10-15	Leases

Sales Incentives

Publication	ASC	ASC Topic
EITF 01-9, *Accounting for Consideration Given by a Vendor to a Customer (Including a Reseller of the Vendor's Products)*	605-50	Revenue Recognition
EITF 02-16, *Accounting by a Customer (Including a Reseller) for Certain Consideration Received from a Vendor*	605-50	Revenue Recognition
EITF 03-10, *Application of Issue No. 02-16 by Resellers to Sales Incentives Offered to Consumers by Manufacturers*	605-50-45	Revenue Recognition
EITF 06-1, *Accounting for Consideration Given by a Service Provider to Manufacturers or Resellers of Equipment Necessary for an End-Customer to Receive Service from the Service Provider*	605-50	Revenue Recognition

Presentation

Publication	ASC	ASC Topic
REG S-X, *Rule 5-03, Income Statements*	225-10-S99-2	Income Statement
SAB Topic 8, *Retail Companies*	605-15-S99-2 and S99-3	Revenue Recognition
SAB Topic 13, *Revenue Recognition*	605-10-S99	Revenue Recognition
EITF 99-19, *Reporting Revenue Gross as a Principal versus Net as an Agent*	605-45	Revenue Recognition
EITF 00-10, *Accounting for Shipping and Handling Fees and Costs*	605-45-45-19	Revenue Recognition
EITF 01-9, *Accounting for Consideration Given by a Vendor to a Customer (Including a Reseller of the Vendor's Products)*	605-50	Revenue Recognition
EITF 01-14, *Income Statement Characterization of Reimbursements Received for "Out-of-Pocket" Expenses Incurred*	605-45-45-22	Revenue Recognition
EITF 02-3, *Issues Involved in Accounting for Derivative Contracts Held for Trading Purposes and Contracts Involved in Energy Trading and Risk Management Activities*	815-10-45-9	Derivatives and Hedging
EITF 02-16, *Accounting by a Customer (Including a Reseller) for Certain Consideration Received from a Vendor*	605-50	Revenue Recognition
EITF 03-10, *Application of Issue No. 02-16 by Resellers to Sales Incentives Offered to Consumers by Manufacturers*	605-50-45	Revenue Recognition

Presentation

Publication	ASC	ASC Topic
EITF 03-11, *Reporting Realized Gains and Losses on Derivative Instruments That Are Subject to FASB Statement No. 133 and Not "Held for Trading Purposes" as Defined in Issue No. 02-3*	815-10-55-62	Derivatives and Hedging
EITF 06-1, *Accounting for Consideration Given by a Service Provider to Manufacturers or Resellers of Equipment Necessary for an End-Customer to Receive Service from the Service Provider*	605-50	Revenue Recognition
EITF 06-3, *How Taxes Collected from Customers and Remitted to Governmental Authorities Should Be Presented in the Income Statement (That Is Gross versus Net Presentation)*	605-45-15-2	Revenue Recognition

INDUSTRY-BASED GUIDANCE

Airlines

Publication	ASC	ASC Topic
AAG-AIR, *Industry Audit Guide for Audits of Airlines*	908-605	Airlines

Agriculture

Publication	ASC	ASC Topic
SOP 85-3, *Accounting by Agricultural Producers and Agricultural Cooperatives*	905-605	Agriculture
AAG-APC, *Audit and Accounting Guide for Audits of Agricultural Producers and Agricultural Cooperatives*	905-605	Agriculture

Broadcasting

Publication	ASC	ASC Topic
FAS-63, *Financial Reporting by Broadcasters*	920-605	Entertainment—Broadcasters

Cable Television

Publication	ASC	ASC Topic
FAS-51, *Financial Reporting by Cable Television Companies*	922-605	Entertainment—Cable Television

Casinos

Publication	ASC	ASC Topic
AAG-CAS, *Audit and Accounting Guide for Audits of Casinos*	924-605	Entertainment—Casinos

Construction Contracts

Publication	ASC	ASC Topic
ARB-45, *Long-Term Construction-Type Contracts*	605-35	Revenue Recognition
SOP 81-1, *Accounting for Performance of Construction-Type and Certain Production-Type Contracts*	605-35	Revenue Recognition
AAG-CON, *Audit and Accounting Guide for Construction Contractors*	910-605	Contractors—Construction

Employee Benefit Plans

Publication	ASC	ASC Topic
SOP 92-6, *Accounting and Reporting by Health and Welfare Benefit Plans*	962 and 965	Plan Accounting—Defined Contribution Pension Plans/Plan Accounting—Health and Welfare Benefit Plans
AAG-EBP, *Audit and Accounting Guide for Audits of Employee Benefit Plans*	960 and 962	Plan Accounting—Defined Contribution Pension Plans/Plan Accounting—Health and Welfare Benefit Plans

Federal Government Contractors

Publication	ASC	ASC Topic
ARB-43, *Restatement and Revision of Accounting Research Bulletins*, Chapter 11, *Government Contracts*	912-605	Contractors—Federal Government
AAG-FGC, *Audit and Accounting Guide for Audits of Federal Government Contractors*	912-605	Contractors—Federal Government

Financial Services

Publication	ASC	ASC Topic
FAS-91, *Accounting for Nonrefundable Fees and Costs Associated with Originating or Acquiring Loans and Initial Direct Costs of Leases, an amendment of FASB Statements No. 13, 60, and 65 and a rescission of FASB Statement No. 17*	310-20	Receivables
FAS-140, *Accounting for Transfers and Servicing of Financial Assets and Extinguishments of Liabilities, a replacement of FASB Statement No. 125*	405-20	Liabilities
FAS-156, *Accounting for Servicing of Financial Assets, an amendment of FASB Statement No. 140*	860-50	Transfers and Servicing
SAB Topic 5DD, *Miscellaneous Accounting—Loan Commitments Accounted for as Derivative Instruments*	815-10-S99	Derivatives and Hedging

Financial Services

Publication	ASC	ASC Topic
FIN-45, *Guarantor's Accounting and Disclosure Requirements for Guarantees, Including Indirect Guarantees of Indebtedness of Others, an interpretation of FASB Statements No. 5, 57, and 107, and rescission of FASB Interpretation No. 34*	460	Guarantees
SOP 01-6, *Accounting by Certain Entities (Including Entities with Trade Receivables) That Lend to or Finance the Activities of Others*	860-50	Transfers and Servicing
SOP 03-3, *Accounting for Certain Loans or Debt Securities Acquired in a Transfer*	310-30	Receivables
AAG-DEP, *Audit and Accounting Guide for Depository and Lending Institutions: Banks and Savings Institutions, Credit Unions, Finance Companies and Mortgage Companies*	942-605	Financial Services— Depository and Lending
AAG-INV, *Audit and Accounting Guide for Audits of Investment Companies*	946	Financial Services— Investment Companies
AAG-BRD, *Audit and Accounting Guide for Brokers and Dealers in Securities*	940-605	Financial Services— Brokers and Dealers
EITF 84-20, *GNMA Dollar Rolls*	860-10	Transfers and Servicing
EITF 85-13, *Sale of Mortgage Service Rights on Mortgages Owned by Others*	860-50-40-10 and 40-11	Transfers and Servicing
EITF 85-20, *Recognition of Fees for Guaranteeing a Loan*	605-20-25-9	Revenue Recognition
EITF 85-24, *Distribution Fees by Distributors of Mutual Funds That Do Not Have a Front-End Sales Charge*	946-605-25-8	Financial Services— Investment Companies
EITF 86-8, *Sale of Bad-Debt Recovery Rights*	860-10-55-73	Transfers and Servicing
EITF 88-22, *Securitization of Credit Card and Other Receivable Portfolios*	860-20-55-16	Transfers and Servicing
EITF 95-5, *Determination of What Risks and Rewards, If Any, Can Be Retained and Whether Any Unresolved Contingencies May Exist in a Sale of Mortgage Loan Servicing Rights*	860-50-40-3 through 40-5	Transfers and Servicing
EITF 97-3, *Accounting for Fees and Costs Associated with Loan Syndications and Loan Participations after the Issuance of FASB Statement No. 125*	310-20-25-19 and 25-20	Receivables
FSP FIN 45-2, *Whether FASB Interpretation No. 45, "Guarantor's Accounting and Disclosure Requirements for Guarantees, Including Indirect Guarantees of Indebtedness of Others," Provides Support for Subsequently Accounting for a Guarantor's Liability at Fair Value*	460-10-35-2	Guarantees

Financial Services

Publication	ASC	ASC Topic
FSP FIN 45-3, *Application of FASB Interpretation No. 45 to Minimum Revenue Guarantees Granted to a Business or Its Owners*	460-10-55-10 and 55-11	Guarantees
FASB Staff Implementation Guide, *A Guide to Implementation of Statement 91 on Accounting for Nonrefundable Fees and Costs Associated with Originating or Acquiring Loans and Initial Direct Costs of Leases: Questions and Answers*	310-20	Receivables
FSP EITF 85-24-1, *Application of EITF Issue No. 85-24, "Distribution Fees by Distributors of Mutual Funds That Do Not Have a Front-End Sales Charge," When Cash for the Right to Future Distribution Fees for Shares Previously Sold Is Received from Third Parties*	946-605	Financial Services— Investment Companies

Franchises

Publication	ASC	ASC Topic
FAS-45, *Accounting for Franchise Fee Revenue*	952-605	Franchisors

Freight

Publication	ASC	ASC Topic
EITF 91-9, *Revenue and Expense Recognition for Freight Services in Process*	605-20- 25-13	Revenue Recognition

Health Care

Publication	ASC	ASC Topic
AAG-HCO, *Audit and Accounting Guide for Health Care Organizations*	954-605	Health Care Entities

Insurance

Publication	ASC	ASC Topic
FAS-60, *Accounting and Reporting by Insurance Enterprises*	944-605	Financial Services— Insurance
FAS-97, *Accounting and Reporting by Insurance Enterprises for Certain Long-Duration Contracts and for Realized Gains and Losses from the Sale of Investments*	944-605	Financial Services— Insurance
FAS-113, *Accounting and Reporting for Reinsurance of Short-Duration and Long-Duration Contracts*	944-605	Financial Services— Insurance
SOP 03-1, *Accounting and Reporting by Insurance Enterprises for Certain Nontraditional Long-Duration Contracts and for Separate Accounts*	944-20 and 944-80	Financial Services— Insurance

Insurance

Publication	ASC	ASC Topic
FTB 90-1, *Accounting for Separately Priced Extended Warranty and Product Maintenance Contracts*	605-20-25-1 through 25-6	Revenue Recognition
FSP FAS 97-1, *Situations in Which Paragraphs 17(b) and 20 of FASB Statement No. 97, "Accounting and Reporting by Insurance Enterprises for Certain Long-Duration Contracts and for Realized Gains and Losses from the Sale of Investments," Permit or Require Accrual of an Unearned Revenue Liability*	944-605-25-8 through 25-11	Financial Services— Insurance

Motion Pictures

Publication	ASC	ASC Topic
SOP 00-2, *Accounting by Producers or Distributors of Films*	926-605	Entertainment—Films

Music

Publication	ASC	ASC Topic
FAS-50, *Financial Reporting in the Record and Music Industry*	928-605	Entertainment—Music

Not-for-Profit Organizations

Publication	ASC	ASC Topic
FAS-116, *Accounting for Contributions Received and Contributions Made*	958-605	Not-for-Profit Entities
AAG-NPO, *Audit and Accounting Guide for Not-for-Profit Organizations*	958-605	Not-for-Profit Entities

Oil and Gas

Publication	ASC	ASC Topic
FAS-19, *Financial Accounting and Reporting by Oil and Gas Producing Companies*	932	Extractive Activities—Oil and Gas
SAB Topic 12, *Oil and Gas Producing Activities*	932-360-S99	Extractive Activities—Oil and Gas
FAS-69, *Disclosures about Oil and Gas Producing Activities, an amendment of FASB Statements 19, 25, 33, and 39*	932-235	Extractive Activities—Oil and Gas
AAG-OGP, *Audit and Accounting Guide for Audits of Entities with Oil and Gas Producing Activities*	932-605	Extractive Activities—Oil and Gas

Real Estate

Publication	ASC	ASC Topic
FAS-66, *Accounting for Sales of Real Estate*	360-20	Property, Plant, and Equipment
FAS-67, *Accounting for Costs and Initial Rental Operations of Real Estate Projects*	970-605-25	Real Estate—General

Real Estate

Publication	ASC	ASC Topic
FAS-98, *Accounting for Leases, an amendment of FASB Statements No. 13, 66, and 91 and a rescission of FASB Statement No. 26 and Technical Bulletin 79-11*	840-40	Leases
FIN-43, *Real Estate Sales, an interpretation of FASB Statement No. 66*	360-20	Property, Plant, and Equipment
SOP 92-1, *Accounting for Real Estate Syndication Income*	970-605	Real Estate—General
SOP 04-2, *Accounting for Real Estate Time-Sharing Transactions*	978-605	Real Estate—Time Sharing Activities
AAG-CIR, *Audit and Accounting Guide for Common Interest Realty Associations*	972-360	Real Estate—Common Interest Realty Associations
EITF 84-17, *Profit Recognition on Sales of Real Estate with Graduated Payment Mortgages or Insured Mortgages*	360-20-40-35	Property, Plant, and Equipment
EITF 85-27, *Recognition of Receipts from Made-Up Rental Shortfalls*	970-360	Real Estate—General
EITF 86-6, *Antispeculation Clauses in Real Estate Sales Contracts*	360-20-40-39	Property, Plant, and Equipment
EITF 86-7, *Recognition by Homebuilders of Profit from Sales of Land and Related Construction Contracts*	970-360-55-4	Real Estate—General
EITF 87-9, *Profit Recognition on Sales of Real Estate with Insured Mortgages or Surety Bonds*	360-20-40-11	Property, Plant, and Equipment
EITF 88-12, *Transfer of Ownership Interest as Part of Down Payment under FASB Statement No. 66*	360-20-55-66	Property, Plant, and Equipment
EITF 88-21, *Accounting for the Sale of Property Subject to the Seller's Preexisting Lease*	840-40-55-37	Leases
EITF 88-24, *Effect of Various Forms of Financing under FASB Statement No. 66*	360-20-40-14	Property, Plant, and Equipment
EITF 07-6, *Accounting for the Sale of Real Estate Subject to the Requirements of FASB Statement No. 66 When the Agreement Includes a Buy-Sell Clause*	360-20-55-21	Property, Plant, and Equipment

Research and Development Arrangements

Publication	ASC	ASC Topic
ASU 2010-17, *Revenue Recognition– Milestone Method*	605-28	Revenue Recognition
FAS-68, *Research and Development Arrangements*	730-20	Research and Development
REG S-X, Rule 5-03, *Income Statements*	225-10-S99-2	Income Statement
SAB Topic 13, *Revenue Recognition*	605-10-S99	Revenue Recognition

Software

Publication	ASC	ASC Topic
SOP 97-2, *Software Revenue Recognition*	985-605	Software
EITF 00-3, *Application of AICPA Statement of Position 97-2 to Arrangements That Include the Right to Use Software Stored on Another Entity's Hardware*	985-605-55-120 through 55-125	Software
ASU 2009-14, *Certain Revenue Arrangements That Include Software Elements*	985-605	Software
FSP FIN 45-1, *Accounting for Intellectual Property Infringement Indemnifications under FASB Interpretation No. 45, "Guarantor's Accounting and Disclosure Requirements for Guarantees, Including Indirect Guarantees of Indebtedness of Others"*	460-10-55-31 through 55-34	Guarantees
TPA 5100, Various AICPA Technical Practice Aids	985-605	Software

Utilities

Publication	ASC	ASC Topic
FAS-71, *Accounting for the Effects of Certain Types of Regulation*	980-605	Regulated Operations
EITF 91-6, *Revenue Recognition of Long-Term Power Sales Contracts*	980-605-25	Regulated Operations
EITF 92-7, *Accounting by Rate-Regulated Utilities for the Effects of Certain Alternative Revenue Programs*	980-605-25	Regulated Operations
EITF 96-17, *Revenue Recognition under Long-Term Power Sales Contracts That Contain both Fixed and Variable Pricing Terms*	980-605-25	Regulated Operations

MISCELLANEOUS ISSUES

Customer Acceptance Provisions

Publication	ASC	ASC Topic
SAB Topic 13, *Revenue Recognition*	605-10-S99	Revenue Recognition
FAS-5, *Accounting for Contingencies*	460-10-25	Guarantees

Equity Received as Compensation in Revenue Transaction

Publication	ASC	ASC Topic
EITF 00-8, *Accounting by a Grantee for an Equity Instrument to Be Received in Conjunction with Providing Goods or Services*	505-50	Equity

Guarantees and Indemnifications

Publication	ASC	ASC Topic
FAS-5, *Accounting for Contingencies*	460-10	Guarantees
FIN-45, *Guarantor's Accounting and Disclosure Requirements for Guarantees, Including Indirect Guarantees of Indebtedness of Others, an interpretation of FASB Statements No. 5, 57, and 107, and rescission of FASB Interpretation No. 34*	460-10	Guarantees
EITF 03-12, *Impact of FASB Interpretation No. 45 on Issue No. 95-1*	460-10-55-17	Guarantees
FSP FIN 45-1, *Accounting for Intellectual Property Infringement Indemnifications under FASB Interpretation No. 45, "Guarantor's Accounting and Disclosure Requirements for Guarantees, Including Indirect Guarantees of Indebtedness of Others"*	460-10-55-31 through 55-34	Guarantees
FSP FIN 45-2, *Whether FASB Interpretation No. 45, "Guarantor's Accounting and Disclosure Requirements for Guarantees, Including Indirect Guarantees of Indebtedness of Others," Provides Support for Subsequently Accounting for a Guarantor's Liability at Fair Value*	460-10-35-2	Guarantees
FSP FIN 45-3, *Application of FASB Interpretation No. 45 to Minimum Revenue Guarantees Granted to a Business or Its Owners*	460-10-55	Guarantees

Installment Method of Accounting

Publication	ASC	ASC Topic
APB-10, *Omnibus Opinion—1966, Installment Method of Accounting*	605-10-25-3 through 25-5	Revenue Recognition

Leases

Publication	ASC	ASC Topic
FAS-13, *Accounting for Leases*	840	Leases
FAS-29, *Determining Contingent Rentals, an amendment of FASB Statement No. 13*	840-10-55-38	Leases
FAS-91, *Accounting for Nonrefundable Fees and Costs Associated with Originating or Acquiring Loans and Initial Direct Costs of Leases, an amendment of FASB Statements No. 13, 60, and 65 and a rescission of FASB Statement No. 17*	310-20	Receivables
FAS-98, *Accounting for Leases, an amendment of FASB Statements No. 13, 66, and 91 and a rescission of FASB Statement No. 26 and Technical Bulletin No. 79-11*	840-40	Leases
SAB Topic 13, *Revenue Recognition*	605-10-S99	Revenue Recognition

Leases

Publication	ASC	ASC Topic
FTB 85-3, *Accounting for Operating Leases with Scheduled Rent Increases*	840-20-25-2	Leases
FTB 88-1, *Issues Relating to Accounting for Leases*	840	Leases
EITF 84-37, *Sale-Leaseback Transaction with Repurchase Option*	840-40-S99	Leases
EITF 85-27, *Recognition of Receipts from Made-Up Rental Shortfalls*	970-360-55	Real Estate—General
EITF 86-17, *Deferred Profit on Sale-Leaseback Transaction with Lessee Guarantee of Residual Value*	840-40-55-26	Leases
EITF 95-1, *Revenue Recognition on Sales with a Guaranteed Minimum Resale Value*	840-10-55-12 through 55-25	Leases
EITF 95-4, *Revenue Recognition on Equipment Sold and Subsequently Repurchased Subject to an Operating Lease*	605-15-25-5	Revenue Recognition
EITF 98-9, *Accounting for Contingent Rent*	840-10-50-5	Leases
EITF 01-8, *Determining Whether an Arrangement Contains a Lease*	840-10-15	Leases
EITF 01-12, *The Impact of the Requirements of FASB Statement No. 133 on Residual Value Guarantees in Connection with a Lease*	840-10-15-20	Leases
EITF 03-12, *Impact of FASB Interpretation No. 45 on Issue No. 95-1*	460-10-55-17	Guarantees
EITF Topic D-107, *Lessor Consideration of Third-Party Residual Value Guarantees*	840-30-S99	Leases
FASB Staff Implementation Guidance, *A Guide to Implementation of Statement 91 on Accounting for Nonrefundable Fees and Costs Associated with Originating or Acquiring Loans and Initial Direct Costs of Leases: Questions and Answers*	310-20	Receivables
FSP FAS-13-2, *Accounting for a Change or Projected Change in the Timing of Cash Flows Relating to Income Taxes Generated by a Leveraged Lease Transaction*	840-30-35-37 through 35-47	Leases

Nonmonetary Transactions

Publication	ASC	ASC Topic
APB-29, *Accounting for Nonmonetary Transactions*	845-10	Nonmonetary Transactions
EITF 87-10, *Revenue Recognition by Television "Barter" Syndicators*	920-845	Entertainment—Broadcasters
EITF 93-11, *Accounting for Barter Transactions Involving Barter Credits*	845-10-30-17 through 30-20	Nonmonetary Transactions
EITF 99-17, *Accounting for Advertising Barter Transactions*	605-20-25-14 through 25-18	Revenue Recognition

Nonmonetary Transactions

Publication	ASC	ASC Topic
EITF 01-2, *Interpretations of APB Opinion No. 29*	845-10	Nonmonetary Transactions
EITF 04-13, *Accounting for Purchases and Sales of Inventory with the Same Counterparty*	845-10-25-4	Nonmonetary Transactions

Rights of Return or Cancellation

Publication	ASC	ASC Topic
FAS-48, *Revenue Recognition When Right of Return Exists*	605-15-25	Revenue Recognition
SAB Topic 13, *Revenue Recognition*	605-10-S99	Revenue Recognition

Sales of Future Revenues

Publication	ASC	ASC Topic
EITF 88-18, *Sales of Future Revenues*	470-10-25	Debt

Warranties

Publication	ASC	ASC Topic
FAS-5, *Accounting for Contingencies*	460-10-25-5 through 25-7	Guarantees
FTB 90-1, *Accounting for Separately Priced Extended Warranty and Product Maintenance Contracts*	605-20-25-1 through 25-6	Revenue Recognition
FIN-45, *Guarantor's Accounting and Disclosure Requirements for Guarantees, Including Indirect Guarantees of Indebtedness of Others, an interpretation of FASB Statements No. 5, 57, and 107, and rescission of FASB Interpretation No. 34*	460-10	Guarantees

REVENUE RECOGNITION UNDER INTERNATIONAL FINANCIAL REPORTING STANDARDS

Another source of revenue recognition literature is International Financial Reporting Standards (IFRS). IFRS is the most commonly used set of accounting standards outside the United States. IFRS has been promulgated by the International Accounting Standards Board (IASB) and its predecessor, the International Accounting Standards Committee (IASC), and their respective interpretive bodies, the IFRS Interpretations Committee (IFRIC) and the Standing Interpretations Committee (SIC).

A detailed discussion of IFRS revenue recognition literature is beyond the scope of this publication. However, it can be useful to refer to IFRS on certain matters (as the book does in several subsequent chapters) to understand how other standard-setters have resolved those issues. This can help in applying relevant U.S. GAAP guidance.

The following pages describe (at a very basic level) IFRS revenue recognition guidance and identify relevant IFRS pronouncements.

It should be noted that the IASB issued an Exposure Draft, *Revenue from Contracts with Customers*, on June 24, 2010, that if adopted, would create a single revenue recognition standard for IFRS that would be applied across various industries and capital markets. The proposed standard would replace IAS 18 *Revenue*, IAS 11 *Construction Contracts* and related interpretations. It was issued jointly with the FASB with a goal of converging standards between U.S. GAAP and IFRS. See further discussion of this joint project in Chapter 13, "Future Expectations."

IFRS Framework

The IASB's framework defines income as "increases in economic benefits during the accounting period in the form of inflows or enhancements of assets and decreases of liabilities that result in increases in equity, other than those relating to contributions from equity participants." The framework goes on to distinguish between the two main components of income—revenue and gains. Revenue arises "in the course of the ordinary activities of an entity." In contrast, gains are "other items that meet the definition of income and *may or may not* arise in the course of the ordinary activities of an entity [emphasis added]." The framework goes on to explain that because gains are not different in nature from revenues, they are not regarded as a separate element.

Although similar to U.S. GAAP in most aspects, the lack of a distinction between revenue and gains is a difference. However, this rarely results in significantly different treatment of particular transactions.

Applicable Standards

The most striking difference between U.S. GAAP and IFRS concerning revenue recognition is the volume of guidance. Although U.S. GAAP, as laid out above, has many standards on revenue recognition, IFRS has very little guidance, and what guidance exists is often so high-level that many different ways of applying the literature have developed.

IAS 18, *Revenue*, is a general statement that addresses revenue recognition for three significant types of revenue: (1) product sales, (2) service transactions, and (3) rights to use assets. IAS 18 defines revenue as the "gross inflow of economic benefits during the period arising from the course of the ordinary activities of the entity when those inflows result in an increase in equity, other than increases resulting from contributions by equity participants." IAS 18 notes that such inflows must be on the entity's own account; revenue does not include amounts collected on behalf of a third party. Three additional IASB standards address, in detail, other significant types of revenue: (1) IAS 11, *Construction Contracts*, (2) IAS 17, *Leases*, and (3) IAS 41, *Agriculture*. Limited revenue recognition guidance for the insurance industry also is provided in IFRS 4, *Insurance Contracts*.

Several interpretations that address revenue recognition topics may also be useful to those using U.S. GAAP, as they address issues or questions that may arise but for which U.S. GAAP is incomplete. These include IFRIC 13, *Customer Loyalty Programmes*, covering the accounting for award credits issued in connection with a revenue transaction; IFRIC 12, *Service Concession Arrangements*, dealing with revenue recognition and many other issues that often arise in public-private infrastructure and service arrangements; and IFRIC 15, *Agreements for the Construction of Real Estate*, which provides guidance on selecting a revenue recognition model for contracts to build and sell real estate.

To the extent that a topic or issue is covered by both U.S. GAAP and IFRS literature, a U.S. company must follow the guidance in U.S. literature. However, if a topic or issue is not covered in U.S. literature but is covered in IASB literature, a U.S. company can refer to IASB literature for accounting guidance and policies that are likely to be acceptable in the U.S. GAAP framework. Referring to IASB literature provides the perspective of a standard-setter that has specifically focused on and addressed an accounting topic or issue. This perspective can be helpful to a U.S. company in determining how to account for a particular topic or issue that is not covered in U.S. GAAP.

Presentation and Other Issues

Presentation of revenue on the income statement is addressed in IAS 1, *Presentation of Financial Statements*. IAS 1 gives preparers of financial statements considerable flexibility on the introduction of additional revenue line items, sub-totaling, and ordering.

IAS 14, *Segment Reporting*, defines "segment result" as "segment revenues less segment expenses" and has definitions of both segment revenues and expenses with specific items to be included or excluded from those amounts. For example, segment revenue includes "an entity's share of profits and losses of associates, joint ventures, or other investments accounted for under the equity method if those items are included in consolidated or total entity revenue" and segment expenses specifically excludes these amounts. This is relevant regarding where such profit and losses should appear on the consolidated statement of income.

Listing of IFRS Revenue Recognition Literature

IAS 18	*Revenue*
IAS 11	*Construction Contracts*
IAS 17	*Leases*
IAS 41	*Agriculture*
IFRS 4	*Insurance Contracts*
SIC 13	*Jointly Controlled Entities—Nonmonetary Contributions by Venturers*
SIC 15	*Operating Leases—Incentives*
SIC 27	*Evaluating the Substance of Transactions Involving the Legal Form of a Lease*
SIC 29	*Service Concession Arrangements—Disclosure*
SIC 31	*Revenue—Barter Transactions Involving Advertising Services*
IFRIC 4	*Determining Whether an Arrangement Contains a Lease*
IFRIC 12	*Service Concession Arrangements*
IFRIC 13	*Customer Loyalty Programmes*
IFRIC 15	*Agreements for the Construction of Real Estate*
IFRIC 18	*Transfers of Assets from Customers*

CHAPTER 3
GENERAL PRINCIPLES

CONTENTS

BACKGROUND

Revenue, which appears on the top line of the income statement, is one of the most important measures of a company's health to preparers, auditors, and users of financial statements. The amount and timing of revenue recognition have a significant effect on the results of a company's operations. The changing nature of business operations (and revenue-generating transactions) suggests that accounting for revenue will continue to generate significant questions. Basic guidance on revenue recognition is addressed in the FASB Concepts Statements, which say that revenue should be recognized when it is both earned and either realized or realizable (CON-5, par. 83).

The following are examples of situations where revenue is earned and realized at, or almost at, the same time:

- A restaurant's revenue generally is earned and realizable after a meal has been eaten and paid for by the diner.
- A retail store's revenue generally is earned and realizable when the customer pays for the merchandise at the cash register.
- A manufacturer's revenue generally is earned and realizable for COD orders upon delivery.
- For plumbers and for providers of lawn care and similar services, revenue generally is earned and realizable as the services are performed and paid for by the customer.

In some cases, revenue is realized before it is earned. For example:

- Magazine subscriptions are often paid for in advance. The revenue is realized before the magazines are delivered and earned when the magazines are delivered.
- Airlines generally require payment when a ticket is purchased, at which time revenue is realized. Revenue is earned when the airline provides the transportation.

In other cases, revenue is earned before it becomes realizable. For example:

- A manufacturer that sells products on credit earns revenue from the sale upon delivery. The revenue may not be immediately realizable if the customer's ability to pay is in question.
- Some retailers provide products to customers on a trial basis, in which case the customer has no commitment to pay for the products unless he or she keeps them for a particular period of time. Although the earnings process may arguably be complete when the product is delivered, the revenue does not become realizable until the trial period lapses.

Because these fundamental concepts are easily applied to many transactions, the accounting standard-setters have not provided much other general guidance. Instead, additional guidance has been focused on the application of the basic concepts to more complex transactions and on how certain issues affect the application of the basic concepts. As discussed in Chapter 2, "A Brief Survey of Revenue-Related Literature," detailed revenue recognition guidance is limited to a small portion of transactions. However, the number and complexity of transactions continues to expand and the basic concepts are not always readily applicable to transactions that are common today.

SURVEY OF ACCOUNTING LITERATURE

The general principles on revenue reporting under U.S. generally accepted accounting principles (GAAP) are set forth in the FASB's Conceptual Framework. The Framework provides a conceptual basis upon which the FASB and other accounting standard-setters can develop detailed accounting standards. As a result, the Concepts Statements are not intended to provide sufficient guidance for preparers to determine the proper accounting treatment in a particular transaction.

The basic principle of revenue accounting as set forth in CON-5, paragraph 83, is that "recognition involves consideration of two factors, (a) being realized or realizable and (b) being earned, with sometimes one and sometimes the other being the more important consideration." This conceptual guidance has been unchanged since it was first issued by the FASB in 1984.

For many revenue transactions, the conceptual guidance is augmented by Statements on Financial Accounting Standards that provide more detailed guidance on applying the basic concepts. Additional general guidance on revenue recognition comes from ASC 605-10-S99 (SAB Topic 13, *Revenue Recognition*).

REVENUE RECOGNITION LITERATURE

ASC	ASC Topic/Subtopic	Publication	Subject
605-10-S99	Revenue Recognition/ Overall	SAB Topic 13	Revenue Recognition
N/A	N/A	CON-5	Recognition and Measurement in Financial Statements of Business Enterprises
605-35	Revenue Recognition/ Construction-Type and Production-Type Contracts	ARB-45	Long-Term Construction-Type Contracts
605-10-25-3	Revenue Recognition/ Overall	APB-10	Installment and Cost Recovery Methods of Revenue Recognition
605-15-25	Revenue Recognition/ Products	FAS-48	Revenue Recognition When Right of Return Exists
470-40-05	Debt/Product Financing Arrangements	FAS-49	Product Financing Arrangements

ASC	ASC Topic/Subtopic	Publication	Subject
928-605-25-2	Entertainment—Music/Revenue Recognition	FAS-50	Music License Fees
360-20	Property, Plant, and Equipment/Real Estate Sales	FAS-66	Accounting for Sales of Real Estate
605-35	Revenue Recognition/Construction-Type and Production-Type Contracts	SOP 81-1	Accounting for Performance of Construction-Type and Certain Production-Type Contracts
985-605	Software/Revenue Recognition	SOP 97-2	Software Revenue Recognition
926-605	Entertainment—Films/Revenue Recognition	SOP 00-2	Accounting by Producers or Distributors of Films
605-20-S99	Revenue Recognition/Services	EITF D-96	Management Fees Based on a Formula
605-50	Revenue Recognition/Customer Payments and Incentives	EITF 01-9 and EITF 06-1	Payments to Customers

SUPPORTING LITERATURE

ASC	ASC Topic/Subtopic	Publication	Subject
460-10-25	Guarantees/Overall	FAS-5	Warranty Obligations Incurred in Connection with the Sale of Goods or Services
450-20-25	Contingencies/Loss Contingencies	FAS-5	Loss Contingencies
840	Leases	FAS-13	Leases
980-605-30	Regulated Operations/Revenue Recognition	FAS-71	Regulated Operations—Revenue Collected Subject to Refund
815-10-15	Derivatives and Hedging/Overall	FAS-133	Definition of a Derivative
405-20	Liabilities/Extinguishment of Liabilities	FAS-140	Extinguishment of Liabilities
840-10-15	Leases/Overall	EITF 01-8	Determining Whether an Arrangement Contains a Lease
N/A	N/A	SEC FRR 23	The Significance of Oral Guarantees to the Financial Reporting Process

OVERVIEW

The two concepts—earned and realized or realizable—are meant to ensure that a company does not recognize revenue (1) until it has performed under the terms of the arrangement, thereby earning the right to receive and retain payment as contractually documented, and (2) unless it will indeed receive and retain (realize) payment in a form that has value to the company.

Earned

As stated in CON-5, "revenues are considered to have been earned when the entity has substantially accomplished what it must do to be entitled to the benefits represented by the revenues." This may be delivering goods, performing services, providing information, or any other activity for which one entity would pay another entity. The acts the seller performs to fulfill the earned criterion constitute the "earnings process."

To meet the earned criterion, the earnings process must be completed, at least in part. Until the company has performed, it should not recognize revenue related to amounts it has been paid in advance or will be paid in return for that performance. In most cases, the point at which revenue is earned is fairly clear from the terms of the transaction. For example:

- An automobile part manufacturer's revenue is earned when it delivers parts to its customers.

- A car rental agency's revenue is earned via the passage of time as it allows a customer to use one of its cars.

- A grocery store's revenue is earned when the customer proceeds through the checkout line with groceries.

In many other transactions, however, it is unclear when revenue has been earned. For example, an executive recruiter performs many activities as part of a search, including contacting potential candidates, setting up interviews, and assisting in salary negotiations. However, it is not until someone has been hired that the customer benefits from all these activities. Similarly, a sales agent performs many activities to line up purchasers of its customer's products. However, it is not until the products are purchased that the customer benefits from these activities. In these situations, it is not immediately clear whether revenue is earned over time (e.g., the period over which the search for candidates or purchasers is performed), or only upon successful completion of all necessary activities (e.g., acceptance by a candidate or orders placed by a purchaser).

Completion of the earnings process also may have nothing to do with the timing of the payments under the contract. For example, the receipt of a deposit or upfront fee in an arrangement does not necessarily indicate that revenue has been earned, even if the deposit or fee is nonrefundable. On the other hand, the fact that payment in an arrangement is not due for some period of time does not necessarily indicate that the revenue has not yet been earned. In some cases, although performance on one component may be complete, revenue may not be recognized if payment for that performance is contingent upon completion of performance on other components of the contract. See Chapter 4, "Multiple-Deliverable Revenue Arrangements," for a discussion of contingent revenue.

Realized or Realizable

Revenue is considered realized or realizable when the seller receives either cash from the customer or an asset, such as a note receivable, that is convertible into cash. In addition, the receipt of nonmonetary assets that are not readily convertible into cash also meets the realizability criterion as long as the assets have value to the seller (see further discussion in Chapter 8, "Miscellaneous Issues").

The requirement that revenue must be realized or realizable before it is recognized should be common sense. If the company has not received a benefit from the arrangement, it would be illogical to recognize the related revenue. Determining whether the realizable criterion has been met can often be fairly easy. In general, this occurs when either a cash payment is received or the customer becomes legally obligated to make such a payment because the seller has fulfilled its responsibilities under the contract.

However, many provisions can exist in arrangements that raise questions about the realizability of revenue. For example, when payment is received but the customer has a right of return, the right of return may make realizability uncertain. In other arrangements, the fee may vary based on one or more events whose outcome will not be known until after initial payment or delivery. In transactions with vendor financing and/or extended payment terms, the fee may not be realizable because of the extent of the seller's involvement with the financing of payments made (or to be made) by the customer.

Four Conditions for Recognition

The accounting literature that has been developed since the conceptual framework guidance was introduced has attempted to provide additional conditions for determining when revenue has been earned and is realizable. As previously mentioned, some of this literature is transaction-specific (e.g., ASC 926-605, on the licensing of motion pictures), while some is issue-specific (e.g., ASC 470-40-05, on product financing arrangements). In contrast, ASC 605-10-S99 (SAB Topic 13) is more general in nature.

Although different pieces of literature use different terms, each generally requires that the following four conditions are met in order for revenue to be both earned and realizable (e.g., ASC 605-10-S99; 985-605-25-3; 926-605-25-1; 928-605-25-2) (e.g., SAB Topic 13A1):

1. Persuasive evidence of an arrangement exists.

2. The arrangement fee is fixed or determinable.

3. Delivery or performance has occurred.

4. Collectibility is reasonably assured.

OBSERVATION: Each of the above four conditions must be met by the end of an accounting period in order to recognize revenue from a particular transaction. If any condition fails to be satisfied, revenue recognition must be delayed until the period in which the final condition is met.[1]

Each of the four criteria will be discussed in this chapter. Generally speaking, the analyses of the collectibility and persuasive evidence criteria do not change significantly based on the type of transaction involved. Therefore, the discussion of these conditions in this chapter applies to all transactions, and there is no material discussion of these conditions in Chapters 4–7 and 9–10, which address specific issues and transaction types.

By contrast, the analyses of the fixed or determinable fee and delivery or performance criteria can differ significantly based on the type of transaction involved. Therefore, the basic discussion of these criteria included in this chapter is supplemented by significant additional discussion by transaction type in Chapters 4–7 and 9–10.

PERSUASIVE EVIDENCE OF AN ARRANGEMENT

To determine whether the "earned" criterion has been met—that is, to assess whether the seller has substantially completed what it has agreed to do—it is necessary to identify what obligations the seller has undertaken. For this reason, revenue cannot be recognized until there is persuasive evidence of an arrangement. The existence of persuasive evidence of an arrangement permits identification of the seller's obligations and facilitates an analysis of whether the seller has fulfilled these obligations and earned the related revenue.

Persuasive evidence of an arrangement also helps ensure that the realizability criterion is met because it provides the legal basis on which the seller can demand payment from the customer. If no arrangement exists under which the buyer has agreed to pay the seller for performing under the contract, any revenue the seller believes he or she is owed may not be realizable and the seller may not have a right to payment under the law.

What Constitutes "Persuasive Evidence"

The accounting literature does not specify the types of evidence that qualify as persuasive evidence of an arrangement. In general, the requirement is that whatever documentation a company normally uses to document a sales transaction be in place before revenue is recognized.

Many companies routinely document sales arrangements by written contracts. For these companies, persuasive evidence of an arrangement generally would exist upon execution of the final contract by both parties. Thus, despite the fact that the seller may have delivered the products or services specified and billed the customer, no revenue should be recognized if the final contract is pending.

---

[1] Meeting the revenue recognition conditions after the end of the period is a "Nonrecognized Subsequent Event," as discussed in ASC 855-10-25-3. Nonrecognized subsequent events "provide evidence with respect to conditions that did *not* exist at the date of the balance sheet but arose after the balance sheet date."

ILLUSTRATION: PERSUASIVE EVIDENCE OF AN ARRANGEMENT

(Adapted from ASC 605-10-S99, A2, ques. 1 (SAB Topic 13A2, ques. 1))

Facts: Company A has product available to ship to customers prior to the end of its current fiscal quarter. Customer Beta places an order for the product, and Company A delivers the product prior to the end of its current fiscal quarter. Company A's normal and customary business practice for this class of customer is to enter into a written sales agreement that requires the signatures of the authorized representatives of the Company and its customer to be binding. Company A prepares a written sales agreement, and its authorized representative signs the agreement before the end of the quarter. However, Customer Beta does not sign the agreement because Customer Beta is awaiting the requisite approval by its legal department. Customer Beta's purchasing department has orally agreed to the sale and stated that the contract will be formally approved the first week of Company A's next fiscal quarter. Company A expects that payment will be made on normal credit terms.

Discussion: In view of Company A's business practice of requiring a written sales agreement for this class of customer, persuasive evidence of an arrangement would require a final agreement that has been executed by the properly authorized personnel of the customer. Customer Beta's execution of the sales agreement after the end of the quarter causes the transaction to be considered a transaction of the subsequent period.

EXAMPLE: PERSUASIVE EVIDENCE OF AN ARRANGEMENT

Citrix Systems Form 10-K—Fiscal Year Ended December 31, 2009

Persuasive evidence of the arrangement exists. The Company recognizes revenue on packaged products and appliances upon shipment to distributors and resellers. For packaged product and appliance sales, it is the Company's customary practice to require a purchase order from distributors and resellers who have previously negotiated a master packaged product distribution or resale agreement. For electronic and paper license arrangements, the Company typically requires a purchase order from the distributor, reseller or end-user (depending on the arrangement) and an executed product license agreement from the end-user. For technical support, product training and consulting services, the Company requires a purchase order and an executed agreement. For online services, the Company requires the customer or the reseller to electronically accept the terms of an online services agreement or execute a contract.

If a company does not have a standard or customary business practice of using written contracts to document a sales arrangement, there would usually be other forms of written or electronic evidence to document the transaction. Such evidence might be as simple as a restaurant check, a cash register receipt, or a click on the "submit order" button on an internet site (ASC 605-10-S99, A2, ques. 1) (SAB Topic 13A2, ques. 1).

The methods used to document sales transactions may vary from location to location within a company, or may vary based on the type of customer (e.g., corporate vs. individual) or transaction (e.g., product vs. service). Therefore, each transaction should be evaluated based upon the documentation that would be expected to exist for the type of transaction.

EXAMPLE: PERSUASIVE EVIDENCE OF AN ARRANGEMENT

8X8, Inc. Form 10-K—Fiscal Year Ended March 31, 2010

For all sales, except those completed via the Internet, we use either a binding purchase order or other signed agreement as evidence of an arrangement. For sales over the Internet, we use a credit card authorization as evidence of an arrangement, and recognize revenue upon settlement of the transaction, if there are no customer acceptance conditions.

In some instances, a company may enter into a transaction in which the documentation is not consistent with the company's standard practice. In these cases, judgment must be applied in assessing whether persuasive evidence of an arrangement exists. For example, if a company that normally uses written contracts to document its arrangements delivers its product and receives payment and acceptance of the product from its customer, persuasive evidence of an arrangement may very well exist, even if the formal contract was never signed due to the customer's desire for quick delivery.

DELIVERY

To ensure that the earned criterion is met, delivery or performance must occur before revenue is recognized. This requirement helps assess whether the obligations undertaken by the vendor have been completed. Each obligation is generically referred to as an element or deliverable. This assessment must be done individually for each deliverable in an arrangement. However, when multiple deliverables exist, certain issues must be considered when allocating the arrangement fee to the individual deliverables. These issues are discussed in Chapter 4, "Multiple-Deliverable Revenue Arrangements."

Basic Models

Delivery occurs when the seller has fulfilled its obligations related to a particular item and the customer has realized value from the seller's performance. Delivery of some deliverables may occur all at once, while delivery of others may occur over a period of time. Although an infinite variety of deliverables can be included in a revenue arrangement, the delivery or performance condition is generally evaluated for accounting purposes using one of two models. The decision of which model to use is based on whether the vendor's obligations are completed and is value transferred to the customer all at once or over a period of time. The first model, referred to in this product as the Completed Performance model, is used when a single point in time can be identified as the point when the vendor completes its obligation and the customer realizes value. The second model, referred to as the Proportional Performance model, is used when the seller fulfills its performance obligation, and the customer receives value, over a period of time.

PRACTICE POINTER: No matter which model is used, the delivery condition is not met until the vendor's obligation to the customer is fulfilled. Therefore, if the vendor hires a third party to fulfill the obligation, revenue cannot be recognized until the third party actually fulfills the obligation. Merely hiring an outside party to provide a deliverable to the customer does not constitute delivery, because hiring a third party does not provide value to the customer. Value is not provided unless and until the customer actually receives the deliverable.

Choosing a Model

The choice of which model to use is a key step toward recognizing revenue. In some cases, the identification of an appropriate model is easy, because the performance pattern is clear. Other situations require significant judgment. Although some generalizations can be made about what kind of deliverables should be evaluated under each model, it is important to review the substance of each deliverable to determine when delivery occurs for that deliverable.

The discussion below focuses on different types of deliverables, since it is necessary to separately assess delivery for each deliverable in an arrangement. When an arrangement includes multiple deliverables, the delivery condition is not met for a particular deliverable if it does not have value to the customer on a standalone basis. This is discussed further in Chapter 4, "Multiple-Deliverable Revenue Arrangements."

Products

The delivery of products generally is evaluated using the Completed Performance model, because the customer realizes all of the value at once—that is, when the product is physically delivered to the customer. At that time, the vendor completes its entire obligation with respect to the deliverable. The Completed Performance model is sometimes referred to as the product model.

Although a manufacturer may take a number of actions related to an arrangement before delivering the product, these actions generally do not provide value to the customer until delivery occurs. Therefore, it is usually not appropriate to recognize revenue using the Proportional Performance Model as the product is being manufactured. However, delivery of a product must be evaluated using the Proportional Performance model when the arrangement qualifies for percentage of completion accounting, as discussed in Chapter 9, "Contract Accounting." Products may also be evaluated under the Proportional Performance model when the arrangement involves a subscription. See Chapter 5, "Product Deliverables," for further discussion on delivery of products.

Services

The delivery of a service generally is evaluated using the Proportional Performance model, because the vendor fulfills a portion of its obligations and the customer receives value as each part of the service is performed. As a result, revenue is earned as each part of the service is performed. For example, a home health service that agrees to visit a patient once a week for a year should recognize a portion of the revenue with each visit (provided the other conditions for revenue recognition have been met). In situations where service is provided over a period of time, delivery may occur ratably throughout that time period. For example, the fee in an arrangement to provide high-speed internet access for one year would be recognized ratably over the year (provided the other conditions for revenue recognition have been met).

The correct model to use for some service transactions, however, is less clear. For example, in certain service transactions, although the service is performed over a period of time, the customer realizes value only if and when the final act of the service is performed. This may be true in the case of installation services, where the customer may not realize any value from the installation until it is completed. Similarly, a sales agent generally would not be considered to have delivered services until the customer makes a purchase from the supplier. These types of services may be most appropriately evaluated under the Completed Performance model.

See Chapter 6, "Service Deliverables," for additional discussion on the delivery of services.

PRACTICE ALERT: Situations may arise where arrangements that purport to cover only the sale of products or the delivery of services actually contain a lease. See ASC 840-10-15, which provides guidance on how to determine whether an arrangement contains a lease. When an arrangement has a lease, the lease component must be accounted for as such using lease accounting guidelines even though the arrangement is characterized as a product sale or a service transaction. Because of the differences in the accounting treatment of product sales, service transactions, and leases, the determination that a lease exists will likely have a significant effect on the amount and timing of revenue recognition. The provisions of ASC 840-10-15 are discussed under "Leases" later in this chapter.

Intellectual Property

Intellectual property licensing presents challenges in determining when delivery occurs. For example, in a transaction involving the right to use copyrighted material for a two-year period, does delivery occur when the license term begins, or does delivery occur ratably over the two-year period? For certain types of intellectual property transactions, industry- or transaction-specific accounting literature provides guidance on which model to use for assessing delivery. However, there is little authoritative guidance for the majority of intellectual property licenses. A detailed discussion of this topic can be found in Chapter 7, "Intellectual Property Deliverables." In addition, delivery of software is discussed in Chapter 10, "Software—A Complete Model."

Leases

For certain transactions, the model to use for evaluating delivery is specified in the accounting literature. One major category of transactions for which significant guidance exists is leasing. Lease transactions are primarily addressed in ASC 840, which specifies that the lessor should treat certain leases as operating leases and others as sales-type leases.[2] In substance, an operating lease is evaluated under the Proportional Performance model, with revenue generally being recognized ratably over the lease term. Conversely, revenue recognition in a sales-type lease is based on the Completed Performance model, with performance deemed complete upon physical delivery of the item being leased.

When an arrangement that purports to be only a sale of products or services in effect contains a lease, the accounting treatment of the lease component will likely have a significant effect on the amount and timing of revenue recognition. As a result, and to add clarity to the definition and determination of whether an arrangement contains a lease, supplemental guidance exists in ASC 840-10-15. This guidance builds upon the fundamental definition of a lease in ASC 840 and requires consideration of the following characteristics in order to determine whether an arrangement contains a lease:

- Only property, plant, or equipment (which includes only land and/or depreciable assets) can be the subject of a lease, and a lease only exists if fulfillment of the arrangement is dependent on the use of specific property, plant, or equipment (the property, plant, or equipment can be either explicitly or implicitly identified) (ASC 840-10-15-5 and 15-6).

- A right to use property, plant, or equipment has been conveyed and, therefore a lease exists, if the purchaser/lessee has the right to control use of the underlying property, plant, or equipment. The right to control the use of the property, plant, or equipment exists if either of the following conditions exist:

  — The purchaser/lessee (a) has the right to operate the subject assets (either itself or through directing others) in a manner it determines, or (b) has the ability or right to control physical access to the subject assets, while obtaining or controlling more than a minor amount of the output or other utility of the subject assets; or

  — It is remote that another party or other parties will take more than a minor amount of the output or other utility of the property, plant, or equipment during the arrangement, and the price the purchaser will pay for the output is neither contractually fixed per unit nor equal to the current market price per unit as of the time of delivery of the output (ASC 840-10-15-6).

ASC 840-10-15-17 also notes that executory costs fall within the scope of ASC 840.

When an arrangement contains a lease, the lease deliverable must be accounted for using ASC 840 even though the overall arrangement is characterized as a product sale or the delivery of services. Separation of the lease element (or elements) from the other elements in the arrangement is discussed in Chapter 4, "Multiple-Deliverable Revenue Arrangements."

---

[2] Lease accounting is not addressed in this product. CCH has other sources of guidance that should be consulted for sales-type vs. operating lease classification.

Construction and Other Long-Term Contracts

Another type of transaction for which U.S. GAAP provides specific guidance on revenue recognition is construction and other long-term contracts. This guidance, in ASC 605-35, provides factors to consider for determining whether to use the Completed Performance or Proportional Performance model. For long-term contracts, the two models are referred to as the Completed Contract and Percentage-of-Completion methods, respectively. Discussion of the scope and application of long-term contract accounting is included in Chapter 9, "Contract Accounting."

ILLUSTRATION: CHOOSING THE APPROPRIATE MODEL FOR ASSESSING DELIVERY OF PRODUCTS AND SERVICES

The following examples illustrate the typical factors that must be taken into account when choosing which model to use.

EXAMPLE 1

Facts: Company A manufactures and sells furniture. It has a standard product line and customers may choose various colors, fabrics, and finishes from Company A's product catalog. Company A manufactures the furniture only after a customer places an order.

Discussion: Company A performs several activities in fulfilling a customer order, including manufacturing the furniture and physically delivering it to the customer. However, the customer only receives value upon the actual delivery of the furniture. Therefore, delivery or performance does not occur while the furniture is manufactured. Company A should evaluate delivery under the Completed Performance model.

EXAMPLE 2

Facts: Company B charges users a fee for nonexclusive access to its web site containing proprietary databases. The fee allows access to the web site for a one-year period. After the customer is provided a user ID, there are no other specific actions Company B must perform related to an individual customer. Rather, Company B must only continue to allow the customer access to the databases.

Discussion: The only specific action Company B performs with respect to a customer is providing the customer a user ID. However, the customer receives value over the course of the year that access to the databases is provided. Therefore, Company B should evaluate delivery under the Proportional Performance model.

EXAMPLE 3

Facts: Company C, a telecommunications service provider, enters into an arrangement to sell its business customer a number of generic telephones and to provide basic telephone service for one year.

Discussion: The customer receives some value from the arrangement when the telephones are delivered and additional value over the year that service will be provided. Company C should therefore evaluate delivery of the telephones under the Completed Performance model and should evaluate delivery of the telephone service under the Proportional Performance model. Chapter 4, "Multiple-Deliverable Revenue Arrangements," should be consulted for purposes of determining whether the telephones and basic telephone service should be treated as separate units of accounting.

EXAMPLE 4

Facts: Company D provides training to corporate boards of directors on carrying out their responsibilities. When Company D gets a new client, it spends time learning about the company, its management personnel, and the industries in which it operates. Company D uses this information to customize the training course for that company's board of directors. Company D then delivers the training to the board during a day-long session.

Discussion: Company D performs several activities in the course of fulfilling its responsibilities, some of which involve the design of customer-specific content. However, the customer receives value only when the final act, the delivery of the training, occurs. Therefore, Company D should use the Completed Performance model to evaluate delivery for its transactions.

EXAMPLE 5

Facts: Company E publishes guidance on accounting for various transactions. Company E updates its materials once per year and prints a hard-copy book after each update. Customers either purchase the most recent hard-copy version of the materials or purchase online access to the information for one year.

Discussion: Customers who buy the hard-copy book receive value from the transaction when the book is delivered, and Company E has no further obligations once the book is delivered. However, online subscribers receive value throughout the year that access is provided, and Company E fulfills a portion of its obligation each day of the year. Therefore, the Completed Performance model is appropriate for sales of books, and the Proportional Performance model is appropriate for sales of online subscriptions.

Applying the Completed Performance Model

As noted above, the Completed Performance model is used when a single point in time can be identified at which the vendor completes its obligation. This should coincide with the point in time that the customer has realized value by obtaining an asset, the results of a service, or other benefits. Under this model, the delivery criterion is met, in total, at that particular point in time. Therefore, the Completed Performance model is used when performance takes place all at once or when it takes place over a period of time, but value is not transferred to the customer until the final act is completed. Because all revenue is recognized at that time, large differences in revenue for a financial reporting period can occur depending on whether delivery occurs just before or just after period-end.

In a product sale, performance generally is completed when the product is delivered to the customer. Determining exactly when that occurs, however, is not always straightforward. For example, when a product is shipped through the mail or by a third-party carrier, delivery may occur when the product leaves the seller's premises or when it arrives at the buyer's location, depending on the shipping terms. In other situations, a seller may retain certain risks and rewards so that performance is not actually complete, despite physical delivery. The resolution of these types of issues and uncertainties is required to apply the Completed Performance model to a product sale appropriately.

When the Completed Performance model is applied to a service transaction, it is generally because the final act of the service is the act that allows the customer to realize the benefits of the service. Therefore, if the Completed Performance model is appropriate for a service, the point at which delivery is deemed to occur (i.e., completion of the final act) must be identified.

In other transactions where the completed performance model is applied, the issues that are likely to be important for determining when to recognize revenue are similar to those in a product sale. The application of the Completed Performance model to various transactions is more fully discussed in Chapters 5–10.

Applying the Proportional Performance Model

In the Proportional Performance model, revenue is recognized as performance occurs, based on the relative value of the performance that has occurred to that point in time. This model is useful when the vendor fulfills its obligation over a period of time, and the customer receives value throughout the performance period.

In applying the Proportional Performance model to a service transaction, the key issue is generally the pattern of performance. For example, if a service transaction involves a specified number of similar acts, such as mowing a lawn once a week for an entire summer, an equal amount of revenue should be recognized upon completion of each act. However, when the acts are not similar, revenue should be allocated based on their relative values. In other situations, value may be transferred to a customer ratably over a period of time, such as when the service is insurance coverage or access to a health club. The application of the Proportional Performance model to various transactions is discussed more fully in Chapters 5–10.

FIXED OR DETERMINABLE FEE

Ensuring that a fee is fixed or determinable prior to revenue recognition is at the crux of the realizability criterion. For example, if the fee is dependent upon future events, it is unclear whether it will indeed be paid. As a result, it is uncertain whether the fee is realizable. However, a fee that is not fixed or determinable may also suggest that revenue has not yet been earned, if the seller is still required to perform in some manner.

Meaning of Fixed or Determinable

Although several pieces of accounting literature, including ASC 985-605, ASC 926-605, and ASC 605-10-S99 (SAB Topic 13), refer to the fixed or determinable fee criterion, there is no clear definition of fixed or determinable fees. Instead, the literature provides examples that illustrate certain concepts relevant to determining whether a fee is fixed or determinable.

Many arrangement terms raise questions about whether the fee is fixed or determinable. For example, customer rights of return or cancellation introduce uncertainty into the arrangement. Similarly, fees subject to change based upon the future success or failure of the work performed may indicate that a fee is not fixed or determinable. In addition, arrangements may have penalty or bonus clauses that introduce potential variability into the arrangements.

Whether a fee is fixed or determinable is not always an "all or nothing" answer. In many arrangements, a portion of the fee is not subject to change for any reason, while another portion may vary based on one or more factors. In these instances, the portion of the fee that is not subject to change should be considered fixed or determinable.

OBSERVATION: The requirement of a fixed or determinable fee refers to whether the fee can vary based upon future events. In certain situations, a fee that cannot change based upon future events may not be quantifiable until certain information related to past events is collated and evaluated. For example, consider an arrangement in which a company provides transaction processing services that are priced based on the number of transactions processed each month for its customers. Although the fee cannot change based on future events, the amount owed by customers at any point in time will only be determined after it has been calculated using activity reports from the company's various locations.

In situations like this, the fact that information about past events must be gathered and analyzed does not preclude a conclusion that the fee is fixed or determinable. Instead, the company should record its best estimate of the revenue at period-end and adjust that estimate when information is completely analyzed to calculate the precise fee amount. If this analysis is completed before the financial statements are released, it should be incorporated into those financial statements.[3]

Evaluating Terms That Allow for Variable Fees

Any term in an arrangement that could change the arrangement fee should be analyzed to determine whether that fee (in whole or in part) is fixed or determinable. Although the accounting literature provides no direct guidance on how to make such a determination, existing guidance and concepts applied in the accounting for related issues can be used to identify the following four categories of factors that might cause a fee to be variable:

1. *Factors within the customer's control.* For example, general return rights and incentive fees based on the customer's usage of a product.

2. *Factors within the seller's control.* For example, certain forms of price protection and bonuses relating to cumulative performance over the term of a contract.

---

[3] The analysis of information about events that occurred before the end of the accounting period is a "Recognized" subsequent event, as discussed in ASC 855-10-25-1. Recognized subsequent events are "subsequent events that provide additional evidence about conditions that existed at the date of the balance sheet, including the estimates inherent in the process of preparing financial statements."

3. *Factors within control of a specified third party.* For example, an agent's fee might be partially refundable based on whether the end customer exercises a right of return; or, a lessor might receive additional payments if the lessee exceeds certain sales levels (in this situation the additional lease payments are in control of the lessee's customers).

4. *Factors based on an index or other underlying.* For example, fees based on investment return as compared to an index, fees that vary with changes in the CPI or the inflation rate, and contingencies based on the weather.

Factors within the Customer's Control

General Rule

If an arrangement fee can be increased by future customer actions, the increase is not fixed or determinable until the customer takes the action. This is the case for a vendor that receives a bonus based on the usage of a delivered product or a licensor of intellectual property that is due a fee for each sale of a product incorporating the licensed technology. Thus, even if most customers do use the product or incorporate the licensed technology in the manner specified, revenue cannot be recognized until that usage or incorporation occurs.

OBSERVATION: Arrangements involving factors within the customer's control may be specified in different ways to achieve the same result. For example, an arrangement could entitle the seller to a $20,000 bonus if the customer uses the product more than 20 times in the first year. Alternatively, an economically similar arrangement could be created if the arrangement started with a $20,000 higher fee and specified that a penalty of $20,000 would occur if the customer did not use the product more than 20 times in the first year. Both of these arrangements should be accounted for as if the $20,000 at risk is not fixed or determinable until the customer uses the product 20 times.

There are other situations in which customer actions or rights could reduce the amount of revenue that will ultimately be realized by the seller. Volume or other rebates and rights of return are examples. When a customer has such a right, the portion of the fee at risk generally should not be considered fixed or determinable until the customer's right has expired.

Exception—Ability to Predict Actions

As noted above, fees subject to change based on customer actions are generally not considered fixed or determinable. However, there are some situations where customers' actions can be predicted. ASC 605-15-25-1 through 25-4, which addresses rights to return products, permit revenue recognition in certain circumstances based on predicted behavior as long as the estimate is reasonable and reliable. This guidance has been used by analogy, extending the application of such estimates to other rights as well. The exception, however, only applies when the customer's future action would reduce the fee. In other words, absent the customer's action, the fee would be higher.

Rights of return. When a customer has the right to receive a full refund by returning a product, the fee may not be fixed or determinable. Indeed, some might also suggest that there is no persuasive evidence of an arrangement under these circumstances. Nevertheless, despite the existence of such rights, revenue can often be recognized before the right of return expires. These rights have been specifically addressed in ASC 605-15-25, which concludes that revenue may be recognized upon delivery as long as a reliable estimate of returns can be made and certain other conditions are met. If a company enters into a large number of homogeneous transactions, a reliable estimate may be developed based on its historical experience. In this situation, the company must defer only revenue in the amount expected to be refunded. Further information about accounting for rights of return, including a discussion of factors that may indicate a reliable estimate of returns cannot be made, is provided in Chapter 5, "Product Deliverables."

Rights to cancel service transactions. In some service transactions, customers have a right (similar to a product return right)—to cancel the remainder of the service and receive a full refund (i.e., not just a refund based on the remaining service to be performed). This is common in the sale of certain memberships (such as warehouse club memberships) and may exist for a limited time in the sales of insurance policies, warranties, and similar items. The ASC does not provide guidance for cancellation rights in service transactions; the scope of ASC 605-15-25-1 through 25-4 is limited to product returns. However, the application of those concepts may allow a company to make reliable estimates of refunds or cancellations. When this is the case, recognition of revenue excluding the amount the company expects to refund is acceptable, although not required.

SEC REGISTRANT ALERT: In ASC 605-10-S99, A4a (question 1 of SAB Topic 13A4a), the SEC staff expressed its view that, while recognition of revenue based on a reliable estimate of cancellations may be acceptable, deferral of all revenue until the refund period ends is preferable in these situations.

Other service transactions may include a right to cancel the remainder of the service for a pro-rata refund (i.e., a refund of only a portion of the fee) based on the proportion of the service remaining to be provided. In these situations, the fee becomes fixed or determinable ratably throughout the service period, as the amount of the refund the customer could receive decreases. Because the service is delivered on a proportional basis throughout the period, these types of cancellation rights generally do not cause further delays in revenue recognition.

Additional information about the accounting for service cancellation rights, including a discussion of factors that may indicate a reliable estimate of refunds cannot be made, is provided in Chapter 6, "Service Deliverables."

Coupons and rebates. Certain revenue arrangements give the customer the ability to send in a form or other documentation of their purchase to obtain a full or partial rebate of the purchase price (e.g., a $20 mail-in rebate found in the box of a computer printer). In other arrangements, a vendor may sell products to a retailer and also issue coupons to the retailers' customers (e.g., a newspaper coupon for 50 cents off a box of cereal). In both of these instances, the fee from the sale can change after the seller has performed under the arrangement. In general, the existence of a coupon or rebate indicates that the purchase price is not fixed or determinable.

Redemption rates on coupons and rebates are much lower than 100%. Therefore ASC 605-50 concludes that revenue potentially subject to rebate or refund may be recognized as long as a reliable estimate of usage can be made. The following factors may impair a company's ability to make a reasonable estimate of coupon or rebate redemptions (ASC 605-15-25-3):

- Significant possibility of external factors, such as obsolescence or regulatory changes, affecting the product;
- A long offer period;
- A lack of relevant historical experience; and
- An absence of a large volume of relatively homogeneous transactions.

Other sales incentives involve an offer to rebate or refund a specified amount of cash only if the customer makes a specified cumulative level of purchases or remains a customer for a minimum time period. Like rebates that are exercisable based on a single purchase, revenue subject to volume rebates may be recognized based on an estimate, as long as the estimate is reasonable and reliable.

If a reliable estimate of the rebate liability cannot be made for either single or volume purchases, the related revenue is not considered fixed or determinable. As a result, this revenue cannot be recognized until the rebate rights lapse.

Further information about the accounting for rebate rights, including a more detailed discussion of factors that may indicate a reliable estimate of rebates cannot be made, is included in Chapter 8, "Miscellaneous Issues."

EXAMPLE: ESTIMATE OF REBATE LIABILITY

Abaxis, Inc. Form 10-K—Fiscal Year Ended March 31, 2011

Distributor and Customer Rebates

We offer distributor pricing rebates and customer incentives, such as cash rebates, from time to time. The distributor pricing rebates are offered to distributors upon meeting the sales volume requirements during a qualifying period and are recorded as a reduction to gross revenues during a qualifying period. Cash rebates are offered to distributors or customers who purchase certain products or instruments during a promotional period and are recorded as a reduction to gross revenues.

The distributor pricing rebate program is offered to distributors in the North America veterinary market, upon meeting the sales volume requirements of veterinary products during the qualifying period. Factors used in the rebate calculations include the identification of products sold subject to a rebate during the qualifying period and which rebate percentage applies. Based on these factors and using historical trends, adjusted for current changes, we estimate the amount of the rebate that will be paid and record the liability as a reduction to gross revenues when we record the sale of the product. Settlement of the rebate accruals from the date of sale ranges from one to nine months after sale. Changes in the rebate accrual at each fiscal year end are based upon distributors meeting the purchase requirements during the quarter. Other rebate programs offered to distributors or customers vary from period to period in the medical and veterinary markets.

The following table summarizes the change in total accrued distributor and customer rebates (in thousands):

Year Ended	Balance at Beginning of Year	Provisions	Payments	Balance at End of Year
March 31, 2011	$ 48	$694	$(331)	$411
March 31, 2010	$ 96	$268	$(316)	$ 48
March 31, 2009	$140	$294	$(338)	$ 96

Other situations. The concept of reliably predicting customer actions has only been addressed in the specific situations discussed above. Analogizing to ASC 605-15-25-1 through 25-4, ASC 605-10-S99, A4a (question 1 of SAB Topic 13A4a), or ASC 605-50 may be appropriate in a limited number of other situations.

However, no amount of evidence is sufficient to allow the recognition of revenue that will be received if a customer takes a specific action in the future. For example, if a fee in a license arrangement is $100 for a three-month license, and the customer has an option to extend the license to one year for an additional $50, the $50 extension fee cannot be considered fixed or determinable until the option is exercised, no matter how likely it is that the extension will be exercised. (Note that although the extension fee is not fixed or determinable, the customer's right to purchase an extension at a seemingly discounted rate is likely a second deliverable in the arrangement, such that a portion of the $100 fee would be allocated to the option. See Chapter 4, "Multiple-Deliverable Revenue Arrangements.")

Factors within the Seller's Control

In some cases, the fee in an arrangement may vary based upon the seller's performance. For example, in an arrangement to deliver a large amount of equipment, there may be fixed fees for the equipment, plus a bonus payment if the seller completes all deliveries (or a penalty if the seller does not complete all deliveries) within a specified period. In other situations, a seller may offer price protection to the buyer by agreeing to return a portion of the arrangement fee if the seller subsequently sells the same product or service to another customer at a lower price.

General Rule

The fee may not be fixed or determinable if it depends on the seller's future actions. For example, if a seller can earn a bonus by completing a service ahead of schedule, that bonus should not be recognized until the service is completed ahead of schedule and the bonus is earned.

> **OBSERVATION:** Arrangements like this may be specified in different ways to achieve the same result. For example, an arrangement could entitle the seller to a $20,000 bonus if the service is completed by a particular date. Alternatively, an economically similar arrangement could be created if it started with a $20,000 higher fee and specified that the seller would be penalized $20,000 if it did not finish by the same date. Both of these arrangements should be accounted for as if the $20,000 at risk is not fixed or determinable until the project is completed by the specified date.

Exception—Ability to Predict or Control Actions

ASC 605-15-25-1 through 25-4 and related literature provide exceptions that permit revenue recognition when future customer actions can change the arrangement fee. Because a seller's actions are easier to predict than a customer's, a lower threshold of evidence is required. However, if a reliable estimate cannot be made—for example, because the arrangement is unique or contains atypical performance criteria—the vendor's future actions should be interpreted such that they result in the least amount of revenue recognized by the vendor. The accounting literature provides specific guidance on this topic in certain situations.

Conditional rights of return. Revenue attributable to delivered items in an arrangement may be refundable if the seller fails to deliver some or all of the other items in the arrangement. The accounting for conditional rights of return in multiple-deliverable arrangements is discussed in Chapter 4, "Multiple-Deliverable Revenue Arrangements."

Price protection based solely on sellers' prices. Sellers may agree to refund a portion of the purchase price to customers if the sellers' standard prices decrease. Because the seller will determine whether to lower its prices, it may be possible to estimate the effect of this price protection. When this is the case, a vendor may conclude that the fee is fixed in whole or in part. However, if the vendor has shown an inability to predict price decreases or an inability to keep its prices at preferred levels (perhaps due to aggressive competition), then the fee should not be considered fixed or determinable (ASC 985-605-25-36).

Exception—Recognition Based on Current Measurements

In some cases, a service provider may agree to a time-based fee arrangement. For example, a hotel manager may agree to compensation based partially on the hotel's operating income for a calendar year or a sales agent may be entitled to a bonus if he or she increases sales by a certain percentage relative to the prior year. In these situations, the question is whether any portion of the incentive fee is fixed or determinable before the end of the measurement period. The SEC staff commented on this situation in ASC 605-20-S99 and indicated that such fees may be considered fixed and determinable at any point in time (using the formula and contract terms at that date) even if the vendor cannot predict the results of its future actions. Nonetheless, the SEC staff noted a preference for the conclusion that the incentive fee is not fixed or determinable until the end of the measurement period.

OBSERVATION: In an arrangement where a bonus or additional fee is earned upon meeting a particular threshold, no part of the bonus or additional fee is fixed or determinable until the threshold is met, even if the progress to date indicates that this will occur. Recognition at interim dates would be acceptable only if there are termination provisions that call for a final measurement based on progress to date (ASC 605-10-S99, A4c) (SAB Topic 13A4c).

DISCLOSURE ALERT: See Chapter 12, "Disclosures," for information about required disclosures.

ILLUSTRATION: ACCOUNTING FOR FEES BASED ON A FORMULA

Facts: Investment Advisor A manages Fund B and is paid a flat fee per month, plus 20% of Fund B's returns in excess of 12% annually. The contract may be terminated by either party with reasonable notice at the end of each quarter. In the event of a termination, the amount due for the incentive fee will be calculated as of the termination date based on the fund returns to date by comparing them with a 12% annual return prorated for the portion of the year that has passed.

Assume that Fund B's returns exceed the annual target by $120,000 in the first quarter, $60,000 in the second quarter, $50,000 in the fourth quarter, and are $80,000 less than the target in the third quarter. Thus, the total return of Fund B for the year exceeds the 12% target return by $150,000. Advisor A's 20% share of the $150,000 is $30,000.

Discussion: Advisor A may choose from two accounting policies. The first is not to recognize incentive fee revenue until the end of the one-year measurement period under the theory that none of it is fixed or determinable until then because future poor performance in a subsequent interim period could decrease the incentive fee revenue earned in a prior interim period. This method, which is preferred by the SEC staff, would result in the recognition of $30,000 in incentive fee income on the last day of the year.

The second method is to record incentive fee revenue as the amount that would be due under the formula at the point in time when the contract could be terminated—in this example, at the end of the quarter. Accordingly, Advisor A would record $24,000 of incentive fee revenue in the first quarter and $12,000 in the second quarter. In the third quarter, however, $16,000 of the previously recognized revenue would be reversed. Finally, $10,000 of incentive fee revenue would be recognized in the fourth quarter.

Factors within Control of a Third Party

Certain contracts have fees that vary based on the actions of a party other than the buyer or seller (e.g., agency contracts). For example, a sales agent may agree to refund its commission if the end customer returns the product. Alternatively, the agent may receive a bonus if a customer the agent introduces to the supplier makes additional purchases from the supplier or renews his or her subscription. Other arrangements, particularly if they are long-term in nature, may contain pricing terms that vary with changes in tax law or industry regulations.

General Rule

Third-party actions are likely to be even more difficult to predict than customer actions. As a result, it is not appropriate to assume that third parties will take actions resulting in additional payments from the customer to the vendor in an arrangement. However, if a third party can take an action that reduces a company's revenue, it is generally appropriate to assume the third party will take such an action.

For example, in an operating lease that provides for additional rent when sales exceed a certain level, the lessor should not recognize this additional amount until the specified level of sales is reached, even if sales trends suggest that this will occur. Similarly, an agent whose fee is at risk if the end customer cancels its arrangement with the seller should generally not recognize the fee as revenue until the end customer's cancellation right lapses.

Exception—Ability to Predict Actions

Third-party cancellation and return rights. Revenue recognition is acceptable in arrangements that include certain third-party return or cancellation rights as long as the amount of refunds can be reliably estimated. The criteria to determine the reliability of these estimates are similar to those required for estimating cancellations in other service transactions (e.g., using the existence of a large pool of homogeneous transactions to derive the estimate). Further discussion on estimating cancellations in these situations is included in Chapter 6, "Service Deliverables."

Price-matching. Certain retailers, such as electronic stores, routinely offer a form of price protection based on their competitors' prices. These retailers offer, for example, to refund the difference between the price paid by a customer and a lower price on the same product offered by a competitor within the next 30 days. Unlike price protection based on the particular vendor's future prices, estimating the effects of a price-matching offer is likely to be very difficult. However, if a sufficient history exists and the competitive environment is stable, it may be possible to estimate the effects of a price-matching policy. If reliable estimates can be made, revenue may be recognized net of the expected price-matching payments. If a reliable estimate cannot be made, as is likely to be the case, no revenue should be recognized until the price-matching period ends.

ILLUSTRATION: THIRD-PARTY ACTIONS AND FIXED OR DETERMINABLE FEES

(Adapted from ASC 605-10-S99, A4a, ques. 2 (SAB Topic 13A4a, ques. 2))

EXAMPLE 1:   A leasing broker's commission from the lessor upon a commercial tenant's signing of a lease agreement is refundable under lessor cancellation privileges if the tenant fails to move into the leased premises by a specified date.

EXAMPLE 2:   A talent agent's fee receivable from its principal (a celebrity) for arranging an endorsement for a five-year term is cancelable by the celebrity if the customer breaches the endorsement contract with the celebrity.

EXAMPLE 3:   An insurance agent's commission received from the insurer upon selling an insurance policy is entirely refundable for the 30-day period required by state law, and it is subsequently refundable on a declining pro rata basis until the consumer has made six monthly payments.

Discussion: In all of these cases, the arrangement fee can vary based upon the actions of a third party named in the contract. Thus, absent a large volume of homogeneous transactions sufficient to allow a reliable estimate of the effects of these rights, the fee in question should only be recognized as the third party takes actions or as the right to take these actions lapses.

Because of the unique nature of the transactions in Examples 1 and 2, it is unlikely that such a large volume of homogeneous transactions would exist to allow for a reliable estimate of cancellations.

However, in Example 3, a sufficient history may exist. Therefore, the company should evaluate whether it has sufficient evidence to make a reliable estimate of cancellations and thereby recognize revenue. If a sufficient history does not exist, no revenue should be recognized until the 30-day full refund period has lapsed. The revenue would then become fixed or determinable on a ratable basis until the customer has made six payments.

Exception—Regulators' Approval of Rate Increases

In some cases, a regulated company, such as a utility, is permitted to bill requested rate increases before the regulator has ruled on the request. The fact that the regulator has the power to deny the request raises a question about whether the possible increased rates are fixed or determinable. The FASB addressed this question in the context of regulated businesses within the scope of ASC 980. The FASB concluded that contingent refundability should be treated as a collectibility issue rather than a fixed or determinable issue. Thus, the criteria in ASC 450-20-25 would determine whether a provision for estimated refunds should be recognized (see "Collectibility" in this chapter).

Exception—Fees at Risk Due to Changes in Law or Regulation

When the third-party action that could change the arrangement fee is a legal or regulatory change, it is generally appropriate to assume that no such change will occur. Thus, revenue should be recognized on the basis of existing laws and regulations. For example, in providing guidance on the effects of potential changes in tax law on income tax calculations, ASC 740, *Income Taxes*; 740-10-25-47, specifically prohibits the assumption of any changes until they are enacted. However, if changes that would result in a reduced fee are considered probable, a reserve for refunds may be required under ASC 450-20-25-2.

Other Exceptions

If unique circumstances make it unlikely that the portion of the fee at risk will actually be lost, it may be possible to conclude that the fee is fixed or determinable, despite the existence of the contingency. Each set of facts and circumstances should be carefully analyzed to determine whether this is the case.

ILLUSTRATION: FEE MAY VARY BASED ON THIRD-PARTY ACTIONS

Facts: Company X acts as a sales representative for Company Y. Company X's commission is earned on a sliding scale such that its commission on the first 10,000 units of Company Y's products sold in a year is $5 per unit and the commission for each unit beyond that is $7 per unit. Company X has been selling Company Y's products for several years and has always sold at least 20,000 units. At the end of the first quarter, Company X has sold 5,000 units of Company Y's product and collected $25,000 from Company Y. Company X believes that it will sell approximately 5,000 units per quarter for the rest of the year.

Discussion: Company X believes that it will eventually realize $120,000 in commissions during the year (10,000 units at $5, plus another 10,000 units at $7), an average of $6 per unit, and has historical experience that supports this estimate. Therefore, Company X may believe that it should record a receivable of $5,000 at the end of the first quarter, in addition to the revenue it has already collected. However, whether Company X meets its estimated sales is at least partially in control of third parties, that is, the customers who purchase Company Y's product. The additional revenue is not fixed or determinable and Company X should only recognize the $25,000 it has collected as revenue in the first quarter. Revenue attributable to additional sales should be recorded only when those sales occur.

Factors Based on an Index

Many leases have rent escalation clauses tied to the inflation rate or consumer price index. Other arrangements, such as those to deliver commodities, may include fees that vary based on the market price of the commodity on a particular date. These are examples of factors unrelated to a specific party's actions that may nonetheless cause an arrangement fee to be variable.

PRACTICE ALERT: Some sales arrangements include embedded rights and obligations that may meet the definition of a derivative in ASC 815-10-15. Depending on their nature and economic relationship to the remainder of the arrangement, these embedded features may have to be accounted for separately, similar to a freestanding derivative. Such an embedded derivative is subject to the same accounting requirements as a freestanding derivative, and the remaining host arrangement is accounted for using applicable revenue recognition principles.

Like the other types of variable fees discussed previously, fees that vary based upon future changes in an index or other underlying may not be fixed or determinable, because it is generally not appropriate to recognize revenue using predictions of future events. However, as noted above, there are situations where it is permissible to recognize revenue based on predictions of future customer, seller, or third-party actions, particularly when a sufficient body of evidence exists such that reliable estimates can be made. This evidence, however, does not usually exist to predict future changes in an index or other underlying. Therefore, revenue should be recognized in these situations based on the then-current measurement, which assumes no future increases or decreases. The effects of changes in the index or underlying should be recognized as soon as such changes occur (ASC 840-10-55-11).

Fees Affected by Multiple Factors

Many arrangements have fees that can vary based on multiple factors, each of which may be under the control of a different party or tied to a different index. In general, each factor should be evaluated separately, with revenue being recognized only if none of the factors preclude the fee from being considered fixed or determinable.

EXHIBIT 3-1: FIXED OR DETERMINABLE FEES

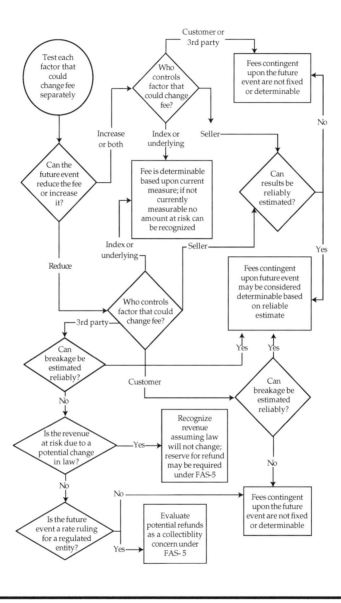

COLLECTIBILITY

The final condition that must be met before revenue can be recognized is that collection of the fee must be reasonably assured. Clearly, when a fee is uncollectible, no revenue should be recognized, as the company will not receive an economic benefit from the arrangement.

The accounting literature, however, does not provide specific criteria that should be used to evaluate whether collection is reasonably assured. The same factors used to develop a bad debt reserve for accounts receivable also should be helpful in determining whether collection of an arrangement fee is reasonably assured. This evaluation should be performed when the other three conditions for revenue recognition are met.

Accounting if Collectibility Is Not Reasonably Assured

If collectibility is not reasonably assured at the time the other three revenue recognition conditions are met, revenue should not be recognized until collection becomes reasonably assured or occurs. In general, the direct costs of the transaction should be expensed as if revenue had been recognized. When collection has been deemed less than reasonably assured, such costs generally will not meet the definition of an asset and should not be capitalized or recorded on the balance sheet.[4]

EXAMPLE: COLLECTIBILITY NOT REASONABLY ASSURED

Bassett Furniture Industries, Inc. Form 10-K—Fiscal Year Ended Nov. 27, 2010

Staff Accounting Bulletin No. 104, *Revenue Recognition* ("SAB 104") outlines the four basic criteria for recognizing revenue as follows: (1) persuasive evidence of an arrangement exists, (2) delivery has occurred or services have been rendered, (3) the seller's price to the buyer is fixed or determinable, and (4) collectibility is reasonably assured. SAB 104 further asserts that if collectability of all or a portion of the revenue is not reasonably assured, revenue recognition should be deferred until payment is received. During fiscal 2010, 2009 and 2008 there were seven, thirteen and five dealers, respectively, for which these criteria were not met and therefore revenue was being recognized on a cost recovery basis. As of November 27, 2010, November 28, 2009, and November 29, 2008 there were two, seven, and five dealers, respectively, that remained on the cost recovery basis. The following table details the total revenue and cost deferred:

	2010	2009	2008
Revenue deferred	$947	$7,149	$2,215
Cost deferred	$663	$5,004	$1,551

Uncollectible Amounts and Bad Debts

It is important to evaluate collectibility before revenue is initially recognized so that collectibility problems existing before revenue recognition can be separated from similar problems that arise later. If collection is not reasonably assured at the inception of the arrangement, no revenue would be recognized. If collection is reasonably assured initially and revenue is recognized but subsequent events require a change in the accounts receivable reserve or write-off, the related bad debt expense should be adjusted accordingly. See Chapter 11, "Presentation," for a discussion of income statement classification of bad debt expense.

---

[4] In rare circumstances, recognition of revenue and costs under the installment or cost recovery methods may be appropriate (ASC 605-10-25-3 and 25-4). However, the use of these methods is usually limited to sales of real estate (ASC 360-20-40-27 through 40-34).

EVALUATING THE REVENUE RECOGNITION CONDITIONS

Arrangement-by-Arrangement Analysis

When evaluating the four conditions discussed in this chapter, it is important to consider all aspects of the arrangement. To accomplish this, the contracts underlying the arrangement should be reviewed in detail to ensure that all contractual terms are properly interpreted. For most companies, this review should begin with the company's standard sales contract. However, any modifications to the standard contract must be evaluated for their effects on revenue recognition. Modifications to standard contracts could require a company to recognize revenue differently for each contract. For example, if a company sells products with different shipping (or FOB) terms, revenue on those shipped FOB Shipping Point may generally be recognized upon shipment, while revenue on those shipped FOB Destination may not be recognized until the customer receives the products. Similarly, different customer acceptance provisions or cancellation rights in various contracts may cause otherwise similar contracts to be accounted for differently.

PRACTICE POINTER: Many provisions can affect the timing of revenue recognition. Therefore, companies should have controls in place to limit the types of provisions that sales personnel can add to the standard contract. In addition, controls should be in place to ensure that all sales contracts are reviewed by accounting personnel who can appropriately evaluate whether any nonstandard terms will affect revenue recognition.

All Contractual Terms Must Be Considered

Some companies use contracts that contain terms that customers generally ignore in practice. For example, a contract may include customer acceptance provisions that allow the customer to have an equipment vendor's engineering staff on-site for a period of time after installation of the equipment. However, as long as installation goes smoothly, customers may not take advantage of this right. In other situations, an arrangement may provide the customer with the right to a certain amount of service, but history may show that customers on average do not use the maximum amount of service to which they are entitled. This often occurs, for example, in wireless telephone plans that provide a basket of monthly minutes.

In most situations, delivery should be evaluated under the assumption that the vendor will have to fulfill all of its obligations under the arrangement, including those that are only to be performed if requested by the customer.

Exception—Ability to Estimate Breakage

However, if the company has significant historical experience with a large volume of homogeneous contracts that include similar terms and that experience allows the company to reliably estimate what portion of the deliverables will not ultimately be requested by the customer, it is acceptable to take this "breakage" into account in recognizing revenue. To support this, there must be significant objective evidence available to support a conclusion that obligations will not have to be fulfilled.

Even if sufficient evidence exists to estimate breakage, it should be an extremely rare occurrence where consideration of breakage results in immediate income recognition. Instead, the arrangement fee should be recognized as the products or services are delivered to the customer over the performance period. For example, consider a situation in which a customer prepays $10,000 for 100 hours of professional services to be provided over the course of one year, but the professional services provider has sufficient history and experience to demonstrate that the customer will ultimately demand only 80 hours of services. In this situation, the professional services provider may adopt an accounting policy that would result in recognizing the $10,000 of revenue over the 80 hours of services as they are rendered—$125 per hour of service rendered. Alternatively, the professional services provider may adopt an accounting policy that would result in recognizing $8,000 of revenue over the 80 hours of services as they are rendered and $2,000 of breakage income upon expiration of the arrangement. However, the professional services provider may not adopt an accounting policy that would result in recognizing $2,000 of breakage income upon initiation of the arrangement and $8,000 of revenue over the 80 hours of services as they are rendered. To do so would be to recognize revenue before performance has occurred.

SEC REGISTRANT ALERT: Generally, the SEC staff has stated that the derecognition guidance of ASC 405-20 governs the accounting treatment for the situation in which a customer might not hold a seller to its obligations under the contract. That would lead to recognizing revenue related to breakage only when the contract expires. However, in a December 5, 2005, speech at the 2005 AICPA National Conference on Current SEC and PCAOB Developments, the SEC staff indicated that derecognition may also be acceptable when the vendor can demonstrate that it is remote that the customer will require performance. The staff discussed the application of this concept to sales of gift cards, some percentage of which would not be redeemed. One policy that would always be acceptable would to recognized breakage only when the potential obligation legally expires. However, the staff indicated that expected breakage could be taken into account before the obligation legally expires if the reporting entity could reliable estimate expected breakage. In that case, breakage could either be recognized by recognizing revenue as expected performance (net of expected breakage) occurs, or when the likelihood of the customer requesting additional performance is considered remote.

EXAMPLE: ESTIMATE OF BREAKAGE

Limited Brands Form 10-K—Fiscal Year Ended January 30, 2010

The Company's brands sell gift cards with no expiration dates to customers. The Company does not charge administrative fees on unused gift cards. The Company recognizes income from gift cards when they are redeemed by the customer. In addition, the Company recognizes income on unredeemed gift cards when it can determine that the likelihood of the gift card being redeemed is remote and that there is no legal obligation to remit the unredeemed gift cards to relevant jurisdictions (gift card breakage). The Company determines the gift card breakage rate based on historical redemption patterns. The Company accumulated enough historical data to determine the gift card breakage rate at Bath & Body Works during the fourth quarter of 2005 and Victoria's Secret during the fourth quarter of 2007. Gift card breakage is included in Net Sales in the Consolidated Statements of Income.

During the fourth quarter of 2007, the Company recognized $48 million in pre-tax income related to the initial recognition of gift card breakage at Victoria's Secret.

EXAMPLE: RELIABLE ESTIMATE OF BREAKAGE

Learning Tree Form 10-K—Fiscal Year Ended October 2, 2009

Revenue Recognition

We offer our customers a multiple-course sales discount referred to as a Learning Tree Training Passport. A Learning Tree Training Passport allows an individual Passport holder to attend up to a specified number of courses over a one- to two-year period for a fixed price. For a Training Passport, the amount of revenue recognized for each course attendance is based upon the selling price of the Training Passport, the list price of the course taken, the weighted average list price of all courses taken and the estimated average number of courses Passport holders will actually attend. Upon expiration of each individual Training Passport, we record the difference, if any, between the revenues previously recognized and that specific Training Passport's selling price. The estimated attendance rate is based upon the historical experience of the average number of course events that Training Passport holders have been attending. The actual Training Passport attendance rate is reviewed at least semi-annually, and if the Training Passport attendance rates change, the revenue recognition rate for active Training Passports and for Training Passports sold thereafter is adjusted prospectively.

We believe it is appropriate to recognize revenues on this basis in order to most closely match revenue and related costs, as the substantial majority of our Passport holders do not attend the maximum number of course events permitted under their Training Passports. We believe that the use of recent historical data is reasonable and appropriate because of the relative stability of the average actual number of course events attended by Passport holders.

The average actual attendance rate for all expired Training Passports has closely approximated the estimated rate we utilize. Although we have seen no material changes in the historical rates as the number of course titles has changed, we monitor such potential effects. In general, determining the estimated average number of course events that will be attended by a Training Passport holder is based on historical trends that may not continue in the future. These estimates could differ in the near term from amounts used in arriving at the reported revenue. If the estimates are wrong, we would record the difference between the revenues previously recognized for that Training Passport and the Training Passport selling price upon expiration of that Training Passport. Thus, the timing of revenue recognition may be affected by an inaccurate estimation, but the inaccuracy would have no effect on the aggregate revenue recognized over the one- to two-year life of each Training Passport.

For newer Passport products for which historical utilization data is not available, we assume that the estimated average number of courses to be attended is equal to the number of courses available on the Passport. This assumed utilization rate may be revised in future periods after sufficient time has passed to amass historical trends.

Multiple Contracts and Side Letters

Most of the time, the boundaries of an arrangement are clearly defined by the contract between the parties. However, to ensure that all appropriate terms are considered prior to revenue recognition, it may be necessary to evaluate multiple contracts as part of a single arrangement. For example, a contract for the sale of products may not specifically provide any rights of return. However, the existence of a master supply agreement with the same customer may grant that customer significant return rights on all purchases.

In other situations, a company may enter into a side letter with the customer that effectively amends the contract between the parties and grants the customer additional rights, requires the seller to provide additional products or services, or alters the payment terms. Any revenue accounting process must consider such a side letter in order to facilitate a thorough analysis.

SEC REGISTRANT ALERT: In early 2003, the SEC staff issued the Report Pursuant to Section 704 of the Sarbanes-Oxley Act of 2002 (Section 704 Report). In compiling the information in the Section 704 Report, the SEC staff studied enforcement actions filed during the period July 31, 1997, through July 30, 2002. The greatest number of enforcement actions related to improper revenue recognition. A common theme in these enforcement actions related to side letters that were not considered, or inappropriately considered, in recognizing revenue. This is a strong indication that more attention should be given to uncovering the existence and understanding the terms of side agreements and the effects they have on revenue recognition. (Also see SEC FRR 23, *The Significance of Oral Guarantees to the Financial Reporting Process.*)

Further guidance on combining contracts for revenue recognition purposes, including factors that should be considered in deciding whether to combine contracts, is included in Chapter 4, "Multiple-Deliverable Revenue Arrangements."

Noncontractual Terms

Although the rights and obligations of both parties to a revenue arrangement are often contractually documented, there are some situations where rights and obligations are established by common business practice, local law, or custom. For example, rights of return are often unspecified in a sales arrangement, but nonetheless offered for a limited time if the customer is not satisfied. Similarly, products that are not covered by a written warranty will often be replaced or repaired by the seller if they do not function properly. All such rights and obligations should be considered in the revenue recognition process.

CHAPTER 4
MULTIPLE-DELIVERABLE REVENUE ARRANGEMENTS

CONTENTS

BACKGROUND

Companies frequently enter into arrangements with their customers that call for multiple actions, such as delivering one or more products, providing services, granting a license or other right, and (or) taking (or refraining from taking) certain actions. Arrangements that obligate the seller to do multiple things are generally referred to as "multiple-deliverable revenue arrangements." These arrangements can be as simple as the sale of a shirt and pants (two product deliverables) or as complex as a hospital construction contract that includes the installation of sophisticated diagnostic tools, the sale of related software and a contract to operate the hospital upon completion.

Multiple-deliverable arrangements where the various performance obligations are delivered at different times give rise to an accounting issue that has generated significant consternation—whether and how to allocate the arrangement consideration among the various deliverables.

SURVEY OF ACCOUNTING LITERATURE

Some industry and transaction-specific areas of GAAP include assistance on how to account for arrangements with multiple deliverables that fall within the scope of that literature. In addition, ASC 605-25, which was originally added to GAAP by EITF 00-21 and then significantly modified by ASU 2009-13, provides guidance on accounting for multiple-deliverable arrangements. All of this literature generally relies on the same underlying principles to determine whether the deliverables can be treated separately for accounting purposes.

REVENUE RECOGNITION LITERATURE

ASC	ASC Topic/Subtopic	Publication	Subject
605-10-S99	Revenue Recognition/Overall	SAB Topic 13	Revenue Recognition
N/A	N/A	CON-5	Recognition and Measurement in Financial Statements of Business Enterprises
N/A	N/A	CON-6	Elements of Financial Statements
952-605	Franchisors/ Revenue Recognition	FAS-45	Accounting for Franchise Fee Revenue
605-15-25-1	Revenue Recognition/ Products	FAS-48	Revenue Recognition When Right of Return Exists
360-20	Property, Plant, and Equipment/Real Estate Sales	FAS-66	Accounting for Sales of Real Estate

ASC	ASC Topic/Subtopic	Publication	Subject
460	Guarantees	FIN-45	Guarantees
460-10-55-31	Guarantees/Overall	FSP FIN 45-1	Licensee Indemnifications
605-20-25-1	Revenue Recognition/ Services	FTB 90-1	Separately Priced Extended Warranty and Product Maintenance Contracts
605-35	Revenue Recognition/ Construction-Type and Production- Type Contracts	SOP 81-1	Accounting for Performance of Construction-Type and Certain Production-Type Contracts
985-605	Software/Revenue Recognition	SOP 97-2, EITF 03-5 and ASU 2009-14	Software Revenue Recognition
926-605	Entertainment— Films/Revenue Recognition	SOP 00-2	Accounting by Producers or Distributors of Films
605-20-25-8	Revenue Recognition/ Services	EITF 85-20	Recognition of Fees for Guaranteeing a Loan
605-25	Revenue Recognition/ Multiple-Element Arrangements	EITF 00-21 and ASU 2009-13	Revenue Arrangements with Multiple Deliverables
985-605-55-4	Software/Revenue Recognition	TPA 5100.39	Combining Separate Software Customer Contracts

SUPPORTING LITERATURE

ASC	ASC Topic/Subtopic	Publication	Subject
450-20	Contingencies/Loss Contingencies	FAS-5	Loss Contingencies
840	Leases	FAS-13	Leases
815	Derivatives and Hedging	FAS-133	Derivatives and Hedging
820	Fair Value Measurements and Disclosures	FAS-157	Define and Measure Fair Value
815-10-15-8 and 15-9	Derivatives and Hedging/Overall	FAS-133 Guide	Combining Separate Financial Contracts
840-10-15	Leases/Overall	EITF 01-8	Determining Whether an Arrangement Contains a Lease

OVERVIEW

CON-5 sets forth the guidance that revenue should be recognized when it is both realized (or realizable) and earned. In discussing the "earned" criterion, CON-5 goes on to say, "revenues are considered to have been earned when the entity has substantially accomplished what it must do to be entitled to the benefits represented by the revenues" (CON-5, par. 83b). While there is usually little doubt as to when this has occurred, the concept is not as easily applied to multiple-deliverable arrangements. A harsh interpretation of the CON-5 discussion would not permit revenue recognition until a seller has completed all of its obligations in a multiple-deliverable arrangement (no matter how long that takes). The accounting literature, however, recognizes that a deliverable *may* represent a separate earnings process that provides value to the customer, even if there are other items in the arrangement. The discussion of separating multiple-deliverable arrangements into different units of accounting focuses on whether conditions are such that separation is appropriate, and, if so, how to allocate the revenue to the separate units.

There are actually a number of different models that are used to determine when to separate deliverables in a multiple-deliverable arrangement and how to allocate revenue to those deliverables if they are separated. Most of the models were developed with a particular kind of transaction in mind, and therefore apply to only very narrow groupings of transactions. For the vast majority of multiple-deliverable arrangements, there was no guidance on separating deliverables in a multiple-deliverable arrangement until 2002 when the EITF finished its deliberations of EITF 00-21. The guidance originally published in EITF 00-21 was updated and amended significantly by the conclusions published in ASU 2009-13. These two pronouncements established the bulk of current guidance on multiple-deliverable revenue arrangements, which is included in ASC 605-25.

ASC 605-25 covers the separation of deliverables in a multiple-element arrangement and the allocation of revenue to the separate units of accounting. However, ASC 605-25 does not replace or override transaction- or industry-based guidance that covers those topics. To the extent such other literature applies and addresses some of the multiple-deliverable questions, that literature should be used to deal with the questions covered and ASC 605-25 should be used for the other issues. This is discussed further in a subsequent section of this chapter titled, "Determining the Model to Apply."

As mentioned above, most arrangements will fall within the scope of ASC 605-25. Under that model, delivered items should be considered a separate unit of accounting to which revenue may be allocated if and only if:

1. The *delivered item(s)* has value to the customer on a standalone basis. Standalone value exists if the deliverable is sold separately by the vendor or if the customer could resell the delivered item on a standalone basis. Satisfaction of this condition does not depend on the existence of an observable market for the deliverable.

2. If the arrangement includes a general right of return related to the delivered item, delivery or performance of the *undelivered item(s)* is considered probable and substantially in the control of the vendor.

If those two criteria are met, the amount of revenue allocated to the delivered item(s) is to be determined based on the relative selling price(s) of the items in the arrangement, with the exception that revenue allocated to delivered items cannot be greater than the amount the vendor would expect to collect (or retain) if the vendor becomes unable to fulfill the remainder of the contract. This chapter goes into further detail about each of these provisions.

DEFINING THE ARRANGEMENT

Generally, each contract is analyzed separately for the purpose of identifying deliverables and determining how to recognize revenue. However, it may be necessary to combine two or more contracts when the *substance of the arrangement* would be distorted by accounting for the contracts separately.

When various deliverables of what is substantively a single arrangement are documented in multiple contracts, these contracts must be combined and evaluated as one multiple-deliverable arrangement. There is a presumption that separate contracts with the same entity or related parties entered into at or near the same time have been negotiated as a package and should therefore be evaluated as a single arrangement (ASC 605-25-25-3).

GAAP provides additional guidance on determining when it is appropriate to combine certain types of contracts. For example, ASC 985-605-55-4 addresses the combination of contracts in software revenue recognition (see Chapter 10, "Software—A Complete Model"). In addition, ASC 815-10-15-8 and 15-9 deal with the combination of separate contracts for the purposes of applying the derivatives and hedging literature.

The underlying principles of these parts of GAAP are logical guidelines to use in evaluating whether separate revenue contracts should be combined and evaluated as one arrangement. Based on those principles, the following is a non-exhaustive list of factors that should be used to determine whether separate contracts should be combined and evaluated as a single multiple-deliverable arrangement:

Timing of the Execution of the Contracts:

1. The contracts or agreements were negotiated or executed within a short time frame of each other or in contemplation of each other (ASC 985-605-55-4 and ASC 815-10-15-8 and 15-9).

Identity of the Customer:

2. The contracts are with the same customer (or affiliates of each other) (ASC 815-10-15-8 and 15-9).

Substance and the Composition of the Contract:

3. The contracts relate to the same deliverables, or what is, in essence, the same project (ASC 985-605-55-4 and ASC 815-10-15-8 and 15-9).

4. The different deliverables are closely interrelated or interdependent in terms of design, technology, or function (ASC 985-605-55-4).

5. One or more deliverables in one contract or agreement are essential to the functionality of a deliverable in another contract (ASC 985-605-55-4).

Arrangement Consideration and the Payment Terms:

6. The fee for one or more contracts or agreements is subject to refund or forfeiture or other concession if another contract is not satisfactorily completed (ASC 985-605-55-4).

7. Payment terms under one contract or agreement coincide with performance criteria of another contract or agreement (ASC 985-605-55-4).

ILLUSTRATION: EVALUATING MULTIPLE CONTRACTS

EXAMPLE 1

Facts: Company G manufactures and sells computer printers. These printers use a proprietary ink cartridge design, such that the cartridges cannot be provided by any other manufacturer. The printers are sold by retailers for $100 each and the ink cartridges sell for $40 each. When a printer is sold, it includes one cartridge. Company G's printers and ink cartridges are readily available from retail distributors of Company G's products. Company G enters into a contract to supply a customer with 100 printers for $80 each. Six months later, Company G signs a contract with the same customer to provide ink cartridges for the printers on an as-needed basis for $30 each for two years.

Discussion: A review of the indicators described above shows that the contracts are with the same customer (indicator 2) and that the "Substance of the Deliverables" indicators (3, 4, and 5) are present, suggesting that the contracts should be combined. However, the "Fee and Payment Terms" indicators (6 and 7) do not exist, and it is not clear that indicator 1 exists. Additional factors that Company G should consider include the fact that ink cartridges can be purchased by the customer from parties other than Company G, and the fact that Company G routinely sells printers and ink cartridges separate from each other. In this situation, Company G would likely conclude that the arrangement for the sale of printers and the arrangement for the sale of ink cartridges should not be combined. However, a slight change in the facts (e.g., if the arrangements were signed less than one month apart) might change this conclusion.

EXAMPLE 2

Facts: Company R owns the rights to a proprietary chemical compound used to make various products. It licenses the right to use the compound in a particular product line to a customer for three years, which is the remaining life of the patent on the compound. However, Company R does not provide the customer with a license to manufacture the proprietary compound or have it manufactured—Company R maintains those rights exclusively until the patent expires. The customer will be responsible for developing the product and marketing it. An initial payment under the license is due at signing, with further payments due ratably over the term of the license. In a separate contract, contemplated at the time of the license, but negotiated and signed three months later, Company R agrees to supply the chemical compound to this customer at market prices for three years.

Discussion: A review of the indicators described above shows that indicators 1 through 5 are present and suggests that the contracts should be combined. However, the "Fee and Payment Terms" indicator 6 does not exist. In this case, Company R would likely conclude that the two contracts should be combined and evaluated as one arrangement for revenue recognition purposes.

DELIVERABLES

One might think that GAAP provides a definition of "deliverable" since there has been so much standard-setting focused on guidance for determining when and how to separate deliverables in a multiple-deliverable revenue arrangement. Unfortunately, it does not, and the absence of a definition means that judgment based on the facts and circumstances is required to determine which terms in an arrangement with a customer should be considered deliverables and therefore relevant to revenue recognition. At its broadest interpretation, any performance obligation undertaken by the seller could be considered a deliverable, and all such obligations should therefore be evaluated. Obligations to, for example, perform services, grant licenses, and deliver products, are almost invariably considered deliverables.

However, it is less clear whether or not other provisions that impose obligations on the seller should be considered deliverables for accounting purposes. For example, in an arrangement involving the sale of a specialized product, the vendor may promise not to sell a similar product to any of the customer's competitors. It is not clear whether the exclusivity provision is a separate deliverable apart from the product deliverable. Similarly, a company licensing its technology may explicitly agree to assist the customer in patent infringement allegations from third parties. In this case, it is not clear whether the obligation to assist a customer in legal defense should be considered a deliverable independent of the licensing deliverable.

In considering whether these and other obligations should be considered deliverables, it is important to consider how the customer would view obligation. That is, if the obligation would have substantive value to the customer distinct from the value provided by other performance obligations, the obligation should likely be treated as a separate deliverable.

Over time, despite the lack of guidance in the accounting literature, accountants have generally become comfortable in identifying deliverables for revenue recognition purposes. Nonetheless, issues are raised from time to time regarding this step in the accounting for revenue. Several examples of these issues are discussed below.

Because the identification of deliverables is both a key driver of the timing of revenue recognition and can be quite subjective, it is important that, where provisions in an arrangement that appear to impose obligations on the seller are *not* considered deliverables for purposes of revenue recognition, the company document its thought process for making this determination.

Inconsequential or Perfunctory Performance Obligations

It is a general tenet of GAAP that non-substantive terms, rights, or obligations should not affect accounting results. In certain arrangements a question may arise regarding whether a deliverable is non-substantive, such that it should not affect the recognition of revenue. The phrase "inconsequential or perfunctory" is frequently used to refer to a performance obligation that is not substantive.

Whether a remaining performance obligation may be viewed as inconsequential or perfunctory is not addressed in ASC 605-25. However, the SEC staff has addressed this question in ASC 605-10-S99 (SAB Topic 13A3c). This guidance is not mandatory for private companies, although they should still consider its application given the absence of other guidance.

In ASC 605-10-S99 (SAB Topic 13A3c), the SEC staff indicates that if the only remaining performance obligation on the part of the vendor is inconsequential or perfunctory, the vendor can still conclude that it has met the delivery or performance criterion necessary to recognize revenue for the delivered items (ASC 605-10-S99) (SAB Topic 13A3c, ques. 1).

Under this guidance, a remaining performance obligation may not be considered inconsequential or perfunctory if (a) it is essential to the functionality of a delivered item, (b) the vendor's failure to fulfill the remaining performance obligation would result in the customer receiving a full or partial refund or rejecting (or a right to a refund or to reject) delivered items, or (c) the vendor does not have a demonstrated history of fulfilling the remaining performance obligation in a timely manner and reliably estimating the remaining costs (ASC 605-10-S99) (SAB Topic 13A3c, ques. 1 and 2).

Essential to the Functionality

The phrase "essential to the functionality" originated in ASC 985-605 to refer to a situation in which a delivered item cannot be used by the customer for its intended purpose until another item is also delivered. In that situation, the undelivered item is "essential to the functionality" of the delivered item. In concept, when an undelivered item is essential to the functionality of a delivered item, that delivered item likely does not have "stand-alone value to the customer," which is a phrase used in ASC 605-25. Therefore, both the "standalone value to the customer" guidance in ASC 605-25 (as discussed later in this chapter) and the "essential to the functionality" guidance in ASC 985-605 (see Chapter 10, "Software—A Complete Model") may be useful in evaluating whether a performance obligation could be inconsequential or perfunctory.

For example, consider an arrangement that includes equipment and installation. If the installation involves significant changes to the features or capabilities of the equipment or building complex interfaces or connections and the installation services are unavailable from other vendors, then the installation is likely essential to the functionality of the equipment. Therefore, the installation could not be considered inconsequential. Conversely, if the equipment were a standard product, the installation did not significantly alter the equipment's capabilities, and other companies were available to perform the installation, then the installation services would not be essential to the product's functionality and such services *might* be inconsequential or perfunctory (ASC 605-10-S99) (SAB Topic 13A3c, ques. 3).

Refund Right

Whether a refund right exists if the remaining performance obligation is not fulfilled is often documented in the sales contract. However, such rights may also exist due to industry practice, company policy, or laws and regulations. In addition, the relationship between the buyer and the seller should be evaluated in full to determine whether unstated refund rights might exist. All rights that exist, whether explicit or implicit, must be considered. If a refund right does exist that can be triggered by non-performance of a particular act, that act cannot be considered inconsequential or perfunctory. The existence of the refund right lends substance to the obligation, and the fact that the parties to the contract decided to include such a right demonstrates that they view the obligation to be substantive.

Other Criteria

Other factors should also be considered in determining whether a remaining performance obligation is inconsequential or perfunctory, including (ASC 605-10-S99) (SAB Topic 13A3c, ques. 2):

- Has the cost or time to fulfill the remaining performance obligation in similar contracts historically varied significantly from one instance to another?

- Are the skills required to fulfill the remaining performance obligation specialized or not readily available in the marketplace?

- Is the cost of fulfilling the remaining performance obligation, or the fair value of that remaining performance obligation, more than insignificant in relation to such items as the contract fee, gross profit, and operating income allocable to the other items in the arrangement?

- Is the period before the remaining performance obligation is fulfilled lengthy?

- Is the timing of payment of a portion of the sales price coincident with fulfilling the remaining performance obligation?

A "yes" answer to any of these questions is an indication that the performance obligation is more than inconsequential or perfunctory.

Accounting for Remaining Performance Obligations Considered Inconsequential or Perfunctory

A vendor should develop a policy that is consistent across similar arrangements and similar performance obligations to determine whether the remaining obligations are inconsequential or perfunctory. The cost of any remaining performance obligation considered inconsequential or perfunctory should be recognized (with the expense recorded as part of cost of sales) when revenue from the arrangement is first recognized (ASC 605-10-S99) (SAB Topic 13A3c, ques. 1).

This evaluation is highly subjective and, as a result, different vendors might reach different conclusions. It is important to keep in mind that a conclusion to treat a performance obligation as a substantive one is almost invariably acceptable, while a conclusion to treat an obligation as inconsequential or perfunctory, and therefore ignore it in evaluating revenue recognition, can be subject to disagreement. As noted above, it is important to document clearly the reasons for a decision to treat any obligation as inconsequential or perfunctory.

DISCLOSURE ALERT: See Chapter 12, "Disclosures," regarding accounting policy disclosure requirements.

EXAMPLE: INCONSEQUENTIAL OR PERFUNCTORY DELIVERABLES

American Science and Engineering, Inc. Form 10-K—Fiscal Year Ended March 31, 2010

We recognize sales for our systems that are produced in a standard manufacturing operation, have minimal customer site installation requirements and have shorter order to delivery cycles, when title passes and when other revenue recognition criteria are met. Management believes the customer's post-delivery acceptance provisions and installation requirements on certain of these systems are perfunctory and inconsequential and the costs of installation at the customer's site are accrued at the time of revenue recognition. We have demonstrated a history of customer acceptance subsequent to shipment and installation of these systems. For systems which entail more significant installation efforts and site work and/or have non-standard customer acceptance provisions, revenue recognition is deferred until installation is complete and customer acceptance has occurred.

Potential Deliverables

Many arrangements that include firm purchase and sale obligations for certain deliverables discuss additional deliverables that may or may not be provided. GAAP does not provide explicit guidance on whether such items should be considered deliverables and analyzed in the context of the original arrangement or, alternatively, should be considered a separate arrangement for the purposes of the revenue recognition guidance in the event that they actually are performed. Nonetheless, there are principles and concepts in GAAP that should be considered in developing an accounting policy for these potential deliverables.

When-and-If Available Deliverables

A when-and-if-available clause requires the seller or licensor to make additional products, services, or upgrades to delivered items available to the buyer or licensee if such products, services, or upgrades become available. For example, if the owner of the rights to a drug licenses those rights to a third party for use in Japan, a when-and-if-available clause may require the company to provide the customer with the results of any work it performs to improve the drug or get it approved in the U.S. to treat additional conditions.

Even though a when-and-if-available clause does not obligate the seller to develop additional products, services, or upgrades, the clause does represent a continuing obligation because, in the event the seller does develop the items subject to the clause, it must provide them to the customer. Whether this obligation should be considered a deliverable in the arrangement, however, depends upon the facts and circumstances.

In most cases, the fact that a when-and-if available clause exists in an arrangement suggests that there is at least a reasonable likelihood that the seller will develop the contemplated products, service, or upgrades. For instance, in the example above, the seller retains the U.S. rights to the drug, and thus would be motivated to improve the drug despite having sold the Japanese rights. If it is probable that the seller will develop the products, services, or upgrades covered by a when-and-if clause and therefore be required to deliver such items to the customer, the when-and-if available obligation should be treated as a deliverable in the arrangement, even if it does not impose substantive costs on the seller.

However, in some cases, it could be unlikely that the seller would develop the additional products, services, or improvements covered by the when-and-if available clause. In these cases, it is possible that the seller could reasonably conclude that the when-and-if-available clause is an inconsequential obligation, as discussed previously in this chapter, and that it should not be treated as a deliverable.

Contingent Deliverables

Contingent performance obligations are obligations that are contemplated in the arrangement, but, depending upon the success of other deliverables or the occurrence of events outside the control of the vendor and customer, may not need to be performed. For example, contingent deliverables arise when a project will be performed in phases, but each phase depends upon the success of earlier phases. In that case, whether the vendor will be required to fulfill its obligations in phase 2 is contingent upon whether phase 1 is successful.

Prior to ASU 2009-13, contingent deliverables like these were generally considered deliverables for purposes of revenue recognition. However, early in the discussion that led to ASU 2009-13, the EITF decided that the question of contingent deliverables had never been discussed and therefore should not be addressed in GAAP. As a result of that decision, a previously existing example (previously ASC 605-25-55-37, now superseded) that treated a contingent performance obligation as a deliverable was removed.

The result of this change is that there is no discussion in GAAP of contingent deliverables. Some have asserted this means that such items now do not need to be considered deliverables if the company elects (as an accounting policy) not to do so. However, the lack of guidance in GAAP should not be perceived to allow a free choice as to whether to consider such items in determining when to recognize revenue.

For example, a deliverable that is contingent on the occurrence of an event that is probable to occur could not reasonably be excluded from the allocation of consideration. In addition, if the contingent deliverable would be provided at a significant incremental discount, the discount, at least, must be taken into account in allocating consideration.

Because of this change, however, contingent obligations that are considered to be unlikely to be fulfilled might be excluded from the allocation. As noted above, it is important that, where provisions in an arrangement that appear to impose obligations on the seller are *not* considered deliverables for purposes of revenue recognition, the company document its thought process for making this determination. That thought process could not reasonably stop at the determination that the obligation is contingent, but should instead substantively consider the implications of the contingent deliverable to the arrangement as a whole.

Optional Purchases

Another type of potential deliverable is an optional purchase. For example, an arrangement might allow the buyer to purchase additional products or services at its option for stated prices. Whether the vendor must fulfill that performance obligation depends upon whether the customer exercises its option. Contracts that include rights to purchase additional items must be evaluated carefully to ensure revenue is allocated to all items of value.

One possibility in these arrangements is that, because the customer, not the vendor, controls whether the additional products or services will be delivered, the contract should be considered a contract for the maximum number of deliverables the vendor can be required to provide, with the possibility that less than the maximum will need to be handled like breakage, as discussed in Chapter 3, "General Principles". This treatment would certainly be appropriate if the purchase price for the "optional" deliverables was so small as to be non-substantive. In those cases, exercise of the option should be presumed, and the "optional" purchases should be considered deliverables in the original arrangement.

Purchases that are contractually optional should also be considered deliverables if the customer has no real choice but to exercise its option. For example, if the optional products or services were necessary to realize the value of the required or previously delivered items, the customer would substantively be compelled to exercise its option. In that case, the "optional" items should be considered deliverables in the original arrangement.

If, however, the arrangement is not such that the customer is substantively or economically compelled to exercise its option in order to realize value from other products or because the purchase price of the optional items is non-substantive, the optional purchases might reasonably be excluded from evaluation as deliverables. In that situation, each purchase by the customer would seem to represent a separate purchasing decision, and therefore could logically be considered a separate arrangement for revenue recognition purposes.

However, when the potential deliverables are not considered part of the original arrangement, the terms of the customer's right to purchase additional items should be evaluated to determine whether a significant discount on future purchases has been provided. If the customer has the right to request an additional product or service at a significantly discounted price for that item, ignoring that fact in recognizing revenue would distort the economics of the arrangement. In that case, some of the arrangement fee would clearly relate to the "purchase" of an option by the customer to receive the additional items at reduced prices. Therefore, a portion of the arrangement fee would be allocated to the option. Further discussion of rights to discounts on future purchases can be found in Chapter 8, "Miscellaneous Issues."

DETERMINING THE MODEL TO APPLY

As mentioned previously, there are several places in GAAP where separating deliverables in a multiple-deliverable arrangement is discussed. For example, ASC 985-605, ASC 605-35, and ASC 840 provide separation and allocation guidance for arrangements within their scope. Guidance other than ASC 605-25 should be followed if it covers the separation of deliverables in a multiple-deliverable arrangement and the allocation of consideration to those separate units of accounting. When there is no other applicable literature, ASC 605-25 should be applied (ASC 605-25-15-3). When there is other applicable literature that addresses some, but not all, of the multiple-deliverable issues, ASC 605-25 should be applied to fill in the gap(s) (ASC 605-25-15-3).

Because different models can lead to different conclusions regarding whether and how to separate deliverables in a particular arrangement, it is important to determine whether the arrangement is covered by a model other than ASC 605-25. A thorough review of other parts of GAAP that address multiple-deliverable arrangements shows a number of levels of guidance. For example, there are ASC topics that address the following issues for particular transactions or industries (with examples of each type of guidance):

- Separation and allocation related only to deliverables within the ASC topic's defined scope, with no discussion about separating deliverables within the ASC topic's scope from other deliverables in the arrangement. In this situation, the guidance in ASC 605-25 should be used to initially separate the deliverables within the scope of the specific literature from those outside its scope:

  — ASC 605-35 on long-term construction contracts (see further discussion in Chapter 9, "Contract Accounting").

  — ASC 985-605 on software arrangements (see discussion in Chapter 10, "Software—A Complete Model").

  — ASC 926-605 on revenue from motion pictures (see discussion Chapter 7, "Intellectual Property Deliverables").

- Separation and allocation related to deliverables within the ASC topic's defined scope, and separation of deliverables within its scope from other deliverables in the arrangement, without guidance on how to allocate consideration between the deliverables within the ASC topic's scope from those outside of that scope. In these situations, the specific guidance should be applied to determine whether the deliverables within and outside its scope should be separated. If the deliverables should be separated, the relative selling price method described in ASC 605-25 must be used to allocate arrangement consideration (ASC 605-25-15-3):

  — ASC 840-20 and 840-30 on leases.

- Separation and allocation related to deliverables within the ASC topic's defined scope, separation of deliverables within its scope from other deliverables, and allocation of consideration to the deliverables within the ASC topic's scope. In this situation, the guidance in the other ASC topic should be used to separate deliverables within its scope from those outside it, and the amount of consideration allocated to the deliverables within its scope should be determined based on the guidance in that ASC topic. The remaining consideration would be allocated to deliverables outside that ASC topic's scope:

— ASC 952-605 on revenue from franchise fees (see discussion in Chapter 7 "Intellectual Property Deliverables").

— ASC 460 on guarantees and indemnifications (see discussion later in this chapter).

— ASC 605-20-25 on extended warranties (see discussion in Chapter 5, "Product Deliverables").

This chapter focuses on the ASC 605-25 model because it applies to the vast majority of situations. As noted above, other chapters address some of the other parts of GAAP that provide multiple-deliverable guidance. No matter which guidance is used to separate deliverables within the scope of a specific ASC topic from other deliverables, further separation of the deliverables within the scope of that other ASC topic is governed by the guidance in that ASC topic, and further separation of other deliverables is governed by ASC 605-25. If, based on the guidance in ASC 605-25, deliverables that fall within the scope of specific guidance cannot be separated from other deliverables, the appropriate recognition of revenue should be determined for these combined deliverables as a single unit of accounting (ASC 605-25-15-3 and 605-25-25-6).

SEC REGISTRANT ALERT: In a December 2003 speech, the SEC staff discussed (a) the scope interaction of ASC 985-605 and ASC 605-25, and (b) the scope interaction of ASC 985-605 and ASC 840. The SEC staff noted that prior to the issuance of ASC 605-25, bundled information technology consulting arrangements including software license, customization, installation, and continuing information technology management services (a service deliverable) were usually accounted for as a single deliverable under ASC 605-35. ASC 605-25 should be applied to bundled arrangements that include significant customization of software to determine whether the ASC 985-605 deliverables should be separated from other deliverables.

The SEC staff also noted that the hardware and executory cost deliverables of a leased customized software arrangement should be unbundled and accounted for separately using ASC 840.

EXAMPLE: ASC 840 AND NON ASC 840 DELIVERABLES

Xerox Corporation Form 10-K—Fiscal Year Ended December 31, 2010

Revenue Recognition under Bundled Arrangements

We sell our products and services under bundled lease arrangements, which typically include equipment, service, supplies and financing components for which the customer pays a single negotiated monthly fixed price for all elements over the contractual lease term. Approximately 40% of our equipment sales revenue is related to sales made under bundled lease arrangements. Typically these arrangements include an incremental, variable component for page volumes in excess of contractual page volume minimums, which are often expressed in terms of price per page. Revenues under these arrangements are allocated, considering the relative fair values of the lease and non-lease deliverables included in the bundled arrangement, based upon the estimated fair values of each element. Lease deliverables include maintenance and executory costs, equipment and financing, while non–lease deliverables generally consist of supplies and non–maintenance services. The allocation for lease deliverables begins by allocating revenues to the maintenance and executory costs plus profit thereon. These elements are generally recognized over the term of the lease as services revenue. The remaining amounts are allocated to the equipment and financing elements, which are subjected to the accounting estimates noted above under "Revenue Recognition for Leases." We perform analyses of available verifiable objective evidence of equipment fair value based on cash selling prices during the applicable period. The cash selling prices are compared to the range of values included in our lease accounting systems. The range of cash selling prices must be reasonably consistent with the lease selling prices, taking into account residual values, in order for us to determine that such lease prices are indicative of fair value.

SEPARATION AND ALLOCATION UNDER ASC 605-25

ASC 605-25 addresses three problematic issues that arise in multiple-deliverable arrangements. The first issue is that the customer might not receive value from a delivered item because the delivered item works together with one of the undelivered items in the arrangement. The second issue stems from the fact that the arrangement fee generally is negotiated for the entire package of deliverables in the contract rather than deliverable-by-deliverable. Therefore, it may not be clear how much revenue is specifically allocable to each deliverable. The third issue arises when a portion of the arrangement fee related to delivered items is contingent in some way upon the delivery of another item in the arrangement.

OBSERVATION: In this discussion, the term "contingent revenue" is used to refer to situations in which the contingency as to whether revenue will be collected or retained is a function of the vendor's performance with respect to *undelivered items.* Other contingencies might also exist, such as customer acceptance requirements (performance or other mutually agreed-upon or subjective criteria) and warranties (conformity with published specifications) that relate to *delivered items.* Those items are discussed elsewhere in this publication, as they are not unique to multiple-deliverable arrangements.

In order to address these concerns, ASC 605-25-25-5 indicates that delivered items should be considered a separate unit of accounting to which revenue may be allocated if and only if:

1. The *delivered item(s)* has value to the customer on a standalone basis. Standalone value exists if the deliverable is sold separately by the vendor or if the customer could resell the delivered item on a standalone basis. Satisfaction of this condition does not depend on the existence of an observable market for the deliverable.

2. If the arrangement includes a general right of return related to the delivered item, delivery or performance of the *undelivered item(s)* is considered probable and substantially in the control of the vendor.

If these two criteria are met, revenue is allocated amongst the deliverables based upon their relative selling prices with the exception that revenue allocated to delivered items may not exceed the amount that the vendor would expect to be paid (or to retain) in the event it was unable to complete its remaining performance obligations.

PRACTICE ALERT: ASU 2009-13 removed another requirement from the allocation guidance—the requirement that there be objective and reliable evidence of the fair value (selling price) of the undelivered items. Before ASU 2009-13, a lack of sufficient evidence of the selling price of the undelivered items prohibited allocation of revenue to delivered items. Therefore, no revenue could be recognized on those items, even if it was clear they provided value to the customer. The prohibition on separating deliverables in a multiple-deliverable arrangement simply because of a lack of sufficient evidence of the selling price of the undelivered items was often cited as a provision that distorted reported results. The removal of this provision significantly increases the likelihood that separation of delivered and undelivered items will occur.

The identification of deliverables in an arrangement should be initially performed at the inception of the agreement. This analysis will help assess whether each condition of the basic model will be met when certain items are delivered. However, the final determination of whether the completion of any particular deliverable should result in the recognition of revenue should be made at the time revenue on that item would otherwise be recognizable, aside from the concerns raised by the existence of undelivered items. Thus, as each item is delivered, the vendor in a multiple-deliverable arrangement should review the conditions based on the status of the arrangement at that time (ASC 605-25-25-4).

DISCLOSURE ALERT: See Chapter 12, "Disclosures," for information about required disclosures.

SEC REGISTRANT ALERT: In early 2003, the SEC staff issued the Report Pursuant to Section 704 of the Sarbanes-Oxley Act of 2002 (Section 704 Report). In compiling the information in the Section 704 Report, the SEC staff studied enforcement actions filed during the period July 31, 1997, through July 30, 2002. The greatest number of enforcement actions brought by the SEC related to improper revenue recognition. One of the common revenue recognition issues highlighted in the Section 704 Report related to improper recognition of revenue from multiple-deliverable arrangements or bundled contracts. One of the two actions discussed in the Section 704 Report in this regard involved improper allocation of arrangement consideration. The other action involved improper separation of interdependent deliverables. This finding is a strong indication that more attention should be given to accounting for multiple-deliverable arrangements.

In addition, in early 2003, the SEC staff issued the Summary by the Division of Corporation Finance of Significant Issues Addressed in the Review of the Periodic Reports of the Fortune 500 Companies (Fortune 500 Report). This report resulted from the SEC's Division of Corporation Finance's (Corp Fin) review of all annual reports filed by Fortune 500 companies. The report provides insight into areas commonly questioned by Corp Fin during its reviews of annual reports. One area specifically mentioned in the Fortune 500 Report relates to accounting for multiple-deliverable arrangements. Corp Fin specifically indicated that companies in the computer software, computer services, computer hardware, and communications equipment industries could improve their disclosures by expanding the discussion related to multiple-deliverable arrangements.

Standalone Value to the Customer

In some cases, it is easy to conclude that delivered items have standalone value. For example, when a purchase from a store's internet site is shipped in multiple packages because one or more items are on backorder, it is almost always the case that the delivered items can be used by the customer as soon as they arrive without waiting for other items. In addition, in a retail environment, it is almost always the case that individual items are routinely offered and sold separately, which proves that each item has standalone value.

In other situations, significant judgment may be required to evaluate whether deliverables have value to the customer on a standalone basis. This is often the case, for example, if the undelivered items and the delivered items work together, or if the undelivered item is a service this is provided in part using products or intellectual property that was previously delivered.

While an item clearly has standalone value if it can be used by the customer without further help or assistance from the vendor, ASC 605-25 also provides that a delivered item (or items) has standalone value if it is sold separately by any vendor or if it could be resold by the customer on a standalone basis. To conclude that a deliverable has standalone value to the customer because the deliverable is sold separately by another vendor, that other vendor should provide the same quality and value to the customer. Factors to consider by way of comparison include (but are not limited to) pricing, functionality, features, quality grades/assessments, ease of installation and delivery, warranty and acceptance provisions, and availability of post-sale support. To conclude that the customer could resell the deliverable on a standalone basis, the company must consider the nature of the market in which the deliverable can be resold, the value to be received on resale, and whether reselling the deliverable would affect its quality or utility. The examples below and those included in ASC 605-25-55 illustrate the application of the concept of "standalone value to the customer" in various situations.

ILLUSTRATION: STANDALONE VALUE TO THE CUSTOMER

The following two examples represent arrangements where the delivered item *does not* have value to the customer on a standalone basis:

Example 1:   The arrangement involves the sale of a satellite television receiver and one year of service. The receiver operates on a proprietary network and therefore can only be used with the service provided by the vendor in the arrangement. In addition, there is no secondary market for separate sales of the satellite television receiver since each receiver is uniquely identified to a particular customer and that customer's service contract. As such, the receiver does not have value to the customer on a standalone basis (i.e., absent the ongoing satellite television service).

Example 2:   The arrangement involves the sale and installation of equipment. The equipment is highly specialized and will not operate until certain adjustments are made during installation. Because of the unique nature and specialization of the equipment, only one vendor manufactures or installs the equipment. This effectively prohibits the customer from reselling the equipment on a standalone basis. As such, the equipment does not have value to the customer on a standalone basis (i.e., absent the installation service).

The following two examples represent arrangements where the delivered item *does* have value to the customer on a standalone basis:

Example 3:   The arrangement involves the sale of office equipment by Vendor D and a contract to provide maintenance on that office equipment. Vendor D, as well as other vendors, sells the office equipment without the maintenance contract. As such, the office equipment has value to the customer on a standalone basis (i.e., absent the maintenance contract).

Example 4:   The arrangement involves the sale of two pieces of manufacturing equipment by Vendor E. Both pieces of equipment are needed to manufacture the intended product. Vendor E only sells the two pieces of equipment together. However, other vendors sell separately equipment that is comparable to, and compatible with, each piece of Vendor E's equipment. This also effectively results in the customer being able to resell Vendor E's equipment on a standalone basis if it chose to do so. As such, each piece of equipment has value to the customer on a standalone basis (i.e., absent the delivery of the other piece of equipment).

EXAMPLES: STANDALONE VALUE TO THE CUSTOMER

Immunogen, Inc. Form 10-Q—Quarterly Period Ended March 31, 2011

Exclusive Licenses

The deliverables under an exclusive license agreement generally include the exclusive license to the Company's TAP technology, and may also include deliverables related to research activities to be performed on behalf of the collaborative partner and the manufacture of preclinical or clinical materials for the collaborative partner.

Generally, exclusive license agreements contain non-refundable terms for payments and, depending on the terms of the agreement, provide that the Company will (i) at the collaborator's request, provide research services which are reimbursed at a contractually determined rate, (ii) at the collaborator's request, manufacture and provide to them preclinical and clinical materials which are reimbursed at the Company's cost, or, in some cases, cost plus a margin, (iii) earn payments upon the achievement of certain milestones and (iv) earn royalty payments, generally until the later of the last applicable patent expiration or 10 to

12 years after product launch. Royalty rates may vary over the royalty term depending on the Company's intellectual property rights. The Company may provide technical assistance and share any technology improvements with its collaborators during the term of the collaboration agreements. The Company does not directly control when any collaborator will request research or manufacturing services, achieve milestones or become liable for royalty payments. As a result, the Company cannot predict when it will recognize revenues in connection with any of the foregoing.

In determining the units of accounting, management evaluates whether the exclusive license has standalone value to the collaborative partner based on the consideration of the relevant facts and circumstances for each arrangement. Factors considered in this determination include the research capabilities of the partner and the availability of TAP technology research expertise in the general marketplace.

Novartis

In October 2010, the Company entered into an agreement with Novartis Institutes for BioMedical Research, Inc. (Novartis). The agreement initially provides Novartis with a research license to test the Company's TAP technology with Novartis' own antibodies and an option to take exclusive development and commercialization licenses to use ImmunoGen's TAP technology to develop therapeutic products for a specified number of individual antigen targets. The initial term of the research license is for three years and it may be extended by Novartis for up to two one-year periods by the payment of additional consideration. The terms of the agreement also require Novartis to exercise its option for the development and commercialization licenses by the end of the research term. The Company received a $45 million upfront payment in connection with the execution of the agreement, and for each development and commercialization license for an antigen target, the Company is entitled to receive milestone payments potentially totaling $200.5 million plus royalties on product sales, if any. The Company also is entitled to receive payments for manufacturing preclinical and clinical materials at the request of Novartis as well as for research and development activities performed on behalf of Novartis. Novartis is responsible for the development, manufacturing and marketing of any products resulting from this agreement.

In accordance with ASU No. 2009-13, the Company identified all of the deliverables at the inception of the agreement. The significant deliverables were determined to be the research license, the exclusive development and commercialization licenses and the research services. The Company has determined that the research license together with the development and commercialization licenses represent one unit of accounting as the research license does not have standalone value from the development and commercialization licenses. The Company has also determined that this unit of accounting does have standalone value from the research services. As a result, the research services are considered a separate unit of accounting. The estimated selling prices for these units of accounting was determined based on market conditions and entity-specific factors such as the terms of the Company's previous collaborative agreements, recent preclinical and clinical testing results of therapeutic products that use the Company's TAP technology, the Company's pricing practices and pricing objectives, and the nature of the research services to be performed for Novartis and market rates for similar services. The arrangement consideration was allocated to the deliverables based on the relative selling price method. The Company will recognize license revenue as each exclusive development and commercialization license is delivered pursuant to the terms of the agreement. The Company does not control when Novartis will exercise its options for development and commercialization licenses. As a result, the Company cannot predict when it will recognize the related license revenue except that it will be within the term of the research license. The Company will recognize research services revenue as the related services are delivered.

NetSuite Inc. Form 10-K—Fiscal Year Ended December 31, 2010

We commence revenue recognition when all of the following conditions are met:

- there is persuasive evidence of an arrangement
- the service is being provided to the customer
- the collection of the fees is reasonably assured
- the amount of fees to be paid by the customer is fixed or determinable

In most instances, revenue from a new customer acquisition is generated under sales agreements with multiple elements, comprised of subscription and support fees from customers accessing our cloud-based application suite and professional services associated with consultation services. We evaluate each element in a multiple-element arrangement to determine whether it represents a separate unit of accounting. An element constitutes a separate unit of accounting when the delivered item has standalone value and delivery of the undelivered element is probable and within our control. Subscription and support have standalone value because we routinely sell it separately. Professional services have standalone value because we have sold professional services separately and there are several third party vendors that routinely provide similar professional services to our customers on a standalone basis.

General Refund Rights

In many arrangements, a customer can exercise certain rights after a product is delivered. For example, general rights of return and standard warranty provisions represent uncertainties and potential future obligations that exist at the time of delivery. Typically, such rights are evaluated for each deliverable in an arrangement, pursuant to the appropriate guidance (e.g., ASC 605-15-25-1 through 25-4 for returns and ASC 460 for warranties).

If general refund rights exist and delivery or performance of the undelivered item(s) is considered probable and substantially in the vendor's control, then those rights should be accounted for as discussed in Chapter 5, "Product Deliverables," and Chapter 6, "Service Deliverables," as appropriate. The existence of these rights would not preclude treating a delivered item in a multiple-deliverable arrangement separately for accounting purposes.

However, if general refund rights exist and delivery or performance of the undelivered item(s) is not probable and substantially in the vendor's control, then the delivered item should not be treated separately for accounting purposes (ASC 605-25-25-5).

Therefore, when such general refund rights exist, an assessment of whether performance of the undelivered item(s) is probable and substantially in the vendor's control is required after *each* deliverable in the arrangement is delivered. The vendor's ability to meet this criterion is a function of the nature of the undelivered items and the specific characteristics of the vendor. Factors that may impact the likelihood of performance of undelivered items include the amount of time to complete, degree of customization, reliance on subcontractors, and the availability of components. The vendor's history of performance and financial condition must also be considered in the assessment.

Distinction Between General and Specific Refund Rights

An important distinction is made between general and specific refund rights in ASC 605-25. The existence of a general refund right creates a connection between the deliverables that must be considered from the perspective of the *vendor*. As a result, the vendor must assess whether performance related to undelivered items is probable and substantially within its control.

By contrast, the existence of a specific refund right creates a connection between the deliverables that the vendor should consider from the *customer's* perspective. A specific refund right expressly connects the deliverables in a multiple-deliverable arrangement because it specifically ties the vendor's right to consideration (or the right to retain consideration) to whether the vendor provides the undelivered items. This express link indicates that there is a stronger connection between deliverables in a multiple-deliverable arrangement containing a specific refund right than in a multiple-deliverable arrangement containing only a general refund right.

To address the accounting implications of this stronger connection, the amount allocated to a delivered item is limited to the lesser of (*a*) the amount otherwise allocable to that item (based on the relative selling price method) or (*b*) the amount that is not contingent upon the delivery of additional items or meeting other specified performance conditions (ASC 605-25-30-5). This treatment of specific refund rights is further discussed below under "Allocation of Arrangement Consideration—Contingent Consideration."

Measurement of Arrangement Consideration

The amount of total arrangement consideration to be allocated to the various deliverables is often clear based on the terms and conditions of the contract, as the contract will state a fixed amount to be paid for all of the deliverables in the arrangement. However, it is not uncommon for contracts to include terms that make the price, or some portion of it, variable. In these instances, the total amount of arrangement consideration may not be fixed or determinable (see the discussion in Chapter 3, "General Principles").

Before revenue is allocated to deliverables under the model in ASC 605-25, such revenue must be fixed or determinable other than with respect to the impact of refund rights and potential performance bonuses (ASC 605-25-30-1). If a portion of the arrangement fee is not fixed or determinable for other reasons, only the portion that is fixed or determinable should be allocated to individual deliverables. As more of the fee becomes fixed or determinable, the allocation should be updated to take into account the additional arrangement consideration.

Allocation of Arrangement Consideration

To a casual observer, it might seem that allocating arrangement consideration to individual deliverables in a multiple-deliverable arrangement should start with determining whether the contract states separate prices for each deliverable. However, it has long been recognized in GAAP that when a contract covers more than one activity, the parties to the contract would generally be indifferent as to whether the individual stated prices were representative of the amount that would be charged in a separate agreement. Therefore, contractually stated prices in a multiple-deliverable agreement are presumed not to be sufficiently meaningful to base the allocation of revenue on them (ASC 605-25-30-7).

Relative Selling Price Method

In general, where the accounting literature discusses arrangements with multiple parts, the objective is to allocate the arrangement consideration to the individual deliverables based on their relative fair values.[1] That principle is also applied in ASC 605-25.

In some cases, a deliverable in a multiple-element arrangement is required by other parts of GAAP to be recognized and subsequently remeasured at its fair value. This could happen, for example, if the performance obligation meets the definition of a derivative in ASC 815. In those cases, that deliverable should be allocated consideration equal to its fair value, and the remaining consideration should be allocated to the other deliverables in the arrangement using the relative selling price method discussed below (ASC 605-25-30-4).

Allocation of arrangement consideration to any other deliverables that should be treated separately is done based on the relative selling prices of the deliverables (ASC 605-25-30-2). Estimated selling prices are used rather than fair value in order to avoid the potential complexity that might come from applying the definition of fair value in ASC 820 and to narrow the focus to a measure that is clearly relevant to revenue transactions. To apply the relative selling price method, the vendor first determines (or estimates) the amount that each deliverable would be sold for on its own. The sum of those prices is then compared to the arrangement consideration, and any difference is applied to the separate deliverables ratably.

A result of applying the relative selling price method is that when a multiple-deliverable arrangement has a total fee that is less than the amount that would be determined by adding up the selling prices of the individual deliverables, the discount is allocated pro rata across each of the deliverables.

---

[1] For example, fair value allocation is discussed in ASC 840, ASC 952-605, ASC 360-20, ASC 460, ASC 605-35, ASC 985-605, and SASC 926-605.

ILLUSTRATION: ALLOCATION OF ARRANGEMENT CONSIDERATION— RELATIVE SELLING PRICE METHOD

General Facts: Company W manufactures equipment that is used to make widgets. The widget-making process involves two pieces of equipment, both of which Company W manufactures. In an arrangement with a new customer, Company W sells both pieces of equipment, along with 10 days of training for the customer's employees, for a total fee of $900,000. Title to each machine transfers upon shipment. Company W does not grant general or specific refund rights to its customers.

VARIATION 1

Additional Facts: Company W also sells each piece of equipment separately. In addition, competitors manufacture machines that perform the same functions as Machine 1 and 2, and machines from different manufacturers are interchangeable. Company W sells Machine 1 separately for $400,000, and Machine 2 separately for $550,000. No amount of the arrangement consideration is contingent upon performance of undelivered components.

Company W sells training services separately to customers who already have equipment installed and want additional training for new employees. Company W charges $5,000 per day for training. However, not all customers purchase training, as Company W includes operating manuals with its equipment.

Company W delivers Machine 1 first, then Machine 2, then the training, using the installed machines to demonstrate the machines' functionality. Payment terms are $400,000 upon delivery of Machine 1, $475,000 upon delivery of Machine 2, and $25,000 upon providing the training.

Discussion: Since Company W and other vendors sell each of the machines separately and since the customer can learn how to operate the machines without buying training from Company W, Machine 1 has value to the customer on a standalone basis (i.e., absent Machine 2 and the training), and Machine 2 has value to the customer on a standalone basis (i.e., absent the training).

The separate selling prices for all three deliverables in the arrangement are evident because Company W sells each one separately. The allocation of the consideration to the three deliverables, using the relative selling price method, is as follows:

Selling Price of Machine 1	$ 400,000	(40% of total)
Selling Price of Machine 2	550,000	(55% of total)
Selling Price of Training	50,000	(5% of total)
Total	$1,000,000	(100% of total)
Less: Arrangement Fee	900,000	
Discount in the Arrangement	$ 100,000	
Discount as a Percentage of Selling Prices	– 10%	
Allocation to Machine 1 = $400,000 – 10% (40% of arrangement fee)	$ 360,000	
Allocation to Machine 2 = $550,000 – 10% (55% of arrangement fee)	495,000	

Allocation to Training = $50,000 – 10% (5% of arrangement fee)	45,000
Total Arrangement Fee	$ 900,000

Company W should recognize the arrangement consideration allocated to each item when the recognition criteria discussed in other chapters of this book (i.e., Chapter 5, "Product Deliverables," for Machines 1 and 2; and Chapter 6, "Service Deliverables," for the training) have been satisfied.

VARIATION 2

Additional Facts: The customer needs the machines to operate in a unique environment. As such, Machines 1 and 2 are manufactured to unique customer specifications. Company W does not sell Machine 1 and Machine 2 separately. Company W's competitors do not manufacture similar machines. Due to the unique customer specifications, there is not a secondary market in which the customer could resell the machines individually. Company W sells Machine 1 and Machine 2 together for $950,000.

Company W sells training services separately to customers who already have equipment installed and want additional training for new employees. Company W charges $5,000 per day for training. However, not all customers purchase training, as Company W includes operating manuals with its equipment. The unique customer specifications related to Machines 1 and 2 do not alter the manner in which training would take place.

Company W delivers Machine 1 first, then Machine 2, then the training, using the installed machines to demonstrate the machines' functionality. Payment terms are $400,000 upon delivery of Machine 1, $475,000 upon delivery of Machine 2, and $25,000 upon providing the training.

Discussion: Machine 1 does not have value absent Machine 2 since (a) machines from different suppliers do not work with each other, (b) Company W does not sell the machines separately, and (c) the customer cannot resell Machine 1 on a standalone basis. Because the customer can learn to operate the machines without buying training from Company W, the combination of Machines 1 and 2 has value to the customer absent delivery of the training. This arrangement therefore has two units of accounting: (1) Machines 1 and 2 (the machines), and (2) training.

The allocation of the consideration to the deliverables would be as follows:

Selling Price of Machines 1 and 2	$ 950,000	(95% of total)
Selling Price of Training	50,000	(5% of total)
Total	$1,000,000	(100% of total)
Less: Arrangement Fee	900,000	
Discount in the Arrangement	$ 100,000	
Discount as a Percentage of Selling Prices	– 10%	
Allocation to Machines 1 and 2 = $950,000 – 10% (95% of arrangement fee)	855,000	
Allocation to Training = $50,000 – 10% (5% of arrangement fee)	45,000	
Total Arrangement Fee	$ 900,000	

Company W should not recognize the arrangement consideration allocated to the machines until the recognition criteria discussed in Chapter 5, "Product Deliverables," have been satisfied for *both* machines. Arrangement consideration allocated to the training should be recognized when the recognition criteria discussed in Chapter 6, "Service Deliverables," have been satisfied.

Separate Selling Prices

In determining (or estimating) the separate selling prices of the deliverables in an arrangement, the vendor should consider all information reasonably available. ASC 605-25-30-2 notes that certain available information about separate selling prices is more objective than other information, and therefore specifies a hierarchy of information to be used in determining the separate selling prices for the purpose of allocating revenue to multiple deliverables.

The top level in the hierarchy is vendor-specific objective evidence (VSOE) of selling price, as discussed in the literature on software revenue recognition (see Chapter 10, "Software—A Complete Model"). VSOE of selling price is limited to (ASC 605-25-30-6A):

- The price charged when the same deliverable is sold separately.

- For a deliverable not yet sold separately, the price established by management, if it is probable that the price, once established, will not change before the separate introduction of the deliverable into the marketplace.

When VSOE does not exist, the next level of the hierarchy is described as third-party evidence of selling price. Third-party evidence of selling price of a deliverable would exist if any other vendor separately sells a product or service that is generally interchangeable with the product or service being evaluated (ASC 605-25-30-6B). For many deliverables, such evidence may not be available because the product or service is unique to the vendor.

When neither VSOE nor third-party evidence exists, the allocation is based on the vendor's best estimate of the price that the deliverable would be sold for if it was sold on a standalone basis (ASC 605-25-30-6C). Other than the requirement that this estimate truly be the "best" estimate the company can make, there is no limitation or specific guidance to be applied in estimating the selling price under this last level of the hierarchy.

PRACTICE POINTER: It is the ability to use the third level of the hierarchy that significantly differentiates the multiple-deliverable revenue guidance after the issuance of ASU No. 2009-13 from the guidance that existed before it. Prior to the change, if no evidence from the first two levels of the hierarchy existed, the value of the deliverable was deemed to be insufficiently reliable to permit allocation of revenue.

Because of the significant consequences of not having VSOE or third-party evidence of the value of a deliverable, vendors often went to great lengths to support the assertion that such evidence did exist. While the consequences of not having VSOE or third-party evidence are not nearly as significant now, vendors must still consider all reasonably available information in determining whether VSOE or third-party evidence of selling prices exists. ASC 605-25 does not permit simply skipping to the third level of the hierarchy without attempting to obtain VSOE or third-party evidence because the top two levels are considered to provide a more reliable estimate.

EXAMPLE: FAIR VALUE EVIDENCE

Apple, Inc. Form 10-K/A—Fiscal Year Ended September 26, 2009

Revenue Recognition for Arrangements with Multiple Deliverables

For multi-element arrangements that include tangible products that contain software that is essential to the tangible product's functionality and undelivered software elements that relate to the tangible product's essential software, the Company allocates revenue to all deliverables based on their relative selling prices. In such circumstances, the new accounting principles establish a hierarchy to determine the selling price to be used for allocating revenue to deliverables as follows: (i) vendor-specific objective evidence of fair value ("VSOE"), (ii) third-party evidence of selling price ("TPE"), and (iii) best estimate of the selling price ("ESP"). VSOE generally exists only when the Company sells the deliverable separately and is the price actually charged by the Company for that deliverable.

For both iPhone and Apple TV, the Company has indicated it may from time-to-time provide future unspecified software upgrades and features free of charge to customers. The Company has identified two deliverables generally contained in arrangements involving the sale of iPhone and Apple TV. The first deliverable is the hardware and software essential to the functionality of the hardware device delivered at the time of sale, and the second deliverable is the right included with the purchase of iPhone and Apple TV to receive on a when-and-if-available basis future unspecified software upgrades and features relating to the product's essential software. The Company has allocated revenue between these two deliverables using the relative selling price method. Because the Company has neither VSOE nor TPE for the two deliverables the allocation of revenue has been based on the Company's ESPs. Amounts allocated to the delivered hardware and the related essential software are recognized at the time of sale provided the other conditions for revenue recognition have been met. Amounts allocated to the unspecified software upgrade rights are deferred and recognized on a straight-line basis over the 24-month estimated life of the related hardware. All product cost of sales, including estimated warranty costs, are generally recognized at the time of sale. Costs for engineering and sales and marketing are expensed as incurred.

For all periods presented, the Company's ESP for the software upgrade right included with each iPhone and Apple TV sold is $25 and $10, respectively. The Company's process for determining its ESP for deliverables without VSOE or TPE considers multiple factors that may vary depending upon the unique facts and circumstances related to each deliverable. The Company believes its customers, particularly consumers, would be reluctant to buy unspecified software upgrade rights related to iPhone and Apple TV. This view is primarily based on the fact that upgrade rights do not obligate the Company to provide upgrades at a particular time or at all, and do not specify to customers which upgrades or features will be delivered in the future. Therefore, the Company has concluded that if it were to sell upgrade rights on a standalone basis, such as those included with iPhone and Apple TV, the selling price would be relatively low. Key factors considered by the Company in developing the ESPs for iPhone and Apple TV upgrade rights include prices charged by the Company for similar offerings, the Company's historical pricing practices, the nature of the upgrade rights (e.g., unspecified and when-and-if-available), and the relative ESP of the upgrade rights as compared to the total selling price of the product. In addition, when developing ESPs for products other than iPhone and Apple TV, the Company may consider other factors as appropriate including the pricing of competitive alternatives if they exist, and product-specific business objectives.

Residual Method No Longer Acceptable

Prior to ASU 2009-13, if no evidence from the first two levels of the hierarchy existed, the value of the deliverable was deemed to be insufficiently reliable to use as a basis for allocation of revenue. However, the previous guidance did provide that so long as If sufficient evidence (i.e., VSOE or third-party evidence) of the selling price of undelivered items existed, revenue could be recognized on the delivered items under the "residual method" (ASC 605-25-30-2 and 30-3, now superseded). Under this method, the amount of arrangement consideration allocated to the delivered items was the total arrangement consideration less the aggregate selling prices (as determined by VSOE or third-party evidence) of the undelivered items. Thus, any potential discount in the arrangement was allocated entirely to the delivered items.

The residual method was allowed mainly because the limitation on acceptable evidence of fair value (selling price) was likely to result in an inability to separate deliverables quite frequently, and the EITF concluded that allowing the residual method would reduce the frequency with which that occurred in a way that would still protect against revenue being recognized too quickly. Because ASU 2009-13 eliminates the requirement that evidence of selling prices meet a particular reliability threshold in order to permit separation, the EITF concluded that there was no longer a need for the residual method. As such, it has been eliminated, except for software deliverables (see Chapter 10, "Software—A Complete Model").

While the elimination of the residual method from ASC 605-25 does not prohibit separation of deliverables, it can result in increased work. Prior to ASU 2009-13, a vendor in a multiple-deliverable arrangement that had sufficient evidence of selling price (fair value) of the undelivered items might have chosen to use the residual method and not attempt to determine or estimate the standalone selling price of the item or items delivered first. That is no longer an option. As a result, vendors in multiple-deliverable arrangements must estimate the standalone selling price for all deliverables, or at least each group of deliverables that is delivered at a different time from other deliverables in the arrangement.

ILLUSTRATION: EFFECT OF ELIMINATION OF RESIDUAL METHOD

Facts: Company X sells Product P and Service Q in a single arrangement to Customer Y. Company X does not grant general or specific refund rights to Customer Y. Total arrangement consideration is $90,000. Based on its facts and circumstances, Company X concludes that Product P has value to the customer on a standalone basis. Product P is a customized product for Customer Y and Company X does not have a standard pricing model for Product P. Service Q is a standard service that normally sells for $20,000. Product P is delivered first.

Discussion: Prior to ASU 2009-13, Company X would likely have used the residual method to allocate revenue between Product P and Service Q, since (a) each of the products has value to the customer on a standalone basis, (b) VSOE exists for the undelivered Service Q, and (c) there is no general right of return to consider. In that case, Company X would have recognized $70,000 in revenue upon delivery of Product P, with $20,000, the amount supported by VSOE, allocated to Service Q. No attempt would be made to determine the value of Product P on a standalone basis.

However, after adopting the changes made by ASU 2009-13, Company X may no longer use the residual method. Instead, Company X will need to estimate the selling price of Product P in a separate transaction. Company X could not simply use the residual method to estimate Product P's separate selling price. Rather, Company X would need to consider all reasonably available information in estimating the separate selling price of Product P.

If Company X determines that its best estimate of the selling price of Product P is $80,000, it would allocate $72,000 to Product X and $18,000 to Service Q, reflecting a pro rata allocation of the $90,000 arrangement fee to the two deliverables with combined selling prices of $100,000.

EXAMPLE: ELIMINATION OF RESIDUAL METHOD

Concurrent Computer Corporation Form 10-Q—Quarterly Period Ended September 30, 2010

In October 2009, the FASB amended the accounting standards for multiple-element revenue arrangements under ASU 2009-13 to:

- provide updated guidance on whether multiple deliverables exist, how the elements in an arrangement should be separated, and how the consideration should be allocated;
- require an entity to allocate revenue in an arrangement using estimated selling prices ("ESP") of each element if a vendor does not have VSOE or TPE; and
- eliminate the use of the residual method and require a vendor to allocate revenue using the relative selling price method.

We adopted this accounting guidance on July 1, 2010 and we elected to apply the guidance on a prospective basis for applicable arrangements entered into or materially modified on or after July 1, 2010.

Prior to the adoption of ASU 2009-13, we were not able to establish VSOE or TPE for all of the elements of a revenue arrangement. As a result, prior to adoption of ASU 2009-13, revenue from multiple-element arrangements was allocated to each of the multiple elements and recognized as follows:

- For our typical multiple-element revenue arrangements, we had established VSOE or TPE for undelivered elements such as maintenance and services, but not for one or more of the delivered elements in the arrangement. For these arrangements, we recognized revenue using the residual method. Under the residual method, all revenue was deferred until all elements for which no VSOE or TPE was available, were delivered. Any discount was applied entirely to the value of the delivered element(s) and the total fair value of the undelivered element(s) was deferred, based upon VSOE or TPE.

- Infrequently, we entered into multiple-element revenue arrangements whereby we had not established VSOE or TPE for undelivered elements. For these arrangements, we typically deferred all revenue until the service was completed, or if the only remaining deliverable for which we did not have VSOE or TPE was maintenance, we recognized the entire value of the arrangement ratably over the maintenance period.

As a result of the adoption of ASU 2009-13, we allocate revenue to each element in an arrangement based on a selling price hierarchy. The selling price for a deliverable is based on its VSOE, if available, TPE, if VSOE is not available, or ESP, if neither VSOE nor TPE is available. We have typically been able to establish VSOE of fair value for our maintenance and services. We determine VSOE of fair value for professional services and maintenance by examining the population of selling price for the same or similar services when sold separately, and determining that the pricing population for each VSOE classification is within a very narrow range of the median selling price. For each element, we evaluate at least annually whether or not we have maintained VSOE of fair value based on our review of the actual selling price of each element over the previous 12 month period.

Our product deliverables are typically complete systems comprised of numerous hardware and software components that operate together to provide essential functionality and we are typically unable to establish VSOE or TPE of fair value for our products. Due to the custom nature of our products, we must determine ESP at the individual component level whereby our estimated selling price for the total system is determined based on the sum of the individual components. ESP for components of our real-time products are typically based upon list price, as we usually sell our real-time product components at list price, and only infrequently sell our real-time products at a discount off of list, of generally not more than 10%. ESP for components of our video products are based upon our most frequent selling price of standalone and bundled sales, based upon a twelve month historical analysis. If a mode selling price is not available, then ESP will be the mean selling price of all such component sales based upon a twelve month historical analysis, unless facts and circumstances indicate that another selling price, other than the mode or mean selling price, is more representative of our estimated selling price. We will update our analysis of mode and average selling price at least annually, unless facts and circumstances indicate that more frequent analysis is required.

Revenue for the three months ended September 30, 2010 was $15,546,000, with the adoption of ASU 2009-13 and ASU 2009-14. This compares with revenue of $14,918,000 for the three months ended September 30, 2010, had we not adopted ASU 2009-13 and ASU 2009-14. The primary driver of the impact was the $621,000 increase in product revenue during the three months ended September 30, 2010. The increase in product revenue primarily resulted from our ability to recognize revenue from a product sale that had an undelivered element for which we are now able to establish an estimated selling price, but that would have required a full deferral of revenue under previous accounting guidance, due to our inability to establish VSOE for the undelivered element. The increase in recognizable product revenue also resulted from allocating discounts on bundled orders to both delivered elements, which typically include products, and undelivered elements, which typically include maintenance and professional services, using the relative selling price method under ASU 2009-13. Prior to adoption of ASU 2009-13 and 2009-14, we used the residual method which required us to allocate the entire discount on bundled arrangements to the delivered elements. As of September 30, 2010, our deferred revenue was $12,193,000, as compared to $12,793,000 had we not adopted ASU 2009-13 and 2009-14.

Contingent Revenue

Even when delivered items do provide standalone value to the customer, it may be the case that the arrangement provides for penalties in the event later deliverables are not accomplished as required in the arrangement. The business reasons for such terms might be as simple as the customer having chosen the particular vendor based on that vendor's ability to supply all of the items in the arrangement vs. having to use multiple vendors. Whatever the reason, the timing of revenue recognition might be altered if an arrangement includes provisions that effectively make some of the revenue allocated to delivered items contingent upon the performance of as-yet-uncompleted obligations.

When contingent revenue exists, it is generally due to either specific refund rights or performance bonuses. Specific refund rights are contractual provisions that provide a customer with the right to return a delivered product for a refund (or to avoid payment for previously delivered items) or would require any other concession if the vendor failed to deliver or provide any remaining undelivered items in the arrangement (ASC 605-25-30-5). For example, the customer may be entitled to return all deliverables for a refund, even if only one of several deliverables is not delivered. In other situations, the customer may have the right to a refund or liquidated damages in the event a particular item is not delivered.

Performance bonuses, by contrast, are payments due from customers only if specified performance conditions are met. For example, the customer may be required to pay additional consideration if the vendor completes performance by a specified date or below specified costs. Performance bonuses should not be considered in the measurement and allocation of arrangement consideration until the performance criteria have been met, as the revenue is not fixed or determinable until then.

OBSERVATION: Rights triggered by nonperformance may result from existing laws or be explicitly stated in the contract. However, rights may also exist as a matter of business practice or by implicit agreement between the parties. All rights should be considered, not merely those that are legally documented. This is consistent with the general notion of accounting for the substance of an arrangement, rather than its form.

The amount *allocated* to a delivered item is limited to the lesser of (a) the amount otherwise allocable to that item (based on the relative selling price method) or (b) the amount that is not contingent upon the delivery of additional items or meeting other specified performance conditions (ASC 605-25-30-5). This limitation has no effect on the allocation of arrangement consideration if the amount that may be withheld or refunded is equal to or less than the amount of arrangement consideration that would otherwise be allocated to the specified undelivered item. If, however, the payment that may be withheld or refunded is greater than the amount of arrangement consideration that would normally be allocated to the specified undelivered item, then some amount of the consideration that would otherwise be allocated to delivered items is contingent upon subsequent performance. Because of this, the amount that is at risk is not fixed or determinable and should not be allocated to the delivered item.

ILLUSTRATION: ALLOCATION OF ARRANGEMENT CONSIDERATION— EFFECTS OF SPECIFIC REFUND RIGHTS

(Adapted from Exhibit A in the SEC staff's frequently asked question and answer document on SAB 101, *Revenue Recognition in Financial Statements*. Although most of this FAQ document was ultimately codified in SAB Topic 13 by way of SAB 104, *Revenue Recognition*, Exhibit A was not included in the codification. The examples included in Exhibit A continue to be used in this product, as adapted, because of their continued relevance in the context of ASC 605-25.)

General Facts: Company A develops, manufactures, and sells complex manufacturing equipment. Company A enters into a sales contract with Customer B to sell and install a specific piece of equipment for $20 million. Company A does not provide Customer B with a general right of return. Company A concludes that the equipment has value to the customer on a standalone basis. Company A has developed its own internal specifications for the model of equipment Customer B ordered and has previously demonstrated that the equipment meets those specifications. There are no special operational specifications in the contract with Customer B and the equipment does not need to be integrated with other equipment. Title to the equipment passes to the customer upon delivery. Company A sells the equipment separately for $19,500,000. In those cases, a general contractor installs the equipment, charging $500,000.

VARIATION 1

Additional Facts: The contract with Customer B includes a customer acceptance provision that obligates Company A to demonstrate that the installed equipment meets its standard criteria before customer acceptance. If customer acceptance is not achieved within 120 days of delivery of the equipment, Customer B can require Company A to remove the equipment and refund all payments. Payment terms are 80% due upon delivery and 20% due after installation and customer acceptance.

Discussion: Company A should treat the equipment and installation as separate deliverables for accounting purposes since the equipment has value to the customer on a standalone basis and there is no general right of return to consider. However, Company A has a specific refund right related to the equipment that becomes exercisable if installation is not successfully completed within 120 days. As such, the amount allocated to the equipment is limited to the lesser of (a) the amount otherwise allocable to the equipment using the relative selling price method or (b) the amount that is not contingent upon performance of the installation. While $19,500,000 is otherwise allocable to the equipment (i.e., absent the specific refund right), 100% of that amount is contingent upon performance of the installation due to the specific refund right. As such, Company A ultimately should not allocate any arrangement consideration to the equipment. All of the arrangement consideration is effectively allocated to the installation service.

The arrangement consideration allocated to installation should not be recognized until the recognition criteria discussed in other chapters of this product (i.e., Chapter 5, "Product Deliverables," for the equipment, and Chapter 6, "Service Deliverables," for the installation) have been satisfied.

VARIATION 2

Additional Facts: Company A is an experienced provider of installation services related to its equipment. It has never failed to install the equipment as required in a contract within 120 days of delivery. The $20,000,000 arrangement fee is due upon delivery of the equipment. However, if installation is not successfully performed within 120 days of delivery of the equipment, Customer B may cancel the installation portion of the contract with Company A and receive a $750,000 refund from Company A. Customer B does not have the right to return the equipment based on Company A's failure to perform installation. In addition, Customer B has no general refund rights.

Discussion: Company A should treat the equipment and installation as separate deliverables for accounting purposes since the equipment has value to the customer on a standalone basis and there is no general right of return to consider. However, Company A has a specific refund right related to the equipment that becomes exercisable if installation is not successfully completed within 120 days. As such, the amount allocated to the equipment is limited to the lesser of (a) the amount otherwise allocable to the equipment using the relative selling price method or (b) the amount that is not contingent upon performance of the installation. While $19,500,000 is otherwise allocable to the equipment (i.e., absent the specific refund right), $250,000 of that amount is contingent upon performance of the installation due to the specific refund right. As such, Company A ultimately should only allocate $19,250,000 of the arrangement consideration to the equipment. This results in $750,000 of the arrangement consideration ultimately being allocated to the installation.

The arrangement consideration allocated to the equipment should be recognized when the recognition criteria discussed in Chapter 5, "Product Deliverables," have been satisfied. The arrangement consideration allocated to the installation should be recognized when the recognition criteria discussed in Chapter 6, "Service Deliverables," have been satisfied.

Customer Cancellation Provisions

In some cases, an arrangement includes a provision that allows the customer to cancel or terminate the arrangement upon payment of a fee. When such a provision exists in a multiple-deliverable arrangement, a company should assume that the customer will not cancel the arrangement for purposes of allocating arrangement consideration among the deliverables. However, to the extent an amount is recorded as an asset for the excess of revenue recognized over the amount of cash received from the customer since the inception of the arrangement, that asset should not exceed the cancellation fee to which the vendor is entitled under the arrangement. In these situations, the vendor's right to the cancellation fee must be legally enforceable, and the vendor should have the intent to enforce its contractual right to collect the cancellation fee for purposes of supporting recognition of the asset (ASC 605-25-30-6).

Deferred Costs

As noted previously, there are instances when revenue in a multiple-deliverable arrangement may not be recognized even though some of the deliverables have already been delivered. This can occur for several reasons, including a delivered item not having standalone value to a customer and the existence of a specific refund right. When revenue cannot be recognized upon delivery of an item, an issue arises regarding how to treat the costs incurred related to that deliverable.

When costs are minimal, this issue is not significant. However, for many deliverables, the related direct and incremental costs are significant. The accounting literature does not provide detailed guidance on the deferral of costs for multiple-deliverable arrangements, although the costs must meet the definition of an asset as defined in CON-6 in order to qualify for deferral. A discussion on this topic is provided in Chapter 8, "Miscellaneous Issues."

RECOGNITION WHEN DELIVERABLES CANNOT BE SEPARATED

In several situations discussed earlier, revenue from a delivered item cannot be recognized due to its interaction with undelivered items. When this occurs, the arrangement consideration allocable to a delivered item(s) that cannot be treated separately for accounting purposes should be combined with the arrangement consideration allocable to the other applicable undelivered item(s) within the arrangement. The appropriate pattern of revenue recognition should then be determined for that bundled group of deliverables (ASC 605-25-25-6). This pattern of recognition may differ depending upon the reason the deliverables in the multiple-deliverable arrangement were not separated for accounting purposes.

Delivered Item Does Not Have Standalone Value to the Customer

When a delivered item does not have value to the customer on a standalone basis, arrangement consideration otherwise allocable to the delivered item should not be recognized. This component of the arrangement consideration should be recognized, assuming all other revenue recognition criteria have been met, when another item(s) has been provided such that the two (or more) items have value to the customer on a standalone basis. At this point, the timing or pattern of recognition will depend on the nature of the items involved.

OBSERVATION: In the situation where a delivered item does not have value to the customer on a standalone basis (i.e., absent the delivery of one or more undelivered items), it is generally the case that there is at least one undelivered item that is essential to the functionality of the delivered item. As a result, when the delivered item does not have value to the customer on a standalone basis absent the undelivered item, the undelivered item should not be considered an inconsequential or perfunctory remaining performance obligation.

General Refund Right Exists and Performance of Undelivered Item(s) Not Probable or Substantially within Vendor's Control

When a general refund right exists and the delivery or performance of the undelivered items is not considered probable or substantially within the control of the vendor, arrangement consideration otherwise allocable to the delivered item should not be recognized. That arrangement consideration should be recognized, assuming all other revenue recognition criteria have been met, at the earlier of (a) the expiration of the general refund right (i.e., the general refund right is no longer a factor in determining whether the delivered item should be treated separately for accounting purposes) or (b) the performance of the undelivered items becoming probable and substantially within the control of the vendor (i.e., the company will have satisfied the separation condition). At this point, the timing or pattern of recognition will depend on the nature of the items involved.

This approach is consistent with the conclusion that would be reached in applying ASC 605-15-25-1 through 25-4. As discussed in Chapter 5, "Product Deliverables," the criterion that must be met to recognize revenue when a right of return exists is the ability to reasonably estimate the amount of future returns. Making reasonable estimates of the amount of future returns would not be possible if performance of an undelivered item is not probable or substantially in the vendor's control. Failure to meet this criterion (or any of the other necessary criteria under ASC 605-15-25-1 through 25-4) results in the deferral of revenue until the earlier of (a) expiration of the return right or (b) subsequently concluding that the criterion is met. Although not explicitly noted, it is this guidance that resulted in the inclusion of the general refund right condition in ASC 605-25.

OBSERVATION: In the situation where a multiple-deliverable arrangement is not separated because a general refund right exists and performance of the undelivered item(s) is not probable or substantially in the vendor's control, it is highly unlikely that the undelivered item(s) could be considered inconsequential or perfunctory because evaluation of many of the "inconsequential or perfunctory" indicators described earlier in this section would not be possible. As a result, the inability to evaluate these indicators would suggest that the undelivered item(s) is more than inconsequential or perfunctory.

RECOGNITION WHEN SPECIFIC REFUND RIGHT EXISTS

When a specific refund right results in some or all of the amount otherwise allocable to a delivered item (the at-risk amount) not being allocated to that item, the at-risk amount should only be recognized, provided the other criteria for recognition have been met, upon the earlier of (a) the expiration of the specific refund right (i.e., the specific refund right is no longer a factor in determining the amount of revenue that should be allocated to the delivered item) or (b) delivery of the undelivered item on which the specific refund right is based (i.e., the basis for the specific refund right no longer exists). The timing or pattern of recognition at this point will depend on the nature of the items involved.

Given the cost deferral issues that may arise when a specific refund right exists, a question may arise regarding recognition of the amount allocated to a delivered item that is not at-risk. For example, assume the following:

1. There are two deliverables in the arrangement;

2. The total arrangement consideration is $100;

3. The amounts otherwise allocable to Deliverable 1 and Deliverable 2 based on their relative selling prices are $70 and $30, respectively;

4. Deliverable 1 is delivered before Deliverable 2;

5. $100 is due upon receipt of Deliverable 1;

6. If Deliverable 2 is not delivered, the vendor must refund $60; and

7. Deliverable 1 and Deliverable 2 meet the separation criteria in ASC 605-25.

In this situation, the amount ultimately allocated to Deliverable 1 is $40. The $70 that would otherwise have been allocable to Deliverable 1 is reduced to $40 because the amount otherwise allocated to the undelivered deliverable ($30) is less than the amount that would be refunded if the undelivered deliverable is not delivered ($60, for a difference of $30).

Depending on the cost of Deliverable 1 and how that cost is recognized, the recognition of $40 of revenue related to Deliverable 1 could result in a negative profit margin. As a result, a question has arisen regarding whether the $40 of revenue ultimately allocated to Deliverable 1 (and the related cost) could be deferred until the revenue ultimately allocated to Deliverable 2 (and the related cost) is recognized. In this situation, it would be inappropriate to defer the $40 of revenue ultimately allocated to Deliverable 1 if it otherwise meets the applicable revenue recognition criteria. To allow deferral of the revenue in this situation would effectively make the conclusion reached based on applying the guidance in ASC 605-25 (i.e., that the deliverables should be treated separately) optional, which was specifically rejected in the deliberations that led to this guidance. Whether some or all of the cost of Deliverable 1 can be deferred in this situation is discussed in Chapter 8, "Miscellaneous Issues."

OBSERVATION: The existence of a specific refund right related to an as-yet-undelivered item precludes treatment of that item as inconsequential or perfunctory since the vendor's failure to fulfill the remaining performance obligation would result in the customer receiving a full or partial refund or rejecting (or a right to a refund or to reject) delivered items.

TRANSITION FOR ASU 2009-13

As discussed throughout this chapter, ASU 2009-13 made significant changes to the model for multiple-deliverable arrangements in ASC 605-25. The new guidance must be applied in fiscal years beginning after June 15, 2010 (2011 for calendar year companies), and applies to revenue arrangements entered into or significantly modified after its adoption (ASC 605-25-65-1a).

In the year of adoption, qualitative (narrative) information regarding any changes applied prospectively is required, including a discussion of changes to units of accounting for similar arrangements and the effect of those changes on the timing and pattern of revenue recognition (ASC 605-25-65-1c). Quantitative information may also be necessary to explain the effects of the new guidance if the difference is significant (ASC 605-25-65-1d).

Companies that wish to do so may apply the guidance in ASU 2009-13 retroactively to the beginning of any fiscal year. Because the changes made by ASU 2009-13 are so significant, retroactive adoption may be difficult. Nonetheless, companies may wish to elect retroactive adoption because the new guidance does, for certain arrangements, allow accounting that more closely matches the economics of the revenue arrangement. Early adoption was also permitted.

EXAMPLES: ADOPTION OF ASU 2009-13

(Also see Concurrent Computer Corporation example earlier in this chapter)

Apple, Inc. Form 10-Q—Quarterly Period Ended December 26, 2009

Retrospective Adoption of New Accounting Principles

In September 2009, the Financial Accounting Standards Board ("FASB") amended the accounting standards related to revenue recognition for arrangements with multiple deliverables and arrangements that include software elements ("new accounting principles"). The new accounting principles permit prospective or retrospective adoption, and the Company elected retrospective adoption during the first quarter of 2010.

Under the historical accounting principles, the Company was required to account for sales of both iPhone and Apple TV using subscription accounting because the Company indicated it might from time-to-time provide future unspecified software upgrades and features for those products free of charge. Under subscription accounting, revenue and associated product cost of sales for iPhone and Apple TV were deferred at the time of sale and recognized on a straight-line basis over each product's estimated economic life. This resulted in the deferral of significant amounts of revenue and cost of sales related to iPhone and Apple TV.

The new accounting principles generally require the Company to account for the sale of both iPhone and Apple TV as two deliverables. The first deliverable is the hardware and software essential to the functionality of the hardware device delivered at the time of sale, and the second deliverable is the right included with the purchase of iPhone and Apple TV to receive on a when-and-if-available basis future unspecified software upgrades and features relating to the product's essential software. The new accounting principles result in the recognition of substantially all of the revenue and product costs from the sales of iPhone and Apple TV at the time of sale. Additionally, the Company is required to estimate a standalone selling price for the unspecified software upgrade rights included with the sale of iPhone and Apple TV and recognizes that amount ratably over the 24-month estimated life of the related hardware device.

The Company had the option of adopting the new accounting principles on a prospective or retrospective basis. Prospective adoption would have required the

Company to apply the new accounting principles to sales beginning in fiscal year 2010 without reflecting the impact of the new accounting principles on iPhone and Apple TV sales made prior to September 2009. Accordingly, the Company's financial results for the two years following adoption would have included the impact of amortizing the significant amounts of deferred revenue and cost of sales related to historical iPhone and Apple TV sales. The Company believes prospective adoption would have resulted in financial information that was not comparable between financial periods because of the significant amount of past iPhone sales; therefore, the Company elected retrospective adoption. Retrospective adoption required the Company to revise its previously issued financial statements as if the new accounting principles had always been applied. The Company believes retrospective adoption provides the most comparable and useful financial information for financial statement users, is more consistent with the information the Company's management uses to evaluate its business, and better reflects the underlying economic performance of the Company.

NetSuite Inc. Form 10-K—Fiscal Year Ended December 31, 2010

In October 2009, the FASB amended the accounting standards for multiple-element revenue arrangements ("ASU 2009-13") to:

- provide updated guidance on whether multiple deliverables exist, how the elements in an arrangement should be separated, and how the consideration should be allocated;

- require an entity to allocate revenue in an arrangement using estimated selling prices ("ESP") of each element if a vendor does not have vendor-specific objective evidence of selling price ("VSOE") or third-party evidence of selling price ("TPE"); and

- eliminate the use of the residual method and require a vendor to allocate revenue using the relative selling price method.

The Company early adopted this accounting guidance on April 1, 2010, for applicable arrangements entered into or materially modified after January 1, 2010 (the beginning of the Company's fiscal year).

Prior to the adoption of ASU 2009-13, the Company was not able to establish VSOE or TPE for all of the undelivered elements. As a result, the Company typically recognized subscription and support, and professional services revenue ratably over the contract period, and allocated subscription and support revenue and professional services revenue based on the contract price.

As a result of the adoption of ASU 2009-13, the Company allocates revenue to each element in an arrangement based on a selling price hierarchy. The selling price for a deliverable is based on its VSOE, if available, TPE, if VSOE is not available, or ESP, if neither VSOE nor TPE is available. As the Company has been unable to establish VSOE or TPE for the elements of its arrangements, the Company establishes the ESP for each element primarily by considering the weighted average of actual sales prices of professional services sold on a standalone basis and subscription and support including various add-on modules when sold together without professional services, and other factors such as gross margin objectives, pricing practices and growth strategy. The consideration allocated to subscription and support is recognized as revenue over the contract period. The consideration allocated to professional services is recognized as revenue on a percentage-of-completion method. The Company has established processes to determine ESP, allocate revenue in multiple arrangements using ESP, and make reasonably dependable estimates of the percentage-of-completion method for professional services.

The total arrangement fee for a multiple element arrangement is allocated based on the relative ESP of each element unless the fee allocated to the subscription and support under this method is less than the fee subject to refund if the performance conditions are not met. In these instances, since the professional services are generally completed prior to completion of the subscription and support, the allocation of the fee for subscription and support is at least equal to the contractual amounts subject to the performance conditions.

Prior to adoption of ASU 2009-13, in multiple element arrangements where the Company determined that a subset of professional services was essential to the customers use of the subscription services ("Essential Professional Services Arrangements"), the Company deferred the commencement of revenue recognition for the entire arrangement until it had delivered the essential professional services component or made a determination that the remaining professional services were no longer essential to the customer. With the adoption of ASU 2009-13, the Company recognizes revenue for subscription and support services in such arrangement over the contract period commencing when the subscription service is made available to the customer and for professional services on a percentage-of-completion method.

Revenue for the twelve months ended December 31, 2010 was $193.1 million with the adoption of ASU 2009-13. This compares with revenue of $189.5 million for the twelve months ended December 31, 2010, had the Company not adopted ASU 2009-13. The primary driver of the impact was an increase of $2.6 million in professional services and other revenue that the Company recognized for the twelve months ended December 31, 2010 resulting from performing the professional services over a shorter period than the subscription contract term. The Company recognized an increase of $972,000 in subscription and support revenue for the twelve months ended December 31, 2010 due to the adoption of ASU 2009-13. The increase in revenue due to the adoption of ASU 2009-13 for the twelve months ended December 31, 2010 includes an increase of $1.6 million as a result of new Essential Professional Services Arrangements entered into by the Company in 2010. As of December 31, 2010, the Company's deferred revenue was $81.1 million, as compared to $84.7 million had the Company not adopted ASU 2009-13.

For single element sales agreements, subscription and support revenue is recognized ratably over the contract term beginning on the provisioning date of the contract. Prior to April 1, 2010, professional services revenue generated under single element sales agreements was immaterial and therefore was recognized when fully delivered. As of April 1, 2010, the date of adoption of ASU 2009-13, the Company recognizes professional services revenue based on percentage-of-completion method for both single and multiple element arrangements since the Company can now separate the professional services revenue from subscription and support revenue. The Company recognized $516,000 in professional services revenue during the twelve months ended December 31, 2010 from single element arrangements as a result of recognizing revenues on a percentage-of-completion method instead of when fully delivered.

GUARANTEES AND INDEMNIFICATIONS

Some entities, such as financial institutions or insurance companies, are in the "business" of providing guarantees or indemnifications. Other entities provide guarantees or indemnifications in connection with their other, primary business activities. This section of the chapter focuses on the accounting considerations for the latter set of entities. Specifically, it focuses on the accounting by entities that enter into multiple-deliverable arrangements where one of the deliverables is a guarantee and the other deliverables relate to their primary activities.

ASC 460 provides initial accounting and disclosure requirements related to guarantees and indemnifications. ASC 460's broad scope makes it applicable to many provisions that are relatively common in revenue arrangements. For example, equipment manufacturers often guarantee the loans their customers obtain from third-party lenders to purchase the manufacturers' equipment. The accounting for such guarantees is covered by ASC 460. Warranties are also within the scope of ASC 460 and are subject to certain disclosure requirements. Chapter 12, "Disclosures," discusses the disclosure requirements related to guarantees.

Scope

As mentioned above, ASC 460 provides a broad definition of "guarantee." Of course, a provision need not be labeled a "guarantee" in order to fall within the scope of ASC 460. Therefore, careful consideration may be required in order to identify provisions in sales arrangements that meet the definition.

Basic Characteristics

If a guarantee or indemnification possesses any of the following basic characteristics, and does not qualify for one of the exceptions discussed below, it falls within the scope of ASC 460 (ASC 460-10-15-4):

- Contracts that contingently require the guarantor to make payments to the guaranteed party based on changes related to an asset, liability, or equity security of the guaranteed party.
- Contracts that contingently require the guarantor to make payments to the guaranteed party based on another entity's failure to perform under an agreement (performance guarantees).
- Indemnification agreements (contracts) that contingently require the indemnifying party (the guarantor) to make payments to the indemnified party (guaranteed party) based on changes related to an asset, liability, or equity security of the indemnified party.
- Indirect guarantees of the indebtedness of others even though the payment to the guaranteed party may not be based on changes in an underlying that is related to an asset, liability, or equity security of the guaranteed party.

These provisions would scope in a number of routine provisions of sales arrangements, including warranties, volume rebate programs, and many others. However, ASC 460 also includes a number of scope exceptions that make its provisions less onerous. The exceptions that are relevant to revenue arrangements are discussed below. Following that is a discussion of how all of these scope provisions apply to a number of common revenue-related guarantees, indemnifications, or other provisions.

Scope Exceptions

The following types of guarantees that may be found in revenue arrangements are excluded from all of the provisions of ASC 460 (i.e., neither the initial recognition and measurement [IR&M] nor disclosure provisions apply to these guarantees), even if they possess one of the basic characteristics discussed above (ASC 460-10-15-7):

- Guarantees of the residual value of leased property at the end of a lease term by the lessee if the lessee accounts for the lease as a capital lease.

- Guarantees involved in leases that are accounted for as contingent rent.

- Vendor rebates where the contract contingently requires the vendor to make payments to the customer based on the customer's sales revenues, number of units sold, or similar events.

- Guarantees (or indemnifications) whose existence prevents the guarantor from being able to either account for a transaction as the sale of an asset or recognize the profit from that sale transaction.

ASC 460 provides additional exclusions from its IR&M provisions. The following types of guarantees or indemnifications that may be found in revenue arrangements are subject to the disclosure provisions of ASC 460, but are not subject to the IR&M provisions (see Chapter 12, "Disclosures" for a discussion of the disclosure requirements) (ASC 460-10-15-9 and ASC 460-10-25-1):

- Guarantees that meet the definition of a derivative and are accounted for at fair value.

- Product warranties related to the product's ability to function but not its value.

- Guarantees by an original lessee when the lease is modified (as discussed in the authoritative literature addressing lease accounting) such that the original lessee becomes secondarily liable instead of being primarily liable (i.e., primary obligor role shifts from original lessee to new party).

Revenue-Related Guarantees and Indemnifications

The application of the scope provisions of ASC 460 to some of the more common guarantees and indemnifications found in sales arrangements follows:

- *A manufacturer's guarantee of a loan obtained by its customer from a third-party lender to buy the manufacturer's product.* Such a guarantee contains one of the basic characteristics of a guarantee because it requires the manufacturer to make payments to the lender if the customer fails to perform under an obligating agreement (i.e., the customer's loan agreement with the third-party lender). This guarantee does not contain any of the characteristics that would exclude it from any of the provisions of ASC 460.

- *A fixed-price trade-in right offered by a vendor to its customer.* Such a right contains one of the basic characteristics of a guarantee because it may require the seller to make a payment to the purchaser based on changes in the price of the asset purchased. This guarantee does not contain any of the characteristics that would exclude it from any of the provisions of ASC 460 unless the existence of such a guarantee prevents revenue recognition.

- *A product warranty.* As noted above, a product warranty is excluded from ASC 460's IR&M provisions, but the disclosure provisions apply (see Chapter 12, "Disclosures," for a discussion of these disclosure requirements).

- *An indemnification in a software licensing agreement that indemnifies the licensee against liability and damages arising from any claims of patent, copyright, trademark, or trade secret infringement by the software vendor's software.* As discussed in ASC 460-10-55-30 through 55-34, such an indemnification is akin to a product warranty. ASC 460's disclosure provisions apply to this indemnification, while its IR&M provisions do not (see Chapter 12, "Disclosures," for a discussion of the disclosure requirements of FIN-45).

- *Vendor rebates based on the volume of purchases made by a customer over a period of time.* Such a provision does not contain any of the basic characteristics of a guarantee because the contingent payment provision relates to an asset of the vendor, not the purchaser. Payment provisions related to a company's own assets are not guarantees covered by ASC 460.

- *Arrangements that provide for contingent payments to the purchaser such that the contingency prevents revenue recognition.* This is a specific scope exclusion from all of ASC 460. Examples include provisions in product sales arrangements that require the transaction to be accounted for as a consignment or a financing (see Chapter 5, "Product Deliverables"), and software arrangements where the software vendor participates in the customer's financing through either (a) indemnifying the financing party against claims beyond the software vendor's standard indemnifications or (b) guaranteeing the customer's loan with the financing party, thus preventing the recognition of revenue when the presumption that the fee is not fixed or determinable cannot be overcome (see Chapter 10, "Software—A Complete Model").

There are many other types of guarantees or indemnifications in revenue arrangements. Companies should be very diligent in evaluating the provisions of their contracts against the criteria in ASC 460. Consultation with auditors or other experts in this regard may be necessary due to the broad and complex nature of the scope provisions.

Initial Recognition and Measurement

In initially accounting for any guarantee or indemnification, ASC 460 concludes that there are two related but distinct liabilities (ASC 460-10-25-2):

1. *Noncontingent liability.* The guarantor's obligation to stand ready to perform under the terms of the guarantee.

2. *Contingent liability.* The guarantor's potential obligation to make payments in the future related to the guarantee.

The "stand-ready" obligation must be initially recognized at its fair value. If the guarantee or indemnification is the only deliverable in the transaction with an unrelated party, the liability recognized is the fee received by the guarantor for providing that guarantee or indemnification. If the guarantee or indemnification is part of a multiple-deliverable arrangement, the liability recognized should be an estimate of the guarantee or indemnification's fair value (ASC 460-10-30-2).

When a guarantee or indemnification that falls within the scope of the IR&M provisions of ASC 460 exists in an arrangement, it must be separated from the other deliverables and recorded at its fair value. The relative selling price method (or other method, if the arrangement falls within scope of another applicable area of GAAP) should then be used to allocate the remaining consideration among the other deliverables in the arrangement.

Accounting for the contingent liability continues to be governed by ASC 450-20. Therefore, a contingent liability should only be recognized when occurrence of the liability becomes probable and the amount is reasonably estimable. It would be unusual for a contingent liability to be recognized initially (i.e., at the same time as the noncontingent liability). However, if this occurs, the total liability recognized for the guarantee or indemnification should be the greater of (a) the noncontingent liability (i.e., the fair value of the guarantee or indemnification) or (b) the probable and reasonably estimable contingent liability (ASC 460-10-30-3).

Subsequent Measurement

Although ASC 460 does not provide any requirements related to the subsequent measurement of the recorded noncontingent liability, it does provide insight regarding the "typical" subsequent accounting. ASC 460 indicates that the noncontingent liability would typically be taken into income as the guarantor's risk is reduced, which would be (a) when the related guarantee or indemnification expires or is settled (settlement approach), (b) over the term of the guarantee or indemnification based on a systematic and rational amortization method (earnings process approach), or (c) over the term of the guarantee as the fair value of the guarantee changes, but only if this approach is supported by other authoritative literature, such as guarantees that meet the definition of a derivative (fair value approach) (ASC 460-10-35-2). Each of these approaches is discussed below. By contrast, subsequent measurement of the contingent liability is governed by ASC 450-20 and is beyond the scope of this publication:

- *Settlement approach.* This approach would result in the elimination of the noncontingent liability when the guarantor's obligation under the guarantee is settled or when it expires based on the terms of the guarantee.

- *Earnings process approach.* This approach results in the reduction of a noncontingent liability over the period the guarantor stands ready to honor the guarantee. In a sense, this method treats the noncontingent liability as a deferred fee for providing a service. ASC 605-20-25-9 indicates that the pattern over which such a fee should be recognized depends on the nature of the guarantee.

- *Fair value approach.* This approach results in an increase or decrease in the guarantee's carrying amount during the period of the guarantee based on periodic remeasurements. As discussed above, a guarantee "qualifies" for this approach only if there is other supporting authoritative literature. For example, a guarantee that meets the definition of a derivative must be accounted for under ASC 815, which requires it to be subsequently remeasured based on its fair value. While guarantees that meet the definition of a derivative in ASC 815 are excluded from the IR&M provisions of ASC 460, they are subject to the disclosure requirements.

The approach that should be used to subsequently measure the noncontingent liability component of a guarantee is a matter of judgment that depends on both the type of guarantee and the facts and circumstances. The approach selected should be disclosed and consistently applied in similar situations.

DISCLOSURE ALERT: See Chapter 12, "Disclosures," regarding accounting policy disclosure requirements.

ILLUSTRATION: MULTIPLE-DELIVERABLE ARRANGEMENT CONTAINING A GUARANTEE

Facts: On January 1, 20X1, Manufacturer A sells product to Company B for $100,000. Company B arranges financing with Lender C. Lender C requests and receives a guarantee from Manufacturer A. The guarantee calls for Manufacturer A to make Lender C whole if Company B defaults on its loan with Lender C. Manufacturer A determines that the fair value of the guarantee is $10,000 on January 1, 20X1. The term of Company B's loan with Lender C is two years. Manufacturer A is released from the guarantee obligation gradually as Company B makes its payments. Manufacturer A determines that the conditions for revenue recognition are met on January 1, 20X1 (including the collectibility condition). Company B makes the scheduled payments to Lender C for the first year of the loan, totaling $50,000. At the end of 20X1, Manufacturer A determines that the fair value of the guarantee is $3,000. Manufacturer A also concludes that recognition of a contingent liability related to the guarantee is not required at December 31, 20X1. Company B defaults on the first payment due in 20X2, at which point Manufacturer A concludes it will have to make Lender C whole for the remaining balance of Company B's loan. For ease of illustration, the effects of interest are not considered.

Accounting: Manufacturer A recognizes receipt of payment, revenue, and guarantee liability on January 1, 20X1:

Cash	$100,000	
Product Revenue		$90,000
Guarantee (Noncontingent) Liability		$10,000

The entries recorded during 20X1 and 20X2 depend on the approach used by Manufacturer A to subsequently measure the noncontingent guarantee liability. As such, the entries under the settlement and earnings process approaches are presented below, with a comparison of both approaches that follow. Manufacturer A may not use the fair value approach since that approach is not supported by other authoritative literature in relation to Manufacturer A's transaction (e.g., the guarantee does not meet the definition of a derivative under ASC 815).

Settlement Approach

During 20X1, Manufacturer A would not reduce the noncontingent guarantee liability, even though it has been released from half of the guarantee obligation, since the guarantee obligation has not expired or been settled.

Upon Company B's default in 20X2, Manufacturer A would record the contingent loss:

Guarantee Loss	$50,000	
Guarantee (Contingent) Liability		$50,000

Upon Manufacturer A's settlement of the guarantee in 20X2, Manufacturer A would record the cash payment to Lender C to pay off Company B's outstanding loan balance and record the noncontingent guarantee liability as guarantee income since it has been settled:

Guarantee (Contingent) Liability	$50,000	
Cash		$50,000
Guarantee (Noncontingent) Liability	$10,000	
Guarantee Income		$10,000

Earnings Process Approach

During 20X1, Manufacturer A would reduce the noncontingent guarantee liability and recognize guarantee income based on the guidance in ASC 605-20-25-8 (assume straight-line amortization for ease of illustration):

Guarantee (Noncontingent) Liability	$5,000	
Guarantee Income		$5,000

Upon Company B's default in 20X2, Manufacturer A would record the contingent loss:

Guarantee Loss	$50,000	
Guarantee (Contingent) Liability		$50,000

During 20X2, Manufacturer A would continue to reduce the noncontingent guarantee liability and recognize guarantee income:

Guarantee (Noncontingent) Liability	$5,000	
Guarantee Income		$5,000

Upon Manufacturer A's settlement of the guarantee in 20X2, Manufacturer A would record the cash payment to Lender C to pay off Company B's outstanding loan balance:

Guarantee (Contingent) Liability	$50,000	
Cash		$50,000

Comparison	Approach	
	Settlement	Earnings Process
Guarantee Liability at 12/31/20X1	$10,000	$5,000
Guarantee Liability upon Company B's Default	$60,000	$55,000
Guarantee Income During 20X1	$0	$5,000
Guarantee Income During 20X2	$10,000	$5,000
Guarantee Loss During 20X2	$50,000	$50,000

The primary difference between the approaches is the timing of the reduction (or changes) in the noncontingent guarantee liability. Under the settlement approach, Manufacturer A does not reduce the noncontingent guarantee liability until it settles the guarantee obligation. However, under the earnings process approach, the noncontingent guarantee liability will change prior to the guarantee's actual settlement since Manufacturer A amortizes the noncontingent guarantee liability over the period it remains obligated to perform—the guarantee period. Under these two approaches, the guarantee income (noncontingent liability) and guarantee loss (contingent liability) are effectively viewed as two separate amounts related to two separate occurrences. Whether the guarantee income and loss are recognized gross or net on the income statement in these two approaches is a matter of judgment that depends on the facts and circumstances.

CHAPTER 5
PRODUCT DELIVERABLES

CONTENTS

BACKGROUND

The most basic (and probably the most common) sales transaction is the sale of a product for cash. Although the transaction may be simple, the accounting for it is not necessarily straightforward. For example, a retail sale in which the customer pays cash for a product at the checkout counter is a simple transaction for which it seems the accounting should be obvious. When the customer leaves the store, the goods have been delivered and paid for, so it would appear that the revenue has been both earned and realized. However, even this simple transaction typically includes terms that can present revenue recognition issues. For example, most retailers grant customers a right of return for a limited period of time. In addition, there may be both explicit and implicit warranties on the products purchased. These and other common sales terms raise questions about the amount and timing of revenue recognition. More complicated product sale arrangements, such as those between a manufacturer and a reseller or between a parts supplier and its major customers, can introduce a myriad of other obligations and terms that further complicate the amount and timing of revenue recognition.

PRACTICE ALERT: Situations may arise where arrangements that purport to cover only the sale of products actually contain a lease. ASC 840, *Leases*; 840-10-15, discussed in Chapter 3, "General Principles," provides guidance to help determine whether an arrangement contains a lease. Regardless of the formal characterization of an arrangement, the portion of the arrangement that represents a lease must be accounted for using lease accounting principles. Separation of the lease element from the other deliverables in the arrangement is discussed in Chapter 4, "Multiple-Deliverable Revenue Arrangements."

This chapter explores significant accounting issues that are common in product transactions. Where a product transaction includes multiple deliverables, these accounting issues must be evaluated separately for each deliverable in the arrangement. As discussed in Chapter 4, "Multiple-Deliverable Revenue Arrangements," the interrelationship between deliverables in a multiple-deliverable arrangement may give rise to issues beyond those that exist in a single-deliverable transaction.

SURVEY OF ACCOUNTING LITERATURE

U.S. generally accepted accounting principles (GAAP) does not comprehensively address general product sale issues. Some general guidance, although far from comprehensive, is found in the FASB Concepts Statements and ASC 605-10-S99 (SAB Topic 13, Revenue Recognition). Despite the lack of general guidance, many pronouncements address specific product transaction issues. For example, ASC 605-15-25 addresses sales with a right of return. Other guidance on product sale transactions has been developed based on industry practice. In addition, International Financial Reporting Standards ("IFRS"), most notably in IAS 18, provide guidance on certain issues not covered in U.S. GAAP. Although companies reporting under U.S. GAAP are not required to follow IFRS, those standards are good sources for policies that may be acceptable within the U.S. GAAP framework.

REVENUE RECOGNITION LITERATURE

ASC	ASC Topic/Subtopic	Publication	Subject
605-10-S-99	Revenue Recognition/Overall	SAB Topic 13	Revenue Recognition
605-15-25-1	Revenue Recognition/ Products	FAS-48	Revenue Recognition When Right of Return Exists
470-40	Debt/Product Financing Arrangements	FAS-49	Product Financing Arrangements
605-20-25	Revenue Recognition/ Services	FTB 90-1	Separately Priced Extended Warranty and Product Maintenance Contracts
815-10-55-12	Derivatives and Hedging/Overall	EITF 95-1	Revenue Recognition on Sales with a Guaranteed Minimum Resale Value
605-15-25-5	Revenue Recognition/ Products	EITF 95-4	Revenue Recognition on Equipment Sold and Subsequently Repurchased Subject to an Operating Lease

SUPPORTING LITERATURE

ASC	ASC Topic/Subtopic	Publication	Subject
835-30	Interest/Imputation of Interest	APB-21	Interest on Receivables and Payables
460	Guarantees (Product Warranties Subsections)	FAS-5	Product Warranties

ASC	ASC Topic/Subtopic	Publication	Subject
460	Guarantees (General Subsections)	FIN-45	Guarantees
840-10-15	Leases	EITF 01-8	Determining Whether an Arrangement Contains a Lease

EXHIBIT 5-1: OVERVIEW OF PRODUCT REVENUE RECOGNITION

This flowchart, which extends over multiple pages, provides a visual representation of the key factors that often affect the timing and amount of revenue recognition on sales of products. Each of the key issues highlighted in the flowchart is discussed further in this chapter.

EXHIBIT 5-1: OVERVIEW OF PRODUCT REVENUE RECOGNITION

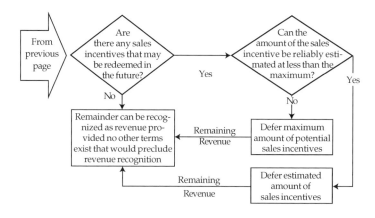

GENERAL CONDITIONS FOR RECOGNITION

As with all revenues, product sales revenue should be recognized when it has been earned and is realized or realizable. Revenue from product sales is generally earned when the products are delivered to the customer. Such revenue is usually considered realizable once the customer has committed to pay for the products and the customer's ability to pay is not in doubt. However, various types of uncertainties may exist that affect *when* (timing) and *how much* (amount) revenue is recognized (CON-5, pars. 83 and 84).

As discussed in Chapter 3, "General Principles," revenue is considered earned and realizable when all of the following conditions are met:

1. Persuasive evidence of an arrangement exists.

2. The arrangement fee is fixed or determinable.

3. Delivery or performance has occurred.

4. Collectibility is reasonably assured.

In addition, the delivery condition in a product sale should generally be evaluated under the Completed Performance model. This means that delivery occurs at a single point in time, rather than over an extended period. Although this point in time usually is when physical delivery of the product occurs, there are many arrangements where this is not the case.

The guidance in this chapter addresses most product deliverables. However, certain contracts to deliver products should be accounted for using contract accounting principles. These contracts are typically for building a customized product that will take an extended period of time to complete. Contract accounting is discussed in Chapter 9, "Contract Accounting."

Risks and Rewards of Ownership

In a product sale, all of the general conditions for revenue recognition are usually present at the time the product is delivered (i.e., when the buyer takes physical possession of the product from the seller). In general, the delivery requirement for purposes of recognizing revenue is satisfied when substantial risks and rewards of ownership of the goods have passed from the seller to the buyer.

The term "risks and rewards of ownership" refers to all of the things that would normally accrue to an owner of products. For example, risks of ownership include a loss of market value, obsolescence, theft, physical damage, and excess inventory. Rewards of ownership include gains due to increases in value, the right to use and restrict the use of the product, the right to sell or otherwise determine the disposition of the product, the right to enhance the existing product, and the ability to grant security interests in the product.

The physical transfer of a product does not always indicate that revenue has been earned. For example, in some transactions, the seller may retain specified risks or benefits after the product has been transferred to the customer; in other transactions, all risks and benefits may be transferred to the buyer before the product is delivered to the buyer. The issues discussed in this chapter generally relate to whether the retention by the seller of a specific risk or reward precludes revenue recognition.

Manufacturers versus Resellers

The same general revenue recognition guidance applies whether the products being sold have been manufactured by the company or were purchased for resale. Thus, the act of manufacturing or building a product is not an earnings event, except in the case of long-term contracts accounted for under the Percentage-of-Completion model (see Chapter 9, "Contract Accounting").

The identity of the customer, however, may have some effect on the revenue recognition analysis. For example, although the principles of revenue recognition are the same whether the customer is an end-user or a reseller, the results of applying those principles (e.g., to rights of return) can vary significantly depending on whether the customer is an end-user or a reseller.

DELIVERY

Transfer of Title

As noted above, physical delivery is often the time when revenue is considered earned, because the risks and rewards of ownership generally rest with the holder of the products and, therefore, pass to the buyer at delivery. However, with rare exceptions (see "Title Retained after Delivery," below), physical delivery must be accompanied by the passage of "title" from the seller to the buyer before revenue can be recognized. "Title" is a term that generally pertains to the ownership of goods in a legal sense. The party that has title to goods is assumed to control their use and be at risk of loss, absent contractual arrangements stating otherwise. Therefore, for accounting purposes, products generally are considered delivered when title passes from the seller to the buyer. In many transactions, such as retail purchases, passage of title is not documented in any formal manner, but the timing of title transfer is clear from the transaction (e.g., title passes at the register when the customer pays for the merchandise).

However, the timing of title transfer is not as clear in many other transactions. For example, without analyzing the specific contract, it is not clear when title transfers for goods delivered by mail; in some cases, title transfers when the goods are put in the mail and in others, title transfers only upon receipt by the buyer. A similar situation exists for manufacturers who ship to their customers by modes of transportation such as truck or train using a third-party shipping agent. Because the transfer of title is basically a legal concept, it may be necessary to consult with legal experts to determine when title transfers. In most situations, however, a basic understanding of local laws and the terms agreed upon by the buyer and seller are enough to determine when title has transferred.

OBSERVATION: Transfer of title is important in revenue recognition for product sales, because it generally determines when the risk of loss and control of the products passes from the seller to the buyer. However, contractual arrangements can separate the transfer of certain risks or rights from the transfer of title. As discussed above, when risks and rewards of ownership remain with the seller, revenue recognition often is not appropriate. This is true even if title has been transferred. For further discussion, see "Consignment Sales" below.

Free-on-Board Terms

Free-on-Board (FOB) terms generally designate which party pays for shipping the products. "FOB shipping point" means that the shipping is paid for by the buyer. "FOB destination" means that the shipping is paid for by the seller. In most cases, the party that pays for shipping owns (i.e., has title to) the products during shipment. Therefore, FOB destination indicates that title to the product passes upon delivery to the customer. FOB shipping point signifies that title passes when the products leave the seller's premises. The FOB terms are usually specified in a contract between the parties, the purchase order, the bill of lading, or some other documentation of the sales transaction.

OBSERVATION: Although rare, some contracts specify that title transfers at a different point during transit—for example, when a particular border is crossed. Other contracts may specify that title transfers either before the goods leave the seller's premises or some time after they are received by the buyer.

If the risks and rewards of ownership transfer at the same time that the title transfers, FOB terms specify the point at which revenue can be considered earned. For accounting purposes, products shipped FOB shipping point can generally be considered delivered when the goods leave the seller's premises. Products shipped FOB destination are considered delivered when the goods reach the customer. As such, FOB terms indicate whether outbound shipments in transit should be recognized as a sale at period-end. FOB shipping point terms result in recognition of revenue and cost of sales at the end of a reporting period for shipments in transit at that date (provided the other criteria for recognition have been met); FOB destination terms result in shipments in transit not being recorded until the subsequent reporting period (ASC 605-10-S99, A3a) (SAB Topic 13A3a).

OBSERVATION: Even when FOB destination terms are used such that title does not transfer until the buyer receives the products, the risk of physical loss on the products may be held by a third-party shipping agent and not the seller. However, this does not allow the seller to recognize revenue before the shipping agent completes delivery to the buyer because the shipper is the seller's agent and the seller will not have fulfilled its obligations to the buyer until the products are delivered.

PRACTICE POINTER: A majority of companies routinely record all sales transactions when they leave the company's premises. This is done even if the goods are shipped FOB destination, because it is far easier to determine the point at which goods are shipped than it is to determine when the customer receives them. When this procedure is used on FOB destination shipments, the company should evaluate the amount of outbound shipments in transit at period-end and reverse the recognition of sales and cost of sales for those transactions if the effects are material.

Local Laws

Because title is essentially a legal concept, laws sometimes specify the point at which title transfers. In certain jurisdictions, these laws can be overridden by contractual language; in others, the laws override any documentation of title transfer. As a result, local laws must be taken into account to determine when title has transferred. This is especially important in transactions where the seller and buyer are in different jurisdictions.

EXAMPLES: DELIVERY

Amazon.com, Inc. Form 10-K—Fiscal Year Ended December 31, 2010

Product sales and shipping revenues, net of promotional discounts, rebates, and return allowances, are recorded when the products are shipped and title passes to customers. Retail sales to customers are made pursuant to a sales contract that provides for transfer of both title and risk of loss upon our delivery to the carrier.

International Paper Company Form 10-K—Fiscal Year Ended December 31, 2009

Revenue is recognized when the customer takes title and assumes the risks and rewards of ownership. Revenue is recorded at the time of shipment for terms designated f.o.b. (free on board) shipping point. For sales transactions designated f.o.b. destination, revenue is recorded when the product is delivered to the customer's delivery site, when title and risk of loss are transferred. Timber and timberland sales revenue is generally recognized when title and risk of loss pass to the buyer.

Subscriptions

When products are sold under a subscription arrangement, the delivery condition should be evaluated under the Proportional Performance model and revenue should be allocated to each product in proportion to its value. In many cases, each item is allocated the same amount of revenue because their individual values do not vary significantly (e.g., a magazine or newspaper subscription). As each item is delivered, revenue allocated to that item should be recognized, unless other terms of the transaction prohibit recognition. Subscription revenue may not be recognized when the subscription is received or billed with an accrual of the estimated costs to fulfill the subscription, even when the subscription price is completely nonrefundable. In this case, revenue is realized at the inception of the subscription, but only earned as the products are delivered.

Delivery to an Alternate Site or Third Party

A seller's performance may generally be considered complete upon delivery to a third party designated by the buyer, unless the seller retains an explicit or implicit obligation to deliver the product to the customer. For example, a company that purchases inventory in excess of its currently available storage space may direct the seller to deliver the products to a third-party warehouse for storage. As long as full payment is due on normal terms upon delivery to the third party, and the customer is responsible for storage costs and transporting the product to its own facilities when needed, the delivery criterion would be met.

However, if a significant portion of the purchase price is not payable until the product reaches the customer, delivery to the third party should not result in revenue recognition, even when the buyer has chosen the third party. The delay in payment until final delivery indicates that the seller retains risk until the customer receives the product at the final delivery point. If this is the case, a partial payment received upon delivery to the third party should be reflected as a liability, rather than as revenue (ASC 605-10-S99, A3a) (SAB Topic 13A3a).

When a product is delivered to a third party selected by the seller, revenue recognition must usually be delayed until the product is delivered to the customer. For example, a mail order catalog company may deliver goods to an outside fulfillment house, which will then package and ship the goods to the customer. In this type of arrangement, revenue should only be recognized upon final delivery to the customer, because the fulfillment house is an agent of the seller. However, if the buyer specifically acknowledges that, upon delivery to the third party, the seller has no further obligation with respect to the transaction and that the buyer must look solely to the third party to obtain final delivery of the products, the delivery criterion will generally be satisfied.

Title Retained after Delivery

In some situations, sellers retain title after goods are delivered. The most common example is in consignment arrangements. Generally, delivery does not occur on a consignment until title passes to the buyer. However, there are instances where the delivery condition is met even though title is retained. In these limited circumstances, all significant risks and rewards of ownership must still transfer to the buyer, even though title does not pass.

One example is when the seller retains title to provide security for the collection of the purchase price and the seller's rights are limited to taking action only in the event of nonpayment. This may occur in countries where local laws and customs do not provide the seller with a security interest in products that have been sold but not yet paid for. If the seller retains title, but its rights are limited to recovering the goods only in the event of nonpayment—that is, the seller cannot, for example, rescind the transaction or prohibit the customer from doing what it wishes with the goods, despite holding title—revenue can be recognized upon delivery provided that the other conditions for revenue recognition have also been met. In the U.S., however, the Uniform Commercial Code provides the seller with a security interest in goods that have not yet been paid for even after passage of title, so title generally need not be retained for this purpose (ASC 605-10-S99, A2, ques. 3) (SAB Topic 13A2, ques. 3).

Other transactions in which the seller retains title after delivery should be analyzed as leasing transactions. If the transaction can be classified as a sales-type lease under the leasing literature, revenue recognition upon delivery may be appropriate.

PRACTICE POINTER: Some companies sell their products pursuant to standard contracts with clauses that enhance the seller's rights to payment for the products sold. Although the clause is included for a sound business purpose, the retention of title generally exposes the seller to certain risks and entitles it to certain rights (in addition to a security interest in the event of nonpayment) that could affect the timing of revenue recognition. Therefore, companies that retain title to products after shipment but before payment should determine the legal effect of such an arrangement. If title retention is solely meant to ensure timely payment by the customer, revenue recognition may still be appropriate. However, if title retention exposes the seller to any additional risks or rights, regardless of whether the seller intends to exercise its rights, the product should not be considered delivered until payment is received and title passes.

EXAMPLE: TITLE RETENTION TO RECOVER PRODUCTS IN EVENT OF CUSTOMER DEFAULT

Unisys Corporation Form 10-K—Fiscal Year Ended December 31, 2009

Revenue from hardware sales with standard payment terms is recognized upon the passage of title and the transfer of risk of loss. Outside the United States, the company recognizes revenue even if it retains a form of title to products delivered to customers, provided the sole purpose is to enable the company to recover the products in the event of customer payment default and the arrangement does not prohibit the customer's use of the product in the ordinary course of business.

DELIVERY WITHOUT A TRANSFER OF RISK

Consignment Sales

A consignment "sale" is not a sale at all. A shipment of goods "on consignment" generally means that payment (and title passage) is expected only when the purchaser resells the inventory to a customer or uses it in production. As a result, the seller retains ownership of the inventory and unsold/unused items may be returned by the purchaser. Because the seller retains title and most risks and rewards of ownership, except perhaps custodial risks (e.g., the risk of physical loss), the shipment of goods on consignment does not constitute delivery for accounting purposes and does not trigger the recognition of revenue (ASC 605-10-S99, A2, ques. 2) (SAB Topic 13A2, ques. 2).

Consignment sales usually are specified in a contract. However, a contract need not be labeled as a consignment to be treated as one for accounting purposes. For example, with rare exception (see "Title Retained After Delivery" above), a purported sale in which title remains with the seller until the buyer resells, pays for, or uses the goods should be treated as a consignment, because the lack of title transfer will usually mean that significant risks and rewards remain with the seller.

Even when title transfers to the buyer upon delivery, the arrangement terms may nonetheless indicate that the transaction is a consignment and should be treated as one. This frequently occurs in situations in which the buyer is essentially acting as a sales or fulfillment agent for the seller. For example, an arrangement in which title passes to the customer upon shipment and the customer has unlimited rights of return and need not pay for the goods until resale occurs is, in substance, a consignment. In these cases, revenue should not be recognized until the goods are resold. However, determining when a transaction is substantively similar to a consignment is a matter of significant judgment. Some factors that may be indicative of an in-substance consignment are as follows:

OBSERVATION: Although these factors may be explicitly detailed in the sales agreement, they can also exist by custom or historical practice between the parties. For example, a small manufacturer whose product is mainly distributed by a large retailer may have little or no leverage to enforce specific terms in the sales agreement and, therefore, agree to accept returns or give sales discounts that are not explicitly documented. In this situation, an evaluation of whether these implicit rights create an in-substance consignment should be conducted.

---

1. *Payment is not due until the goods have been resold.* The buyer has no risk of loss.

2. *The buyer lacks substance, or uses financing or guarantees from the seller to purchase the products.* In this situation, the seller retains the risk of loss through its financing-related commitments.

OBSERVATION: If the seller guarantees debt incurred by the buyer to purchase the seller's products and the arrangement is not a consignment or product financing (see below), the seller has entered into a multiple-deliverable arrangement with the buyer. The deliverables in this arrangement consist of the product and the guarantee. The application of ASC 460 to this situation is discussed in Chapter 4, "Multiple-Deliverable Revenue Arrangements."

3. *The buyer has, in substance, an unlimited right of return.* This removes the buyer's risk of loss because the product can be returned if the item is not resold.

4. *The buyer pays more than other customers or makes purchases above and beyond its normal needs.* This indicates that some type of side arrangement may exist between the seller and buyer.

5. *The seller imposes constraints on the buyer's sales, pricing, credit, and advertising policies.* This indicates that the seller has retained some control over the use and disposition of the product and, therefore, not enough risks and rewards of ownership have passed to the buyer to permit revenue recognition.

6. *The seller agrees to take returns from the buyer if the buyer gets returns from its customers.* This removes some of the buyer's risk for the product and may indicate that the buyer is essentially acting as the seller's agent.

7. *The seller agrees to assume the credit risk that exists in the buyer/reseller's sales to end customers.* The reseller may, in substance, be acting as the seller's agent.

8. *The payment due the seller varies based on its customer's success in reselling the product.* The reseller may, in substance, be acting as the seller's agent.

OBSERVATION: None of the factors discussed above definitively indicate that an arrangement should be accounted for as a consignment. However, all transactions with any of the above characteristics should be carefully evaluated to determine their substance. It is also important to analyze a company's history of ultimately resolving these transactions. For example, if the buyer/reseller has a long right of return but payment for the products is made promptly and returns are small and predictable, this right of return may not be indicative of an arrangement that is, in substance, a consignment. Conversely, if payment is not due until the end of a long return period or if significant returns frequently occur just before the return period lapses, the arrangement would appear to be an in-substance consignment.

SEC REGISTRANT ALERT: In early 2003, the SEC staff issued the Report Pursuant to Section 704 of the Sarbanes-Oxley Act of 2002 (Section 704 Report). In compiling the information in this report, the SEC staff studied enforcement actions filed during the period July 31, 1997, through July 30, 2002. The greatest number of enforcement actions related to improper revenue recognition, and one of the issues highlighted in the report was the accounting for consignment sales. The SEC staff noted that the accounting for consignment sales (and other contingency sales) "generally failed to meet the criteria under U.S. GAAP for recognizing revenue because the seller had not actually assumed the risks and rewards of ownership, the terms of the sale were modified, or the revenue was otherwise not realized (or realizable) and earned." This finding is a strong indication that more attention should be given to the identification of and accounting for consignment sales.

EXAMPLES: IN-SUBSTANCE CONSIGNMENTS

Advanced Micro Devices, Inc. Form 10-K—Fiscal Year Ended December 26, 2009

The Company recognizes revenue from products sold directly to customers, including original equipment manufacturers (OEMs), when persuasive evidence of an arrangement exists, the price is fixed or determinable, delivery has occurred and collectibility is reasonably assured. Estimates of product returns, allowances and future price reductions, based on actual historical experience and other known or anticipated trends and factors, are recorded at the time revenue is recognized. The Company sells to distributors under terms allowing the distributors certain rights of return and price protection on unsold merchandise held by them. The distributor agreements, which may be cancelled by either party upon specified notice, generally contain a provision for the return of those of the Company's products that the Company has removed from its price book or that are not more than twelve months older than the manufacturing code date. In addition, some agreements with distributors may contain standard stock rotation provisions permitting limited levels of product returns. Accordingly, the Company defers the gross margin resulting from the deferral of both revenue and related product costs from sales to distributors with agreements that have the aforementioned terms until the merchandise is resold by the distributors and reports such deferred amounts as "Deferred income on shipments to distributors" on its consolidated balance sheet. Products are sold to distributors at standard published prices that are contained in price books that are broadly provided to the Company's various distributors. Distributors are then required to pay for this product within the Company's standard commercial terms, which are typically net 30 days. The Company uses reserves to record price protection given to distributors and customer rebates in the period of distributor re-sale. The Company determines these reserves based on specific contractual terms with its distributors. Price reductions generally do not result in sales prices that are less than the Company's product cost. Gross margin resulting from the deferral of both revenue and related product costs on shipments to distributors is revalued at the end of each fiscal period based on the change in inventory units at distributors, latest published prices, and latest product costs.

The Company also sells its products to distributors with substantial independent operations under sales arrangements whose terms do not allow for rights of return or price protection on unsold products held by them. In these instances, the Company recognizes revenue when it ships the product directly to the distributors.

Silicon Image, Inc. Form 10-K—Fiscal Year Ended December 31, 2009

For products sold to distributors with agreements allowing for price concessions and stock rotation rights/product returns, we recognize revenue based on when the distributor reports that it has sold the product to its customer. Our recognition of such distributor sell-through is based on point of sales reports received from the distributor which establishes a customer, quantity and final price. Revenue is not recognized upon our shipment of product to the distributor, since, due to certain forms of price concessions, the sales price is not substantially fixed or determinable at the time of shipment. Price concessions are recorded when incurred, which is generally at the time the distributor sells the product to its customer. Additionally, these distributors have stock rotation rights permitting them to return products to us, up to a specified amount for a given period of time. When the distributor reports that it has sold product to its customer, our sales price to the distributor is fixed. Once we receive the point of sales reports from a distributor, it has satisfied all the requirements for revenue recognition with respect to the product reported as sold and any product returns/stock rotation and price concession rights that the distributor has under its distributor agreement with Silicon Image lapsed at that time. Pursuant to our distributor agreements, older, end-of-life and certain other products are generally sold with no right of return and are not eligible for price concessions. For these products, revenue is recognized upon shipment and title transfer assuming all other revenue recognition criteria are met.

At the time of shipment to distributors, we record a trade receivable for the selling price since there is a legally enforceable right to payment, relieve inventory for the carrying value of goods shipped since legal title has passed to the distributor and, until revenue is recognized, record the gross margin in "deferred margin on sale to distributors," a component of current liabilities in our consolidated balance sheets. Deferred margin on the sale to distributor effectively represents the gross margin on the sale to the distributor. However, the amount of gross margin we recognize in future periods will be less than the originally recorded deferred margin on sales to distributor as a result of negotiated price concessions. We sell each item in our product price book to all of our distributors worldwide at a relatively uniform list price. However, distributors resell our products to end customers at a very broad range of individually negotiated price points based on customer, product, quantity, geography, competitive pricing and other factors. The majority of our distributors' resale is priced at a discount from list price. Often, under these circumstances, we remit back to the distributor a portion of their original purchase price after the resale transaction is completed. Thus, a portion of the "deferred margin on the sale to distributor" balance represents a portion of distributors' original purchase price that will be remitted back to the distributor in the future. The wide range and variability of negotiated price concessions granted to distributors does not allow us to accurately estimate the portion of the balance in the deferred margin on the sale to distributors line item that will be remitted back to the distributors. In addition to the above, we also reduce the deferred margin by anticipated or determinable future price protections based on revised price lists, if any.

Product Financing Arrangements

In the consignment arrangements discussed above, payment to the vendor is delayed until the products are used or resold. When payment is due upon delivery or shortly thereafter, a transaction would generally not be considered a consignment. However, certain terms included in the sales agreement may indicate that, substantively, the sale is actually a financing arrangement—that is, a secured borrowing with the inventory serving as collateral. Sales of inventory should be analyzed as financing arrangements when payment is due under normal terms but the risks and rewards of ownership have not been transferred to the purchaser.

ASC 470-40 addresses product financing arrangements and specifies that a financing, rather than a sale, exists if the following two conditions are met (ASC 470-40-15-2):

1. *The arrangement requires the seller to repurchase the product (or a substantially identical product), or processed goods that the product is a component of, at specified prices, and the prices are not subject to change except for fluctuations due to financing and holding costs.* This condition indicates that the seller has retained risks related to the market value of the product, because it will be forced to repurchase the product, regardless of market demand.

2. *The amount the seller will pay to repurchase the products covers (or will be adjusted to cover) the buyer's purchasing and holding costs (including interest).* This indicates that the buyer's return from the transaction is essentially a financing return, rather than one a company would expect from purchasing and reselling inventory.

The above terms need not be explicitly stated for the arrangement to be treated as a product financing. ASC 470-40-15-2 notes that a repurchase obligation substantively exists in any of the following situations:

- The seller agrees to make up any difference between certain specified resale prices and the actual resale price for products when they are sold by the buyer.

- The seller has an option, but not an obligation, to repurchase the product, but there is a significant incentive for the seller to exercise the repurchase option. An example is an arrangement that provides for a significant penalty if the seller does not exercise its option.

- The buyer has a put option whereby it can require the seller to repurchase the product.

OBSERVATION: Many product financing arrangements can be difficult to identify. However, these transactions all share a common characteristic—they are largely motivated by the seller's immediate need for cash, even when responsibility for the products being sold is retained by the seller. As a result, product financing arrangements can often be identified by determining whether the seller retains the responsibility (either in real or financial terms) for the products, even after they are paid for by the buyer. Similarly, a buyer's motivation in a product financing arrangement is to earn a return from the seller (that is similar to what a lender would receive) on the money it spends to purchase and hold the product. For example, a sales transaction in which the buyer has a right of return that enables it to recover more than the purchase price (plus any processing costs) of the inventory items may be indicative of a financing arrangement. In addition, a purported sale to a financial institution may very well be, in-substance, a product financing arrangement.

When an arrangement is accounted for as a product financing, payments received from the "customer" should be recorded as a liability and generally classified as debt (see Chapter 11, "Presentation") and the inventory delivered to the buyer should remain on the seller's books. As the buyer incurs holding costs (such as insurance) and processing costs, the seller should record a payable to the buyer as if the buyer had incurred the costs on the seller's behalf. The seller should then account for the costs consistent with their nature and the seller's normal policies. Repurchase payments in excess of the original debt recorded and the accrued holding and processing costs should be treated as interest expense.

ILLUSTRATION: PRODUCT FINANCING ARRANGEMENT

Facts: The Grenache Co. sells 100 cases of its 2005 vintage Grenache to AMS Cellars for $500 per case, receiving $50,000 cash upon delivery. The Grenache Co. agrees to repurchase any unsold cases of the 2005 Grenache from AMS in six months at $525 per unit. The Grenache Co. estimates, based on its history of selling Grenache to AMS, that AMS will resell 94 of the 100 cases within six months and, therefore, The Grenache Co. believes it will repurchase six cases in six months at $525 per case. Market interest rates are approximately 10% for secured borrowings. AMS sells 50 of the 100 cases of the 2005 Grenache to a third party three months later and sells another 44 cases just before the six months are up. The remaining six units are sold back to The Grenache Co. at the stipulated $525 per case price. Holding costs for the 2005 Grenache are negligible.

Accounting: Because The Grenache Co. has granted AMS the right to put unsold inventory back to it at a price that equals the original sales price increased by an amount that represents a financing rate of return, the transaction should be treated as a product financing arrangement. Therefore, no revenue can be recognized upon delivery, despite The Grenache Co.'s ability to estimate its ultimate obligation under the arrangement. Because no revenue is recognized, the inventory remains on The Grenache Co.'s books. The accounting is as follows:

- At the inception of the arrangement, The Grenache Co. records the cash received:

Cash	$50,000	
Debt		$50,000

- For three months, The Grenache Co. records interest on the entire debt ($50,000 × 10% effective rate × $\frac{1}{4}$ of a year = $1,250)

Interest Expense	$1,250	
Interest Payable		$1,250

- When AMS sells the first 50 units, The Grenache Co. recognizes revenue and eliminates that portion of the debt:

Debt	$25,000	
Interest Payable	$625	
Revenue		$25,625

- For the remaining three months, The Grenache Co. records interest on the remaining debt ($25,000 × 10% effective rate × $1/4$ of a year = $625):

Interest Expense	$625	
Interest Payable		$625

- When AMS sells the next 44 units, The Grenache Co. recognizes revenue and eliminates that portion of the debt:

Debt	$22,000	
Interest Payable	$1,100	
Revenue		$23,100

- The Grenache Co. records the repurchase of the remaining six units:

Debt	$3,000	
Interest Payable	$150	
Cash		$3,150

The accounting is the same as if The Grenache Co. borrowed $25,000 for three months and another $25,000 for six months at a 10% interest rate, and then sold 50 cases of the 2005 Grenache at $512.50 per unit in three months and another 44 cases of the 2005 Grenache at $525 per cases in the next three months. This is consistent with the conclusion that the original transaction is essentially a financing transaction, rather than a true product sale.

REVENUE RECOGNITION BEFORE DELIVERY

"Bill and Hold" Sales

In certain situations, revenue may be recognized before shipment if delivery is delayed at the buyer's request and the buyer takes title and agrees to pay for the goods in advance. This type of transaction is called a "bill and hold" sale. Both the SEC and the IASB have addressed these sales transactions; they have not been addressed by a U.S. accounting standard-setter. As a result, private companies preparing financial statements under U.S. GAAP are not subject to any specific requirements. Nonetheless, private companies should adopt a consistent accounting policy and the SEC and IFRS models provide the best policy frameworks available. The IFRS model is found in IAS 18, par. 14 and appendix par. 1, while the SEC model is found in ASC 605-10-S99, A3a (SAB Topic 13A3a).

Both models attempt to ensure that revenue is only recognized if the substance of the transaction (apart from the physical location of the goods) is exactly the same as if the products had been shipped to the buyer. The criteria are, therefore, restrictive and generally result in recognition only upon delivery to the buyer. This is particularly the case with the SEC model, which must be used by public companies preparing U.S. GAAP financial statements. Details of both models are as follows:

1. *(IFRS and SEC) Risks of ownership must have passed to the buyer.* This is a standard criterion that must be met before recognizing revenue in any product sale transaction.

2. *(IFRS) The amount of revenue can be measured reliably.* This is a standard criterion that must be met before recognizing revenue in any transaction.

   (SEC) Although the SEC's position on bill and hold sales does not specifically include a similar requirement, the requirement that the fee be fixed or determinable (see Chapter 3, "General Principles") covers this point.

3. *(IFRS) The seller does not continue to exercise managerial responsibility or control over the products.* If the seller retains control or involvement, this indicates that the risks and rewards did not transfer as they would if the products had been delivered.

   (SEC) The seller cannot retain any specific performance obligations such that the earnings process is not complete. Although the SEC focuses on the risks of continuing involvement rather than the control that such involvement provides, the intent is similar. If the seller has any performance obligations remaining, the revenue has not been earned.

4. *(IFRS) It is probable that the seller will realize revenue on the sale.* This is a standard criterion that must be met before recognizing revenue in any sale.

   (SEC) The customer must have made a fixed commitment to purchase the goods, preferably in writing. The SEC states the same provision more definitively because the staff is concerned that any conditions or contingencies may indicate that the transaction has not yet been consummated. Thus, revenue recognition on a bill and hold transaction would be precluded if, for example, the customer has a right of return.

5. *(IFRS) Any costs to be incurred related to the sale can be measured reliably.* If the seller expects to incur costs of an uncertain amount, it is difficult to conclude that all of the seller's significant obligations have been fulfilled.

   (SEC) The goods must be complete and ready for shipment. This effectively prohibits the incurrence of any future costs, other than those related to delivery.

6. *(IFRS) It is probable that delivery will be made.* If delivery is not probable, the existence of the transaction is called into question, especially if payment has not yet been received.

   (SEC) There must be a fixed delivery schedule that is consistent with the buyer's business purpose. The SEC believes that the delivery date (s) must be set before revenue can be recognized, a more restrictive requirement than the comparable IFRS requirement.

7. *(IFRS) The goods are on hand, identified, and ready for delivery.* If the goods are not currently available for delivery, revenue recognition is not appropriate because delivery cannot yet be fulfilled.

   (SEC) The goods must be segregated from remaining inventory so that they cannot be used to fill orders for others. This criterion, which requires that the goods be treated as if they have been delivered to the customer, is somewhat more explicit than the comparable IFRS criterion.

8. *(IFRS) The buyer specifically acknowledges the deferred delivery instructions.* Without this acknowledgement, it is difficult to substantiate that a contractual arrangement for the sale exists.

(SEC) The buyer, not the seller, must request (typically in writing) that the transaction be on a bill and hold basis and the buyer must have a substantial business purpose for ordering on a bill and hold basis. The SEC's model is more restrictive because the SEC believes that bill and hold provisions must be acknowledged and requested by the buyer and that the reason for the request should be disclosed.

9. *(IFRS) The usual payment terms apply.* Deferred payment terms may indicate that payment is tied to delivery and that the substance of the transaction is a purchase upon shipment.

(SEC) The date by which the seller expects payment and whether the seller has modified its normal billing and credit terms for this buyer. If the seller has modified its normal billing and credit terms, the transaction should be evaluated to determine whether payment terms have been extended and the seller should determine whether payment is unlikely or specifically tied to delivery. The latter would indicate that it is a bill and hold transaction for which revenue recognition is inappropriate.

If the seller determines that revenue recognition is appropriate, the SEC model requires assessment of whether the related receivable should be discounted in accordance with ASC 835-30.

SEC REGISTRANT ALERT: In early 2003, the SEC staff issued the Report Pursuant to Section 704 of the Sarbanes-Oxley Act of 2002 (Section 704 Report). In compiling the information in the Section 704 Report, the SEC staff studied enforcement actions filed during the period July 31, 1997, through July 30, 2002. The greatest number of enforcement actions related to improper revenue recognition and one of the issues highlighted in the report was the accounting for bill and hold transactions. The SEC staff noted that, "Improper accounting for bill-and-hold transactions usually involves the recording of revenue from a sale, even though the customer has not taken title of the product and assumed the risks and rewards of ownership of the products specified in the customer's purchase order or sales agreement. . . . These transactions may be recognized legitimately under U.S. GAAP when special criteria are met, including being done pursuant to the buyer's request." This finding underscores the requirement that the above conditions be met prior to recognizing revenue on a bill and hold transaction. It also indicates common shortcomings in bill and hold transactions from a revenue recognition perspective, including items 1 and 8 as discussed above.

The criteria discussed above have been specifically identified by the IASB and the SEC and must be met to recognize revenue on a bill and hold basis. However, other factors might also be useful in assessing whether the substance of the bill and hold agreement is that of a consummated transaction for which revenue recognition is appropriate, or that of a (potential) future transaction for which revenue should not yet be recognized. For example, ASC 605-10-S99, A3a

(SAB Topic 13A3a) identifies a number of examples of additional factors that might be relevant:

- *Past experiences with bill and hold transactions.* If payments in past transactions were received late or not at all, the substance of the transactions may have been agreements to make purchases at a later date or upon delivery.

- *Whether the buyer bears the risk of loss in the event of a decline in the market value of the goods.* If the buyer does not bear this risk, all the risks of ownership have not been transferred. This may occur if the transaction has a price-protection clause.

- *Whether the seller's custodial risks are insurable and insured.* If the risk of holding the product is so high that insurance is unavailable or prohibitively expensive, the custodial risk may be too high to conclude that all substantive risks of ownership have passed to the buyer.

- *Whether the buyer's business reasons for the bill and hold have introduced a contingency to the buyer's commitment.* For example, if the buyer requests a bill and hold transaction because it does not yet have a license to own or take custody of the products, this might indicate that the transaction will never be completed.

PRACTICE POINTER: Any company that enters into bill and hold transactions should ensure that it has very strong controls over the process of negotiating and signing contracts with customers, because small changes to a contract can cause the arrangement to fail the bill and hold criteria. For example, if a salesperson negotiates extended payment terms or a right of return, the timing of revenue recognition on a bill and hold transaction would likely be affected, even though such clauses might not affect revenue recognition on a standard sales transaction. A company's internal controls should also ensure that revenue from a bill and hold transaction is limited to transactions where the arrangement was specifically requested by the customer, rather than suggested by the salesperson.

The SEC staff has also cautioned companies not to attempt to get around the bill and hold requirements by arguing that a contract for manufacture and delivery of a product is a multiple-element arrangement, with production and delivery (or manufacture and packaging) representing separate deliverables for accounting purposes.

SEC REGISTRANT ALERT: In December 2005, an SEC release on vaccine bill and hold transactions allowed vaccine stockpile participants to recognize revenue despite not meeting bill and hold requirements. This guidance may not be analogized to for any other type of bill and hold transaction.

DISCLOSURE ALERT: See Chapter 12, "Disclosures," for information about disclosures that may be required.

EXAMPLE: SEC ENFORCEMENT ACTION RELATED TO BILL AND HOLD SALES

Excerpts Taken from Accounting and Auditing Enforcement Release No. 1911—November 13, 2003

Improper Bill-and-Hold Sale

Gateway also solicited an arrangement with one of its larger customers, a rent-to-own consumer leasing company, in mid-September 2000.

On September 21, 2000, Gateway's sales representative sent an e-mail to the consumer leasing company confirming that the consumer leasing company would issue a purchase order for $16.5 million of PCs, for which it would receive a 5% discount, that the consumer leasing company would be billed by September 30, 2000, and would take the PCs by October 31, 2000. The e-mail did not reference warehousing arrangements. The parties agreed the consumer leasing company would not take the product until the fourth quarter, after it issued subsequent purchase orders from individual stores, as had been its practice. They also agreed that the consumer leasing company would be invoiced and pay on subsequent store purchase orders, not the $16.5 million purchase order.

On September 21, 2000, the consumer leasing company issued a purchase order for $16.5 million in PCs and peripherals. The purchase order provided that the equipment would be shipped to "local warehousing for subsequent distribution," and stated that the order was FOB destination. Gateway then "shipped" the products by segregating them in the third-party warehouses located adjacent to Gateway's manufacturing facilities. . . . The consumer leasing company did not make any arrangements with the warehouses, or have any contact with the warehouses.

Gateway improperly recognized revenue of $16.5 million on the third quarter purported sale (and also failed to apply the 5% discount on the sale until the fourth quarter). Thus, Gateway increased its third quarter reported revenue by $16.5 million.

The transaction failed to satisfy three critical GAAP criteria for revenue recognition on a bill-and-hold transaction.[4] First, revenue recognition was inappropriate because the consumer leasing company lacked any substantial business purpose for ordering the goods on bill-and-hold basis. Second, Gateway had specific performance obligations concerning the purchase order that it did not discharge during the third quarter, including (1) upon receipt of a second purchase order from the consumer leasing company, an obligation to remove the product from the warehouse inventory, send it back to Gateway's manufacturing facility for re-entry into Gateway's computer system, and then ship the product to the individual store specified on the order; and (2) an obligation to reverse the September 21, 2000, sale of the PC out of its system and issue a second invoice to the consumer leasing company. These specific performance obligations precluded revenue recognition. Third, revenue recognition was inappropriate because the consumer leasing company did not request that the transaction be on a bill-and-hold basis and did not pay the cost for warehousing the inventory.

---

[4] *Footnote Omitted.*

Layaway Sales

Layaway sales are a type of bill and hold transaction. In a layaway transaction, a buyer makes a partial payment (typically nonrefundable) on an item to be delivered in the future upon payment of the remaining purchase price, and the seller sets the buyer's item aside for a period of time. However, if the buyer does not make the remaining payment within the required period, the initial deposit will be forfeited and the seller may sell the item to another customer.

Layaways are bill and hold transactions because the seller collects a portion of the purchase price without delivering the item. It is clear that under the SEC's bill and hold model, a layaway transaction could not qualify for revenue recognition before the last payment is received and the product is delivered. This is because the buyer has not made a final commitment to purchase the goods, as he or she may elect to cease making payments and thereby not purchase the goods (ASC 605-10-S99, A3e) (SAB Topic 13A3e).

Because this specific condition is only included in the SEC's bill and hold model, nonpublic companies may be able to justify revenue recognition on a layaway sale if they can show that the basic revenue recognition criteria have been met. IAS 18 specifically allows recognition of revenue on layaway transactions if the first five requirements of the IAS bill and hold accounting model are met (see prior discussion) and both of the following conditions exist:

1. *A significant deposit is received* (IAS 18, App. par. 3). The buyer in a layaway transaction has the right to stop making payments under the arrangement. Therefore, the buyer's risk of loss due to a decline in market value is limited to the dollar amount of payments to date. As a result, some of the risk of a market price decline remains with the seller and might only be partially covered by the forfeited payments. Therefore, the size of the initial deposit must be carefully considered to ensure that it effectively transfers enough of the risk of loss to the buyer.

2. *Experience indicates that most layaway transactions are eventually consummated* (IAS 18, App. par. 3). Without historical evidence that most customers complete required payments and take delivery, it is difficult to conclude that a sale has occurred.

Payments received before revenue can be recognized should be recorded as deposit liabilities, and the related inventory should remain on the books. In the event that initial payments are forfeited because the buyer does not complete the required payments, the deposit liability should be eliminated and income credited by the same amount. This credit generally should not be classified as revenue because no earnings event occurred. Instead, it should be reflected as a gain classified below gross margin.

POST-DELIVERY PRODUCT-RELATED OBLIGATIONS

Customer Acceptance Provisions

Customer acceptance provisions allow the customer to cancel an arrangement when the product delivered does not meet the customer's needs or desires. The existence of such provisions raises questions as to whether the earnings process is complete at the time of shipment or only after customer acceptance has been obtained. When products are sold subject to these provisions, the nature of the provisions should be analyzed to determine which accounting model applies to the transaction. Generally, customer acceptance provisions and the related accounting take one of the four forms discussed below.

Product Shipped for Trial or Evaluation Purposes

In these arrangements, the seller delivers a product (before finalizing a sales agreement) and allows the customer to evaluate it prior to acceptance. When products are shipped on this basis, a purchase is consummated only upon customer acceptance. In some cases, acceptance occurs as long as the customer does not reject the product within a specified period of time. For example, a book club may ship its members a book every month for a 14-day trial period. If the member does not return the book within the trial period, the member is deemed to have accepted the book and is obligated to pay for it.

In other cases, an affirmative acceptance from the customer is necessary to trigger a purchase obligation. This is more common if the product is equipment that is intended for a specific use.

Regardless of whether title passes upon shipment, these arrangements do not constitute a sale until acceptance occurs. This is because until acceptance, there is no persuasive evidence of an arrangement. Accordingly, in arrangements where products are delivered for trial or evaluation purposes, revenue should not be recognized until acceptance occurs, either by notification from the customer or by passage of time without rejection, provided the other conditions for revenue recognition have been met (ASC 605-10-S99, A3b, ques. 1) (SAB Topic 13A3b, ques. 1).

PRACTICE POINTER: The reason shipment on a trial basis or for evaluation purposes does not trigger revenue recognition is because the arrangement does not even purport to be a sale until acceptance occurs. Therefore, historical experience at estimating how many of these shipments will ultimately result in sales, no matter how accurate, cannot be used to justify revenue recognition prior to acceptance. By contrast, subjective customer acceptance clauses and rights of return (discussed later in this chapter) do not absolutely preclude revenue recognition during the return period because a sale agreement is in place before the products are delivered. Since rights of return provide many of the same protections as an arrangement with a trial or evaluation period, companies may wish to change their sales contracts accordingly. This may allow a company to recognize revenue at an earlier point in time.

Subjective Right of Return

Certain customer acceptance provisions give the buyer a right to reject the product if he or she is dissatisfied for any reason. An example of such a provision is one that allows the customer to return a product with "no questions asked." Acceptance provisions based on wholly subjective terms are, in substance, general rights of return. Thus, this class of acceptance provisions should be accounted for in accordance with ASC 605-15-25 and related interpretations. (See ASC 605-10-S99, A3b, ques. 1 (SAB Topic 13A3b, ques. 1) and "Rights of Return" in this chapter.)

Customer Acceptance Based on Meeting Standard Seller-Specified Performance Criteria

These provisions give the customer a right of return or replacement if the delivered product is defective, fails to meet advertising claims, or does not meet the *vendor's* published specifications for the product. In some cases, the seller may have the right to refund the purchaser's money or repair the product rather than provide a replacement. This type of acceptance provision is generally used in a situation where identical rights are granted to every customer of a particular class and involves seller-specified performance criteria that the seller is reasonably certain the product will meet. If the seller has previously demonstrated that the product meets these criteria, the customer acceptance provision is no different from a product warranty. Under these circumstances, the customer acceptance provision should be accounted for as a warranty (see "Product Warranties" in this chapter).

However, if the seller has not previously demonstrated that the delivered product meets the stated specifications, warranty accounting is not appropriate, because it is uncertain whether the company has delivered the product specified in the arrangement. Therefore, revenue should be deferred until the specifications have been achieved or the customer has accepted the product (ASC 605-10-S99, A3b, ques. 1 and 2) (SAB Topic 13A3b, ques. 1 and 2).

Customer Acceptance Based on Customer-Specified or Negotiated Criteria

This type of customer acceptance provision is the most difficult to analyze. Provisions like these are common in sales of equipment to be used in manufacturing, and in sales of industrial goods designed for a specific location, such as an air conditioning system designed for a particular building. Prior to installation and product testing at the customer's location, it is often unclear whether the product meets the specified criteria. This is because, no matter how much testing is done before shipment, it may not be possible to replicate the conditions of the customer's environment. These types of arrangements usually allow the seller a period of time after installation and testing to resolve any problems that might exist in meeting the criteria. As a result, the seller may need to perform additional work after installation in order to meet the specifications. If a substantive amount of additional work is likely to be required, revenue recognition upon shipment is inappropriate because the seller has not met its obligations.

Therefore, when an arrangement has customer-specified acceptance provisions, the seller must be able to reliably demonstrate that the delivered product meets these specified criteria before revenue can be recognized. If the criteria are sufficiently objective and the seller can replicate conditions under which the customer will operate the product, it may be possible to objectively demonstrate compliance with the acceptance provisions prior to shipment. In this case, revenue may be recognized upon delivery, provided that all other revenue recognition conditions have been met.

However, if unique aspects of the customer's environment could affect the assessment of whether the product meets the criteria or if other circumstances exist that prohibit the seller from verifying compliance with the acceptance provisions until delivery or installation, revenue should not be recognized until compliance can be verified. Verification often consists of a formal customer sign-off to indicate that the acceptance provisions have been met. However, if the seller can verify that the product meets the acceptance criteria and, thereby, believes it would be able to enforce a claim for payment even though formal customer sign-off has not occurred, revenue may be recognized because the seller has fulfilled all terms of the contract. As with other accounting that is based on a legal interpretation, consultation with legal experts may be necessary to determine the appropriate treatment (ASC 605-10-S99, A3b, ques. 1) (SAB Topic 13A3b, ques. 1).

EXHIBIT 5-2: CUSTOMER ACCEPTANCE PROVISIONS

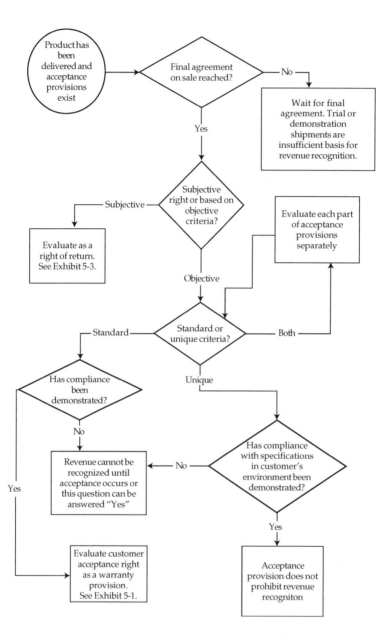

EXAMPLE: CUSTOMER ACCEPTANCE PROVISIONS

GT Solar International, Inc. Form 10-K—Fiscal Year April 2, 2011

Revenue Recognition

We recognize revenue when title and risk of loss have passed to the customer, evidence of an arrangement exists, fees are contractually fixed or determinable, collectability is reasonably assured through historical collection results and regular credit evaluations, and there are no uncertainties regarding customer acceptance. The application of our revenue recognition policies for established products differ from our newer products. Our revenue recognition policies are described in further detail below.

For arrangements containing products that we consider to be "established," we recognize upon delivery revenue equal to the lesser of the amount allocated to the equipment or the contractual amount due (typically 90%) with the remainder recognized upon completion of installation. For arrangements containing products considered to be "new," or containing customer acceptance provisions that are deemed to be more than perfunctory, revenue is recorded upon customer acceptance or at the time the product is determined to be "established." For the standard DSS contract, a portion of the total sales price (typically 10%) is not due until installation and customer acceptance occurs. For other arrangements, a portion of the total sales price is due upon reaching certain performance metrics and customer acceptance of such specifications.

Products are classified as "established" products if post-delivery acceptance provisions and the installation process have been determined to be routine, due to the fact that the acceptance provisions are generally a replication of pre-shipment procedures. The majority of our products and subcomponents are manufactured to a standard specification. To ensure contractual performance levels are satisfied, the products or subcomponents are often are tested at either our manufacturing facility or that of our third party manufacturer prior to shipment. To the extent that customers' conditions cannot be replicated in our facilities, or if there is not a demonstrated history of meeting newer customer specifications, then the product is treated as "new" for revenue recognition purposes, as customer acceptance would be considered an element in these transactions.

In determining when a "new" product is considered "established," we consider several factors, including the stability of the product's technology, the ability to test the product prior to shipment, successful installations at customers' sites and the performance results once installed. We generally believe that satisfaction of these factors, coupled with a minimum of three to five successful customer installations and acceptances, is necessary to support the conclusion that there are no uncertainties regarding customer acceptances and that the installation process can be considered perfunctory. These factors, as well as the consideration of the ease of installation in different customer environments, are all taken into consideration in determining whether a product should be classified as "established."

OBSERVATION: Acceptance provisions based on specific criteria must be evaluated on a contract-by-contract basis. As a result, the timing of revenue recognition may differ for otherwise similar contracts. For example, in an arrangement to deliver multiple machines, each of which operate to identical specifications, it may not be possible to determine whether the first machine meets the specifications until it is tested in the customer's plant. Therefore, revenue recognition would need to be deferred on the first machine until after installation and testing. However, if the other machines in the order are identical to the first and any modifications that were necessary on the first machine are made to the others before shipment, revenue recognition on these machines may be appropriate upon shipment. If the contract specified unique acceptance provisions for each machine delivered, the analysis of the timing of revenue recognition would be different for each machine.

DISCLOSURE ALERT: See Chapter 12, "Disclosures," for information about disclosures that may be required.

SEC REGISTRANT ALERT: In early 2003 the SEC staff issued the Summary by the Division of Corporation Finance of Significant Issues Addressed in the Review of the Periodic Reports of the Fortune 500 Companies (Fortune 500 Report). This report resulted from the SEC's Division of Corporation Finance's (Corp Fin) review of all annual reports filed by Fortune 500 companies. The report provides insight into areas commonly questioned by Corp Fin during its reviews of annual reports. One area specifically mentioned in this report relates to customer acceptance clauses. Corp Fin noted that the quality of disclosures on these provisions requires improvement, particularly in the capital goods, semiconductor, and electronic instruments and controls industries.

ILLUSTRATION: EFFECTS OF CUSTOMER ACCEPTANCE PROVISIONS ON REVENUE RECOGNITION

(Adapted from ASC 605-10-S99, A3b, ques. 3 through 5 (SAB Topic 13A3b, ques. 3 through 5))

Facts: Company E is an equipment manufacturer whose main product is generally sold in a standard model. The contracts for sale of that model provide for customer acceptance to occur after the equipment is received and tested by the customer. The acceptance provisions state that if the equipment does not perform to Company E's published specifications, the customer may return the equipment for a full refund or a replacement unit, or may require Company E to repair the equipment so that it performs up to published specifications. Customer acceptance is indicated by either a formal sign-off by the customer or by the passage of 90 days without a claim under the acceptance provisions. Title to the equipment passes upon delivery to the customer. Company E does not perform any installation or other services on the equipment it sells and tests each piece of equipment against its specifications before shipment. Payment is due under Company E's normal payment terms for that product—30 days after customer acceptance.

EXAMPLE 1

Additional Facts: Company E receives an order from a new customer for a standard model of its main product. Based on the customer's intended use of the product, location, and other factors, there is no reason that the equipment would operate differently in the customer's environment than it does in Company E's facility.

Discussion: Although the arrangement includes a customer acceptance provision, acceptance is based on meeting Company E's published specifications for a standard model. Because Company E demonstrates that the equipment shipped meets the specifications before shipment, and the equipment is expected to operate the same in the customer's environment as it does in Company E's, Company E should evaluate the customer acceptance provision as a warranty under ASC 460. If Company E can reasonably and reliably estimate the amount of warranty obligations, Company E should recognize revenue upon delivery of the equipment (provided the other criteria for recognition are met) with an appropriate liability for probable warranty obligations.

EXAMPLE 2

Additional Facts: Company E enters into an arrangement with a new customer to deliver a version of its standard product modified as necessary to fit into a space of specific dimensions while still meeting all of the published vendor specifications with regard to performance. In addition to the customer acceptance provisions relating to the standard performance specifications, the customer may reject the equipment if it does not conform to the specified dimensions. Company E creates a testing chamber of the exact same dimensions as specified by the customer and makes simple design changes to the product so that it fits into the testing chamber. The equipment still meets all of the standard performance specifications.

Discussion: The contract effectively includes two customer acceptance clauses—one based on a customer-specific criterion and one based on standard performance specifications. For the customer acceptance clause based on the customer-specific criterion, Company E demonstrates that the equipment shipped meets that objective criterion before shipment. As such, there are no uncertainties related to that customer acceptance clause that affect revenue recognition. For the customer acceptance clause based on the standard performance specifications, Company E demonstrates that the equipment shipped meets those specifications before shipment as well. This customer acceptance clause should be evaluated under ASC 460 as a warranty obligation. If Company E can reasonably and reliably estimate the amount of warranty obligations, it should recognize revenue upon delivery of the equipment with an appropriate liability for probable warranty obligations (provided the other criteria for recognition are met).

EXAMPLE 3

Additional Facts: Company E enters into an arrangement with a new customer to deliver a version of its standard product modified as necessary to be integrated into the customer's new assembly line while still meeting all of the standard published vendor specifications with regard to performance. The customer may reject the equipment if it fails to meet the standard published performance specifications or cannot be satisfactorily integrated into the new line. Company E has never modified its equipment to work on an integrated basis in the type of assembly line the customer has proposed. In response to the request, Company E designs a version of its standard equipment that is modified as believed necessary to operate in the new assembly line. The modified equipment still meets all of the standard published performance specifications, and Company E believes the equipment will meet the requested specifications when integrated into the new assembly line. However, Company E is unable to replicate the new assembly line conditions in its pre-shipment testing.

Discussion: This contract includes a customer acceptance clause based, in part, on a customer-specific criterion and Company E cannot demonstrate that the equipment shipped meets that criterion before shipment. Accordingly, Company E may not recognize revenue before the product is successfully integrated at its customer's location and meets the customer-specific criterion.

Product Warranties

Many product sale arrangements include a warranty provision that provides the purchaser with some protection in the event the product does not perform as expected or requires post-sale servicing. Under a normal warranty, the seller assumes an obligation to repair or replace the product if it fails to perform as advertised or according to published specifications. However, not all warranty provisions involve the same type of obligation and it is important to understand the substance of these obligations to facilitate the proper accounting. For example, if the seller commits to ensure that the product will meet certain specifications that have not yet been demonstrated, revenue should not be recognized until compliance with these specifications is achieved. Furthermore, if the warranty is based on meeting criteria specific to a particular customer or product sale, the warranty obligation should be evaluated as a customer acceptance provision based on customer-specified criteria (see "Customer Acceptance Provisions" above).

In addition, certain warranties may include obligations other than ensuring that the product continues to operate according to specifications. For example, a warranty provision in a software arrangement may include the right to upgrades or updates to the product or a warranty on an automobile may include oil changes and other preventative maintenance during the warranty term. Neither of these specific provisions should be accounted for as part of the warranty. Rather, the sale of a product, along with a promise to provide upgrades or services after the sale, should be treated as a multiple-deliverable arrangement (see Chapter 4, "Multiple-Deliverable Revenue Arrangements"). Therefore, a portion of the sales prices in these situations generally should be allocated to the additional deliverables and deferred until the seller fulfills its obligations to provide the other products or services.

Most warranty provisions, however, merely require that the seller repair or replace the item if it fails to perform in the way it was designed and manufactured to perform. These provisions are usually explicitly identified in the documentation that comes with the product, but warranties may also be implied or required by laws or regulations (e.g., the "lemon laws" that cover automobiles in many states are a type of warranty). Because of a warranty commitment, the seller's involvement with the product may not end after delivery. At a minimum, the seller must be prepared to honor the warranty for whatever period of time it is in force.

One method of accounting for a product sale with a warranty would be to treat it as a multiple-deliverable arrangement; the product would be one deliverable and the warranty another. Revenue would be allocated between the product and the warranty, with the amount allocated to the warranty recognized as revenue over the warranty period, consistent with other service transactions. Another possible method of accounting for a warranty would be to treat it as a part of the product and not account for it separately. If analyzed this way, a question arises as to whether the warranty obligation is significant enough to prevent revenue recognition on the product. If the obligation is significant, revenue would not be recognized until the warranty expires. Conversely, if the warranty obligation were deemed insignificant, all revenue would be attributed to the product and recognized upon delivery (or when all revenue recognition criteria are met). U.S. GAAP recognizes the merit of both accounting approaches, depending on the facts and circumstances.

OBSERVATION: Although warranties are conceptually within the scope of ASC 460, they are exempted from its accounting requirements.

Standard Warranties

In many cases, a sale of goods in the normal course of business includes a standard warranty for all buyers of the product. This warranty is not treated as a separate service; rather, it is considered an integral part of the product sale. Revenue may be recognized upon product delivery when a standard warranty is included in the transaction, provided that the costs of honoring the warranty can be reliably estimated and that the other conditions for revenue recognition have been met. The estimated costs of honoring the warranty must be accrued to cost of sales when revenue is recognized, and these costs should be updated as estimates change.

However, if the costs of honoring the warranty cannot be reliably estimated and the potential range of loss is wide, revenue should be deferred until either a reliable estimate of the costs can be made or the warranty period expires (ASC 460-10-25-6). Indicators that costs may not be reliably estimable include (a) the introduction of new products or significant modifications that have been made to old products, (b) the extension of the scope of a warranty beyond what has normally been given in the ordinary course of business, and (c) undertaking new obligations.

DISCLOSURE ALERT: See Chapter 12, "Disclosures" for information about required disclosures.

Separately Priced Extended Warranty and Product Maintenance Contracts

The preceding discussion applies only to standard warranties offered to all purchasers of a product without an extra charge. Revenue from separately priced extended warranty and product maintenance contracts should be deferred and recognized in income over the contract period. A warranty is priced separately any time a customer may purchase the product with or without the warranty. For example, assume that all purchasers of a particular model of television receive a one-year warranty and can purchase a three-year warranty for an added charge. The arrangement should be accounted for as having a one-year standard warranty and a two-year separately priced extension. As such, the fee paid for the two-year extension should be deferred and recognized as revenue after the television is delivered in years two and three. The purchase price of the television with the standard one-year warranty should be recognized as revenue upon delivery as long as all other revenue recognition conditions are met and the costs of honoring the one-year warranty can be reliably estimated.

The recognition pattern for revenue attributable to a separately priced extended warranty contract should be on a straight-line basis, unless historical evidence indicates that the costs of performing services under the contract are incurred on other than a straight-line basis. If costs are incurred on other than a straight-line basis, revenue should be recognized over the contract period in proportion to the costs expected to be incurred in performing services under the contract (ASC 605-20-25-1 through 25-6).

DISCLOSURE ALERT: See Chapter 12, "Disclosures" for information about required disclosures.

EXAMPLES: WARRANTIES

Dell, Inc. Form 10-K—Fiscal Year Ended January 28, 2011

Warranty Liability and Related Deferred Service Revenue

NOTE 9—WARRANTY AND DEFERRED EXTENDED WARRANTY REVENUE

Dell records liabilities for its standard limited warranties at the time of sale for the estimated costs that may be incurred. The liability for standard warranties is included in accrued and other current and other non-current liabilities on the Consolidated Statements of Financial Position. Revenue from the sale of extended warranties is recognized over the term of the contract or when the service is completed, and the costs associated with these contracts are recognized as incurred. Deferred extended warranty revenue is included in deferred services revenue on the Consolidated Statements of Financial Position. Changes in Dell's liabilities for standard limited warranties and deferred services revenue related to extended warranties are presented in the following tables:

	Fiscal Year Ended		
	January 28, 2011	January 29, 2010	January 30, 2009
Warranty liability:			
Warranty liability at beginning of period	$ 912	$1,035	$ 929
Costs accrued for new warranty contracts and changes in estimates for pre-existing warranties[a][b]	1,046	987	1,180
Service obligations honored	(1,063)	(1,110)	(1,074)
Warranty liability at end of period	$ 895	$ 912	$1,035

	Fiscal Year Ended		
	January 28, 2011	January 29, 2010	January 30, 2009
Current portion	$ 575	$ 593	$ 721
Non-current portion	320	319	314
Warranty liability at end of period	$ 895	$ 912	$1,035

	Fiscal Year Ended		
	January 28, 2011	January 29, 2010	January 30, 2009
	(in millions)		
Deferred extended warranty revenue:			
Deferred extended warranty revenue at beginning of period	$5,910	$5,587	$5,233
Revenue deferred for new extended warranties[b]	3,877	3,481	3,470
Revenue recognized	(3,371)	(3,158)	(3,116)
Deferred extended warranty revenue at end of period	$6,416	$5,910	$5,587
Current portion	$2,959	$2,906	$2,601
Non-current portion	3,457	3,004	2,986
Deferred extended warranty revenue at end of period	$6,416	$5,910	$5,587

[a] Changes in cost estimates related to pre-existing warranties are aggregated with accruals for new standard warranty contracts. Dell's warranty liability process does not differentiate between estimates made for pre-existing warranties and new warranty obligations.

[b] Includes the impact of foreign currency exchange rate fluctuations.

Products Shipped Subject to Other Conditions

Product sales can include various other conditions. For example, products may be sold subject to installation or performance of other services. When a product is sold together with post-delivery services, the arrangement should be accounted for as a multiple-deliverable arrangement. If the product and service deliverables meet the requirements for separate accounting treatment, the revenue allocated to the product deliverable should be recognized at the appropriate time, without regard to the service deliverable. However, if the deliverables do not meet the requirements for separate accounting treatment, no revenue should be recognized until the product is delivered *and* the service has been performed. See Chapter 4, "Multiple-Deliverable Revenue Arrangements," for further discussion.

RIGHTS OF RETURN

Return rights are very common in product transactions. For example, almost any retail purchase can be returned for a limited period of time. Resellers and distributors are often granted rights of return to reduce their risk of loss if the product is difficult to resell. Similarly, sales of commercial products may have rights of return related to quality, performance testing, or other factors.

PRACTICE POINTER: Return rights are often documented in the sales contract. However, such rights may also exist due to industry practice, company policy, or laws and regulations. In addition, the relationship between the buyer and seller should be evaluated in full to determine whether unstated rights of return might exist. For example, a large customer of a company may have enough leverage to return goods beyond the limited period stated in the contract. Although the seller may be within its rights to deny such returns, it is common for a seller to accept such a return from an important customer. Therefore, all rights of return, whether or not explicitly stated in a contract, must be considered.

General Rights of Return

ASC 605-15 provides accounting guidance for a subjective right of return, such as a "100% satisfaction guarantee," that may be exercised at will by the purchaser. This guidance prohibits recognition of revenue if there is significant uncertainty as to whether, or to what extent, the return right will be exercised.

Rights of Return vs. Rights of Exchange

The guidance regarding rights of return does not apply to rights given to ultimate customers (i.e., end users) to exchange one item for another of the same kind, quality, and price. These "like-kind" exchange rights are not treated as returns for accounting purposes and generally should have no effect on revenue recognition (ASC 605-15-15-2). Instead, the estimated costs of fulfilling those exchange rights expected to be exercised should be accrued at the time of sale.

This exception applies only to sales to end-users, not resellers. Therefore, if a manufacturer of a product provides "stock rotation rights" to distributors or retailers that allow the reseller-customer to return products for credits towards other purchases, that right must be evaluated as a right of return, no matter how similar the products the credit can be used towards are to the original products.

In addition, the evaluation of whether the exchange represents an exchange of a product for one of the same kind-quality, and price must be made considering the condition of the product to be returned. For example, a right to exchange product that is accidentally damaged by the customer for an undamaged product would not represent a like-kind exchange. Such a right would be considered a right of return.

Similarly, a right offered by a drug manufacturer to allow its customer to return product that gets close to its expiration date for "fresh" product is not a like-kind exchange, as the fresh product is clearly more useful than the product close to its expiration date. In addition, such rights, when offered, are almost invariably offered to distributors of the drug, not to patients who will take the drug, and therefore are not being offered to ultimate customers. For both reasons, this kind of right, even when limited to getting fresh inventory of the same drug, must be evaluated as a right of return.

Accounting for Rights of Return

Although a return right creates a question as to whether the transaction has been completed, the seller records revenue upon delivery if the terms of the arrangement make it clear that a sale has occurred, there are no other contingencies, and the likelihood of the customer exercising the right of return can be estimated.

Specifically, revenue should be recognized at the time of sale, net of estimated returns, only if all of the following conditions (and the remaining general conditions for revenue recognition) are met (ASC 605-15-25-1):

1. *The sales price to the buyer is fixed or determinable.* This shows that the return period is not just part of the transaction's pricing negotiations. If the arrangement does not meet this criterion, no revenue should be recognized because a fixed or determinable fee is one of the prerequisites to recognizing revenue.

2. *Payment is not contractually or otherwise excused until the product is resold.* If payment is not required until the product is resold, the transaction takes on characteristics of a consignment, for which no revenue should be recognized.

OBSERVATION: Although payment may contractually be due within a specified period of time, a company may have a business practice of not pursuing payment until the customer actually resells the products. If this is the case, the business practice must be considered in the evaluation, and revenue may not be recognized until the right of return expires or payment is received.

---

3. *The buyer holds the risks of destruction, damage, or theft of the property.* If the buyer does not hold these risks, then all of the risks and rewards of ownership have not passed, and revenue recognition is prohibited.

4. *The buyer has economic substance apart from the seller.* A sale with a right of return to a company with little substance raises significant questions about the buyer's ability to pay. In this case, the buyer would appear to be acting as a sales agent for the seller, rather than as a substantive purchaser. As a result, the seller should not record any sale to the nonsubstantive purchaser.

5. *The seller does not have significant obligations for future performance relating to the resale of the product by the buyer.* If the seller is required to assist the buyer in the product's resale, the seller has not completed its obligations under the arrangement until resale has occurred and should not recognize revenue until then, provided the other conditions for recognition have been met.

6. *The amount of future returns and costs expected in connection with any returns can be reasonably predicted.* This criterion requires the most judgment and is the one that most often cannot be met. See below for further discussion.

Estimating Returns

Determining whether a reasonable estimate of returns can be made is sometimes quite easy. For example, a product that has been sold to the same group of customers and has generated a consistent rate of return for many years can probably be expected to have the same level of returns in the future, as long as there are no external changes that might affect customers' return habits. On the other hand, a start-up company selling a newly invented product that is not similar to any other product on the market may quickly conclude that it cannot estimate the level of returns that will occur (ASC 605-10-S99, A4a, ques. 4) (SAB Topic 13A4a, ques. 4).

OBSERVATION: There is no specific level of returns that would prohibit recognition of revenue on sales with a right of return. The accounting literature focuses entirely on the ability of a company to estimate returns in determining whether revenue may be recognized upon delivery. When the percentage of customers exercising return rights is high, it may be more difficult to estimate the rate of returns, but this is just one of many factors a company would take into account in determining whether it can make a reliable estimate of returns (ASC 605-10-S99, A4a, ques. 5) (SAB Topic 13A4a, ques. 5).

When evaluating whether a reasonable estimate of returns can be made, all available information should be considered. The following factors, the existence of any of which may cause the seller to conclude that returns cannot be reasonably predicted, should be considered by a seller when estimating the amount of returns:

1. *The product is susceptible to significant external factors, such as technological obsolescence or changes in demand* (ASC 605-15-25-3). When the return period is lengthy, it may be difficult to predict the economic and technological life of (i.e., demand for) the product. It may also be harder to forecast competitors' actions and customers' responses to market factors.

2. *The return period is long* (ASC 605-15-25-3). The longer the return period, the more difficult it becomes to predict the level of returns. Whether a return period is long should be determined based on the nature of the product, industry practice, and the type of customer.

3. *The absence of relevant historical experience* (ASC 605-15-25-3). Without historical experience to reference, predicting customer actions is virtually impossible. However, in the absence of company-specific experience, industry experience may be relevant.

4. *The absence of a large volume of relatively homogeneous transactions* (ASC 605-15-25-3). It is generally difficult to predict the actions of a particular

customer. However, it is much easier to predict, on average, the actions of a large number of similar customers.

5. *Increases in or excess levels of inventory at distributors, or a lack of information about the levels of inventory at distributors* (ASC 605-10-S99, A4b, ques. 1) (SAB Topic 13A4b, ques. 1). Either of these situations indicates that historical experience is less likely to have sufficient predictive ability to guide future actions given the problems with inventory management.

6. *Importance of sales by and to a particular distributor to the reporting entity (overall or to a specific reportable segment)* (ASC 605-10-S99, A4b, ques. 1) (SAB Topic 13A4b, ques. 1). Trends in sales by and to an important distributor or significant changes in inventory levels at a new distributor may have implications for the vendor's ability to estimate returns.

7. *Expected introductions of new products* (ASC 605-10-S99, A4b, ques. 1) (SAB Topic 13A4b, ques. 1). If the product subject to the return right is near the end of its life due to the planned introduction of a new or upgraded version, it is possible that more returns will occur as customers opt for the new or upgraded version.

8. *The product is new* (ASC 605-10-S99, A4b, ques. 1) (SAB Topic 13A4b, ques. 1). The newer the product, the less likely it is that relevant return experience exists. Depending upon the circumstances, return experience with other, similar, products may be useful.

OBSERVATION: The ability to estimate returns could vary from product to product, location to location, customer to customer, and arrangement to arrangement. In addition, it may be possible for a company to estimate returns for certain transactions but not others. Thus, a company that sells various products or serves different market segments whose return rates are expected to vary should develop different return estimates for each type of product or market segment.

EXHIBIT 5-3: RIGHTS OF RETURN

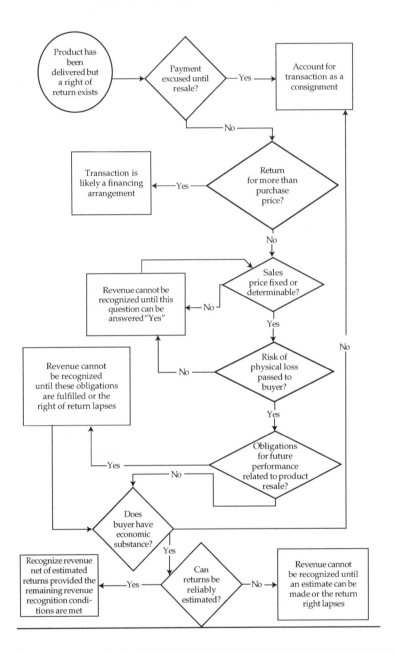

PRACTICE POINTER: U.S. GAAP requires a reliable estimate of returns before any revenue can be recognized. Some have suggested that, even in the absence of a good estimate, revenue recognition should be allowed if a company assumes an unusually conservative (i.e., high) level of returns that is unlikely to be exceeded. However, this treatment is not consistent with the accounting literature. Therefore, it is critical that the company develop and sustain the ability to reliably estimate returns to recognize any revenue at delivery (ASC 605-10-S99, A4b, ques. 5) (SAB Topic 13A4b, ques. 5).

In some arrangements, however, a company may sell a large number of products to a single customer with a capped right of return. For example, if the customer is only permitted to return up to 20% of the products shipped, revenue may be recognized upon delivery for the 80% to which the return rights do not apply, assuming all other revenue recognition criteria are met. The 20% of products to which the rights of return do apply should be evaluated to determine whether revenue may be recognized upon delivery.

EXAMPLE: INABILITY TO ESTIMATE RETURNS

Dell, Inc. Form 10-K—Fiscal Year Ended January 30, 2009

During Fiscal 2008, we began selling our products through retailers. Sales to our retail customers are generally made under agreements allowing for limited rights of return, price protection, rebates, and marketing development funds. We have generally limited the return rights through contractual caps. Our policy for sales to retailers is to defer the full amount of revenue relative to sales for which the rights of return apply as we do not currently have sufficient historical data to establish reasonable and reliable estimates of returns, although we are in the process of accumulating the data necessary to develop reliable estimates in the future. All other sales for which the rights of return do not apply are recognized upon shipment when all applicable revenue recognition criteria have been met. To the extent price protection and return rights are not limited, all of the revenue and related cost are deferred until the product has been sold by the retailer, the rights expire, or a reliable estimate of such amounts can be made.

Accounting for Rights of Return

When revenue is not recognized at the time of sale because an estimate of returns cannot be made, the seller should delay recognition until the earlier of when the return privilege has expired or information allowing the company to make a reasonable estimate of returns becomes available, provided the other conditions for revenue recognition have been met (ASC 605-15-25-1). In this situation, the inventory "sold" should remain on the company's books, and any cash collected should be reflected as a liability, rather than as revenue. The inventory should be evaluated for impairment under the assumption that the customer will return the products to the company and consider any anticipated repackaging or other costs to put the merchandise in saleable condition.

OBSERVATION: U.S. GAAP is clear that when an estimate of returns cannot be made, no revenue can be recognized. To be consistent with this approach, no cost of sales should be recognized. It is not appropriate in such a situation to merely defer the margin on the sale by recognizing revenue equal to cost of sales. While deferring only the gross margin ensures that net income is not overstated, it results in the recognition of revenue for a transaction that is, essentially, incomplete (ASC 605-10-S99, A4b, ques. 1) (SAB Topic 13A4b, ques. 1). It also misrepresents various balance sheet components.

When a transaction meets all of the criteria for revenue recognition upon delivery despite the existence of a return right, revenue and cost of sales should be recognized net of the expected returns. Any inventory expected as a return should be evaluated for impairment and this evaluation should consider any anticipated repackaging or other costs to put the merchandise in saleable condition. As estimates of returns change, the anticipated refund liability should be adjusted to reflect this new information.

DISCLOSURE ALERT: See Chapter 12, "Disclosures," for information about disclosures that may be required.

SEC REGISTRANT ALERT: In early 2003 the SEC staff issued the Summary by the Division of Corporation Finance of Significant Issues Addressed in the Review of the Periodic Reports of the Fortune 500 Companies (Fortune 500 Report). This report resulted from the SEC's Division of Corporation Finance's (Corp Fin) review of all annual reports filed by Fortune 500 companies. The report provides insight into areas commonly questioned by Corp Fin during its reviews of annual reports. One area specifically mentioned in this report relates to rights of return. Corp Fin noted that the quality of disclosures on rights of return requires improvement, particularly in the capital goods, semiconductor, electronic instruments and controls, and pharmaceutical industries.

ILLUSTRATION: PRODUCT SOLD WITH RIGHT OF RETURN

Facts: Example Company sells 100 units of Product A at $100 per unit. Product A has an inventory cost of $87 per unit, and repackaging any returned units for resale will cost $15 per unit. Customers get a 30-day right of return on Product A and, ultimately, 5 of the 100 units are returned. The right of return is the only issue that can affect when revenue should be recognized.

EXAMPLE 1

Additional Facts: Example Company determines at the time of sale that it cannot estimate the amount of returns it will receive.

Accounting:

Upon delivery:

- No revenue is recognized and the inventory remains on the company's books.
- The inventory is evaluated for impairment, under the assumption it will be returned. As the inventory cost plus anticipated repackaging costs ($87 + $15 = $102/unit) exceeds the anticipated sales price of the products ($100/unit), an impairment of $2 per unit, or $200 total, is recorded.

Cost of Sales (Impairment)	$200	
Inventory		$200

- Payment is received.

Cash	$10,000	
Deposit Liability		$10,000

At the end of the return period:

- Revenue for products not returned is recognized.

Deposit Liability	$9,500	
Revenue		$9,500

- Inventory is reduced and cost of sales recorded for products not returned.

Cost of Sales	$8,075	
Inventory ($85 × 95 units)		$8,075

- Cash is refunded on the returned products.

Deposit Liability	$500	
Cash		$500

- Repackaging costs are incurred on the returned products.

Inventory	$75	
Cash		$75

EXAMPLE 2

Additional Facts: Example Company determines that it can estimate the amount of returns and this estimate is initially determined to be 6% of sales.

Accounting:

Upon delivery:

- Revenue is recognized for products not expected to be returned and a refund liability is recorded for products expected to be returned.

Cash	$10,000	
Revenue		$9,400
Deposit Liability		$600

- Cost of sales is recognized for products not expected to be returned.

Cost of Sales ($87 × 94 units)	$8,178	
Inventory		$8,178

- Units expected to be returned are evaluated for impairment, taking repackaging costs into account. An impairment of $2 per unit is calculated.

Cost of Sales	$12	
Inventory		$12

At the end of the return period:

- Additional revenue and cost of sales are recognized because returns were less than expected.

Deposit Liability	$100	
Revenue		$100
Cost of Sales	$85	
Inventory		$85

- Cash refunds are made for returned products.

Deposit Liability	$500	
Cash		$500

- Repackaging costs on returned products are incurred.

Inventory	$75	
Cash		$75

SALES WITH MARKET VALUE PROTECTION

Certain clauses in a product sales arrangement mitigate some of the buyer's risk of a decline in market value of the goods. However, when these clauses cause the seller to retain a substantial amount of the risks and rewards of ownership, sale accounting will be precluded.

Price Protection

A price protection clause provides the buyer a credit (either in cash or as a discount on future purchases) if there is a price decrease during a specified period of time or until the buyer resells the goods. Some price protection clauses (sometimes called "Most Favored Nation" clauses) require a payment only if the seller lowers its prices during the price protection period. Other terms result in a direct payment to the customer if a competitor offers the same or a similar product at a lower price. Retailers in competitive market segments, such as appliances and electronics, commonly offer the latter form of price protection.

The accounting for price protection depends on whether the seller can estimate the amount of refunds to be granted under the price protection terms. If the seller can develop a reasonable and reliable estimate, revenue should be recognized upon delivery (assuming all other revenue recognition criteria are met) net of a provision for estimated price protection refunds. If the seller cannot develop a reasonable and reliable estimate, revenue should not be recognized until either such an estimate can be made or the price protection period ends. When the price protection clause allows for refunds based on the actions of a competitor, it may be difficult to make a reasonable and reliable estimate because the payments can be triggered by a third party rather than the seller. At a minimum, the factors discussed under "Rights of Return" should be considered in these situations.

DISCLOSURE ALERT: See Chapter 12, "Disclosures," for information about disclosures that may be required.

SEC REGISTRANT ALERT: In a December 2001 speech, the SEC staff indicated that it would focus on the accounting for price protection clauses. Specifically, the staff suggested that it will be highly skeptical in a situation where a company has developed an estimate of payments to be granted without relevant historical experience. In addition, in early 2003, the SEC staff issued the Summary by the Division of Corporation Finance of Significant Issues Addressed in the Review of the Periodic Reports of the Fortune 500 Companies (Fortune 500 Report). This report resulted from the SEC's Division of Corporation Finance's (Corp Fin) review of all annual reports filed by Fortune 500 companies. The report provides insight into areas commonly questioned by Corp Fin during its reviews of annual reports. One area specifically mentioned in this report relates to price protection clauses. Corp Fin noted that the quality of disclosures on price protection clauses requires improvement, particularly in the capital goods, semiconductor, and electronic instruments and controls industries.

EXAMPLES: PRODUCT RETURNS AND PRICE PROTECTION

Intel Corporation Form 10-K—Fiscal Year Ended December 25, 2010

We recognize net product revenue when the earnings process is complete, as evidenced by an agreement with the customer, transfer of title, and acceptance, if applicable, as well as fixed pricing and probable collectability. We record pricing allowances, including discounts based on contractual arrangements with customers, when we recognize revenue as a reduction to both accounts receivable and net revenue. Because of frequent sales price reductions and rapid technology obsolescence in the industry, we defer product revenue and related costs of sales from sales made to distributors under agreements allowing price protection or right of return until the distributors sell the merchandise. The right of return granted generally consists of a stock rotation program in which distributors are able to exchange certain products based on the number of qualified purchases made by the distributor. Under the price protection program, we give distributors credits for the difference between the original price paid and the current price that we offer. We record the net deferred income from product sales to distributors on our balance sheet as deferred income on shipments to distributors. We include shipping charges billed to customers in net revenue, and include the related shipping costs in cost of sales.

Activision Blizzard, Inc. Form 10-K—Fiscal Year Ended December 31, 2009

We may permit product returns from, or grant price protection to, our customers under certain conditions. In general, price protection refers to the circumstances in which we elect to decrease the wholesale price of a product by a certain amount and, when granted and applicable, allows customers a credit against amounts owed by such customers to us with respect to open and/or future invoices. The conditions our customers must meet to be granted the right to return products or price protection include, among other things, compliance with applicable trading and payment terms, and consistent return of inventory and delivery of sell-through reports to us. We may also consider other factors, including the facilitation of slow-moving inventory and other market factors. Management must make estimates of potential future product returns and price protection related to current period product revenue. We estimate the amount of future returns and price protection for current period product revenue utilizing historical experience and information regarding inventory levels and the demand

and acceptance of our products by the end consumer. The following factors are used to estimate the amount of future returns and price protection for a particular title: historical performance of titles in similar genres; historical performance of the hardware platform; historical performance of the franchise; console hardware life cycle; sales force and retail customer feedback; industry pricing; weeks of on-hand retail channel inventory; absolute quantity of on-hand retail channel inventory; our warehouse on-hand inventory levels; the title's recent sell-through history (if available); marketing trade programs; and competing titles. The relative importance of these factors varies among titles depending upon, among other items, genre, platform, seasonality, and sales strategy. Significant management judgments and estimates must be made and used in connection with establishing the allowance for returns and price protection in any accounting period. Based upon historical experience, we believe that our estimates are reasonable. However, actual returns and price protection could vary materially from our allowance estimates due to a number of reasons including, among others, a lack of consumer acceptance of a title, the release in the same period of a similarly themed title by a competitor, or technological obsolescence due to the emergence of new hardware platforms. Material differences may result in the amount and timing of our revenue for any period if factors or market conditions change or if management makes different judgments or utilizes different estimates in determining the allowances for returns and price protection. For example, a 1% change in our December 31, 2009 allowance for returns and price protection would impact net revenues by approximately $3 million.

Guaranteed Resale or Residual Value

To induce a purchaser to buy its product, a company may offer what amounts to a blanket guarantee on the value of the product for some period of time after delivery. Such guarantees can take several forms. For example, the company may agree to repurchase the product from its customer for a set price after several years of use. Alternatively, a company could agree to make up the difference between the actual selling price when its customer resells the product and the guaranteed price. These kinds of price guarantees must be evaluated as part of the original sale transaction, rather than as a separate purchase transaction or loss contingency.

The accounting for a resale price or residual value guarantee generally depends on whether the purchaser (i.e., the beneficiary of the guarantee) intends to use the products or resell them. If the purchaser is a reseller, the seller should account for the transaction as a product financing arrangement (see the discussion earlier in this chapter).

When the purchaser intends to use the products, the seller should account for the transaction as a lease. This is because the purchaser has essentially agreed to pay the difference between the initial purchase price and the guaranteed residual value for use of the product during the guarantee period.

Unless the residual value guarantee is less than 10% of the original sales price or the term of the guarantee is at least 75% of the useful life of the product, the lease accounting literature will classify this type of arrangement as an operating lease, rather than a sales-type lease. As a result, the asset will remain on the seller's books and be depreciated, the cash received will be recorded as a liability, and the difference between the initial sales price and the guaranteed residual value will be recognized as revenue over the guarantee period. If the guarantee can be exercised at various dates, with amounts declining over time, each decrease in guaranteed value should be considered rental income for the applicable period. If the residual value guarantee expires, any remaining liability should be recognized as revenue at that time, and the remaining asset value should be treated as cost of sales (ASC 840-10-55-12 through 55-25).

OBSERVATION: The residual value guarantee in a sales arrangement does not fall within the scope of ASC 460 because ASC 460 does not apply to a guarantee for which the underlying is related to an asset of the guarantor. For example, if a sales arrangement with a residual value guarantee is deemed an operating lease based on applying the guidance in ASC 840-10-55-12 through 55-25, the equipment (i.e., the underlying) will remain on the lessor's books, which exempts the guarantee from the scope of ASC 460. If a sales arrangement with a residual value guarantee is deemed a sales-type lease, the lessor continues to recognize the guaranteed equipment's (the underlying's) residual value as an asset through its net investment in the lease (ASC 460-10-55-17), which also exempts the guarantee from the scope of ASC 460.

ILLUSTRATION: RESIDUAL VALUE GUARANTEE ON USED EQUIPMENT

Facts: Equipment Co. sells Product X for $100,000. It also offers its customer a residual value guarantee on Product X that is exercisable three years after the original sale. The guaranteed value is $55,000 after three years. Product X has a cost basis of $60,000, and an estimated useful life of ten years. Equipment Co. generally uses straight-line depreciation. Since the residual value guarantee is more than 10% of the original sales price and the term of the guarantee is less than 75% of the useful life of the product, Equipment Co. concludes that the agreement should be treated as an operating lease.

EXAMPLE 1

Additional Facts: The customer uses the equipment for three years, and then sells it to a third party for $50,000. Equipment Co. therefore makes a $5,000 payment related to the residual value guarantee.

Accounting:

Original Sale:

- Equipment Co. recognizes the receipt of payment, but no revenue.

Cash	$100,000	
Deposit Liability		$100,000

Each of the three years following the original sale:

- Equipment Co. recognizes the difference between the original sales price and the first residual value guarantee amount as lease income as follows:

Original sales price	$100,000
Residual value guarantee in three years	55,000

Income to recognize over three years		$ 45,000
Income to recognize each year		$ 15,000
Deposit Liability	$15,000	
Lease Revenue		$ 15,000

- Equipment Co. records depreciation expense on Product X based on Product X's carrying value of $60,000 and a ten-year life.

Depreciation Expense	$6,000	
Accum. Depreciation— Product X		$6,000

At the end of year three:

- Equipment Co. records its payment under the guarantee.

Deposit Liability	$5,000	
Cash		$5,000

- Equipment Co. records the remaining liability as revenue, along with cost of sales for the remaining carrying value of Product X.

Deposit Liability	$50,000	
Product Sale Revenue		$50,000
Cost of Sales	$42,000	
Accum. Depreciation— Product X	$18,000	
Historical Cost— Product X		$60,000

EXAMPLE 2

Additional Facts: The customer keeps the equipment longer than three years. Equipment Co. therefore makes no payment on its residual value guarantee.

Accounting:

Original sale and each of the three years following the original sale:

- See Example 1.

At the end of year three:

- Equipment Co. records the remaining liability as revenue, along with cost of sales for the remaining carrying value of Product X.

Deposit Liability	$55,000	
Product Sale Revenue		$55,000
Cost of Sales	$42,000	
Accum. Depreciation— Product X	$18,000	
Historical Cost— Product X		$60,000

Sales with Fixed-Price Trade-In Rights

One variant on a guaranteed residual value is a fixed-price trade-in right, which allows the customer to exchange the purchased product for a specified credit toward another of the manufacturer's products after some period of time. This type of right is a guarantee under ASC 460. As a result, the fixed-price trade-in right should be initially recognized and measured at fair value provided that it does not prohibit revenue recognition on the arrangement in general. In effect, a sales contract that includes a fixed-price trade-in right is a multiple-deliverable arrangement; one deliverable is the sale of the product and the other is the trade-in right or guarantee. Multiple-deliverable arrangements and ASC 460 are discussed in more detail in Chapter 4, "Multiple-Deliverable Revenue Arrangements."

SELLER-PROVIDED FINANCING AND GUARANTEES

Sales with Extended Payment Terms

Some sellers elect to finance their customers' purchases by agreeing to receive fixed payments over an extended period of time, rather than receiving the purchase price per normal payment terms shortly after delivery. Except in the sale of software products (see Chapter 10, "Software—A Complete Model"), U.S. GAAP does not provide specific guidance about when extended payment terms should prevent revenue recognition. However, extended payment terms can affect two of the four basic conditions for revenue recognition—a fixed or determinable fee and that collectibility is reasonably assured.

Extended Payment Terms and Fixed or Determinable Fees

Extended payment terms raise the risk that the seller will agree to provide additional products or services or reduce the arrangement fee to ensure payment according to the stated terms, even for a creditworthy customer. Consider the example of a customer who is dissatisfied with the product but does not have a warranty or return right. The customer may instead elect to withhold payments and require the seller to negotiate to receive additional amounts that are due. Therefore, extended payment terms should be carefully considered along with warranty, return, customer acceptance, and other terms in the arrangement to determine whether they result in a conclusion that the arrangement fee is not fixed or determinable.

OBSERVATION: The above discussion applies only to payment terms that are fixed at the time of delivery. Terms that are extended until the products are used or resold generally indicate the existence of a consignment arrangement, as previously discussed in this chapter.

Extended Payment Terms and Collectibility

The longer the payment terms, the more difficult it is to conclude that collection is reasonably assured. Significant judgment must be applied in these situations. If a seller concludes that collection is not reasonably assured, no revenue or receivable should be recorded. It is not acceptable in these instances to record revenue and a selling expense for the anticipated bad debt because the threshold criteria for revenue recognition were never met.

Discounting Long-Term Receivables

When products are sold on extended payment terms and it is acceptable to recognize revenue upon delivery, ASC 835-30-25-7 requires the long-term receivable and, therefore, the revenue, to be recorded at the present value of the payments, rather than at the nominal value. Interest income should then be accrued on the receivable until all payments are made. Therefore, when extended payment terms are stated at their nominal values, a portion of the payments will be attributed to interest income, as opposed to revenue (ASC 835-30-25-10).

Guaranteeing a Loan in Connection with a Sale of Products

Some companies agree to guarantee the loan a buyer uses to purchase the seller's products. Although the company has collected the purchase price in cash, the probability of ultimately realizing the purchase price is the same as if it had sold the product on extended payment terms per the loan terms. Therefore, before recognizing any revenue, the company should evaluate whether collectibility is reasonably assured as if it were the lender under the loan.

If the company still concludes that collection is reasonably assured and that all other revenue recognition criteria have been met, ASC 460 requires the transaction to be treated as a multiple-deliverable arrangement; one deliverable is the product sale and the other is the loan guarantee. This type of multiple-deliverable arrangement is discussed in more detail in Chapter 4, "Multiple-Deliverable Revenue Arrangements."

DISCLOSURE ALERT: See Chapter 12, "Disclosures," for information about required disclosures.

Sale/Repurchase/Lease Transactions

In certain situations, especially those involving a manufacturer that sells its products through a dealer network, the manufacturer will provide financing to the end users of the product. The manufacturer (or its finance affiliate) may accomplish this by (re)purchasing the product from the dealer and leasing it to the end user. If the manufacturer recognizes revenue on the original sale to the dealer and then also recognizes revenue from the lease to the end user, it will recognize revenue twice on the same physical product. In ASC 605-15-25-5, the EITF concluded that this is acceptable and that the manufacturer may recognize a sale at the time the product is transferred to the dealer, despite the possibility it will repurchase the product to lease it to an end user, if all of the following conditions exist:

1. The dealer is a substantive and independent enterprise that transacts business separately with the manufacturer and end users.

2. The manufacturer has delivered the product to the dealer and the risks and rewards of ownership, including responsibility for the ultimate sale of the product, insurability, theft, or damage, have passed to the dealer.

3. An end user's failure to enter into a lease with the finance affiliate (or manufacturer) would not allow the dealer to return the product to the manufacturer.

4. The finance affiliate (or manufacturer) has no legal obligation to provide a lease arrangement to a potential end user.

5. The end user may choose to obtain financing from parties unaffiliated with the manufacturer, and it is feasible for the end user to do so.

CHAPTER 6
SERVICE DELIVERABLES

CONTENTS

BACKGROUND

Although the U.S. economy was once largely product-based, service-based deliverables have become an integral part of the economy over the past several decades. The number of businesses that offer services to the public continues to increase and the range of these services has consistently expanded. Personal services include those provided by health clubs, lawn care companies, retirement homes, and painters. Business services include architectural and engineering services, outsourcing of functions such as payroll and information technology, advertising, sales and marketing, and storage. Businesses charge for these services using various methods, such as calculating fees based on time, activity and success.

This chapter explores accounting issues that are common in but unique to service transactions. When a service transaction includes multiple deliverables, these accounting issues must be evaluated separately for each deliverable in the arrangement. As discussed in Chapter 4, "Multiple-Deliverable Revenue Arrangements," the interrelationship between deliverables in a multiple-deliverable arrangement may give rise to issues beyond those that exist in a single-deliverable transaction.

PRACTICE ALERT: Some arrangements that purport to cover only the sale of services may contain lease deliverables. See Chapter 3, "General Principles" for a discussion of ASC 840, *Leases*; 840-10-15 which provides guidance on how to determine whether an arrangement contains a lease. When an arrangement contains lease deliverables, the lease components must be accounted for as such. This is the case even though the arrangement is not formally characterized as a lease. Separation of the lease element from the other deliverables in an arrangement is discussed in Chapter 4, "Multiple-Deliverable Revenue Arrangements."

SURVEY OF ACCOUNTING LITERATURE

U.S. GAAP addresses certain service specific transactions in some detail. Additional general guidance has been derived from the FASB Concepts Statements and ASC 605-10-S99 (SAB Topic 13, *Revenue Recognition*). This chapter provides a discussion of both the specific and the applicable general guidance.

In the late 1970s, the AICPA and the FASB attempted to develop standards on common accounting issues in service transactions. The AICPA developed an exposure draft of a proposed SOP, which was subsequently issued as an FASB Invitation to Comment in 1978. Although this document is sometimes referenced for suggested accounting guidance, it never went beyond the Invitation to Comment stage and, therefore, is not authoritative literature.

REVENUE RECOGNITION LITERATURE

ASC	ASC Topic/Subtopic	Publication	Subject
605-10-S99	Revenue Recognition/Overall	SAB Topic 13	Revenue Recognition
N/A	N/A	CON-5	Recognition and Measurement in Financial Statements of Business Enterprises
605-15-25	Revenue Recognition/ Products	FAS-48	Revenue Recognition When Right of Return Exists
730-20	Research and Development/ Research and Development Arrangements	FAS-68	Research and Development Arrangements
605-20-25	Revenue Recognition/ Services	FTB 90-1	Separately Priced Extended Warranty and Product Maintenance Contracts
605-35	Revenue Recognition/ Construction-Type and Production-Type Contracts	SOP 81-1	Construction-Type and Certain Production-Type Contracts
980-605-25	Regulated Operations/Revenue Recognition	EITF 91-6	Long-Term Power Sales Contracts
605-20-25-13	Revenue Recognition/ Services	EITF 91-9	Revenue and Expense Recognition for Freight Services
605-25	Revenue Recognition/ Multiple-Element Arrangements	EITF 00-21 and ASU 2009-13	Revenue Arrangements with Multiple Deliverables
605-28	Revenue Recognition/ Milestone Method	ASU 2010-17	Milestone Method of Revenue Recognition

SUPPORTING LITERATURE

ASC	ASC Topic/Subtopic	Publication	Subject
835-30	Interest/Imputation of Interest	APB-21	Interest on Receivables and Payables
460 (Product Warranties Subsections)	Guarantees	FAS-5	Warranties
460 (General Subsections)	Guarantees	FIN-45	Guarantees
405-20	Liabilities/ Extinguishment of Liabilities	FAS-140	Extinguishments of Liabilities
470-10-25	Debt/Overall	EITF 88-18	Sales of Future Revenues
840-10-15	Leases/Overall	EITF 01-8	Determining Whether an Arrangement Contains a Lease

GENERAL CONDITIONS FOR REVENUE RECOGNITION

Revenue from service transactions should be recognized when it has been earned and is realized or realizable. Revenue from services is generally earned either as the services are performed or when they are complete and is usually considered realizable once the customer has committed to pay for the services and the customer's ability to pay is not in doubt. However, many uncertainties may exist in service transactions that affect the amount and timing of revenue recognition (CON-5, pars. 83 and 84).

As discussed in Chapter 3, "General Principles," revenue is considered earned and realizable when all of the following conditions are met:

1. Persuasive evidence of an arrangement exists.

2. The arrangement fee is fixed or determinable.

3. Delivery or performance has occurred.

4. Collectibility is reasonably assured.

The analysis of the first and fourth conditions does not change significantly based on the type of transaction involved. See Chapter 3, "General Principles," for discussion of the persuasive evidence and collectibility conditions. The balance of this chapter focuses on the analysis of the performance and fixed or determinable fee conditions in service transactions.

PERFORMANCE

The evaluation of a service transaction requires an understanding of the pattern of delivery or performance. Performance determines the extent to which the earnings process is complete and whether the customer has received value from the service. The key question in service transactions is whether performance involves single or multiple acts. As discussed in Chapter 3, the Proportional

Performance model often is applied to service transactions because delivery or performance occurs over time. However, the pattern of delivery or performance is not always clear or determinative. In certain service transactions, the customer does not receive any value from the service until it is completed. In these cases, revenue recognition should occur pursuant to the Completed Performance model.

Performance Is a Single Act

In some service transactions, performance consists of a single act. For example, a customer may pay a stylist for a haircut. Determining when performance has occurred for this type of transaction is not difficult and using either the Completed Performance or Proportional Performance model will result in the recognition of the same amount of revenue at essentially the same time.

Performance Involves Multiple Acts

When performance involves multiple acts, it is necessary to determine whether the Completed Performance model or Proportional Performance model should be used to evaluate when the delivery criterion has been met and revenue earned. When the performance of multiple acts spans more than one accounting period, this determination will affect the amount and timing of revenue recognized in each period.

The Proportional Performance model is often appropriate for service transactions because the customer typically receives value as the services are performed. For example, when a company purchases transaction-processing services for one year, it receives value each time a transaction is processed. Similarly, a company that purchases data warehousing services receives a benefit each time data are stored on the service provider's hardware.

However, the Completed Performance model should be used if services are performed in more than a single act, but the final act is so significant in relation to the overall transaction that the transfer of value to the customer only takes place when the final act is completed. For example, a real estate agent hired to sell a house performs many acts—running advertisements in newspapers, scheduling showings, assisting in contract negotiations, and coordinating open houses. However, the final act—actually closing on the sale—is so significant that revenue should generally only be recognized at that time, even if a nonrefundable fee was collected when the house was first listed (see the discussion of "Advance Fees" in this chapter).

Determining whether to use the Completed Performance model or the Proportional Performance model requires significant judgment. However, the following factors, if present in a service arrangement, may indicate that the Completed Performance model should be used:

1. *If the seller fails to perform the final act, the customer (or the customer's new service provider) would need to "start over," rather than just pick up where the original vendor left off.* If revenue is truly earned as services are provided, neither the customer nor the customer's new service provider should

have to reperform activities or services already completed by the original vendor.

2. *Payment terms indicate that no payment is due until the final act is performed.* This may indicate that the parties have agreed that the final act is particularly significant.

3. *The final act is significantly different in nature from the other acts to be performed.* This may indicate that the other acts are simply performed to allow the final and important act to be performed.

4. *The contracts underlying the transaction specify only the final act (i.e., completion of service) and other acts are performed at the seller's discretion.* If the interim acts are not discussed in the contracts, they are unlikely to be important to the customer.

5. *There is significant uncertainty as to whether the vendor can complete all of the acts in the arrangement.* If the vendor is uncertain of its ability to complete the final act or acts, this may indicate that these acts are more difficult and potentially more significant to the arrangement.

ILLUSTRATION: CHOOSING THE DELIVERY MODEL IN A SERVICE TRANSACTION

(Adapted from ASC 605-10-S99, A4d (SAB Topic 13A4d))

Facts: Company M performs claims processing and medical billing services for healthcare providers. In this role, Company M is responsible for preparing and submitting claims to third-party payers, tracking outstanding billings, and collecting amounts billed. Company M's fee is a fixed percentage (e.g., 5%) of the amount collected. If no collections are made, no fee is due to Company M. Company M has historical evidence indicating that the third-party payers pay 85% of the billings submitted with no further effort by Company M.

Discussion: Company M must wait until collections occur before recognizing revenue. Despite the fact that Company M estimates it will not need to put forth any further efforts in 85% of the billings, the fact remains that the final act—collecting on the receivables—is of such significance that revenue should not be recognized until it is completed. The importance of collection, as compared to sending the bills and the other acts Company M performs, is evidenced by the fact that payment is not due until collection occurs.

Applying the Completed Performance Model

Revenue Recognition

When the Completed Performance model is used to assess the delivery criterion, a specific act provides evidence that performance is complete. Revenue is earned at the time this act is completed, provided all other revenue recognition criteria are met.

Recognition of Direct and Incremental Costs

When revenue is not recognized until performance is completed, a question arises about how to account for the direct and incremental costs related to performance. These costs are similar to the costs incurred by a manufacturer to produce inventory for sale. Inventory costs are capitalized when incurred and expensed as cost of sales as revenues on the product sales are earned and recognized.

When the Completed Performance model is used, costs similar to inventory costs can generally be capitalized (provided they are realizable) and recognized as an expense when the related revenue is recognized. Costs that can generally be capitalized include those that are (a) directly related to the performance of services under the arrangement and (b) incremental to costs that the vendor would have incurred if it did not need to fulfill the contract in question. For additional discussion of cost recognition in these and other situations, see Chapter 8, "Miscellaneous Issues."

Applying the Proportional Performance Model

When delivery in a service transaction is evaluated using the Proportional Performance model, the pattern of performance must be determined. This determination should focus on the pattern of service provided to the customer, rather than on when resources or effort are expended by the service provider.

PRACTICE ALERT: The application of the Proportional Performance model (as discussed in this chapter) should not be confused with the percentage-of-completion method of accounting. As discussed later in this section under "Recognition of Direct Costs," the percentage-of-completion method results in a constant gross margin percentage. This is not necessarily the case when the Proportional Performance model is used. The percentage-of-completion method should only be applied to service contracts that fall within the scope of ASC 605-35. Such contracts are limited to architectural or engineering design services and construction consulting services.

ILLUSTRATION: RECOGNITION BASED ON PATTERN OF SERVICE, NOT PATTERN OF COSTS

(Adapted from ASC 605-10-S99, A3f, ques. 1 (SAB Topic 13A3f, ques. 1))

Example 1: A company charges users a fee for nonexclusive access to its web site, which contains proprietary databases. The fee allows access to the web site for a one-year period. After the customer is provided with an identification number and trained in the use of the database, there are no incremental costs that will be incurred in serving this customer.

Example 2: An Internet company charges a fee to users for advertising a product for sale or auction on certain pages of its web site. The company agrees to maintain the listing for a period of time. The cost of maintaining the advertisement on the web site for the stated period is minimal.

Example 3: A company charges a fee to host another company's web site for one year. The arrangement does not involve exclusive use of any of the hosting company's servers or other equipment. Almost all of the projected costs will be incurred upon the initial loading of information on the host company's Internet server and setting up appropriate links and network connections.

Discussion: In these instances, some argue that revenue should be recognized when the initial setup is completed because the ongoing obligation involves minimal cost or effort and is therefore perfunctory or inconsequential. However, the substance of each of these transactions indicates that the purchaser pays for a service that is delivered over time. As a result, revenue recognition should also occur over time, reflecting the pattern of provision of service rather than in proportion to the costs incurred or efforts expended.

Identifying the Acts That Trigger Revenue Recognition

Acts that actually provide value to the customer are the only ones that should trigger revenue recognition in a service transaction. Setup or administrative activities generally should not trigger revenue recognition. The following factors may indicate that a particular task is insufficient to trigger revenue recognition:

1. *The task is not identified in the service contract.* In general, an unspecified task is less likely to represent an item that provides value to the customer and more likely to be an internal process of the vendor.

2. *The task relates to building the vendor's infrastructure or training its employees to be able to perform services for the customer.* These are tasks that are performed to allow the provision of service during the contract term. They generally do not independently provide value to the customer.

3. *The task is purely administrative in nature.* Administrative tasks, such as setting up a customer account, billing the customer, and responding to routine information requests are only *indirectly* related to providing the contracted-for service.

4. *The customer would not be aware that the task was performed.* Tasks that provide value to the customer and thus appropriately trigger revenue recognition should generally be visible to the customer.

There is not necessarily a link between the level of costs incurred related to a particular act and whether that act should trigger revenue recognition. For example, if an act results in the incurrence of substantive costs, that fact alone should not result in the conclusion that the act triggers revenue recognition (ASC 605-10-S99, A3f, ques. 1) (SAB Topic 13A3f, ques. 1). That determination should be based on whether value is provided to the customer, not on the level of costs associated with the act.

OBSERVATION: Selecting which acts in a service arrangement should trigger revenue recognition is very similar to identifying the various deliverables in a multiple-deliverable arrangement (see Chapter 4, "Multiple-Deliverable Revenue Arrangements"). In fact, service transactions with multiple activities are, in substance, multiple-deliverable arrangements. Whether the contract is analyzed as a multiple-deliverable arrangement or not, the result should be the same—

actions that do not contribute toward providing value to the customer should not trigger revenue recognition.

Pattern of Revenue Recognition

Once the acts triggering revenue recognition have been identified, it is necessary to determine the pattern of revenue recognition as these acts are performed.

DISCLOSURE ALERT: See Chapter 12, "Disclosures," for information about disclosures that may be required.

Specified number of similar acts. If the transaction involves a specified number of identical or similar acts (e.g., the processing of bi-weekly payroll checks by a payroll processor), an equal amount of revenue should be recognized for each act. Even if the cost to provide each act varies—for example, because of a learning curve faced by the service provider—the same amount of revenue should be recognized each time the act is performed.

In some arrangements, the customer does not take advantage of all of the service to which it is entitled. This is referred to as "breakage." For example, if the arrangement is to process mortgage payments for the life of a mortgage, the service provider may be able to estimate, based on typical early payoff experience, that the mortgage will last for much less than its stated 30-year term. A service provider that believes it will actually perform fewer acts than the maximum number specified in the arrangement may also believe that revenue should be recognized based on this lower estimate, thereby allocating more revenue to each act. In certain circumstances, this is permissible. See the discussion in the "Evaluating the Revenue Recognition Conditions" Section of Chapter 3, "General Principles," for more information.

Specified number of non-similar acts. Some service transactions involve multiple dissimilar acts. For example, consider a lawn care company offering complete landscaping services on an annual basis. The service includes mowing, watering, fertilizing, trimming, and replanting. When a service transaction involves a specified number of defined acts that are not identical or similar, revenue should be allocated on the basis of the relative value of each act. In substance, this type of transaction is a multiple-deliverable arrangement (see Chapter 4, "Multiple-Deliverable Revenue Arrangements"). If the acts are interrelated such that individual acts do not provide standalone value to the customer, revenue should be recognized on a systematic and rational basis over the estimated period (generally the service or contract term) during which the acts will be performed. Where no systematic and rational basis well represents the pattern in which performance takes place, revenue might be recognized on a straight-line basis, so long as value is continuously being transferred to the customer throughout the period.

If, however, an arrangement includes two separate *services* that do not individually provide standalone value, revenue recognition is unlikely to be appropriate until the performance period for *both* services has begun. This situation must be analyzed as a multiple-deliverable arrangement, as discussed in Chapter 4. Determining whether a situation involves a single service with multiple acts or multiple services requires judgment. For example, a vendor that replaces transmissions performs two or more acts in doing so (e.g., removes old transmission, installs new transmission). However, the replacement of the transmission is generally viewed as one service. Conversely, a vendor that replaces a transmission and changes the oil is clearly providing two services.

OBSERVATION: When a service provider constructs assets that it will own and operate to provide contractual services, these assets should not be considered separate deliverables. As discussed earlier, the construction of these assets represents a setup activity that the service provider must perform in order to provide the contractual services. Therefore, these acts should not trigger revenue recognition.

SEC REGISTRANT ALERT: In a December 2002 speech, the SEC staff discussed service contract revenue recognition. The SEC staff stressed that registrants should consider whether service contracts contain multiple deliverables that should be evaluated for separation in accordance with ASC 605-25. As a result, registrants should not default to treating a service contract as one bundled arrangement for revenue recognition purposes.

Unspecified number of similar acts for a specified period. If a service transaction involves an unspecified number of identical or similar acts with a fixed period of performance (e.g., a maintenance contract on office equipment), revenue should be recognized ratably over the specified period during which the acts will be performed, unless evidence suggests that some other method is more representative of the pattern in which performance takes place. The seasonality of service or prior experience regarding the pattern of performance may constitute such evidence. For example, an annual contract to provide road maintenance in a cold-weather location would likely involve a higher percentage of services provided during winter months compared with the summer.

Unspecified number of similar acts for an unspecified period. Some service contracts provide for a service to continue indefinitely or for the lifetime of the service provider or the customer. For example, a muffler shop may offer a lifetime guarantee on its service for an extra fee. This unlimited extended warranty could require the muffler shop to perform an unspecified amount of additional work over a long period of time. Similarly, a health club may offer a lifetime membership in exchange for a large one-time fee (either with or without ongoing periodic fees).

In these situations, the contractual service period is indefinite. When this is the case, it is generally appropriate to recognize revenue over an estimated service period. To the extent that sufficient data exists to estimate the expected service period or the amount of service that will be provided, revenue should be allocated to each act or time period based on these estimates.

However, if there is no basis upon which to estimate either the service period or the amount of service that will be provided, revenue should only be recognized when performance is complete, or when breakage actually occurs (e.g., the health club member terminates his or her membership).

Recognition of Direct and Incremental Costs

Long-term service contracts are fairly common and are frequently used in outsourcing arrangements. For example, a business may hire a service provider to manage its information technology or transportation functions. Long-term service contracts are also used in the management of certain projects, such as testing programs for new drugs and health care products.

As discussed in Chapter 9, "Contract Accounting," long-term contracts to deliver products or equipment are accounted for under the percentage-of-completion method, a particular application of the Proportional Performance model, if the scope criteria in ASC 605-35-15 are met. Except in the case of engineering or architectural design and construction consulting services, percentage-of-completion accounting should not be applied to service contracts. The main difference between contract accounting and the Proportional Performance model is that ASC 605-35 requires that expected costs and expected revenues be recognized in a way that generates a consistent gross margin throughout the life of the contract. As such, it provides guidance for both cost and revenue recognition.

For contracts outside of ASC 605-35, costs of performing services for which revenue is recognized under a Proportional Performance model must generally be recognized as incurred. Therefore, although the application of the Proportional Performance model to service transactions frequently results in revenue recognition based on the percentage of completion of the service, it is not appropriate to recognize costs in the same manner. Direct and incremental costs of services accounted for under the Proportional Performance model should, instead, be recognized as incurred, even if they are not incurred ratably as services are provided.

SEC REGISTRANT ALERT: In a December 2002 speech, the SEC staff discussed the issue of applying percentage-of-completion accounting to service contracts that are outside the scope of ASC 605-35. The SEC staff stressed that ASC 605-35 and, therefore percentage-of-completion accounting, should not be applied to service contracts that do not fall within its scope. The only service contracts that fall within the scope of ASC 605-35 are those for architectural or engineering design services and construction consulting services.

In many long-term service contracts, the service provider expects the contract to be more profitable later in the contract term because productivity is expected to increase over the course of the contract. If the percentage-of-completion method as described in ASC 605-35 were applied, gross margin would be recognized based on the estimated revenues and costs over the term of the contract. However, for a service contract not covered by ASC 605-35, this method of accounting is not acceptable. Direct and incremental costs of providing the service should be expensed as incurred, rather than spread over the contract term. Therefore, margins are likely to vary over the course of a long-term service contract; however, the varying margins appropriately reflect performance in the different periods.

PRACTICE POINTER: Because the costs in a long-term service contract are likely to be higher in the initial years, some service providers structure their contracts to have higher payments in the early years (or require a significant upfront payment or incorporate liquidated damages clauses) in order to balance the contract's cash inflows and cash outflows. However, changes in the timing of customer payments do not result in a similar change to the pattern of revenue recognition. In general, revenue should still be recognized ratably over the service period unless the service to the customer is also greater in the beginning of the contract.

Recognition of Initial and Setup Costs

As discussed earlier, vendors sometimes perform acts that do not trigger revenue recognition. For example, a company that agrees to manage a database may incur costs to convert the data into a format that works with its systems. Other companies may incur costs related to contract procurement, such as a sales commission. Under certain conditions, these costs may be capitalized as an asset and expensed as revenue is recognized over the term of the service arrangement. For a detailed discussion on this topic, see Chapter 8, "Miscellaneous Issues."

EXAMPLE: COSTS OF SETUP ACTIVITIES

Phase Forward Incorporated Form 10-K—Fiscal Year Ended December 31, 2009

Revenues resulting from *InForm* and *OutcomeLogix* application hosting services consist of three stages for each clinical trial: the first stage involves application set up, including design of electronic case report forms and edit checks, installation and server configuration of the system; the second stage involves application hosting and related support services; and the third stage involves services required to close out, or lock, the database for the clinical trial. Revenues resulting from *Phase Forward IRT* and *Covance IVRS/IWRS* application hosting services also consist of three stages for each clinical trial: the first stage involves application set up, including design and set up for the subject randomization and medication inventory management, installation and server configuration of the system; the second stage involves application hosting and related support services; and the third stage involves services required to close out, or lock, the database for the clinical trial. Services provided for *InForm*, *Phase Forward IRT*, *OutcomeLogix* and *Covance IVRS/IWRS* for the first and third stages are provided on a fixed fee basis based upon the complexity of the trial and system requirements. Services for the second stage are charged separately as a fixed monthly fee. We recognize revenue from all stages of the *InForm*, *Phase Forward IRT*, *OutcomeLogix* and *Covance IVRS/IWRS* hosting service ratably over the hosting period. Fees charged and costs incurred for the trial system design, set up and implementation are deferred as applicable, until the start of the hosting period and then amortized and recognized, as applicable, ratably over the estimated hosting period. The deferred costs include incremental direct costs with third parties and certain internal direct costs related to the trial and application set up. These costs include salary and benefits associated with direct labor costs incurred during trial set up, as well as third-party subcontract fees and other contract labor costs. Work performed outside the original scope of work is contracted for separately as an additional fee and is generally recognized ratably over the remaining term of the hosting period. Fees for the first and third stages of the services are billed based upon milestones. Fees for application hosting and related services in the second stage are billed quarterly in advance. Bundled into this revenue element are the revenues attributable to the software license used by the customer.

ADVANCE FEES

Service Fee Paid in Advance

Service providers may require payment in advance. The advance payment may be either refundable (i.e., the customer may cancel the arrangement and receive a refund) or nonrefundable (i.e., the customer is not entitled to cancel the arrangement and receive a refund). In the case of a refundable advance fee, revenue should not be recognized upon collection of the fee because the fee is neither earned nor realizable.

When a nonrefundable advance fee is paid, the realizability condition for revenue recognition is satisfied. However, the fact that an advance payment is nonrefundable does not overcome the fact that performance has not yet occurred. Therefore, revenue should not be recognized until performance occurs and the revenue is earned.

PRACTICE POINTER: Some contracts that include a fee to be paid upon signing specify that the fee is intended to compensate the service provider for services rendered prior to contract execution. In general, it is not appropriate to allocate a fee in a service arrangement to activities that occurred before the arrangement was signed.

Initiation and Installation Fees

A service transaction may require a nonrefundable initiation fee with subsequent periodic payments for future services (e.g., an activation fee for a cellular telephone with monthly payments based on usage) or a nonrefundable fee for installation of equipment essential to providing the future services with subsequent periodic payments for the services (e.g., a fee charged to install and connect a security alarm with monthly payments for the ongoing security monitoring).

Initiation and installation services may be services in and of themselves. This is the case when installation or initiation services meet the conditions necessary for separation from the other services in the contract, pursuant to the model discussed in Chapter 4, "Multiple-Deliverable Revenue Arrangements." If these conditions are met, revenue allocated to the initiation or installation services may be recognized when these services are provided as long as the other conditions for revenue recognition have been met. If the initial fee is greater than the amount allocated to initiation or installation services, the difference should be treated as an advance fee for the other services in the arrangement and recognized as these services are provided.

In other instances, no separate services are provided at the outset of the arrangement in return for the initiation or installation fee, or, if services are performed, they do not meet the separation conditions discussed in Chapter 4, "Multiple-Deliverable Revenue Arrangements" (e.g., the services do not provide standalone value to the customer). When this is the case, the fee charged for the installation or initiation service should be deferred and recognized as the other services in the arrangement are performed. In substance, the initial fee is an advance charge for future services, rather than a charge for a separate service.

The period over which the deferred upfront fee should be recognized should extend beyond the initial contractual period if the relationship with the customer is expected to extend beyond the initial term and the customer continues to benefit from the payment of the upfront fee (e.g., if subsequent renewals do not include a similar fee) (ASC 605-10-S99, A3f, ques. 1) (SAB Topic 13A3f, ques. 1). In addition, customers may pay a higher upfront fee for additional services, custom features, or functionality. Upon renewal, the customers would continue to benefit from these incremental services, features, or functionality. Therefore, it would be appropriate to recognize the upfront fees over the *expected* customer relationship term rather than the initial term.

EXAMPLES: SERVICE AND ACTIVATION FEES PAID IN ADVANCE

Acxiom Corporation Form 10-K—Fiscal Year Ended March 31, 2009

The Company provides database management and IT management services under long-term arrangements. These arrangements may require the Company to perform setup activities such as the design and build of a database for the customer under the database management contracts and migration of the customer's IT environment under IT management contracts. In the case of database management contracts, the customer does not acquire any ownership rights to the Company's intellectual property used in the database and the database itself provides no benefit to the customer outside of the utilization of the system during the term of the database management arrangement. In some cases, the arrangements also contain provisions requiring customer acceptance of the setup activities prior to commencement of the ongoing services arrangement.

Upfront fees billed during the setup phase for these arrangements are deferred and setup costs that are direct and incremental to the contract are capitalized and amortized on a straight-line basis over the service term of the contract. Revenue recognition does not begin until after customer acceptance in cases where contracts contain acceptance provisions. Once the setup phase is complete and customer acceptance occurs, the Company recognizes revenue over the remaining service term of the contract. In situations where the arrangement does not require customer acceptance before the Company begins providing services, revenue is recognized over the contract period and no costs are deferred.

Cincinnati Bell Inc. Form 10-K—Fiscal Year Ended December 31, 2009

Initial billings for Wireline service connection and activation are deferred and amortized into revenue on a straight-line basis over the average customer life. The associated connection and activation costs, to the extent of the upfront fees, are also deferred and amortized on a straight-line basis over the average customer life.

Data center and managed services consist primarily of recurring revenue streams from collocation, interconnection, and managed infrastructure services. These recurring revenue streams are billed monthly and recognized ratably over the term of the contract. Data center and managed services can also include revenues from non-recurring revenue streams such as installation revenues. Certain non-recurring installation fees, although generally paid in lump sum upon installation, are also deferred and recognized ratably over the term of the contract.

License or Processing Fees

Fees may be received in exchange for a license or other intangible right or for the performance of certain administrative tasks related to a future service (e.g., processing a health club membership application). In many cases, the license provided or the services performed do not constitute deliverables that a customer would pay for, absent an ongoing service arrangement. In these situations, the upfront deliverables do not result in revenue recognition upon delivery, because they do not have value to the customer on a standalone basis (see Chapter 4, "Multiple-Deliverable Revenue Arrangements," for further discussion). Like initiation or installation fees that cannot be separately accounted for, these fees should also be deferred and recognized over the performance period of the remaining services in the arrangement. As noted above, this period may extend beyond the initial contractual performance period if renewals are expected and the customer continues to benefit from payment of the up front fee.

ILLUSTRATION: UPFRONT FEES

(Adapted from ASC 605-10-S99, A3f, ques. 1 and 2 (SAB Topic 13A3f, questions 1 and 2), and questions 11 and 12 in the SEC staff's frequently asked question and answer document on SAB 101, *Revenue Recognition in Financial Statements*. Although not codified in SAB Topic 13 presently, the examples continue to be relevant in understanding the accounting for upfront fees.)

Facts: An arrangement provides a lifetime membership to a health club. An initiation payment compensates the health club for processing the application, providing a membership kit to the member and assigning the member a locker. The member then pays a monthly fee for continued access to the facility. Assume that this arrangement is a single unit of accounting under ASC 605-25 (see Chapter 4, "Multiple-Deliverable Revenue Arrangements").

Discussion: This transaction should be accounted for under the Proportional Performance model, because service is provided throughout the term of the arrangement. The customer receives no separate value from the application processing and the membership kit and would not pay for them absent the contract to use the club. Therefore, these acts do not trigger revenue recognition. Instead, the fee charged should be deferred and recognized as the rest of the services (health club access) are provided.

Because the arrangement is a lifetime membership, the upfront fee that is deferred should be recognized over the estimated customer relationship period, assuming that this period can be estimated. If it cannot be estimated, the initiation fee should be deferred until the relationship period can be estimated or the customer's membership terminates because he or she stops making monthly payments.

Facts: An arrangement involves the installation of an additional telephone jack at a residence and the activation and provision of local phone service to the new owners. The installation of the additional jack may be performed at the same time as activation of phone service or at a different time. The customer pays an activation fee, a fee to install the additional jack, and a monthly fee for the local telephone service.

Discussion: The provision of telephone service should be accounted for under the Proportional Performance model. The activation services do not provide the customer with any value absent the ongoing telephone service and therefore no revenue should be recognized upon activation. The activation services and ongoing telephone service represent a single unit of accounting under ASC 605-25 (see Chapter 4, "Multiple-Deliverable Revenue Arrangements"). The additional telephone jack, however, provides added value to the homeowner (by increasing the value of his or her home), regardless of the provision of service. Therefore, revenue may be recognized upon the installation of the additional jack. The amount allocated to the installation of the additional telephone jack should be determined using the guidance in Chapter 4, "Multiple-Deliverable Revenue Arrangements." Any amount received upfront in excess of the amount allocated to the installation of the additional telephone jack (perhaps some or all of the amount labeled an activation fee) should be deferred and recognized over the period that telephone service will be provided. Because this period is unspecified, the deferred fee should be recognized over the estimated service period, assuming this period can be estimated.

Facts: Company A provides its customers with activity tracking or similar services (e.g., tracking of property tax payment activity, sending delinquency letters on overdue accounts) for a ten-year period. Company A requires customers to prepay for all of the services for the term specified in the arrangement. The ongoing services to be provided are generally automated after the initial customer setup. At the outset of the arrangement, Company A performs setup procedures to facilitate delivery of its ongoing services to customers. These procedures consist primarily of establishing the necessary records and files in Company A's pre-existing computer systems. Once the initial customer setup activities are complete, Company A provides its services in accordance with the arrangement. Company A is not required to refund any portion of the fee if the customer terminates the services or does not utilize all of the services to which it is entitled. Assume that this arrangement is a single unit of accounting under ASC 605-25 (see Chapter 4, "Multiple-Deliverable Revenue Arrangements").

Discussion: The customer cannot, and would not, separately purchase the setup services without the ongoing services. The customer contracted for the ongoing activity tracking service, not for the setup activities. Provided all other revenue recognition criteria are met, service revenue should be recognized on a straight-line basis, unless evidence suggests that the revenue is earned or obligations are fulfilled in a different pattern over the contractual term of the arrangement or the expected period during which those specified services will be performed, whichever is longer.

POST-PERFORMANCE OBLIGATIONS

Customer Acceptance Provisions

Customer acceptance provisions generally allow the customer to cancel the arrangement if the service does not meet expectations. The existence of such provisions raises questions as to whether the earnings process is complete when the service is performed, or only after customer acceptance has been obtained. When services are subject to customer acceptance, the terms of these provisions determine what accounting model to apply. Generally, customer acceptance provisions and the related accounting take one of the four forms discussed below (for a flow chart on evaluating customer acceptance provisions, see Exhibit 5-2 in Chapter 5, "Product Deliverables").

Service Performed for Trial or Evaluation Purposes

Sellers often provide their services on a trial basis to potential customers to facilitate an evaluation. For example, a health club may offer a trial period during which the customer has access to all the benefits of membership before being obligated to pay for membership.

Demonstration or trial arrangements do not constitute sales and no revenue can be recognized prior to acceptance by the customer. The passage of a specified interval without rejection or affirmative acceptance by the customer is required to trigger a purchase obligation and provide persuasive evidence of an arrangement. Revenue may be recognized after acceptance provided the other conditions for revenue recognition have been met (ASC 605-10-S99, A3b, ques. 1) (SAB Topic 13A3b, ques. 1).

PRACTICE POINTER: No amount of evidence of the ability to develop reasonable and reliable estimates of the percentage of demonstration or trial arrangements that result in sales will permit revenue recognition prior to acceptance because a trial or demonstration arrangement is not a sale. By contrast, subjective customer acceptance clauses and refund rights do not absolutely preclude revenue recognition because a sales agreement is in place before the services are performed. Because these rights provide customers with protections similar to those in a trial or evaluation period, companies may want to change their trial contracts accordingly. This may allow a company to recognize revenue at an earlier point in time.

Subjective Refund Right

Certain customer acceptance provisions permit the buyer to request a refund or refuse payment in the event he or she is dissatisfied with the service for any reason. An example of such a provision is a "100% satisfaction guarantee." Acceptance provisions based on wholly subjective terms are, in substance, general cancellation rights. Thus, this class of acceptance provisions should be accounted for similar to a cancellation right, as discussed in "Cancellation or Refund Rights" later in this chapter).

Customer Acceptance Based on Meeting Standard Seller-Specified Performance Criteria

These provisions give customers the right to a refund or to withhold payment for a service that is ineffective, fails to meet advertising claims, or does not meet the vendor's published specifications. For example, an internet service provider may guarantee that certain up-time targets will be met, which would give a customer the right to cancel the arrangement and receive a refund if they are not. In other cases (e.g., a car repair with a guarantee), the seller may perform the service a second time, rather than refund the purchaser's money.

This type of acceptance provision is usually offered (a) when the seller is reasonably certain the service will meet the applicable specifications, and (b) to every customer of a particular class. If the seller has previously demonstrated its ability to meet the specified criteria, the customer acceptance provision should be accounted for as a warranty (see "Service Warranties" in this chapter).

However, revenue recognition (and warranty accounting) is not appropriate when the seller has not previously demonstrated that it can perform the service to the stated specifications because it is not yet clear that the specified service has been delivered. Revenue should be deferred until the specifications have been achieved or the customer accepts the service (SAB Topic 13A3b, ques. 1) (ASC 605-10-S99, A3b, ques. 1).

Customer Acceptance Based on Customer-Specified or Negotiated Criteria

This type of acceptance provision, which is the most complex, is generally included in arrangements with customized services. These provisions usually give the seller a period of time after initially performing the service to resolve any problems that might exist in meeting the criteria. Because the service provider must continue to work until the performance conditions are satisfied, it may not be possible to conclude that obligations under the arrangement have been substantially performed until these specifications are met.

Therefore, when customer-specified acceptance provisions exist, the seller must be able to reliably demonstrate that the service meets (or will meet upon completion, if revenue on the service is to be recognized using the Proportional Performance model) the acceptance criteria prior to revenue recognition. This may be possible if the criteria are objective or if the company has provided similar services to the customer in the past.

However, if unique aspects of the customer's environment could affect whether the service meets the specified criteria, or if other circumstances exist that prohibit the seller from verifying compliance with the acceptance provisions until the service has been completed, revenue should not be recognized until compliance can be verified. Verification often consists of formal customer sign-off that the acceptance provisions have been met. However, if the seller can verify that the service meets the acceptance criteria and therefore believes it would be able to enforce a claim for payment even though formal customer sign-off has not occurred, revenue may be recognized because the seller has fulfilled all terms of the contract. As with any accounting treatment that is based on a legal interpretation, consultation with legal experts may be necessary to determine the appropriate treatment (ASC 605-10-S99, A3b, ques. 1) (SAB Topic 13A3b, ques. 1).

OBSERVATION: Acceptance provisions based on criteria specific to a particular contract or customer must be evaluated on a contract by contract basis. Therefore, the timing of revenue recognition may not be the same for different contracts.

DISCLOSURE ALERT: See Chapter 12, "Disclosures," for information about disclosures that may be required.

SEC REGISTRANT ALERT: In early 2003, the SEC staff issued the Summary by the Division of Corporation Finance of Significant Issues Addressed in the Review of the Periodic Reports of the Fortune 500 Companies (Fortune 500 Report). This report resulted from the SEC's Division of Corporation Finance's (Corp Fin) review of all annual reports filed by Fortune 500 companies and provides insight into areas commonly questioned by the SEC staff during its reviews of annual reports. One area specifically mentioned in this report relates to customer acceptance clauses. The SEC staff noted that the quality of disclosures related to customer acceptance clauses requires improvement.

Service Warranties

Many service arrangements include a warranty provision that gives the purchaser some protection in the event the service does not provide the expected benefits. Automobile mechanics, carpenters, and electricians are among the service providers that often provide these warranties. Usually, a service warranty requires the vendor to perform the service a second time if the work does not produce the expected results. Because warranty provisions may involve different types of obligations, it is important to understand the substance of these obligations in order to properly account for the warranty. For example, if the seller commits to ensure that the service will meet certain specifications beyond those that it usually meets, the seller will likely be unable to determine how much performance will be required to meet the specifications. In these cases, revenue should only be recognized when the specifications are achieved.

In addition, certain warranties may include obligations other than ensuring that the service continues to meet specifications. These additional deliverables should not be accounted for as part of the warranty. Rather, an arrangement that includes the right to future additional products or services should be accounted for as a multiple-deliverable arrangement (see Chapter 4, "Multiple-Deliverable Revenue Arrangements"). Therefore, a portion of the arrangement fee in these situations should be allocated to the additional deliverables and deferred until the seller fulfills its obligations related to the additional products or services.

As noted above, most service warranty provisions merely require that the seller perform the service a second time if it does not provide the intended results (and fix any damage caused, if applicable). Warranty obligations are usually explicit in the service contract, but may also be implied or required by laws or regulations (e.g., many states require certain licensed service providers to provide a limited warranty with their services). Because of an explicit or implicit warranty commitment, the seller's performance obligation may not end when the initial service is completed. At the very least, the seller must stand ready to honor the warranty for whatever period of time it is in force.

One possible method of accounting for a sale with a warranty would be to treat it as a multiple-deliverable arrangement with the initial service and the warranty as separate deliverables. The amount of revenue allocated to the warranty would then be recognized over the warranty period. Another method would be to consider the warranty part of the original service, rather than as a separate service. If analyzed this way, a question arises as to whether the warranty obligation is significant enough to prevent revenue recognition on the original service. If it is significant, then revenue could not be recognized until the warranty expires. Conversely, if the warranty obligation were deemed insignificant, all revenue would be attributed to the original service and recognized when that service is performed, assuming all other revenue recognition criteria are met.

U.S. generally accepted accounting principles (GAAP) recognizes the merit in both of these approaches. When a standard warranty is given to all customers, it is considered inseparable from the service. However, when the warranty is separately priced so that some customers may opt to pay for it while others do not, the warranty is considered a separate service (i.e., a separate deliverable) consistent with the way it is sold.

Standard Warranties

When a service provider offers a standard warranty to all of its customers, the warranty is not treated as a separate service. Instead, it is considered an integral part of providing the service under the arrangement. Revenue may be recognized as the service is performed (assuming other revenue recognition conditions are also met) when a standard warranty is included in the transaction, provided that the costs of honoring the warranty can be reliably estimated. In these cases, the estimated costs of honoring the warranty must be accrued as a cost of sales when revenue is recognized. Accrued costs should be updated as estimates change.

However, if the costs of honoring the warranty cannot be reliably estimated and the potential range of loss is wide, revenue should be deferred until either a reliable estimate of the costs can be made or the warranty period expires (ASC 460-10-25-4). Indicators that costs may not be reliably estimable include (a) the service is new or is being provided by new personnel, (b) the scope of a warranty has been extended beyond what has normally been given in the ordinary course of business, and (c) new obligations have been undertaken.

DISCLOSURE ALERT: See Chapter 12, "Disclosures," for information about required disclosures.

Separately Priced Extended Warranty and Product Maintenance Contracts

Revenue from separately priced extended warranties and product maintenance contracts should be deferred and recognized over the contract period. A warranty is priced separately any time a customer has the option to buy the service with or without the warranty. For example, assume that everyone who has their brakes replaced at a national chain gets a one-year warranty on the work, but that three-year protection is available for an additional charge. The arrangement should be accounted for as having a one-year standard warranty and a two-year separately priced extension. As a result, the fee paid for the two-year extension should be deferred and recognized as revenue in years two and three after the brake job has been performed. The charge for the brake job with the standard one-year warranty should be recognized as revenue when the job is completed, as long as the other revenue recognition conditions are met *and* the costs of honoring the one-year warranty can be reliably estimated.

Revenue attributable to a separately priced extended warranty contract should be recognized on a straight-line basis unless historical evidence indicates that the costs of performing services under the contract are incurred on other than a straight-line basis. If costs are incurred on other than a straight-line basis, revenue should be recognized over the contract period in proportion to the costs expected to be incurred in performing services under the contract (ASC 605-25-25-3).

OBSERVATION: A company that sells an extended warranty may purchase insurance to cover its potential losses. Although purchasing insurance may transfer the risk of loss under the contract to the insurance company, the seller remains liable for the warranty obligation in the event that the insurance company cannot or will not honor the insurance coverage. Because the seller has neither fulfilled its obligation nor been released by the buyer from that obligation (i.e., the buyer was not a party to the insurance contract), purchasing insurance to cover the risk of loss under a warranty contract should not trigger revenue recognition. The accounting for the warranty contract and the accounting for the insurance should be considered separately.

DISCLOSURE ALERT: See Chapter 12, "Disclosures," for information about required disclosures.

EXAMPLE: SERVICE WARRANTIES

Midas, Inc. Form 10-K—Fiscal Year Ended January 1, 2011

Recognition of Warranty Costs

Customers are provided a written warranty from MDS on certain Midas products purchased from Midas shops in North America, namely brake friction, mufflers, shocks and struts. The warranty will be honored at any Midas shop in North America and is valid for the lifetime of the vehicle, but is voided if the vehicle is sold. The Company maintains a warranty accrual to cover the estimated future liability associated with outstanding warranties. The Company determines the estimated value of outstanding warranty claims based on: (1) an estimate of the percentage of all warranted products sold and registered in prior periods at retail that are likely to be redeemed; and (2) an estimate of the cost of redemption of each future warranty claim on a current cost basis. These estimates are computed using actual historical registration and redemption data as well as actual cost information on current redemptions.

Annual warranty activity is summarized as follows (in millions):

Fiscal Year	2010	2009	2008
Accrued warranty expense at beginning of period	$13.3	$16.5	$24.8
Warranty benefit, net	(0.3)	(0.3)	(2.7)
Changes in foreign currency exchange rate	0.1	0.5	(1.1)
Warranty credit issued to franchisees (warranty claims paid)	(2.3)	(3.4)	(4.5)
Accrued warranty expense at end of period	10.8	13.3	16.5
Less current portion	1.7	2.0	2.4
Accrued warranty—non-current	$ 9.1	$11.3	$14.1

Warranty expense (benefit) is included in operating costs and expenses in the statements of operations. A portion of warranty expense incurred is also paid as claims within the same fiscal year. Warranty expense was reduced by $0.3 million, $0.6 million and $3.4 million in fiscal 2010, 2009 and 2008, respectively, due to changes in estimated warranty redemptions.

As of January 1, 2008, the Company changed how the Midas warranty obligations are funded in the United States. From June 2003 through December 2007, product royalties received from the Company's preferred supply chain vendors were recorded as revenue and substantially offset the cost of warranty claims. Beginning in fiscal 2008, the Midas warranty program in the United States is funded directly by Midas franchisees. The franchisees are charged a fee for each warranted product sold to customers. The fee is charged when the warranty is registered with the Company. The fee billed to franchisees is deferred and is recognized as revenue when the actual warranty is redeemed and included in warranty expense. This fee is intended to cover the Company's cost of the new warranty program, thus revenues under this program will match expenses and the new warranty program will have no impact on the results of operations. In connection with this change, beginning in 2008 Midas system franchisees in the United States started receiving rebates on their purchases from the Company's preferred supply chain vendors and MDS no longer receives product royalties on Midas franchisee purchases in the United States. Because the Company's U.S. supply chain partners are responsible for the warranty of parts during the first 12 months, MDS did not begin to record revenues or expenses under the new program until fiscal 2009.

As of July 1, 2009, the Company changed how the Midas warranty obligations are funded in Canada to match the U.S. program. As a result, beginning in July 2009 Midas system franchisees in Canada started receiving rebates on their purchases from the Company's preferred supply chain vendors and MDS no longer receives product royalties on Midas franchisee purchases in Canada. Because the Company's Canadian supply chain partners are responsible for the warranty of parts during the first 12 months, MDS did not begin to record revenues or expenses under the new Canadian program until fiscal 2010.

Annual activity for the deferred warranty obligation related to this new program is summarized as follows (in millions):

Fiscal Year	2010	2009	2008
Deferred warranty obligation at beginning of period	$ 5.3	$ 3.0	—
Warranty fees charged to franchisees and company-operated shops	2.8	2.8	3.0
Warranty credits to company-operated shops	(0.1)	—	—
Warranty credits to franchisees (recognized as revenue and expense)	(1.2)	(0.5)	—
Deferred warranty obligation at end of period	$ 6.8	$ 5.3	3.0

Other Post-Performance Obligations

Service providers may assume obligations that continue after the main service has been completed. For example, a transaction processor may agree to provide information about the transactions it processes over a specified period. Whenever a service provider agrees to perform multiple services, or takes on continuing performance obligations, the arrangement should be accounted for as multiple-deliverable arrangement. See Chapter 4, "Multiple-Deliverable Revenue Arrangements," for further discussion.

CANCELLATION OR REFUND RIGHTS

In product sales, customers often have the right to return a product and receive a full refund if they are not satisfied. Although not as common, service transactions may have similar provisions. For example, membership warehouse clubs typically charge an annual fee that is wholly refundable for some period of time after the beginning of the term. Other service providers may offer "100% satisfaction guarantee or your money back." The accounting for product return rights is addressed in ASC 605-15-25, which allows revenue recognition when a return right exists, provided that certain conditions are met (see Chapter 5, "Product Deliverables"). However, this guidance does not apply to service transactions (ASC 605-15-15-3).

OBSERVATION: The guidance in this section applies to service transactions with full refund rights. However, some service transactions may have cancellation provisions that reduce the refundable amount as time passes or as service is provided. These refund rights only need to be considered if some revenue that would be recognizable absent the refund right is potentially subject to refund. Because refund rights in these situations generally expire ratably and the service is usually delivered ratably, such rights do not usually limit revenue recognition.

PRACTICE POINTER: Cancellation or refund rights are often documented in the sales contract. However, these rights may also exist due to industry practice, company policy, or federal, state, and local laws and regulations. In the evaluation of cancellation or refund rights, all rights, whether or not explicitly stated, must be considered.

Potential Accounting Treatments

Although ASC 605-15-15 specifically excludes service transactions from its scope, many companies have applied similar accounting to refundable service transactions. As a result, revenue is recognized upon performance of the service and an estimate of refunds is accrued. Some, however, believe this treatment is not acceptable for service transactions.

There are strong arguments on both sides of this issue. Supporters of the analogy to ASC 605-15-15 note that the standard allows revenue recognition on a product sale even though a right of return exists in situations where the vendor has fulfilled its obligations and the amount of revenue is reasonably estimable. They believe the same conditions often exist in a service transaction with refund rights.

Those who believe the analogy is inappropriate argue that the differences between product and service transactions warrant different treatment of refund rights. They also believe that a refund obligation is within the scope of ASC 405-20, which only allows financial liabilities to be derecognized if (1) the debtor pays the creditor and is relieved of its obligation for the liability (*paying the creditor* includes delivery of cash, other financial assets, goods or services, or reacquisition by the debtor of its outstanding debt securities) or (2) the debtor is legally released from being the primary obligor under the liability (ASC 405-20-40). Since a refund obligation is only relieved when it is paid or expires, such an analysis would result in no amount potentially subject to refund being recognized as revenue. A second argument is that unlike a product refund wherein the product is returned to the seller, a service transaction cannot be undone once it has been performed. Thus, the customer ultimately keeps the results of the service without paying for it.

In the end, the decision regarding which model to apply to refundable service transactions is an accounting policy decision that a company must make (ASC 605-10-S99, A4a, ques. 3) (SAB Topic 13A4a, ques. 3).

DISCLOSURE ALERT: Companies should disclose their choice of accounting policy for service transactions with a right of refund. See Chapter 12, "Disclosures," for additional discussion of accounting policy disclosures.

Applying ASC 605-15-25 by Analogy

If a company elects to apply a policy similar to the accounting specified in ASC 605-15-25, it must determine whether the applicable requirements have been met. The criteria of ASC 605-15-25-1, are as follows, as they would be applied to a service transaction:

1. *The sales price to the buyer is fixed or determinable.* This shows that the refund period is not part of the transaction's pricing negotiations. If the arrangement does not meet this criterion, no revenue should be recognized because a fixed or determinable price is a prerequisite to revenue recognition.

2. *The buyer has economic substance apart from the seller.* A sale to a company with little substance (or primarily that provided by the seller) raises significant questions about the buyer's ability to pay. In such a case, the seller should not record the sale.

3. *The seller does not have significant obligations for future performance relating to the refundable service.* If the seller is required to continue performing additional work for the customer until the refund right lapses, the performance criterion may not have been met.

4. *The amount of future cancellations and refunds can be reasonably predicted.* This is the most subjective criterion and is often not met. See below for further discussion.

Estimating Refunds

It is often easy to determine whether a reasonable estimate of refunds can be made. For example, if a service has been provided to the same group of customers and has generated a consistent rate of refund requests for many years, this rate can be expected to continue in the future, provided there are no external factors that might change this experience. By contrast, a start-up company or one that sells a new service may not be able to estimate the level of refunds. The following factors should be considered in the evaluation of whether an estimate of refunds can be reasonably made (ASC 605-15-25-3):

1. *The service is susceptible to significant external factors, such as the introduction of competitors' services with superior technology or greater expected market acceptance, that affect market demand for the seller's service offerings.* When the cancellation period is lengthy, it may be difficult to predict the economic and technological life of (i.e., demand for) the service. It may

also be harder to forecast competitors' actions and customers' responses to market factors.

2. *The cancellation period is long.* The longer the cancellation or refund period, the more difficult it becomes to predict the level of refund requests. The determination of length should be based on the nature of the service, industry practice, and the type of customer.

3. *The absence of relevant historical experience.* Without historical experience to reference, customer actions may be impossible to predict. In the absence of company-specific experience, industry experience may be relevant. However, because the identity of the service provider may greatly affect customer satisfaction, industry experience may be less relevant in service transactions than in product transactions.

4. *The absence of a large volume of relatively homogeneous transactions.* It is generally difficult to predict the actions of a particular customer. However, it is easier to predict the actions of a large number of customers.

5. *The service is new.* The newer the service offering, the less specific refund experience that exists. Depending upon the circumstances, refund experience for similar services may be relevant.

OBSERVATION: The ability to estimate refunds may vary from location to location, customer to customer, and arrangement to arrangement. Thus, it is possible that a company may be able to estimate refunds for certain transactions but not others. In addition, when a company sells various types of services or serves market segments whose cancellation rates are expected to vary, the company should develop different estimates for each type of service or market segment.

SEC REGISTRANT ALERT: The SEC staff believes that it is preferable to apply ASC 405-20 to refundable service transaction fees and thereby defer revenue recognition until the refund period expires (ASC 605-10-S99, A4a, ques. 4) (SAB Topic 13A4a, ques. 4). However, the SEC staff will accept an analogy to ASC 605-15-25 if the criteria discussed above under are satisfied. With respect to estimating the refunds to be provided, the staff believes all of the following must be true for an acceptable estimate to be made (ASC 605-10-S99, A4a, ques. 1) (SAB Topic 13A4a, ques. 1):

- The estimates of terminations or cancellations and refunded revenues are being made for a large pool of homogeneous items (e.g., membership or other service transactions with the same characteristics such as terms, periods, class of customers, nature of service).

- There is a sufficient company-specific historical basis upon which to estimate the refunds and the company believes that such historical experience is predictive of future events. The SEC staff generally believes that a company introducing new services or servicing a new class of customer should wait until it has at least two years of experience before concluding that sufficient company-specific historical evidence exists.

- Reliable estimates of the expected refunds can be made on a timely basis. The SEC staff considers any of the following to be indicative of an inability to make reliable estimates:

  — There are recurring, significant differences between actual experience and estimated cancellation or termination rates (e.g., an actual cancellation rate of 40% versus an estimated rate of 25%) even if the effect of the difference on the amount of estimated refunds is not material to the consolidated financial statements.

  — There are recurring variances between the actual and estimated amount of refunds that are material to either revenue or net income in quarterly or annual financial statements.

  — There is more than a remote chance that material adjustments (both individually and in the aggregate) to previously recognized revenue would be required.

  — The customer's termination or cancellation and refund privileges exceed one year.

DISCLOSURE ALERT: See Chapter 12, "Disclosures," for information about required disclosures.

Accounting for Refund Rights

If revenue is not recognized when the service is performed because of the inability to estimate refunds, the seller should defer revenue recognition until either the cancellation period has expired or information allowing the company to make a reasonable estimate becomes available (ASC 605-15-25-1). In this situation, any cash collected should be reflected as a liability, rather than as revenue. Costs related to providing the service should still be recognized as incurred, because unlike refund rights in product transaction, the seller cannot reclaim anything of value from the customer in the event the customer requests a refund.

When a company chooses the ASC 605-15-25 method of accounting, it must meet the conditions discussed earlier to recognize revenue net of estimated refunds. Although revenue is reduced for the amount of estimated refunds, a similar reduction is generally not reflected in cost of sales. If revenue is recognized in earnings over the service period, adjustments for changes in estimated refunds should be recorded by adjusting the revenue, deferred revenue, and refund obligations at each financial statement date to the amounts that are appropriate based on the latest refund estimate (ASC 605-10-S99, A4a, ques. 1) (SAB Topic 13A4a, ques. 1).

ILLUSTRATION: SERVICE SOLD WITH RIGHT OF REFUND

Facts: Marketing Company sells 100 memberships to its travel club at $120 per membership. Customers may cancel their membership at any time during the one-year term of the membership. Any customer who does so receives a full refund of the membership fee. Ten customers request a refund after three months and 30 others request a refund just before the end of the membership period.

EXAMPLE 1

Additional Facts: Marketing Company has a policy of waiting until the refund period expires before recognizing revenue, thereby treating the refund provision as a monetary liability pursuant to ASC 405-20.

Accounting:

Upon sale:

- Payment is received, but no revenue is recognized.

Cash	$12,000	
Deposit Liability		$12,000

After three months:

- Cash is refunded to the 10 customers that request refunds.

Deposit Liability	$1,200	
Cash		$1,200

At the end of the year:

- Cash is refunded to the 30 customers that requested refunds.

Deposit Liability	$3,600	
Cash		$3,600

- Revenue on the remaining memberships is recognized in full because the refund period has expired and performance has occurred.

Deposit Liability	$7,200	
Revenue		$7,200

EXAMPLE 2

Additional Facts: Marketing Company follows a policy of recognizing revenue on sales of memberships with a refund right as long as refunds can be estimated. This is similar to the accounting treatment under ASC 605-15-25 for product sales with a right of return. Because this travel club is a new offering, Marketing Company concludes that it cannot reliably estimate the amount of refunds.

Accounting:

Same as in Example 1.

EXAMPLE 3

Additional Facts: Marketing Company follows a policy of recognizing revenue on sales of memberships with a refund right as long as refunds can be estimated. In this case, Marketing Company originally estimates a 30% refund rate, but changes the estimate to 40% when 10 customers request a refund after three months. Marketing Company has sufficient evidence to support its refund estimates.

Accounting:

Upon sale:

- Payment is received, but no revenue is recognized because performance has not occurred. Based on its estimates of expected refunds, Marketing Company records both deferred revenue and a monetary liability.

Cash	$12,000	
Deferred Revenue		$8,400
Deposit Liability		$3,600

During the first three months of the membership:

- Revenue is recognized ratably on those memberships for which refunds are not expected.

Deferred Revenue	$2,100	
Revenue		$2,100

After three months:

- Cash is refunded to the 10 customers that request refunds.

Deferred Liability	$1,200	
Cash		$1,200

- Based on its new estimate of refunds, Marketing Company adjusts the remaining deferred revenue and deposit liability balances, as well as the revenue recognized in the three months that have elapsed.

Deferred Revenue	$900	
Revenue		$300
Deposit Liability		$1,200

During the remaining nine months of the membership:

- Revenue is recognized ratably on those memberships for which refunds are not expected.

Deferred Revenue	$5,400	
Revenue		$5,400

- Cash is refunded to the 30 customers that request refunds.

Deposit Liability	$3,600	
Cash		$3,600

SELLER-PROVIDED FINANCING AND GUARANTEES

Sales with Extended Payment Terms

Some sellers may provide financing for their customers' purchases by agreeing to receive fixed payments over a long period of time, rather than in advance (see "Advance Fees") or in accordance with normal payment terms. Except in sales of software products, (see Chapter 10, "Software—A Complete Model"), U.S. GAAP does not provide specific guidance on when extended payment terms should prevent revenue recognition. However, extended payment terms can affect two of the four conditions for revenue recognition: (1) a fixed or determinable fee and (2) collectibility is reasonably assured.

Extended Payment Terms and Fixed or Determinable Fees

Extended payment terms raise the risk that the service provider will offer additional products or services or reduce the arrangement fee to ensure payment according to the stated terms, even for a creditworthy customer. For example, a dissatisfied customer who does not have a warranty may withhold payment and require the seller to renegotiate the terms of the arrangement. Therefore, extended payment terms should be evaluated, along with warranty, refund, customer acceptance, and similar provisions, to determine whether the arrangement fee is fixed or determinable. If both the payment terms and performance of the service are extended such that the payment terms mirror the performance, revenue recognition may not be delayed. However, if the payment terms extend beyond completion of the service or are disproportionately delayed until the end of a long service period, the timing of revenue recognition may be affected.

Extended Payment Terms and Collectibility

The longer the payment terms, the more difficult it is to conclude that collection is reasonably assured. If collection is not reasonably assured, no revenue or receivable should be recorded. It is unacceptable to record revenue and a selling expense for the anticipated bad debt because the threshold criteria for revenue recognition have not been met.

Discounting Long-Term Receivables

When services are sold on terms that extend significantly beyond the point in time that revenue is recognized, the long-term receivable, and therefore the revenue, should be recorded at the present value of the payments, rather than the nominal value. Interest income would be accrued on the receivable until all payments are made. Therefore, when extended payment terms are stated at their nominal values, a portion of the payments will be attributed to interest income, as opposed to revenue (ASC 835-30-25). However, if the payment terms are extended but merely reflect the proportional performance of the contract, no discounting is required.

Guaranteeing a Loan in Connection with a Sale of Services

A company may agree to guarantee amounts borrowed (from third-party lenders) by a customer to buy the company's services. Although the company has collected cash, it has effectively sold the services on extended payment terms pursuant to the loan terms. Therefore, prior to recognizing any revenue, the company should evaluate whether collectibility is reasonably assured as if it were the lender in the transaction.

If the company concludes that collection is reasonably assured and all other revenue recognition criteria have been met, ASC 460 requires the transaction to be treated as a multiple-deliverable arrangement—the deliverables are the sale of services and the loan guarantee. This type of multiple-deliverable arrangement is discussed in Chapter 4, "Multiple-Deliverable Revenue Arrangements."

DISCLOSURE ALERT: See Chapter 12, "Disclosures," for information about required disclosures.

REVENUE RECOGNITION FOR SPECIFIC TRANSACTIONS

Accounting standard-setters have addressed the application of the general revenue recognition guidance (specifically, whether and when revenue has been earned) to certain service transactions. This guidance also provides insight, by analogy, into how the general guidance might be applied to other types of service transactions. The discussion below focuses on two types of service transactions that are addressed in the literature. For a comprehensive listing of the literature that addresses specific transactions, see Chapter 2, "A Brief Survey of Revenue-Related Literature."

Transportation Revenues

Some argue that the delivery condition in a freight or shipping business should be assessed using the Proportional Performance model because the goods get closer to their destination as they progress in the shipping process. However, an argument in favor of assessing the delivery condition using the Completed Performance model is the fact that the customer will not receive value until the goods are delivered to their destination.

Revenue recognition for freight providers in discussed in ASC 605-20-25-13. The EITF concluded that the following four methods of accounting for freight services are acceptable:

1. *Revenue is recognized when freight is received from the shipper or when freight leaves the carrier's terminal with accrual of the estimated direct costs to complete delivery.* This method is considered least preferable by the SEC staff because revenue is recognized before performance. This outcome is also inconsistent with the general revenue recognition principles. Although freight carriers may use this method, other companies should not analogize to this guidance to support revenue recognition before performance.

2. *Revenue and direct costs are recognized when the shipment reaches its destination.* This method applies the Completed Performance model and treats costs as an asset when they are incurred. As a result, costs are recognized at the same time as revenue.

3. *Revenue is recognized when shipment is completed with expenses recognized as incurred.* This method also applies the Completed Performance model, but does not treat costs incurred as an asset. Although acceptable, this method does not match revenue and expenses and may therefore distort results.

4. *Revenue is recognized based on relative transit time in each reporting period with expenses recognized as incurred.* This method applies the Proportional Performance model to the transaction.

DISCLOSURE ALERT: Because freight companies may adopt any of the above four revenue recognition policies, the choice of policy should be disclosed. See Chapter 12, "Disclosures," for additional discussion of accounting policy disclosures.

EXAMPLES: FREIGHT REVENUES

Union Pacific Corporation Form 10-K—Fiscal Year Ended December 31, 2010

We recognize freight revenues as freight moves from origin to destination. The allocation of revenue between reporting periods is based on the relative transit time in each reporting period with expenses recognized as incurred. Other revenues, which include revenues earned by our subsidiaries, revenues from our commuter rail operations, and accessorial revenue, are recognized as service is performed or contractual obligations are met. Customer incentives, which are primarily provided for shipping a specified cumulative volume or shipping to/from specific locations, are recorded as a reduction to operating revenues based on actual or projected future customer shipments.

United Parcel Service, Inc. Form 10-K—Fiscal Year Ended December 31, 2010

U.S. Domestic and International Package Operations—Revenue is recognized upon delivery of a letter or package.

Forwarding and Logistics—Freight forwarding revenue and the expense related to the transportation of freight are recognized at the time the services are performed. Material management and distribution revenue is recognized upon performance of the service provided. Customs brokerage revenue is recognized upon completing documents necessary for customs entry purposes.

Freight—Revenue is recognized upon delivery of a less-than-truckload ("LTL") or truckload ("TL") shipment.

We utilize independent contractors and third party carriers in the performance of some transportation services. In situations where we act as principal party to the transaction, we recognize revenue on a gross basis; in circumstances where we act as an agent, we recognize revenue net of the cost of the purchased transportation.

Swift Transportation Co., Inc. Form 10-K—Fiscal Year Ended December 31, 2006

Cumulative Effect Adjustments

The Company previously recognized operating revenues and related direct costs as of the date freight is picked up for shipment. This revenue recognition policy was consistent with method two under EITF 91-9. Historically, the Company evaluated the materiality of revenue recognition in accordance with method two of EITF 91-9 as compared to a more preferable method (i.e. method three or five) on both a quarterly and annual basis utilizing the rollover method. The Company believes the prior years quarterly and annual consolidated financial statements derived from the application of method two do not differ materially from the results that would have been derived under method three discussed within EITF 91-9 due to the Company's relatively short length of haul, under the rollover method. Pursuant to SAB 108, the Company assessed the materiality using both the rollover and iron-curtain methods. Under the iron-curtain method, the difference between method two under EITF 91-9 and the more preferable method three under EITF 91-9 was considered material to our consolidated financial statements as of and for the year ended December 31, 2006. Accordingly, the Company recorded an adjustment to reduce the opening 2006 retained earnings by $10.2 million to reflect the implementation of SAB 108.

Research and Development Arrangements

Companies often provide research and development (R&D) services in various types of arrangements. In some cases, a customer owns all rights to the results of the R&D. In other cases, the customer funds all or a portion of the R&D and receives some rights to the results of the activities. Certain arrangements also give the company that performs the R&D a right or the obligation to purchase the results of the R&D from the customer.

Because these arrangements are complex, it may be difficult to determine whether revenue should be recognized as R&D is performed or only upon its successful completion. Indeed, because of the existence of a purchase option as described above, it may be unclear whether the payments from the funding party are merely loans, rather than payments for services. Even if it is determined that the payments are for services, the pattern of revenue recognition may still be unclear, particularly if some payments are contingent upon reaching future milestones. Many of the issues on R&D arrangements were addressed in ASC 730-20. Other issues were addressed in ASC 605-10-S99 (SAB Topic 13) and through the development of industry practice. Guidance on milestone payments was provided in 2010 with the issuance of ASU No. 2010-17.

DISCLOSURE ALERT: See Chapter 12, "Disclosures," for information about disclosures that are required for companies that perform research and development for others.

Determining the Nature of the Obligation

Payments received from the funding party may be recognized as revenue (using the Proportional Performance model) as R&D services are performed, if the company determines that it has undertaken an obligation to provide services, rather than to repay a loan or to provide a developed product (i.e., an obligation not only to provide services, but to succeed in doing whatever the R&D hopes to do). To reach this conclusion, it must be clear that the funding party bears the risk of the R&D not producing the expected results.

If the company performing the R&D is obligated to repay any of the funds provided by the other parties regardless of the outcome of the research and development, all or part of the risk has not been transferred. The following are examples in which an entity has committed to repay (ASC 730-20-25-4):

- The company guarantees, or has a contractual commitment that assures, repayment of the funds provided by the other parties, regardless of the outcome of the research and development.

- The other parties can require the entity to purchase their interests in the research and development, regardless of the outcome.

- The other parties automatically will receive debt or equity securities of the entity on termination or completion of the research and development, regardless of the outcome.

In each of these cases, it is clear that the "customer" is only lending the company money to fund the R&D, rather than paying the company to perform it, because the "customer" has the ability to get its money back if the R&D fails.

Even if written agreements under the arrangement do not require the entity to repay any funding, other conditions may indicate that the entity is likely to bear the risk of failure. If these conditions suggest that it is probable[1] the company will repay the funding if the R&D fails, there is a presumption that the entity has such an obligation. As discussed under "Cancellation or Refund Rights" in this chapter, refundable service fees should not be recognized as revenue unless the potential refunds can be reliably estimated. Given the customer-specific nature of R&D arrangements, it is unlikely that reliable estimates can be made. The following conditions create the presumption that the entity will repay the other parties if the R&D fails (ASC 730-20-25-6):

- *The entity has indicated the intent to repay all or a portion of the funds provided.*

- *The entity would suffer a severe economic penalty if it failed to repay any of the funds provided to it, regardless of the outcome of the research and development.* An economic penalty is considered "severe" if, in the normal course of business, an entity would probably choose to pay the other parties rather than incur the penalty. For example, if the entity would lose valuable rights to existing products in the event it did not purchase the funding party's interest in the R&D, the funds received should be considered a loan rather than payment for services.

- *A significant related-party relationship between the entity and the parties funding the research and development exists at the time the entity enters into the arrangement.* This indicator is particularly strong if the entity also has the right to purchase the results of the R&D on anything other than a fair value basis. See Chapter 8, "Miscellaneous Issues," for further discussion of related-party revenue transactions.

- *The entity has essentially completed the project before entering into the arrangement.* In this case, it would appear that the funding party is purchasing the results of the R&D, rather than contracting with the company to perform R&D. The payment received is effectively a prepayment for future R&D results if that R&D is successful.

- *The entity is required to make royalty payments to the funding party based on the revenues from products other than (or in addition to) those stemming from the products developed with the funds provided by that party.* In this situation, it would appear that the funding party is purchasing a future payment stream, rather than merely purchasing R&D services. Payments for a

---

[1] Probable is used here consistent with its use under ASC 450, to mean repayment is likely.

future payment stream are generally accounted for as debt (ASC 470-10-25).

Accounting If There Is Deemed to Be an Obligation to Repay the Funding

If the company has an obligation to repay the funding, revenue should not be recognized using the Proportional Performance model. Instead, a liability to repay the funding should be recognized. Revenue might, in these cases, be appropriately recognized under the Completed Performance model if the liability is repaid by delivery of the successful results of the R&D, instead of by paying cash to the funding party.

Accounting If the Obligation Is to Perform R&D Services

If the repayment of any funds provided by the funding parties depends solely on success of the R&D (e.g., royalty payments), the contract should be considered a contract to perform R&D services and provide access to the related intellectual property. This is likely a multiple-deliverable arrangement, with the license or other rights in the intellectual property being one deliverable, and the R&D services being another. Such an arrangement should be evaluated under ASC 605-25 (see Chapter 4, "Multiple-Deliverable Revenue Arrangements") to determine whether the deliverables should be treated as one unit of accounting or separated into multiple units.

Whether the license to the underlying intellectual property and the ongoing R&D services can be separated will usually depend on whether the license has stand-alone value to the customer. For example, if the intellectual property is unique, the customer may not sublicense or otherwise transfer its right to the technology, and the seller is either contractually or practically the only company that can provide R&D services that are essential in order to derive value from the technology, the license would not have stand-alone value to the customer and would be combined with the R&D services in one unit of accounting. All of the revenue would then likely be recognized over the period that the services are performed under a Proportional Performance model.

However, if the R&D services could contractually and feasibly be provided by other vendors or if the customer could perform the remaining R&D itself, the license might have standalone value, in which case the arrangement would be separated into multiple units of accounting. In this instance, it might be possible to recognize the revenue properly allocated to the license element immediately under a Completed Performance model, while the revenue allocated to the services would be recognized under a Proportional Performance model.

Once any revenue properly allocable to a separate intellectual property unit of accounting has been allocated, the entity should assess performance of the services under the Proportional Performance model and recognize the related revenue as services are performed, assuming that all other revenue recognition criteria have been met. However, determining the pattern of performance is not always straightforward. In addition, payments may not mirror the pattern of performance, because they are often triggered only when (and if) specific milestones are reached. Such payments are not fixed or determinable until these milestones are achieved and, as a result, the amount of revenue that may be recognized is limited.

Three methods are generally accepted for purposes of determining the pattern of revenue recognition in R&D arrangements.

SEC REGISTRANT ALERT: In a December 2007 speech, the SEC Staff discussed whether a vendor's participation on a joint steering committee (to monitor progress on the R&D) established through a collaborative arrangement constitutes a deliverable. The SEC Staff noted that if a contract requires the vendor to participate on such a committee or if the failure to do so would question the vendor's performance under the arrangement, then a presumption exists that participation is obligatory and, therefore, it should be evaluated as a potential deliverable. This can be important to the revenue recognition period, because such steering committees generally are intended to continue in operation long after the product has been approved, sometimes for the product's entire life.

SEC REGISTRANT ALERT: The SEC Staff has stated that a nonrefundable upfront payment in an arrangement involving the license of intellectual property and performance of R&D activities, may not be recognized up front (ASC 605-10-S99, A3f, ques. 1) (SAB Topic 13A3f, ques. 1). Although this guidance may appear to be definitive in stating that the license deliverable could never be treated as a separate unit of accounting, the SEC staff clarified in a 2009 speech that revenue could appropriately be allocated to a technology license that has stand-alone value as discussed in ASC 605-25.

Performance-Based Methods

Two of the methods rely on the model in ASC 980-605-25. An analogy is appropriate because the transactions addressed therein also involve situations in which payments under the contract do not mirror performance. The model in ASC 980-605-25 mandates the recognition of revenue based on the lesser of the amount calculated using the proportional performance to date and the amount due under the terms of the contract for work that has already been performed. Thus, if 60% of the service has been provided, but only 55% of the total fee is due, revenue is limited to 55% of the total fee. Conversely, if 60% of the service has been provided, but 65% of the total fee is due, only 60% of the total fee may be recognized.

As noted above, ASC 980-605-25 is the basis for two methods of accounting for R&D service contracts. One of the methods—the Expected Revenue method—uses total expected revenue in applying the model. This calculation bases the estimate of the amount of revenue earned at any point in time on the total revenue the company expects to earn from the contract, including payments that have not yet become due because the milestones to which they relate have not yet been reached. The other method—the Payments Received method—only uses upfront payments and payments related to milestones already reached. Both methods limit the amount of revenue recognized at any point in time to amounts that have become due (and are nonrefundable) under the terms of the contract.

The following steps illustrate the application of these two performance-based methods to R&D contracts:

1. Estimate the percentage of total services that have already been provided.

OBSERVATION: Over time, the estimate of total effort to be expended may change. If this happens, the change in estimate should be accounted for using either the cumulative catch-up method or the prospective method. The cumulative catch-up method effectively provides for a true-up to the new estimate in the current period by calculating revenue as if the new estimate were used all along. The prospective method effectively provides for revenue to be recognized in the current and future periods using the remaining fees to be recognized and the remaining effort to be expended.

PRACTICE POINTER: As discussed earlier in this chapter, there may be situations in which the total amount of service to be provided is not estimable, either from a time-based or efforts-based perspective. In these cases, it is not possible to recognize any revenue under the ASC 980-605-25 based methods until performance is complete or the amount of performance that will be required can be reliably estimated. However, the milestone method, discussed below, may be appropriate in these situations.

---

2. Multiply that percentage by either the total expected payments (Expected Revenue method), or the nonrefundable payments to-date (including those that are contractually due, but have not yet been made, as long as collectibility is reasonably assured) (Payments Received method), depending on which method is to be used.

3. Compare the result of step 2 with the nonrefundable payments received to date (including payments that are contractually due but not yet paid, as long as collectibility is reasonably assured). The lesser of the two is the amount of revenue that should be recognized, cumulatively, on the contract.

An illustration of these methods follows the discussion of the milestone method.

EXAMPLES: INITIAL FEE IN A RESEARCH ARRANGEMENT

Immunogen, Inc. Form 10-K—Fiscal Year Ended June 30, 2009

Generally, upfront payments on single-target licenses are deferred over the period of our substantial involvement during development. The determination of the length of this period is subject to judgment and estimation and can have an impact on the amount of revenue recognized in a given period. Our employees are available to assist our collaborators during the development of their products. We estimate this development phase to begin at the inception of the collaboration agreement and conclude at the end of non-pivotal Phase II testing. We believe this period of involvement is, depending on the nature of the license, on average six and one-half years. Quarterly, we reassess our periods of substantial involvement over which we amortize our upfront license fees. In the event that a single-target license were to be terminated, we would recognize as revenue any portion of the upfront fee that had not previously been recorded as revenue, but was classified as deferred revenue at the date of such termination.

We defer upfront payments received from our broad option agreements over the period during which the collaborator may elect to receive a license. These periods are specific to each collaboration agreement, but are between three and 12 years. If a collaborator selects an option to acquire a license under these agreements, any option fee is deferred and is recorded over the life of the option, generally 12 to 18 months. If a collaborator exercises an option and we grant a single-target license to the collaborator, we defer the license fee and account for the fee as we would an upfront payment on a single-target license, as discussed above. Upon exercise of an option to acquire a license, we would recognize any remaining deferred option fee over the period of our substantial involvement under the license acquired. In the event a broad option agreement were to be terminated, we would recognize as revenue any portion of the upfront fee that had not previously been recorded as revenue, but was classified as deferred revenue at the date of such termination. In the event a collaborator elects to discontinue development of a specific product candidate under a single-target license, but retains its right to use our technology to develop an alternative product candidate to the same target or a target substitute, we would cease amortization of any remaining portion of the upfront fee until there is substantial preclinical activity on another product candidate and our remaining period of substantial involvement can be estimated.

Milestone Method

The milestone method separates, rather than combines, the upfront and milestone payments. Because the upfront fee does not relate to a discrete earnings process, it should be recognized over the performance period on a systematic and rational basis. If information on efforts expended and total efforts to be expended is available, a percentage-of-efforts based method should most likely be used. If this information is not available, the most likely systematic and rational basis would be a time-based method where the upfront fee is recognized ratably over the performance period. The milestone payments, however, are deemed to relate to the portion of the performance period that is dedicated to achieving the specific milestone. As a result, each milestone is, in substance, treated as if it were a separate contract to be evaluated using a Completed Performance model.

Until recently, there was no guidance in U.S. GAAP on which to base the application of the milestone method. Instead, the method had been developed and refined informally based on discussions amongst companies, their auditors, and the SEC staff. Despite this, there were continuing questions about whether the milestone method was acceptable, because its result is similar to bifurcation of each milestone into a separate unit of accounting, even though the separate milestones would not qualify for separation under ASC 605-25.

ASU 2010-17 added ASC 605-28 to U.S. GAAP, confirms that the milestone method is an acceptable accounting method for certain contracts, and provides guidance on its application. Even where the milestone method is acceptable, it is not required. However, the method described in ASC 605-28 is the only acceptable method of accounting that results in the recognition of milestone consideration in its entirety when the milestone is achieved (ASC 605-28-25-1).

The milestone method may only be applied to milestones that are substantive and where the payment triggered by achieving the milestone relates solely to past performance (ASU 605-28-20 and 605-28-25-2).

A milestone may only qualify for the accounting in ASC 605-28 if it meets several criteria, as evaluated at the inception of the arrangement:

1. *There is substantive uncertainty when the arrangement is signed about whether the specified target or event will be achieved.* The mere fact that a vendor believes it will achieve the milestone doesn't mean that there is no substantive uncertainty. However, an event that is routinely performed cannot be considered a substantive milestone, even if its achievement triggers a payment.

2. *The event can only be achieved based on the vendor's performance or an outcome resulting from that performance.* Therefore, a payment triggered by changes in a market index is not a substantive milestone. Similarly, payments contingent only upon passage of time, or a customer's use of the research and development, are not substantive milestones.

3. *The payment to be made upon achievement of the milestone is commensurate with either the vendor's level of effort or the increase in value of the customer's rights that occur because of the achievement of the milestone.* A payment clearly in excess of the value of the services provided or the increase in value of the customer's rights in the research and development is evidence that the payment is not solely related to the performance that has already occurred. In this case, the payment may relate in part to future performance, rather than past performance.

4. *The payment to be made upon achievement of the milestone is reasonable in the context of the arrangement.* A payment that appears to be too large in relation to the work performed or in relation to other items in the arrangement may not relate solely to the vendor's performance in reaching the milestone.

If a particular milestone or the related payment does not meet the above criteria, the payment cannot be recognized in its entirety upon achievement of the milestone. In that case, one of the methods previously discussed in this section should be used to account for that payment, or it may be treated similar to an up-front payment. The fact that one milestone in a contract is considered non-substantive does not, however, mean that all milestones must be treated as non-substantive. Rather, each milestone should be evaluated individually (ASC 605-28-285-3).

DISCLOSURE ALERT: See Chapter 12, "Disclosures," for information about disclosures that may be required.

Comparison of Methods

ILLUSTRATION: COMPARISON OF PERFORMANCE-BASED AND MILESTONE-BASED MODELS

Facts: Biotech Company (Biotech) enters into an agreement with Pharmaceutical Company (Pharma) to license Compound A to Pharma for a period of three years. In addition, Biotech agrees to perform research and development for Pharma with the goal of using Compound A to develop a medicinal treatment for acne. Biotech receives $100,000 up front and $200,000 as it meets each of two milestones. For purposes of this example, assume that the milestones are substantive and meaningful. None of these payments ($500,000 in total) are refundable under any circumstances once received. No other continuing performance obligations exist. Biotech estimates that it will spend $50,000, $40,000, and $60,000 of labor costs in Years 1, 2, and 3, respectively, in performing R&D for Pharma. During Year 2, the first milestone is reached. Biotech incurs $50,000 and $40,000 of labor costs in Years 1 and 2, respectively.

Accounting: The license of Compound A and the R&D services are two deliverables in a multiple-deliverable arrangement. Biotech concludes that these deliverables cannot be separated because the interrelated nature of the license and the research and development activities result in the license not having standalone value to the customer. Biotech calculates revenue for Year 1 and Year 2 using the two performance-based methods and the milestone-based method as follows:

	Year 1	Year 2
Labor Dollars Expended to Date	$ 50,000	$ 90,000
Total Expected Labor Dollars	150,000	150,000
Percent Complete at End of Year	33%	60%
Upfront Payment Received	100,000	100,000
Milestone Payments Received (Cumulative)	—	200,000
Total Payments Received to Date	100,000	300,000
"Earned" Amount Using the Payments Received Method (Cumulative)	33,333	180,000
Amount to be Recognized Using Payments Received Method (lesser of "earned" amount and payments received) (Cumulative)	**33,333**	**180,000**
Total Expected Payments	500,000	500,000
"Earned" Amount Using the Expected Revenue Method (Cumulative)	166,667	300,000
Amount to be Recognized Using the Expected Revenue Method (lesser of "earned" amount and payments received) (Cumulative)	**100,000**	**300,000**

	Year 1	Year 2
Amount to be Recognized using Milestone-Based Method (All milestone payments received plus a portion of upfront payment based on percent complete at the end of year) (Cumulative)	33,333	260,000

Therefore, Biotech calculates revenue for Year 1 and Year 2 using each of the three methods as follows.

	Expected Revenue	Payments Received	Milestone
Year 1	$100,000	$ 33,333	$ 33,333
Year 2	200,000	146,667	226,667
Cumulative through Year 2	$300,000	$180,000	$260,000

Each of the three methods results in a different pattern of revenue recognition over the two-year period. The different patterns result from each method being more or less reliant on certain facts. The performance-based—expected revenue—method's variations are tied primarily to level of effort. However, if the milestone payments do not keep pace with the level of effort expended, the method's variance may also be dependent on the timing of milestone payments. The performance-based—payments received—method's variations are tied primarily to level of effort and timing of milestone payments. The timing of milestone payments affects this method because revenue is calculated based on receipts. This also results in a greater amount of backended revenue (i.e., recognized towards the end of the service period). The milestone method's variations depend in part on the approach used to recognize the upfront fee. If an efforts-based approach is used to recognize the upfront fee (as is the case in the illustration above), the milestone-based method's variations will be caused by both level of effort and timing of milestone payments. If a time-based approach is used to recognize the upfront fee, then the milestone-based method's variations will be due solely to the timing of milestone payments.

Which of these methods is preferable depends to a certain extent on the facts and circumstances.

PRACTICE POINTER: The method selected to account for R&D contracts is considered an accounting policy choice. As a result, any change from this method to another must be treated as a change in accounting principle. Such change would have to be considered preferable in order to be effected.

EXAMPLE: MILESTONE METHOD

Medivation, Inc. Form 10-K—Fiscal Year Ended December 31, 2009

Milestone Payments

Under both the Pfizer and Astellas Collaboration Agreements, we are entitled to receive milestone payments based on achievement of specified development, regulatory and commercial events. Management evaluated the nature of the events triggering these contingent payments, and concluded that these events- except for (a) those relating to regulatory activities in Europe, development and regulatory activities in Japan, and commercial activities, all of which are areas in which we have no pertinent contractual responsibilities, and (b) the initiation of the second Phase 3 clinical trial under the Astellas Collaboration Agreement, an event which management deemed to be reasonably assured at the inception of the Astellas collaboration-constituted substantive milestones. This conclusion was based primarily on the facts that (i) each triggering event represents a specific outcome that can be achieved only through successful performance by us of one or more of our deliverables, (ii) achievement of each triggering event was subject to inherent risk and uncertainty and would result in additional payments becoming due to us, (iii) each of these milestones was substantive, based primarily on the facts that the payments they trigger are non-refundable, (iv) achievement of the milestone entails risk and was not reasonably assured at inception of the Collaboration Agreement, (v) substantial effort is required to complete each milestone, (vi) the amount of each milestone payment is reasona- ble in relation to the value created in achieving the milestone, (vii) a substantial amount of time is expected to pass between the up-front payment and the potential milestone payments, and (viii) the milestone payments relate solely to past performance. Based on the foregoing, we will recognize any revenue from these milestone payments under the substantive milestone method in the period in which the underlying triggering event occurs.

For the contingent payments triggered by events that do not constitute substan- tive milestones, management concluded that the appropriate revenue recogni- tion treatment depends on whether the triggering event occurs during or after the performance period of the applicable Collaboration Agreement. Where the trig- gering event occurs during the applicable performance period, we will amortize any revenue from this event on a straight-line basis over the period beginning on the date the event occurs and ending at completion of the applicable perform- ance period. Where the triggering event occurs after the applicable performance period, we will recognize the associated revenue in the period in which the event occurs.

CHAPTER 7
INTELLECTUAL PROPERTY DELIVERABLES

CONTENTS

BACKGROUND

Many companies earn revenue by permitting others to use their assets. Some examples include:

- A car rental agency.
- A computer software developer that licenses software products to customers.
- A movie production company that licenses film rights.
- A franchisor that allows customers to use its name and processes.
- A life sciences company that allows a pharmaceutical company to sell a drug.

The accounting for transactions in which one company receives payment in exchange for the right to use its assets has been debated for many years. However, this debate has not produced a universally applicable model. This is the result of key differences across transaction types, including:

- The term of the arrangement (i.e., limited or in perpetuity);
- The nature of the asset (i.e., tangible versus intangible);
- Whether the right to use is exclusive or nonexclusive;
- Variable or fixed fees; and
- Cancellation and modification provisions.

Certain licenses of intangible assets are addressed in the accounting literature (see "Revenue Recognition for Specific Intellectual Property Transactions" later in this chapter), but many others are not. When a company licenses intellectual property that is not the subject of a specific authoritative pronouncement, the company must consider the license's specific facts and circumstances, the general revenue recognition guidance contained in the FASB Concepts Statements, and the individual pieces of topic-specific guidance that address accounting for the sale of rights to use specific types of assets. SEC registrants must (and private companies might) also consider the guidance provided in ASC 605-10-S99 (SAB Topic 13, *Revenue Recognition*).

This chapter explores significant accounting issues that are common in but unique to the sale or licensing of intellectual property assets. Where an intellectual property asset transaction includes multiple deliverables, these accounting issues must be evaluated separately for each deliverable in the arrangement. As discussed in Chapter 4, "Multiple-Deliverable Revenue Arrangements," the interrelationship between deliverables in a multiple-deliverable arrangement may give rise to issues beyond those that exist in other transactions.

SURVEY OF ACCOUNTING LITERATURE

The accounting literature that addresses the sale or licensing of intellectual property assets is almost entirely transaction- or industry-based. For example, there is a significant amount of guidance on leasing tangible assets and licensing motion picture rights. Conversely, with the exception of ASC 605-10-S99 (SAB Topic 13), which addresses several narrow issues on intellectual property licenses in general, there is little or no implementation guidance for transactions that fall outside the scope of the industry- or transaction-based literature.

ASC	ASC Topic/Subtopic	Publication	Subject
	REVENUE RECOGNITION LITERATURE		
605-10-S99	Revenue Recognition/Overall	SAB Topic 13	Revenue Recognition
605-30	Revenue Recognition/Rights to Use	N/A	Rights to Use
952-605	Franchisors/ Revenue Recognition	FAS-45	Franchise Fee Revenue
605-15-25	Revenue Recognition/ Products	FAS-48	Revenue Recognition When Right of Return Exists
985-605	Software/Revenue Recognition	SOP 97-2 and ASU 2009-14	Software Revenue Recognition
926-605	Entertainment— Films/Revenue Recogition	SOP 00-2	Accounting by Producers or Distributors of Films
928-605	Entertainment— Music/Revenue Recognition	FAS 50	Licenses of Music
605-25	Revenue Recognition/ Multiple-Element Arrangements	EITF 00-21 and ASU 2009-13	Revenue Arrangements with Multiple Deliverables
808	Collaborative Arrangements	EITF 07-1	Accounting for Collaborative Arrangements

SUPPORTING LITERATURE

ASC	ASC Topic/Subtopic	Publication	Subject
835-30	Interest/Imputation of Interest	APB-21	Interest on Receivables and Payables
840	Leases	FAS-13	Leases
460	Guarantees	FIN-45	Guarantees
460-10-55-30	Guarantees/Overall	FSP FIN 45-1	Intellectual Property Infringement Indemnifications

GENERAL CONDITIONS FOR RECOGNITION

As with all revenue transactions, revenue from intellectual property transactions should be recognized when it has been earned and is realized or realizable. Revenue is generally earned at either the beginning or throughout the license term, depending upon the nature of the license and the other obligations taken on by the licensor. Such revenue is usually considered realizable once the customer has committed to pay for the license, provided the customer's ability to pay is not in doubt. In licenses of intellectual property, it is common to only have a commitment to make partial payments at the inception of the license, with the customer becoming obligated to make additional payments based on performance milestones, use of the property, or the passage of time. These and other uncertainties may determine the amount and timing of revenue recognition.

As discussed in Chapter 3, "General Principles," revenue is considered earned and realizable when all of the following conditions are met:

1. Persuasive evidence of an arrangement exists.

2. The arrangement fee is fixed or determinable.

3. Delivery or performance has occurred.

4. Collectibility is reasonably assured.

The analysis of the first and fourth conditions above does not change significantly based on the type of transaction involved. Therefore, this chapter primarily focuses on the analysis of the fixed or determinable and delivery conditions in intellectual property transactions.

DELIVERY

The most significant revenue recognition issue in intellectual property arrangements is whether delivery occurs when the lease or license term begins (Completed Performance model) or throughout the term of the lease or license (Proportional Performance model). To make this determination, it is necessary to assess whether the arrangement is, in substance, the sale of an asset. If the transaction is deemed a sale, such that control and substantially all of the risks and rewards of the asset are transferred, the Completed Performance model should be applied.

However, in most licenses or leases of intellectual property, the rights transferred involve only a portion of the rights embodied in the asset. For example, licenses are often non-exclusive, such that the property can be licensed to many customers. In addition, rights to use property can be for a limited period of time, restricted to a particular jurisdiction or industry, or limited as to the amount of usage. In all of these situations, it is clear that the transaction is not a complete sale of the asset, calling into question whether the Completed Performance model is appropriate. On the other hand, the seller/licensor's performance may be essentially complete once the license begins, making application of the Proportional Performance model seem unusual as well.

Each arrangement and asset type can have unique characteristics that make the assessment of whether revenue should be recognized at the beginning of the license term or over the license term difficult. In addition to the specific rights encompassed in the right to use, other issues that can make the assessment difficult include various kinds of continuing involvement of the seller/licensor in helping the licensee realize value from its right to use, uncertainty surrounding the value and usefulness of the intellectual property being licensed, and complicated formulas for determining the payment due to the seller/licensor.

OBSERVATION: Software and other types of intellectual property are often delivered via a tangible medium. This, however, does not change the fact that the value to the customer is the intellectual property. For example, computer software delivered on a compact disc is actually the sale or license of the software program. The compact disc is merely the tangible medium used to provide the customer access to the intangible computer software program.

Possible Analogies in the Accounting Literature

The accounting literature addresses several types of transactions involving rights to use assets. These transactions include leases, licenses to software, and motion pictures and franchise arrangements. The existing literature discusses when to apply the Completed Performance or Proportional Performance model to assess delivery.

Leases

The sale of the right to use one or more tangible assets is a lease. Detailed guidance is provided in the accounting literature on how to determine whether the Completed Performance or Proportional Performance model applies to a lease. ASC 840 has been amended and supplemented repeatedly over the years. A detailed listing of the relevant authoritative pronouncements addressing a lessor's accounting for lease revenue is included in Chapter 2, "A Brief Survey of Revenue-Related Literature."

This guidance may also be useful, by analogy, in accounting for sales of the right to use intangible assets (i.e., intellectual property licenses) because it focuses on which party (lessor or lessee) holds the risks and rewards of ownership. The basic model in ASC 840 requires a lessor to determine whether the substance of the lease is the sale of the asset by focusing on which party (the lessee or lessor) holds the risks and rewards of ownership. If a lease transaction is essentially the sale of an asset, the analysis of delivery should be analogous to that in a product sale (Completed Performance model). If the lease effectively conveys the lessee the right to use the asset for a limited time, delivery should be evaluated as it is in many service transactions (Proportional Performance model).

A lessor uses the following decision tree to determine the appropriate delivery model for a lease:

EXHIBIT 7-1: LEASE FLOW CHART

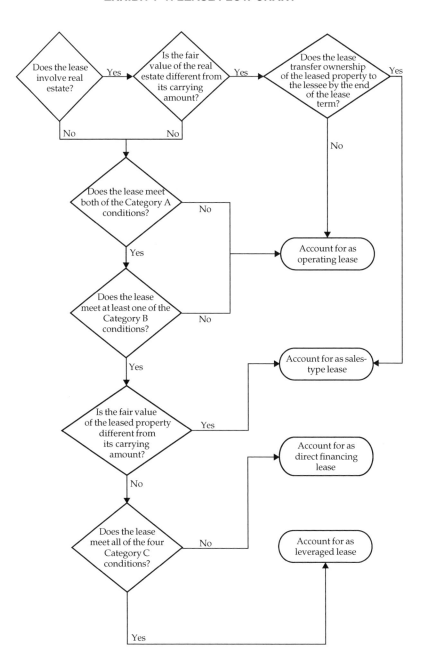

Category A Conditions (ASC 840-10-25-42)

1. Collections of rentals must be reasonably predictable

2. Significant risks or commitments beyond those related to usual sales warranties cannot be retained or undertaken

Category B Conditions (ASC 840-10-25-1)

1. Title to the leased asset transfers to lessee at the end of the lease term

2. Lessee has option to purchase leased asset at a bargain price

3. Lease term is 75% or more of the estimated useful life of the property subject to the lease

4. Present value of minimum lease payments is 90% or more of the fair value of the leased property less any investment tax credit retained by the lessor

Category C Conditions (ASC 840-10-25-43)

1. Lease involves at least three parties: lessee, long-term creditor, and lessor

2. Long-term creditor financing is substantial and nonrecourse to lessor

3. Lessor's net investment declines during the early years and increases during the later years of the lease term

4. Lessor accounts for any retained investment tax credit as cash flow component of lease

---

The criteria (Category A, B, and C Conditions) focus on whether the lessor has transferred the significant risks and rewards of ownership to the lessee. If the lessor retains the significant risks and rewards, the lease must be treated as an operating lease—that is, the lessor must apply the Proportional Performance model whereby the operating lease payments are recognized as revenue over the lease term. If the lessor transfers the significant risks and rewards of ownership to the lessee, the Completed Performance model should be used. The lease is treated as a sales-type, direct financing, or leveraged lease, as appropriate. Each of these methods results in the application of a variation of the Completed Performance model.

Franchises, Software, Music, and Motion Pictures

Franchise fee revenue recognition is discussed in ASC 952-605; software revenue recognition in ASC 985-605; music licensing revenue in ASC 928-605, and recognition of revenue from the licensing of films in ASC 926-605. In general, the Completed Performance model is used to evaluate the delivery condition unless certain factors exist. Further discussion of arrangements involving franchises and motion pictures is included later in this chapter. Software revenue recognition is discussed fully in Chapter 10, "Software—A Complete Model."

Choosing the Right Model

The software, music, and motion picture models are comparable because the nature of the licensed property is similar. The franchise model, however, is different, because these arrangements invariably involve a continuing relationship between the parties. Certain characteristics of the ASC 840 lease model set it apart from each of the above models.

The determination as to which of these models is the best analogy for intellectual property licenses depends on the type of intellectual property involved. For example, content is central to both a manuscript for a novel and a film. Although the content is presented differently, the nature of the intellectual property involved is the same. As a result, the company trying to sell or license the manuscript should consider applying the guidance in ASC 926-605 to determine when the fees received from sale or licensing should be recognized.

Finding the appropriate analogy for other types of intellectual property is not quite as easy. For example, the value in the formula for a candy bar is realized through the product that the formula produces. ASC 926-605 would be a difficult analogy because there are no significant similarities between a candy bar formula and a film. The nature of the candy bar formula, however, is somewhat similar to a software program since a computer code works much like a formula. However, the value provided by the software program is completely different from the value provided by a candy bar formula. As a result, ASC 985-605 may not be easily applied. A franchise agreement may include the rights to food or other formulas. However, there is much more involved in a franchise than merely the transfer of rights to intellectual property such as a candy bar formula. In this instance, ASC 952-605 is not a clean analogy. A candy bar formula is clearly intellectual property and not a tangible asset. It is, therefore, difficult to apply the ASC 840 model.

While analogizing to a particular part of the literature can help answer questions that arise, all facts and circumstances related to the intellectual property license must be analyzed in the context of the general revenue recognition concepts and conditions discussed above (see "General Conditions for Recognition") to determine when delivery occurs under the license.

Key Factors in Evaluating Delivery of Intellectual Property

Delivery generally occurs when value is transferred to the customer. In intellectual property transactions, it may be unclear whether value transfers all at once or over time as the right to use the asset is provided. The factors discussed below should be used to determine which model applies and when to begin recognizing revenue.

Commencement of License Term

The earliest point at which delivery can occur is the first day of the license term. For example, if a license arrangement is consummated on March 15, but the license term begins on April 1, the licensor may not recognize any revenue prior to April 1. This approach is consistent with one of the general conditions that must be met to recognize revenue from the sale or license of software, music, and films. This point applies to intellectual property transactions under either the Completed Performance model or the Proportional Performance model. In both cases, no revenue should be recognized until the beginning of the license term

(ASC 605-10-S99, A3d and ASC 985-605-55-103) (SAB Topic 13A3d and TPA 5100.70).

Risks and Rewards of Ownership

Intellectual property is sometimes delivered on a physical medium. When this is the case, many of the considerations typically involved in product sales are relevant to recognition of revenue from the intellectual property license. For example, intellectual property on a physical medium (e.g., a CD, a book, or printed data) is generally not considered delivered until title transfers, along with the related risks and rewards of ownership of the physical medium containing the intellectual property. See Chapter 5, "Product Deliverables," for discussion of these issues. Chapter 10, "Software—A Complete Model," also discusses how these issues are addressed in the software revenue recognition literature.

Exclusivity

Rights to use tangible assets can be fundamentally different from rights to use intangible assets. A specific tangible asset may be used by only one user at a time, whereas an intangible asset can be used concurrently by many users. Consider an automobile and computer software. The automobile (the tangible asset) may only be rented to and used by one driver at a time, whereas the computer software (the intangible asset) may be licensed to and operated by many users at the same time. This basic distinction has resulted in the development of different accounting models for the sale of rights to use tangible and intangible assets.

An arrangement that provides exclusive rights to intellectual property is comparable to a similar transaction involving a tangible asset because it can only be licensed (or sold) once. An arrangement that provides non-exclusive rights to intellectual property, however, is similar to the software license described above because it can be sold to more than one concurrent user. Therefore, the leasing literature might be used to determine when delivery occurs in an arrangement with exclusivity and the software literature might be used to determine when delivery occurs in a non-exclusive arrangement.

Duration of the Arrangement

Comparing the term of the arrangement with the life of the intellectual property enables the licensor to evaluate whether the arrangement is more similar to the outright sale of a product or a short-term operating lease.

Arrangement term. Because licenses of intellectual property (other than those discussed above) are not addressed in the authoritative literature, there is no guidance on how to determine the life of an arrangement that has options or potential extensions. For example, the stated term of the arrangement may be five years. However, provisions in the arrangement may automatically (or on achievement of certain milestones or targets, for example, if neither party has defaulted) extend the term in perpetuity. In this situation, the seller or licensor should carefully consider whether the term of the arrangement is effectively the life of the intellectual property.

Intellectual property life. The life of the intellectual property is the time period over which it provides benefits to its owner or users. To understand the life of the intellectual property, the seller or licensor should consider the nature of (1) the legal rights it possesses to the intellectual property and (2) the intellectual property itself. For example, if the intellectual property rights are subject to a patent, the seller or licensor should consider when the patent will expire and whether it will or can be renewed. In addition, the seller or licensor should consider whether the intellectual property rights relate to a technology susceptible to obsolescence, which could result in the economic life being shorter than the legal life.

An arrangement whose duration is for the life of the intellectual property has an attribute similar to a product sale—neither the customer's right to use the intellectual property nor its ownership of the product revert back to the owner after a limited period of time. Duration of the arrangement is also relevant in lease accounting. One of the conditions that qualify an arrangement for sales-type lease treatment is a lease term that is 75% or more of the estimated useful life of the property subject to the lease.

An arrangement whose duration is shorter than the life of the intellectual property has attributes similar to an operating lease because the rights to use the property will lapse before the end of the property's useful life. The primary benefit of considering the duration of the arrangement arises when it is evaluated in conjunction with exclusivity.

Exclusivity/Duration Matrix

Different combinations of exclusivity and duration affect the analysis of which model—Competed Performance or Proportional Performance—is most appropriate. The following matrix outlines which model(s) can be justified in accounting for the sale or license of intellectual property based on the confluence or divergence of exclusivity and duration:

	Term equal to life of intellectual property	Term less than life of intellectual property
Exclusive	**Quadrant I** **Completed Performance**	**Quadrant II** **Proportional Performance**
Non-exclusive	**Quadrant III** **Completed or Proportional Performance**	**Quadrant IV** **Completed or Proportional Performance**

Quadrant I

When intellectual property is licensed to a customer for the duration of its life and on an exclusive basis, it is very similar to an outright product sale. Therefore, a Completed Performance model is generally most appropriate. In an outright product sale, except for normal rights of return that are accounted for separately in accordance with ASC 605-15-25, the product will not revert to the seller. Similarly, the right to use the intellectual property will not revert to the seller or licensor during the intellectual property's life if the license is exclusive and its term is equal to the intellectual property's remaining useful life. Furthermore, as in an outright product sale where the specific product is sold only to one customer, intellectual property sold on an exclusive basis is only licensed to one customer.

OBSERVATION: Intellectual property may be licensed on an exclusive basis for use in either specific geographic areas or specific applications. For example, a specific medical compound may be licensed exclusively to one researcher for use in developing a treatment for one medical condition and also exclusively licensed to a second researcher for use in developing a treatment for a different medical condition. Similarly, a candy bar formula may be licensed exclusively to one company for the North American region and licensed exclusively to a second company for the European region.

Quadrant II

When intellectual property is licensed to a customer for less than the duration of its life and on an exclusive basis, a Proportional Performance model is generally most appropriate, because the license is similar to an operating lease. In an operating lease, the right to use the asset will revert to the lessor at the end of the lease term. Similarly, the right to use the intellectual property will revert to the seller or licensor at the end of the license arrangement term if the term is less than the life of the intellectual property. The presumption, in both cases, is that the leased asset or licensed intellectual property will have value to the lessor or licensor at that point in time. Furthermore, in an operating lease the asset is only leased to one customer. Likewise, the intellectual property is only licensed to one customer when the terms are exclusive.

OBSERVATION: Although transactions with these characteristics appear similar to operating leases, both ASC 985-605 and ASC 926-605 generally require the use of a Completed Performance model in these situations. Therefore, the operating lease analogy should not be applied to all intellectual property licenses that are exclusive and limited in duration. Each license should be analyzed carefully to reach an appropriate conclusion.

Quadrants III and IV

When a sale or license of intellectual property is non-exclusive, it is not clear whether a Completed Performance model or a Proportional Performance model should be applied. For instance, non-exclusivity is prevalent in software and motion picture arrangements and a Completed Performance model is generally used in both cases. However, the leasing literature requires certain conditions to be met (which are unlikely in the typical intellectual property licensing arrangement) in order to treat the right to use a tangible asset as a sale. This is because ownership of the intellectual property does not usually transfer to the licensee at the end of the arrangement term, the licensee does not usually have the option to purchase the intellectual property at a bargain price, and it is usually not possible to determine whether the present value of the payments under the arrangement are 90% or more of the fair value of the intellectual property due to the complexity of deriving a fair value for these assets. If the term of the arrangement represents 75% or more of the estimated life of the intellectual property, one of the criteria may be satisfied. If this is the case, a Completed Performance model may be the most appropriate.

In many of the Quadrant III and IV situations, a legitimate case might be made for using either the Completed Performance model or the Proportional Performance model. As a result, a seller should determine which model best fits the specific facts and circumstances and select it as the accounting policy for the arrangement (and other similar arrangements). If neither model is clearly the best analogy, a seller or licensor of intellectual property will have to choose one of the models to use as its accounting policy in these (and other similar) situations.

PRACTICE POINTER: Companies in this situation should determine their accounting policy choice after careful consideration. Any change to this policy (i.e., going from a Proportional Performance model to a Completed Performance model or vice versa) is treated as a change in accounting principle. See ASC 250, *Accounting Changes and Error Corrections*, for the appropriate accounting treatment.

DISCLOSURE ALERT: See Chapter 12, "Disclosures," for information about disclosures that may be required.

FIXED OR DETERMINABLE FEES

Variable Fees

It is common for the fee in a license of intellectual property to depend upon how the property is used by the customer. For example, the fee related to a drug under development may increase if the customer receives FDA approval to begin the next stage of testing. Similarly, fees that result from licensing a customer list may be tied to a specific amount of sales that the licensee generates. These fees, like other fees that depend upon the occurrence of a future event (e.g., receipt of FDA approval), are not fixed or determinable. Chapter 3, "General Principles," includes a general discussion on this topic.

Refund, Return, and Cancellation Rights

General Model

Intellectual property licenses often include rights of return, cancellation, or refund. These rights are generally included in arrangements where intellectual property is licensed to many end customers. For example, the purchase of a movie on DVD usually includes a limited time right of return and the purchase of an annual license to view internet content may include a right that allows a full refund if the purchaser cancels within the first 30 days. Other intellectual property transactions may have specially designed refund or return rights. For example, a license of the rights to a technology being developed may be cancelable by the customer for a full or partial refund if certain milestones in the development of the technology are not reached.

PRACTICE POINTER: Return rights are often documented in the sales contract. However, such rights may also exist due to industry practice, company policy, or federal, state, and local laws and regulations. In addition, the relationship between the buyer and seller should be evaluated to determine whether unstated rights of return might exist and whether the company has a practice of accepting returns that it is not required to by the contract. All rights of return, whether or not explicitly stated, must be considered. See the return rights Examples in Chapter 5.

Both ASC 985-605 and ASC 926-605 specifically require the use of the guidance in ASC 605-15-25 when accounting for returns on sales of software and movies. By analogy, ASC 605-15-25 may be applied to sales of other intellectual property when a right of return exists.

Although a return right creates a question as to whether the transaction has been completed, the seller records revenue upon delivery if the terms of the arrangement make it clear that a sale has occurred, there are no other contingencies, and the likelihood of the customer exercising the right of return can be estimated. Specifically, revenue should be recognized at the time of sale, net of estimated returns, only if all of the following conditions are met (ASC 605-15-25-1):

1. The sales price to the buyer is fixed or determinable.

2. Payment is not contractually or otherwise excused until the product is resold.

3. The buyer holds the risks of destruction, damage, or theft of the property. If not, all of the risks and rewards of ownership have not passed to the buyer and revenue recognition is prohibited.

4. The buyer has economic substance apart from the seller.

5. The seller does not have significant obligations for future performance relating to the resale of the product by the buyer.

6. The amount of future returns and costs expected in connection with any returns can be reasonably predicted.

A detailed discussion of these criteria is provided in Chapter 5, "Product Deliverables." Except for the sixth criterion, the analysis is effectively the same in an intellectual property transaction as it would be in a product sale. The third criterion is relevant in intellectual property transactions when the intellectual property is provided on a physical medium, such as a compact disc. The right-of-return analysis in these situations is essentially the same as in a product sale, including the need to consider whether the buyer holds the "physical risks" related to the tangible medium on which the intellectual property is provided. However, analysis of the sixth criterion in an intellectual property license presents unique challenges, which are discussed below.

Estimating Returns

As discussed in Chapter 5, "Product Deliverables," a large volume of homogeneous transactions is required to estimate the extent to which customers will exercise return or refund rights. In certain types of intellectual property transactions, such as the sales of computer software or videotapes to end-users, there may be a large volume of homogeneous transactions on which an estimate of returns can be based.

However, other licenses of intellectual property, such as licenses to use technology to develop products, or rights to access data such as membership or customer lists, are unlikely to have the requisite large volume of homogeneous transactions. Instead, these transactions are more likely to be "one-off" transactions that include mostly customized terms. To the extent that fees paid by the licensee in these types of arrangements are refundable, they are not recognizable, because a reasonable and reliable estimate of returns cannot be made.

Even when a large volume of homogeneous transactions does exist, other factors might affect the ability to make a reliable estimate of the number of customers that will exercise their rights. These factors are discussed in detail in Chapter 5.

CONTINUING PERFORMANCE OBLIGATIONS

Regardless of the delivery model used to account for the sale or licensing of intellectual property, the seller or licensor must understand the nature of any continuing performance obligations whether related to the license of intellectual property or in separate agreements, such as research and development or contract manufacturing arrangements. Unless the continuing performance obligation meets the requirements to be treated as a separate deliverable, the existence of such an obligation affects the timing of revenue recognition. Chapter 4, "Multiple-Deliverable Revenue Arrangements," provides an in-depth discussion of the conditions that must be met to conclude that multiple deliverables can be separated for accounting purposes. Two continuing performance obligations that are common in intellectual property licenses are discussed below.

When-and-If-Available Deliverables

A when-and-if-available clause requires the seller or licensor to make enhancements or other information related to the licensed intellectual property available to the buyer or licensee if it becomes available. For example, if the owner of the rights to a drug licenses them to a third party for use in Japan, a when-and-if-available clause may require the company to provide the customer with the results of any work it performs to improve the drug or get it approved in the U.S. to treat additional conditions.

If delivery of any additional rights or information is required under a when-and-if-available clause, a continuing performance obligation exists in the arrangement. However, in some cases, a when-and-if-available clause is included in an arrangement, but the seller/licensor has no intent to improve upon the product or to develop additional information.

Because a when-and-if-available clause is considered an incremental deliverable, the license agreement must be evaluated as a multiple-deliverable arrangement, as discussed in Chapter 4, "Multiple-Deliverable Revenue Arrangements,"

When-and-if available deliverables generally can be separated for accounting purposes from the initially licensed intellectual property, as the existing intellectual property usually provides standalone value without the when-and-if available upgrades or additions. As a result, the estimated selling price of the rights to when-and-if-available upgrades or enhancements would be allocated to that deliverable. Estimating the selling price of those rights may be difficult, as it is unlikely the similar rights would ever actually be separately sold, but that difficulty is not, in and of itself, a reason to conclude that when-and-if available deliverable should not separated for accounting purposes from the initial intellectual property license.

In some situations, it is possible for the licensor to conclude that a when-and-if-available clause is an inconsequential obligation. If the only remaining obligation is inconsequential, the licensor may determine that it has met the delivery or performance criterion necessary to recognize revenue (ASC 605-10-S99, A3c, ques. 1) (SAB Topic 13A3c, ques. 1). The factors that must be considered are discussed in Chapter 4, "Multiple-Deliverable Revenue Arrangements."

A when-and-if-available clause should not be considered inconsequential simply because it does not result in any incremental costs to the licensor. Instead, the analysis should be based on whether any delivery requirements or other obligations (e.g., refunds or concessions) are expected to result from it. If the likelihood that any substantive items will be delivered is remote, then the when-and-if-available clause should be considered inconsequential. In addition, the seller or licensor should be able to explain why the when-and-if-available clause deemed inconsequential was negotiated into the arrangement.

OBSERVATION: ASC 985-605 provides guidance on how to determine when post-contract customer support, including unspecified upgrades and enhancements, may be considered inconsequential. ASC 985-605-25-73 states that:

A determination that unspecified upgrades/enhancements offered during the PCS arrangement are expected to be minimal and infrequent should be evidenced by the patterns of minimal and infrequent unspecified upgrades/enhancements offered in previous PCS arrangements. A conclusion that unspecified upgrades/enhancements are expected to be minimal and infrequent, should not be reached simply because unspecified upgrades/enhancements have been, or are expected to be, offered less frequently than on an annual basis. Regardless of the vendor's history of offering unspecified upgrades/enhancements to initial licensees, PCS should be accounted for separately from the initial licensing fee if the vendor expects to offer upgrades/enhancements that are greater than minimal or more than infrequent to the users or resellers of the licensed software during the PCS arrangement.

DISCLOSURE ALERT: See Chapter 12, "Disclosures," for information about disclosures that may be required.

Combined License and Research and Development Arrangements

Arrangements that involve licensing intellectual property and providing related research and development services are increasingly common. The licensor typically receives nonrefundable upfront fees, milestone payments, royalties, or a combination of all three. These transactions are multiple-deliverable arrangements. Whether the intellectual property license and R&D services may be accounted for separately should be determined using the guidance of ASC 605-25 (see Chapter 4, "Multiple-Deliverable Revenue Arrangements").

This determination to whether the intellectual property can be separated from the R&D services will usually depend on whether the license has stand-alone value to the customer. For example, if the intellectual property is unique, the customer may not sublicense or otherwise transfer its right to the technology, and the seller is either contractually or practically the only company that can provide R&D services that are essential in order to derive value from the technology, the license would not have stand-alone value to the customer and would be combined with the R&D services in one unit of accounting. When the deliverables in this type of arrangement cannot be separated, any initial payment received (often termed a license payment) should be treated like an advance payment for the services and recognized over the performance period (determined based on all of the items in the arrangement).

However, if the R&D services could contractually and feasibly be provided by other vendors or if the customer could perform the remaining R&D itself, the license might have standalone value, in which case the arrangement would be separated into multiple units of accounting. In that case, it might be possible to recognize the revenue properly allocated to the license element immediately under a Completed Performance model, while the revenue allocated to the services would be recognized under a Proportional Performance model.

Revenue recognition for R&D services is discussed in detail in Chapter 6, "Service Deliverables."

SEC REGISTRANT ALERT: In a December 2007 speech, the SEC Staff discussed whether a vendor's participation on a joint steering committee (to monitor progress on the R&D) established through a collaborative arrangement constitutes a deliverable. The SEC Staff noted that if a contract requires the vendor to participate on such a committee or if the failure to do so would question the vendor's performance under the arrangement, then a presumption exists that participation is obligatory, and, therefore, it should be evaluated as a potential deliverable. This can be important to the revenue recognition period, because such steering committees generally are intended to continue in operation long after the product has been approved, sometimes for the product's entire life.

SEC REGISTRANT ALERT: The SEC Staff has stated that a nonrefundable upfront payment in an arrangement involving the license of intellectual property and performance of R&D activities, may not be recognized up front (ASC 605-10-S99, A3f, ques. 1) (SAB Topic 13A3f, ques. 1). Although this guidance may appear to be definitive in stating that the license deliverable could never be treated as a separate unit of accounting, the SEC staff clarified in a 2009 speech that revenue could appropriately be allocated to a technology license that has stand-alone value as discussed in ASC 605-25.

DISCLOSURE ALERT: See Chapter 12, "Disclosures," for information about disclosures that may be required.

EXAMPLE: COMBINED LICENSE AND RESEARCH AND DEVELOPMENT ARRANGEMENTS

Immunogen, Inc. Form 10-Q—Quarterly Period Ended March 31, 2011

Exclusive Licenses

The deliverables under an exclusive license agreement generally include the exclusive license to the Company's TAP technology, and may also include deliverables related to research activities to be performed on behalf of the collaborative partner and the manufacture of preclinical or clinical materials for the collaborative partner.

Generally, exclusive license agreements contain non-refundable terms for payments and, depending on the terms of the agreement, provide that the Company will (i) at the collaborator's request, provide research services which are reimbursed at a contractually determined rate, (ii) at the collaborator's request, manufacture and provide to them preclinical and clinical materials which are reimbursed at the Company's cost, or, in some cases, cost plus a margin, (iii) earn payments upon the achievement of certain milestones and (iv) earn royalty payments, generally until the later of the last applicable patent expiration or 10 to 12 years after product launch. Royalty rates may vary over the royalty term depending on the Company's intellectual property rights. The Company may provide technical assistance and share any technology improvements with its collaborators during the term of the collaboration agreements. The Company does not directly control when any collaborator will request research or manufacturing services, achieve milestones or become liable for royalty payments. As a result, the Company cannot predict when it will recognize revenues in connection with any of the foregoing.

In determining the units of accounting, management evaluates whether the exclusive license has standalone value to the collaborative partner based on the consideration of the relevant facts and circumstances for each arrangement. Factors considered in this determination include the research capabilities of the partner and the availability of TAP technology research expertise in the general marketplace.

Novartis

In October 2010, the Company entered into an agreement with Novartis Institutes for BioMedical Research, Inc. (Novartis). The agreement initially provides

Novartis with a research license to test the Company's TAP technology with Novartis' own antibodies and an option to take exclusive development and commercialization licenses to use ImmunoGen's TAP technology to develop therapeutic products for a specified number of individual antigen targets. The initial term of the research license is for three years and it may be extended by Novartis for up to two one-year periods by the payment of additional consideration. The terms of the agreement also require Novartis to exercise its option for the development and commercialization licenses by the end of the research term. The Company received a $45 million upfront payment in connection with the execution of the agreement, and for each development and commercialization license for an antigen target, the Company is entitled to receive milestone payments potentially totaling $200.5 million plus royalties on product sales, if any. The Company also is entitled to receive payments for manufacturing preclinical and clinical materials at the request of Novartis as well as for research and development activities performed on behalf of Novartis. Novartis is responsible for the development, manufacturing and marketing of any products resulting from this agreement.

In accordance with ASU No. 2009-13, the Company identified all of the deliverables at the inception of the agreement. The significant deliverables were determined to be the research license, the exclusive development and commercialization licenses and the research services. The Company has determined that the research license together with the development and commercialization licenses represent one unit of accounting as the research license does not have standalone value from the development and commercialization licenses. The Company has also determined that this unit of accounting does have standalone value from the research services. As a result, the research services are considered a separate unit of accounting. The estimated selling prices for these units of accounting was determined based on market conditions and entity-specific factors such as the terms of the Company's previous collaborative agreements, recent preclinical and clinical testing results of therapeutic products that use the Company's TAP technology, the Company's pricing practices and pricing objectives, and the nature of the research services to be performed for Novartis and market rates for similar services. The arrangement consideration was allocated to the deliverables based on the relative selling price method. The Company will recognize license revenue as each exclusive development and commercialization license is delivered pursuant to the terms of the agreement. The Company does not control when Novartis will exercise its options for development and commercialization licenses. As a result, the Company cannot predict when it will recognize the related license revenue except that it will be within the term of the research license. The Company will recognize research services revenue as the related services are delivered.

Patent Defense and Maintenance

Intellectual property licenses often require the licensor to defend the validity and legality of underlying intellectual property (patent, trademark, etc.) against future claims. This ongoing obligation might be thought to impact revenue recognition for two reasons. First, it could be considered a separate deliverable in the arrangement. The SEC staff, however, accepts that, although the promise to defend against legal challenges is an obligation, it does not represent a separate deliverable because the licensee receives no additional value from these actions beyond that which was delivered initially. As a result, the presence of such a provision does not, in and of itself, require the licensor to use a Proportional Performance model to account for the arrangement (ASC 605-10-S99, A3g) (SAB Topic 13A3g).

Alternatively, the promise to defend against legal challenges could affect revenue recognition because it appears to be a guarantee within the scope of ASC 460. However, because the guarantee relates to the performance of an asset of the customer, it scoped out of ASC 460 for recognition and measurement purposes (ASC 460-10-55-33). The disclosure requirements of ASC 460 apply, however.

OBSERVATION: If, at the time the license is entered into, the licensor believes that its patent may not be valid or aware that its ownership of the intellectual property may not be legal, it should consider whether revenue should be deferred.

DISCLOSURE ALERT: See Chapter 12, "Disclosures," regarding the disclosure requirements of ASC 952-605.

Warranties and Customer Acceptance Clauses

Some intellectual property licenses may include warranties and customer acceptance clauses. For example, a customer acceptance clause may allow the customer to cancel the license for a full refund if the technology does not perform to specifications in the license arrangement.

When these clauses are included, their effect on revenue recognition should be evaluated in the same manner as similar clauses in a product sale arrangement. Chapter 5, "Product Deliverables," provides detailed guidance on the accounting for these clauses.

DISCLOSURE ALERT: See Chapter 12, "Disclosures," for information about disclosures that may be required.

SELLER-PROVIDED FINANCING AND GUARANTEES

Licenses with Extended Payment Terms

Some licensors provide financing for their customers' purchases by agreeing to receive fixed payments over a long period of time, rather than full payment at the inception of the license. Except in the sale of software products (see Chapter 10, "Software—A Complete Model"), U.S. generally accepted accounting principles (GAAP) does not provide specific guidance about when extended payment terms should preclude revenue recognition. However, extended payment terms can affect the evaluation of two conditions for revenue recognition: (1) a fixed or determinable fee and (2) collectibility.

Extended Payment Terms and Fixed or Determinable Fees

Extended payment terms raise the risk that, in order to ensure payment according to the stated terms, the licensor will agree to extend the license or otherwise provide the licensee with additional rights related to the intellectual property. For example, a customer that earns less revenue than expected from the licensed technology because of increased competition might withhold a license payment in the hope of terminating the license early, or receiving additional value from the licensor.

If the combination of extended payment terms and risks inherent in the license create a significant likelihood of concessions, payments should only be considered fixed or determinable as they are made. Therefore, revenue related to future payments under extended payment terms would not be recognized, even if delivery has already occurred.

OBSERVATION: ASC 985-605 specifically addresses extended payment terms in the context of software arrangements. The presumption is that the fee is not fixed or determinable if payment terms extend beyond the earlier of the expiration of the license term or one year after delivery. Although no similar presumption exists outside of software arrangements, the guidance in ASC 985-605-25-33 through 25-35 may be a useful analogy for other intellectual property licenses. See Chapter 10, "Software—A Complete Model," for a complete discussion.

Extended Payment Terms and Collectibility

The longer the payment terms, the more difficult it is to conclude that collection is reasonably assured. If collection is not reasonably assured, no revenue or receivable should be recorded. It is unacceptable in these instances to record revenue and a selling expense for the anticipated bad debt because the threshold criteria for revenue recognition have not been met.

Discounting Long-Term Receivables

When intellectual property is licensed on terms that extend significantly beyond the point in time that revenue is recognized, the long-term receivable and the related revenue should be recorded at the present value of the payments, rather than the nominal value. Interest income should be accrued on the receivable until all payments are received. Therefore, when extended payment terms are stated at their nominal values, a portion of the payments will be attributed to interest income, as opposed to revenue (ASC 835-30-25-7). In effect, product or service revenue is earned on delivery and as other criteria are satisfied. The recognition of interest income acknowledges the financing provided to the customer. If the payment terms are extended but merely reflect the proportional performance of the contract, no discounting is required. In this case, the extended payments are earned as services are delivered over time; no financing has been provided to the customer.

Guaranteeing a Loan in Connection with a License

A company may agree to guarantee amounts borrowed by a customer to license the company's intellectual property. Although the company has collected cash in this situation, it has effectively licensed the property on extended payment terms pursuant to the loan terms. Therefore, prior to recognizing any revenue, the company should evaluate whether collectibility is reasonably assured as if it were the lender in the loan transaction.

If the company concludes that collection is reasonably assured and all other revenue recognition criteria have been met, ASC 460 requires the transaction to be treated as a multiple-deliverable arrangement. The two deliverables are the intellectual property license and the loan guarantee. This type of arrangement is discussed in Chapter 4, "Multiple-Deliverable Revenue Arrangements."

DISCLOSURE ALERT: See Chapter 12, "Disclosures," for information about required disclosures.

REVENUE RECOGNITION FOR SPECIFIC INTELLECTUAL PROPERTY TRANSACTIONS

As noted in the introductory sections of this chapter, revenue recognition for certain intellectual property transactions is addressed in the accounting literature. These models are generally consistent because revenue is recognized when the four basic conditions for recognition are met. However, because each model was developed to address a narrow set of transactions, the analysis of when the conditions are met is somewhat different in each instance.

Collaborative Arrangements

Significant operating and financial risks of developing and successfully marketing products and services based on intellectual property (as well as other assets) have resulted in the proliferation of the use of collaborative arrangements to share these risks in the biotechnology, pharmaceutical, motion picture, software, and computer hardware industries. The collaborative arrangements involve a wide range of activities from research and development to marketing and distribution and are often conducted through a "virtual joint venture" that does not always include the formation of a legal structure. Within this "virtual joint venture," however, specific activities or operations in certain geographic locations may be conducted through legal structures. Contractual terms governing the sharing of operating responsibilities and the allocation of revenues, expenses, and profits or losses between participants in the arrangement vary widely across arrangements.

Financial reporting of these arrangements is diverse. The diversity often leads to a lack of comparability of arrangements across companies within the same industry. Revenues, reimbursements, and expenses are variously classified and reported either gross or net in the income statements of participants. Some arrangements have been reported under the equity method using ASC 323, *Investments—Equity Method and Joint Ventures*.

In ASC 808, a collaborative arrangement is defined as a contractual arrangement between two or more parties involving a joint operating activity conducted wholly or partly through a legal entity wherein the parties have the following two significant characteristics:

1. They are active participants in the arrangement, with each party doing significantly more than just providing financial resources.

2. They are exposed to significant risks and rewards that are based on the success of the endeavor.

A collaborative arrangement may be subject to ASC 808 even when it is partially conducted through a separate legal entity. The requirements of ASC 810, ASC 323, or other related accounting standards may apply to the part of the arrangement conducted through a legal entity.

DISCLOSURE ALERT: The disclosure requirements of ASC 808 apply to the *entire* collaborative arrangement even if a part of the arrangement is conducted through a legal entity.

The financial reporting requirements of ASC 808 do not apply to arrangements within the scope of other authoritative accounting literature. This Issue also does not provide any guidance related to recognition and measurement issues (for example, determination of the appropriate units of accounting, the appropriate recognition requirements, or when recognition criteria are satisfied) related to collaborative arrangements.

Participants should evaluate the substance of contractual arrangements at inception to determine whether they are collaborative arrangements. A reconsideration of this assessment would be required whenever changes in the facts and circumstances change either the role of the participants or their exposure to risks and rewards of the arrangement. However, a collaboration agreement can begin at any point in the life cycle of an operating activity.

The determination of whether an entity is (1) an active participant in, and (2) exposed to significant risks and rewards of a collaborative arrangement, and therefore subject to the requirements of ASC 808, calls for significant judgment and is a function of the facts and circumstances specific to the arrangement, including, but not limited to, the terms and conditions of the arrangement.

ASC 808-10-15-8 provides the following indicators (not intended to be an exhaustive list) of active participation:

- Directing and conducting the activities of the joint operating activity,

- Sharing responsibilities of a steering committee or other governance mechanism, and

- Ownership or control of a contractual or other legal right to the underlying intellectual property.

The following terms and conditions may indicate that the participants are not subject to significant risks and rewards of the arrangement (ASC 808-10-15-11):

- Compensation for services provided is commensurate with market rates,

- The arrangement permits recovery of all (or substantially all) of the cumulative economic contribution to date in the event a participant quits the arrangement without cause,

- A single participant receives all of the initial profits, and

- A participant is subject to limit risks and/or rewards.

The stage in the life cycle of the endeavor and the expected duration or extent of the participants' financial participation in the arrangement relative to the endeavor's aggregate expected life or total expected value are other factors that should be evaluated in determining whether a participant is exposed to significant risks and benefits of a collaborative arrangement (ASC 808-10-15-12).

The guidance in ASC 605-45 should be used to determine whether revenues generated and costs incurred in transactions with third parties should be reported gross or net on the income statement. All revenues and costs that are subject to other authoritative accounting literature should be accounted for in accordance with that literature.

The income statement characterization of payments between participants in a collaborative arrangement should be based on:

- The nature and contractual terms of the arrangement,

- The nature of each participant's business operations, and

- Whether the payments are subject to other authoritative literature on income statement characterization.

Payments subject to other authoritative literature should be reported pursuant to that literature. The income statement characterization of payments not subject to other authoritative literature should be based on analogy to authoritative literature or a reasonable and rational accounting policy election that must be consistently applied.

Participants in a collaborative arrangement should disclose the following in the initial period and annually thereafter (ASC 808-10-50):

- Information about the nature and the purpose of its collaborative arrangements,

- Its rights and obligations in the collaborative arrangements,

- The accounting policy for collaborative arrangements per ASC 235, *Notes to Financial Statements*; 235-10, and

- The income statement classification and amounts attributable to transactions between the participants in the arrangement for each period an income statement is presented.

Separate disclosure is required of information related to individually significant collaborative arrangements.

EXAMPLE: COLLABORATIVE ARRANGEMENTS

Time Warner, Inc. Form 10-K—Fiscal Year Ended December 31, 2010

Accounting for Collaborative Arrangements

The Company's collaborative arrangements primarily relate to arrangements entered into with third parties to jointly finance and distribute theatrical productions ("co-financing arrangements") and an arrangement entered into with a third party television network to acquire the rights to broadcast certain sports programming in the United States from 2011 through 2024. This sports programming arrangement did not have a material impact to the Company's results of operations as of and for the year ended December 31, 2010.

In most cases, the form of the co-financing arrangement is the sale of an economic interest in a film to an investor. The Filmed Entertainment segment generally records the amounts received for the sale of an economic interest as a reduction of the costs of the film, as the investor assumes full risk for that portion of the film asset acquired in these transactions. The substance of these arrangements is that the third-party investors own an interest in the film and, therefore, in each period the Company reflects in the consolidated statement of operations either a charge or benefit to costs of revenue to reflect the estimate of the third-party investor's interest in the profits or losses incurred on the film. The estimate of the third-party investor's interest in profits or losses incurred on the film is determined using the film forecast computation method. For the years ended December 31, 2010, 2009 and 2008, net participation costs of $508 million, $321 million and $584 million, respectively, were recorded in costs of revenues.

Software

ASC 985-605 provides two models—Completed Performance and Proportional Performance—to account for software revenue. The correct model to use is dictated by whether the software sold or licensed involves significant production, modification, or customization (collectively referred to as significant changes). If no significant changes are required, a Completed Performance model is used. If significant changes to the software are required, ASC 985-605 requires the use of contract accounting, which generally results in the application of a Proportional Performance model. Software revenue recognition is discussed in Chapter 10, "Software—A Complete Model."

Franchises

ASC 952-605 provides guidance on the recognition of franchise fee revenue. A franchisor earns franchise fee revenue from the franchisee pursuant to the terms of the franchise agreement. The franchise agreement generally conveys rights to the franchisee such as the right to operate a business using the franchisor's name, the right to use the franchisor's processes, and the right (or requirement) to purchase products or services from the franchisor.

Scope

The arrangement must possess certain characteristics to meet the definition of a franchise agreement in U.S. GAAP.[1] Any arrangement that has these characteristics is a franchise agreement, regardless of whether it is labeled as such and regardless of whether the company in question considers itself to be in the franchising business (ASC 952-605-20):

- The agreement must be written and establish the rights and responsibilities of the franchisor and franchisee for a defined period of time.

- The agreement must have as its purpose the distribution of a product or service, or an entire business concept, within a particular market area.

- The agreement must provide for the franchisor and franchisee to contribute resources for establishing and maintaining the franchise.

- The agreement must outline and describe the specific marketing practices to be followed, specify the contribution of each party to the operation of the business, and set forth certain operating procedures with which both parties agree to comply.

- The agreement must establish the franchised outlet as a business entity requiring and supporting the full-time business activity of the franchisee (i.e., if the outlet is merely an authorized distributor or representative to sell a particular good or service, it is not a franchise).

- The agreement must establish a common identity for the franchisor and franchisee.

PRACTICE POINTER: It is common for a purported franchise agreement to be missing one or more of the characteristics described above. For example, a trademark license agreement may not require the licensor to do anything other than transfer the trademark to the licensee. As a result, the trademark licensing arrangement would not be considered a franchise agreement for accounting purposes. Other agreements may have the purported franchisee enter into an agency relationship with the franchisor to sell the franchisor's products, or to identify potential franchisees. To the extent that a license agreement does not possess *all* of the characteristics listed above, it is not considered a franchise agreement under ASC 952-605. In such cases, revenue should be recognized using the general guidance for intellectual property or service transactions, depending upon the nature of the arrangement.

Franchise Fees

Franchise fees are generally characterized as either initial or continuing. The initial fees are usually paid up front in conjunction with the transfer of intellectual property rights, the performance of initial services, and the sale of proprietary equipment. The continuing fees are usually paid over the life of the franchise agreement. These fees may be paid as the franchisor sells products or services to

---

[1] The need for such an agreement to be in place fulfills the persuasive evidence of an arrangement condition that is a part of all revenue recognition analyses.

the franchisee or can be based on a percentage of the franchisee's revenues or another quantitative operating measure. In most cases, the franchise agreement specifies a combination of some or all of these types of fees.

DISCLOSURE ALERT: See Chapter 12, "Disclosures," for information about disclosures that may be required.

EXAMPLE: TYPES OF FRANCHISE FEES

Buffalo Wild Wings, Inc. Form 10-K—Fiscal Year Ended December 27, 2009

Our franchise agreements have terms ranging from 10 to 20 years. These agreements also convey extension terms of 5 or 10 years depending on contract terms and if certain conditions are met. We provide training, preopening assistance and restaurant operating assistance in exchange for area development fees, franchise fees and royalties of 5% of the franchised restaurant's sales. Franchise fee revenue from individual franchise sales is recognized upon the opening of the restaurant when we have performed all of our material obligations and initial services. Area development fees are dependent upon the number of restaurants granted in the agreement as are our obligations under the area development agreement. Consequently, as our obligations are met, area development fees are recognized in relation to the expenses incurred with the opening of each new restaurant and any royalty-free periods. Royalties are accrued as earned and are calculated each period based on reported franchisees' sales.

Allocation of Initial Franchise Fees

Initial franchise fees compensate the franchisor for providing a bundle of deliverables. These deliverables may include the transfer of rights to certain intellectual property (e.g., restaurant name, logos, formulas) and services necessary to assist the franchisee in opening a franchised outlet (e.g., training, site identification). Specific equipment, products, or supplies may also be included. The initial franchise fee does not necessarily only relate to these initial deliverables. A portion of the fee may also relate to products or services that will be provided to the franchisee in the future. The key to correctly recognizing (with respect to the amount and timing) an initial franchise fee is to allocate it to the various products and services provided.

The initial franchise fee should be allocated based on the following sources of value for each deliverable:

Deliverable	Source of Value
Equipment, supplies and products to be furnished initially	Fair value of the assets
Products to be sold in the future	Either the selling price of the same product to other customers or the cost of the product plus a reasonable profit on the sale
Services to be provided in the future	Cost of providing the service plus a reasonable profit margin
Services and intellectual property rights provided initially	Residual

The method used to allocate the initial franchise fee in a franchise agreement is a residual method. This type of method starts with the total amount to be allocated (the initial franchise fee) and subtracts the values of some, but not all, of the deliverables (equipment, supplies, and products to be provided initially, products to be sold in the future, and services to be provided in the future), leaving the residual to represent the value of the remaining items (services and intellectual property rights to be provided initially).

ILLUSTRATION: INITIAL FRANCHISE FEE ALLOCATION

Facts: Franchisor Inc. (Franchisor) enters into a franchise agreement with Franchisee Co. (Franchisee). This agreement meets the conditions of ASC 952-605-20 and is considered a franchise agreement for accounting purposes. The franchise agreement conveys the right to open a franchised outlet that bears Franchisor's trademark name and that produces and sells Franchisor's secret recipe breads. The term of the agreement is five years. The franchise agreement requires Franchisee to make the following payments to Franchisor: (1) an initial fee of $1,000,000, (2) royalty payments equal to 2% of Franchisee's sales, (3) $50,000 per year for 50,000 pounds of unique organic flours, and (4) $60,000 per year for four seasonal marketing campaigns. The franchise agreement requires Franchisor to provide the following to Franchisee: (1) rights to use its trademark and secret recipes, (2) initial services, including site-selection and site-design assistance and employee training on baking methods, (3) equipment necessary for Franchisee to produce the secret recipe breads, including a specifically designed oven and oven implements, (4) 50,000 pounds annually of unique organic flours, and (5) four seasonal marketing campaigns. The fair value of the specifically designed oven and oven implements is $140,000. The selling price of 50,000 pounds of the unique organic flours to other customers is $60,000. The cost of providing the four seasonal marketing campaigns plus a reasonable profit margin is $75,000.

Allocation: The $1,000,000 initial fee is allocated as follows:

Franchise Element		Amount of Initial Fee Allocated
Oven and oven implements (equipment)		$140,000
Products (organic flours) to be sold in the future		
Selling price to other customers over the term of the franchise agreement ($60,000 per year for 5 years)	$300,000	
Selling price to Franchisee ($50,000 per year for 5 years)	250,000	50,000
Future services (marketing campaigns)		
Cost plus a reasonable profit margin ($75,000 per year for 5 years)	375,000	
Selling price to Franchisee ($60,000 per year for 5 years)	300,000	75,000
Initial services and rights to use trademark and secret recipes (residual)		$735,000

Recognition of Fees Related to Initial Services and Intellectual Property Rights

The portion of the initial franchise fee allocated to the initial services and intellectual property rights should be recognized when the franchisor has substantially performed or satisfied its obligations under the franchise agreement. The franchisor must consider the following questions when assessing whether it has substantially performed:

1. Does the franchisor have any obligation or intent to refund cash received or forgive notes or receivables due from the franchisee?

2. Has the franchisor performed less than substantially all of the initial services required under the franchise agreement?

3. Are there any remaining material conditions or obligations that would preclude the franchisor from concluding that it has substantially performed?

4. Does the franchise agreement include an option for the franchisor to purchase the franchisee's business that the franchisor expects to exercise?

If the answer to any of these questions is "yes," the franchisor has not substantially performed. For example, answering "yes" to the first question indicates that a portion of the initial franchise fee is refundable. When any portion of the fee is refundable, it should not be recognized. Answering "yes" to the last question means that the initial fee is effectively a reduction of the future purchase price of the business. In this case, the initial fee should not be recognized as revenue at all.

It is presumed that the earliest point a franchisor can achieve substantial performance is upon commencement of operations by the franchisee. This presumption can only be overcome if the franchisor can demonstrate that all obligations, both explicit and implicit, have been fulfilled before the franchisee starts its operations (ASC 952-605-25-3).

OBSERVATION: In answering the questions above, a franchisor must determine whether there are any services that the franchisor is expected to perform, either as a matter of practice or due to regulatory considerations, even if these services are not explicit in the franchise agreement. If these obligations exist, the franchisor does not achieve substantial performance until these services are either performed or no longer required.

EXAMPLE: RECOGNITION OF INITIAL FEES

Wendy's/Arby's Group, Inc. Form 10-K—Fiscal Year Ended January 3, 2010

"Franchise revenues" include royalties, franchise fees, and rental income. Royalties from franchised restaurants are based on a percentage of net sales of the franchised restaurant and are recognized as earned. Initial franchise fees are recorded as deferred income when received and are recognized as revenue when a franchised restaurant is opened since all material services and conditions related to the franchise fee have been substantially performed by the Company upon the restaurant opening. Renewal franchise fees are recognized as revenue when the license agreements are signed and the fee is paid since there are no material services and conditions related to the renewal franchise fee. Franchise commitment fee deposits are forfeited and recognized as revenue upon the termination of the related commitments to open new franchised restaurants. Rental income from locations owned by the Company and leased to franchisees is recognized on a straight-line basis over the respective operating lease terms.

There are many different types of services and intellectual property rights provided by a franchisor as part of the initial services. However, franchisors are precluded from allocating the residual amount of the initial franchise fee to any individual initial services or intellectual property rights provided (even if separate prices are stated in the franchise agreement) unless there have been separate sales of the individual services. This restriction exists because initial services and intellectual property rights are often so interrelated and interdependent that assigning individual values would be difficult and essentially meaningless (ASC 952-605-25-11). Therefore, a Completed Performance model is used for the initial services and intellectual property rights and delivery of both must occur before revenue attributable to either may be recognized.

> **OBSERVATION:** The conclusion in ASC 952-605 is that neither initial services nor rights to be delivered have value to the franchisee on a standalone basis (e.g., absent the other initial services and rights). This is consistent with the general guidance for multiple-deliverable transactions discussed in Chapter 4, "Multiple-Deliverable Revenue Arrangements."

Recognition of Fees Related to Equipment, Supplies, and Products

Revenue from the sale of equipment, supplies, and products delivered either initially or in the future should be recognized when these products meet the requirements for revenue recognition as discussed in Chapter 5, "Product Deliverables."

Recognition of Fees Related to Future Services to Be Provided

Continuing franchise fees should be recognized when earned and realized or realizable (ASC 952-605-25-12). For royalty-based fees, this will generally occur when the royalties accrue and become receivable to the franchisor. For services that are not part of the initial services, consult Chapter 6, "Service Deliverables," for guidance on how to determine when such fees are earned and realized or realizable. Any initial franchise fee allocated to future services (i.e., services that are not part of the initial services) should be deferred and recognized over the life of the franchise (ASC 952-605-25-4).

> **PRACTICE POINTER:** When franchisors sell inventory, equipment, or continuing services to franchisees, the role of the franchisor must be understood to determine whether such sales should be recognized gross or net in the income statement. To the extent the franchisor acts as an agent in these sales, no revenues and expenses should be recognized. For example, a franchisor may

place orders for equipment on behalf of its franchisees. In this situation the franchisor should *not* recognize equipment sales and cost of equipment sales. Instead, this transaction should be accounted for on the balance sheet using receivables and payables. Additional guidance on recognizing revenue and expenses gross or net in the income statement can be found in Chapter 11, "Presentation."

ILLUSTRATION: FRANCHISE FEE RECOGNITION

Facts: Assume the same facts as those in the earlier Initial Franchise Fee Allocation illustration. In addition, Franchisee's revenues for Year 1 under the franchise agreement were $5,000,000.

Accounting: The accounting for the initial and continuing franchise fees in Year 1 is as follows:

- At the inception of the franchise agreement, Franchisor records the initial franchise fee received:

Cash or Receivable	$1,000,000	
Deferred Revenue		$1,000,000

- Upon achieving substantial completion related to the initial services and intellectual property rights, Franchisor recognizes the portion of the initial franchise fee allocated to those initial deliverables:

Deferred Revenue	$735,000	
Initial Franchise Fee Revenue		$735,000

- Upon delivery of the specifically designed oven and oven implements and transfer of title to Franchisee, Franchisor recognizes the portion of the initial franchise fee allocated to that equipment:

Deferred Revenue	$140,000	
Equipment Sales		$140,000

- During Year 1, upon delivery of the unique organic flours and transfer of title to Franchisee, Franchisor recognizes one-fifth of the initial franchise fee allocated to that deliverable and the incremental amount paid by or due from Franchisee for those deliveries:

Deferred Revenue	$10,000	
Cash or Receivable	$50,000	
Product Sales		$60,000

- During Year 1, upon earning the revenue related to the four seasonal marketing programs, Franchisor recognizes one-fifth of the initial franchise fee allocated to that deliverable and the incremental amount paid by or due from Franchisee for those services:

Deferred Revenue	$15,000	
Cash or Receivable	$60,000	
Service Fees		$75,000

- During Year 1, upon earning the royalties and the royalties becoming receivable from Franchisee, Franchisor recognizes royalty revenues:

Cash or Receivable	$100,000	
Royalty Revenues		$100,000

Area Franchise Fees

Area franchise agreements grant rights that allow a franchisee to open multiple franchised outlets within a defined geographic area. The key questions to answer before recognizing the initial franchise fee are:

- Do the franchisor's substantial obligations under the area franchise agreement relate to the area franchise as a whole?

- Are the effort and cost of the initial services to be provided under the area franchise agreement significantly independent of the number of individual franchises to be established?

If the answer to both of these questions is "yes," then the initial franchise fee under the area franchise agreement should be treated similarly to the initial franchise fee under an individual franchise agreement. However, if the answer to either or both questions is "no," the franchisor must allocate the initial franchise fee to each franchised outlet based on the expected total number. This method effectively breaks down an area franchise agreement into individual franchise agreements.

ILLUSTRATION: AREA FRANCHISE FEE

Facts: Franchisor M enters into an area franchise agreement with Franchisee D. This agreement meets the definition in ASC 952-605-20 and is considered a franchise agreement for accounting purposes. The area franchise agreement conveys Franchisee D the right to open up to ten franchised outlets in the metropolitan Detroit area, as defined in the franchise agreement. Each of these franchised outlets will bear Franchisor M's trademark name and sell Franchisor M's specialized baby products. The term of the agreement is five years. The franchise agreement requires Franchisee D to make an initial franchise fee payment of $5,000,000. The initial services and intellectual property rights to be provided by Franchisor M include transferring trademarks and providing site-selection and site-design assistance. Franchisee D expects to open all ten franchise outlets.

Assessment: The effort and cost relating to the site-selection and site-design assistance are significantly dependent on the number of individual franchises to be established. Each incremental franchised outlet to be opened by Franchisee D results in Franchisor M having to put forth the effort and expend the cost necessary to select and design a site. As a result, Franchisor M concludes that it must allocate the initial franchise fee among the ten franchised outlets Franchisee D expects to open. This results in the allocation of the $500,000 initial franchise fee ($5,000,000 total initial franchise fee divided by ten expected franchised outlets) to each franchised outlet. Each franchised outlet will be treated as an individual franchise agreement for purposes of recognizing the $500,000.

As previously noted, allocating an initial franchise fee under an area franchise agreement often involves estimating the number of franchised outlets to be opened by the franchisee. If this estimate is subsequently revised due to a change in circumstances, the remaining fees should be recognized as revenue in proportion to the remaining services to be performed.

Refund rights attached to an initial franchise fee in an area franchise agreement are treated the same as refund rights in an individual franchise agreement. As a result, the franchisor may not recognize revenue from any portion of an initial franchise fee that may be refunded to the franchisee. Under an area franchise agreement, refund rights may not mirror the method used to allocate the initial franchise fee (e.g., more revenue is refundable at any given point in time than the amount that otherwise can be considered earned). This underscores the need to ensure that refund rights have been appropriately considered in an area franchise agreement.

Motion Pictures

Arrangements to license or sell films are varied. They may include the rights to a single film or many films. They may allow exploitation on an exclusive or non-exclusive basis in defined or undefined geographic regions. They may provide the customer with only limited control over the actual distribution of a film. Fees under these agreements may be paid up front or over time and may be fixed, variable, or a combination of fixed and variable. Understanding the terms of an arrangement to license or sell films is an integral part of determining when fees should be recognized as revenue. ASC 926 provides such guidance.

The provisions of ASC 926-605 apply to sales or licenses of film rights by producers and distributors of films who own or control these rights. The definition of films includes feature or animated films, television specials, television series, or similar products. Films may be housed on a variety of media including film, video tape, and that used to provide digitized content (e.g., DVDs).

A producer or distributor of films should recognize revenue related to the sale or license of films only when all of the following conditions have been met (ASC 926-605-25-1):

1. There is persuasive evidence of a sale or licensing arrangement with a customer;

2. The film is complete and, in accordance with the terms of the arrangement, has been delivered or is available for immediate and unconditional delivery;

3. The license period of the arrangement has begun and the customer can begin its exploitation, exhibition, or sale;

4. The arrangement fee is fixed or determinable; and

5. Collection of the arrangement fee is reasonably assured.

These conditions are similar to those required in most transactions, although they are modified slightly to address the unique characteristics of film licenses and sales.

Persuasive Evidence of an Arrangement

The evaluation of the persuasive evidence condition is generally no different for films than it is for any other revenue arrangement. However, regardless of the form of the documentation for an arrangement, such documentation must be in place and legally enforceable before any revenue is recognized (ASC 926-605-25-4). For additional discussion, see Chapter 3, "General Principles."

Completion

ASC 926-605 requires the use of a Completed Performance model for evaluating when revenue is earned. This evaluation is fairly straightforward. However, any modification to the film that must be made before it is ready for the customer should be evaluated to determine whether it is significant. If the modifications are significant, the film is not considered complete and revenue cannot be recognized (ASC 926-605-25-8).

Significant modifications are those changes that add new or additional content to a film. Thus, modifying a film by reshooting a scene or adding special effects would be considered significant because content is added or changed. On the other hand, modifying a film by inserting subtitles, formatting it to fit a television screen, or adjusting it to allow the insertion of a commercial would not be considered significant, as none of these actions add content to the film itself (ASC 926-605-20).

Delivered or Available for Delivery

Revenue should not be recognized prior to physical delivery when a licensing arrangement calls for or is silent about delivery (ASC 926-605-25-6); also see Chapter 5, "Product Deliverables," for a discussion of physical delivery). Some licensing arrangements may directly or indirectly (through a film laboratory access letter) grant the customer immediate and unconditional access to a film print. In this type of arrangement, the delivery criterion is satisfied when the film is complete and immediately available (ASC 926-605-25-7).

OBSERVATION: While the exception discussed above allows for revenue recognition before delivery in some circumstances, U.S. GAAP rarely permits this. As such, this provision should generally not be analogized to. See Chapter 5, "Product Deliverables" for another exception to the delivery requirement with regards to bill-and-hold transactions that meet very restrictive criteria.

License Period Has Begun

This condition prohibits revenue recognition until the license period of the arrangement has started and the customer is free to begin exploitation, exhibition, or sale of the film. A common restriction in a film license or sales arrangement is the inclusion of a street date. A street date generally restricts a customer from exploiting, exhibiting, or selling a film prior to the date the producer or distributor plans to market the film on a broader basis. For example, a distributor may ship copies of a hit movie on DVD to a reseller in September, but restrict their sale until October 1, to synchronize availability throughout the country and tie that availability to a marketing program. Revenue related to the DVDs shipped in September may not be recognized before the street date of October 1 (ASC 926-605-25-10).

Many producers enter into arrangements where they license the rights to market film-related products. These arrangements are often entered into well before the release date of the related film. However, producers should not recognize revenue from these types of arrangements prior to the release of the related film (ASC 926-605-25-30). Until this occurs, the license period on the film-related products has not substantively begun.

EXAMPLE: SATISFACTION OF AVAILABILITY CONDITION

Viacom, Inc. Form 10-K—Fiscal Year Ended December 31, 2009

Revenue we earn in connection with the exhibition of feature films by our *Filmed Entertainment* segment is recognized in accordance with the accounting guidance for producers or distributors of films. Our *Filmed Entertainment* segment principally earns revenue from the exhibition of feature film content based upon theatrical exhibition, home entertainment and various television markets (e.g., network, pay, syndication, basic cable). We recognize revenue from theatrical distribution of motion pictures upon exhibition. We recognize revenue from home entertainment product sales, net of anticipated returns, including rebates and other incentives, upon the later of delivery or the date that these products are made widely available for sale by retailers. We recognize revenue from the licensing of feature films and original programming for exhibition in television markets upon availability for airing by the licensee. We recognize revenue for video-on-demand and similar pay-per-view arrangements as the feature films are exhibited based on end-customer purchases as reported by the distributor.

Allocation of Fees in Multiple-Film Arrangements

A producer or distributor often licenses or sells multiple films to customers in one arrangement. These films may or may not be produced or completed upon commencement of the arrangement. In these situations, any fee received must be allocated among the individual films. The allocation of a fee among the individual films in a multiple-film arrangement is based on refundable amounts for incomplete or unproduced films and estimated relative fair values for complete films (ASC 926-605-25-12).

OBSERVATION: Each film in a multiple-film arrangement is, in substance, a separate deliverable. The process of allocating a flat fee between films in a multiple-film arrangement is similar to the allocation methodology used in other multiple-deliverable arrangements. See Chapter 4, "Multiple-Deliverable Revenue Arrangements." However, one significant difference exists. This relates to using the amount that is refundable if an unproduced film is ultimately not produced for purposes of allocating a portion of the flat fee to the unproduced film. This methodology is used to address specific factors often present in film arrangements and should not be used in other multiple-deliverable transactions.

ILLUSTRATION: ALLOCATION OF FLAT FEE TO MULTIPLE FILMS

Facts: Producer B enters into a license agreement with Customer K. The license agreement grants exploitation and exhibition rights to Customer K for three separate films. Two of the films, *Action-Packed* and *Romance,* are complete. The remaining film, *Political Thriller,* is not yet complete. The license agreement requires Customer K to pay a flat fee of $10,000,000. If Producer B does not complete *Political Thriller,* it must refund $2,500,000. The fair values of the exploitation and exhibition rights related to *Action-Packed* and *Romance* are $6,000,000 and $4,000,000, respectively.

Allocation: The $10,000,000 flat fee is first allocated to *Political Thriller* based on the refundable amount of $2,500,000. The remaining $7,500,000 is allocated based on the relative fair values of *Action-Packed* and *Romance,* resulting in 60% of that amount, or $4,500,000, being allocated to *Action-Packed,* and 40%, or $3,000,000, being allocated to *Romance.*

When available, a producer or distributor should use the quoted market price of each completed film as its fair value for allocation purposes. If a quoted market price is not available, the producer or distributor should use the best available information to determine fair value. One valuation technique often used in this situation is a discounted cash flow methodology (ASC 926-605-25-16).[2]

If a producer or distributor concludes that it cannot determine the fair value for an individual completed film, it is prohibited from recognizing any of the flat fee until it can determine fair value and complete the allocation.

Fixed or Determinable Fees

Flat fees. Flat fees are payable regardless of the success or failure of the film and are neither contingent upon future performance by the producer or distributor nor subject to change based on rights held by the customer. Flat fees are considered fixed and determinable because the amount of the fee is not dependent upon any future events (ASC 926-605-25-11).

Variable fees. Variable fees are those based on some measure of the film's performance, such as a percentage of a customer's revenue from exploiting or exhibiting a film. These fees are considered fixed or determinable as the customer exhibits or exploits the film (ASC 926-605-25-18). Until then, the fees are not fixed or determinable because they are dependent upon future events.

Nonrefundable minimum guarantees. The fee in some arrangements can be essentially variable, except to the extent that the customer guarantees it will pay some minimum amount. Generally, the nonrefundable minimum guarantees are treated as flat fees and any amounts over and above this minimum are treated as variable fees. However, in some arrangements, the nonrefundable minimum

---

[2] ASC 926-605 includes guidance on the application of a discounted cash flow methodology to estimate fair value. Additional guidance may be found in ASC 820, *Fair Value Measurements and Disclosures.*

guarantee is cross-collateralized (i.e., it can be applied to a number of films, territories, and/or markets and the exploitation results (revenues) for all applicable films, territories, and/or markets are aggregated for purposes of determining the variable fees payable to the producer or distributor under the arrangement). To the extent that a nonrefundable guaranteed minimum exists in an arrangement that has been cross-collateralized, the nonrefundable minimum guarantee is effectively the same as a variable fee and is only considered fixed and determinable as the customer exhibits or exploits the films, or at the end of the license (ASC 926-605-25-20).

Returns and price concessions. A producer or distributor should account for returns and price concessions based on the provisions of ASC 605-15-25. To recognize revenue net of estimated product returns and price concessions, the following conditions must be met (ASC 605-15-25-1):

1. The seller's price to the buyer is substantially fixed or determinable at the date of sale.

2. The buyer has paid the seller, or the buyer is obligated to pay the seller and the obligation is not contingent on resale of the product.

3. The buyer's obligation to the seller would not be changed in the event of theft or physical destruction or damage of the product.

4. The buyer acquiring the product for resale has economic substance apart from that provided by the seller.

5. The seller does not have significant obligations for future performance to directly bring about resale of the product by the buyer.

6. The amount of future returns and price concessions can be reasonably estimated.

The producer or distributor must consider both the contract terms and its customary business practices when identifying return rights or price concession obligations. If the producer or distributor does not meet all of the foregoing conditions, the fees under the arrangement are not fixed or determinable. For additional discussion of these conditions, see Chapter 5, "Product Deliverables."

Arrangement Modifications

It is not uncommon for film arrangements to be modified for various reasons. For example, the term of the arrangement may be extended, the territory expanded, the number of allowable showings increased, or the basis on which the fee is calculated changed. The type of modification determines the appropriate accounting.

If an arrangement modification solely involves extending the term of an existing arrangement, fees related to the modification should be recognized after the modification has been finalized, based on the type of fee involved (e.g., flat, variable) as discussed above (ASC 926-605-25-23 through 25-25).

All other modifications make the revised arrangement a new arrangement. To the extent any refunds or concessions are granted by the producer or distributor through the arrangement modifications, previously reported revenue in the amount of the refunds or concessions should be reversed (ASC 926-605-25-26).

OBSERVATION: The accounting for refunds or concessions in a modified arrangement effectively results in the producer or distributor recognizing revenue as if the new financial terms had been in place at the beginning of the original arrangement. As a result, a cumulative catch-up adjustment is recorded in the year of the modification for the difference between cumulative revenue recognized under the old financial terms and cumulative revenue that would have been recognized under the new financial terms.

ILLUSTRATION: ARRANGEMENT MODIFICATION INVOLVING CONCESSION

Facts: Producer T had a license agreement with Customer D. Only one film was involved in the license agreement. The original license agreement had a term of three years and provided a flat fee of $50,000 and variable fees of 10% based on Customer D's gross receipts. Customer D's gross receipts in Year 1 were $1,000,000. In Year 1, Producer T recognized the $50,000 flat fee and $100,000 of variable fees as revenue. At the beginning of Year 2, Producer T and Customer D modified the terms of the original license agreement. The modified license agreement changed the flat fee to $20,000 and the variable fee rate to 12%.

Accounting: At the beginning of Year 2, Producer T should reverse $10,000 of revenue. This is based on the following calculation:

Revenue recognized in Year 1	
Flat fee	$ 50,000
Variable fee	100,000
Total	150,000
Revenue that would have been recognized in Year 1 under the modified terms	
Flat fee	20,000
Variable fee	120,000
Total	140,000
Concession	$ 10,000

CHAPTER 8
MISCELLANEOUS ISSUES

CONTENTS

OVERVIEW

Chapters 4–7 have provided a detailed discussion of specific types of revenue transactions. This chapter addresses issues that are related to revenue recognition but arise because of the interaction of the accounting for revenue with accounting for other aspects of an arrangement. Included in this chapter are sections on:

1. Costs of revenue transactions;

2. Sales incentives;

3. Related-party sales;

4. Nonmonetary transactions; and

5. Deferred revenue in a business combination.

COSTS OF REVENUE TRANSACTIONS

The majority of costs of product sales are typically recognized when the related revenue is recognized. These costs are typically included in a caption entitled "Cost of goods sold" or "Cost of sales." Until that point in time, costs of products to be sold are carried on the balance sheet as inventory.

Costs of service transactions are typically recognized as incurred when revenue is being recognized under the Proportional Performance model as services are performed. If revenue is not recognized until service in completed, then the costs of providing those services are typically deferred and recognized along with the related revenue.

While these treatments are fairly well-established and cover the bulk of costs of revenue transactions, there are many other costs for which the accounting is not so well-defined. In some cases, certain costs may be deferred and recognized along with revenue from the transaction to which the costs relate.

In addition, there are certain situations in which the accounting described in the previous two paragraphs might result in unusual relationships of the recognition of costs and revenues. Again, such costs may sometimes be deferred until the related revenue is recognized.

LISTING OF APPLICABLE LITERATURE

ASC	ASC Topic/Subtopic	Publication	Subject
605-10-S99	Revenue Recognition/Overall	SAB Topic 13	Revenue Recognition
N/A	N/A	CON-6	Elements of Financial Statements
330-10	Inventory/Overall	ARB-43, Ch. 4	Inventory Pricing
944	Financial Services— Insurance	FAS-60	Accounting and Reporting by Insurance Enterprises
310-20	Receivables/ Nonrefundable Fees and Other Costs	FAS-91	Nonrefundable Fees and Costs Associated with Originating or Acquiring Loans and Initial Direct Costs of Leases

ASC	ASC Topic/Subtopic	Publication	Subject
605-20-25	Revenue Recognition/ Services	FTB 90-1	Accounting for Separately Priced Extended Warranty and Product Maintenance Contracts
340-10	Deferred Costs and Other Assets/Overall	EITF 99-5	Accounting for Pre-Production Costs Related to Long-Term Supply Arrangements
605-25	Revenue Recognition/ Multiple-Element Arrangements	EITF 00-21 and ASU 2009-13	Revenue Arrangements with Multiple Deliverables

The accounting for many costs associated with revenue transactions is well established. U.S. generally accepted accounting principles (GAAP) addresses the following types of costs:

ASC	ASC Topic/Subtopic	Publication	Subject
720-35	Other Expenses/ Advertising Costs	SOP 93-7	Advertising Costs
340-20	Other Assets and Deferred Costs/ Capitalized Advertising Costs	SOP 93-7 and PB-13	Direct-Response Advertising Costs
720-15	Other Expenses/ Start-Up Costs	SOP 98-5	Costs of Start-Up Activities
330	Inventory	ARB-43, Chapter 4	Inventory Costs
340-10	Other Assets and Deferred Costs/ Overall	EITF 99-5	Pre-Production Costs of Long-Term Supply Arrangements
985-20	Software/Costs of Software to be Sold, Leased, or Marketed	FAS-86	Costs of Software Developed for Sale or Licensing
350-40	Intangible-Goodwill and Other/Internal-Use Software	SOP 98-1	Costs of Internal-Use Software
350-50	Intangible-Goodwill and Other/Website Development Costs	EITF 00-2	Internet Site Development Costs
926-20	Entertainment-Films/ Other Assets-Film Costs	SOP 00-2	Costs of Producing and Marketing Films
970	Real Estate-General	FAS-67	Real Estate Development Costs
944	Insurance	FAS-60	Insurance Enterprise Costs

Despite the guidance noted above that covers specific kinds of costs, there is no guidance on how to account for many costs in revenue transactions. There is little debate over the accounting for the largest portion of the costs of revenue transactions—those costs directly associated with providing goods or services to the customer. For example, the costs of providing services are recognized as incurred, which is generally consistent with the pattern of revenue recognition.

However, the accounting for costs indirectly associated with customer contracts is much in debate. Certain costs (e.g., the cost of soliciting a customer, negotiating the terms of a contract, and paying a sales commission) may be incurred before the contract with the customer is signed. Other costs are incurred before performance begins, during the setup phase of a service transaction, or during delivery of a component in a multiple-deliverable arrangement that cannot be treated separately for accounting purposes. In these cases, recognizing costs as expenses when they are incurred results in cost recognition before the related revenue may be recognized. Because of this, some accountants believe that costs should be deferred, or capitalized, in these situations. In general, the following cost categories are often considered candidates for deferral or capitalization:

- *Solicitation costs*—Costs incurred by a vendor to solicit or acquire a *specific* customer or revenue stream (excluding advertising). An example of a solicitation cost is a sales commission.

- *Direct origination costs*—Direct costs incurred to consummate a specific revenue transaction. Examples of origination activities include the evaluation of a customer's credit rating, negotiation of the sales contract, and preparation and processing documentation of the transaction.

- *Multiple-deliverable costs*—Costs related to a delivered item in a multiple-deliverable arrangement, where the delivered item either (1) cannot be treated separately for accounting purposes, or (2) should be treated separately but the amount of revenue allocated to it is restricted because all or a portion of the revenue for that item is contingent upon performance on an undelivered item. For example, if a vendor sells equipment subject to installation but concludes that the equipment does not have value to the customer absent the installation (that is, on a standalone basis), no revenue can be recognized upon delivery of the equipment. The cost of the equipment is an example of a multiple-deliverable cost.

- *Setup and other direct and incremental costs of installation*—Costs related to activities that enable a vendor to perform under the terms of the arrangement. These activities (a) are performed (and the related costs incurred) at the inception of an arrangement, (b) do not represent a separate earnings process, and (c) are arrangement specific. An example of setup and installation costs are those incurred by a vendor in a human resource outsourcing contract for conversion of the customer's historical data to the vendor's software platform.

The key issue with regard to these costs is whether the costs may be capitalized or deferred until revenue is recognized. The accounting literature answers this question for some transactions and certain types of costs. For example, ASC 944-30 provides guidance for insurance companies, ASC 310-20 provides guidance on the deferral of loan origination costs, and ASC 605-20 provides guidance on deferral of costs related to the sale of extended warranties.

However, this guidance is narrow in scope and does not address the majority of situations in which costs are incurred before revenue is recognized.

The question of cost deferral has arisen more frequently since the issuance of ASC 605-10-S99 (SAB Topic 13, *Revenue Recognition*), which underscored the SEC staff's view that the incurrence of costs should not necessarily result in revenue recognition, thereby leading to more situations in which costs are incurred before revenue can be recognized. ASC 605-10-S99 (SAB Topic 13) directly addresses cost deferral by suggesting that in certain arrangements, the models in ASC 310-20 and ASC 605-20 may be appropriate.

EXAMPLES: SETUP COSTS

Acxiom Corporation Form 10-K—Fiscal Year Ended March 31, 2010

The Company provides database management and IT management services under long-term arrangements. These arrangements may require the Company to perform setup activities such as the design and build of a database for the customer under the database management contracts and migration of the customer's IT environment under IT management contracts. In the case of database management contracts, the customer does not acquire any ownership rights to the Company's intellectual property used in the database and the database itself provides no benefit to the customer outside of the utilization of the system during the term of the database management arrangement. In some cases, the arrangements also contain provisions requiring customer acceptance of the setup activities prior to commencement of the ongoing services arrangement.

Upfront fees billed during the setup phase for these arrangements are deferred and setup costs that are direct and incremental to the contract are capitalized and amortized on a straight-line basis over the service term of the contract. Revenue recognition does not begin until after customer acceptance in cases where contracts contain acceptance provisions. Once the setup phase is complete and customer acceptance occurs, the Company recognizes revenue over the remaining service term of the contract. In situations where the arrangement does not require customer acceptance before the Company begins providing services, revenue is recognized over the contract period and no costs are deferred.

Computer Sciences Corp. Form 10-K—Fiscal Year Ended April 2, 2010

Outsourcing Contract Costs

Costs on outsourcing contracts, including costs incurred for bid and proposal activities, are generally expensed as incurred. However, certain costs incurred upon initiation of an outsourcing contract are deferred and expensed over the contract life. These costs represent incremental external costs or certain specific internal costs that are directly related to the contract acquisition or transition activities. Such capitalized costs can be separated into two principal categories: contract acquisition costs and transition/set-up costs. The primary types of costs that may be capitalized include labor and related fringe benefits, subcontractor costs, travel costs, and asset premiums.

The first principal category, contract acquisition costs, consists mainly of due diligence activities after competitive selection as well as premiums paid. Premiums are amounts paid to clients in excess of the fair market value of acquired assets. Fixed assets acquired in connection with outsourcing transactions are capitalized at fair value and depreciated consistent with fixed asset policies described above. Premiums are capitalized as outsourcing contract costs and amortized over the contract life. The amortization of outsourcing contract cost premiums is accounted for as a reduction in revenue. The second principal category of capitalized outsourcing costs is transition/set-up costs. Such costs are primarily associated with installation of systems and processes and are amortized over the contract life.

In the event indications exist that an outsourcing contract cost balance related to a particular contract may be impaired, undiscounted estimated cash flows of the contract are projected over its remaining term and compared to the associated asset group including the unamortized outsourcing contract cost balance. If the projected cash flows are not adequate to recover the unamortized cost balance of the asset group, the balance would be adjusted based on the contract's fair value in the period such a determination is made. The primary indicator used to determine when impairment testing should be performed is when a contract is materially underperforming, or is expected to materially underperform in the future, as compared to the original bid model or subsequent annual budgets.

Definition of an Asset

The conceptual framework makes clear that costs should not be deferred if they do not create or add value to an asset. Assets are defined as " . . . probable future economic benefits obtained or controlled by a particular entity as a result of past transactions or events" (CON-6, par. 25). The costs addressed in this section do not independently result in the creation of any tangible assets. Furthermore, internally-generated intangible assets that do not arise from legal or contractual rights, such as customer relationships, skilled workforce, etc., generally may not be capitalized. For this reason, advertising costs (with the limited exception of direct-response advertising costs as defined in ASC 730 (SOP 93-7)), employee training costs, product and service development costs, and other such general costs of a business cannot be capitalized unless they result in creation of an asset separate from customer contracts or relationships.

However, when the costs are attributable to a particular revenue-generating arrangement, the arrangement itself could be considered an asset because the revenue provides a future economic benefit and the arrangement is controlled by the company and legally binding. Thus, costs that can be related to a specific revenue arrangement may be capitalized in some instances (ASC 605-10-S99, A3f, ques. 3) (SAB Topic 13A3f, ques. 3) as, essentially, the cost of acquiring an intangible asset, that asset being the contract with the customer.

Solicitation and Origination Costs

Solicitation and contract origination costs are incurred before performance for the customer begins. These are costs directly related to obtaining and administering the contract, and generally thought of as both normal and necessary to earn revenue. Because of that, many have argued that such costs should be capitalized when incurred and expensed when revenue is recognized. GAAP addresses these costs in several narrow areas, allowing for capitalization, but with some restrictions.

ASC 310-20 addresses the accounting for loan solicitation and direct origination costs, and allows such costs to be capitalized. Costs eligible for deferral are those that relate directly to a specific loan and are either: (1) incremental direct costs incurred with third parties, or (2) certain internal direct costs related to origination activities. Internal direct costs are limited to a portion of the salaries and benefits of employees involved in the origination process (ASC 310-20-20). This amount is calculated by multiplying the percentage of the employees' time spent on origination activities and the employee's total compensation (salary plus commissions plus benefits). Commissions paid to internal salespeople may be capitalized to the extent that the salesperson performs origination (as opposed to just solicitation) activities.

ASC 605-20 addresses the accounting for costs to acquire separately priced extended warranty and product maintenance contracts. It specifies that only incremental direct costs incurred for a specific contract should be deferred (ASC 605-20-25-4). This would appear to be slightly inconsistent with the costs allowed to be deferred under the ASC 310-20 model, as discussed above, as it effectively precludes the deferral of any portion of employee salaries and benefits.

Choosing an Accounting Policy

The capitalization of customer acquisition costs, and other costs incurred before performance begins, is generally not required. Expensing as incurred is always acceptable for such costs that are not covered explicitly in the accounting literature (ASC 605-10-S99, A3f, ques. 3) (SAB Topic 13A3f, ques. 3). However, it is also generally acceptable to analyze these costs using a model similar to that described in ASC 310-20 or ASC 310-20-20. The objective would be to defer costs that are directly related to the transaction until the revenue is recognized. In some cases, a company may believe that a model other than those described here best meets this objective. This may be appropriate depending on the nature of costs incurred. The policy should be selected based on an analysis of the arrangements and the costs incurred, rather than on a goal of capitalizing (or expensing) a certain amount of costs.

OBSERVATION: Direct costs of a delivered product that cannot be treated separately from the undelivered items in the arrangement (see Chapter 4, "Multiple-Deliverable Revenue Arrangements," for additional information) should be capitalized, subject to the realizability test discussed subsequently. Expensing these costs, which are actually costs of performance rather than acquisition or setup, would be inconsistent with the guidance in ASC 330-10-05-3 (paragraph 4 of ARB-43, Ch. 4), which states: "the inventory at any given date is the balance of costs applicable to goods on hand remaining after the matching of absorbed costs with concurrent revenues. This balance is appropriately carried to future periods provided it does not exceed an amount properly chargeable against the revenues expected to be obtained from ultimate disposition of the goods carried forward." The costs associated with this situation should not be confused with those that arise when a delivered item should be treated separately, but the amount of revenue allocated to it is restricted because all or a portion of the payment for that delivered item is contingent upon delivery of an undelivered item. See the section entitled, "Special Considerations for Certain Multiple-Deliverable Costs," for a discussion of this type of cost.

DISCLOSURE ALERT: Companies should disclose their choice of accounting policy related to the capitalization or expensing of customer acquisition and other costs addressed in this section. See Chapter 12, "Disclosures," for additional discussion of accounting policy disclosures.

EXAMPLE: SOLICITATION AND ORIGINATION COSTS

salesforce.com, inc. Form 10-K—Fiscal Year Ended January 31, 2010

Accounting for Deferred Commissions. We defer commission payments to our direct sales representatives. The commissions are deferred and amortized to sales expense over the non-cancelable terms of the related subscription contracts with our customers, which are typically 12 to 24 months. The commission payments, which are paid in full the month after the customer's service commences, are a direct and incremental cost of the revenue arrangements. The deferred commission amounts are recoverable through the future revenue streams under the non-cancelable customer contracts. We believe this is the preferable method of accounting as the commission charges are so closely related to the revenue from the non-cancelable customer contracts that they should be recorded as an asset and charged to expense over the same period that the subscription revenue is recognized.

During fiscal 2010, we deferred $82.3 million of commission expenditures and we amortized $63.9 million to sales expense. During the same period a year ago, we deferred $63.7 million of commission expenditures and we amortized $58.7 million to sales expense. Deferred commissions on our consolidated balance sheet totaled $75.5 million at January 31, 2010 and $57.1 million at January 31, 2009.

Set-Up Costs

This category of costs covers activities that are performed after the customer contract is signed, but do not provide goods or services to customer. Rather, they are activities that must be undertaken in order to allow the company to provide goods or services to its customer. These are generally one-time activities related to setting up customer accounts, accumulating and converting data, and similar activities. Outsourcing contracts typically involve a significant amount of set-up activities to allow the company taking over the outsourced function to take over the activity.

Because set-up costs in certain arrangements are significant, some believe that revenue should be recognized upon the performance of set-up activities. However, unless the set-up activities themselves provide value to the customer, they do not constitute a separate deliverable and therefore should not trigger revenue recognition (ASC 605-10-S99, A3f, ques. 1 and 2) (SAB Topic 13A3f, ques. 1 and 2).

However, as the costs relate directly to a specific customer arrangement, both practice and the SEC staff accept capitalization of incremental direct set-up and similar costs incurred after a contract is obtained (ASC 605-10-S99, A3f, ques. 3) (SAB Topic 13A3f, ques. 3).

Multiple-Deliverable Costs

When specific refund rights exist in a multiple-deliverable arrangement, the amount of revenue allocable to a delivered item is limited to the lesser of: (a) the amount otherwise allocable to that item (on the basis of the relative selling price method), or (b) the amount that is not contingent upon the delivery of additional items or meeting other specified performance conditions (ASC 605-25-30-5) (see Chapter 4, "Multiple-Deliverable Revenue Arrangements"). These situations raise the question of the proper accounting treatment for the costs associated with the delivered item (referred to in this section as the delivered item costs).

This discussion can be illustrated with the following numerical examples:

Common Facts: There are two deliverables in the arrangement—Item 1 and Item 2. Total arrangement consideration is $100. The amounts otherwise allocable to Item 1 and Item 2 based on their relative selling prices are $70 and $30, respectively. Vendor delivers Item 1 before Item 2. The cost of Item 1 is $50. The cost of Item 2 is $10. Item 1 and Item 2 otherwise meet the separation criteria in ASC 605-25. All of the revenue recognition conditions have been met for Item 1 upon its delivery.

Example 1 Additional Facts: $100 is due upon delivery of Item 1. Vendor must refund the entire amount if Item 2 is not delivered.

Example 1 Discussion

In this example, no revenue should be allocated to Item 1 because the entire amount of arrangement consideration is refundable if Item 2 is not delivered. The question is whether the cost of Item 1 ($50) should be deferred or expensed upon delivery of Item 1. Deferring the $50 until delivery of Item 2 (assuming this occurs) would result in revenue of $100, costs of $60, and a profit margin of $40 for the entire transaction, all recognized at the same point in time. Expensing the $50 upon delivery of Item 1 results in a negative profit margin of $50 for the Vendor upon delivery of Item 1 and a higher positive profit margin of $90 upon delivery of Item 2.

Example 2 Additional Facts: $100 is due upon delivery of Item 1. If Item 2 is not delivered, Vendor must refund $60.

Example 2 Discussion

In this example, $40 of revenue is allocated to Item 1. The $70 that would otherwise have been allocated to Item 1 is reduced to $40 (a reduction of $30) because the amount otherwise allocated to the undelivered item ($30) is less than the amount that would be refunded if the undelivered item is not delivered ($60, for a difference of $30). The question is how the cost of Item 1 should be treated and whether this treatment is affected by the fact that some amount of revenue is allocated to Item 1.

In Example 2, the cost of Item 1 ($50) exceeds the revenue allocated to it ($40) by $10. In this situation, deferring the entire cost of Item 1 would not be appropriate. It would also be inappropriate to defer the $40 of revenue allocated to Item 1 because the conditions for revenue recognition have been met (see Chapter 4, "Multiple-Deliverable Revenue Arrangements"). However, because expensing the entire $50 upon delivery of Item 1 would result in negative profit margin of—$10 for Vendor on Item 1, should some portion of Item 1's cost be deferred? If so, how should this be determined?

Accounting for Delivered Item Costs

The fact patterns in Examples 1 and 2 are relatively straightforward. However, the treatment of Item 1's cost in these Examples is not easily resolved. Consider the additional complexities that would be introduced if the cost of Item 1 were $40 or $30, or if a third item delivered after Item 2 had additional specific refund rights. Unfortunately, there is no accounting literature that specifically addresses these issues.

Different approaches have been discussed on how to determine whether any delivered item costs in a particular set of facts and circumstances should be capitalized for accounting purposes.

As always, in order to capitalize any costs, the company must determine that it has obtained or controlled future economic benefits as a result of the partially-completed revenue transaction. Otherwise, there is no asset to recognize. In making this determination, the company should consider the contract it has with the customer to deliver a second item at a potentially higher profit margin than it otherwise would have. Presuming that the reporting company believes an asset does exist, the next question becomes how to determine the "cost" of that asset—(i.e., how much of the cost of the delivered item should be attributed to "buying" the asset represented by the contract). This requires the consideration of factors such as the margin that will be earned on the final deliverable and the margin that will be earned on the final deliverable in comparison to the margin that would typically be earned on this item if it were sold on a standalone basis.

Possible outcomes and the explanations for them include:

- *Expense the delivered item costs upon delivery*—In Example 1, this would result in $50 expense on delivery of Item 1 with no revenue. In Example 2, this would result in the recognition of $40 of revenue and $50 of cost of goods sold upon the delivery of Item 1. This treatment would be the appropriate for either situation if the vendor concludes that delivery of Item 1 does not create an asset. Such a conclusion would be required if, for example, there were significant doubt about Vendor's ability to complete Item 2.

- *Capitalize the delivered item costs upon delivery*—Example 1, a $50 asset would be recorded upon delivery of Item 1. All of the revenue and costs of sales would then be recognized upon delivery of Item 2. This analysis would be appropriate if Vendor concludes the contract which gives it the right to $100 upon the delivery of Item 2 is an asset because, for example, Item 2 would normally be sold separately for much less than $100.

  In the case of Example 2, this would result in the recognition of $40 of revenue and no costs upon the delivery of Item 1. This treatment would therefore seem unacceptable in Example 2 as it allows recognition of all of the profit on the transaction upon delivery of Item 1.

- *Expense delivered item costs up to the amount of revenue allocated to the delivered item and capitalize the delivered item costs in excess of the amount of revenue allocated to the delivered item (i.e., capitalize the delivered item costs to the extent of any loss) upon delivery*—For Example 1, this results in capitalizing all of the costs of Item 1 upon delivery, similar to the discussion above. In the case of Example 2, this would result in the recognition of $40 of revenue, $40 of cost of goods sold, and $10 of deferred costs upon delivery of Item 1. This treatment suggests that any costs incurred in excess of the amount of revenue allocated to the delivered item are implicitly an investment in the rest of the contract.

- *Expense/Capitalize the costs of Item 1 on a pro rata basis upon delivery (i.e., costs would be expensed based on the proportion of revenue allocated to the delivered item and revenue that otherwise would have been allocated to the delivered item)*—Again, for Example 1, this would result in capitalizing all of the costs of Item 1. In the case of Example 2, this would result in the recognition of $40 of revenue, $29 ($40 ÷ $70 × $50) of cost of goods sold, and $21 of deferred costs upon delivery of Item 1. This model essentially concludes that similar gross margins should be recognized on each deliverable, and allocates costs accordingly. This would be appropriate if the deliverables would reasonably be expected to have similar profit margins, but may be inappropriate otherwise.

SEC REGISTRANT ALERT: In a December 2003 speech, the SEC staff provided the following examples of situations where it may be appropriate to conclude that delivered item costs represent an asset: (1) the arrangement is effectively a consignment (in which case the delivered items would represent consignment inventory), (2) the loss incurred is considered an investment in the remainder of the contract, supported by the fact that the revenue allocated to the remaining deliverables is greater than the estimated selling prices of these deliverables, or (3) the costs incurred are contractually guaranteed reimbursable costs (similar to those costs discussed in ASC 340-10). In these examples, the application of Step 1 in the approach discussed above results in the conclusion that an asset exists. In addition, under the second approach discussed above, an analysis of the potential accounting treatments would likely result in the conclusion that some or all of the delivered item costs should be capitalized.

When a decision is made to recognize delivered item costs as an asset, a key issue for the SEC staff involves the method selected to evaluate the asset for impairment. Other issues include (1) the nature of the costs that should be considered in calculating the loss on a delivered item and (2) how and over what periods the asset should be amortized.

In this speech, the SEC staff acknowledged that there is no one-size-fits-all solution to the treatment of these costs. Given the analytical complexities and level of judgment required to determine whether these costs should be deferred, the SEC staff encouraged registrants to discuss the approaches they have taken with the SEC staff.

EXAMPLE: DEFERRED COSTS

salesforce.com, inc. Form 10-K—Fiscal Year Ended January 31, 2010

If a consulting arrangement does not qualify for separate accounting, we recognize the consulting revenue ratably over the remaining term of the subscription contract. Additionally, in these situations we defer the direct costs of the consulting arrangement and amortize those costs over the same time period as the consulting revenue is recognized. The deferred cost on our consolidated balance sheet totaled $19.1 million at January 31, 2010 and $17.3 million at January 31, 2009. Such amounts are included in prepaid expenses and other current assets and other assets.

ILLUSTRATION: COST DEFERRAL

Facts: Satellite TV Company (Satellite) sells receivers and satellite dishes and provides satellite television programming to customers. Satellite enters into a transaction with Customer M (M) where M purchases a satellite dish and receiver and signs a contract to receive one year of satellite programming. M installs the satellite dish and receiver itself. Amounts to be paid by M include a $50 upfront, nonrefundable fee and $30 per month for the duration of the contract. If the customer cancels the contract early, a $200 cancellation fee is due to Satellite. The costs incurred by Satellite include:

- $150 related to its purchase of the receiver and satellite dish from a third party
- $15 of origination costs (allocated employee costs for one-quarter hour spent by an employee to perform a credit check and process paperwork)
- $25 of setup costs (allocated employee costs for one-half hour spent activating the receiver and satellite dish to receive Satellite's signals)
- $100 commission paid to an internal employee dedicated solely to selling activities

Satellite has concluded that it should not separate the sale of the receiver and satellite dish from the satellite programming services. Furthermore, Satellite has concluded that the upfront fee should be deferred over a period of three years (expected customer relationship period) using the straight-line method.

Discussion: Each of the costs listed above should be evaluated as follows:

- Receiver and satellite dish—The costs of the receiver and satellite dish are incremental direct costs paid to a third party. They are eligible for deferral.
- Performing credit check and processing paperwork—The amounts related to an internal employee performing a credit check and processing paperwork are direct internal origination costs. These costs are generally eligible for deferral.
- Activating receiver and satellite dish—The amount related to an internal employee activating the receiver and satellite dish to receive Satellite's signals represents direct payroll-related costs incurred in connection with setup activities. These costs are generally eligible for deferral.
- Commission—The commission paid to an internal employee dedicated solely to selling activities is likely eligible for deferral as long as the commission is paid only for successful efforts—that is, only when a contract is generated.

Based on this evaluation, the total amount of potentially capitalizable costs is $290. As discussed above, the receiver and dish costs would be required to be capitalized. Satellite could elect to capitalize the other costs or expense them as incurred. In addition, Satellite might conclude that capitalizing only some of the setup, commission and/or origination costs would provide the most transparent presentation to investors and could likely justify a policy reflecting that judgment. For example, Satellite might decide to capitalize only the incremental costs of a new contract, which would cause Satellite to expense the setup and origination costs, but capitalize the sales commissions.

Realizability Test

Like all assets, deferred costs must be evaluated for realizability. Both ASC 310-20 and ASC 605-20-25 (FTB 90-1) require the deferral of costs due to the existence of a contractual revenue stream against which these costs must be matched. As a result, the nature of the terms of arrangements that fall within the scope of these statements supports the realizability of the deferred costs.

Outside of these arrangements, if a company adopts a policy of capitalizing certain costs of revenue transactions, there should similarly be a revenue stream to support that capitalization. For example, the following questions should be considered to determine whether such costs are realizable:

- Has any nonrefundable revenue related to the specific transaction been deferred?

- Is there a clause in the contractual arrangement that management intends to enforce (e.g., a liquidated damages clause) that would facilitate recovery of the deferred costs?

Deferrable costs up to the amount of nonrefundable deferred revenue are considered realizable because the recognition of the deferred revenue will offset the recognition of deferred costs. If deferrable costs are in excess of nonrefundable deferred revenue (or if there is no deferred revenue), these excess costs should only be considered realizable if there is a legally enforceable contract that obligates the customer to make payments that will cover any future costs and leave enough margin to cover the deferred costs as well.

One question that arises in applying this test is whether any revenue in addition to contractual minimums should be included. For example, in the satellite television arrangement discussed above, the customer may be able to purchase additional services, such as premium movie channels or special event programming. It may be appropriate to include these additional revenues (and related costs) in the realizability test if the additional amounts are probable and objectively supportable. However, companies should be judicious when adopting a policy that considers revenues in excess of minimum contractual revenues to estimate net margins for purposes of the realizability test.

OBSERVATION: Some companies have essentially eliminated the need for a realizability test by adopting a policy of deferring costs only to the extent of deferred revenues. This policy is less preferable than one that adopts a full cost deferral model or expenses all costs as incurred. However, a policy of deferring direct costs to the extent of deferred revenues is acceptable, if applied consistently.

EXAMPLE: LIMITING DEFERRED COSTS TO DEFERRED REVENUES

Qwest Communications International Inc. Form 10-K—Fiscal Year Ended December 31, 2009

We recognize revenue for services when the related services are provided. Recognition of certain payments received in advance of services being provided is deferred until the service is provided. These advance payments include activation fees and installation charges, which we recognize as revenue over the expected customer relationship period, which ranges from one to four years. We also defer costs for customer acquisitions. The deferral of customer acquisition costs is limited to the amount of revenue deferred on advance payments. Costs in excess of advance payments are recorded as expense in the period such costs are incurred. Expected customer relationship periods are estimated using historical experience. Termination fees or other fees on existing contracts that are negotiated in conjunction with new contracts are deferred and recognized over the new contract term.

ILLUSTRATION: APPLICATION OF THE REALIZABILITY TEST

Facts: Assume the same facts and conclusions as those presented earlier in the examples involving Satellite TV Company (Satellite). In addition, assume the following:

- The monthly costs incurred by Satellite to provide programming services to M are $12.

- Satellite has received a letter from its external legal counsel indicating that its programming services contracts are legally enforceable.

- Satellite has a history of enforcing its contracts and intends to enforce its contract with M.

Also, Satellite does not have a policy of including revenues expected in excess of contractual minimums (e.g., specialty programming fees) when determining whether deferred costs are realizable.

Application: Based on its accounting policies, Satellite has determined that $290 of costs are deferrable in the arrangement it has with M. An amount equal to the upfront nonrefundable fee of $50 is considered realizable. Satellite also expects net margins of $216 during the contract period ($360 of contractual revenue [$30 per month for 12 months] less $144 of related direct costs ([$12 per month for 12 months]). Satellite can support its expectations of $216 in net margins under this contract with a large volume of company-specific history for similar contracts. An additional $216 of deferrable costs are also considered realizable since (a) this amount represents probable and objectively supportable net margins, (b) Satellite's contract with M is legally enforceable, (c) Satellite intends to enforce its contract with M, and (d) Satellite's intentions are reasonable in light of its demonstrable history of enforcing its contracts.

Based on this analysis, the amount of deferrable costs that are realizable is $266 ($50 supported by the upfront nonrefundable fee and $216 supported by probable and objectively supportable net margins). The remainder of the deferrable costs, $24 ($290 total deferrable costs less $266 realizable deferrable costs), should be expensed as incurred.

Amortization

Deferred costs should generally be amortized as revenue related to the applicable contract is recognized. Thus, if the deferred costs are equal to or less than deferred revenue related to the same contract, the costs should be amortized over the same period and in the same manner as the related deferred revenue (ASC 605-10-S99, A3f, ques. 5) (SAB Topic 13A3f, ques. 5). If there are no deferred revenues, or if the amount of deferred costs exceeds the related deferred revenues, the cost, or excess costs, should be amortized in proportion to the revenue realized during the base contract term, excluding extensions. In these situations, the pattern of recognition for deferred costs should generally mirror the revenue to be recognized under the contract and if no pattern of revenue recognition can be predicted, the costs should be amortized on a straight-line basis over the contract period.

ILLUSTRATION: AMORTIZATION OF DEFERRED COSTS

Facts: Assume the same facts and conclusions as those presented earlier in the examples involving Satellite TV Company (Satellite).

Amortization: Satellite should amortize $50 of deferred costs over the same period and in the same manner that the $50 upfront nonrefundable fee will be recognized as revenue. This results in the recognition of $50 of deferred costs on a straight-line basis over a three-year period. The remaining $216 of deferred costs should be amortized on a straight-line basis over the one-year contract period.

Summary: Revenues and costs recognized over the expected period of the customer relationship (assuming that the revenue recognition criteria have been met) is as follows:

	Year 1	Year 2	Year 3	Total
Revenue:				
Amortization of upfront nonrefundable fee	$ 17	$ 17	$ 16	$ 50
Monthly programming fees	360	360	360	1,080
Total	377	377	376	1,130
Costs:				
Amortization of deferred costs				
$50 over three years	17	17	16	50
$216 over one year	216			216
Excess of deferrable costs over realizable costs	24	—		24
Monthly programming costs	144	144	144	432
Total	401	161	160	722
Net margin	$(24)	$216	$216	$408

SALES INCENTIVES

Many companies offer incentives to induce sales. Some common incentives include:

- Coupons and rebates in a single purchase transaction.
- Rights to discounts on future purchases.
- Volume discounts resulting in a cash rebate when a cumulative level of purchases is reached.
- "Free" products or services with the purchase of one or more products or services.
- "Points" (or "Miles") that can be accumulated and exchanged for free products or services, sometimes including products or services provided by parties other than the vendor.

This section discusses recognition of the costs of these incentives.[1]

LISTING OF APPLICABLE LITERATURE

ASC	ASC Topic/ Subtopic	Publication	Subject
605-10-S99	Revenue Recognition/ Overall	SAB Topic 13	Revenue Recognition
405-20	Liabilities/ Extinguishment of Liablities	FAS-140	Extinguishments of Liabilities
605-25	Revenue Recognition/ Multiple-Element Arrangements	EITF 00-21 and ASU 2009-13	Revenue Arrangements with Multiple Deliverables
605-50	Revenue Recognition/Sales Incentives	EITF 01-9 and EITF 02-16	Customer Payment and Incentives
985-605-55-82	Software/ Revenue Recognition	TPA 5100.50	Definition of More-Than-Insignificant Discount
985-605-55-83	Software/ Revenue Recognition	TPA 5100.51	Accounting for Significant Incremental Discounts

Coupons and Rebates

Coupons (e.g., a newspaper coupon for 50 cents off a box of cereal) and rebates (e.g., a $20 mail-in rebate found in the box of a computer printer) are examples of sales incentives that can be used by the beneficiary of the offer in a single purchase transaction. In many cases, the coupon or rebate user may not be the

---

[1] Proper classification of the costs of these incentives is also important. Classification is discussed in Chapter 11, "Presentation."

direct customer of the entity that offers the incentive. For example, newspaper coupons and mail-in rebates are generally offered by product manufacturers, but are redeemed by consumers who buy the product from a retail store. The retail store (or a distributor that acted as an intermediary) is the product manufacturer's direct customer; the end-user (consumer) is an indirect customer of the product manufacturer. The estimated cost of a single-purchase sales incentive must be recognized at the later of the date at which the related sale is recorded by the vendor or the date at which the sales incentive is offered (ASC 605-50-25-3). The rationale underlying this requirement stems from the possibility that the manufacturer may have sold the product to the vendor (or distributor) prior to offering the sales incentive.

Redemption rates on coupons and rebates are much lower than 100%. In fact, newspaper coupon redemption rates rarely exceed single-digit percentages. Therefore, if a company can reasonably estimate the expected redemption amount, it can record this estimate as a reduction in revenue. As estimates change, the accrual for the potential refund should also be adjusted. If reasonable estimates cannot be made, a liability should be recognized for the maximum potential amount of sales incentives that could be exercised or awarded. The following factors might impair a company's ability to make a reasonable estimate of coupon or rebate redemptions (ASC 605-50-25-4):

1. *The offer period is long.* The longer the offer period, the more difficult it becomes to predict the response rate. Whether an offer period is long should be determined based on the nature of the product, industry practice, and the type of customer.

2. *The absence of relevant historical experience.* Without historical experience to reference, predicting customer actions is virtually impossible. However, in the absence of company-specific experience, industry experience may be relevant.

3. *The absence of a large volume of relatively homogeneous transactions.* It is generally difficult to predict the actions of a particular customer. However, it is easier to predict the actions of a large number of customers.

OBSERVATION: These factors are similar to those required for estimating product returns (see Chapter 5, "Product Deliverables") or service cancellations (see Chapter 6, "Service Deliverables") because, in both cases, the company is attempting to predict the actions of its customers.

EXAMPLE: CUSTOMER REBATES

McAfee, Inc. Form 10-K—Fiscal Year Ended December 31, 2009

We reduce revenue for estimates of sales incentives and sales returns. We offer sales incentives, including channel rebates, marketing funds and end-user rebates for products in our corporate and consumer product lines. Additionally, end users may return our products, subject to varying limitations, through distributors and resellers or to us directly for a refund within a reasonably short period from the date of purchase. We estimate and record reserves for sales incentives and sales returns based on our historical experience. In each accounting period, we must make judgments and estimates of sales incentives and potential future sales returns related to current period revenue. These estimates affect our "net revenue" line item on our consolidated statements of income and comprehensive income and affect our "accounts receivable, net", "deferred revenue" or "other accrued liabilities" line items on our consolidated balance sheets.

At December 31, 2009, our allowance for sales returns and incentives was $68.8 million compared to $61.2 million at December 31, 2008. If our allowance for sales returns and incentives were to increase by 10%, or $6.9 million, our net revenue would decrease by $1.5 million and our deferred revenue would decrease by $5.4 million for the year ended December 31, 2009.

Volume Rebates

Other sales incentives involve an offer to rebate or refund a specified amount of cash if the customer reaches a specified cumulative level of purchases or remains a customer for a certain time period. The cost of these incentives should be recognized as each of the required revenue transactions that results in progress by the customer toward earning the rebate occurs (ASC 605-50-25-7). The accrued cost should be limited to the estimated rebates potentially due, as long as an estimate can be made. If an estimate cannot be made, the maximum rebate potentially due customers should be accrued (ASC 605-50-25-8).

Changes in the estimated amount of rebates or refunds and retroactive changes by a vendor to a previous offer should be recognized using a cumulative catch-up adjustment (ASC 605-50-25-9). For example, if a vendor introduces a volume rebate program three months into the fiscal year that will be calculated based on purchases for the entire year, an accrual related to the estimate of rebates that will be due related to transactions that occurred during the first three months of the year should be recorded immediately.

OBSERVATION: Although estimating the amount of incentives to be used by a large group of consumers may be possible because of historical experience, estimating volume rebates to be earned by a specific customer may be more difficult. This is particularly the case when the incentive plan is tailored for a specific customer. Therefore, companies that offer incentives to a small number of large customers are more likely to have difficulty estimating the amounts to be earned than companies that offer incentives to a large number of small customers.

Similar accounting should be followed by the customer receiving the volume rebate. The customer should recognize a reduction in cost of sales as each of the required revenue transactions that results in progress toward earning the rebate occurs, provided the rebate is (a) payable pursuant to a binding arrangement and (b) probable and reasonably estimable. If the rebate or refund is not probable and reasonably estimable, it should be recognized as the milestones are achieved (ASC 605-50-25-10). Changes in the estimated amount of rebates or refunds and retroactive changes by a vendor to a previous offer should be recognized using a cumulative catch-up adjustment (ASC 605-50-25-12). See the SEC Registrant Alert in the Chapter 7 section entitled, "Combined License and Research and Development Arrangements."

EXAMPLE: VOLUME REBATES

BJ's Wholesale Club, Inc. Form 10-K—Fiscal Year Ended January 30, 2010

Vendor Rebates and Allowances

We receive various types of cash consideration from vendors, principally in the form of rebates, based on purchasing or selling certain volumes of product, time-based rebates or allowances, which may include product placement allowances or exclusivity arrangements covering a predetermined period of time, price protection rebates and allowances for retail price reductions on certain merchandise, and salvage allowances for product that is damaged, defective or becomes out-of-date. We recognize such vendor rebates and allowances based on a systematic and rational allocation of the cash consideration offered to the underlying transaction that results in progress by BJ's toward earning the rebates and allowances, provided the amounts to be earned are probable and reasonably estimable. Otherwise, rebates and allowances are recognized only when predetermined milestones are met. We recognize product placement allowances as a reduction of cost of sales in the period in which we complete the arranged placement of the product. Time-based rebates or allowances are recognized as a reduction of cost of sales over the performance period on a straight-line basis. All other vendor rebates and allowances are recognized as a reduction of cost of sales when the merchandise is sold or otherwise disposed.

We also receive cash consideration from vendors for demonstrating their products in the clubs and for advertising their products, particularly in the *BJ's Journal*, a publication sent to a subset of BJ's members periodically throughout the year. In both cases, such cash consideration is recognized as a reduction of selling, general and administrative ("SG&A") expenses to the extent it represents a reimbursement of specific, incremental and identifiable SG&A costs incurred by BJ's to sell the vendors' products. If the cash consideration exceeds the costs being reimbursed, the excess is characterized as a reduction of cost of sales. Cash consideration for product demonstrations is recognized in the period during which the demonstrations are performed. Cash consideration for advertising vendors' products is recognized in the period in which the advertising takes place.

Manufacturers' Incentives Tendered by Consumers

We record consideration from manufacturers' incentives (such as rebates or coupons) in net sales when the incentive is generic and can be tendered by a consumer at any reseller and we receive direct reimbursement from the manufacturer, or clearinghouse authorized by the manufacturer, based on the face value of the incentive. If these conditions are not met, we record such consideration as a decrease in cost of sales.

Discounts on Future Purchases

A vendor may offer a discount on future purchases in conjunction with a current sales transaction. Some of these discounts may only be applied to future purchases of a particular product. Others may be applied to any future purchases during a defined time period.

The Software Model

The accounting for discounts offered on future purchases is addressed in the software revenue recognition literature (see Chapter 10, "Software—A Complete Model"). The software model requires a determination of whether the discount is incremental and *more-than-insignificant.* Revenue accounting for a transaction is affected only when the discount is deemed incremental and more-than-insignificant. In that case, a proportionate amount of the discount must be allocated to all the deliverables in the arrangement based on the relative fair value (selling price) of each deliverable. Although the software model does not apply to non-software transactions, it presents one view of the appropriate accounting for discounts that should be considered by companies outside the software industry.

DISCLOSURE ALERT: Companies should disclose their choice of accounting policy for discounts offered to a customer in a current transaction that can be used for future purchases. See Chapter 12, "Disclosures," for additional discussion of accounting policy disclosures.

More-than-insignificant Incremental discounts. A future discount on purchases is considered a more-than-insignificant incremental discount if it meets all of the following criteria (ASC 985-605-15-3):

- *The future discount is incremental to the range of discounts reflected in the pricing of the other elements (deliverables) of the arrangement.* If the customer was able to negotiate a 30% discount on the items in the current arrangement, offering a 30% discount on additional items does not grant the customer anything that would not otherwise have been available.

- *The future discount is incremental to the range of discounts typically given in comparable transactions.* Discounts typically given in comparable transactions do not confer any value to the customer not currently available to the customer.

- *The future discount is significant.*

A future discount that does not meet all of these criteria should not receive any accounting recognition.

Accounting for more-than-insignificant incremental discounts. The basic principle for more-than-insignificant incremental discounts calls for a proportionate amount of the discount to be allocated to all the items in the arrangement based on the relative fair value (selling price) of each item. The application of this principle is straightforward when: (1) the products or services to which the discount applies are specified, and (2) there is sufficient evidence of the fair values (selling prices) of those products or services.

However, when either the products or services to which the discount applies are not specified, the accounting treatment is more complex and depends on whether the maximum amount of the discount can be quantified. When that maximum amount can be quantified, it should be allocated to the current and future purchases on the assumption that the customer will purchase the minimum amount necessary to be eligible for the maximum discount. The portion of the current transaction fee deferred is recognized proportionately as future purchases are delivered or provided (assuming that all other revenue recognition criteria are satisfied) ensuring that a consistent discount rate is applied. Any remaining deferred revenue is recognized when the discount expires.

When the maximum amount of the discount cannot be quantified (for example, when the quantity of future products or services to which the discount may apply is not specified), revenue allocated to current and future purchases should be net of the discount (note that revenue related to the initial purchase is deferred and, on future purchases, cash received determines the amount recognized as revenue). The portion of the fee deferred in conjunction with the current sales transaction should be recognized as revenue ratably over the discount period.

ILLUSTRATION: MORE-THAN-INSIGNIFICANT INCREMENTAL DISCOUNTS

EXAMPLE 1

Facts: Manufacturer X sells Product Y for $100 (its fair value) along with a right to a discount of $50 on Product Z, whose price and fair value is $150. The $50 discount is considered a significant incremental discount.

Accounting: Manufacturer X should allocate the $50 discount across Products Y and Z based on an overall discount rate of 20%. The overall discount rate is calculated as the ratio of the discount ($50) to the total of the fair values of Product Y and Z ($100 + $150 = $250). The amount of revenue that should be recognized for Product Y is $80 ($100 less the 20% discount) and $120 for Product Z ($150 minus the 20% discount). When the revenue recognition criteria have been met for the sale of each product, Manufacturer X will record the following journal entries:

- Upon sale of Product Y:

Cash or Receivable	$100	
Product Revenue		$80
Deferred Revenue		$20

- Upon sale of Product Z:

Cash or Receivable (sales price of $150 less $50 discount)	$100	
Deferred Revenue	$ 20	
Product Revenue		$120

EXAMPLE 2

Facts: Manufacturer L sells Product M for $250 (its fair value) along with a right to a discount of $100 that can be used on any of Manufacturer L's other Products—Products N through Z. The list prices of Products N through Z range from $150 to $350. The $100 discount is considered a significant incremental discount. Three months after the purchase of Product M, the customer uses the discount to purchase Product V, whose list price and fair value is $300.

Accounting: Manufacturer L should allocate the $100 discount across Product M and the future product purchase using the fair value of Product M and the lowest possible fair value of the future purchase on which the discount may be used ($150). The overall discount rate is 25%, calculated as the ratio of the discount ($100) to the total fair values of Product M and the lowest fair value ($250 + $150 = $400). The amount of revenue that should be recognized for Product M is $187.50 ($250 reduced by 25%) and for Product V is $262.50 ($300 sales price less the $100 discount plus the $62.50 deferred in connection with the Product M sale). When the revenue recognition criteria have been met for the sale of each product, Manufacturer X will record the following journal entries:

- Upon sale of Product M:

Cash or Receivable	$250.00	
Product Revenue		$187.50
Deferred Revenue		$ 62.50

- Upon sale of Product V:

Cash or Receivable (sales price of $300 less $100 discount)	$200.00	
Deferred Revenue	$62.50	
Product Revenue		$262.50

EXAMPLE 3

Facts: Service Provider F sells Service G for $100 (its fair value) along with a right to a discount of 50% off all future purchases of Services H through W, with a maximum discount of $200. The 50% discount is considered a significant incremental discount by Service Provider F. Three months after the purchase of Service G, the customer uses the discount to purchase Service T, whose list price and fair value is $300.

Accounting: Service Provider F should assume that the customer will purchase the level of services necessary to take advantage of the maximum discount. This level of future purchases is $400 ($200 maximum discount divided by 50% discount rate). The overall discount rate is 40%, calculated as the ratio of the maximum discount ($200) to the total of the fair value of Service G and the level of future purchases necessary to earn the maximum discount ($100 + $400 = $500). The amount of revenue that should be recognized related to Service G is $60 ($100 reduced by 40%) and Service T is $180 ($300 sales price reduced by 40%, or $300 sales price less $150 cash discount plus 75% ($300 ÷ $400) of the $40 deferred in connection with the Service G sale). When the revenue recognition criteria have been met related to the sale of each service, Service Provider F records the following journal entries:

- Upon sale of Service G:

Cash or Receivable	$100	
Service Revenue		$60
Deferred Revenue		$40

- Upon sale of Service T:

Cash or Receivable (sales price of $300 less $150 discount)	$150	
Deferred Revenue	$30	
Service Revenue		$180

The remaining deferred revenue of $10 would be recognized upon future purchases totaling at least $100 or expiration of the discount.

Additional Examples: Additional examples of accounting for discounts on future purchases can be found in Chapter 10, "Software—A Complete Model."

Breakage

As described above and in Chapter 10, the software literature does not allow breakage (the portion of customers that will not use an offered discount) to be considered in the accounting for discounts on future purchases. This is due to the difficulty in making reasonable and reliable estimates of the breakage factor, as software transactions tend to be unique.

There are other areas of revenue accounting, however, in which the use of breakage is allowed, as long as reasonable and reliable estimates can be made. Several of these areas are discussed in Chapter 3, "General Principles." Companies that enter into a high volume of homogeneous transactions that include offers of discounts on future purchases may be able to make reliable estimates of breakage related to those offers. In these cases, it would likely be acceptable to use these estimates in the accounting for the offer.

SEC REGISTRANT ALERT: In a December 2002 speech, the SEC staff discussed breakage in situations where customers make a nonrefundable prepayment for services or goods that they ultimately do not demand. The SEC staff observed that ASC 405-20 requires either performance or legal release to extinguish a liability. Because a prepayment for future delivery of services or goods creates a liability, the application of ASC 405-20 would result in no income recognition until the end (or expiration) of the performance period for products or services paid for, but not demanded, by the customer. Alternatively, the SEC staff indicated that it will not object to revenue recognition prior to the expiration of the performance period provided both the following conditions exist:

1. Management can demonstrate that the demand for future performance is remote based on a large population of homogeneous transactions; and

2. There is objective reliable historical evidence supporting the estimate of breakage.

The SEC staff also indicated that (a) it would be skeptical of an accounting model that results in immediate income for breakage and (b) whether breakage represents revenue or a gain (i.e., other income) depends on the facts and circumstances.

In a December 2002 speech, the SEC staff discussed breakage in situations where customers make a nonrefundable prepayment for services or goods that they ultimately do not demand. The SEC staff observed that ASC 405-20 requires either performance or legal release to extinguish a liability. Because a prepayment for future delivery of services or goods creates a liability, the application of ASC 405-20 would result in no income recognition until the end (or expiration) of the performance period for products or services paid for, but not demanded, by the customer. Alternatively, the SEC staff indicated that it will not object to revenue recognition prior to the expiration of the performance period provided both the following conditions exist:

1. Management can demonstrate that the likelihood of a demand for future performance is remote; and

2. There is objective reliable historical evidence supporting the estimate of breakage.

The SEC staff also indicated that: (a) it would be skeptical of an accounting model that results in immediate income for breakage, and (b) whether breakage represents revenue or a gain (i.e., other income) will depend on the facts and circumstances.

The SEC staff used gift card redemption as an example, noting that recognition of breakage (the percentage of gift cards that will not be redeemed) on sale of the gift card is unacceptable (the delivery criterion is not satisfied at the inception of the arrangement). Gift card breakage can be recognized as the vendor is released from its obligation (e.g., at redemption or expiration) or when redemption is deemed remote. Another method recognizes breakage in proportion to actual redemption. In order to use this method, the vendor needs objective and reliable estimates of (1) breakage and (2) the period of gift card redemption. Registrants were encouraged to discuss specific facts and circumstances with the SEC staff.

Point and Loyalty Programs

Point and loyalty programs come in all shapes and sizes. Some programs involve a company granting points to their customers for every purchase with those points being redeemable in the future for goods or services provided by the company. The best known examples are airline frequent flyer programs.

There are also entities that specialize in operating point and loyalty programs. These entities (referred to as program operators) administer point and loyalty programs as a main revenue producing activity. Program operators sell points in their programs to third parties, and the third parties grant those points to their customers, employees, or others. These points are usually redeemable for a variety of goods or services. The program operator's obligations to its customers under these arrangements may solely involve redeeming the points. However, more often the program operator also provides a variety of administrative services to its customers such as tracking the point accumulation and redemption by the customer's participants in the program.

Some programs combine these basic elements. For example, in addition to granting "miles" to their customers based on purchases, many airlines also sell miles. The purchasers may be consumers who will redeem the points themselves or they may be other service providers, such as hotels or car rental agencies that will issue the miles to their customers.

The accounting considerations for these types of arrangements vary depending on the nature of the specific point and loyalty program. The more common considerations relate to (1) points granted to customers in connection with a current sales transaction, (2) points sold to third parties, (3) program operators, and (4) breakage.

DISCLOSURE ALERT: Companies should disclose their accounting policy for the point and loyalty programs they offer and/or administer. See Chapter 12, "Disclosures," for additional discussion of accounting policy disclosures.

Points Granted as Part of Current Sales Transaction

The simplest point programs are those in which a customer earns points from purchases that are redeemable for additional products or services. In this transaction, the vendor has effectively sold two items to the customer: (1) the product or service delivered to the customer as part of that sales transaction, and (2) a portion of a product or service that will be provided in the future upon the redemption of the points issued. The fact that multiple items have been sold suggests that the arrangement should be accounted for as a multiple-deliverable arrangement.

As discussed in Chapter 4, "Multiple-Deliverable Revenue Arrangements," ASC 605-25 provides criteria that must be met prior to treating items in a multiple-deliverable arrangement separately for accounting purposes. Although point and loyalty programs integrated with current sales transactions are multiple-deliverable arrangements, they have specifically been excluded from the scope of ASC 605-25 due to their unique nature. However, companies may elect to apply ASC 605-25 to these types of arrangements. If points are treated as a separate unit of accounting under ASC 605-25, revenue allocated to the points must be deferred and recognized when the points are redeemed.

OBSERVATION: Many companies that issue points to their customers in programs such as the ones discussed do not follow the guidance in ASC 605-25. In practice, they use an accounting policy that results in: (1) no revenue allocation to the points, and (2) an accrual of associated costs at the point when revenue is recognized for the other items in the arrangement. The measurement of the accrued liability varies across industries and companies within the same industry. Some companies have changed their measurement over time as well.

Points Sold

As discussed above, a company may sell points to customers on a standalone basis. In other transactions, the points are included with a product or service, but are treated as a separate deliverable for accounting purposes. In both situations, the sale of points does not represent separate earnings processes, as the customer would not pay for points without the ability to redeem them for valuable items.[2] Therefore, the earnings process related to the sale of points must be evaluated using a Completed Performance model, with performance only considered complete when the points are redeemed.

EXAMPLES: INSIGNIFICANT DELIVERABLE

AMR Corp. Form 10-K—Fiscal Year Ended December 31, 2009

Frequent flyer program

American uses the incremental cost method to account for the portion of its frequent flyer liability incurred when AAdvantage members earn mileage credits by flying on American or its regional affiliates.

The Company considers breakage in its incremental cost calculation and recognizes breakage on AAdvantage miles sold over the estimated period of usage for sold miles that are ultimately redeemed. The Company calculates its breakage estimate using separate breakage rates for miles earned by flying on American and miles earned through other companies who have purchased AAdvantage miles for distribution to their customers, due to differing behavior patterns. Management considers historical patterns of account breakage to be a useful indicator when estimating future breakage. Future program redemption opportunities can significantly alter customer behavior from historical patterns with respect to inactive accounts. Such changes may result in material changes to the deferred revenue balance, as well as recognized revenues from the program.

American includes fuel, food, passenger insurance and reservations/ticketing costs in the calculation of incremental cost. These estimates are generally updated based upon the Company's 12-month historical average of such costs. American also accrues a frequent flyer liability for the mileage credits expected to be used for travel on participating airlines based on historical usage patterns and contractual rates.

Revenue earned from selling AAdvantage miles to other companies is recognized in two components. The first component represents the revenue for air transportation sold and is valued at fair value. This revenue is deferred along with revenue related to expected breakage of sold miles and recognized over the period the mileage is expected to be used, which is currently estimated to be 28 months. The second revenue component, based on the residual method and representing the marketing services sold, is recognized as related services are provided.

The Company's total liability for future AAdvantage award redemptions for free, discounted or upgraded travel on American, American Eagle or participating airlines, as well as unrecognized revenue from selling AAdvantage miles to other

---

[2] In certain programs, the issuer of points may be able to discontinue the program or change its terms without any liability to the point-holder. Even in these situations, the company has the obligation to redeem points presented for redemption before the terms are changed or the program is abandoned. Therefore, the accounting should reflect the redemption obligation.

companies, was approximately $1.5 billion and $1.7 billion at December 31, 2009 and 2008, respectively (and is recorded as a component of Air traffic liability in the consolidated balance sheets), representing 19.2 percent and 18.2 percent of AMR's total current liabilities, at December 31, 2009 and 2008, respectively.

The approximate number of free travel awards used for travel on American and American Eagle was 5.2 million one-way travel awards in 2009 (or 2.6 million round trip awards) and 6.2 million one-way travel awards in 2008 (or 3.1 million round trip travel awards) representing approximately 8.9 and 9.7 percent of passengers boarded in each year, respectively. The Company believes displacement of revenue passengers is minimal given the Company's load factors, its ability to manage frequent flyer seat inventory, and the relatively low ratio of free award usage to total passengers boarded.

Changes to the percentage of the amount of revenue deferred, deferred recognition period, percentage of awards expected to be redeemed for travel on participating airlines, breakage or cost per mile estimates could have a significant impact on the Company's revenues or incremental cost accrual in the year of the change as well as in future years.

ILLUSTRATION: SALE OF PRODUCT AND POINTS

Facts: Company A sells a variety of household products. For each dollar of purchases, Company A's premier customers earn one point. The points may be accumulated and redeemed for a variety of Company A's household products. Point values are assigned to each of the household products for redemption purposes. Company A sells $50,000 of household products to Premier Customer D. As a result, Premier Customer D earns 50,000 points. The sales price of the household products to non-premier customers is $50,000. Company A regularly sells points on a standalone basis for $.25 per point. For purposes of this example, assume that Company A concludes that it should treat the sale of the household products separate from the sale of the points. Customer D eventually redeems the points for household products having a carrying amount of $6,000.

Accounting: Company A allocates revenue to the points based on the following calculation:

Selling price of household products	$50,000
Selling price of points (50,000 points @ $.25 per point)	12,500
Total	62,500
Arrangement consideration	50,000
Portion allocable to household products based on relative selling prices	80%
Consideration allocated to household products	40,000
Portion allocable to points based on relative selling prices	20%
Consideration allocated to points	$10,000

Company A records the following journal entries:

- Upon meeting the revenue recognition criteria related to the sale of the household products to Customer A:

Cash or Receivable	$50,000	
Product Revenue		$40,000
Unredeemed Points Liability	$10,000	

- Upon redemption of the points by Customer A:

Unredeemed Points Liability	$10,000	
Product Revenue		$10,000
Cost of Goods Sold	$ 6,000	
Product Inventory		$ 6,000

Program Operators

Program operators may agree to provide several deliverables to their customers, including the issuance and redemption of points as well as the provision of administrative services. Although these arrangements are specifically excluded from the scope of ASC 605-25, they may still be evaluated as multiple-deliverable arrangements, with the sale and redemption of the points considered one deliverable and the administrative services as one or more additional deliverables. See Chapter 4, "Multiple-Deliverable Revenue Arrangements," for guidance regarding separation of multiple-deliverable arrangements.

If the administrative services are treated separately, the earnings process for the services will most likely be evaluated using a Proportional Performance model, with revenue recognized throughout the performance period. The revenue allocated to the points, however, would be recognized when the points are redeemed using a Completed Performance model. If the services and points are combined and treated as a single unit of accounting, the revenue recognition accounting policy should take into consideration all of the program operators' obligations.

Breakage

As previously discussed, breakage is a term commonly used to describe the portion of customers that will not use all of the rights they obtain in a transaction. For point and loyalty programs, breakage refers to the points that will never be redeemed. This occurs because point holders may not accumulate a sufficient amount of points for redemption purposes, they may lose track of their points, or they may decide it is not worth their time or effort to redeem the points. Breakage presents a unique accounting issue—when should revenue be recognized for points that are not expected to be redeemed?

As discussed earlier, ASC 605-50 addresses breakage related to the redemption of rebate offers. Under that guidance, a company may take breakage into consideration when accruing the liability related to redemption of rebate offers if reasonable and reliable estimates of the expected level of rebate redemptions can be made. Similar analyses allow breakage to be considered when accounting for rights of return or cancellation (see Chapter 5, "Product Deliverables," and

Chapter 6, "Service Deliverables"). If a similar analysis yields a reliable estimate of breakage in a point program, that estimate may generally be taken into account in allocating revenue to points issued.

Even if sufficient evidence exists to estimate breakage, this should not result in immediate income recognition from points that are expected to go unredeemed. Instead, the sales price related to the points should be recognized based on the number of points expected to be redeemed by the customer over the redemption period.

ILLUSTRATION: FACTORING IN BREAKAGE

Facts: Airline J sells 1,000,000 miles to Customer D for $500,000. Airline J can make reasonable and reliable estimates of breakage and consequently determines that only 800,000 of these miles will ultimately be redeemed. During Airline J's first quarter, 250,000 of these miles are redeemed and used by Customer D.

Accounting: Airline J calculates the following amount of revenue that should be recognized for each mile as it is redeemed:

Arrangement consideration	$ 500,000
Reasonable and reliable estimate of miles to be redeemed	800,000
Revenue per mile	$ 0.625

Airline J records the following journal entries:

- Upon receiving cash from Customer D:

Cash or Receivable	$500,000	
Unredeemed Miles Liability		$500,000

- Upon redemption and use of miles by Customer D in first quarter (250,000 miles redeemed at $.625 of revenue per mile):

Unredeemed Miles Liability	$156,250	
Service Revenue		$156,250

PRACTICE POINTER: In the above illustration, breakage was not factored into the revenue accounting by recognizing $100,000 ($500,000 arrangement consideration × [200,000 miles not expected to be redeemed/1,000,000 miles sold]) of revenue upon the sale of the miles. This approach is inappropriate because Airline J has not yet provided any services to earn that revenue.

If a company cannot make reasonable and reliable estimates of point redemption levels, it must assume that all of the points will eventually be redeemed for accounting purposes. This maximum point redemption liability is reduced over time as points are redeemed or as points expire unused. If points do not have an expiration date or if a company has a policy of honoring expired points, revenue might be deferred for a longer period of time, until the company is able to reliably estimate what percentage of points will ultimately be redeemed.

RELATED-PARTY SALES

Transactions reflected in financial statements are presumed to have been consummated on an arm's-length basis. This presumption is not justified when transactions are with related parties—even if the transactions are consummated on the same terms as those with unrelated parties—because the transactions may be the result of the relationship and may not have taken place without it. Accordingly, transactions with related parties require disclosure and, in certain cases, special accounting treatment.

General

In general, sales to related parties should be evaluated under the same general principles as other transactions. However, the fact that the customer is a related party can affect the judgment applied to many uncertainties that may otherwise exist in the transaction.

For example, sales to related parties with rights of return might not reasonably be expected to have the same return experience as other sales with rights of return. Therefore, reliable estimates of returns on these sales may not be available. Consignment arrangements with related parties, price protection clauses, warranties, acceptance provisions, and other uncertainties in related party transactions also warrant special consideration.

Noncontractual Terms

Every related party contract and transaction should be reviewed to determine whether, in substance, the rights and obligations (of both the customer and the vendor) are different from the rights and obligations in sales to unrelated parties.

Transactions That Lack Substance

The financial reporting system recognizes transactions when they have a substantive business purpose. Special accounting treatments are prescribed for transactions lacking a substantive business purpose.

Related party transactions should be carefully evaluated to establish the underlying business or economic rationale. For example, a sale with a limited right of return to a related party may, in substance, be an arrangement in which the "buyer" is acting as a sales agent for the "seller" or the right of return may be substantively unlimited, because the seller would accept returns from the related party beyond the contractual limitations. The accounting treatment for transactions lacking substance or a business purpose should reflect that fact, either by not recognizing the transaction at all (e.g., treat the arrangement as a shipment on consignment) or by altering the way it is treated (e.g., as one with an unlimited right of return, rather than a limited right of return).

Disclosures

The accounting literature requires specific disclosures about related party transactions. All parties in a related party transaction should ensure that the disclosures enable financial statement users to understand the magnitude of the transactions, the risks associated with them, and the reasons for them. Specific required disclosures for related party transactions are discussed in Chapter 12, "Disclosures."

SEC REGISTRANT ALERT: In early 2003, the SEC staff issued the Report Pursuant to Section 704 of the Sarbanes-Oxley Act of 2002 (Section 704 Report). In compiling the information in the Section 704 Report, the SEC staff studied enforcement actions filed during the period July 31, 1997, through July 30, 2002. One of the areas of improper accounting where a significant number of enforcement actions were brought by the SEC related to the disclosure of related party transactions. The SEC staff noted in the Section 704 Report that "Failure to disclose related party transactions hides material information from shareholders and may be an indicator of weaknesses in internal control and corporate governance procedures." This finding is a strong indication that more attention should be given to identifying and disclosing related party transactions. See Chapter 12 for a detailed discussion of required disclosures.

NONMONETARY TRANSACTIONS

A nonmonetary transaction involves an exchange of goods or services with little or no cash (or a financial instrument) changing hands. In general, any transaction in which less than 25% of the fair value is paid for with monetary consideration (i.e., cash or a financial instrument) should be considered a nonmonetary transaction. Although there are many types of nonmonetary transactions, this discussion focuses on nonmonetary transactions that may affect a company's revenues. In these cases, a company transfers products, services, or other revenue-generating items that constitute its ongoing major or central operations[3] in exchange for a nonmonetary asset. In most monetary transactions, measuring the total value of the transaction is not difficult because one of the parties in the transaction pays cash or another financial instrument. Because nonmonetary transactions involve little or no cash consideration, they raise measurement issues with respect to the value that should be assigned to the transaction.

OBSERVATION: Nonmonetary revenue transactions do not affect the timing of revenue recognition, only the amount of revenue recognized.

PRACTICE POINTER: In certain situations, purchase and sales agreements are entered into concurrently with the same party. In some cases these agreements require the transfer of cash between the parties. The substance of

---

[3] Other nonmonetary transactions may result in the recognition of a gain or loss, but not revenue. See Chapter 11, "Presentation," for a discussion of the difference between revenues and gains.

such agreements must be scrutinized to determine whether these agreements effectively represent a nonmonetary exchange transaction. For example, Company A agrees to sell $1,000,000 of inventory to Company B. Company B must make a payment to Company A in the amount of $1,000,000. At the same time, Company A agrees to purchase $1,000,000 of inventory from Company B. Company A must make a payment to Company B in the amount of $1,000,000. The sales and purchase agreements in this example effectively represent a nonmonetary transaction. The fact that cash was exchanged between the parties is meaningless in this transaction.

SEC REGISTRANT ALERT: Round-trip transactions have received a significant amount of attention from the SEC staff. Round-trip transactions were an area of focus in the SEC staff's Report Pursuant to Section 704 of the Sarbanes-Oxley Act of 2002 (Section 704 Report), issued in early 2003. The SEC staff studied enforcement actions filed during the period July 31, 1997, through July 30, 2002. In addition, round-trip transactions have also been a focus in recent SEC staff speeches. The SEC staff characterizes round-trip transactions in the Section 704 Report as transactions that "involve simultaneous pre-arranged sales transactions often of the same product in order to create a false impression of business activity and revenue." The SEC staff cited a number of enforcement actions in the Section 704 Report where registrants inappropriately used round-trip transactions to boost revenue. Essentially, the types of round-trip transactions identified by the SEC staff in the Section 704 Report should be treated as nonmonetary transactions. Nonmonetary transactions that lack substance should not result in the recognition of revenue. Registrants should carefully consider the accounting for such transactions and provide appropriate disclosure.

LISTING OF APPLICABLE LITERATURE

ASC	ASC Topic/Subtopic	Publication	Subject
N/A	N/A	CON-5	Recognition and Measurement in Financial Statements of Business Enterprises
845-10	Nonmonetary Transactions/Overall	APB-29 and FAS-153	Nonmonetary Transactions
845-10-30-17	Nonmonetary Transactions/Overall	EITF 93-11	Barter Transactions Involving Barter Credits
605-20-25	Revenue Recognition/ Products	EITF 99-17	Accounting for Advertising Barter Transactions

ASC	ASC Topic/Subtopic	Publication	Subject
505-50	Equity/Equity-Based Payments to Nonemployees	EITF 00-8	Accounting by a Grantee for an Equity Instrument to Be Received in Conjunction with Providing Goods or Services
845-10-15-6	Nonmonetary Transactions	EITF 04-13	Accounting for Purchases and Sales of Inventory with the Same Counterparty

Basic Accounting Model

The first question that arises in a nonmonetary sale is whether any revenue should be recognized, as it is not clear that the "realized or realizable" criterion (see Chapter 3, "General Principles") can be met. CON-5 states:

> If product, services, or other assets are exchanged for nonmonetary assets that are not readily convertible into cash, revenues . . . may be recognized on the basis that they have been earned and the transaction is completed. Recognition . . . depends on the provision that the fair values involved can be determined within reasonable limits (CON-5, par. 84f).

An exchange (or exchange transaction) is a reciprocal transfer between entities where one entity obtains assets or services or incurs a liability by transferring assets or services or incurring other obligations to the other entity (ASC 845-10-20) (APB-29, par. 3(c)).

Consistent with the guidance in CON-5, revenue is generally recognized in a nonmonetary transaction if the fair values of the goods and services exchanged in the transaction can be determined. U.S. GAAP requires recognition of non-monetary transactions at the fair value of the assets or services given up or those received, whichever is more readily determinable (ASC 845-10-30-1) (APB-29, par. 18). There are, however, exceptions to this treatment that may be relevant in a nonmonetary revenue transaction.

The recorded amount (carrying amount adjusted for impairment) of the nonmonetary asset(s) surrendered, rather than the fair values of the assets exchanged, must be used to measure a nonmonetary exchange under any of the following conditions (ASC 845-10-30-3) (APB-29, par. 20):

- Neither the fair value of the asset or service received nor the fair value of the asset or service given up is readily determinable.

- The exchange is of product or property held for sale in the ordinary course of business for product or property that will be sold in the same line of business to customers other than the parties to the exchange.

- The transaction has no commercial substance.

OBSERVATION: If these exceptions did not exist, companies could artificially inflate earnings with transfers of inventory. Consider the situation where Company A transfers inventory to Company B in exchange for Company B's inventory. Both companies plan on selling the inventory they receive in the exchange to third-party customers in the normal course of their businesses. In the absence of these exceptions, both companies would be grossing up revenues and cost of sales by exchanging inventory for inventory. Grossing up these amounts is not appropriate if the exchange does not result in sales to third-party customers or change expected future cash flows.

PRACTICE POINTER: Even in a nonmonetary exchange that is to be recognized based on the historical cost of the asset given up, a loss should be recognized if the transaction indicates that the fair value of the asset is less than its recorded amount. The loss in these instances is required to be recorded because the market price of the inventory has been shown to be less than its cost (ASC 330-10-35) (ARB-43, Chapter 4, Statement 7).

DISCLOSURE ALERT: See Chapter 12, "Disclosures," for information about disclosures required for nonmonetary transactions.

Commercial Substance

An exchange with commercial substance is a transaction that is expected to significantly change the entity's future cash flows. A transaction has a substantive effect on the entity's expected future cash if either of the following conditions are satisfied (ASC 845-10-30-4) (APB-29, par. 21):

1. The amount, timing, and risk of the future cash flows of the assets surrendered and those of the asset(s) received are significantly different.

2. The entity-specific values of the assets surrendered and those of the asset(s) received are significantly different and that difference is significant relative to the fair values of the assets exchanged. (CON-7 defines entity-specific values with reference to the economics and business activities of a specific entity (CON-7, par. 24(b).)

Inventory-for-Inventory Exchange

Purchase and sale transactions with the same counterparty are required to be combined for the purpose of applying ASC 845-10 (APB-29) in certain circumstances.

1. Two or more inventory purchase and sales transactions with the same counterparty that were entered into in contemplation of each other, and

2. One transaction is *legally* contingent upon the performance of another inventory transaction with the same counterparty (ASC 845-10-15-6).

The effect of combining these transactions is that they are likely to be looked at as an inventory-for-inventory exchange that must be recorded at the carrying amount of the inventory transferred. The EITF noted that the issuance of invoices and the exchange of offsetting cash consideration does not affect this consensus. Where a transaction is not legally contingent upon the performance of another inventory transaction, certain factors (the list is not exhaustive and no single factor is likely to be determinative) may indicate that the two transactions were entered into in contemplation of each other (ASC 845-10-25-4):

- The transactions between the counterparties are subject to a specific (as opposed to a master netting arrangement) legal right of offset of obligations;

- These transactions are entered into the inventory purchase and sales transactions simultaneously;

- Inventory purchase and sales transactions were entered into at off-market terms; and

- There is relative certainty that the reciprocal inventory transactions will occur.

A transaction in which one entity transfers finished goods in a nonmonetary exchange for raw materials or work-in-process inventory within the same line of business does not qualify as an exchange transaction that facilitates sales to customers for the transferor of finished goods (ASC 845-10-30-15) (see paragraph 20(b) of APB Opinion 29). As a result, this type of transaction should be measured at fair value if:

- Fair value is determinable within reasonable limits; and

- The transaction has commercial substance (as discussed above).

The counterparties are required to disclose the revenues and costs (or gains and losses) related to this class of inventory transactions. All other nonmonetary exchanges of inventory in the same line of business must be reported at the carrying amount of the inventory transferred.

ILLUSTRATION: EXCHANGE OF INVENTORY FOR FIXED ASSET

Facts: Manufacturer A and Manufacturer B enter into a transaction where Manufacturer A provides inventory to Manufacturer B in exchange for a fixed asset that it intends to use in its production process. No cash or other monetary consideration is exchanged in this transaction. The readily determinable fair value of the inventory is $25,000 and it is recorded on Manufacturer A's books at $20,000.

Accounting: As the transaction is not an inventory-for-inventory exchange and the fair value can be readily determined, Manufacturer A should account for this transaction based on the fair value of the inventory surrendered. This results in the following journal entries being recorded by Manufacturer A upon consummation of the transaction:

Journal Entry	Debit	Credit
Fixed assets	$25,000	
Revenue		$25,000
Cost of goods sold	$20,000	
Inventory		$20,000

Fair Value Considerations

To account for a revenue-generating nonmonetary transaction based on fair value, the fair value must be readily determinable within reasonable limits (ASC 845-10-30-1). All evidence should be considered to determine the fair value of the transaction. In most cases, a nonmonetary transaction involving inventory or services that a company sells in its major ongoing central line of business can be valued based on the normal selling prices of such items. Other evidence might include quoted market prices or appraisals of the assets received in the transaction.

However, companies involved in a nonmonetary transaction should also consider whether the prices charged to others are indeed relevant measures of the value of the items exchanged in the instant transaction. For example, the parties should consider whether the products or services in the exchange are really usable to their full extent by the counterparties to the arrangement. If not, it may be inappropriate to value the transaction based on prices charged to customers who can use the products or services more effectively. In some instances, transactions in which it is not clear that the counterparties can actually use the products exchanged should be recorded the historical cost of the assets surrendered as transactions that lack commercial substance. Even if the transaction is substantive, if major uncertainties exist related to recoverability of the fair value assigned to an asset received in a nonmonetary transaction, such fair value should not be considered readily determinable within reasonable limits (ASC 845-10-30-8).

One common type of nonmonetary transaction involves an exchange of advertising space. This is more common among Internet-based companies, but is observed in other industries as well. Companies engaging in advertising barter transactions should recognize revenue (and expense) at the fair value of the advertising space given up in the exchange transaction, provided that the fair value of that advertising space is determinable. If the fair value is not determinable, the transaction is recorded at the book value of the advertising space given up, which will generally be zero. The EITF has provided guidance on the development of fair value evidence. Fair value of advertising space surrendered must be based on recent historical cash transactions for the sale of similar advertising space to unrelated third parties (ASC 605-20-25-14 through 25-18).

Historical cash transactions. Only cash, marketable securities, or other consideration readily convertible to cash transactions occurring within the last six months may be considered for purposes of determining the fair value of the advertising surrendered. In addition, a company should consider whether there are any internal or external factors that would suggest that six months is too long of a period to look back to for purposes of finding representative cash transactions. Once a historical cash transaction has been used to substantiate the fair value of one advertising barter transaction, it may not be used to substantiate the fair value of another advertising barter transaction.

Similar advertising. Advertising space surrendered in a nonmonetary transaction is deemed similar to advertising space sold in a cash transaction, only if both advertising spaces (ASC 605-20-25-17):

1. Use the same media (e.g., a nonmonetary transaction where space is surrendered);

2. Use the same vehicle (e.g., a nonmonetary transaction where advertising space in Newspaper A is surrendered is not considered similar to a monetary transaction where advertising space in Newspaper B is surrendered); and

3. Are similar with respect to:

   a. Circulation, exposure, or saturation within an intended market;

   b. Timing (time of day, day of week, daily, weekly, 24 hours a day/7 days a week, and season of the year);

   c. Prominence (page on web site, section of periodical, location on page, and size of advertisement);

   d. Demographics of readers, viewers, or customers; and

   e. Duration (length of time advertising will be displayed).

DISCLOSURE ALERT: See Chapter 12, "Disclosures," for information about required disclosures.

EXAMPLE: BARTER TRANSACTIONS

Sinclair Broadcast Group, Inc. Form 10-K—Fiscal Year Ended December 31, 2010

Certain program contracts provide for the exchange of advertising airtime in lieu of cash payments for the rights to such programming. The revenues realized from station barter arrangements are recorded as the programs are aired at the estimated fair value of the advertising airtime given in exchange for the program rights. Program service arrangements are accounted for as station barter arrangements, however, network affiliation programming is excluded from these calculations. Revenues are recorded as revenues realized from station barter arrangements and the corresponding expenses are recorded as expenses recognized from station barter arrangements. In conjunction with the 2009 termination of our MyNetworkTV affiliation agreements described in *Note 10. Commitments and Contingencies*, in September 2009 our relationship with MyNetworkTV changed to a program service arrangement and is accounted for as a station barter arrangement.

We broadcast certain customers' advertising in exchange for equipment, merchandise and services. The estimated fair value of the equipment, merchandise or services received is recorded as deferred barter costs and the corresponding obligation to broadcast advertising is recorded as deferred barter revenues. The deferred barter costs are expensed or capitalized as they are used, consumed or received and are included in station production expenses and station selling, general and administrative expenses, as applicable. Deferred barter revenues are recognized as the related advertising is aired and are recorded in revenues realized from station barter arrangements.

Barter Credits

Nonmonetary transactions may involve barter credits that entitle the holder to receive goods or services in the future. The entity that redeems the barter credits may be the counterparty to the nonmonetary transaction or it may be a party whose business is operating barter credit programs. The basic nonmonetary transaction accounting model should be applied to nonmonetary transactions involving barter credits. Special considerations when applying this model to nonmonetary transactions involving barter credits include (ASC 845-10-30-17 through 30-19):

- A presumption exists that the fair value of the nonmonetary asset exchanged is not greater than its carrying amount. This presumption can only be overcome if there is persuasive evidence to the contrary.

- The fair value of the nonmonetary asset in the transaction is generally considered to be more determinable than the fair value of the barter credits. The exception to this is if the barter credit can be exchanged for cash or for items with independent quoted market prices (e.g., oil, gold).

- To record the transaction at fair value, there must be the expectation that the barter credits will be redeemed in a reasonable period of time and that the party that will provide goods or services upon the redemption of the barter credits will be in existence to honor its commitment.

ILLUSTRATION: EXCHANGE OF INVENTORY FOR BARTER CREDITS

Facts: Manufacturer C receives barter credits from Company Z in exchange for inventory. The carrying value of the inventory is $5,000. The fair value of the inventory is $4,500. Manufacturer C has received barter credits in previous nonmonetary transactions and has always redeemed these barter credits after a short period of time. The barter credits may not be redeemed for cash. Assume for purposes of this example that the barter credits will not be redeemed for inventory to be sold in the same line of business.

Accounting: Manufacturer C should account for this transaction based on the fair value of the inventory exchanged for the barter credits. This results in the following journal entries being recorded by Manufacturer A upon consummation of the transaction:

Journal Entry	Debit	Credit
Impairment loss on inventory	$ 500	
Inventory		$ 500
Cost of goods sold	$4,500	
Inventory		$4,500
Barter credits	$4,500	
Revenue		$4,500

Once barter credits have been recorded as part of a nonmonetary transaction, an impairment loss on the remaining amount of barter credits should be recognized if either (1) the fair value of the barter credits drops below their carrying amount or (2) the holder of the barter credits does not believe it is probable that it will redeem the barter credits (ASC 845-10-30-19).

Receipt of Some Monetary Consideration

When both monetary and nonmonetary consideration is received in a transaction whose accounting should be based on fair values, the monetary consideration paid or received becomes part of the fair value determination.

When both monetary and nonmonetary consideration is received in a transaction whose accounting would otherwise not be based on fair values, the effect of the monetary consideration on the accounting for the transaction depends on the magnitude of the monetary consideration. As noted earlier, if the monetary consideration received in such a transaction is 25% or more of the fair value of the transaction, then the transaction should be accounted for as a monetary transaction. Monetary transactions are recorded at fair value.

If the monetary consideration is less than 25%, its effects depend on whether the company receives or pays the monetary consideration. If the company receives monetary consideration, the transaction should, in substance, be treated as a monetary transaction (at fair value) to the extent of the monetary consideration, and a nonmonetary transaction (at historical cost) for the balance. If the company is paying monetary consideration, it should not recognize any income. The recorded amount of the asset received in the nonmonetary transaction is based on the monetary consideration paid in the transaction plus the carrying amount of the asset surrendered in the transaction (ASC 845-10-30-6) (APB-29, par. 22).

ILLUSTRATION: MONETARY CONSIDERATION LESS THAN 25% OF TRANSACTION'S FAIR VALUE

Facts: Manufacturer A and Manufacturer B enter into a transaction involving the exchange of inventory. Manufacturer A and Manufacturer B operate in the same line of business and plan on selling the inventory received in the exchange to end-users. Additional facts related to the transaction are as follows:

	Manufacturer	
	A	B
Fair value of inventory provided	$15,000	$12,000
Fair value of inventory received	$12,000	$15,000
Recorded amount of inventory provided	$8,000	$7,000
Cash consideration received	$3,000	None
Cash consideration paid	None	$3,000

Accounting: Since this is an inventory-for-inventory exchange in the same line of business and the monetary consideration is less than 25% of the fair value of the transaction, it should not be accounted for as a monetary transaction.

Since Manufacturer A is receiving monetary consideration, it should account for the transaction as follows:

Monetary consideration received	$ 3,000	$ 3,000
Fair value of transaction	15,000	
Percentage of the transaction that is monetary	20%	
Recorded cost of inventory transferred	8,000	
Cost of sales for the portion of the inventory "sold" for monetary consideration		1,600
Profit to be recognized		$ 1,400

Journal Entry	Debit	Credit
Cost of Sales	$1,600	
Inventory		$1,600
Cash	$3,000	
Revenue		$3,000

These entries result in the inventory received by Manufacturer A having an initial carrying amount of $6,400. Manufacturer A only records revenue to the extent of cash consideration since this is an inventory-for-inventory exchange.

Since Manufacturer B is paying monetary consideration, it should account for the transaction as follows:

Journal Entry	Debit	Credit
Inventory	$3,000	
Cash		$3,000

No revenue or cost of sales results from this transaction for Manufacturer B since it is an inventory-for-inventory exchange where Manufacturer B is paying cash consideration.

EXAMPLE: NONMONETARY TRANSACTION ACCOUNTING POLICY

FreightCar America, Inc. Form 10-K—Fiscal Year Ended December 31, 2009

Pursuant to ASC 845, *Nonmonetary Transactions* (formerly Accounting Principles Board ("APB") Opinion No. 29, *Accounting for Non-Monetary Transactions*, and Emerging Issues Task Force ("EITF") Issue No. 01-2, *Interpretations of APB No. 29*, revenue is recognized for the entire transaction on transactions involving used railcar trades when the cash consideration is in excess of 25% of the total transaction value and on a pro-rata portion of the total transaction value when the cash consideration is less than 25% of the total transaction.

Payment in the Form of Equity Securities

One type of nonmonetary transaction that is somewhat common is the sale of products, services, or intellectual property for equity of the customer. In many cases, this transaction raises no questions other than those that exist in most nonmonetary transactions. However, an additional question that arises in certain sales for equity securities is what date to use in measuring the fair value of the equity instruments received. The question often arises because the instrument only vests as performance occurs or upon its completion. Thus, until that point, there is some question as to whether the vendor will ever receive the benefits embodied in the equity instrument.

In this situation, the vendor should measure the fair value of the equity instruments as of the earlier of the following dates (ASC 505-50-30-18):

1. The date the parties come to a mutual understanding of the terms of the equity-based compensation arrangement and a performance commitment is reached. A performance commitment is a commitment under which performance by the seller to earn the equity instruments is probable because of sufficiently large disincentives for nonperformance. Neither the forfeiture of the equity instruments, nor the ability to sue for nonperformance, in and of themselves, represents a sufficiently large disincentive.

2. The date the vendor completes the performance necessary to earn the equity instruments (i.e., the vesting date).

If, after the measurement date described above, the quantity or any of the terms of the equity instruments are dependent on the achievement of performance conditions, the initial measurement should be the one with the lowest value possible, as any amount above that would not be considered fixed or determinable. Changes in the fair value of the equity instrument that result from an adjustment to the instrument upon the achievement of a performance condition should be measured as additional revenue from the transaction by calculating the increase in the fair value of the instrument due to the changes (ASC 505-50-35-14).

OBSERVATION: The instruments in these transactions may also experience changes in fair value after the measurement date for various other reasons. Changes in fair value of the equity instruments after the measurement date unrelated to the achievement of performance conditions should be accounted for in accordance with the relevant literature on the accounting and reporting for investments in equity instruments, and should not affect the amount of revenue recognized.

DISCLOSURE ALERT: See Chapter 12, "Disclosures," for information about required disclosures.

SEC REGISTRANT ALERT: As discussed earlier, round-trip transactions are receiving a significant amount of attention by the SEC staff. One round-trip transaction discussed by the SEC staff in a speech in December 2002 involved a vendor delivering cash and products or services and concurrently receiving cash and an equity interest in the customer. The substance of this transaction may be that the vendor is delivering products or services in exchange for an equity interest. If this is the substance of the transaction, the vendor should (a) record the investment in the counter-party at the fair value of either the shares received or the goods or services sold, whichever is more readily determinable, (b) record the net cash outlay or receipt, and (c) recognize as revenue the difference between the value of the investment received and the net cash outlay. The SEC staff has been clear that the substance of round-trip transactions should govern form. To the extent a registrant enters into round-trip transactions, the accounting for such transactions should be carefully considered and the details of such transactions should be appropriately disclosed.

BUSINESS COMBINATIONS

Business combinations almost invariably give rise to many accounting issues. From determining the fair values of the assets acquired to accounting for contingencies to aligning accounting and reporting systems, business combinations are almost always a headache for the accounting department of the acquirer. There are multiple books much longer than this one that provide guidance on accounting for business combinations. However, several revenue-related issues that are common in business combinations merit some discussion here.

Accounting Policies and Procedures

It is not uncommon for the acquirer and acquiree in a business combination to have previously used different accounting policies for similar transactions. Perhaps more commonly, the acquirer and acquiree will have the same policy, but apply that policy in a different manner. In the revenue area, this can appears in many ways. For example:

- The two entities may have different thresholds for determining whether "collectibility is reasonably assured."

- The acquiree may base its measurement of progress under the Proportional Performance method on a different factor that the acquirer.

- The acquirer and acquiree may use different shipping terms on products, affecting when title transfers and therefore when revenue should be recognized.

- The two entities may have different policies with relation to which costs of revenue transactions are deferred.

- Different processes used by the two entities may make historical experience from before the combination not predictive of post-combination events in areas such as returns, breakage, etc.

The potential examples are endless. However, all of these differences need to be identified quickly, because it is generally inappropriate for a company to have different accounting policies across the organization, and it is also inappropriate for a company to make different judgments about the effect of certain factors based simply on whether the factor shows up in the pre-acquisition acquirer or target's operations.

Deferred Revenue of the Target

The assets and liabilities of the target company are, with only a few exceptions, recognized at fair value on the acquisition date by the acquirer. One of those liabilities to be recognized might very well be deferred revenue, which should be recognized if the combined company will need to complete performance of an obligation taken on by the target before the acquisition. In most cases, the fair value of the deferred revenue liability will be very small, particularly if payment for the goods or services has not yet been provided. In that case, the fair value of the obligation taken on in the acquisition would take into account the right to payment as well. Presuming that prices had not changed significantly since the target entered into the contract, the value of the obligation and the value of the right to payment are likely to almost completely offset.

However, in some instances, the deferred revenue liability could be significant, particularly if payment was received in advance by the target before the acquisition. In such a situation, it is important that the acquirer ensure that a deferred revenue liability is only established in purchase accounting for the fair value of the remaining performance, which may be very different than the deferred revenue recorded on the target's books. In fact, the deferred revenue balance recorded by the target is essentially irrelevant in determining the appropriate deferred revenue liability to be recorded by the acquirer in its initial accounting for the acquisition.

A few more common situations in which a significant change from the target's deferred revenue balance may be necessary include:

- If the target has partially performed on a contract, but recognized no revenue because the delivered items do not have stand-alone value, only the fair value of the obligation to provide the undelivered items should be recorded.

- If the target had deferred revenue due to a concern about collectibility or because the fee was not fixed or determinable even though the goods or services had already been provided, no deferred revenue should be recorded in the initial accounting for the acquired entity, as there is no remaining performance obligation.

- Up-front fees in licensing, development, or long-term supply agreements typically must be deferred by the seller and recognized over the license, development or supply period. If a business combination occurs at a significantly later date, the fair value of the obligation to provide services is unlikely to bear any relation to the remaining amount of deferred revenue on the target's books.

In many of these situations, the acquirer will record less deferred revenue in its initial accounting for the combination than the target had recorded pre-acquisition. As a result, some revenue will essentially never be recognized, but will essentially disappear in the accounting for the combination.

EXAMPLES: DEFERRED REVENUE IN A BUSINESS COMBINATION

Deltek, Inc. Form 10-K—Fiscal Year Ended December 31, 2010

As a component of our acquisitions, we acquired maintenance and subscription obligations (and the associated deferred revenue) with our acquisitions. We valued acquired deferred revenue based on estimates of the cost of providing solution support services plus a reasonable profit margin. Upon each acquisition, the acquired deferred revenue balances were recorded at an average of 40% of their book value on the date of acquisition. This reduced deferred revenue amount is recognized as revenue over the remaining contractual period of the obligation, generally no more than one year from the date of acquisition. Changes in the estimates used in determining these valuations could result in more or less revenue being recorded.

ANSYS, Inc. Form 10-K—Fiscal Year Ended December 31, 2010

In valuing deferred revenue on the Ansoft balance sheet as of the acquisition date, the Company applied the fair value provisions applicable to the accounting for business combinations. Although this purchase accounting requirement had no impact on the Company's business or cash flow, the Company's reported revenue under accounting principles generally accepted in the United States, primarily for the first 12 months post-acquisition, was less than the sum of what would otherwise have been reported by Ansoft and ANSYS absent the acquisition. Acquired deferred revenue of $7.5 million was recorded on the Ansoft opening balance sheet. This amount was approximately $23.5 million lower than the historical carrying value. There was no meaningful impact on reported revenue for the year ended December 31, 2010. The impact on reported revenue for the year ended December 31, 2009 was $1.1 million for lease license revenue and $7.0 million for maintenance revenue. The impact on reported revenue for the year ended December 31, 2008 was $1.7 million for lease license revenue and $13.0 million for maintenance revenue.

****

Purchase accounting for deferred revenue and its related tax impact. The Company acquired Ansoft Corporation on July 31, 2008. In accordance with the fair value provisions applicable to the accounting for business combinations, acquired deferred revenue of approximately $7.5 million was recorded on the opening balance sheet, which was approximately $23.5 million lower than the historical carrying value. Although this purchase accounting requirement had no impact on the Company's business or cash flow, it adversely impacted the Company's reported GAAP revenue primarily for the first twelve months post-acquisition. In order to provide investors with financial information that facilitates comparison of both historical and future results, the Company has provided non-GAAP financial measures which exclude the impact of the purchase accounting adjustment. The Company believes that this non-GAAP financial adjustment is useful to investors because it allows investors to (a) evaluate the effectiveness of the methodology and information used by management in its financial and operational decision-making and (b) compare past and future reports of financial results of the Company as the revenue reduction related to acquired deferred revenue will not recur when related annual lease licenses and software maintenance contracts are renewed in future periods.

CHAPTER 9
CONTRACT ACCOUNTING

CONTENTS

SURVEY OF APPLICABLE LITERATURE

Accounting for construction contracts is one of the few areas in which a comprehensive model for revenue recognition exists. The basic model was first provided in 1955. However, there was not much guidance on the application of the basic model or its scope. Standard-setters eventually determined that ARB-45 had not kept pace with the changing times and additional guidance was needed. As a result, SOP 81-1 was issued in 1981 and applies to both construction-type and certain production-type contracts.

The audit and accounting guides for construction contractors (AAG-CON) and federal government contractors[1] (AAG-FGC) provide supplemental application guidance.

LISTING OF APPLICABLE LITERATURE

ASC	ASC Topic/Subtopic	Publication	Subject
912	Contractors—Federal Government	ARB-43, Ch. 11 and AAG-FGC	Government Contracts
605-35	Revenue Recognition/Construction-Type and Production-Type Contracts	ARB-45 and SOP 81-1	Performance of Construction-Type and Certain Production-Type Contracts
450-20	Contingencies/Loss Contingencies	FAS-5	Loss Contingencies
985-605	Software/Revenue Recognition	SOP 97-2	Software Revenue Recognition
605-25	Revenue Recognition/Services	EITF 00-21	Revenue Arrangements with Multiple Deliverables
910	Contractors—Construction	AAG-CON	Audit and Accounting Guide for Construction Contractors
210-10-S99	Balance Sheet/Overall	REG S-X, Rule 5-02	Financial Statement Requirements, Commercial and Industrial Companies, Balance Sheets

OVERVIEW

Throughout this book, one of the most important questions affecting the timing of revenue recognition has been whether to use the Completed Performance or Proportional Performance model to determine when revenue has been earned. As noted in Chapter 3, "General Principles," product sales are generally analyzed

---

[1] This audit and accounting guide is no longer published.

under the Completed Performance model, such that revenue is not considered earned until the product is complete and delivered to the customer.

However, certain product transactions have characteristics that may make the use of the Proportional Performance model appropriate. This category of transactions calls for the delivery of a product that is built or constructed to the customer's specifications, rather than through the vendor's normal manufacturing and operating processes. Products built or constructed to customer specifications are generally not useful to the vendor apart from fulfilling the applicable contract, and the customer often has rights related to the products being constructed even before they are completed. Revenue in these transactions is considered earned during production, rather than only upon delivery of the completed product, as long as certain conditions are met.

The contract accounting literature generally specifies that costs should be recognized along with revenue on a proportional (or ratable) basis throughout the term of the contract. This is very much unlike other applications of the Proportional Performance model where costs are recognized as incurred.

Also, unlike other areas of the accounting literature, ASC 605-35 includes very specific guidance on issues such as changes in estimates and changes in the terms of contracts.

SCOPE

Because of the significant differences in the way revenue and costs are recognized under contract accounting, it is important to carefully evaluate contracts to determine which guidance applies. Revenue from a product sale that does not fall within the scope of ASC 605-35 may not be recognized under a Proportional Performance model. Further, while revenue on a service transaction is typically recognized under a Proportional Performance model, costs on a contract that does not fall within the scope of the contract accounting literature should be recognized as incurred, rather than smoothed over the contract's term.

The guidance in this chapter applies to construction-type and certain production-type contracts where facilities are built, goods are manufactured, or certain defined, related services are performed by a contractor[2] to customer specifications. However, contracts where a company uses its standardized manufacturing processes or regular marketing channels generally do not fall within the scope of ASC 605-35 even if the subject of the contract is manufactured or performed by the company to customer specifications. This includes sales of goods from inventory or from homogeneous continuing production processes. Service contracts, other than those related to the construction industry, do not fall within the scope of ASC 605-35.

SEC REGISTRANT ALERT: As discussed above, it is generally not appropriate to analogize to ASC 605-35 with respect to linking revenue and cost

---

[2] "Contractor" will be used throughout this chapter to describe the selling party in a contract that falls within the scope of this chapter's guidance.

recognition. In a December 2002 speech, the SEC staff stressed that percentage-of-completion accounting should not be applied to service contracts that are outside the scope of ASC 605-35. Service contracts that fall within the scope of ASC 605-35 are limited to contracts for architectural or engineering design services and construction consulting services (ASC 605-35-15-3).

Arrangements that fall within the scope of ASC 605-35 must be supported with legally enforceable, binding agreements between the customer and contractor.[3] The duration of a contract (i.e., the period of time to construct, produce, or provide) is not a defining factor for purposes of determining whether a contract falls within the scope of ASC 605-35. However, it may be a factor in determining whether the percentage-of-completion or completed-contract method should be used to account for the contract.

Examples of contracts that fall within the scope of this chapter include (ASC 605-35-15-3):

- Construction contracts, such as those of general building, heavy earth moving, dredging, demolition, design-build contractors, and specialty contractors (e.g., mechanical, electrical, or paving) and related service contracts, such as contracts for construction consulting services (e.g., agency contracts or construction management agreements), and contracts performed by architects, engineers, or architectural or engineering design firms.
- Contracts to design and build ships and transport vessels.
- Contracts to design, develop, manufacture, or modify complex aerospace or electronic equipment to a customer's specifications or to provide services related to the performance of such contracts.

Software and software-related arrangements that involve significant production, modification, or customization of software (ASC 985-605-15-3) are also accounted for under the guidance of ASC 605-35. See Chapter 10, "Software—A Complete Model" for a comprehensive discussion of this class of arrangements.

As noted previously, contracts outside the scope of ASC 605-35-15-6 include those involving the sale of products produced using the contractor's standardized manufacturing process (even if produced to the customer's specifications) and marketed using the contractor's regular marketing channels.

OBSERVATION: Understanding the nature of the contract and determining whether or not the contract falls within the scope of ASC 605-35 is an important exercise because it could have a significant effect on the recognition of the related revenues and costs. A contract to build a piece of equipment that falls within the scope of ASC 605-35 may be accounted for using a Proportional Performance model (percentage-of-completion method) resulting in the recognition of revenues as work is performed, and recognition of costs in proportion to revenues. However, if this contract is outside the scope of ASC 605-35, the

[3] This is equivalent to the "persuasive evidence of an arrangement" condition that is generally required in order to recognize revenue on other transactions.

related revenue and costs may be recognized only at a single point in time under a Completed Performance model. Whether an arrangement is within the scope of ASC 605-35 also has other important consequences for the amount and timing of revenue (e.g., different treatment of incentives) and cost (or, more precisely, expense) recognition.

ACCOUNTING METHODS

ASC 605-35 describes two accounting methods—the percentage-of-completion method and the completed-contract method. Other methods, such as those where revenue is recognized based on progress billings or receipts and costs are recognized when incurred, are not acceptable. Under the percentage-of-completion method, contract revenues and contract costs should be recognized using a Proportional Performance model (i.e., as the contractor performs under the contract). By contrast, the completed-contract method specifies that contract revenues and contract costs should be recognized under a Completed Performance model (i.e., when the contract is complete or substantially complete). These two methods are not interchangeable for the same set of facts and circumstances. The decision about which method to apply must be based on an analysis of the arrangement using the specific criteria in ASC 605-35; the determination is not a policy choice to be made by the contractor.

Circumstances of Use—Percentage-of-Completion

Percentage-of-completion is considered the model that best reflects the economics of most construction contracts. This is because, while not required in order to use percentage-of-completion accounting, these contracts (as well as certain other contracts) generally transfer ownership to the customer over time, as the asset is being built or manufactured. The percentage-of-completion method generally synchronizes revenue recognition and transfer of ownership. Furthermore, the contractor is usually compensated as the work is performed (through progress payments).

The percentage-of-completion method applies to contracts with the following characteristics (ASC 605-35-25-56 and 25-57):

- The contractor can consistently make reasonably dependable estimates of contract revenues, contract costs, and progress towards completion.
- The contract spells out the specific rights and obligations of the customer and contractor, the contractor's compensation, and settlement terms.[4]
- The customer and contractor are both expected to satisfy their contractual obligations.

Ability to Make Estimates

The presumption is that the contractor can make reasonably dependable estimates in order to enter into profitable contracts and sustain its business model.

---

[4] This point is generally consistent with the "fixed or determinable fee" condition generally required to recognize revenue on other transactions.

This presumption can only be overcome if persuasive evidence exists to support the conclusion that it cannot make such estimates (ASC 605-35-25-58).

OBSERVATION: When the ability to make estimates can affect revenue recognition, the accounting literature generally presumes that estimates cannot be made, unless persuasive evidence indicates they are reliable. As noted above, the contract accounting literature begins from a different perspective. The principle is the same—estimates should only be used if they are judged to be reasonable and reliable. However, the threshold of reliability for estimates used in percentage-of-completion is lower, resulting in estimates being used more often than they are in other situations.

Estimates, by their very nature, may deviate from actual results. However, when the deviation is consistently significant, the contractor should evaluate whether the estimates are reasonably dependable. This evaluation should attempt to (1) establish why the estimates are consistently and significantly different from actual results and (2) correct the estimation process, before discontinuing use of the percentage-of-completion method.

A contractor that can otherwise make reasonably dependable estimates may not be able to do so in isolated instances due to the existence of particular circumstances that inhibit the ability to make estimates on individual contracts. These "inherent hazards" may cast doubt on the ability of a customer or contractor to satisfy obligations under the contract and are different from normal recurring business risks. Examples of inherent hazards include contracts where completion is questionable due to external factors (e.g., pending legislation or litigation) and contracts where the item being manufactured or built is physically at risk due to external developments (e.g., condemnation or expropriation). Given the unique nature of inherent hazards, there must be specific, persuasive evidence that the existence of such a hazard prevents the development of reasonably dependable estimates (ASC 605-35-25-65).

Circumstances of Use—Completed Contract

The completed-contract method may be used where the results would not differ materially from using the percentage-of-completion method, and it must be used where reasonably dependable estimates of contract revenues, contract costs, or progress towards completion cannot be made (ASC 605-35-25-90 through 25-93).

A short-term contract is a situation where the application of the completed-contract method would not result in a materially different outcome from using the percentage-of-completion method. Therefore, if the contractor enters into predominantly short-term contracts, adopting the completed-contract method as its accounting policy would be appropriate. However, the contractor should carefully evaluate the effect of this reporting policy decision on interim financial statements.

When the completed-contract method is used because the contractor cannot make reasonably dependable estimates of contract revenues, contract costs, or progress toward completion, this method must be applied for the duration of the contract. As a result, the contractor may not change to the percentage-of-completion method if reasonably dependable estimates of contract revenues, contract costs, and progress toward completion can subsequently be made.

Basic Accounting Policy

A company will generally determine its basic accounting model for contracts within the scope of ASC 605-35 based on its standard agreements. However, a company may subsequently enter into a contract that is unique or atypical. In these situations, the company should consider whether a departure from its basic accounting model is necessary to account for the unique or atypical facts and circumstances. If a departure from its basic accounting model is necessary for such a contract, the contractor should disclose that departure (ASC 605-35-25-61; 605-35-25-95; 605-35-50-3; 605-35-50-5).

OBSERVATION: A departure from the usual accounting model to account for a unique or atypical contract does not constitute a change in accounting policy. The contractor is merely using a different accounting policy for a different type of contract.

Other factors that may cause a contractor to depart from its basic accounting model include (1) the determination that reasonably dependable estimates cannot be made for a specific contract or (2) the existence of an inherent hazard related to a specific contract. These departures from the basic accounting model should also be disclosed.

EXAMPLES: COMPLETED CONTRACT METHOD—BASIC MODEL

Crown Castle International Corp. Form 10-K—Fiscal Year Ended December 31, 2009

To a lesser extent, we provide network services, such as antenna installations and subsequent augmentation, network design and site selection, site acquisition services, site development and other services. Network services revenues are generally recognized using the completed contract method. Under the completed contract method, revenues and costs for a particular project are recognized in total at the completion date. When using the completed contract method of accounting for network services revenues, we must accurately determine the completion date for the project in order to record the revenues and costs in the proper period. For antenna installations, we consider the project complete when the customer can begin transmitting its signal through the antenna. Although we don't typically incur losses on our network services because we typically enter into cost-plus profit contracts, we must also be able to estimate losses on uncompleted contracts, as such losses must be recognized as soon as they are known. We use the completed contract method for our network services projects, because our projects have a short duration (generally less than one year). We do not believe that our use of the completed contract method for network services projects produces financial position and operating results that differ substantially from the percentage-of-completion method.

Intelligent Systems Corporation Form 10-K—Fiscal Year Ended December 31, 2010

At present, we use the completed contract method to account for our contracts as we do not have an adequate historical basis on which to prepare reliable estimates of percentage-of-completion for these contracts. Moreover, there are inherent hazards with early software implementations, such as changes in customer requirements or software defects, that make estimates unreliable.

Accordingly, software revenue related to the license and the specified service elements (except for PCS) in the initial contract are recognized at the completion of the contract, when (i) there are no material uncertainties regarding customer acceptance, (ii) cancellation provisions, if any, have expired and (iii) there are no significant obligations remaining.

COMBINING OR SEGMENTING CONTRACTS

Prior to applying either the percentage-of-completion or completed-contract method, the contractor must determine the proper unit of accounting. Normally, the unit of accounting is an individual contract. However, in certain situations, it may be appropriate to combine a group of contracts and account for them as if they were a single agreement. Conversely, a situation may arise where it is appropriate to segment a contract or group of contracts into two or more units of accounting and separately account for each unit of accounting as if it were an individual contract. Specific criteria have been developed to determine when contracts should be combined or segmented.

Combining Contracts

It is generally appropriate to combine contracts when accounting for them separately would misrepresent the economic substance of the arrangements as well as the amount and timing of the earned revenues, costs of earned revenues, and gross profit. Because of this interrelationship, the combined gross profit from the contracts should be recognized as the work is performed.

The following questions (based on the criteria in ASC 605-35-25-5 through 25-8) must be considered by a contractor to determine whether contracts should be combined for accounting purposes:

1. *Were the contracts negotiated as a single package in the same economic environment with an overall profit objective?* The time period between the negotiation of individual contracts should be reasonably short to lead to the conclusion that they were negotiated in tandem. If not, the likelihood that the contracts were negotiated in the same economic environment is diminished.

2. *Do the contracts, in essence, represent an agreement to perform a single project?* The elements, phases, or units of output of a group of contracts must be interrelated and interdependent to be considered a single project. The interrelationship and interdependence should extend to the design, technology, function, or ultimate purpose or use of the output from each contract.

3. *Do the contracts require closely related construction activities with substantial common costs that cannot be separately identified with, or reasonably allocated to, the individual contracts?* Where two or more contracts have substantial

costs in common, they may, in substance, be part of the same arrangement.

4. *Are the contracts performed concurrently or in a continuous sequence under the same project management at the same location or at different locations in the same general vicinity?*

5. *Do the contracts, in substance, constitute an agreement with a single customer?* An assessment of the other conditions that must be met to combine contracts should be considered in this context. The following questions are relevant:

   a. Did the different parties negotiate the contracts together?

   b. Do the different parties operate in the same economic environment?

   c. Is it reasonable to conclude that the contracts represent a single project that will benefit both parties?

   In determining whether the contracts were effectively negotiated with a single customer, it is important to consider the mutual relationship and intentions of each party. For example, the more distant the relationship between the parties, the less likely it is that the contracts were negotiated with a single customer.

If the answer to each of the foregoing questions is "yes," a group of construction- or production-type contracts may be combined for accounting purposes. If the answer to any of the foregoing questions is "no" for a group of *construction-type* contracts, the contracts may not be combined for accounting purposes. If the answer to any of the questions is "no" when dealing with a group of *production-type* contracts, the contracts may still be combined into groupings such as production lots or releases for the purposes of accumulating and allocating production costs to units produced or delivered on the basis of average unit costs, if the following two conditions are met (ASC 605-35-25-9):

1. The contracts are with one or more customers for the production of substantially identical units of a basic item produced concurrently or sequentially, and

2. Revenue on the contracts is recognized under the percentage-of-completion method using the units-of-delivery approach discussed later in this chapter.

Segmenting a Contract or Group of Contracts

A contract or group of contracts may contain various elements or phases that have different profit margins. In addition, the contractor may agree to perform the various elements or phases independent of one another. In this situation, treating such a contract or group of contracts as a single unit for accounting purposes may distort the true economics of each element or phase. To address this situation, three sets of specific criteria have been established to determine whether a contract or group of contracts may be segmented for accounting purposes.

The first set of criteria allows a contract or group of contracts to be segmented if the following three actions were taken during the negotiations, were documented, and are verifiable (ASC 605-35-25-12):

1. The contractor submitted bona fide proposals on the separate components of the project and on the entire project;

2. The customer had the right to accept the proposals on either basis; and

3. The aggregate amount of the proposals on the separate components approximated the amount of the proposal on the entire project.

If documentation is lacking, or if these steps were not taken, the contract or group of contracts may still be segmented if all of the following criteria (second set) are met (ASC 605-35-25-13):

1. The terms and scope of the contract or project clearly call for separable phases or elements;

2. The separable phases or elements of the project are often bid or negotiated separately;

3. The market assigns different gross profit rates to the segments because of factors such as different levels of risk or differences in the relationship of the supply and demand for the services provided in the different segments;

4. The contractor has a significant history of providing similar services to other customers under separate contracts for each significant segment to which a profit margin higher than the overall profit margin on the project is ascribed;

5. The significant history with customers who have contracted for services separately is relatively stable in terms of pricing policy rather than unduly weighted by erratic pricing decisions;

6. The excess of the sum of the prices of the separate elements over the price of the total project is clearly attributable to cost savings incident to combined performance of the contract obligations; and

7. The similarity of services and prices in the contract segments and the prices of such services to other customers contracted separately should be documented and verifiable.

If neither the first nor second set of criteria has been satisfied for a *construction-type* contract or group of contracts, no segmentation is allowed. However, a *production-type* contract or group of contracts that do not meet either the first or second set of criteria may still be segmented into groupings such as production lots or releases for the purposes of accumulating and allocating production costs to units produced or delivered on the basis of average unit costs, when the following two conditions are met (ASC 605-35-25-14):

1. The contracts are with one or more customers for the production of substantially identical units of a basic item produced concurrently or sequentially; and

2. Revenue on the contracts is recognized under the percentage-of-completion method using the units-of-delivery approach (discussed later in this chapter).

A production-type contract that does not satisfy any of the three sets of conditions provided herein may not be segmented.

OBSERVATION: The segmentation criteria above are a specific methodology for separating elements in a multiple-deliverable arrangement. The criteria are more restrictive and significantly different from the criteria applicable to other situations. Only the criteria discussed herein may be applied to segment contracts within the scope of the contract accounting literature.

PRACTICE ALERT: As discussed in more detail in Chapter 4, "Multiple-Deliverable Revenue Arrangements," ASC 605-25 does not apply to arrangements that fall within the scope of ASC 605-35. However, if an arrangement includes elements that fall within the scope of ASC 605-35 *and* elements that fall outside the scope of ASC 605-35, ASC 605-25 (or whatever other literature is applicable) should be applied to separate the ASC 605-35 elements from the other elements.

Discussion of Accounting Methods

Throughout the remainder of this chapter, it is assumed that the unit of accounting is an individual contract. This does not change the fact that when contracts are combined or segmented, the combined group of contracts or individual contract segment is the appropriate unit of accounting. It is to these units of accounting (in their combined or segmented form) that either the percentage-of-completion or completed-contract method should be applied.

PERCENTAGE-OF-COMPLETION METHOD

The use of the percentage-of-completion method results in the recognition of revenues and costs as the contractor performs under the contract. This method requires the contractor to estimate progress toward completion and calculate the amount of revenues, costs, or gross profit to be recognized in each accounting period. This characteristic of the percentage-of-completion method raises the following questions:

- What happens if the contractor cannot make reasonably dependable estimates?
- How may the contractor measure its progress toward completion?
- How should the contractor determine or calculate revenues, costs, or gross profit to be recognized in each accounting period?

Estimates of Contract Amounts

Contract revenues, contract costs, and progress toward completion must be estimated by the contractor to determine the amount of revenues, costs, or gross profits to recognize in a particular period. Normally, the contractor is able to determine and use its best estimates of these amounts. However, in some cases, the contractor may only be able to (1) determine a range of estimated amounts or (2) determine that it will not incur a loss. In extreme situations, the contractor may be unable to make any reasonably dependable estimates or even determine that it will not incur a loss. As discussed above, the completed-contract method must be used in these situations.

Range of Amounts

When a contractor can only estimate a range of revenues and costs, the most likely estimate within the range should be used. If the contractor cannot determine which estimate in the range is most likely, the amounts within the ranges that would result in the lowest profit margin (the lowest contract revenue estimate and the highest contract cost estimate) should be used (ASC 605-35-25-60).

ILLUSTRATION: LOWEST PROBABLE PROFIT MARGIN

Facts: Contractor A enters into a contract with Customer X to construct a unique building. This is the largest building by far that Contractor A has ever agreed to construct for a customer. Consequently, Contractor A is only able to estimate the range of revenues and costs expected under the contract. Contractor A estimates that its total contract revenues will range from $5.2 million to $5.5 million and that its total contract costs will range from $4.5 million to $4.8 million. Because of the lack of similarity between this contract and other contracts into which Contractor A has entered, Contractor A is not able to determine which point within these ranges is most likely to occur. At the end of the first reporting period, Contractor A has incurred $1.2 million of contract costs and estimates that the project is 25% complete.

Accounting: Because Contractor A cannot determine which amounts within the contract revenue and cost ranges are most likely to occur, it should use the combination of amounts that results in the lowest profit margin. Consider the following possibilities:

	(in thousands)			
Contract Revenues	Highest		Lowest	
Contract Costs	Highest	Lowest	Highest	Lowest
Percentage complete	25%	25%	25%	25%
Contract revenues	$ 5,500	$ 5,500	$ 5,200	$ 5,200
Calculated revenues	1,375	1,375	1,300	1,300
Contract costs	4,800	4,500	4,800	4,500
Calculated costs	1,200	1,125	1,200	1,125
Calculated profit margin	$ 175	$ 250	$ 100	$ 175

The combination of the lowest contract revenues and highest contract costs results in the lowest overall profit margin. As a result, these are the amounts

Contractor A should use to calculate revenues earned under the percentage-of-completion method.

No Loss Incurrence

In some situations, it may be impractical for the contractor to estimate either specific amounts or ranges of contract revenues and costs. However, if the contractor can at least determine that it will not incur a loss, a zero profit model should be used. The zero profit model results in the recognition of an equal amount of revenues and costs. This method should only be used if more precise estimates cannot be made and its use must be discontinued when such estimates are obtainable. Once a contractor has more precise estimates, the change should be treated as a change in an accounting estimate (ASC 605-35-25-60; 605-35-25-67 through 25-69).

OBSERVATION: If in the previous example, Contractor A was not able to determine a range of contract revenues and costs, but could at least ascertain that it would not incur a loss on the contract, Contractor A would recognize $1.2 million of revenue in the first reporting period affected by the contract.

PRACTICE POINTER: Before switching from the percentage-of-completion method to the completed-contract method (due to the inability to estimate), the contractor should review the contractual terms to determine whether there is protection from incurring a loss. If there is such a provision (e.g., contract terms provide for the contractor to be compensated on a cost-plus basis), the contractor should continue to use the percentage-of-completion method but with a zero profit model. To illustrate the significance of this decision, consider the previous example. Use of the percentage-of-completion method with a zero profit model results in the recognition of $1.2 million of revenue and expense in the first reporting period affected by the contract. By contrast, no revenue or expense would be recognized if Contractor A used the completed-contract method.

EXAMPLE: DIFFERENT MODELS FOR DIFFERENT CONTRACTS

McDermott International, Inc. Form 10-K—Fiscal Year Ended December 31, 2009

Contracts and Revenue Recognition. We determine the appropriate accounting method for each of our long-term contracts before work on the project begins. We generally recognize contract revenues and related costs on a percentage-of-completion method for individual contracts or combinations of contracts under the guidelines of FASB Topic Revenue Recognition. The use of this method is based on our experience and history of being able to prepare reasonably dependable estimates of the cost to complete our projects. Under this method, we recognize estimated contract revenue and resulting income based on costs incurred to date as a percentage of total estimated costs. Certain costs may be excluded from the cost-to-cost method of measuring progress, such as significant costs for materials and major third-party subcontractors, if it appears that such exclusion would result in a more meaningful measurement of actual contract progress and resulting periodic allocation of income. Total estimated costs, and resulting contract income, are affected by changes in the expected cost of materials and labor, productivity, scheduling and other factors. Additionally, external factors such as weather, customer requirements and other factors outside of our control may affect the progress and estimated cost of a project's completion and, therefore, the timing of revenue and income recognition. We routinely review estimates related to our contracts, and revisions to profitability are reflected in the quarterly and annual earnings we report.

For contracts as to which we are unable to estimate the final profitability except to assure that no loss will ultimately be incurred, we recognize equal amounts of revenue and cost until the final results can be estimated more precisely. For these deferred profit recognition contracts, we recognize revenue and cost equally and only recognize gross margin when probable and reasonably estimable, which we generally determine to be when the contract is approximately 70% complete. We treat long-term construction contracts that contain such a level of risk and uncertainty that estimation of the final outcome is impractical except to assure that no loss will be incurred as deferred profit recognition contracts.

Fixed-price contracts are required to be accounted for under the completed-contract method if we are unable to reasonably forecast cost to complete at start-up. For example, if we have no experience in performing the type of work on a particular project and were unable to develop reasonably dependable estimates of total costs to complete, we would follow the completed-contract method of accounting for such projects. Our management's policy is not to enter into fixed-price contracts without an accurate estimate of cost to complete. However, it is possible that in the time between contract execution and the start of work on a project, we could lose confidence in our ability to forecast cost to complete based on intervening events, including, but not limited to, experience on similar projects, civil unrest, strikes and volatility in our expected costs. In such a situation, we would use the completed-contract method of accounting for that project. We did not enter into any contracts that we have accounted for under the completed-contract method during 2009 or 2008.

For all contracts, if a current estimate of total contract cost indicates a loss on a contract, the projected loss is recognized in full when determined.

Measuring Progress Toward Completion

A variety of acceptable methods have evolved to measure progress toward completion. These methods can be categorized as either input or output measures. Input measures are generally based on costs incurred or effort put forth. Output measures are generally based on units delivered or units of work performed (ASC 605-35-25-70). Because output measures directly measure the progress of fulfillment of the contract, they are regarded as better measures of progress toward completion than input measures. However, reliable measures of output are often unavailable (ASC 605-35-25-71). Therefore, input measures are more commonly used.

A contractor must exercise significant judgment in choosing the method it uses to measure progress toward completion for each type of contract. Once the method is selected, it should be consistently applied to contracts with similar characteristics. However, a contractor should use different methods to measure progress toward completion if doing so will provide the best estimates. Progress toward completion should be substantiated periodically through physical observation.

Input Measures

Cost-based measures are the most commonly used input measures. Costs incurred divided by total costs expected to be incurred provides the percentage-complete measure. This measure assumes that there is a relationship between project progress and the incurrence of costs (i.e., an additional dollar of contract cost incurred leads to increased productivity). This may not actually be the case, depending on the facts and circumstances. For example, if a contract has high initial costs related to the use of specialized labor but lower labor costs for the balance of the project, it may not be appropriate to measure progress based on the labor costs incurred.

An important component of a cost-to-cost calculation is determining what costs to include. The general rule requires all contract costs (including those related to subcontractors) to be included in the calculation (components of contract costs are discussed in more detail later in this chapter). When determining the amount of contract costs incurred that should be included, payments for work not yet performed and significant amounts of uninstalled materials not specifically produced or manufactured for the project should not be included (ASC 605-35-25-75 through 25-77). Instead, these costs should be included in costs incurred only when the materials are installed or the prepaid work is performed.

ILLUSTRATION: COST-TO-COST MEASURE

Facts: Contractor B enters into a contract with Customer Y to construct a unique building. Contractor B determines that this contract falls within the scope of ASC 605-35. Contractor B also concludes that it can use the percentage-of-completion method because reasonably dependable estimates of contract revenues, costs, and progress towards completion are determinable. Based on the information available, Contractor B decides to use a cost-to-cost method to estimate progress towards completion. Payments for contract costs through the end of the accounting period totaled $1.7 million. These payments included the following:

- $0.2 million to Subcontractor 1 for work already performed;
- $0.1 million of advance payments to Subcontractor 2 for work not yet performed;
- $1.0 million of standard materials purchased from third parties, $0.6 million of which has been used in the construction process and $0.4 million of which has not been used in the construction process; and
- $0.4 million of other contract costs relating primarily to labor and equipment.

Contractor B estimates that total contract costs expected to be incurred are $6.0 million.

Accounting: Progress toward completion using a cost-to-cost measure should be based on $1.2 million of the $1.7 million contract cost payments made through the end of the period. The advance payments to Subcontractor 2 for work not yet performed ($0.1 million) and the payments for standard materials purchased from third parties that have not yet been used in the construction process ($0.4 million) should be excluded from the calculation of progress toward completion. The percentage-complete at the end of the period is calculated as follows:

$1.2 million of contract costs / $6.0 million of total expected
contract costs
= 20% of contract is complete

Another commonly used input measure is based on efforts expended. The unit of measure in an efforts-based model may be labor dollars, labor hours, machine hours, material quantities, or any other unit of measure that reflects the usage of effort. The percentage complete is calculated based on total efforts expended (e.g., labor hours spent) divided by total efforts expected to be expended (e.g., total labor hours expected to be spent). Generally, an efforts-based model can be more closely linked to productivity than a cost-to-cost model. However, inefficiencies and other factors may weaken the link between efforts expended and productivity. When using an efforts-based measure, the contractor should include the efforts of subcontractors. If the efforts of subcontractors cannot be reasonably determined in the unit of measure necessary (e.g., labor hours), an efforts-based model should not be used (ASC 605-35-25-72 and 73).

Output Measures

Output measures base progress toward completion on results achieved. The most common output measures are units produced or units delivered. Other output measures focus on value added to the project and achievement of contract milestones. Generally, output measures are regarded as better measures of progress toward completion than input measures. However, reliable measures of output are often unavailable (ASC 605-35-25-71). For example, in a contract to produce a single piece of equipment or construct a single house, there is not likely to be any output measure on which progress toward completion can be measured.

The most common output measure is a units delivered approach, which results in the recognition of revenue as each unit of output is delivered. Costs are allocated to the delivered units based on an average unit cost, which may be based on costs incurred to date or costs expected to be incurred over the contract period. This method should be used in situations where products are manufactured or produced to the customer's specifications on a continuous or sequential basis (ASC 605-35-25-55). Use in other situations would generally be inappropriate.

An example of an output measure based on units delivered is a contract where the contractor has agreed to pave a stretch of road. In this situation, the distance of road paved in divided by total distance to be paved under the contract would give an output measure of the percentage of completion.

EXAMPLE: USE OF UNITS-OF-DELIVERY AND COST-TO-COST

Lockheed Martin Corp. Form 10-K—Fiscal Year Ended December 31, 2009

Contract Accounting / Revenue Recognition

Approximately 80% of our net sales are derived from long-term contracts for design, development, and production activities (also referred to as DD&P contracts). Our remaining net sales are derived from contracts to provide other services that are not associated with design, development, or production activities. We consider the nature of our contracts and the types of products and services provided when we determine the proper accounting method for a particular contract.

Accounting for Design, Development, and Production Contracts

For long-term, fixed-price DD&P contracts that, among other factors, require us to provide a number of similar items produced in a stable production environment, we record sales on a percentage of completion basis using units-of-delivery as the basis to measure progress toward completing the contract. For example, we use this method of revenue recognition on our C-130J tactical transport aircraft program and Multiple Launch Rocket System program. For certain other long-term, fixed-price DD&P contracts that, along with other factors, require us to deliver minimal quantities over a longer period of time or to perform a substantial level of development effort in comparison to the total value of the contract, sales are recorded when we achieve performance milestones or using the cost-to-cost method to measure progress toward completion. Under the cost-to-cost method of accounting, we recognize sales based on the ratio of costs incurred to our estimate of total costs at completion. As an example, we use this methodology for our Aegis Weapon System program.

In some instances, long-term production programs may require a significant level of development and/or a low rate of initial production in their early phases, but will ultimately require delivery of increased quantities in later, full-rate production stages. In those cases, the revenue recognition methodology may change from the cost-to-cost method to the units-of-delivery method as new contracts for different phases of a program are received after considering, among other factors, program and production stability. As we incur costs under cost-reimbursement-type contracts, we record sales and an estimated profit. Cost-reimbursement-type contracts include time and materials and other level-of-effort-type contracts. Examples of this type of revenue recognition include the F-35 Lightning II Joint Strike Fighter development and low-rate initial production contracts, and the THAAD missile defense program. Most of our long-term contracts are denominated in U.S. dollars, including contracts for sales of military products and services to foreign governments conducted through the U.S. Government (*i.e.*, foreign military sales).

As a general rule, we recognize sales and profits earlier in a production cycle when we use the cost-to-cost and milestone methods of percentage of completion accounting than when we use the units-of-delivery method. In addition, our profits and margins may vary materially depending on the types of long-term contracts undertaken, the costs incurred in their performance, the achievement of other performance objectives, and the stage of performance at which the right to receive fees, particularly under award and incentive fee contracts, is finally determined.

Output measures should not be based on comparisons of progress billings to total expected billings or cash receipts to total expected cash receipts. Payment terms are established by contract and bear no direct relationship to the actual progress toward completion. Milestones, as stated in a contract, may not reflect output completed. Milestones often better reflect negotiated payment schedules and the budgetary or financial needs of a customer and/or the contractor. When using milestones as the basis of the output measure, it is important to ensure (by documentation and by noting verifiable evidence) that milestones are substantively correlated with output.

Determining Revenues and Costs to Be Recognized

One of two alternatives may be used to calculate earned revenue and costs of earned revenue under the percentage-of-completion method. A contractor should select one of the alternatives and apply it consistently to all contracts. Guidance on what constitutes contract revenues and contract costs for purposes of applying these alternatives is provided later in this chapter.

Alternative A

Under this alternative, both revenues and costs of sales are recognized based on the measure of progress toward completion. More specifically, revenue for any period equals total expected contract revenue multiplied by the percentage complete at the end of the period in question, less the amount of revenue recognized in prior periods. Similarly, cost of sales for any period equals total expected contract costs multiplied by the percentage complete at the end of the period in question, less the amount of contract costs recognized in prior periods (ASC 605-35-25-83).

Alternative B

Under this alternative, gross profit is the only measure based on progress toward completion. Cost of sales is based on actual costs incurred to date; revenues are then recorded in an amount equal to costs incurred plus the gross profit calculated based on the percentage complete. More specifically, cost of sales for any period equals the contract costs incurred in that period. Gross profit for any period equals total expected revenues less total expected costs, multiplied by the percentage complete at the end of the period in question, less gross profit recognized in prior periods. Revenue is merely the sum of the cost of sales for the period plus the gross profit for the period (ASC 605-35-25-84).

Comparison of Alternatives

The same amount of gross profit should result in any given period, regardless of the alternative selected. However, revenues and costs may vary given the different calculation methods under each alternative. As a result, the gross profit percentage may also vary.

Neither of the two methods applies the Proportional Performance model as it is applied in service and other transactions that are outside the scope of ASC 605-35. For these transactions, the Proportional Performance model generally results in the recognition of revenues on a ratable basis and the recognition of costs as incurred. By contrast, Alternative A results in the ratable recognition of both revenues and costs, while Alternative B results in ratable recognition of gross profit, but not costs or revenues.

PRACTICE POINTER: Because the application of Alternatives A and B can produce significantly different results from the Proportional Performance model in certain service transactions (see Chapter 6, "Service Deliverables"), it is very important to understand which transactions are within the scope of the contract accounting literature.

The similarities and differences between Alternatives A and B can best be illustrated through a numerical example.

ILLUSTRATION: COMPARISON OF ALTERNATIVES A AND B

Facts: Contractor C enters into a contract with Customer K to construct an office building. Assume for purposes of this example that contract accounting applies and that Contractor C meets the conditions to apply the percentage-of-completion method. The construction period is expected to span two years. The total amount due from Customer K under the contract is $10 million. The initial estimate of costs to construct the office building is $9 million. Other information necessary to determine earned revenues and costs of earned revenues for Year 1 and Year 2 of the contract is provided below.

	Year 1	Year 2
Total Expected Revenues	$10,000,000	$10,000,000
Total Expected Contract Costs	9,000,000	9,000,000
Total Expected Gross Profit	1,000,000	1,000,000
Current Period Actual Costs	4,000,000	5,000,000
Percent Complete	40%	100%
Progress Billings	$ 3,500,000	$6,500,000

Comparison of Alternatives: The amount of Current Period Revenues and Current Period Cost of Sales under Alternatives A and B for Years 1 and 2 are shown below.

Alternative A	Year 1	Year 2
Cumulative Revenues:		
Total Expected Revenues	$10,000,000	$10,000,000
Percent Complete	40%	100%
Cumulative Revenues	4,000,000	10,000,000
Current Period Revenues:		
Cumulative Revenues	4,000,000	10,000,000
Revenue Recognized in Prior Periods	—	4,000,000
Current Period Revenues	4,000,000	6,000,000
Cumulative Cost of Sales:		
Total Expected Contract Costs	9,000,000	9,000,000

Alternative A	Year 1	Year 2
Percent Complete	40%	100%
Cumulative Cost of Sales	3,600,000	9,000,000
Current Period Cost of Sales:		
Cumulative Cost of Sales	3,600,000	9,000,000
Cost of Sales Recognized in Prior Periods	—	3,600,000
Current Period Cost of Sales	3,600,000	5,400,000
Current Period Gross Profit	$ 400,000	$ 600,000
Current Period Gross Profit Percentage	10%	10%

Under Alternative A, at the end of Year 1, the following amounts would be reflected as assets on Contractor C's balance sheet: (a) $500,000 of Unbilled Revenues ($4,000,000 Current Period Revenues, less $3,500,000 of Progress Billings), and (b) $400,000 of Costs of Uncompleted Contracts ($4,000,000 of Current Period Actual Costs incurred, less $3,600,000 Current Period Cost of Sales).

Alternative B	Year 1	Year 2
Cumulative Gross Profit:		
Total Expected Gross Profit	$1,000,000	$1,000,000
Percent Complete	40%	100%
Cumulative Gross Profit	400,000	1,000,000
Current Period Gross Profit:		
Cumulative Gross Profit	400,000	1,000,000
Gross Profit Recognized in Prior Periods	—	400,000
Current Period Gross Profit	400,000	600,000
Current Period Revenues:		
Current Period Cost of Sales	4,000,000	5,000,000
Current Period Gross Profit	400,000	600,000
Current Period Revenues	$4,400,000	$5,600,000
Current Period Gross Profit Percentage	9%	11%

Under Alternative B, at the end of Year 1, $900,000 of Unbilled Revenues ($4,400,000 Current Period Revenues less $3,500,000 of Progress Billings) would be reflected as an asset on Contractor C's balance sheet.

OBSERVATIONS:

1. Current Period Gross Profit is the same under each alternative in both Years 1 and 2. This should always be the case.

2. Current Period Gross Profit Percentages are not consistent between the alternatives in either Year 1 or Year 2. This will generally be the case given that revenues are calculated differently under each alternative.

3. Current Period Gross Profit Percentage is the same in both years under Alternative A. This is the case if there are no changes in estimates

between periods. If there are changes in estimates between periods, the Current Period Gross Profit Percentage will be different year-over-year under Alternative A.

4. Current Period Gross Profit Percentage is different in both years under Alternative B. This is the case if a method other than cost-to-cost is used to measure progress towards completion.

5. The total debit reflected on Contractor C's balance sheet at the end of Year 1 is the same under both alternatives. This should always be the case.

COMPLETED-CONTRACT METHOD

Contract revenues and expenses are recognized under the completed-contract method when the contract is considered complete or substantially complete just as they are in any other application of a Completed Performance model (see Chapter 3, "General Principles"). In the interim, costs incurred and progress billings are reported on the balance sheet (ASC 605-35-25-88).

A contract is complete if there are no remaining costs or potential risks. A contract is substantially complete if any remaining costs or potential risks are considered insignificant. A contractor should use objective criteria to assess the completeness of a contract. These criteria should provide consistency in the contractor's determination of when a contract is complete. Factors that may be considered by the contractor include delivery of the product, acceptance by the customer, departure from the site, and compliance with performance specifications (ASC 605-35-25-96; 605-35-25-97). These criteria are similar to those that would be used in other applications of a Completed Performance model.

To the extent that a contractor recognizes revenues and costs upon substantial completion, the contractor should provide an accrual for the estimated remaining costs to be incurred and for the estimated settlement of any outstanding claims or disputes that could result in payments. These accruals should be evaluated as contingencies using the guidance in ASC 450-20.

REVENUE AND COST ELEMENTS

Contracts within the scope of this chapter can have many different revenue and cost elements. For example, contract revenues are often derived from the following pricing or billing mechanisms:

- Basic contract price
- Customer-furnished materials
- Contract options and additions
- Change orders
- Claims

Cost elements can include both direct and indirect costs of performance, as well as costs incurred before performance begins. A discussion of how these elements affect the recognition of revenues and costs under both the percentage-of-completion and the completed-contract method is provided below.

Basic Contract Price

In many instances, determining the basic contract price is relatively simple. For example, contracts are often structured such that the price will remain fixed even if the contractor's cost experience or performance is not as originally expected. In this type of a contract, the contractor bears all risks related to cost overruns or performance difficulties. As a result, a contractor may attempt to negotiate one or more of the following pricing elements in its basic fixed-price contracts to mitigate these risks (ASC 605-35-25-15 through 25-33):

- Economic price adjustments
- Prospective periodic redetermination of price
- Retroactive redetermination of price
- Firm target cost incentives
- Successive target cost incentives
- Performance incentives
- Level of effort adjustments

Other contracts include variable pricing components such as those based on time and materials. Total revenue under a time-and-materials priced contract varies based on time incurred, materials used, and any mark-up rates applied to these amounts. When revenues are determined based on costs, the contract may call for reimbursement of costs plus an incremental amount. That incremental amount may be fixed or variable based on the performance or ability to meet cost or performance targets.

Estimating the basic contract price requires an analysis of both the fixed and variable pricing elements. Given the amount of judgment involved, estimates of the basic contract price should be evaluated periodically to determine if any adjustments are necessary.

Subcontractor Involvement

When a subcontractor performs activities under a cost-type contract, a question arises as to whether the costs of the subcontractor should be included in the general contractor's income statement on a gross (as contract revenues and contract costs) or net (no net effect on contract revenues or contract costs if the general contractor does not mark up the subcontractor's costs) basis. The factors to consider in making this determination are (1) whether the general contractor acts as a principal or an agent vis-à-vis the subcontractor's costs and (2) the extent to which the general contractor bears the risks related to these costs. Generally, if the general contractor acts as a principal, it likely bears a substantive portion of the risks associated with these costs. In such a situation, the subcontractor costs should be reflected on a gross basis in the general contractor's income statement. Amounts paid to subcontractors should be recorded as contract costs and reimbursements of such amounts received from customers should be included in contract revenues. When the general contractor acts as an agent vis-à-vis the subcontractor's costs, it does not bear a substantive portion of the risks associated with these costs. As a result, the subcontractor costs should be reflected on a net basis in the general contractor's income statement. In other words, subcontractor costs should not be considered contract costs and reimbursements of such costs should not be considered contract revenues (ASC 605-35-25-20; 605-35-25-21).

OBSERVATION: Gross versus net reporting is addressed for arrangements not within the scope of ASC 605-35 in ASC 605-50. Although that guidance is more detailed than the guidance in ASC 605-35, the framework for assessing whether revenue should be recognized gross or net considers the same two key issues discussed above—the role of the entity (principal or agent) and the risks assumed by the entity. Thus, the guidance in ASC 605-50 would generally provide useful additional guidance in determining how to address subcontracted costs. See Chapter 11, "Presentation" for further discussion.

Customer-Furnished Materials

In certain instances, a customer may purchase materials for the contractor to use for a specific project. Whether the contractor should include the value of the materials in contract revenues and costs depends on the risks borne by the contractor relative to these materials. If the contractor is responsible for the nature, type, characteristics, or specifications of such materials, or if the contractor is ultimately responsible for the acceptability of the performance of such materials in the context of the overall project, the value of those materials should be included in contract revenues and contract costs (ASC 605-35-25-22 through 25-24).

EXAMPLE: CUSTOMER-FURNISHED MATERIALS AND SUBCONTRACTOR COSTS

Fluor Corporation Form 10-K—Fiscal Year Ended December 31, 2009

The company recognizes engineering and construction contract revenue using the percentage-of-completion method, based primarily on contract cost incurred to date compared to total estimated contract cost. Customer-furnished materials, labor and equipment and, in certain cases, subcontractor materials, labor and equipment, are included in revenue and cost of revenue when management believes that the company is responsible for the ultimate acceptability of the project.

Contract Options and Additions

In some cases, a contract is changed after performance has begun. Such changes can provide for additional deliverables or changes to the originally contemplated deliverables. Whether contract options and additions should be treated as: (1) a separate contract, (2) part of the original contract, or (3) a change order depends on the facts and circumstances.

A contract option or addition is treated as a separate contract if any of the following circumstances exist (ASC 605-35-25-29):

1. The product or service to be provided differs significantly from the product or service provided under the original contract;

2. The price of the new product or service is negotiated without regard to the original contract and involves different economic judgments; or

3. The products or services to be provided under the exercised option or amendment are similar to those under the original contract, but the contract price and anticipated contract cost relationship are significantly different.

When these criteria are not met, a contract option or addition must be treated as a change order. In addition, a contract option or addition should only be combined with the original contract if it meets the criteria for combining contracts discussed earlier in this chapter.

Change Orders

Change orders are modifications of an original contract that effectively change the provisions of the contract without adding new provisions (ASC 605-35-25-25). Some change orders are approved by the contractor and customer on a timely basis, while others are not approved until after completion of the project. The timing of approval is often determined by the amount of uncertainty in a change order. The accounting treatment of change orders depends on whether the scope and pricing of the order have been approved by both the customer and the contractor. When the scope but not the pricing of the change order has been defined, the appropriate accounting treatment will depend on whether the contractor is using the completed-contract or percentage-of-completion method to account for the contract.

Approved Change Orders

If a change order has been approved with respect to both its scope and its pricing, the price of the change order should be included in contract revenues and the costs of the change order should be included in contract costs (ASC 605-35-25-27). Therefore, a change in estimate of both contract costs and contract revenues would occur at the time a change order is approved. This would generally result in a remeasurement of both the percentage complete and the recognized costs and expenses (see "Changes in Estimates" in this chapter).

Partially-Approved Change Orders

As noted above, the scope of a change order may be defined even though the pricing is not. The treatment of these unpriced change orders varies depending on whether the contractor is using the completed-contract or percentage-of-completion method to account for the contract.

Completed-contract method (ASC 605-35-25-98). The costs related to an unpriced change order should be deferred as contract costs if it is probable that total contract costs, including costs attributable to change orders, will be recovered from contract revenues. In making the judgment as to whether recovery is probable, the contractor should consider its historical ability to recover costs under change orders and the specific facts and circumstances surrounding the change order under review.

Percentage-of-completion method (ASC 605-35-25-87). The inclusion of costs and revenues related to change orders in the computation of earned revenues and costs depends, in part, on the contractor's assessment of whether change order costs will be recovered. If the contractor determines that it is *not* probable that the change order costs will be recovered through a change in the basic contract price, then the change order costs should be included in the percentage-of-completion computation related to the overall contract. Effectively, this assumes that the change order costs will be absorbed, or recovered, by the basic contract price. Therefore, a change in the estimate of contract costs would occur when the scope of a change order is defined.

If the contractor determines that it *is* probable that change order costs will be recovered through a change in the basic contract price, the contractor has the following options:

1. Defer the change order costs (and recognition of any revenue) until agreement on price has been reached; or

2. Treat the change order costs as contract costs in the period they are incurred for purposes of computing costs of earned revenues for that period and recognize contract revenues to the extent of these change order costs.

A contractor should select and consistently follow one of these options to account for unpriced change orders.

To the extent it is probable that the change order will be priced at an amount that exceeds the change order costs, the additional probable contract revenue in excess of the change order costs should only be included in contract revenues for purposes of computing earned revenues under the percentage-of-completion method if realization of that incremental amount is assured beyond a reasonable doubt (ASC 605-35-25-87).

Unapproved Change Orders

A change order in dispute or whose scope and price have not been approved should be evaluated as a claim for purposes of determining whether it should be included in contract revenues and contract costs (see discussion below) (ASC 605-35-25-28).

Claims

The basic contract price is negotiated using a set of project assumptions. When a contractor's experience differs from these assumptions (e.g., due to errors in customer specifications, delays caused by the customer), the contractor will often seek additional compensation from the customer. This additional compensation is sought either through a formal change order or through a claims process. As noted above, unapproved or contested change orders are accounted for as claims because they are substantively equivalent.

A contractor may adopt a policy where claims revenue is only recognized when a claim has been received or awarded. Alternatively, the contractor may adopt an accounting policy that includes claim amounts in contract revenues if,

(a) it is probable that the claim will result in additional contract revenue and (b) this amount can be reliably estimated. Both of these requirements can only be met if all of the following conditions exist (ASC 605-35-25-30; 605-35-25-31):

1. The contract or other evidence provides a legal basis for the claim; or a legal opinion has been obtained, stating that under the circumstances there is a reasonable basis to support the claim;

2. Additional costs are caused by circumstances that were unforeseen at the contract date and are not the result of deficiencies in the contractor's performance;

3. Costs associated with the claim are identifiable or otherwise determinable and are reasonable in view of the work performed; and

4. The evidence supporting the claim is objective and verifiable, not based on management's "feel" for the situation or unsupported representations.

When these conditions are met, revenue from a claim may be recognized up to the extent of costs incurred related to the claim. However, if the estimate of the claim amount is greater than the costs incurred related to the claim, the excess amount should not be recognized as revenue until the claim is settled. This amount, as well as claims that do not meet the above conditions, represents contingent assets, which may not be recognized until they are realized (ASC 605-35-25-31).

Costs incurred related to a claim should be treated as costs of contract performance.

EXAMPLE: ACCOUNTING FOR CLAIMS

Fluor Corporation Form 10-K—Fiscal Year Ended December 31, 2009

Claims arising from engineering and construction contracts have been made against the company by clients, and the company has made claims against clients for cost incurred in excess of current contract provisions. The company recognizes, under ASC 605-35-25, certain significant claims for recovery of incurred cost when it is probable that the claim will result in additional contract revenue and when the amount of the claim can be reliably estimated. Recognized claims amounted to $247 million and $202 million as of December 31, 2009 and 2008, respectively. Unapproved change orders are accounted for in revenue and cost when it is probable that the cost will be recovered through a change in the contract price. In circumstances where recovery is considered probable, but the revenue cannot be reliably estimated, cost attributable to change orders is deferred pending determination of the impact on contract price.

Contract Costs

The identification of contract costs is important given the way costs are accounted for under the percentage-of-completion method (i.e., costs are recognized as the contractor performs) and completed-contract method (i.e., costs are deferred until the contractor is substantially complete). The general rule is that contract costs should only include direct costs related to the contract and indirect costs specifically identifiable or allocable to the contract. The following table lists different types of costs and whether these costs would be considered contract costs (ASC 605-35-25-34 through 25-38).

Cost	Contract Cost?	
	% of Compl.	Compl. Contract
Direct materials	Yes (Note 7)	Yes (Note 7)
Direct labor	Yes	Yes
Direct subcontracting costs	Yes (Note 8)	Yes (Note 8)
Indirect labor	Yes (Note 1)	Yes (Note 1)
Contract supervision	Yes (Note 1)	Yes (Note 1)
Tools and equipment	Yes (Notes 1, 6)	Yes (Notes 1, 6)
Supplies	Yes (Notes 1, 7)	Yes (Notes 1, 7)
Quality control	Yes (Note 1)	Yes (Note 1)
Inspection	Yes (Note 1)	Yes (Note 1)
Insurance	Yes (Note 1)	Yes (Note 1)
Repairs and maintenance	Yes (Note 1)	Yes (Note 1)
Depreciation	Yes (Note 1)	Yes (Note 1)
Amortization	Yes (Note 1)	Yes (Note 1)
Support costs	Yes (Note 1)	Yes (Note 1)
General and administrative	No (Note 2)	Accounting Policy (Note 3)
Selling costs	No (Note 4)	No (Note 4)
Interest	No (Note 5)	No (Note 5)

Note 1:   These costs are indirect costs and are only considered contract costs if they are specifically identifiable with or allocable to the contract. The allocation methods used must be systematic and rational.

Note 2:   General and administrative costs should be expensed as incurred under the percentage-of-completion method.

Note 3:   General and administrative costs may be allocated to a contract and treated as contract costs when using the completed-contract method. The contractor should elect an accounting policy to either expense these costs as incurred or treat them as contract costs. This policy must be consistently followed for all contracts under the completed-contract method.

Note 4:   Selling costs should be expensed as incurred, unless they qualify as precontract costs (see "Precontract Costs" in the next section).

Note 5:   Interest is not considered a contract cost. Interest capitalization is addressed in ASC 835, *Interest*; ASC 835-20.

Note 6:   The cost of equipment purchased for use on a contract should be allocated over the period of its expected use unless title to the equipment is transferred to the customer by terms of the contract (ASC 605-35-25-77).

Note 7:   Inventoriable costs (such as direct materials and supplies not yet used in the construction process) should not be carried at amounts, that when added to the estimated cost to complete, are greater than the estimated realizable value of the related contracts (ASC 605-35-25-37).

Note 8:   Whether subcontracting costs should be reflected in the general contractor's income statement gross or net is discussed earlier in this chapter under "Subcontractor Involvement."

The guidelines above apply to all contracts that fall within the scope of ASC 605-35, including those that compensate the contractor based on costs. Whether a contractor is compensated for a specific type of cost in a cost-type contract does not affect whether it is considered a contract cost.

Precontract Costs

Precontract costs are costs incurred in anticipation of a contract. The nature of the cost and the probability of its recovery are important factors to consider when determining the appropriate accounting treatment. A list of various precontract costs and the appropriate accounting treatment for each is provided below (ASC 605-35-25-41).

Cost	Treatment

Costs (excluding start-up costs) incurred for a specific anticipated contract that will result in a benefit only if the contract is consummated	• Not initially included in contract costs or inventory
	• May be deferred if recoverability from specific contract is probable
	  — If deferred, and contract is consummated, include in contract costs
	  — If deferred, and contract is not consummated or recovery is no longer probable, expense
	  — If not deferred, and contract is subsequently consummated, do not reverse previously expensed costs

Costs incurred for assets (e.g., for the purchase of materials, production equipment, or supplies) in anticipation of a specific contract	• Capitalize cost of the asset subject to the recovery of the cost being probable
Costs incurred to acquire or produce goods in excess of the amounts required for an existing contract in anticipation of future orders for the same item	• Treat as inventory subject to the recovery of the cost being probable
Start-up costs (including training or learning costs) incurred in conjunction with an existing or anticipated contract	• Expense as incurred

Estimate of Costs to Complete

Estimates of costs to complete are important in accounting for a contract under both the percentage-of-completion and completed-contract methods. Such estimates are important under the percentage-of-completion method because total costs to complete (actual-to-date plus estimates to complete) are an integral factor in (1) the cost-to-cost method of measuring progress toward completion, (2) determining the costs of earned revenue recognized in any given period, and (3) determining whether a loss contract exists (also important under the completed-contract method).

Estimates of costs to complete should (ASC 605-35-25-44):

- *Be performed consistently across all contracts.* This requires having standard procedures in place.
- *Be reviewed periodically and compared to actual costs to complete.* This will enable the contractor to determine whether its estimation procedures require revision.

- *Contain the same complement of costs included in actual accumulated contract costs.* For example, if indirect labor is included in actual contract costs, it should be factored into the estimate of costs to complete.

- *Take into consideration expected cost increases.* If labor rates are expected to increase as a result of a new union contract, the higher rates should be used in the estimation process.

PRACTICE POINTER: At any given point in time, contract costs are both costs that have been incurred and those that have yet to be incurred. Because both types of costs are important when accounting for contract revenues and contract costs, the contractor must ensure that it has adequate systems and processes in place to accumulate costs incurred and estimate costs of completion for each contract. This is necessary because costs are not always expensed at the time they are incurred and revenues are not usually recognized when billings occur. The nature or complexity of these systems and processes depends on many factors including:

- The number of open contracts the contractor has at any point in time (e.g., a larger number of open contracts may require computerized cost accumulation and estimation processes whereas a smaller number of open contracts may only require manual cost accumulation and estimation processes); and

- The nature of the contractor's operations (e.g., if the contractor constructs very large, high-tech, complex pieces of equipment, a more elaborate cost accumulation and estimation process may be necessary).

The basic objective is to have systems and processes that provide adequate and consistent cost accumulation and estimation. Adequacy is measured by whether the information produced allows the contractor to properly account for each contract.

EXAMPLE: CONTRACT REVENUE AND COST ESTIMATION

Foster-Wheeler AG Form 10-K—Fiscal Year Ended December 31, 2009

Revenues and profits on long-term contracts are recorded under the percentage-of-completion method.

Progress towards completion on fixed price contracts is measured based on physical completion of individual tasks for all contracts with a value of $5,000 or greater. For contracts with a value less than $5,000, progress toward completion is measured based on the ratio of costs incurred to total estimated contract costs (the cost-to-cost method).

Progress towards completion on cost-reimbursable contracts is measured based on the ratio of quantities expended to total forecasted quantities, typically man-hours. Incentives are also recognized on a percentage-of-completion basis when the realization of an incentive is assessed as probable. We include flow-through costs consisting of materials, equipment or subcontractor services as both operating revenues and cost of operating revenues on cost-reimbursable contracts when we have overall responsibility as the contractor for the engineering specifications and procurement or procurement services for such costs. There is no contract profit impact of flow-through costs as they are included in both operating revenues and cost of operating revenues.

Contracts in process are stated at cost, increased for profits recorded on the completed effort or decreased for estimated losses, less billings to the customer and progress payments on uncompleted contracts.

At any point, we have numerous contracts in progress, all of which are at various stages of completion. Accounting for revenues and profits on long-term contracts requires estimates of total estimated contract costs and estimates of progress toward completion to determine the extent of revenue and profit recognition. We rely extensively on estimates to forecast quantities of labor (man-hours), materials and equipment, the costs for those quantities (including exchange rates), and the schedule to execute the scope of work including allowances for weather, labor and civil unrest. Many of these estimates cannot be based on historical data, as most contracts are unique, specifically designed facilities. In determining the revenues, we must estimate the percentage-of-completion, the likelihood that the client will pay for the work performed, and the cash to be received net of any taxes ultimately due or withheld in the country where the work is performed. Projects are reviewed on an individual basis and the estimates used are tailored to the specific circumstances. In establishing these estimates, we exercise significant judgment, and all possible risks cannot be specifically quantified.

The percentage-of-completion method requires that adjustments or re-evaluations to estimated project revenues and costs, including estimated claim recoveries, be recognized on a project-to-date cumulative basis, as changes to the estimates are identified. Revisions to project estimates are made as additional information becomes known, including information that becomes available subsequent to the date of the consolidated financial statements up through the date such consolidated financial statements are filed with the SEC. If the final estimated profit to complete a long-term contract indicates a loss, provision is made immediately for the total loss anticipated. Profits are accrued throughout the life of the project based on the percentage-of-completion. The project life cycle, including project-specific warranty commitments, can be up to approximately six years in duration.

The actual project results can be significantly different from the estimated results. When adjustments are identified near or at the end of a project, the full impact of the change in estimate is recognized as a change in the profit on the contract in that period. This can result in a material impact on our results for a single reporting period. We review all of our material contracts on a monthly basis and revise our estimates as appropriate for developments such as earning project incentive bonuses, incurring or expecting to incur contractual liquidated damages for performance or schedule issues, providing services and purchasing third-party materials and equipment at costs differing from those previously estimated and testing completed facilities, which, in turn, eliminates or confirms completion and warranty-related costs. Project incentives are recognized when it is probable they will be earned. Project incentives are frequently tied to cost, schedule and/or safety targets and, therefore, tend to be earned late in a project's life cycle.

Changes in estimated final contract revenues and costs can either increase or decrease the final estimated contract profit. In the period in which a change in estimate is recognized, the cumulative impact of that change is recorded based on progress achieved through the period of change. There were 43, 33 and 38 separate projects that had final estimated contract profit revisions whose impact on contract profit exceeded $1,000 in fiscal years 2009, 2008 and 2007, respectively. The changes in final estimated contract profit resulted in a net increase of

$69,000, $26,700 and $35,100 to reported contract profit for fiscal years 2009, 2008 and 2007, respectively, relating to the revaluation of work performed on contracts in prior periods. The changes in fiscal year 2009 included $24,300 for positive settlements on two projects in our Global E&C Group, of which $14,800 was associated with the receipt of a payment on a long outstanding arbitration award. The impact on contract profit is measured as of the beginning of each fiscal year and represents the incremental contract profit or loss that would have been recorded in prior periods had we been able to recognize in those periods the impact of the current period changes in final estimated profits.

LOSS ON CONTRACTS

Regardless of the method used to account for the contract, a loss should be recognized when the current estimate of total contract revenue is less than the current estimate of total contract costs. This determination should be based solely on that contract's revenues and costs after combining or segmenting contracts into appropriate units of accounting, as discussed earlier in this chapter. A loss on one contract (or, if applicable, one segment of a contract) cannot be deferred because the expected income from another contract (or contract segment) will absorb or "cover" that loss (ASC 605-35-25-45).

The loss on a contract should be treated as part of the contract cost, not as a reduction of contract revenues or non-operating expense. The amount of the loss does not need to be broken out separately on the income statement unless it is material, unusual, or infrequent in nature. To the extent the loss is separately presented on the income statement, it should be reflected as a component of gross profit (ASC 605-35-45-1).

When a contract loss is recorded, the credit reflected on the balance sheet should be treated as an offset to costs accumulated, if any exist, or as a current liability. The current liability should be shown as a separate line item on the balance sheet if the amount is significant (ASC 605-35-45-2).

EXAMPLE: LOSS CONTRACTS AND CHANGES UNCERTAINTY DUE TO ESTIMATES

Viasat, Inc. Form 10-K—Fiscal Year Ended April 1, 2011

A substantial portion of our revenues is derived from long-term contracts requiring development and delivery of complex equipment built to customer specifications. Sales related to these contracts are accounted for under the authoritative guidance for the percentage-of-completion method of accounting (ASC 605-35). Sales and earnings under these contracts are recorded either based on the ratio of actual costs incurred to date to total estimated costs expected to be incurred related to the contract or as products are shipped under the units-of-delivery method.

The percentage-of-completion method of accounting requires management to estimate the profit margin for each individual contract and to apply that profit margin on a uniform basis as sales are recorded under the contract. The estimation of profit margins requires management to make projections of the total sales to be generated and the total costs that will be incurred under a contract. These projections require management to make numerous assumptions and estimates relating to items such as the complexity of design and related development costs, performance of subcontractors, availability and cost of materials, labor productivity and cost, overhead and capital costs, and manufacturing efficiency. These contracts often include purchase options for additional quantities and customer change orders for additional or revised product functionality. Purchase options and change orders are accounted for either as an integral part of the original contract or separately depending upon the nature and value of the item. For contract claims or similar items, we apply judgment in estimating the amounts and assessing the potential for realization. These amounts are only included in contract value when they can be reliably estimated and realization is considered probable. Anticipated losses on contracts are recognized in full in the period in which losses become probable and estimable. During fiscal years 2011, 2010 and 2009, we recorded losses of approximately $12.1 million, $9.3 million and $5.4 million, respectively, related to loss contracts.

Assuming the initial estimates of sales and costs under a contract are accurate, the percentage-of-completion method results in the profit margin being recorded evenly as revenue is recognized under the contract. Changes in these underlying estimates due to revisions in sales and future cost estimates or the exercise of contract options may result in profit margins being recognized unevenly over a contract as such changes are accounted for on a cumulative basis in the period estimates are revised. We believe we have established appropriate systems and processes to enable us to reasonably estimate future cost on our programs through regular quarterly evaluations of contract costs, scheduling and technical matters by business unit personnel and management. Historically, in the aggregate, we have not experienced significant deviations in actual costs from estimated program costs, and when deviations that result in significant adjustments arise, we disclose the related impact in Management's Discussion and Analysis of Financial Condition and Results of Operations. However, these estimates require significant management judgment and a significant change in future cost estimates on one or more programs could have a material effect on our results of operations. A one percent variance in our future cost estimates on open fixed-price contracts as of April 1, 2011 would change our income before income taxes by approximately $0.5 million.

CHANGES IN ESTIMATES

Estimation is an integral part of contract accounting, particularly when using the percentage-of-completion method. The percentage-of-completion method requires estimates of total contract revenues, total contract costs, and progress toward completion. Changes in estimates should be accounted for under ASC 250, *Accounting Changes and Error Corrections* using the cumulative catch-up method. The cumulative catch-up method effectively provides for a true-up to the new estimate in the current period by calculating revenues, costs, and gross profit as if the new estimate were used from day one of the contract (ASC 605 35-25-86).

ILLUSTRATION: CHANGES IN ESTIMATES

Facts: Contractor J enters into a contract with Customer V to construct an office building. Performance under the contract is expected to span three years. Assume for purposes of this example that the contract falls within the scope of SOP 81-1 and that Contractor J meets the conditions required to apply the percentage-of-completion method and has decided to use Alternative A to calculate earned revenues and costs of earned revenue. The total amount initially due from Customer V under the contract is $10 million. The initial estimate of costs to construct the office building is $9 million. During Year 2, a change order is approved that results in an additional $500,000 of revenue under the contract. In addition, the combination of increased costs related to the change order as well as decreased costs due to construction efficiencies results in a net increase of $200,000 in the estimate of costs to construct the building. Other information necessary to determine earned revenues and costs of earned revenues for Year 1 and Year 2 of the contract is provided below.

	Year 1	Year 2
Total Expected Revenues	$10,000,000	$10,500,000
Total Expected Costs of Revenues	9,000,000	9,200,000
Total Expected Gross Profit	1,000,000	1,300,000
Expected Gross Profit Percentage	10%	12%
Percent Complete (calculated using an efforts-based input measure)	25%	70%

Accounting: The amount of Current Period Revenues and Current Period Costs using Alternative A for Years 1 and 2 are shown below.

	Year 1	Year 2
Revenues:		
Total Expected Revenues	$10,000,000	$10,500,000
Percent Complete	25%	70%
Cumulative Revenues	2,500,000	7,350,000
Revenues Earned in Prior Periods	—	2,500,000
Current Period Revenues	2,500,000	4,850,000
Costs of Revenues:		
Total Expected Costs	9,000,000	9,200,000
Percent Complete	25%	70%
Cumulative Costs of Revenues	2,250,000	6,440,000
Costs Recognized in Prior Periods	—	2,250,000
Current Period Costs	2,250,000	4,190,000
Current Period Gross Profit	250,000	660,000
Current Period Gross Profit Percentage	10%	14%
Cumulative Gross Profit Percentage	10%	12%

At the end of Year 2 the Cumulative Gross Profit Percentage is equal to the Expected Gross Profit Percentage. This is due to the cumulative catch-up adjustment effectively booked in Year 2. This adjustment resulted in a higher Current Period Gross Profit Percentage than the Cumulative Gross Profit Percentage in Year 2. The catch-up adjustment that was booked in Year 2 resulted in an additional $125,000 of revenues ($10,500,000 × 25% − $2,500,000), $50,000 of costs of revenues ($9,200,000 × 25% − $2,250,000) and $75,000 of gross profit in Year 2.

BALANCE SHEET PRESENTATION

The contract accounting literature, in contrast to the accounting for all other customer arrangements, allows balance sheet amounts that relate to costs and balance sheet amounts that relate to revenues to be offset against each other. In fact, while accounts receivable from billings under the contract are recognized separately, all other balance sheet entries related to a contract are typically made to a single balance sheet account.

Percentage-of-Completion Method

As costs are incurred, they are typically recorded in an asset account, with a descriptive caption such as "contracts in progress." As costs and revenues are recognized in the income statement, this account would be increased by the recognized gross profit. As billings occur, the "contracts in progress" asset would be reduced, and could, if billings occur in advance of the recognition of revenue, result in a "contract in progress" liability (ASC 605-35-45-3). Liabilities recorded due to estimated contract losses should similarly be offset against related contract assets (ASC 605-35-45-2). Contract assets and liabilities from different contracts should not be offset in the balance sheet.

As noted above, any accounts receivable from billings under the contract should be separately recorded, as the receivable represents a financial asset that is no longer tied to the contract accounting.

Completed-Contract Method

Under the completed-contract method, costs are accumulated on the balance sheet until the contract is complete or substantially complete. Similarly, amounts billed to customers are also deferred until the contract is complete or substantially complete. To the extent that the amount of accumulated costs exceeds the amount of advance (or progress) payments received or billed by the contractor, the excess should be reflected on the balance sheet as a current asset, separate from inventory. To the extent that the amount of advance (or progress) payments received or billed by the contractor exceeds the amount of accumulated costs, the excess should be reflected as a liability on the balance sheet (ASC 605-35-45-4 and 5).

PRACTICE POINTER: The contract accounting literature specifies that costs incurred but not yet expensed and revenues billed but not yet recognized should be offset against one another. This is generally inappropriate for other transactions. In those situations, inventory or deferred costs and deferred revenue must be reported separately in most revenue arrangements.

SEC REGISTRANT ALERT: For receivables due under long-term contracts, SEC registrants must state separately in the balance sheet, or disclose in the notes to the financial statements, the following (ASC 210-10-S99) (REG S-X, Rule 5-02):

1. Balances billed but not paid by customers under retainage provisions (i.e., retainage receivables);

2. Amounts representing the recognized sales value of performance and such amounts that have not been billed and were not billable to customers at the date of the balance sheet; and

3. Billed or unbilled amounts representing claims or other similar items subject to uncertainty concerning their determination or ultimate realization.

CHAPTER 10
SOFTWARE—A COMPLETE MODEL

CONTENTS

SURVEY OF APPLICABLE LITERATURE

ASC 985-605 comprehensively addresses revenue recognition for companies that sell, license, lease, or otherwise earn revenue from computer software. Because revenue accounting for software is so thoroughly covered, companies generally need not look to ASC 605-10-S99 (SAB Topic 13, *Revenue Recognition*) for guidance, except on a limited number of issues. The software revenue accounting model was largely promulgated in SOP 97-2, with certain important elements added by the EITF. Significant software revenue implementation guidance was also provided by a Task Force organized by the AICPA. All of this guidance is included in the FASB Accounting Standards Codification™ (ASC).

LISTING OF APPLICABLE LITERATURE

ASC	ASC Topic/ Subtopic	Publication	Subject
985-605	Software/ Revenue Recognition	SOP 97-2	Software Revenue Recognition
605-35	Revenue Recognition/ Construction-Type and Production-Type Contracts	ARB-45 and SOP 81-1	Construction-Type and Certain Production-Type Contracts
845-10	Nonmonetary Transactions/ Overall	APB-29	Nonmonetary Transactions
450-20	Contingencies/ Loss Contingencies	FAS-5	Loss Contingencies
605-15-25	Revenue Recognition/ Products	FAS-48	Revenue Recognition When Right of Return Exists
985-20	Software/Costs of Software to be Sold, Leased or Marketed	FAS-86	Costs of Computer Software to Be Sold, Leased, or Otherwise Marketed
460	Guarantees	FIN-45	Guarantees
460-10-55-30 through 55-34	Guarantees/ Overall	FSP FIN 45-1	Accounting for Intellectual Property Infringement Indemnifications
470-10-25	Debt/Overall	EITF 88-18	Sales of Future Revenues
985-605-15-3	Software/ Revenue Recognition	EITF 00-3	Arrangements That Include the Right to Use Software Stored on Another Entity's Hardware
605-25	Revenue Recognition/ Multiple-Element Arrangements	EITF 00-21 and ASU 2009-13	Revenue Arrangements with Multiple Deliverables

ASC	ASC Topic/ Subtopic	Publication	Subject
605-50	Revenue Recognition/ Customer Payments and Incentives	EITF 01-9	Accounting for Consideration Given by a Vendor to a Customer (Including a Reseller of the Vendor's Products)
985-605-15	Software/ Revenue Recognition	ASU 2009-14 (EITF 09-3)	Certain Revenue Arrangements That Include Software Elements
605-10-S99	Revenue Recognition/ Overall	SAB Topic 13	Revenue Recognition
985-605-25-9 and 55-94	Software/ Revenue Recognition	TPA 5100.38	Determination of Vendor-Specific Objective Evidence After the Balance Sheet Date
985-605-55-4	Software/ Revenue Recognition	TPA 5100.39	Indicators that Multiple Contracts Should be Viewed as Single Arrangements
985-605-55-15	Software/ Revenue Recognition	TPA 5100.41	Effect of Prepayments on Revenue Recognition
985-605-55-77 and 55-78	Software/ Revenue Recognition	TPA 5100.43	Promises to Correct Software Errors (Bug Fixes)
985-605-55-99	Software/ Revenue Recognition	TPA 5100.45	License Mix Arrangements
985-845	Software/ Revenue Recognition	TPA 5100.46 & .47	Nonmonetary Exchanges Involving Software
985-605-55-74	Software/ Revenue Recognition	TPA 5100.49	Post-Contract Customer Support When Contract Accounting Is Applied
985-605-15-3	Software/ Revenue Recognition	TPA 5100.50	Definition of More-Than-Insignificant Discount
985-605-55-85	Software/ Revenue Recognition	TPA 5100.51	Significant Incremental Discounts
985-605-55-57	Software/ Revenue Recognition	TPA 5100.52	Fair Value of PCS in a Perpetual License
985-605-55-59	Software/ Revenue Recognition	TPA 5100.53	Fair Value of PCS in a Short-Term Time-Based License
985-605-55-62	Software/ Revenue Recognition	TPA 5100.54	Fair Value of PCS in a Multi-Year Time-Based License
985-605-55-68	Software/ Revenue Recognition	TPA 5100.55	Fair Value of PCS with a Consistent Renewal Percentage (But Varying Renewal Dollar Amount)

ASC	ASC Topic/ Subtopic	Publication	Subject
985-605-55-18	Software/ Revenue Recognition	TPA 5100.56	Concessions
985-605-55-22	Software/ Revenue Recognition	TPA 5100.57	Overcoming Presumption of Concessions in Extended Payment Term Arrangements
985-605-55-31	Software/ Revenue Recognition	TPA 5100.58	Effect of Prepayments on Software Revenue Recognition—Transfer of Receivable Without Recourse
985-605-55-26	Software/ Revenue Recognition	TPA 5100.59	Subsequent Cash Receipt in an Extended Payment Term Arrangement
985-605-55-34	Software/ Revenue Recognition	TPA 5100.60	Customer Financing with No Software Vendor Participation
985-605-55-36	Software/ Revenue Recognition	TPA 5100.61	Effect of Prepayments on Software Revenue Recognition When Vendor Participates in Customer Financing
985-605-55-40	Software/ Revenue Recognition	TPA 5100.62	Indicators of Incremental Risk and Their Effect on the Evaluation of Whether a Fee Is Fixed or Determinable
985-605-55-42	Software/ Revenue Recognition	TPA 5100.63	Overcoming the Presumption that a Fee Is Not Fixed or Determinable When Vendor Participates in Customer Financing
985-605-55-46	Software/ Revenue Recognition	TPA 5100.64	Indicators of Vendor Participation in Customer Financing That May Not Result in Incremental Risk
985-605-55-79	Software/ Revenue Recognition	TPA 5100.67	Customer Acceptance
985-605-55-64	Software/ Revenue Recognition	TPA 5100.68	Fair Value of PCS in Perpetual and Multi-Year Time-Based Licenses
985-605-55-97	Software/ Revenue Recognition	TPA 5100.69	Delivery Terms
985-605-55-101	Software/ Revenue Recognition	TPA 5100.70	Effect of Commencement of an Initial License Term
985-605-55-105	Software/ Revenue Recognition	TPA 5100.71	Effect of Commencement of an Extension/Renewal License Term

ASC	ASC Topic/ Subtopic	Publication	Subject
985-605-55-110	Software/ Revenue Recognition	TPA 5100.72	Effect of Additional Product(s) in an Extension/ Renewal of License Term
985-605-55-115	Software/ Revenue Recognition	TPA 5100.73	Arrangement Containing an Option to Extend a Time- Based License Indefinitely
985-605-55-201	Software/ Revenue Recognition	TPA 5100.74	Effect of Discounts on Future Products on the Residual Method
985-605-55-70	Software/ Revenue Recognition	TPA 5100.75	Fair Value of PCS Renewals Based on Users Deployed
985-605-55-5	Software/ Revenue Recognition	TPA 5100.76	Fair Value in Multiple- Element Arrangements that Include Contingent Usage- Based Fees

OVERVIEW

Transfers of rights to software are generally accomplished by licenses rather than by outright sales to provide additional legal protection to software vendors. Software sales take many forms and vary in complexity. Although software licenses may have terms similar to a lease, such as a limited term and periodic payments, the rights transferred under software licenses are substantially the same as those transferred in many product sales. Therefore, in many cases, delivery of a license to use software is evaluated under the Completed Performance model (see Chapter 3, "General Principles").

Certain software sales involve significant production, modification, or customization of software. These types of software sales should be accounted for under the long-term construction-type contract model (see "Contract Accounting for Software Arrangements" later in this chapter).

Revenue from each software or software-related element in an arrangement that does not involve significant production, modification, or customization of software should be recognized when the vendor has vendor-specific objective evidence (VSOE) of the fair value of all of the undelivered elements and all of the following criteria have been met for the delivered element (see the "Multiple-Element Arrangements" section of this chapter for a discussion of when elements in a multiple-element arrangement involving software should be separated and if so, the allocation of revenue to each element in the arrangement):

1. Persuasive evidence of an arrangement exists.

2. The arrangement fee is fixed or determinable.

3. Delivery or performance has occurred.

4. Collectibility is reasonably assured.

These four criteria are the same criteria that must be met to recognize revenue in any transaction (see Chapter 3, "General Principles"). ASC 985-605 provides a significant amount of guidance on how to apply the criteria in a software transaction.

SCOPE

ASC 985-605 provides comprehensive guidance on software revenue recognition and was developed to address factors unique to the software industry. For example, one unusual factor of the software industry is that delivering additional units of the product (i.e., a piece of software) involves virtually no cost. As a result, some of the guidance in ASC 985-605 is not consistent with that of other revenue recognition literature. Therefore, determining whether an arrangement is within the scope of ASC 985-605 is extremely important.

ASC 985-605 applies to revenue-producing activities that involve the licensing, sale, leasing, or other marketing of computer software (ASC 985-605-15-3). The scope guidance focuses on the transaction rather than the type of company entering into it. Therefore, any company engaging in a software transaction should apply the guidance in this chapter.

Software-Related Elements

ASC 985-605 applies only to software and software-related elements, as defined in ASC 985-605-15-3c, 985-605-15-4, and 985-605-15-4A (ASU 2009-14, pars. 2 through 4). Pursuant to this guidance, tangible products are not accounted for under the software guidance (ASC 985-605-15-4Ad) (ASU 2009-14, par. 3). In addition, software that works with a tangible product to deliver the tangible product's essential functionality is not accounted for under the software guidance either (ASC 985-605-15-4e) (ASU 2009-14, par. 3), and services related to such software are also not considered software-related elements (ASC 985-605-15-4f) (ASU 2009-14, par. 3).

PRACTICE ALERT: Prior to the changes made by ASU 2009-14, tangible products that required software to deliver their essential functionality were considered software-related elements and both the product and the related software were accounted for under the software guidance (ASC 985-605-15-3, now superseded). As a result, many companies that did not consider themselves to be software companies were nonetheless required to recognize revenue under the provisions of ASC 985-605.

Because ASC 985-605 requires VSOE of fair value (as further discussed in this chapter) in order to separate elements in a multiple-element arrangement for purposes of revenue recognition, many multiple-element software arrangements do not qualify for separation. In those instances, no revenue is recognized for delivered items. When the delivered item is a tangible product and revenue cannot be recognized, the question of what to do with the costs of that product is quite difficult (that question generally doesn't arise if the delivered product is software, as the incremental costs are minimal). Furthermore, in an arrangement involving the delivery of a tangible product containing software, it is often the case that software is useless on its own, and that the tangible product provides most of the value.

Accounting for these arrangements under the software literature therefore generated results that many believed distorted the economics of the transactions. For that reason, the EITF determined that the software guidance should only be applied to software that functions separate from a specific piece of hardware, as well as services related to those software products.

This represents a very significant change in the revenue recognition literature that results in many fewer arrangements being within the scope of ASC 985-605. Combined with the changes made by ASU 2009-13 (see discussion in Chapter 4, "Multiple-Deliverable Revenue Arrangements"), these changes will result in faster revenue recognition for sales of many products that work with software.

In determining whether software (and related services) sold together with a tangible product is essential to the functionality of that tangible product (and therefore excluded from ASC 985-605), the following guidance applies.

- If the tangible product is only infrequently sold without the software, there is a rebuttable presumption that the software is essential to the tangible product's functionality, and therefore should be excluded from ASC 985-605. If, however, the tangible product is frequently sold without software, then any software sold with it in a particular transaction may not be essential to its functionality, and therefore might be within the scope of ASC 985-605.

- When software (and related services) is sold without a tangible product, that sale will be within the scope of ASC 985-605. However, the fact that software is sometimes sold on a standalone basis does not necessarily mean that it is not essential to a tangible product's functionality when it is sold with a tangible product. The question is not whether software can function on its own, but whether the hardware (tangible product) can function without the software.

- Software need not be embedded in the tangible product to be essential to its functionality.

- A tangible product that is simply a mechanism for delivering software should not be accounted for separate from the software. Instead, such items are considered software elements and are covered by ASC 985-605.

EXAMPLE: ADOPTION OF ASU 2009-14

Sensus Form 8-K—Dated May 7, 2010

Retrospective Adoption of Amended Accounting Standards

In October 2009, the Financial Accounting Standards Board ratified Emerging Issues Task Force (EITF) Issue 08-1 and EITF Issue 09-3, resulting in the issuance of accounting standard updates ASU 2009-13 and ASU 2009-14. Sensus elected to adopt the new standards during the fourth quarter of fiscal 2010. The revisions to the Company's financial statements for the fiscal years ended March 31, 2008 and 2009 resulting from this change in accounting standards will be reflected in the Company's Form 10-K for the fiscal year ended March 31, 2010. The Form 10-K for the fiscal year ended March 31, 2010 will also include selected quarterly financial schedules reflecting the impact of retrospective adoption of these accounting standards.

The new accounting principles result in the Company's recognition of substantially all of the revenue and product cost for FlexNet systems when those products are delivered to customers. Under historical accounting principles, the Company was required to account for sales of FlexNet systems over the life of the contracts. Revenue and associated product cost of sales for FlexNet systems were deferred at the time of sale and recognized on a straight-line basis over each contract's life. This resulted in the deferral of significant amounts of revenue and cost of sales related to FlexNet systems.

The Company retrospectively adopted the new accounting principles as if the new accounting principles had been applied in all prior periods from fiscal 2007 through fiscal 2010. Consequently, the financial results of each quarter through fiscal 2010 have been revised. The Company believes retrospective adoption provides analysts and investors with the most comparable and useful financial information and better reflects the underlying performance of the Company's business. For additional information, refer to the Company's Annual Report on Form 10-K for the fiscal year ended March 31, 2010.

ILLUSTRATION: ARRANGEMENTS THAT INCLUDE TANGIBLE PRODUCTS AND SOFTWARE ELEMENTS

(Adapted from ASC 985-605-55-211 through 55-234 (ASU 2009-14, par. 7))

EXAMPLE 1

Facts: Vendor sells a personal computer that includes an operating system that, along with the hardware, provides the basic functionality of a personal computer, including the ability to: (a) manage the computer and its hardware functions; (b) manage and interact with a range of hardware peripherals; and (c) communicate through a variety of types of computer networks. This arrangement has no undelivered elements.

Case A: Vendor rarely sells the computer without the operating system.

Case B: Vendor commonly sells the computer without the operating system.

Case C: Vendor rarely sells the computer without an operating system, but there are multiple operating systems that vendor sells with the computer.

Discussion: In Case A, because the computer is only infrequently sold without the operating system, the operating system would be essential to the functionality of the computer. As such, both the computer and the operating system are excluded from ASC 985-605.

In Case B, because the computer is commonly sold without the operating system, the operating system is not essential to the computer's functionality. The computer is still excluded from ASC 985-605) because it is a tangible product, but the operating system would be a separate deliverable accounted for under the software guidance.

In Case C, although there are multiple operating systems that can be used, the fact that the computer is only infrequently sold without an operating system indicates that the operating system in the particular transaction is essential to the computer's functionality. As such, both the computer and the operating system are outside the scope of ASC 985-605.

The analysis of each of these situations in unaffected by whether the operating system is frequently sold separately from the computer. The critical assessment is whether the computer and the operating system in one transaction are both necessary to provide the computer's essential functionality, not whether the operating system could also be used by another computer.

However, the operating system would be considered a software element in a transaction in which it is sold separately from the computer.

EXAMPLE 2

Facts: Vendor sells a personal computer that includes an operating system that, along with the hardware, provides the basic functionality of a personal computer, including the ability to: (a) manage the computer and its hardware functions; (b) manage and interact with a range of hardware peripherals; and (c) communicate through a variety of types of computer networks. Vendor also provides a specified upgrade right for the next version of its operation, along with post-contract customer support (PCS) related to both the computer and the operating system.

Case D: Vendor rarely sells the computer without the operating system.

Case E: Vendor commonly sells the computer without the operating system.

Discussion: In Case D, consistent with the analysis in Case A above, the computer and operating system are determined to be a single nonsoftware deliverable because the operating system is essential to the computer's functionality. All deliverables related to the computer and operating system are therefore also nonsoftware deliverables. Therefore, the PCS and upgrade right would also be excluded from ASC 985-605.

In Case E, the operating system would be considered to be a software deliverable within the scope of ASC 985-605, consistent with the analysis in Case B above. Therefore, the upgrade right is also a software element within the scope of ASC 985-605. Because the PCS relates to both the software deliverable (i.e., operating system) and nonsoftware deliverable (i.e., computer), it must be bifurcated into its software and nonsoftware components.

EXAMPLE 3

Facts: Vendor sells networking equipment that provides its energy company customers with the ability to remotely monitor and manage their customers' energy use. Vendor sells an integrated package of equipment and software that consists of a monitoring device that is placed at the end customer's location to collect data that it then relays back to the energy company and software that allows the energy company to analyze the data and interface with its billing system. The software is installed on the energy company's computer system, which is not purchased from Vendor. The equipment does not have functionality without the software, and the software does not have functionality without the equipment. Vendor's customers will initially purchase all of these components together; however, they also can separately purchase replacement or expansion equipment or updated versions of the software at a subsequent time.

Discussion: The equipment and software would all be considered nonsoftware elements outside the scope of ASC 985-605. The monitoring and relay equipment work together with the software (though not as a physically combined unit) to deliver the product's essential functionality. Although Vendor does sell the equipment separately without the software, it only does so in replacement situations or as the customer base of the energy company expands. The customer would have needed to previously acquire the software for the replacement equipment to function.

OBSERVATION: Companies should periodically reevaluate the relationship between tangible products and software. In some cases, changes in business models may result in software that was once essential to the functionality of a tangible product no longer being so. In other cases, functionality that used to be provided by a tangible product in conjunction with software may become entirely software-driven, with the hardware serving mainly as a mechanism to deliver the software. In either of those situations, the software that was not previously within the scope of ASC 985-605 would become subject to that guidance after the change in business model.

Incidental Software

Software that is incidental to a product should not be accounted for under ASC 985-605. Indicators of whether software is incidental to a product as a whole include, but are not limited to (see ASC 985-605-15-3 and 15-4):

1. *Whether the software is a significant focus of the marketing effort or is sold separately.* When a company makes software a significant focus of the marketing effort or sells such software separately, it indicates that the software has significant functionality and importance to the product as a whole. The evaluation of the significance of software in the marketing effort should consider representations made in product literature, websites, communications with the customer (including contract negotiations), and other advertising channels.

2. *Whether the vendor will provide software upgrades or telephone support to users relating to the operation of the software.* The obligation to provide these types of post-sale services may indicate that the software is more than incidental. The nature and relative significance of post-sale support services to the overall functionality of the product requires judgment and careful evaluation in making this determination. The distinction between warranties and post-sale support often is a critical component of this evaluation.

3. *Whether the vendor incurs significant costs that are within the scope of ASC 985-20.* Logically, if the company incurs significant costs in developing the software portion of the product, software would be a significant component of the product or service. Another component of this evaluation is the cost of developing and providing post-sale support.

4. *Whether the software and/or post-sale support is sold separately or the customer acquires title to the software.* Such sales and the transfer of title would establish both separability and value to the customer independent of the functionality and features of the remainder of the product or service. The separate subsequent sale or renewal of post-sale support would be a very strong indicator of the significance of software.

ILLUSTRATION: INCIDENTAL SOFTWARE

EXAMPLE 1   (Adapted from ASC 985-605-55-126 through 55-129)

Facts: An automobile includes software that assists in the electronic fuel injection process and helps to run the electronic dashboard. This software is used solely in connection with operating the automobile and is not sold or marketed separately. Once installed, the software may or may not be updated for new versions (models) that the manufacturer subsequently develops. The automobile manufacturer's costs for the development and subsequent updates of the software are insignificant relative to the other development and production costs of the automobile.

Discussion: The sale of the car should not be accounted for in accordance with the literature on software revenue recognition because the software is incidental to the product as a whole. Although the software may be critical to the operation of the automobile, the software *enables* or assists in the operation rather than drives the automobile. The software itself is not the focus of the marketing effort, nor is it what the customer believes he or she is buying.

EXAMPLE 2

Facts: A company produces maps previously distributed in hard copy, but now puts the data on a CD along with software that allows the customer to generate customized maps of his or her route, including identification of key attractions, hotels, and the like along the route. These features are mentioned prominently in the promotional literature for the interactive atlas.

Discussion: The software revenue recognition literature is applicable because the software is not incidental to the product. Although some might argue that the product is maps, not software, the marketing of the product focuses on the interactive features made possible by the software. In this situation, the conclusion would not change, even if the software development costs were small and no post-sale upgrade or technical support were provided.

EXAMPLE 3

Facts: Company A manufactures a handheld personal organizer that includes a calendar, address book, calculator, and game modules. The personal organizer operates using a proprietary software operating system, for which upgrades are periodically made available on Company A's website. The operating system allows users to download other programs to the personal organizer to enhance its capabilities. The main points of differentiation between Company A's products and those of the competitors, aside from minor styling details, are the features and functionality of the operating system, including the number of additional programs that run on the system. Company A spends considerable time and effort in maintaining and upgrading its operating system so that it remains better than the competitors' systems.

Discussion: The software revenue recognition literature is applicable because the software is not incidental to the product. The operating system is a key point of differentiation between Company A's product and the competitors' products, and Company A spends time and effort to keep its product leading edge. In addition, upgrades are made available to users from time to time. All of this indicates that the software is more than incidental to the personal organizer.

> **OBSERVATION:** Companies should periodically reevaluate the significance of embedded software to existing products. This is important because the evolution of additional features and functionality could make software that was once incidental significant to a product as a whole and thereby subject to the guidance in ASC 985-605.

EXAMPLE: INCIDENTAL SOFTWARE

Pitney Bowes, Inc. Form 10-K—Fiscal Year Ended December 31, 2009

We sell equipment with embedded software to our customers. The embedded software is not sold separately, it is not a significant focus of the marketing effort and we do not provide post-contract customer support specific to the software or incur significant costs that are subject to capitalization. Additionally, the functionality that the software provides is marketed as part of the overall product. The software embedded in the equipment is incidental to the equipment as a whole such that the software revenue recognition accounting guidance is not applicable.

Software Used to Provide a Service

A company may provide a customer with services that require the use of software. As a result, it may be difficult to determine whether the transaction should be accounted for as the provision of a service, to which software revenue recognition guidance does not apply, or as the sale of software. The answer depends on whether the rights to use the software remain solely with the company or are transferred to the customer as part of the transaction. When these rights transfer to the customer, the transaction should be accounted for in accordance with ASC 985-605.

ILLUSTRATION: DETERMINING WHETHER A TRANSACTION IS A SOFTWARE OR SERVICE TRANSACTION

Facts: Company I provides tax preparation services. Its services are based on a sophisticated software package that gathers and processes all of the necessary information to prepare a tax return. Customers may use Company I's software in two ways. A customer may purchase a copy of the software from Company I, download the software onto their computer, input the necessary information, and generate their tax return. If the customer chooses this option, he or she obtains a copy of the software that remains on his or her computer.

Alternatively, a customer may log on to Company I's website and for a fee, set up a user account and input the necessary information in an online form. Through an automated process, that information is then input into a version of Company I's software running on Company I's system and a tax return is generated, which the customer may then download and file online. If the customer chooses this option, he or she does not obtain a copy of the software and is only entitled to use the online tax preparation service.

Discussion: The first type of transaction above represents the sale of software and should be accounted for under ASC 985-605 because the customer obtains the right to use the software. However, in the second transaction, the customer does not obtain the right to use the software. Instead, the customer only has the right to obtain a service provided by Company I.

Hosted Software Arrangements

In recent years, there has been significant growth in "Software as a Service" (SaaS). In a SaaS arrangement, users do not take possession of the software. Rather, the software application and/or data resides on the vendor's or a third party's hardware and the customer accesses and uses the software on an as-needed basis through what has colloquially been termed "the Cloud." These arrangements are sometimes called hosting or application service provider arrangements, and may or may not include a license to the software and the customer may or may not have an option to take delivery of the software.

Because the customer in a hosted software arrangement does not install the software on its own computer system, it is not clear whether the customer has purchased software or merely the right to a service. The EITF concluded that a SaaS or hosting arrangement is only considered a sale of software if all of the following are true (ASC 985-605-15-3):

1. The customer has the contractual right to take possession of the software at any time during the hosting period;

2. The customer will not incur a significant penalty (in terms of cost and value in use) if it exercises its right to take possession of the software; and

3. It is feasible for the customer to either run the software on its own hardware or contract with another party unrelated to the vendor to host the software.

An arrangement meeting the above criteria should be accounted for as a multiple-element arrangement (see "Multiple-Element Arrangements" later in this chapter), the two elements being the software product and the hosting service (ASC 985-605-55-124). The multiple-element arrangement guidance in ASC 985-605 should be applied to this type of arrangement, because the hosting services are considered software-related (see "Software-Related Elements" later in this chapter).

OBSERVATION: Even in this situation, revenue should not be recognized upon delivery of the software unless VSOE exists for the hosting element (at inception, the undelivered element) in the arrangement. Unless the company sells hosting services separately, VSOE of fair value likely does not exist (see "Multiple-Element Arrangements" later in this chapter for further discussion).

A hosting arrangement that does not meet all three of the above criteria should be accounted for as a contract to provide a service, not as a sale of software (see Chapter 6, "Service Deliverables"). This makes it unlikely that any revenue will be recognized at the inception of the arrangement.

Even if the customer has the option to take delivery of the software, the seller must still account for the transaction as the provision of a service unless it is "feasible" for the customer to take delivery and thus end the hosting arrangement, without a "significant penalty." The EITF noted that a significant penalty exists if the customer does not have the ability to take delivery of the software without incurring significant cost or has that ability but would experience a significant diminution in utility or value of the software if the hosting arrangement were ended (ASC 985-605-55-122).

The following are some examples of situations in which it is either not feasible for the customer to take possession of the software or a "significant penalty" exists:

- The vendor's software runs only on specialized hardware and most individual customers need to use only a small portion of the hardware's capacity. In addition, no significant third parties provide hosting services using this specialized hardware. In this instance, it is not feasible for most customers to take delivery because it would not be economical for the customer to purchase the hardware.

- The hosting arrangement has a three-year term and may not be cancelled without payment of the remaining hosting fees. Assuming the fair value of the hosting is significant either on its own or in relation to the overall arrangement, the requirement to continue paying for hosting not being received would be a significant penalty.

- A customer is entitled to upgrades of the software if it pays to have the seller host the software and is not entitled to those upgrades (and cannot purchase them) if it ends the hosting arrangement. If upgrades are expected to be important to the customer, the fact that it can obtain them only if it pays for hosting constitutes a significant penalty for ending the hosting arrangement.

- To use a key function of the software, it is necessary that the user communicate with other users of the same software and that communication is facilitated through the hosted environment. Although the customer may have the right to take delivery of the software and cancel the hosting arrangement, it would lose access to the online community if it chooses to cancel the hosting.

EXAMPLE: HOSTING ARRANGEMENTS

Computer Programs and Systems, Inc. Form 10-K—Fiscal Year Ended December 31, 2009

The Company accounts for ASP contracts in accordance with the requirements of the *Hosting Arrangement* section under the *Software* topic and *Revenue Recognition* subtopic of the FASB Codification. The Codification states that the software element of ASP services should not be accounted for as a hosting arrangement "if the customer has the contractual right to take possession of the software at any time during the hosting period without significant penalty and it is feasible for the customer to either run the software on its own hardware or contract with another party related to the vendor to host the software." Each ASP contract includes a system purchase and buyout clause, and this clause specifies the total amount of the system buyout. In addition, a clause is included which states that should the system be bought out by the customer, the customer would be required to enter into a general support agreement (for post-contract support services) for the remainder of the original ASP term. Accordingly, the Company has concluded that ASP customers do not have the right to take possession of the system without significant penalty (i.e. the purchase price of the system), and thus ASP revenue of CPSI falls within the scope of the *Hosting Arrangement* section of the Codification. In accordance with SEC regulations, revenue is recognized when the services are performed.

PERSUASIVE EVIDENCE OF AN ARRANGEMENT

The evaluation of the persuasive evidence of an arrangement criterion is the same in a software environment as in any other revenue transaction. Software companies, like non-software entities, should evaluate this criterion based on their standard business practices. If obtaining written contracts is the software vendor's customary business practice, the persuasive evidence of an arrangement criterion has been met only when both parties have signed and executed the written contract (ASC 985-605-25-16). Regardless of how an arrangement is documented, the documentation must be in place before any revenue can be recognized. For an additional discussion, see Chapter 3, "General Principles."

Documentation of persuasive evidence can take on added significance for a software vendor, because a sale of software generally results in almost zero cost of sales. Therefore, any revenue recognized has nearly a 100% corresponding effect on margins and both operating and pre-tax income.

PRACTICE POINTER: Software companies that sell large software packages are likely to have a small number of individual transactions, each of which is significant to the company's revenue and net income. Because of the significant effect that a revenue transaction may have on net income, these vendors (and their salespeople) may feel pressured to close a transaction before the end of a fiscal quarter or fiscal year, especially if the company is publicly traded. Therefore, companies should have strong internal controls to ensure that appropriate documentation is received before the end of the period for all transactions from which revenue is recognized.

FIXED OR DETERMINABLE FEES AND COLLECTIBILITY

In most cases, the fixed or determinable fees and collectibility criteria are applied to software arrangements in the same manner they are applied to product or service transactions. Thus, if a portion of the fee is contingent upon future events, such as the software helping the customer achieve cost reductions, the contingent portion of the fee should not be recognized until the contingency is resolved.

Transaction-Based Pricing Arrangements

A simple example of a software arrangement with a contingent fee is one where some, or all, of the fee is based on the volume of transactions or amount of information processed. For example, a banking software package may be sold for a fixed fee of $1,000,000 plus an additional payment of one cent for every processed transaction. In this case, the $1,000,000 fixed fee may be recognized upon delivery (provided all other criteria have been met), but the additional one cent per transaction fee cannot be recognized until the transactions are actually processed. This is the case even if the vendor has no further obligations and can reasonably estimate the number of transactions that will be processed.

Extended Payment Terms

ASC 985-605 specifically discusses the application of the fixed or determinable criterion to software arrangements with extended payment terms. Although such terms must be evaluated in any revenue transaction to determine whether they introduce a contingency or raise the risk of nonpayment, extended payment terms in a software environment raise the risk that a concession, such as an additional software product or user license, will be granted to ensure payment of the previously agreed-upon amount. This risk is especially high in the software industry because of rapid technological change and the fact that the cost of providing a concession may be insignificant. As a result, software sales that include extended payment terms must be critically evaluated to determine whether they meet the fixed or determinable criterion.

Because of the higher risk of concessions in software arrangements, ASC 985-605 specifies that a presumption exists that the fee in a software transaction is not fixed or determinable if a significant portion of the payment is due beyond the earlier of the expiration of the license or one year following delivery (ASC 985-605-25-33 and 25-34).

EXAMPLE: EXTENDED PAYMENT TERMS

Metastorm, Inc. and Subsidiaries Financial Statements Filed as an Exhibit to Internet Capital Group, Inc. Form 10-K—Fiscal Year Ended December 31, 2009

License revenues include fees from the sale of software developed and licensed by the Company. Off-the-shelf software sold by the Company is recognized when persuasive evidence of an arrangement exists, delivery has occurred, the fee is fixed and determinable and collection is probable. The Company does not offer any rights of return or price protection either through direct or indirect sales. The Company's payment terms for typical software sales require payment within three months. In certain sales in which customers make large-scale purchase and deployment of software, payment terms could extend beyond three months but in no case beyond twelve months. The Company considers all arrangements with payment terms extending beyond three months for typical software sales and beyond twelve months for sales involving large-scale deployment of software not to have fees that are fixed and determinable. The following are examples of situations where the Company determines the fee to not be fixed or determinable:

- If a significant portion of the fee is due after the Company's established payment terms, revenue recognition is deferred until payment has been received from the customer.

- If a transaction is subject to customer acceptance provisions where delivery is uncertain, revenue recognition is deferred until evidence of the customer's acceptance of the product is received.

- If the price is subject to refund or forfeiture, concession or other adjust-ment, revenue recognition is deferred until these rights expire.

The presumption, however, may be overcome if persuasive evidence dem-onstrates that the vendor has a business practice of using extended payment terms and has been successful in collecting under the original terms, without providing any concessions. If the presumption cannot be overcome due to a lack of such evidence, revenue should be recognized as payments become due, assuming that all other revenue recognition criteria have been met (ASC 985-605-25-34 and 25-35).

OBSERVATION: Because of the conclusion that payment terms exceeding one year create a presumption that the fee is not fixed or determinable, a company with no history of successfully collecting under such arrangements must recognize revenue as payments become due, even though delivery has occurred and the customer is creditworthy. In fact, strong creditworthiness does not help a company overcome this presumption because the concern is that a concession will be provided, not that the customer will become unable to pay.

PRACTICE POINTER: These provisions are often misinterpreted to permit immediate recognition, upon delivery, of any payments due within one year, even if other payments extend beyond one year. The basis for conclusions that was published when SOP 97-2 was issued makes clear that recognition of *any* revenue is prohibited until payments become due unless the presumption dis-cussed above is overcome.

ILLUSTRATION: ONE-YEAR PRESUMPTION

Facts: Vendor S sells a perpetual license to one of its software products for a fee of $10,000,000. Payment terms are $2,500,000 upon delivery and another $2,500,000 every six months thereafter. Thus, $2,500,000 of the fee (the final payment) is due more than one year after delivery. Vendor S does not have a history of using extended payment term arrangements, but the customer in this arrangement is very creditworthy and has used Vendor S's products for a long time without complaints. There are no return, acceptance, or other provisions in the arrangement that raise additional questions regarding the customer's obliga-tion to pay the license fee.

Discussion: Because Vendor S has no history of using extended payment terms, the fact that a significant (25%) portion of the fee is due more than one year after delivery means that Vendor S may only recognize revenue as pay-ments become due. Thus, Vendor S may only recognize $2,500,000 upon delivery, even though $7,500,000 is due within one year of delivery. The creditworthiness of the customer and Vendor S's strong relationship with the customer do not change this conclusion.

Overcoming the Presumption That the Fee in an Extended Payment Term Arrangement Is Not Fixed or Determinable

To overcome this presumption, a company must have persuasive evidence, based on historical practice, of its ability to collect under the original terms of extended payment arrangements without granting concessions.

Concessions by a software vendor may take many forms. Essentially, any change to an arrangement that reduces the total revenue to be recognized, extends the payment terms, increases the customer's rights, or increases the vendor's obligations constitutes a concession. For example, the following would all be considered concessions (ASC 985-605-55-18 through 55-21):

- Extending payment due dates in the arrangement;
- Decreasing total payments due under the arrangement;
- Paying financing fees on a customer's financing arrangement that were not contemplated in the original arrangement;
- Accepting returns beyond those provided for in the terms of the original arrangement;
- Providing discounted or free PCS that was not included in the original arrangement;
- Providing other discounted or free services, upgrades, or products that were not included in the original arrangement;
- Extending the timeframe for a reseller to sell the software or an end user to use the software; and
- Extending the geographic area in which a reseller is allowed to sell the software, or the number of locations in which an end user can use the software.

To have a history of successfully collecting under the original payment terms without making concessions, a vendor must have collected all payments as due under comparable arrangements without providing concessions. For example, a vendor that sells software with three-year payment terms, but has only been doing so for the past year, could not have sufficient history, even if it has yet to encounter any difficulties.

In order to determine whether the company's historical experience is based on sufficiently similar arrangements, the following factors should be considered (ASC 985-605-55-22 through 55-25):

- *Type or class of customer.*
- *Types of products.*
- *Stage of product life cycle.* The later in a product's life cycle that an arrangement is entered into, the higher the likelihood of the product becoming technologically obsolete during the payment period.
- *Elements included in the arrangement.* The inclusion of significant rights to services or discounts on future products in some arrangements, but not others, could indicate that there is a significant difference between these arrangements. For example, an arrangement that does not include bun-

dled PCS and rights to additional software products would not be comparable to arrangements that included these rights.

- *Length of payment terms.*

- *Economics of license arrangement.* License arrangements that include significant discounts from list prices may not be comparable to those that do not.

Revenue Recognition When Payments Become Due

If, at the inception of an arrangement, a fee in a software arrangement with extended payment terms is not deemed fixed or determinable (e.g., if the presumption cannot be overcome), revenue must be recognized as payments become due. However, if the payment terms are changed, it may not be clear when revenue should be recognized.

If a customer makes payments early (e.g., to avoid financing costs), revenue should be recognized when the payments are received, because the fact that the customer has received payments indicates that the fee is now fixed or determinable (ASC 985-605-55-15).

However, the presumption that the licensing fee is not fixed or determinable is *not* overcome if the vendor receives cash from selling the receivable under the extended payment term arrangement to a third party, even if the sale is without recourse to the vendor. The difference between this situation and the one in the previous paragraph is that the transfer of the extended payment term arrangement does not change the nature or structure of the transaction between the vendor and customer. Therefore, the presumption that the fee is not fixed or determinable is not overcome by any transaction between the vendor and a third party. Instead, the sale of the right to receive payments from the customer should be accounted for under ASC 470-10-25 (see Chapter 11, "Presentation") (ASC 985-605-55-31; 985-605-55-32).

Cash Received after Balance Sheet Date

The determination of whether the fee in an extended payment term arrangement is fixed or determinable must be made at the outset of the arrangement. Subsequent cash receipts do not change this conclusion. Thus, a payment (even a full payment) received after the end of a reporting period cannot be used to justify the recognition of revenue in that reporting period. Instead, a payment received after period end should be recognized in the next period (i.e., the period the payment was made) (ASC 985-605-55-26 through 55-30).[1]

Customer Financing with Software Vendor Participation

To receive payment on normal terms, a software vendor may help the customer obtain financing from a third party. If the vendor's participation results in incremental risk that a refund or concession will be provided to either the end-

---

[1] Collecting a payment after the end of the period is a "Nonrecognized Subsequent Event," as discussed in ASC 855. Nonrecognized subsequent events "provide evidence with respect to conditions that did *not* exist at the date of the balance sheet but arose after the balance sheet date."

user or financing party, the financing arrangement should be evaluated to determine whether it creates extended payment terms. For example, if the financing arrangement between the company and the third-party lender extends for greater than one year after delivery, a presumption would exist that the fee is not fixed or determinable. If the software vendor cannot overcome this presumption, revenue should be recognized as payments become due and payable from the customer to the financing party, provided all other revenue recognition requirements have been met. Therefore, a payment received by the vendor at contract inception would be reported as deferred revenue until the customer's payments to the financing party become due.

Any one of the following conditions or actions results in incremental risk and a presumption that the fee is not fixed or determinable (ASC 985-605-55-38 through 55-41):

1. Provisions that require the software vendor to indemnify the financing party against claims (when such indemnifications are greater than similar indemnifications included in the company's standard arrangements with customers).

2. Provisions that require the software vendor to make representations to the financing party related to customer acceptance of the software that are above and beyond any written acceptance documentation that the software vendor has already received from the end user customer.

3. Provisions that obligate the software vendor to take actions against the customer on behalf of the financing party, or to refuse further business from the customer, in the event that the customer defaults under the financing arrangements, unless, as part of the original arrangement, the customer explicitly authorizes the software vendor to take such actions without penalty.

4. Provisions that require the software vendor to guarantee, certify, or otherwise attest to the financing party that the customer meets the financing party's qualification criteria.

5. Provisions that require the software vendor to guarantee the customer's indebtedness to the financing party.

6. The software vendor has previously provided concessions to customers or financing parties to facilitate or induce payment.

When a software arrangement involves an indemnification or a guarantee as discussed in items 1 and 5 above, the provisions of ASC 460 may apply. This depends on whether the existence of the indemnification or guarantee precludes revenue recognition. If the indemnification or guarantee leads to a conclusion that the fee is not fixed or determinable, the provisions of ASC 460 do not apply. However, if the presumption can be overcome (i.e., the fee is fixed or determinable despite the existence of the indemnification or guarantee), the provisions of ASC 460 should be considered.

When the presumption related to an indemnification can be overcome, ASC 460-10-55-30 through 55-34 indicates that a software licensing agreement that indemnifies the licensee against liability and damages (including legal defense costs) arising from any claims of patent, copyright, trademark, or trade secret infringement by the software vendor's software falls within the scope of ASC 460 from a disclosure perspective, but not from an initial recognition and measurement perspective. As a result, although the indemnification must be disclosed, its fair value should not be initially recognized nor should it be treated as a separate element in a multiple-element arrangement (see Chapter 12, "Disclosures").

In other situations in which the presumption is overcome, all of the provisions of ASC 460 may apply. In this case, the arrangement may contain two elements: the software and the guarantee. Further analysis is required to determine whether the guarantee is a separable element. (See Chapter 4, "Multiple-Deliverable Revenue Arrangements," regarding the scope of ASC 460 and the accounting for multiple-element arrangements where one of the elements is a guarantee. Also, see Chapter 12 for the disclosure requirements of ASC 460.)

GAAP also identifies several actions that the vendor may take that do not result in any incremental risk (ASC 985-605-55-46) (TPA 5100.64):

- The software vendor introduces the customer and financing party, facilitates their discussions, provides the financing party with information on behalf of the customer, and assists the customer in filling out applications, as long as the vendor does not attest in any manner that the customer meets the financing party's qualification criteria.

- The software vendor makes representations to the financing party similar to representations included in the arrangement with the customer.

- The vendor takes actions that were explicitly authorized by the customer in the original arrangement to terminate the license agreement and/or any related services, or to not enter into another arrangement for the same or similar product.

- The vendor grants customary recourse provisions to its customer related to warranties for defective software.

Cancellation and Customer Acceptance Clauses

Cancellation clauses should be evaluated to determine their substance. For example, a cancellation clause that is short-term and subjective in nature should be evaluated as a right of return (see "Rights to Exchange or Return Software" later in this chapter). However, a clause that allows a customer to cancel the arrangement only if the software does not meet standard specifications should be evaluated as a warranty. The treatment of warranties in a software transaction is the same as it is in the sale of any other product (see Chapter 5, "Product Deliverables") (ASC 985-605-25-37).

Certain cancellation and customer acceptance clauses may raise uncertainty about whether the transaction is complete. After delivery, if uncertainty exists about customer acceptance of the software, license revenue should not be recognized until acceptance occurs. This will often be the case when a customer acceptance clause is based on customer or arrangement-specific criteria that cannot be evaluated until the software is installed and operating in the customer's environment (ASC 985-605-25-21). For further information on these and other customer acceptance clauses, see Chapter 5.

EXAMPLE: ACCEPTANCE PROVISIONS

Oracle Corporation Form 10-K—Fiscal Year Ended May 31, 2011

Substantially all of our software license arrangements do not include acceptance provisions. However, if acceptance provisions exist as part of public policy, for example, in agreements with government entities where acceptance periods are required by law, or within previously executed terms and conditions that are referenced in the current agreement and are short-term in nature, we generally recognize revenues upon delivery provided the acceptance terms are perfunctory and all other revenue recognition criteria have been met. If acceptance provisions are not perfunctory (e.g. , acceptance provisions that are long-term in nature or are not included as standard terms of an arrangement), revenues are recognized upon the earlier of receipt of written customer acceptance or expiration of the acceptance period.

If a software sale is cancelable after delivery, the fixed or determinable condition is not met until the cancellation privileges lapse. If the cancellation privileges lapse ratably, then the fee becomes fixed or determinable ratably. For example, software sold on a three-year term license, with payments due at the beginning of each year, might have a cancellation provision that enables the customer to terminate its license after two years and avoid making the license fee payment for year 3. If this is the case, revenue related to year 3 cannot be recognized until the cancellation right lapses, even if the vendor has sufficient history to overcome the presumption that the fee is not fixed or determinable because of extended payment terms.

Price Protection

Price protection is common in software arrangements, particularly arrangements with resellers. Price protection typically provides the buyer with a credit for any price decreases that occur during a specified period of time or until the buyer resells the products. In these situations, revenue should be recognized net of the estimated amount to be refunded under the price protection, assuming the refund amount can be reasonably and reliably estimated and that the other conditions for revenue recognition have been met. When there are significant uncertainties related to the seller's ability to maintain its prices, refunds may not be reasonably and reliably estimable. If refunds cannot be reliably estimated, revenue should not be recognized until reliable estimates can be made or the price protection lapses (ASC 985-605-25-36). This is accounting is the same in a software arrangement as it is in any other arrangement.

DELIVERY

Products

The primary software product element is the license which is usually delivered on a disk, tape, or other storage media. Software elements may also be delivered electronically, via e-mail or the internet. Generally, the product element in a software arrangement is fairly easy to identify and will be accounted for in the same manner as any non-software product (i.e., delivery of software generally occurs when the product is transferred to the customer). Exceptions to this fundamental principle are also the same as in other product transactions and include consignment shipments, bill and hold sales, and product financing arrangements. When software is to be delivered on a physical storage medium such as a disk, tape, or hard drive, the financial reporting provisions relating to title or delivery to an alternate site also apply. For information on all these topics, see Chapter 5, "Product Deliverables." Special considerations related to the delivery of software are discussed further below.

Electronic Delivery

When software is delivered electronically, the delivery criterion is considered to have been met when the customer either downloads the software, or has been provided with access codes that permit the immediate possession of the software on the customer's hardware pursuant to an agreement or purchase order for the software (ASC 985-605-25-18).

Multiple Licenses of the Same Product

Some software arrangements involve multiple copies or licenses of the same software. These arrangements may specify the number of copies the customer may use, or allow the customer to use an unlimited number of copies (a site license). As long as the arrangement does not have a variable fee arrangement (i.e., one based on the number of copies ordered), delivery of all copies of a particular piece of software occurs when the first copy or product master is delivered to the customer. In these arrangements, duplication, even if it is to be performed by the vendor, is incidental to the arrangement, and the fee is payable even if no additional copies are requested. The estimated costs of duplication should be accrued at the time revenue is recognized if the vendor is responsible for duplication (ASC 985-605-25-23).

Multiple-copy software arrangements may also be structured so that, although the customer has the right to multiple (or perhaps unlimited) copies of the software, the fee varies based on the number of copies the customer deploys as an end-user, or sells to end-users as a reseller. As a result, delivery only occurs as the copies are made by the user or sold by the reseller. In this type of arrangement, the fee for the additional copies is not fixed or determinable until the copies are made or sold (ASC 985-605-25-24).

Authorization Codes or Keys

Some vendors use electronic "locks" to prevent unauthorized users from accessing the software. Thus, a user must not only have a copy of the software, but also have the correct authorization code, or "key," to use the software. Typically, software installed without a permanent key will work for a short period of time before it becomes locked. In software arrangements involving the use of keys, delivery of all keys is not necessarily required to satisfy the delivery condition. The software may be considered delivered as long as the customer has a version that is fully functional except for the permanent key or additional keys necessary for reproduction and the customer's payment obligation is not contingent in any way upon the delivery of additional keys. However, if a vendor only uses keys selectively, this may be evidence that collectibility is questionable or that the product has only been delivered for demonstration purposes (ASC 985-605-25-27 through 25-29).

ILLUSTRATION: AUTHORIZATION CODES

EXAMPLE 1

Facts: A vendor includes 20 optional functions on a CD which contains its licensed software product. Keys control access to the optional functions and are provided if and when the customer orders and agrees to pay for these functions. The vendor estimates that the customer will purchase three optional functions.

Discussion: Revenue for each optional function should be recognized when evidence of an order exists and the key is delivered to the user. Although the user has received a fully functional version of the licensed software, the user has not agreed to license the additional functions. Therefore, no evidence of an arrangement exists, and revenue for the optional functions may not be recognized when the CD-ROM is delivered.

EXAMPLE 2

Facts: A software vendor's product requires an authorization code to work after being installed on a new computer. The code necessary to activate the software changes daily. The vendor enters into a license arrangement with a user and delivers a disk containing the product. The customer will handle installation of the product and is instructed to contact the vendor for the daily key on the day of installation. The customer is required to pay for the software 30 days after delivery, whether or not it has installed the software.

Discussion: The version of the software that has been delivered is fully functional except for the installation key, and the customer's payment obligation is not contingent upon either installation of the software or delivery of the key. Therefore, revenue may be recognized upon delivery of the software assuming all other revenue recognition conditions have been met.

Delivery before License Period Begins

If software is physically delivered and all other revenue recognition criteria are met, but the customer's license to use the software has not yet begun, revenue should not be recognized because the customer does not yet have the legal right to use the software. Effective delivery does not occur in these situations until the license term begins (ASC 985-605-55-101 through 55-104; 605-10-S99, A3d) (SAB Topic 13A3d).

"Delivery" When License Period Is Extended

When an active term license is extended and no additional products will be provided, the vendor should recognize the fee when the extension is executed, even if that date is before the extension period begins.

When a term license has lapsed (i.e., it is inactive), any purported extension of that license should be treated as a new initial arrangement, not an extension of an existing arrangement. In these situations, the guidance in the section, "Delivery before License Period Begins," should be followed.

When an active term license is extended and an additional product will be provided, the extension fee should be allocated between the software product that was the subject of the original license (original product) and the software product added in the extension (new product) based on the guidance in the "Multiple-Element Arrangements" section of this chapter. The vendor should recognize the amount allocated to the original product when the extension arrangement is executed if all other revenue recognition criteria have been met. The vendor should recognize the amount allocated to the new product when all of the revenue recognition criteria have been met related to that new product (ASC 985-605-55-105 through 55-114).

OBSERVATION: Arrangements may contain an option to extend a time-based license indefinitely for an additional fee. This fee is essentially the same as the additional fee related to an extension/renewal of a license. The right associated with each fee is the same—the right to continue to use the product the customer already has access to as part of the original or base arrangement. Therefore, the additional fee related to the option should be accounted for the same way as a fee received in connection with the extension/renewal of a license. However, if exercise of the option requires another delivery of the software media (e.g., due to a self-destruct or similar mechanism in the original software media delivered), then delivery of the software media must occur before the revenue related to the extension/renewal can be recognized (ASC 985-605-55-115 through 55-118).

Delivery of a Beta Version or an Earlier Release

When the version of the software ordered by the customer is not immediately available because it is still in development or testing before commercial release, the vendor may deliver a beta (or test) version of the product, or an earlier release (e.g., version 5.5 instead of 6.0) so that the customer has a product to use until the ordered version becomes available.

Delivery of a beta version or earlier release does not constitute delivery of the product the customer ordered. As a result, the vendor may not recognize revenue because it has not substantially completed its obligations under the arrangement.

Upgrades

ASC 985-605 defines an upgrade as: "An improvement to an existing product that is intended to extend the life or improve significantly the marketability of the original product through added functionality, enhanced performance, or both." Upgrades are often a key aspect of a software arrangement because software products are often upgraded over time (e.g., from version 1.0 to version 2.0). The accounting for upgrades depends upon whether the upgrade is specified or unspecified.

Specified upgrades are treated as separate elements of the arrangement (see guidance later in this chapter under "Multiple-Element Arrangements" for purposes of determining whether specified upgrades should be treated separately for accounting purposes). Delivery of specified upgrades can generally be determined in the same manner as delivery of products. Unspecified upgrades are discussed below under "Post-Contract Customer Support (PCS)."

Post-Contract Customer Support (PCS)

In contrast to specified upgrades, unspecified upgrades are treated as a component of PCS. PCS includes telephone support, correction of errors (bug fixing or debugging), and unspecified (when- and if-available) product upgrades and enhancements developed by the vendor during the period in which the PCS is provided. These services and upgrades are generally described in the PCS arrangement. Sometimes, a limited period of PCS is included with the purchase of a license to software. This initial period of PCS, even though it may be provided to all purchasers, is considered an element in a multiple-element arrangement (see guidance later in this chapter under "Multiple-Element Arrangements" for purposes of determining whether PCS should be treated separately for accounting purposes).

OBSERVATION: Although an arrangement to provide unspecified upgrades and enhancements is accounted for as PCS, an arrangement that only requires the vendor to provide "bug fixes" that correct errors in the operation of the software should be accounted for as a warranty, pursuant to ASC 450 (ASC 985-605-55-77 and 55-78) (see Chapter 5, "Product Deliverables").

The portion of the fee allocated to PCS should be recognized as revenue ratably over the term of the PCS arrangement because there is generally no better estimate of the manner in which such services will be provided. However, revenue should be recognized in proportion to the expenses expected to be incurred for the PCS services if sufficient vendor-specific historical evidence exists demonstrating that costs to provide PCS are incurred on other than a straight-line basis (ASC 985-605-25-67 and 25-68).

OBSERVATION: Because predicting the costs to be incurred in developing unspecified upgrades is extremely difficult, PCS is almost always recognized on a straight-line basis over the PCS period.

In rare circumstances, PCS is considered insignificant to the arrangement and delivery is not required to recognize the revenue allocated to it. PCS revenue may be recognized at the same time as the portion of the fee allocated to the software product if *all* of the following conditions are met (ASC 985-605-25-71):

1. *The PCS fee is included with the initial licensing fee.* Arrangements where PCS fees are charged for an optional period do not qualify.

2. *The PCS included with the initial license is for one year or less.* This condition is met if the arrangement includes post-delivery telephone support for

an unspecified period of time, but the vendor's history shows that substantially all of the support is provided within the first year after delivery.

3. *The estimated cost of providing PCS during the arrangement is insignificant.* Historical experience in providing PCS to similar customers on similar software products is necessary to reach this conclusion.

4. *If unspecified upgrades are included in the PCS arrangement, such upgrades historically have been and are expected to continue to be minimal and infrequent.* This determination should consider the content of the upgrades in addition to the number.

If PCS revenue is recognized upon the delivery of the software, the vendor must accrue all estimated costs of providing the PCS at the same time (ASC 985-605-25-72).

EXAMPLE: DESCRIPTION OF PCS

Oracle, Corporation Form 10-K—Fiscal Year Ended May 31, 2010

The vast majority of our software license arrangements include software license updates and product support contracts, which are entered into at the customer's option and are recognized ratably over the term of the arrangement, typically one year. Software license updates provide customers with rights to unspecified software product upgrades, maintenance releases and patches released during the term of the support period. Product support includes internet access to technical content, as well as internet and telephone access to technical support personnel. Software license updates and product support contracts are generally priced as a percentage of the net new software license fees. Substantially all of our customers renew their software license updates and product support contracts annually.

Subscriptions

A software vendor may agree to deliver one or more software products or licenses currently and unspecified additional software products in the future. For example, the vendor may agree to deliver all new products to be introduced over the next three years. Such arrangements are treated as subscriptions and are conceptually similar to a magazine or other subscription. A subscription is different from a PCS arrangement (that includes unspecified upgrades and enhancements) because the future deliverables include or are products with their own functionality, rather than upgrades to already existing products.

In a subscription, the customer is entitled to the delivery of products made available during some period of time. Delivery (use by the customer) occurs ratably throughout the period once the first product has been provided to the customer. As a result, no allocation of revenue should be made to any of the software products. Even if the vendor has no obligation to develop additional products and in fact does not intend to develop any products, delivery under a subscription still occurs and revenue is recognized ratably, beginning with the delivery of the first product (ASC 985-605-25-58 and 25-59).

> **OBSERVATION:** Because a subscription typically involves rights to future software products that have not yet been developed, VSOE of fair value of these unspecified products would not exist at the outset of the arrangement. In the absence of these special provisions for subscriptions, no revenue would be recognized until the end of the subscription term.

Software-Related Services

Software-related services other than PCS may also exist in an arrangement and include training, installation, or consulting. Consulting services often involve implementation support, software design or development, and customization or modification of licensed software. When software-related services meet the criteria to be accounted for separately (see "Multiple-Element Arrangements" below), they are considered delivered as the services are performed. If no pattern of performance is discernable, software-related services are considered delivered ratably as they are provided.

> **OBSERVATION:** As discussed above, PCS may be considered incidental to the arrangement under limited circumstances, such that revenue allocated to it may be recognized when the software product is delivered. This exception does not apply to any other software-related services.

MULTIPLE-ELEMENT ARRANGEMENTS

As in other types of arrangements, it is common for software transactions to involve more than one deliverable. For example, software arrangements often include multiple software products, upgrades, enhancements, training, consulting services, and PCS, amongst other deliverables. Of course, the deliverables may also include non-software related products and services, such as hardware and services related to that hardware. As discussed previously, software that is essential to the functionality of hardware is also considered a non-software deliverable.

The issues raised by multiple-element software arrangements are the same as those raised by multiple-element (deliverable) arrangements in other industries. Those issues involve considerations of whether delivered items have provided value to the customer, and how to allocate arrangement consideration between the delivered and undelivered items in the arrangement. However, the software literature addresses these issues differently in some situations, and therefore it is critical to appropriately determine which deliverables are software deliverables that must be accounted for under the software multiple-element model in ASC 985-605, rather than the multiple-deliverable model in ASC 605-25.

Defining the Arrangement When Multiple Contracts Exist

A number of requirements in software revenue recognition affect multiple-element arrangements, but not single-element arrangements. In addition, there are times when the inclusion or exclusion of an element within an arrangement can significantly affect the accounting for the other elements of the arrangement (e.g., one undelivered element for which VSOE (see below) of fair value does not exist prohibits recognition of revenue upon delivery of, or completion of performance for, other elements). For these reasons, it is important to properly identify the "arrangement" (i.e., identify all the elements of deliverables), which is the starting point for allocating revenue to individual elements.

Even if different elements are documented in multiple contracts, contracts should be evaluated together when they are, in substance, part of one arrangement. Some indicators or factors that might indicate that multiple contracts are substantively part of the same arrangement include (ASC 985-605-55-4):

- *Timing of execution of the contracts:*
  - The contracts or agreements are negotiated or executed within a short time frame of each other.

- *Substance and the composition of the contract:*
  - The contracts relate to the same elements or what is, in essence, the same project.
  - The different elements are closely interrelated or interdependent in terms of design, technology, or function.
  - One or more elements in one contract or agreement are essential to the functionality of an element in another contract.

- *Arrangement consideration and payment terms:*
  - The fee for one or more contracts or agreements is subject to refund or forfeiture or other concession if another contract is not completed satisfactorily.
  - Payment terms under one contract or agreement coincide with performance criteria of another contract or agreement.

- *Definition of contract and customer:*
  - The negotiations are conducted jointly with two or more parties (e.g., from different divisions of the same company) to do what, in essence, is a single project.

EXAMPLE: DEFINING THE ARRANGEMENT

Cadence Design Systems, Inc. Form 10-K—Fiscal Year Ended January 2, 2010

A multiple element arrangement, or MEA, is any arrangement that includes or contemplates rights to a combination of software or hardware products, software license types, services, training or maintenance in a single arrangement. From time to time, we may include individual deliverables in separately priced and separately signed contracts with the same customer. We obtain and evaluate all known relevant facts and circumstances in determining whether the separate contracts should be accounted for individually as distinct arrangements or whether the separate contracts are, in substance, a MEA. Significant judgment can be involved in determining whether a group of contracts might be so closely related that they are, in effect, part of a single arrangement.

> **OBSERVATION:** ASC 605-35 also contains guidance to aid in the determination as to when two or more contracts should be segregated or combined. See Chapter 9, Contract Accounting.⁴⁰

Determining the Model to Apply

As discussed in Chapter 4, "Multiple-Deliverable Revenue Arrangements," arrangements that consist only of software and software-related deliverables are not subject to the requirements of ASC 605-25, because ASC 985-605 includes comprehensive guidance on multiple-element arrangements. However, when an arrangement has elements that fall within the scope of ASC 985-605 and elements that do not, ASC 605-25 should be applied to separate the software elements and the non-software elements. Further separation of the software elements is governed by the software multiple-element model (ASC 985-605-25-10f) (ASU 2009-14, par. 5), while further separation of the non-software elements would be governed by ASC 605-25.

EXAMPLE: ALLOCATION BETWEEN SOFTWARE AND OTHER ELEMENTS

Oracle Corporation Form 10-K—Fiscal Year Ended May 31, 2011

We also enter into multiple-element arrangements that may include a combination of our various software related and nonsoftware related products and services offerings including hardware systems products, hardware systems support, new software licenses, software license updates and product support, consulting, Cloud Services and education. In such arrangements, we first allocate the total arrangement consideration based on the relative selling prices of the software group of elements as a whole and to the nonsoftware elements. We then further allocate consideration within the software group to the respective elements within that group following the guidance in ASC 985-605 and our policies as described above. After the arrangement consideration has been allocated to the elements, we account for each respective element in the arrangement as described above.

To ensure that the proper multiple-element guidance is applied to an arrangement involving software and/or software-related elements, it is essential to understand whether the elements fall within the scope of ASC 985-605 or other literature. The following discussion addresses the various types of software and software-related elements that may be included in a multiple-element arrangement and how to determine which guidance is applicable.

Incidental Software

Incidental software, as discussed earlier in this chapter, does not fall within the scope of ASC 985-605 and should not be considered an element in the arrangement. In other words, arrangements including only incidental software are not subject to the software revenue model at all.

Software Products

Software that does not involve significant production, modification, or customization generally falls within the scope of ASC 985-605. However, when software is essential to the functionality of a tangible product in the arrangement, neither the tangible product nor the essential software is considered a software-related element (ASC 985-605-15-3d and 15-3e) (ASU 2009-14, par. 3).

Software Requiring Significant Production, Modification, or Customization

This type of software is still within the scope of ASC 685-605, but the software and the related production, modification, or customization services is accounted for using the contract accounting guidance of ASC 605-35, which is discussed in detail in Chapter 9, "Contract Accounting." In this situation, the software itself and the production, modification or customization services, are together considered a single element.

If a multiple-element arrangement includes both software that must be accounted for using contract accounting and other software-related elements within the scope of ASC 985-605 (e.g., other software products, PCS, training services), the software multiple-element model should be applied to determine whether the elements should be treated separately for accounting purposes. On the other hand, if an arrangement includes software requiring significant customization and another element(s) that would not fall within the scope of ASC 985-605, then ASC 605-25 should be applied to determine whether these elements should be treated separately for accounting purposes (see Chapter 4, "Multiple-Deliverable Revenue Arrangements").

SEC REGISTRANT ALERT: In a December 2003 speech, an SEC staff member communicated that "the consensus reached by the EITF requires that the ASC 605-25 criteria be applied in bundled arrangements involving significant customization of software to determine whether ASC 605-35 deliverables should be separated from the [other] deliverables." This conclusion is different from the one in ASC 985-605-55-74; 985-605-55-75 (TPA 5100.49), which effectively indicates that the multiple-element model in ASC 985-605 should be applied to separate PCS-related services from a multiple-element arrangement including software that involves significant production, modification, or customization and PCS. We believe that although software requiring significant production, modification, or customization must be accounted for under contract accounting, the software remains a ASC 985-605 element. Therefore, the guidance in ASC 605-25 would apply to multiple-element arrangements, including software (regardless of whether significant production, modification, or customization is needed) and one or more non-software elements.

PCS

In most instances, PCS would be treated as a software deliverable. However, if the software to which the PCS relates is not treated as a software deliverable because it works together with a tangible product to provide the tangible product's essential functionality, the PCS is not considered a software element either.

Whether PCS is considered a software element or not, its inclusion in an arrangement generally would not prohibit recognition of revenue on delivery of the software, because PCS is rarely essential to the functionality of the software to which it relates (and the software generally has value to the customer on a standalone basis absent the PCS). Absent any unusual terms that would render the software not fully-functional without PCS, PCS should typically be treated as a separate element for accounting purposes provided appropriate fair value evidence exists to allocate arrangement consideration between the PCS and the other elements in the arrangement.

Other Software-Related Elements

Other software elements may include training, consulting services, installation, specified upgrades, and implementation services. In general, the model to apply to these services follows the model that will be applied to the software to which they relate. For example, upgrades to a software product that is considered a software element are considered also to be software elements, while upgrades to a product that is not considered a software element (because, for example, it works together with hardware to deliver the hardware's essential functionality), are not considered software elements. Similarly, services that relate to the customization, modification, or production of software are accounted for under contract accounting guidance, together with the software.

ILLUSTRATION: DETERMINING THE APPROPRIATE MULTIPLE-ELEMENT ARRANGEMENT GUIDANCE TO APPLY

EXAMPLE 1

Facts: A multiple-element arrangement includes off-the-shelf software (i.e., software that is more than incidental but does not require significant production, modification, or customization) and computer hardware. The off-the-shelf software is not essential to the functionality of the computer hardware.

Discussion: Since the software falls within the scope of ASC 985-605 and the hardware does not, the multiple-element model in ASC 605-25 should be applied to determine whether the two elements should be treated separately for revenue recognition purposes.

EXAMPLE 2

Facts: A multiple-element arrangement includes off-the-shelf software (i.e., software that is more than incidental but does not require significant production, modification, or customization) and computer hardware. The off-the-shelf software is essential to the functionality of the computer hardware.

Discussion: The software is not considered a software-related element in this arrangement because the software is essential to the tangible product's functionality. Since both elements therefore fall outside the scope of ASC 985-605, the multiple-element model in ASC 605-25 should be applied to determine whether the two elements should be treated separately for revenue recognition purposes.

EXAMPLE 3

Facts: A multiple-element arrangement includes software that will be significantly modified and customized as part of the multiple-element arrangement and computer hardware. The significantly modified and customized software is not essential to the functionality of the computer hardware and the computer hardware is not essential to the functionality of the significantly modified and customized software.

Discussion: The arrangement effectively has three deliverables: (1) the software that will be significantly modified and customized, (2) the services that will be performed to significantly modify and customize the software, and (3) the computer hardware. The software and services to significantly modify and customize the software would be treated as a single element (that must be accounted for in accordance with ASC 605-35) if the software does not have standalone value to the customer without the modification and customization, because the software is not essential to the functionality of the computer hardware. The computer hardware is not a software-related element. As one element falls within the scope of ASC 985-605 and one element does not, the multiple-element arrangement model in ASC 605-25 should be applied to determine whether the software element and the computer hardware should be treated separately for revenue recognition purposes.

DISCLOSURE ALERT: See Chapter 12, "Disclosures," for information about required disclosures.

SEC REGISTRANT ALERT: In early 2003, the SEC staff issued a Report Pursuant to Section 704 of the Sarbanes-Oxley Act of 2002 (Section 704 Report). In compiling the information in the Section 704 Report, the SEC staff studied enforcement actions filed during the period July 31, 1997, through July 30, 2002. The greatest number of enforcement actions brought by the SEC related to improper revenue recognition. One of the common revenue recognition issues highlighted in the Section 704 Report related to improper recognition of revenue from multiple-element arrangements or bundled contracts. One of the two actions discussed in the Section 704 Report in this regard involved improper allocation of arrangement consideration and the other involved improper separation of interdependent elements. This finding is a strong indication that more attention should be given to accounting for multiple-element arrangements.

In addition, in early 2003, the SEC staff issued the Summary by the Division of Corporation Finance of Significant Issues Addressed in the Review of the Periodic Reports of the Fortune 500 Companies (Fortune 500 Report). This report resulted from the SEC's Division of Corporation Finance's (Corp Fin) review of all annual reports filed by Fortune 500 companies. The report provides insight into areas commonly questioned by Corp Fin during its reviews of annual reports. One area specifically mentioned in the Fortune 500 Report relates to accounting for multiple-element arrangements. Corp Fin specifically indicated that companies in the computer software, computer services, and computer hardware industries could improve their disclosures by expanding the discussion related to multiple-element arrangements.

The remainder of this section discusses the software multiple-element model.

Allocating Revenue Among Elements

For elements covered by ASC 985-605, if VSOE of fair value (as discussed below) exists for all elements, the arrangement consideration should be allocated to the individual elements based on their relative fair values. However, the full fair value of a specified upgrade right should be allocated to that right, regardless of any discount inherent in the total arrangement. The remainder of the arrangement consideration (total fee or arrangement consideration less the full fair value of the upgrade right) is allocated on the basis of the relative fair values (as supported by VSOE) of each of the individual elements. The discount is therefore allocated pro rata across each of the other elements (ASC 985-605-25-8). The discount is not allocated to the upgrade right.

If VSOE of fair value exists for all undelivered elements, but does not exist for one or more delivered elements, the arrangement consideration should be allocated to the various elements of the arrangement under the residual method. Under this method, the amount of arrangement consideration allocated to the delivered elements should be the total arrangement consideration less the aggregate fair values of the undelivered elements. Thus, any potential discount on the arrangement taken as a whole is allocated entirely to the delivered elements. This ensures that the amount of revenue recognized at any point in time is not overstated. If the sum of the fair values of the undelivered elements is greater than the total arrangement consideration, no revenue may be recognized, despite the fact that one or more elements have already been delivered (ASC 985-605-25-10 and 25-11).

OBSERVATION: The residual method works in only one direction. It works only when VSOE of fair value exists for all undelivered elements. If VSOE of fair value exists for delivered elements, but does not exist for one or more undelivered elements, the residual method cannot be used because it is not possible, in the absence of VSOE of fair value of the undelivered elements, to ensure that all of the potential discount in the arrangement is allocated to the delivered elements. See ASC 985-605-55-88 through 55-92.

EXAMPLE: RESIDUAL METHOD

Oracle Corporation Form 10-K—Fiscal Year Ended May 31, 2011

We often enter into arrangements with customers that purchase both software related products and services from us at the same time, or within close proximity of one another (referred to as software related multiple-element arrangements). Such software related multiple-element arrangements include the sale of our software products, software license updates and product support contracts and other software related services whereby software license delivery is followed by the subsequent or contemporaneous delivery of the other elements. For those software related multiple-element arrangements, we have applied the residual method to determine the amount of software license revenues to be recognized pursuant to ASC 985-605. Under the residual method, if fair value exists for undelivered elements in a multiple-element arrangement, such fair value of the undelivered elements is deferred with the remaining portion of the arrangement consideration recognized upon delivery of the software license or services arrangement. We allocate the fair value of each element of a software related multiple-element arrangement based upon its fair value as determined by our vendor specific objective evidence (VSOE—described further below), with any remaining amount allocated to the software license.

Once the fee in an arrangement has been allocated among elements based on the appropriate method, the allocation should not be subsequently changed, even if the company changes its pricing (ASC 985-605-25-7).

If VSOE of fair value does not exist for one or more undelivered elements, no revenue from the arrangement may be recognized until either sufficient VSOE exists to allocate revenue based on one of the methods described above or the last element in the arrangement is delivered. Establishment of VSOE (e.g., by separately selling an element) after the end of an accounting period but before financial statements are prepared is not sufficient to permit revenue recognition during the accounting period in question (ASC 985-605-25-9 and ASC 985-605-55-94).[2]

OBSERVATION: Some software arrangements are very complex and include a large number of elements. If VSOE of fair value of even one undelivered element does not exist, no revenue may be recognized until VSOE of fair value for that element does exist, or the element is delivered.

Multiple-Product and Multiple-Copy Fixed-Fee Arrangements

Some software arrangements provide customers with the right to reproduce or obtain copies, at specified prices per copy, of several software products for a fixed fee. In these arrangements, the fixed fee is payable regardless of the number of copies of the various products that are eventually used and payment is not tied to deployment or use of the copies. Although the price per copy is fixed at the inception of the arrangement, the arrangement fee cannot be allocated to the individual products because the revenue allocable to each software product depends on the choices to be made by the customer in the future regarding how many of each product will be used (or resold, if the customer is a reseller). These arrangements may also include the rights to select copies of products that are not available at the inception of the arrangement.

Because the minimum fee is fixed in these arrangements and is not dependent upon duplication or the selection of the number of copies of each product to be used, all revenue should be recognized when the first or master copy of all products that are part of the arrangement has been delivered, provided all other revenue recognition criteria have been met. Until then, revenue should be recognized as copies of delivered products are made.

---

[2] Establishing VSOE after period-end is a nonrecognized subsequent event, as discussed in footnote 1.

> **OBSERVATION:** In this case, the stated contract prices are used to recognize revenue, regardless of the fair value of each product and regardless of whether VSOE of fair value exists. This is a unique feature of the accounting for fixed minimum, multi-product, multi-copy arrangements in which the customer chooses how many copies of each product to use. This use of contractually stated amounts to recognize revenue may not be analogized to for other types of arrangements.

Certain arrangements may impose a maximum on the number of copies of a particular product that the customer may select. If all undelivered products in an arrangement are subject to such maximums, any revenue in excess of the specified prices per copy multiplied by the applicable maximums should be recognized as revenue provided all other revenue recognition criteria have been met (ASC 985-605-25-52 through 25-57).

ILLUSTRATION: PER COPY PRICES IN A MULTIPLE-PRODUCT, MULTIPLE-COPY, FIXED-FEE ARRANGEMENT

(Adapted from ASC 985-605-55-134 through 55-144)

EXAMPLE 1

Facts: A vendor enters into an arrangement under which a customer has the right to make copies of Product A at $100 a copy, copies of Product B at $200 a copy, or copies of Product C at $50 a copy until such time as the customer has made copies aggregating $100,000 based on the per copy prices. The customer is obligated to pay the $100,000 immediately, without regard to when it makes copies of the three products. The first copy of Products A and B are delivered immediately, but Product C is not available yet. No portion of the fee allocable to copies made of Products A and B is refundable if Product C is not delivered, nor is there any obligation to deliver Product C if copies of Products A and B aggregating $100,000 have been made. None of the products are essential to the functionality of any of the other products. The maximum number of copies of Product C that can be made is 500.

Discussion: Because the first copy of Product C has not yet been delivered, the maximum amount of the fee that may be used for Product C must be deferred. Thus, $25,000 (500 copies × $50 per copy) must be deferred. The remaining $75,000 of revenue should be recognized when the first copies of Products A and B are delivered to the customer. The $25,000 allocated to Product C would be recognized upon delivery of the first copy of that product. If the customer duplicates enough copies of Products A and B such that the revenue allocable to those products exceeds $75,000, the additional revenue should be recognized as the additional copies are made.

EXAMPLE 2

Facts: Assume the same facts as in the preceding example, except the arrangement does not state a maximum number of copies of Product C that can be made.

Discussion: Because no limit on the number of copies of Product C exists, the customer could, in theory, use the entire fixed fee to purchase copies of Product

C. Therefore, revenue should only be recognized as copies of Products A ($100 of revenue per copy) and B ($200 of revenue per copy) are made, until the first copy of Product C is delivered, at which point, any remaining revenue should be recognized.

License Mix Arrangements

In some cases, a fixed fee, multi-product, multi-copy arrangement may allow a user to change or alternate its use of multiple products or licenses (license mix) even after the customer makes its initial choice.

Software sold under a license mix arrangement is considered delivered for accounting purposes once the first or master copy of each product is delivered. In addition, remixing is not considered an exchange or a return of software because the master or first copy of all products has been licensed and delivered and the customer has the right to use them. Nor is a remix right considered the right to obtain additional products or licenses, as long as the remix rights do not allow the customer to increase the aggregate value of the licenses it uses at a particular time. Therefore, as long as all other revenue recognition criteria are met, revenue from a remix arrangement may be recognized upon delivery of the first or master copy of each product (ASC 985-605-55-99 and 55-100).

However, if the remix provisions allow the customer to receive the rights to use products that do not exist at the initiation of the arrangement, the arrangement should be treated as a subscription (see "Subscriptions" earlier in this chapter).

ILLUSTRATION: REMIX RIGHTS

EXAMPLE 1

Facts: A vendor enters into an arrangement under which a customer has the right to make copies of Product A at $100 a copy, copies of Product B at $200 a copy, or copies of Product C at $50 a copy until such time as the customer has made copies aggregating $100,000 based on the per copy prices. The customer is obligated to pay the $100,000 immediately, without regard to when it makes copies of the three products. The customer initially selects 200 copies of Product B ($40,000), 250 copies of Product A ($25,000), and 700 copies of Product C ($35,000).

After the initial selection, the customer has the right, for three years, to change its use of Products A, B, and C by giving up licenses of one in exchange for licenses of another based on the ratio of the prices stated in the arrangement. For example, the customer can give up one copy of Product B in exchange for two copies of Product A or four copies of Product C.

Discussion: Once a copy of each of the products has been delivered, the remix rights do not affect the recognition of revenue under the contract since the remix rights do not extend to any additional products and the aggregate value of the software under the arrangement is limited to the $100,000 fee.

EXAMPLE 2

Facts: Same as Example 1, except that the customer may exchange each copy of Product B it initially chooses for five copies of Product C.

Discussion: In this case, the customer can obtain additional value based on exercising its remix rights. The 1,000 copies of Product C that could be obtained by giving up 200 copies of Product B have a value of $50,000, while the 200 copies of Product B that would be given up have a value of $40,000. Thus, the additional value that the customer can realize is $10,000. That amount should be deferred to account for these rights when revenue is recognized under the arrangement.

EXAMPLE 3

Facts: Same as Example 1, except that the remix rights will also pertain to any other products that the vendor develops during the remix period, based on the list prices of these products as compared to the contractual prices of Products A, B, and C.

Discussion: Because the remix rights apply to future products, the arrangement should be treated as a subscription, meaning that the $100,000 fee should be recognized ratably over three years.

Vendor-Specific Objective Evidence (VSOE) of Fair Value

General

ASC 985-605 limits the information that a company may use to establish the fair value of a particular element. This information, which is called vendor-specific objective evidence (VSOE) of fair value, is limited to:

1. The price charged when the same element is sold separately.
2. For an element not yet being sold separately, the price established by management having the relevant authority; it must be probable that the price, once established, will not change before the separate introduction of the element into the marketplace.

Separate prices stated in an arrangement are not relevant in determining the fair value of the individual elements, because such prices, having been negotiated as part of the arrangement as a whole, do not necessarily represent bargained-for prices for each individual element. As such, they may not represent fair value (ASC 985-605-25-6).

The definition of VSOE also prohibits the use of surrogate prices, such as prices charged by a competitor for similar products or industry averages, to determine fair value. This is because software produced by different vendors, even if they are designed for the same purpose, invariably has inherent differences. Using competitor prices as evidence of fair value would essentially result in those differences being ignored. For that reason, the evidence must be vendor-specific.

ASC 985-605 also prohibits the use of methods such as "cost plus a normal profit margin" to support fair value. In part, this is because it is difficult to establish both "cost" and a "normal profit margin" in a software environment. The direct cost of software products is very low because almost all of the cost is incurred as the software is developed. Once the software has been developed, additional copies can be produced at almost no cost. Therefore, the notion of a "normal profit margin" is virtually nonexistent.

Allocating revenue to each element based on the combined profit margin in the arrangement is also unacceptable. This type of allocation would not result in the correct assignment of fair value to individual elements, because each element is normally expected to have a different profit margin. For example, software products have an almost nonexistent direct cost component, but services have a significant direct cost component.

Although many other methods for allocating the arrangement fee to the individual elements were suggested during the development of ASC 985-605, none of them are currently allowed. Therefore, software vendors often conclude that insufficient evidence exists (i.e., there is no VSOE of fair value) to allocate the arrangement fee to the individual elements.

EXAMPLE: VSOE OF FAIR VALUE

BMC Software, Inc. Form 10-K—Fiscal Year Ended March 31, 2011

Revenue Recognition

Software license revenue is recognized when persuasive evidence of an arrangement exists, delivery of the product has occurred, the fee is fixed or determinable, collection is probable and vendor-specific objective evidence (VSOE) of the fair value of undelivered elements exists. As substantially all of our software licenses are sold in multiple-element arrangements that include either maintenance or both maintenance and professional services, we use the residual method to determine the amount of license revenue to be recognized. Under the residual method, consideration is allocated to undelivered elements based upon VSOE of the fair value of those elements, with the residual of the arrangement fee allocated to and recognized as license revenue. We have established VSOE of the fair value of maintenance through independent maintenance renewals. These demonstrate a consistent relationship of pricing maintenance as a percentage of either the net license fee or the discounted or undiscounted license list price. VSOE of the fair value of professional services is established based on daily rates when sold on a stand-alone basis, as well as management approved pricing for certain new professional services offerings.

We are unable to establish VSOE of fair value for all undelivered elements in certain arrangements that include multiple software products for which the associated maintenance pricing is based on a combination of undiscounted license list prices, net license fees or discounted license list prices. We are also unable to establish VSOE of fair value for all undelivered elements in certain arrangements that include unlimited licensing rights and certain arrangements that contain rights to future unspecified software products as part of the maintenance offering. If VSOE of fair value of one or more undelivered elements does not exist, license revenue is deferred and recognized upon delivery of those elements or when VSOE of fair value exists for all remaining undelivered elements, or if the deferral is due to the factors described above, license revenue is recognized ratably over the longest expected delivery period of undelivered elements in the arrangement, which is typically the longest maintenance term.

In our time-based license agreements, we are unable to establish VSOE of fair value for undelivered maintenance elements because the contractual maintenance terms in these arrangements are the same duration as the license terms and VSOE of fair value of maintenance cannot be established. Accordingly, license fees in time-based license arrangements are recognized ratably over the term of the arrangements.

Matrix Pricing

In some cases, pricing may be based on combinations of multiple factors. For example, certain arrangements are priced based on the type of customer or the number of users that will be granted access to the licensed products. In these arrangements, a software vendor may, as part of its standard pricing policy, offer a reduced per user price to companies purchasing a greater number of user licenses or a greater number of products. ASC 985-605 does allow these types of pricing policies to be taken into account when determining the fair value of an element in an arrangement (ASC 985-605-25-7).

ILLUSTRATION: VSOE OF FAIR VALUE BASED ON MULTIPLE FACTORS

Facts: A software vendor generally sells a single license to its product for $100. However, as part of its standard price list, not-for-profit entities receive a 10% discount on every license. In addition, any customer purchasing over 100 licenses at once receives a 10% discount off of the otherwise applicable price.

Discussion: Standard discounts imply that the vendor is selling to different classes of customers. Therefore, the vendor really has a matrix of VSOE of fair values for its product. Because the discounts are standard, they should be considered in assessing the VSOE of fair value. This vendor's VSOE of fair value is as follows:

	Not-for-Profits	Other Customers
Less than 100 licenses	$90 per license	$100 per license
100 licenses or more	$81 per license	$90 per license

Specified Upgrades

Specified upgrades are treated as separate elements in an arrangement. Therefore, VSOE of fair value for an undelivered specified upgrade must exist before any revenue may be recognized. VSOE of fair value for a specific upgrade is the fee charged to existing users of the software product who separately purchase the upgrade. However, if the software vendor provides the upgrade free of charge to all users of the product (e.g., by providing a free download on its Internet site) regardless of whether the users have a contractual right to the upgrade, VSOE is zero and revenue need not be deferred when rights to the upgrade are specifically included in an arrangement.

PRACTICE POINTER: Many upgrades are neither sold separately nor provided free of charge to all users, regardless of the contractual arrangements. Instead, customers generally obtain such rights by purchasing PCS (see the next section for the accounting for such arrangements) or negotiating these rights in the original license arrangement. As a result, VSOE of fair value for a specified upgrade often does not exist. Many companies, as a matter of policy, do not include specific upgrade rights in their arrangements to sell software. However, each contract should be reviewed to determine whether specific upgrade rights are granted. It is also important to determine whether the vendor has a history of providing and charging for upgrades regardless of whether the upgrades are included in its arrangements.

ASC 985-605 contains two special provisions on the allocation of the arrangement fee to a specified upgrade. First, no portion of any discount in a multiple-element arrangement should be allocated to a specified upgrade right. Therefore, if an arrangement includes a specified upgrade for which VSOE of fair value exists, the full fair value must be allocated to the upgrade. This is similar to the application of the residual method when VSOE of fair value does not exist for one or more delivered elements. Second, when sufficient vendor-specific experience exists to reasonably estimate breakage (the percentage of customers that are not expected to exercise the upgrade right), the fee allocated to the upgrade right should be reduced to reflect that estimated breakage (ASC 985-605-25-45).

OBSERVATION: The concept of reducing the amount allocated to an undelivered element to reflect expected breakage is an issue that arises frequently in multiple-element arrangements. Although there is some judgment that can be applied in non-software arrangements (see Chapter 3, "General Principles"), ASC 985-605 only allows the application of breakage in the context of specified upgrades. Therefore, when an arrangement includes an additional product, rather than an upgrade, revenue must be allocated to the additional product as if all users will request it, even if the vendor reasonably believes that some will not (i.e., no breakage may be incorporated in the allocation of revenue).

PCS

A limited period of PCS is often included with a software license. As discussed earlier, if PCS is included in an arrangement with software, the software multiple-element arrangement model should be applied to determine whether the software and PCS should be treated separately for accounting purposes. PCS should be treated as a separate element for accounting purposes when VSOE of its fair value exists. Determining whether VSOE of fair value exists for PCS is discussed below. PCS should be analyzed in this manner even though it may be provided to all purchasers. In rare circumstances, however, PCS is considered insignificant to the arrangement and delivery is not required to recognize the revenue allocated to it (see additional discussion of this issue in the section above, "Post-Contract Customer Support (PCS)").

In general, an arrangement that includes software (including software that requires significant production, modification, or customization) and an initial PCS period will also stipulate that the customer may purchase additional periods of PCS, at a specified renewal rate, when the initial "free" period expires. The specified renewal rate provides VSOE of fair value of the PCS services, unless the renewal rate is not substantive (ASC 985-605-25-67).

ILLUSTRATION: ALLOCATION OF ARRANGEMENT FEE BETWEEN LICENSE AND PCS

For purposes of these examples, assume that the software does not involve significant production, modification, or customization.

EXAMPLE 1

Facts: A vendor licenses software to a user along with one year of PCS for $90,000. VSOE of fair value for the software is $ and PCS is renewable on an annual basis for $15,000 per year.

Discussion: The PCS renewal rate is considered substantive and provides VSOE of fair value for the PCS. Therefore, there is sufficient VSOE to allocate the fee between the software and the PCS. The fair value of the two elements is $100,000, meaning there is a 10% discount in the arrangement. This discount should be allocated across the two elements as follows:

	License	PCS	Total
Fair Value	$85,000	$15,000	$100,000
Less: 10% Discount	–8,500	–1,500	–10,00
Revenue	$76,500	$13,500	$90,000

EXAMPLE 2

Facts: A vendor licenses software to a user along with one year of PCS for $90,000. PCS is renewable on an annual basis for $15,000 per year. The vendor does not have VSOE of fair value for the software because it is never sold separately (it is always sold with PCS).

Discussion: The PCS renewal rate is substantive and considered to be VSOE of fair value for the PCS. Therefore, there is sufficient VSOE to allocate the fee using the residual method. In this case, $15,000 of the arrangement fee is deferred, representing the full fair value of the undelivered element, PCS. The remaining $75,000 is allocated to the software element.

Note that there is no way to determine the size of the discount in this example.

EXAMPLE 3

Facts: A software vendor typically prices annual PCS at 13% of its standard perpetual license fee. The VSOE of fair value for the software is $100,000. The vendor enters into an arrangement that includes a perpetual license to its software and one year of PCS for $102,000. The stated renewal rate for PCS is $2,000.

Discussion: The $2,000 should not be considered to be VSOE of fair value for the PCS, as the renewal rate is not substantive. In this situation, the company should look to its standard renewal rates that are used in other arrangements to find VSOE of fair value. Therefore, the fair value of PCS is $13,000 per year. In allocating the license fee, the vendor would need to estimate how many years of discounted PCS the customer would be expected to buy. Typically, the estimate used would be the remaining product life of the software product. Thus, if the product has a five-year remaining life, revenue would be allocated as follows:

	Payments	Fair Value
Software	$102,000	$100,000
Expected Five Years of PCS	8,000	65,000
Total	$110,000	$165,000

This results in an implied discount in the arrangement of 33.33%. Therefore, when revenue is recognized on the sale of software, $66,667 should be recognized. The remainder of the upfront fee ($110,000 − $66,667 = $43,333 or $65,000 less a 33.33% discount) should be deferred and recognized over the anticipated five-year PCS period ($43,333/5, or $8,666.60 of PCS revenue will be recognized each year).

An arrangement may include two different pricing methodologies related to PCS renewals. For example, an arrangement may include (1) a perpetual software license with a three-year unlimited deployment period and (2) PCS where the renewal fee is fixed in the second and third year of the arrangement, but varies in the fourth year and thereafter, depending on the number of software copies deployed. In this situation, a vendor should consider whether there is any basis to determine which of the PCS renewal pricing methodologies represents VSOE of fair value. Much of the time, no basis upon which to make such a determination will exist. However, if sufficient objective evidence exists to support the assertion that the renewal rate in the fourth year and thereafter is more likely than not (i.e., a likelihood of greater than 50%) to approximate or be less than the amount charged in the second and third years, the PCS renewal rates for the second and third years would constitute VSOE of fair value of PCS (ASC 985-605-55-70 through 55-73).

Implied PCS arrangements. When an arrangement does not explicitly include rights to PCS, but the vendor has a historical pattern of providing (or an intention to provide) the customer with support services and/or unspecified upgrades, an implied PCS arrangement exists and should be considered an element in the arrangement.

In other situations, the arrangement may include a period of PCS that begins some time after product delivery, presumably to coincide with the installation or deployment of the product by the customer. However, because such arrangements almost invariably entitle the customer to unspecified upgrades introduced during the intervening period and because other support is generally provided during this period as well, an arrangement with a delayed PCS commencement date should be considered to include PCS during the intervening period. For example, an arrangement that includes one year of PCS that begins three months after product delivery (with no charge for those three months) should be accounted for as an arrangement that includes 15 months of PCS. The arrangement fee should be allocated accordingly (ASC 985-605-55-70 and 55-71).

Renewal rates based on a percentage of license fee. Some vendors have a practice of charging for PCS renewals at a rate calculated as a consistent percentage of the net license fee, which may vary from arrangement to arrangement. Thus, the PCS renewal rates, expressed in terms of actual dollars rather than percentages, will be different across arrangements. As long as each of the arrangements includes a renewal fee based on a consistent percentage of the license fee that is substantive, that renewal rate may be treated as VSOE of fair value for the arrangement (ASC 985-605-55-68 and 55-69).

VSOE of PCS for term licenses. Although perpetual licenses are the more common type of software license arrangement, term licenses are also used. In a term license, the software product can only be used for a limited period of time. In order to continue using the product after the term expires, the customer must enter into a new license (or extend the old one). Many term licenses of software include PCS for the entire period. In these licenses, there is no renewal rate for PCS and VSOE of fair value for PCS does not exist. Although the company might look to its standard PCS renewal rate in perpetual licenses of the same product as evidence of fair value, the fair value for PCS in a term license is likely to be different because of the period during which any upgrades or technical advice will be useful to the customer. Therefore, PCS in a term license and PCS in a perpetual license of the same product are not considered the same element. As a result the separate sales price (renewal rate) of PCS in a perpetual license is not VSOE of fair value for PCS in a term license of the same product (ASC 985-605-55-64 through 55-67).

PRACTICE POINTER: Several other TPAs address PCS issues in term licenses. These TPAs apply to limited circumstances and are not discussed here. However, the guidance has been incorporated into the ASC.

EXAMPLE: VSOE of PCS

Verint System, Inc. Form 10-K—Fiscal Year Ended January 31, 2010

PCS revenues are derived from providing technical software support services and software updates and upgrades to customers on a when-and-if-available basis. PCS revenue is recognized ratably over the term of the maintenance period, which in most cases is one year. When PCS is included within a multiple-element arrangement, we utilize either the substantive renewal rate approach or the bell-shaped curve approach to establish VSOE of the PCS, depending upon the business operating segment, geographical region, or product line.

Under the bell-shaped curve approach of establishing VSOE, we perform a VSOE compliance test to ensure that a substantial majority (75% or over) of our actual PCS renewals are within a narrow range of plus or minus 15% of the median pricing. Under the substantive renewal rate approach, we believe it is necessary to evaluate whether both the support renewal rate and term are substantive, and whether the renewal rate is being consistently applied to subsequent renewals for a particular customer. We establish VSOE under this approach through analyzing the renewal rate stated in the customer agreement and determining whether that rate is above the minimum substantive VSOE renewal rate established for that particular PCS offering. The minimum substantive VSOE rate is determined based upon an analysis of revenue associated with historical PCS contracts. Typically, renewal rates of 15% for PCS plans that provide when-and-if-available upgrades, and 10% for plans that do not provide for when-and-if-available upgrades, would be deemed to be minimum substantive renewal rates. For contracts that do not contain a stated renewal rate, revenue associated with the entire bundled arrangement is recognized ratably over the PCS term. Contracts that have a renewal rate below the minimum substantive VSOE rate are deemed to contain a more than insignificant discount element, for which VSOE cannot be established. We recognize revenue for these arrangements over the period that the customer is entitled to renew their PCS at the discounted rate, but not to exceed the estimated economic life of the product. We evaluate many factors in determining the estimated economic life of our products, including the support period of the product, technological obsolescence, product roadmaps, and customer expectations. We have concluded that our software products have estimated economic lives of from five to seven years.

For certain of our products, we do not have an explicit obligation to provide PCS but as a matter of business practice have provided implied PCS. The implied PCS is accounted for as a separate element for which VSOE does not exist. Arrangements that contain implied PCS are recognized over the period the implied PCS is provided, but not to exceed the estimated economic life of the product.

Services

VSOE of fair value for service elements is more easily determined because services can usually be purchased separately. For example, many software vendors offer training and consultation services on system integration that can be purchased for a specific amount after the software has been delivered or installed. Other services, such as software customization, however, may not have VSOE of fair value, because they are undertaken only as part of a comprehensive arrangement to design, develop, and deliver a customized software package. As discussed below, the existence of such services in an arrangement may require the use of contract accounting.

Elements Essential to the Functionality of One Another

In general, once revenue is allocated to each of the elements in an arrangement, revenue recognition for that element is evaluated without regard to the other elements. However, in determining whether an element in a multiple-element arrangement has been delivered, the delivery of an element is considered not to have occurred if there are undelivered elements that are essential to the functionality of the delivered element, because the customer would not have the full use of the delivered element (ASC 985-605-25-12). For example, no revenue should be recognized upon delivery of a software upgrade if the base package has not yet been delivered.

Service Elements Essential to the Functionality of Software

An important factor to consider in determining whether services are essential to the functionality of any other element is whether the software included in the arrangement is considered core or off-the-shelf software. Core software is software that a vendor uses in creating other software. It is not sold as is because customers cannot use it unless it is customized to meet system objectives or customer specifications. Design and customization services are almost always essential to the functionality of core software included in the same arrangement (ASC 985-605-25-81 through 25-83).

In contrast, off-the-shelf software is software the customer can use with no significant changes in the underlying code. In some instances, an arrangement may include delivery of off-the-shelf software along with integration or other services that do not affect the operation of the off-the-shelf software. In these cases, the services may not be essential to the functionality of the software. However, if significant modifications or additions to software that is normally considered off-the-shelf software are necessary to meet the customer's purpose (e.g., changing or making additions to the software because it would not be usable in its off-the-shelf form in the customer's environment), the software should be considered core software for purposes of that arrangement. As such, the services included in the arrangement would be considered essential to the functionality of the software (ASC 985-605-25-81 through 25-83).

A service element should only be separately accounted for if it is separately identified in the arrangement such that the arrangement fee would be expected to vary based on whether it was included (ASC 985-605-25-78). For example, assume that an arrangement calls for the delivery of a software package that interfaces with a certain report writer system and that the off-the-shelf version of the software does not interface with that report writer. Because the arrangement does not specifically identify the development of the interface as a separate implementation service, this service cannot be accounted for separately. Instead, the service and the product must be accounted for on a combined basis under contract accounting. However, if the arrangement had called for the delivery of the off-the-shelf product and implementation services to build the interface to the report writer, the product and service could possibly be accounted for separately.

Other factors should also be considered in evaluating whether a service element is essential to the functionality of the other elements of an arrangement. For example, the following factors are indicative of services that are essential to the functionality of other elements (ASC 985-605-25-84):

1. *Building complex interfaces is necessary for the vendor's software to be functional in the customer's environment.* If the software is not sold by third parties, there may be no party other than the vendor that can design and develop such complex interfaces.

2. *The timing of payments for the software is coincident with performance of the services.* This would seem to indicate that the customer does not have full use of the software until the services are complete. This factor only indicates that services are essential to the software's functionality if the dollar amount of payments whose timing is tied to the services is greater than the amount of revenue allocated to the services.

3. *Milestones or customer-specific acceptance criteria affect the realizability of the software-license fee.* If the customer has negotiated the right to reject the software if the services are not performed to its satisfaction, this would seem to indicate that the customer believes the services are essential to the functionality of the software.

Conversely, the following factors are indicative that the services are not essential to the functionality of the software (ASC 985-605-25-85):

1. *The services are available from other vendors.* If this is true, then the customer could have obtained any services necessary to use the software for its purposes without the involvement of the vendor.

2. *The services do not carry a significant degree of risk or unique acceptance criteria.* Services that are routine in nature are not likely to be essential to the software's functionality.

3. *The software vendor is an experienced provider of the services.* This indicates a low risk related to the provision of the services.

4. *The vendor is providing primarily implementation services that do not affect the operation of the software.* Services such as loading of software, training of customer personnel, data conversion, report writing and the documentation of procedures, are not generally essential to operating the software.

5. *Customer personnel are dedicated to participate in the services being performed.* The dedication of customer personnel may indicate that services from the vendor are not absolutely necessary.

If a service element is determined to be essential to the functionality of the software in an arrangement, the software product and service elements should be accounted for on a combined basis, using contract accounting. The application of contract accounting to a software arrangement is discussed later in this chapter.

Nonservice Elements

Except for undelivered service elements, U.S. GAAP does not provide significant guidance on how to determine whether one element is essential to the functionality of another. However, many of the same concepts that are relevant in determining whether an undelivered service is essential to the functionality of a delivered element are also relevant when the undelivered element is a product. If an undelivered element other than a service is essential to the functionality of a delivered element, revenue from the delivered element should be deferred until the element essential to its functionality is also delivered.

EXAMPLES: SOFTWARE AND SERVICES

Oracle Corporation Form 10-K—Fiscal Year Ended May 31, 2011

Many of our software arrangements include consulting implementation services sold separately under consulting engagement contracts and are included as a part of our services business. Consulting revenues from these arrangements are generally accounted for separately from new software license revenues because the arrangements qualify as services transactions as defined in ASC 985-605. The more significant factors considered in determining whether the revenues should be accounted for separately include the nature of services (i.e. consideration of whether the services are essential to the functionality of the licensed product), degree of risk, availability of services from other vendors, timing of payments and impact of milestones or acceptance criteria on the realizability of the software license fee. Revenues for consulting services are generally recognized as the services are performed. If there is a significant uncertainty about the project completion or receipt of payment for the consulting services, revenues are deferred until the uncertainty is sufficiently resolved. We estimate the proportional performance on contracts with fixed or "not to exceed" fees on a monthly basis utilizing hours incurred to date as a percentage of total estimated hours to complete the project. If we do not have a sufficient basis to measure progress towards completion, revenues are recognized when we receive final acceptance from the customer that the services have been completed. When total cost estimates exceed revenues, we accrue for the estimated losses immediately using cost estimates that are based upon an average fully burdened daily rate applicable to the consulting organization delivering the services. The complexity of the estimation process and factors relating to the assumptions, risks and uncertainties inherent with the application of the proportional performance method of accounting affects the amounts of revenues and related expenses reported in our consolidated financial statements. A number of internal and external factors can affect our estimates, including labor rates, utilization and efficiency variances and specification and testing requirement changes.

Our Cloud Services offerings are comprised of Oracle Cloud Services and Advanced Customer Services and are also a part of our services business. Oracle Cloud Services are offered as standalone arrangements or as a part of arrangements to customers buying new software licenses or hardware systems products and services. Oracle Cloud Services are designed to provide comprehensive software and hardware management and maintenance services for customers hosted at our Oracle data center facilities, select partner data centers or physically on-site at customer facilities. Advanced Customer Services provides support services, both onsite and remote, to Oracle customers to enable increased performance and higher availability of their products and services. Depending upon the nature of the arrangement, revenues from Cloud Services are recognized as services are performed or ratably over the term of the service period, which is generally one year or less.

Education revenues are also a part of our services business and include instructor-led, media-based and internet-based training in the use of our software and hardware products. Education revenues are recognized as the classes or other education offerings are delivered.

If an arrangement contains multiple elements and does not qualify for separate accounting for the product and service transactions, then new software license revenues and/or hardware systems products revenues, including the costs of hardware systems products, are generally recognized together with the services based on contract accounting using either the percentage-of-completion or completed-contract method. Contract accounting is applied to any bundled software, hardware systems and services arrangements: (1) that include milestones or customer specific acceptance criteria that may affect collection of the software license or hardware systems product fees; (2) where consulting services include significant modification or customization of the software or hardware systems product or are of a specialized nature and generally performed only by Oracle; (3) where significant consulting services are provided for in the software license contract or hardware systems product contract without additional charge or are substantially discounted; or (4) where the software license or hardware systems product payment is tied to the performance of consulting services. For the purposes of revenue classification of the elements that are accounted for as a single unit of accounting, we allocate revenues to software and nonsoftware elements based on a rational and consistent methodology utilizing our best estimate of fair value of such elements.

Refund Provisions Based on Undelivered Elements

Revenue allocated to a delivered element is not considered collectible to the extent that it is subject to forfeiture, refund, or other concession in the event of non-performance on other elements in the arrangement. These forfeiture provisions may or may not be explicitly documented in the arrangement. Nonetheless, revenue should be considered subject to forfeiture, refund, or other concession, unless management does not intend to accept returns or grant concessions under these circumstances. In addition, a review of all available evidence should persuasively support this position.

If the vendor has a historical pattern of making refunds or granting concessions on delivered elements not required under the original provisions of its arrangements due to non-delivery of other elements, no other evidence is persuasive enough to reach a conclusion that revenue in current arrangements with similar elements is not subject to forfeiture. Therefore, no revenue should be recognized until all of the elements are delivered (ASC 985-605-25-13).

ILLUSTRATION: TIMING OF REVENUE RECOGNITION WHEN SPECIFIED DAMAGES ARE INCLUDED IN A MULTIPLE-ELEMENT ARRANGEMENT

Facts: Company X enters into a contract to deliver two off-the-shelf software elements, A and B, for $1,000,000. Company X appropriately allocates $600,000 of the fee to Element A and $400,000 to Element B based on VSOE of fair value. The agreement stipulates that Company X must pay a $550,000 penalty if it does not deliver Element B by a specified date. Element A has already been delivered, but Element B has not.

Accounting: The portion of the fee allocated to Element A that is subject to forfeiture if Element B is not delivered is not considered collectible until Element B is delivered. Therefore, Company X may only recognize revenue upon the delivery of Element A to the extent that revenue is not refundable. In this case, the penalty for failing to deliver Element B on a timely basis ($550,000) exceeds the portion of the fee allocated to Element B ($400,000) by $150,000. Therefore, only $450,000 of the $600,000 otherwise allocable to Element A may be recognized. If Company X receives payments of greater than $450,000 before Element B is delivered, the excess should be reflected as deferred revenue.

RECOGNITION WHEN ELEMENTS ARE ACCOUNTED FOR TOGETHER

There are several situations discussed above in which revenue from two separate deliverables cannot be separated for recognition purposes. The appropriate recognition pattern for such situations depends on the mix of elements in the multiple-element arrangement or portion of a multiple-element arrangement that cannot be further separated.

Multiple-Element Arrangement Includes Software Elements and Non-Software Elements

As discussed earlier in this chapter, separation of a multiple-element arrangement that includes software elements and non-software elements should be based on the guidance in ASC 605-25. If the application of ASC 605-25 results in a conclusion that the elements should not be separated, the general revenue recognition principles apply to the bundled arrangement. In other words, software accounting guidance should not be applied to determine when revenue should be recognized because the bundled group of elements falls outside the scope of ASC 985-605. Additional recognition guidance for elements subject to ASC 605-25 that should not be treated separately for accounting purposes is provided in Chapter 4, "Multiple-Deliverable Revenue Arrangements."

Multiple-Element Arrangement Includes Software Elements Requiring Significant Production, Modification, or Customization and Non-Software Elements

The guidance in ASC 605-25 applies to the separation of the deliverables in a multiple-element arrangement that includes software requiring significant production, modification, or customization, other software-related elements and non-software elements. If the application of ASC 605-25 results in a conclusion that the elements should not be separated, it is usually appropriate to apply general revenue recognition principles to the bundled arrangement. It is generally inappropriate to apply contract accounting to the bundled group of elements for purposes of determining when revenue should be recognized because some the elements fall outside the scope of ASC 605-35. Additional recognition guidance for elements subject to ASC 605-25 that should not be treated separately for accounting purposes is provided in Chapter 4, "Multiple-Deliverable Revenue Arrangements."

Multiple-Element Arrangement Includes Only Software Elements Requiring Significant Production, Modification, or Customization and Software-Related Elements

The software multiple-element model should be used to separate the deliverables in a multiple-element arrangement that includes only software requiring significant production, modification, or customization and software-related elements. If application of the guidance in ASC 985-605 results in a conclusion that the elements should not be separated, the revenue recognition principles in ASC 605-35 should be applied to the bundled group of elements. The general provisions of ASC 605-35 are discussed in detail in Chapter 9, "Contract Accounting," and specific issues related to the application of these provisions to software arrangements are discussed in the following section entitled "Contract Accounting for Software Arrangements."

Multiple-Element Arrangement Includes Only Software and Software-Related Elements

The accounting for a multiple-element arrangement that includes only software and software-related elements should be based on the software multiple-element model. If application of this model results in a conclusion that the elements should not be separated, the revenue recognition principles in ASC 985-605 should be applied to the bundled group of elements.

When the elements cannot be separated for accounting purposes, revenue recognition for the bundled group of deliverables must be based on the reason for inability to separate the elements. Some of these reasons and the effects they have on recognizing revenue are explained below.

Sufficient VSOE of Fair Value Does Not Exist

When sufficient VSOE of fair value does not exist to allocate revenue among software and software-related elements, revenue is generally recognized upon delivery of the final element for which VSOE of fair value does not exist, presuming that all other revenue recognition criteria have been met. Upon delivery of the final element, either the seller's performance under the arrangement will be complete or all of the remaining items will be those for which VSOE of fair value exists. This will allow the company to apply the residual method.

Thus, if an arrangement consists of only software and PCS and there is insufficient VSOE of fair value to allocate revenue among the elements, revenue from the entire arrangement must be recognized as the PCS is delivered—in most cases, ratably over the PCS period. Similarly, if the only undelivered element in an arrangement is a software-related service that is not essential to the functionality of the software, all revenue from the arrangement would be recognized as the service is performed, or, if no pattern of performance can be discerned, on a straight-line basis over the period during which the service is performed (ASC 985-605-25-10).

If the final element to be delivered is a software-related product or specified upgrade for which VSOE of fair value does not exist, all revenue from the arrangement must be deferred until this final product or upgrade is delivered, even if the vendor believes that the product's value is not material to the arrangement.

An Element Is Essential to the Functionality of Another Element

When an undelivered software or software-related element is essential to the functionality of a delivered element, revenue allocated to the delivered element may not be recognized. If the delivered element is a software product and the undelivered element essential to the product's functionality is a software-related service, contract accounting for the product and service must be used (ASC 985-605-25-77) (see "Contract Accounting for Software Arrangements" below). When an undelivered software or software-related product is essential to the functionality of a delivered software or software-related product, revenue allocated to both products should be recognized, assuming all other revenue recognition criteria have been met, when the second product is delivered.

CONTRACT ACCOUNTING FOR SOFTWARE ARRANGEMENTS

If an arrangement to deliver software, either alone or together with other software-related products or services, requires significant production, modification, or customization of software, the service element cannot be accounted for separately. In these cases, the arrangement should be accounted for using long-term contract accounting, in conformity with the relevant guidance in ASC 605-35. Contract accounting is discussed in detail in Chapter 9, "Contract Accounting." However, the application of contract accounting to software arrangements presents unique issues, which are discussed here.

PRACTICE POINTER: Unlike the software revenue recognition guidance, the percentage-of-completion method of contract accounting permits revenue recognition before complete delivery occurs. Therefore, the use of contract accounting might be attractive to a company that enters into an arrangement to sell a software product that is not yet complete. However, transactions that normally are accounted for as product sales may not be accounted for under contract accounting to avoid the delivery requirements normally associated with product sales (ASC 985-605-25-88).

Measuring Progress under the Percentage-of-Completion Method

The diverse approaches used to measure progress toward completion under the percentage-of-completion method may be grouped into two broad categories: (1) input measures, which are measurements made in terms of efforts devoted to the contract, such as costs, labor hours or other inputs, and (2) output measures, which are indices of results achieved, such as units produced or contract milestones.

Output Measures

Output measures are not easily applied to software arrangements because it is difficult to establish relevant measures. However, if the transaction requires delivery of multiple modules, output may be measured based on delivery of individual modules. If reliable output measures cannot be established, input measures should be used (ASC 985-605-25-96).

Input Measures

Although costs incurred may be a good measure of progress on a software arrangement, labor hours often are the best measure of progress for projects involving labor-intensive software customization. When input measures based on costs incurred are used, the contract accounting guidance notes that only costs that relate to contract performance should be included in the measurement. For example, software customization projects begin with core software. As the software was not produced for the purpose of the particular contract, no value should be assigned to it in measuring progress-toward completion (ASC 985-605-25-97 through 25-100).

RIGHTS TO EXCHANGE OR RETURN SOFTWARE

As part of an arrangement, a software vendor may provide the customer with a right to return or exchange software. The accounting for return rights in a software arrangement is generally similar to that used for return rights on any other product, and that accounting is addressed in ASC 605-15-25. The accounting for exchange rights depends on whether the right is limited to an exchange for a product of similar price, features, and functionality. An exchange right that meets these criteria does not receive accounting recognition because it is not considered substantive. However, any other exchange right should be accounted for as a return right.

Distinguishing Among Return, Exchange, and Additional Product Rights

In certain situations, a return or exchange right allows the customer to obtain a new software product and retain the right to use the original product. This is not an exchange or return right at all, but is instead a right to an additional software product. The additional product should be treated as an additional element of the arrangement (ASC 985-605-25-60).

When the customer is not contractually entitled to continue using the original software product, the right is either an exchange or a return right. Although it is sometimes difficult to determine which of the two it is, the following situations are clear:

1. If the customer with the return or exchange right is a reseller rather than an end-user, the right is accounted for as a right of return.

2. If the right allows an end-user to return the software and get anything in exchange other than another software product (e.g., services or PCS), the right is accounted for as a right of return.

Rights that allow an end-user to exchange the software for another software package are accounted for as exchange rights if the software the user is entitled to receive has similar price, functionality and features as the software the user will give up. Whether this is the case is a matter of judgment. However, if the product that is available to the user in the exchange has not yet been developed and the company expects to incur significant costs in development of that product, it should not be considered to have similar price, features, and functionality to the product delivered to the customer (ASC 985-605-25-61).

The most common situation that qualifies for accounting as an exchange is a platform-transfer right, which is the right to exchange a software product for a product marketed under the same name that operates on a different operating system or on different hardware, but otherwise has the same features and functionality (ASC 985-605-25-62; 985-605-25-63).

Accounting for Exchange Rights

The existence of a right that allows an end-user to exchange software for software of similar price, features and functionality does not affect the accounting for a software arrangement. As a result, revenue may be recognized when each of the revenue recognition criteria is met with respect to the original software product deliverable.

Accounting for Return Rights

Like return rights in non-software arrangements, a right to return software should be evaluated to determine its substance. If the return right is limited to situations where the software does not operate according to published specifications, it should be treated as a warranty. Warranties on software products are treated the same as warranties on any other products (see Chapter 5, "Product Deliverables").

A right to return software that does not meet customer- or arrangement-specific operating specifications should be treated as a customer acceptance clause. A return right that is of sufficient length to be something other than a period that allows the customer to determine whether software is functional for the customer's purpose should be treated as a cancellation clause (see "Fixed or Determinable Fees and Collectibility" in this chapter for discussion of the accounting for each of these clauses).

Other return rights on software should generally be accounted for in the same manner as similar rights in product arrangements. Information on how to account for these rights can be found in Chapter 5, "Product Deliverables." However, to recognize revenue when a right of return exists, the vendor must be able to reasonably estimate the amount of returns. Due to the rapid introduction and replacement of software products, historical experience may not be relevant in estimating returns on current sales. In this situation, it is unlikely that returns can be estimated and revenue could not be recognized upon delivery.

EXAMPLE: STOCK BALANCING RIGHTS

Citrix Systems, Inc. Form 10-K—Fiscal Year Ended December 31, 2009

In the normal course of business, we are not obligated to accept product returns from our distributors under any conditions, unless the product item is defective in manufacture, but we do provide most of our distributors with stock balancing and price protection rights. Stock balancing rights permit distributors to return products to us up to the 45th day of the fiscal quarter, subject to ordering an equal dollar amount of our other products prior to the last day of the same fiscal quarter. Price protection rights require that we grant retroactive price adjustments for inventories of our products held by distributors or resellers if we lower our prices for such products. Product items returned to us under the stock balancing program must be in new, unused and unopened condition. We establish provisions for estimated returns for stock balancing and price protection rights, as well as other sales allowances, concurrently with the recognition of revenue. The provisions are established based upon consideration of a variety of factors, including, among other things, recent and historical return rates for both, specific products and distributors, estimated distributor inventory levels by product, the impact of any new product releases and projected economic conditions. Actual product returns for stock balancing and price protection provisions incurred are, however, dependent upon future events, including the amount of stock balancing activity by our distributors and the level of distributor inventories at the time of any price adjustments. We continually monitor the factors that influence the pricing of our products and distributor inventory levels and make adjustments to these provisions when we believe actual returns and other allowances could differ from established reserves. Our ability to recognize revenue upon shipment to our distributors is predicated on our ability to reliably estimate future stock balancing returns. If actual experience or changes in market condition impairs our ability to estimate returns, we would be required to defer the recognition of revenue until the delivery of the product to the end-user. Allowances for estimated product returns amounted to approximately $1.6 million at December 31, 2009 and 2008. We have not reduced and have no current plans to reduce our prices for inventory currently held by distributors or resellers. Accordingly, there were no reserves required for price protection at December 31, 2009 and December 31, 2008. We also record reductions to revenue for customer programs and incentive offerings including volume-based incentives, at the time the sale is recorded. We could take actions to increase our customer incentive offerings, which could result in an incremental reduction to our revenue at the time the incentive is offered.

SALES INCENTIVES

General

Companies that sell packaged software to consumers, either directly or through retailers, often use sales incentives such as rebates. The accounting for such incentives has been addressed in ASC 605-50. The EITF's conclusions in this area are discussed in detail in Chapter 8, "Miscellaneous Issues," and Chapter 11, "Presentation." The application of these conclusions to software arrangements does not pose any unique issues.

Discounts on Future Purchases

In connection with the licensing of an existing product, a vendor might offer a discount (coupon) on future purchases of additional licenses of the same product or on other products or services. If this discount is insignificant, it does not require accounting recognition. However, if the discount is more than insignificant, it creates a presumption that there is an additional element in the arrangement. The authoritative guidance covers a number of issues regarding the accounting for discounts on future purchases.

Significant Incremental Discounts

A discount with respect to future purchases that is provided in a software arrangement indicates that another element is present in a software arrangement if the discount meets all of the following criteria (ASC 985-605-15-3; 985-605-55-87):

1. *It is incremental to the range of discounts reflected in the pricing of the other elements of the arrangement.* If the customer was able to negotiate a 30% discount on the price of the elements in the current arrangement, offering a 30% discount on additional elements does not appear to grant the customer anything that would not otherwise have been available.

2. *It is incremental to the range of discounts typically given in comparable transactions.* A discount that is not incremental to discounts typically

given in comparable transactions (e.g., volume purchase discounts comparable to those generally provided in comparable transactions) does not confer any additional value to the customer other than what was already given.

3. *It is significant.* Judgment is required when assessing whether an incremental discount is significant.

4. *It is not limited to additional copies of products licensed by and delivered to the customer under the same arrangement.* As discussed above under "Delivery," additional copies of delivered software are not considered undelivered element. Rather, this situation should be accounted for as an arrangement in which the fee depends upon the number of copies ordered and duplicated. The amount of the fee contingent upon future duplication should not be recognized until the contingency is resolved. However, there need not be any deferral of the initial licensing fee to recognize the discount on the additional copies.

Accounting for Significant Incremental Discounts

The overriding concept in a software arrangement that includes the right to a significant incremental discount on a future purchase of products or services is that a proportionate amount of this discount should be applied to each element in the arrangement based on the relative fair value. Applying this guidance when all of the elements are known and have VSOE of fair value is relatively straightforward.

However, if either the future elements to which the discount applies are not specified in the arrangement (e.g., a customer is allowed a discount on any future purchases) or VSOE of fair value of the future elements does not exist, the concept in the preceding paragraph becomes difficult to apply. In these situations, if the maximum amount of the incremental discount on the future purchases is quantifiable, this amount should be allocated to the elements in the current arrangement and the future purchases, assuming that the customer will purchase the minimum amount necessary to utilize the maximum discount.

If the maximum amount of the significant incremental discount on future purchases is not quantifiable (e.g., the discount can be used on all purchases within a specified period of time and there is no limit on the amount of purchases), revenue allocated to each element in the arrangement should be reduced by the rate of the discount.

If the residual value method is used to allocate arrangement consideration in a multiple-element arrangement that includes a discount on future purchases, the discount offered in the initial arrangement should be computed by comparing the published list price of the delivered elements to the residual value attributable to these elements. If the discount on future purchases is significant and incremental to the discount computed for the initial arrangement, the software vendor should apply the significant and incremental discount on future purchases to the initial arrangement (ASC 985-605-55-88 through 55-91).

The portion of the fee that is deferred as a result of the significant incremental discount on future purchases should be recognized as revenue proportionately as the future purchases are delivered (assuming all other revenue recognition criteria are met) so that a consistent discount rate is applied to all purchases under the arrangement. If the future purchases are not limited by quantity of product(s) or service(s), the portion of the fee that is deferred as a result of the presence of a significant incremental discount should be recognized as revenue as a subscription (ASC 985-605-55-85).

ILLUSTRATION: SIGNIFICANT INCREMENTAL DISCOUNTS

(Adapted from ASC 985-605-55-185 through 55-203)

(For purposes of these examples, VSOE of fair value equals list price and all of the software products do not involve significant production, modification, or customization.)

EXAMPLE 1

Facts: A software vendor sells Product A for its list price of $40 along with a right to a discount of $30 on another of its software products, Product B, which has a list price of $60. The $30 discount on Product B is a significant incremental discount that would not normally be given in comparable transactions.

Accounting: The vendor should allocate the $30 discount across Product A and Product B. The overall discount is 30%, calculated as the ratio of the discount ($30) to the fair values of the products ($40 + $60 = $100). Therefore, upon the delivery of Product A, the vendor would recognize $28 (a 30% discount off of $40) of revenue and defer $12. If the customer uses the discount and purchases Product B, the vendor would recognize $42 in revenue upon delivery of Product B ($30 in cash received plus the $12 previously deferred). If the discount expires unused, the $12 in deferred revenue would be recognized at that time.

EXAMPLE 2

Facts: A software vendor sells Product A for its list price of $40 along with a right to a discount of $20 on any one of its other software products, Products B through Z. The list prices of Products B through Z range from $40 to $100. The $20 discount is a significant incremental discount that would not normally be given in comparable transactions.

Accounting: The vendor should allocate the $20 discount across Product A and the assumed purchase of whichever of Product B through Z has the lowest fair value ($40). The overall discount is 25% ($20/$80). Therefore, upon delivery of Product A, the vendor would recognize $30 in revenue, and defer $10. If the customer uses the discount and purchases the additional product with a fair value of $40, the vendor would recognize $30 in revenue upon its delivery (the $10 previously deferred and the additional cash license fee due of $20). If the discount expires unused, the $10 in deferred revenue would be recognized at that time.

EXAMPLE 3

Facts: A software vendor sells Product A for its list price of $40 along with a right to a discount of 50% off list price on any future purchases of its other software products, Products B through Z, with a maximum cumulative discount of

$80. The 50% discount is a significant incremental discount that would not normally be given in comparable transactions.

Accounting: The vendor should assume that the customer will purchase additional products worth $160 in order to use the maximum $80 discount. Therefore, the vendor would allocate the $80 discount across Product A and the assumed additional products to be purchased. The overall discount is 40% ($80/$200). Therefore, upon the delivery of Product A, the vendor would recognize $24 of revenue and defer $16. If the customer uses the discount by purchasing additional products with fair values totaling $160, the vendor would recognize $96 in revenue upon delivery of those products ($80 in cash received plus the $16 previously deferred). If the discount expires unused, the $16 in deferred revenue would be recognized at that time.

EXAMPLE 4

Facts: A software vendor sells Product A for $60, which represents a 40% discount off its list price (VSOE) of $100. In the same transaction, it also provides the right to a discount of 50% off of the list price (VSOE) on any future purchases of units of Product B for the next six months with a maximum discount of $200. The discount of 50% on future purchases of units of Product B is a discount not normally given in comparable transactions.

Accounting: Because the discount offered on future purchases of Product B is not normally given in comparable transactions and is both significant and incremental in relation to the 40% discount, it must be accounted for as part of the original sale consistent with Example 3 above. The vendor should assume that the customer will make $400 in purchases of Product B in order to use the maximum discount of $200. Therefore, the vendor would allocate the $240 discount ($40 on Product A and $200 maximum on future purchases) across Product A and the assumed additional products to be purchased. The overall discount is 48% ($240/$500). Therefore, upon the delivery of Product A, the vendor would recognize $52 (a 48% discount off of Product A's fair value of $100) of revenue and defer $8. If the customer uses the discount by purchasing additional products with fair value totaling $400, the vendor would recognize $208 in revenue upon delivery of those products ($200 in cash received plus the $8 previously deferred). If the discount expires unused, the $8 in deferred revenue would be recognized at that time.

EXAMPLE 5

Facts: A software vendor sells Product A for its list price of $40 along with a right to a discount of 50% off list price on any future purchases of its other software products with no maximum cumulative discount. The 50% discount is a significant incremental discount that would not normally be given in comparable transactions.

Accounting: The vendor should apply the 50% discount to Product A and all future products purchased using the discount. Therefore, upon the delivery of Product A, the vendor would recognize $20 of revenue and defer $20. If the customer purchases additional products using the discount, the vendor would recognize revenue equal to the cash received upon the delivery of those products. The previously deferred $20 should be accounted for as a subscription and recognized pro rata over the discount period or, if no period is specified in the arrangement, over the estimated period during which additional purchases will be made.

EXAMPLE 6

Facts: A software vendor sells Product A, which has a list price of $100, for $30 along with the right to a discount of 70% off list price (VSOE) on any future purchases of its other software products for the next six months with no maximum cumulative discount.

Accounting: As the discount offered on future purchases over the next six months is equal to the discount offered on the current purchase (70%), there is no accounting necessary in the original sale for the discount offered on future purchases.

EXAMPLE 7

Facts: A software vendor sells Product A, which has a list price of $100, for $80. One year of PCS is included in the arrangement, and the customer may renew PCS following the initial year at a rate of $15. As part of the transaction, the customer receives the right to a 55% discount off of published list prices for the purchase of all new products released by the software vendor for two years, with no maximum cumulative discount. The software vendor does not have VSOE of fair value for Product A, as Product A is never sold separately.

Accounting: The residual value allocated to Product A is $65 ($80 arrangement fee less $15 PCS renewal rate). The discount on Product A is 35% ($35 discount on Product A ($100 list price less $65 allocated residual value) divided by $100 list price). The incremental discount offered on future purchases is 20% (55% discount on future purchases less 35% computed discount on Product A). If the software vendor concludes that this 20% incremental discount is significant, it will recognize revenue of $45 upon delivery of Product A, provided all other revenue recognition criteria have been met. The $45 ultimately allocated to Product A represents the $80 arrangement fee reduced by (a) $20 of additional discount (20% significant incremental discount off of $100 list price), and (b) $15 PCS renewal rate. The $20 additional discount is deferred and recognized pro rata over the two-year discount period. If the customer purchases additional products using the 55% discount, the software vendor should recognize revenue equal to the net fee attributable to those products when all of the revenue recognition criteria have been met.

NONMONETARY EXCHANGES INVOLVING SOFTWARE

Nonmonetary exchanges involving software are generally treated the same way as those involving other products or services. The guidance in ASC 845-10 (APB-29) is applied to determine whether the transaction should be recorded at historical cost or at fair value. If the transaction should be reported at fair value, then the software revenue recognition guidance is applied to determine whether the measured fair value can be recognized as revenue, or must be deferred until remaining obligations are completed (ASC 985-845).

OBSERVATION: In an exchange in which either or both parties to the agreement do not plan to use or sell the products (or rights) they receive in the exchange, fair value is considered zero, because the transaction does not appear to have economic substance. Therefore, no revenue can ever be recognized in such a transaction.

Exchanging Software for Technology or Product to Be Sold

ASC 985-845-25-3 (APB-29) states that an exchange of inventory for inventory to be sold in the same line of business does not culminate an earnings process. Therefore, if a software vendor exchanges one or more software licenses (which are considered inventory for the purposes of applying this guidance) and receives in return the rights to technology or products that are to be sold, licensed, or leased in the same line of business as the software licenses delivered in the exchange, then the software vendor should record the exchange at historical cost, which is likely to be zero.

However, if the technology or products received by the software vendor in the exchange are to be sold, licensed, or leased in a different line of business from the software licenses delivered, the exchange should be recorded at fair value, as long as VSOE of fair value exists. If VSOE of fair value does not exist, the transaction should be recorded at historical cost, because ASC 985-845-25-5 (APB-29) indicates that historical cost must be used if fair value cannot be reasonably determined and ASC 985-605 limits the determination of fair value of software to VSOE.

OBSERVATION: ASC 845-10 (APB-29) requires that the fair value of a nonmonetary transaction be determinable within reasonable limits. VSOE of fair value is the only way to satisfy this requirement for software and software-related elements included in a nonmonetary transaction.

Exchanging Software for Technology to Be Used Internally

When a software vendor licenses its externally sold software to a customer in exchange for a license to the customer's technology, which the software vendor intends to utilize internally (i.e., the software received will not be sold but instead used in the vendor's operations), the transaction should be recorded at fair value (provided that VSOE exists) because the exchange is one of inventory for a long-term asset, which should not be accounted for at historical cost under ASC 985-845-25-7 (APB-29).

DEFERRED COSTS

Revenue from a software sale may have to be deferred for a number of reasons. In many instances, the issue of whether related direct costs should be deferred is unimportant, because these costs are minimal. However, in certain arrangements, especially those involving payment of sales commissions, the direct and incremental costs of a software sale are significant. Because the deferral of costs is not addressed in ASC 985-605 or any other software-specific guidance, the considerations are the same as in non-software transactions. See the discussion in Chapter 8, "Miscellaneous Issues," for information.

ADDED CONSIDERATIONS IN RESELLER TRANSACTIONS

Consignment Arrangements

When a software vendor has a relationship with a reseller, terms of the arrangement or the customary business practices between the parties may indicate that a contractual sale actually functions more like a consignment, from which revenue should not be recognized. The factors that might result in a software transaction with a reseller being treated as a consignment are similar to those discussed in the "Consignment Sales" section of Chapter 5, "Product Deliverables." In these cases, revenue would not be recognized until the reseller sells the product to an end-user. This is commonly referred to as recognizing revenue upon "sell-through."

EXAMPLE: SELL-THROUGH REVENUE

Isilon Systems, Inc. Form 10-K—Fiscal Year Ended December 31, 2008

On sales to channel partners, we evaluate whether fees are considered fixed or determinable by considering a number of factors, including our ability to estimate returns, the geography in which a sales transaction originates, payment terms, and our relationship and past history with the particular channel partner. If fees are not considered fixed or determinable at the time of sale to a channel partner, revenue recognition is deferred until there is persuasive evidence indicating product has sold through to an end-user. Persuasive evidence of sell-through may include reports from channel partners documenting sell-through activity, copies of end-user purchase orders, data indicating an order has shipped to an end-user, cash payments or letters of credit guaranteeing cash payments or other similar information.

PCS Granted by Resellers

Some transactions give the reseller a right to upgrades or enhancements introduced between the time the reseller arrangement is entered into and the time the reseller sub-licenses the product to end-users. This right is often included even when upgrades and technical support will not be provided to the end-user. Such an arrangement, in which the reseller has the right to provide unspecified upgrades to its customers, is an implied PCS arrangement between the vendor and the reseller. Therefore, the arrangement fee must be allocated, based on VSOE of fair value, between the software product and the implied PCS arrangement. If VSOE of fair value for PCS does not exist, the entire arrangement fee should be recognized over the expected PCS term, which would generally be the period over which the reseller has the right to sell licenses to its customers that include unspecified upgrades developed before the sublicense is entered into (ASC 985-605-25-75).

TRANSITION FOR ASU 2009-14

As discussed throughout this chapter, ASU 2009-14 made significant changes to the scope of ASC 985-605. The new guidance must be applied in fiscal years beginning after June 15, 2010 (2011 for calendar year companies), and applies to revenue arrangements entered into or significantly modified after its adoption (ASC 985-605-65-1a) (ASU 2009-14, par. 8a).

In the year of adoption, qualitative (narrative) information regarding any changes applied prospectively is required, including a discussion of changes to units of accounting for similar arrangements and the effect of those changes on the timing and pattern of revenue recognition. Quantitative information may also be necessary to explain the effects of the new guidance if the difference is significant (ASC 605-25-65-1d) (ASU 2009-13, par. 30d).

Companies that wish to apply the new guidance earlier may do so, but only as of the beginning of a fiscal year. In addition, companies that wish to do so may apply the guidance in ASU 2009-14 retroactively to the beginning of any fiscal year. Because the changes made by ASU 2009-14 are so significant, early or retroactive adoption may be difficult. Nonetheless, companies may wish to elect early or retroactive adoption because the new guidance does, for certain arrangements, allow accounting that more closely matches the economics of the revenue arrangement. Obviously, affected companies should carefully consider whether to elect these optional methods of adoption.

EXAMPLE: ADOPTION OF ASU 2009-14

Hewlett-Packard Company Form 10-K—Fiscal Year Ended October 31, 2009

In October 2009, the FASB issued Accounting Standards Update ("ASU") No. 2009-13, "Multiple-Deliverable Revenue Arrangements" ("ASU 2009-13"). The new standard changes the requirements for establishing separate units of accounting in a multiple element arrangement and requires the allocation of arrangement consideration to each deliverable to be based on the relative selling price. Concurrently to issuing ASU 2009-13, the FASB also issued ASU No. 2009-14, "Certain Revenue Arrangements That Include Software Elements" ("ASU 2009-14"). ASU 2009-14 excludes software that is contained on a tangible product from the scope of software revenue guidance if the software is essential to the tangible product's functionality.

HP early adopted these standards as of the beginning of fiscal 2009 for new and materially modified deals originating after November 1, 2008; therefore, the previously reported quarterly results have been restated to reflect the impact of adoption. As a result of the adoption, fiscal 2009 net revenues and net earnings were higher by $255 million and $55 million, respectively. The impact was due to the recognition of revenue previously deferred for certain deliverables bundled in multiple element arrangements where the arrangements also included services for which HP was unable to demonstrate fair value pursuant to the previous standards. The new standards allow for deliverables for which revenue was previously deferred to be separated and recognized as delivered, rather than over the longest service delivery period as a single unit with other elements in the arrangement. HP is not able to reasonably estimate the effect of adopting these standards on future financial periods as the impact will vary based on the nature and volume of new or materially modified deals in any given period.

For fiscal 2009 and future periods, pursuant to the guidance of ASU 2009-13, when a sales arrangement contains multiple elements, such as hardware and software products, licenses and/or services, HP allocates revenue to each element based on a selling price hierarchy. The selling price for a deliverable is based on its vendor specific objective evidence ("VSOE") if available, third party evidence ("TPE") if VSOE is not available, or estimated selling price ("ESP") if neither VSOE nor TPE is available. In multiple element arrangements where more-than-incidental software deliverables are included, revenue is allocated to each separate unit of accounting for each of the non-software deliverables and to the software deliverables as a group using the relative selling prices of each of the deliverables in the arrangement based on the aforementioned selling price hierarchy. If the arrangement contains more than one software deliverable, the arrangement consideration allocated to the software deliverables as a group is then allocated to each software deliverable using the guidance for recognizing software revenue, as amended.

CHAPTER 11
PRESENTATION

CONTENTS

BACKGROUND

Accounting standard setters have provided little guidance on income statement and balance sheet classification. However, the increasing emphasis on more sophisticated financial analysis has made it important for financial statement preparers to correctly classify income and cost items within the income statement, even when this does not change the reported gross margin, operating income or net income. In addition, the "deferred revenue" caption on the balance sheet has also received more attention because it is a liability usually settled by performance rather than a transfer of cash, which results in an increase in equity rather than a decrease in assets.

SURVEY OF APPLICABLE LITERATURE

Conceptual guidance on income statement classification is provided in CON-6, which distinguishes between (1) revenue and gains, and (2) expenses and losses. In addition, the SEC has issued guidelines for various income statement captions, including revenues, in ASC 225, *Income Statement*; 225-10-S99-2 (REG S-X, Rule 5-03). However, until late 1999, this constituted the only guidance that addressed financial statement classification.

Since then, the EITF has addressed income statement classification in a number of consensuses that are broadly applicable to a wide range of revenue transactions and industries. These issues address questions such as: (1) classification of payments from a company to its customers, (2) classification of taxes collected from customers and remitted to government authorities, (3) whether a company should recognize revenue on a gross or net basis, and (4) whether coupons, rebates, and other discounts should be reported as expenses or as reductions of revenue.

LISTING OF APPLICABLE LITERATURE

ASC	ASC Topic/ Subtopic	Publication	Subject
N/A	N/A	CON-5	Recognition and Measurement in Financial Statements of Business Enterprises
N/A	N/A	CON-6	Elements of Financial Statements
840	Leases	FAS-13	Accounting for Leases
952-605	Franchisors	FAS-45	Franchise Fees
225-10-S99-2	Income Statement/Overall	REG S-X, Rule 5-03	Financial Statement Requirements, Commercial and Industrial Companies, Income Statements
470-10-25	Debt/Overall	EITF 88-18	Sales of Future Revenues
605-45	Revenue Recognition/ Principal Agent Considerations	EITF 99-19	Reporting Revenue Gross as a Principal versus Net as an Agent

ASC	ASC Topic/ Subtopic	Publication	Subject
605-45-45-19	Revenue Recognition/ Principal Agent Considerations	EITF 00-10	Shipping and Handling Fees and Costs
605-45-45-22	Revenue Recognition/ Principal Agent Considerations	EITF 00-14	Income Statement Characterization of Reimbursements Received for "Out-of-Pocket" Expenses Incurred
605-45-50-3	Revenue Recognition/ Principal Agent Considerations	EITF 06-3	Presentation of Taxes Collected from Customers and Remitted to Governmental Authorities
932-330-35	Extractive Activities—Oil and Gas/Inventory	EITF 02-3	Accounting for Derivative Contracts Held for Trading Purposes
605-50	Revenue Recognition/ Customer Payments and Incentives	EITF 01-9 and EITF 06-1	Payments from a Vendor to a Customer
605-50	Revenue Recognition/ Customer Payments and Incentives	EITF 02-16 and EITF 03-10	Accounting by a Customer (Including a Reseller) for Certain Consideration Received from a Vendor
815-10-55-62	Derivatives and Hedging/Overall	EITF 03-11	Reporting Realized Gains and Losses on Derivative Instruments That Are Not "Held for Trading Purposes"
605-15-S99-2	Revenue Recognition/ Products	SAB Topic 8A	Retail Companies—Sales of Leased or Licensed Departments
605-10-S99	Revenue Recognition/ Overall	SAB Topic 13	Revenue Recognition
985-605-55-32	Software/ Revenue Recognition	TPA 5100.58	Effect of Prepayments on Software Revenue Recognition—Transfer of Receivable without Recourse
924-605-45	Entertainment— Casinos/Revenue Recognition	AAG-CAS	Promotional Allowances

ASC	ASC Topic/ Subtopic	Publication	Subject
954-605	Health Care Entities/ Revenue Recognition	ASU 2010-23	Measuring Charity Care
720-50	Other Expenses—Fees Paid to the Federal Government by Pharmaceutical Manufacturers	ASU 2010-27	Recognition and Presentation of Annual Fee Paid By Pharmaceutical Manufacturers that Participate in Government Programs

REVENUES VERSUS GAINS

One of the key issues in income statement classification is whether a transaction that contributes to income should be reported as revenue or as a gain. CON-6 addresses the difference between revenues and gains by noting that "Revenues . . . result from an entity's ongoing major or central operations and activities. . . " while "Gains . . . result from entities' peripheral or incidental transactions" (CON-6, par. 87). CON-5 depicts revenues as a result of an "earnings process" involving activities specifically targeted toward bringing in that revenue, while "Gains commonly result from transactions and other events that involve no 'earnings process,' and for recognizing gains, being earned is generally less significant than being realized or realizable" (CON-5, par. 83b).

The application of this guidance depends on the unique facts and circumstances of a company's operations. In practice, it is generally easy to identify an entity's "ongoing major or central operations and activities." These activities usually include a company's main productive efforts and most of its transactions with other companies. For example, a manufacturer hires employees, buys raw materials, rents or purchases land, buildings, and equipment, and sells its output to customers. Its manufacturing operations convert purchased materials using production processes and facilities into a product that is sold at a price higher than the combined cost of the inputs. Other companies incur expenses and generate revenues differently—for example, retailers and distributors buy, transport, market, and sell goods, insurers charge customers to assume risks, and banks pay interest to depositors to have funds available to provide loans that earn greater interest (CON-6, par. 88).

Some companies engage in many different ongoing major or central activities. Any activity that the company performs repeatedly, expects to continue performing, and on which it focuses its resources and efforts may be an ongoing major line of business and, hence, an activity that generates revenues and expenses, rather than gains and losses.

Transactions that are not part of a company's ongoing major or central operations typically involve activities that are ancillary, but are still necessary. For example, a company that owns its office building may rent excess space to another entity. This rental income should not be reported as revenue. Similarly, a manufacturing or service company will typically invest cash rather than have it sit idle. The interest income earned should not be reported as revenue, even if it was earned on funds obtained from customer prepayments. Other transactions that produce gains (or losses) can be identified because they result from events over which the company has little control, such as currency fluctuations, strikes, natural disasters and related insurance recoveries, as well as changes in the fair value of assets and liabilities.

OBSERVATION: Many companies enter into arrangements that can result in the receipt of payments even though nothing of value is ever provided to the customer. This occurs when a customer returns a product or cancels a service but is required to pay a termination fee. In these and similar situations, the payments should be reported as a gain, rather than as revenue, because no earnings process occurred.

SEC REGISTRANT ALERT: In a December 2002 speech, the SEC staff highlighted the fact that revenues exclude equity in net income of investees, net gains or losses on sales of fixed assets or investments, and "other income."

EXAMPLE: CATEGORIES OF REVENUE AND REVENUES VERSUS GAINS

International Business Machines Corporation, Inc. Form 10-K—Fiscal Year Ended December 31, 2009

OBSERVATION: IBM's Consolidated Statement of Earnings separates revenue into three categories and reports intellectual property and custom development income (IP&CDI), as well as asset sales and other nonrecurring gains (components of Other (income) and expense) under the caption Expense and Other Income.

For the year ended December 31:	Notes	2009	2008
Revenue:			
Services		$55,128	$58,892
Sales		38,300	42,156
Financing		2,331	2,582
Total revenue		95,758	103,630
Cost			
Services		37,146	40,937
Sales		13,606	15,776
Financing		1,220	1,256
Total cost		51,973	57,969
Gross profit		43,785	45,661
Expense and other income:			
Selling, general and administrative		20,952	23,386
Research, development and engineering	Q	5,820	6,337

Intellectual property and custom development income		(1,177)	(1,153)
Other (income) and expense		(351)	(298)
Interest expense	K&L	402	673
Total expense and other income		25,647	28,945
Income from continuing operations before income taxes		18,138	16,715
Provision for income taxes	P	4,713	4,381
Income from continuing operations		13,425	12,334
Discontinued operations:			
Income/(loss) from discontinued operations, net of tax		—	—
Net income		$13,425	$12,334
Earnings/(loss) per share of common stock:			
Assuming dilution:			
Continuing operations	R	$10.01	$8.89 *
Discontinued operations	R	—	—
Total	R	$10.01	$8.89 *
Basic:			
Continuing operations	R	$10.12	$9.02 *
Discontinued operations	R	—	—
Total	R	$10.12	$9.02 *
Weighted-average number of common shares outstanding:			
Assuming dilution		1,341,352,754	1,387,797,198 *
Basic		1,327,157,410	1,369,367,069 *

Intellectual Property and Custom Development Income

The company licenses and sells the rights to certain of its intellectual property (IP) including internally developed patents, trade secrets and technological know-how. Certain transfers of IP to third parties are licensing/royalty-based and other transfers are transaction-based sales and other transfers. Licensing/royalty-based fees involve transfers in which the company earns the income over time, or the amount of income is not fixed or determinable until the licensee sells future related products (i.e., variable royalty, based upon licensee's revenue). Sales and other transfers typically include transfers of IP whereby the company has fulfilled its obligations and the fee received is fixed or determinable at the transfer date. The company also enters into cross-licensing arrangements of patents, and income from these arrangements is recorded only to the extent cash is received. Furthermore, the company earns income from certain custom development projects for strategic technology partners and specific clients. The company records the income from these projects when the fee is realized or realizable and earned, is not refundable and is not dependent upon the success of the project.

GROSS VERSUS NET PRESENTATION OF REVENUE

General

ASC 605-45 addresses a question that frequently arises for product resellers—should the entire amount received from an end-user be recorded as revenue and the amount paid to the supplier as cost of sales or just the net amount as revenue? The correct response, from a financial reporting standpoint, depends on (1) which party in the transaction (i.e., supplier or company) holds all or substantially all of risks and benefits related to the product or service, and (2) an evaluation of the contractual arrangements. Gross reporting treats the transaction as if the company purchased a product or service (thereby acquiring all or substantially all of the related risks and benefits) from the supplier and then sold that product or service to the end-user. Under net reporting, the transaction is recorded as if the end-user made a purchase from the supplier, with the company acting as a sales agent.

This question is common for companies that sell goods or services over the internet. Many internet resellers do not stock inventory and arrange for third-party suppliers to drop-ship merchandise on their behalf. These companies may also sell services that will be provided by a third party. The difficulty in making the determination of gross versus net reporting is that many companies do not assume (a) all the risks and rewards of ownership of the products they sell before entering into the sales transaction or (b) all of the responsibility to provide the services they sell. Through contracts or by operation of the business, some or all of these risks and responsibilities remain with the supplier of the goods or services.

ASC 605-45 applies to all industries and transaction types unless guidance is specifically provided in other authoritative literature.[1] The EITF's consensus on this question does not draw bright lines or provide objective answers. Rather, the guidance identifies a number of indicators that a company should evaluate to determine whether it has taken on enough risks to be considered the principal in the transaction.

PRACTICE ALERT: The EITF has also addressed two gross versus net issues involving derivative instruments. For derivative instruments "held for trading purposes", gains and losses must be shown net in the income statement, regardless of whether the derivative instrument is physically settled (ASC 932-330-35). For derivative contracts *not* "held for trading purposes", the determination of whether realized gains and losses should be reported on a gross or net basis is a matter of judgment that depends on the relevant facts and circumstances. In analyzing these facts and circumstances, the guidance in ASC 605-45 and ASC 845-10, should be considered (ASC 815-10-55-62).

---

[1] For example, ASC 952-605, ASC 952-605, ASC 932-330-35 and ASC 815-10-55-62 and the AICPA Audit and Accounting Guides for Casinos (ASC 924-605-45), include guidance on presenting revenue on a gross versus a net basis.

Indicators of Gross Revenue Reporting

1. *The company is the primary obligor in the arrangement.* The primary obligor is the party responsible for delivering the product or providing service to the customer. In substance, the primary obligor is the party to whom the customer looks for fulfillment and to ensure satisfaction. If this party is the company and not the supplier, the company is at risk for the full amount of the contract, not just a commission. Representations made by a company during marketing and the terms of the sales contract generally will provide evidence as to whether the company or the supplier is the primary obligor (ASC 605-45-45-4).

2. *The company has general inventory risk.* This risk exists when a company buys inventory to resell for a profit. Front-end inventory risk exists if a reseller maintains inventory of a product after taking title and assuming all risks and rewards of ownership *before* the product is ordered by a customer. Back-end inventory risk exists if the customer has a right of return and the reseller will take title to and assume the risks and rewards of ownership if the product is returned. In a service transaction, a similar risk exists if the reseller commits to purchase the service from its supplier before it has found customers. General inventory risk not mitigated by terms of the arrangement between the reseller and supplier is a strong indicator that the reseller should record revenue on a gross basis. However, factors that mitigate general inventory risk must be considered as well. For example, a company's risk may be reduced significantly or essentially eliminated if it has the right to return unsold products or receives inventory price protection from the supplier. Similarly, back-end inventory risk is mitigated if the company has the right to return any products returned by the customer to the supplier (ASC 605-45-45-5; 605-45-7).

3. *The company has the ability to determine the price at which it sells the product or service.* When a company has reasonable latitude to establish prices for the products and services, it is an indication that the company is acting as a principal, rather than as another company's agent (ASC 605-45-45-8).

4. *The company changes the product or performs part of the service.* If a company physically changes the product (beyond its packaging) or performs part of the service ordered by a customer, the company does not appear to act solely as an agent. In addition, this fact may indicate that the company is partially or fully responsible for fulfillment, potentially making it the primary obligor in the arrangement (ASC 605-45-45-9).

PRACTICE POINTER: Transporting or repackaging the goods or providing marketing services does not demonstrate that this indicator of gross reporting exists, even when these actions add value to the product or service.

---

5. *The company has discretion in supplier selection.* When a company has multiple suppliers for a product or service ordered by a customer and

discretion to select the supplier that will provide the product or service ordered by a customer, it is an indication that the company is acting as a principal (ASC 605-45-45-10).

6. *The company is involved in the determination of product or service specifications.* If a company must determine the nature, type, characteristics, or specifications of the product or service ordered by the customer, that fact might indicate that the company is primarily responsible for fulfillment (ASC 605-45-45-11).

7. *The company has physical loss inventory risk (after customer order or during shipping).* Physical loss inventory risk exists if the reseller holds title to the product at some point between the time an order is placed and the product is delivered. Because the risk of physical loss during this period is low, it is a weak indicator of gross reporting (ASC 605-45-45-12).

8. *The company has credit risk.* If a company assumes credit risk for the amount billed to the customer, that fact may provide evidence that the company has risks and rewards as a principal in the transaction. Credit risk exists if a company is responsible for collecting the sales price from a customer but must pay the supplier regardless of whether the sales price is fully collected. A requirement that a company return or refund only the net amount it earned in the transaction, if the transaction is cancelled or reversed, is not evidence of credit risk for the gross transaction. In some cases, credit risk may be mitigated such that this indicator is virtually meaningless—for example, if a customer pays by credit card and a company obtains authorization for the charge in advance of product shipment or service performance, credit risk has been substantially mitigated (ASC 605-45-45-13; 605-45-45-14).

Indicators of Net Revenue Reporting

1. *The supplier is the primary obligor in the arrangement.* If the supplier is responsible for fulfillment and customer satisfaction, the company may not have risks and rewards as a principal in the transaction and should therefore recognize only its net fee as revenue. Representations made by a company during marketing and the terms of the sales contract will generally provide evidence as to a customer's understanding of whether the company or the supplier is responsible for fulfillment (ASC 605-45-45-16).

2. *The amount the company earns per transaction is fixed (in dollars or as a percentage of the arrangement fee).* When a company earns a fixed dollar amount per customer transaction or a stated percentage of the amount billed to a customer, this may indicate that the company is acting as an agent of the supplier (ASC 605-45-45-17).

3. *The supplier has credit risk.* If credit risk exists (i.e., the sales price has not been fully collected prior to delivering the product or service) but the supplier assumes that risk, the company may be acting as an agent of the supplier (ASC 605-45-45-18).

Evaluating the Indicators

Strong and Weak Indicators

The identity of the primary obligor in the transaction and front-end general inventory risk are strong indicators of the nature of the transaction. They help identify the bearer of key risks, such as the risk of market price declines, customer satisfaction, obsolescence, and excess inventory.

By contrast, physical loss inventory risk and credit risk are considered weak indicators. Because they relate to lower risks that are easily mitigated through the use of insurance or well-designed business practices, these indicators are rarely useful.

The importance of certain indicators depends on the specific facts and circumstances in a transaction. For example, back-end general inventory risk may be important when products with high values have low turnover and are often returned or rejected. This risk, however, may be a less significant indicator for low value products with high turnover, because one product can be used to fill a subsequent order.

PRACTICE POINTER: By providing indicators of gross versus net reporting, ASC 605-45 attempts to answer two basic questions.

First, who does the end-customer believe it is buying from? If the end-customer believes it is buying from the company, the company is most likely the primary obligor and should report revenue on a gross basis. If the end-customer believes it is buying from the supplier, it is likely that net reporting for the company is appropriate.

Second, is the company's customer the end-customer or the supplier? If the company's contracts refer to it as an agent or to the product supplier as the customer, it is likely that reporting on a net basis is appropriate.

Answering these questions, however, does not eliminate the requirement that a company review the indicators in ASC 605-45.

Transaction-by-Transaction Analysis

A company may operate as a principal (gross reporting) in some transactions and as an agent (net reporting) in others. For example, an office products company may maintain inventories of products of which large quantities are sold, such as pens, paper, and printer cartridges, but have other products, such as furniture and computers, drop-shipped from the supplier. In this instance, general inventory risk may only exist for the high-volume products. This distinction could result in different conclusions as to how to report these transactions.

EXAMPLE: GROSS VERSUS NET CONCLUSION DIFFERS FOR DIFFERENT TRANSACTIONS

Express Scripts, Inc. Form 10-K—Fiscal Year Ended December 31, 2009

Revenues related to the distribution of prescription drugs by retail pharmacies in our networks consist of the prescription price (ingredient cost plus dispensing fee) negotiated with our clients, including the portion to be settled directly by the member (co-payment), plus any associated administrative fees. These revenues are recognized when the claim is processed. When we independently have a contractual obligation to pay our network pharmacy providers for benefits provided to our clients' members, we act as a principal in the arrangement and we include the total prescription price as revenue in accordance with applicable accounting guidance. Although we generally do not have credit risk with respect to retail co-payments, the primary indicators of gross treatment are present. When a prescription is presented by a member to a retail pharmacy within our network, we are solely responsible for confirming member eligibility, performing drug utilization review, reviewing for drug-to-drug interactions, performing clinical intervention, which may involve a call to the member's physician, communicating plan provisions to the pharmacy, directing payment to the pharmacy and billing the client for the amount they are contractually obligated to pay us for the prescription dispensed, as specified within our client contracts. We also provide benefit design and formulary consultation services to clients. We have separately negotiated contractual relationships with our clients and with network pharmacies, and under our contracts with pharmacies we assume the credit risk of our clients' ability to pay for drugs dispensed by these pharmacies to clients' members. Our clients are not obligated to pay the pharmacies as we are primarily obligated to pay retail pharmacies in our network the contractually agreed upon amount for the prescription dispensed, as specified within our provider contracts. These factors indicate we are a principal as defined by applicable accounting guidance and, as such, we record the total prescription price contracted with clients in revenue.

If we merely administer a client's network pharmacy contracts to which we are not a party and under which we do not assume credit risk, we record only our administrative fees as revenue. For these clients, we earn an administrative fee for collecting payments from the client and remitting the corresponding amount to the pharmacies in the client's network. In these transactions we act as a conduit for the client. Because we are not the principal in these transactions, drug ingredient cost is not included in our revenues or in our cost of revenues. In retail pharmacy transactions, amounts paid to pharmacies and amounts charged to clients are always exclusive of the applicable co-payment. Retail pharmacy co-payments, which we instructed retail pharmacies to collect from members, of $3.1 billion, $3.2 billion and $3.6 billion for the years ended December 31, 2009, 2008, and 2007, respectively, are included in revenues and cost of revenues. We changed our accounting policy for member co-payments during the third quarter of 2008 to include member co-payments to retail pharmacies in revenue and cost of revenue. Retail pharmacy co-payments decreased in the years ended December 31, 2009, 2008, and 2007 as compared to prior periods due to the expected loss of discount card programs and other low margin clients. Additionally, the decrease is due to the increase in generic utilization.

priceline.com Incorporated Form 10-K—Fiscal Year Ended December 31, 2009

Merchant Revenues and Cost of Merchant Revenues

Name Your Own Price® Services:

Merchant revenues and related cost of revenues are derived from transactions where priceline.com is the merchant of record and, among other things, selects suppliers and determines the price it will accept from the customer. The Company recognizes such revenues and costs if and when it fulfills the customer's non-refundable offer. Merchant revenues and cost of merchant revenues include the selling price and cost, respectively, of the travel services and are reported on a gross basis. In very limited circumstances, priceline.com makes certain customer accommodations to satisfy disputes and complaints. The Company accrues for such estimated losses and classifies the resulting expense as adjustments to merchant revenue and cost of merchant revenues. Pursuant to the terms of the Company's hotel service, its hotel suppliers are permitted to bill the Company for the underlying cost of the service during a specified period of time. In the event that the Company is not billed by its hotel supplier within the specified time period, the Company reduces its cost of revenues by the unbilled amounts.

Merchant Price-Disclosed Hotel Service:

Merchant revenues for the Company's merchant price-disclosed hotel service are derived from transactions where its customers purchase hotel room reservations from hotel suppliers at disclosed rates which are subject to contractual arrangements. Charges are billed to customers at the time of booking and are included in deferred merchant bookings until the customer completes the stay. Such amounts are generally refundable upon cancellation prior to stay, subject to cancellation penalties in certain cases. Merchant revenues and accounts payable to the hotel supplier are recognized at the conclusion of the customer's stay at the hotel. The Company records the difference between the selling price and the cost of the hotel room reservation as merchant revenue.

Agency Revenues

Agency revenues are derived from travel related transactions where the Company is not the merchant of record and where the prices of the services sold are determined by third parties. Agency revenues include travel commissions, customer processing fees and global distribution system ("GDS") reservation booking fees and are reported at the net amounts received, without any associated cost of revenue. Such revenues are generally recognized by the Company when the customers complete their travel.

Financial Statement Presentation

Companies with Both Gross and Net Transactions

When a company records some transactions gross and others net, it is likely necessary to report revenue for each type of transaction separately and break out cost of sales in a similar fashion. This enables financial statement users to properly evaluate gross margins on the two types of transactions.

In addition, SEC registrants are also required to report revenue from the sale of products and from the provision of services separately (ASC 225-10-S99-2) (REG S-X, Rule 5-03(b)(1)). Because commissions and fees earned from activities reported net are service revenues, separate presentation of revenues from transactions reported gross (product revenues) and transactions reported net (service revenues) may be required.

EXAMPLE: DISCLOSURE OF REVENUE RECOGNIZED NET

Best Buy Co., Inc. Form 10-K—Fiscal Year Ended February 26, 2011

We sell extended warranties and other service contracts that typically have terms ranging from three months to four years. We also receive commissions for customer subscriptions with various third parties, notably from mobile phone network operators. In instances where we are deemed to be the obligor on the service contract or subscription, the service and commission revenue is deferred and recognized ratably over the term of the service contract or subscription period. In instances where we are not deemed to be the obligor on the service contract or subscription, commissions are recognized in revenue when such commission has been earned, primarily driven by customer activation. Commissions from the sale of extended warranties represented 2.0%, 2.0% and 2.0% of revenue in fiscal 2011, 2010 and 2009, respectively.

Disclosure of Gross Activity for Transactions Reported Net

The EITF noted that although disclosure of gross transaction volume for revenues reported net is not required by U.S. generally accepted accounting standards (GAAP), it may be useful to financial statement users. However, if the gross amounts are disclosed, they should not be characterized as revenues. In addition, the presentation should not result in the gross activity being presented in the income statement such that it begins a column that sums to net income or loss (ASC 605-45-50-1).

Leased Departments

Department stores and other retailers customarily lease portions of their store space to specialty retailers. For example, higher-end department stores often lease space to companies that specialize in displaying and selling cosmetics, or designing and selling wedding dresses. Smaller retailers may allow vending machines owned by another party to be placed in their stores. The store (lessor) typically receives a lease payment from the company leasing the space (lessee). Revenue from the leased part of the store goes to the lessee (which is also responsible for the costs of running its leased portion of the store).

Because the store/lessor has virtually no involvement in product purchasing, pricing, or sales, these types of arrangements generally require the lessee to record sales on a gross basis, with the store only recording its net lease receipts as revenue. Furthermore, these arrangements generally meet the definition of a lease and are therefore within the scope of ASC 840. The department store or other retailer should include only the rental income, if the arrangement is a lease, or service revenue, if the arrangement is not a lease, as part of its revenues (ASC 605-15-S99-2) (SAB Topic 8A).

ILLUSTRATION: ASSESSMENT OF GROSS VERSUS NET REPORTING INDICATORS

EXAMPLE 1

Facts: Company A runs a catalog business that sells home products, such as rugs, sheets, and towels. Company A does not manufacture any of these products, but has instead compiled products from various manufacturers in its catalog. Each product in the catalog identifies the unique supplier, because the identity of the supplier is a factor that customers use to select products to order.

Company A does not maintain inventories but does take title to the products ordered by customers at the point of shipment from suppliers. Title is passed to the customer upon delivery. The gross sales price is charged to the customer's credit card prior to shipment and Company A is the merchant of record. Company A must pay its suppliers even if the credit card amount cannot be collected. Suppliers determine product sales prices and Company A retains a fixed percentage of the sales price and remits the balance to the supplier. The catalog and sales contracts clearly indicate that Company A is not responsible for the quality or safety of the products and that the customer must contact the supplier directly regarding complaints, warranty issues, and returns.

Discussion: Although indicators of gross reporting exist for physical loss inventory risk (during shipping) and credit risk (for collecting amounts charged to credit cards), these indicators do not overcome the stronger indicators that revenues should be reported net. The critical indicators of net reporting are that the supplier, not the company, is the primary obligor and that the amount earned by the company is a fixed percentage of the sales price.

EXAMPLE 2

Facts: Same as in Example 1, except that (1) Company A sets product sales prices, and thereby earns a profit on any amounts in excess of its agreed-upon purchase price with the supplier, and (2) although Company A does not offer a warranty on the products it sells, it does provide a "Satisfaction Guaranteed or Your Money Back" right of return, even when it has no similar right of return with its suppliers.

Discussion: In addition to physical loss inventory risk (during shipping) and credit risk (for collecting amounts charged to credit cards) that exists in Example 1, other gross indicators include both back-end general inventory risk and the pricing latitude of Company A. In addition, the right of return provisions make less clear the identity of the primary obligor. Therefore, gross reporting is appropriate for Company A.

EXAMPLE 3

Facts: Company B is a travel consolidator that negotiates with major airlines to obtain access to airline tickets at reduced rates that are not available to travelers who buy tickets directly from the airlines. Company B determines the prices at which it will sell the airline tickets. The reduced rate paid to an airline by Company B for each ticket sale is negotiated and agreed to in advance and Company B commits to purchase a specific number of tickets for specific flights. Company B must pay for these tickets regardless of whether it is able to resell them. Customers pay for airline tickets using credit cards and Company B is the merchant of record. Although credit card charges are pre-authorized, there are occasional losses that result from disputed charges for which Company B bears the risk of loss. Company B utilizes electronic ticketing and, therefore, no risk of physical loss exists. Company B facilitates the resolution of customer complaints if the customer is dissatisfied with the airline, but Company B's responsibility ends at successfully booking the reservation. The airline is responsible for fulfilling all obligations associated with the ticket.

Discussion: Company B should use gross reporting because it has general inventory risk (a strong indicator of gross reporting) by committing to purchase tickets before it resells them. Company Bs latitude to set ticket prices, also suggests gross reporting because the amount it earns will vary. In addition,

Company B has credit risk for collecting customer credit card charges, although this is a weak indicator of gross reporting. An indicator of net reporting also exists because the airlines provide the transportation and are the primary obligors. However, the gross reporting indicators in this case outweigh the fact that the supplier is the primary obligor.

EXAMPLE 4

Facts: Same as Example 3, except that Company B is only required to pay for tickets that it resells to customers.

Discussion: Company B should report revenues net. As in Example 3, the fact that the airline is the primary obligor is a strong indicator of net reporting. There are two indicators of gross reporting in this example—pricing latitude and credit risk. However, these indicators do not overcome the strong net indicator of the supplier being the primary obligor. The strong indicator of gross reporting—general inventory risk—present in Example 3 is not present here.

PAYMENTS FROM A VENDOR TO A CUSTOMER

When a vendor makes a payment to one of its customers, questions often arise as to the substance of the arrangement. Of course, the payment could be because the vendor is purchasing a product or service from its customer (i.e., the two parties are customers of one another). However, in many instances, the payment is substantively a sales incentive, the main purpose of which is to convince the customer to purchase (or continue purchasing) the vendor's products or services. Payments may include, for example, cash discounts, coupons, rebates, "free" products or services, or equity instruments. In some cases, a vendor will make payments to its customer's customer (an indirect customer of the vendor). For example, the manufacturer of a grocery product may issue coupons that are redeemed by a consumer, even though the manufacturer's customer is the grocery store.

Other common arrangements that involve payments from vendors to customers include:

- Cooperative advertising arrangements, in which a vendor agrees to make payments to its customer if the customer features the vendor's products in its advertising.

- Slotting fees, in which a vendor makes a payment to a retailer so that the retailer will stock the manufacturer's product in its stores, sometimes in a particular location.

- Buydowns, in which a vendor makes a payment to a retailer that makes some amount of purchases at agreed-upon prices.

- Rebates, in which a customer, usually an indirect customer, may send in a form to request a return of a portion of the purchase price of the product or service.

Vendor Classification

Regardless of the way the payment is documented or whether it is contractually linked to any sales contract, all payments from a vendor to a customer must be evaluated as if they may be sales incentives, and therefore reductions of revenue. In addition, the guidance applies whether the consideration is given to direct or indirect customers of the vendor, and whether the consideration is in the form of cash, equity, or a product or service. Furthermore, it applies to payments made to customers who will alter the product before reselling it (e.g., a cooperative advertising payment from a computer chip manufacturer to one of its PC manufacturer customers).

OBSERVATION: The model developed in ASC 605-50 must be applied to payments made to both direct and indirect (i.e., further down the distribution chain) customers to prevent a vendor from changing the reporting of a sales incentive without changing its substance. For example, a vendor could achieve essentially the same result by (1) selling its product at a $1 discount to list price, (2) selling the product at list price and providing a $1 rebate to its direct customer, or (3) selling the product at list price and providing a $1 rebate to a customer further down the distribution chain. An approach that requires revenue reduction in some, but not all, of these arrangements would result in different income statement characterization for sales incentives that are essentially the same.

SEC REGISTRANT ALERT: Round-trip transactions have received a significant amount of attention by the SEC staff and were an area of focus in the SEC staff's Report Pursuant to Section 704 of the Sarbanes-Oxley Act of 2002 (Section 704 Report), issued in early 2003. In compiling the information in the Section 704 Report, the SEC staff studied enforcement actions filed during the period July 31, 1997, through July 30, 2002. In addition, round-trip transactions have also been a focus in recent SEC staff speeches. The Section 704 Report describes round-trip transactions as transactions that "involve simultaneous pre-arranged sales transactions often of the same product in order to create a false impression of business activity and revenue." A payment from a vendor to its customer should be analyzed carefully to ensure that the payment is not merely one leg in a round-trip transaction. See Chapter 8, "Miscellaneous Issues," for additional discussion regarding nonmonetary transactions.

Consideration in the Form of Cash or Equity

ASC 605-50 begins with the presumption that a cash or equity payment by a vendor to a customer (as noted above, "customer" includes both direct and indirect customers) should be accounted for as a reduction in revenues. However, the presumption is overcome if both of the following are true (ASC 605-50-45-2):

1. The vendor receives, or will receive, an identifiable benefit (goods or services) in exchange for the consideration. To meet this condition, the identified benefit must be sufficiently separable from the customer's purchase of the vendor's products such that the vendor could have purchased the identified benefit from somebody other than one of its customers.

2. The vendor can reasonably estimate the fair value of the benefit identified under the first condition.

OBSERVATION: The first criterion is meant to ensure that the two transactions (the sale to the customer and the purchase from it) are separable. The second criterion ensures that the net fee can be appropriately allocated to the events, based on relative fair values. These two criteria are similar to the criteria necessary to separate items in a multiple-deliverable arrangement (see Chapter 4, "Multiple-Deliverable Revenue Arrangements").

If both criteria are met, the lesser of the amount paid to the customer and the fair value of the benefit received may be classified as an expense when recognized in the income statement, while any amount paid in excess of the fair value of the benefit received must be characterized as a reduction of revenue (ASC 605-50-45-2). Any amount that can appropriately be characterized as an expense when recognized in the income statement should be included in an expense caption based on the nature of the identifiable benefit received. For example, if the identifiable benefit is advertising, the amount characterized as an expense should be included in a sales and marketing expense (or similar) caption.

If either of the two criteria is not met, the entire payment must be characterized as a reduction of revenue. Determining whether the criteria are met requires analysis of all available information.

PRACTICE POINTER: When the payment from the vendor is in the form of equity instruments, a question arises about the date to use in valuing the instruments. Regardless of whether the cost of the instruments should be treated as an expense or a reduction of revenues, the value should be measured based on the guidance of ASC 505, *Equity*, 505-50.

Consideration in the Form of "Free" Products or Services

If the sales incentive is a free product or service, the cost of the free product or service should be classified as an expense when recognized in the income statement. The "free" item is considered an additional deliverable in the exchange transaction and not a refund of any amount charged to the customer (ASC 605-50-45-3). The cost of the "free" products or services should be classified as part of cost of sales.

In some situations, a sales incentive in the form of free products or services may be offered after the revenue related to the original products or services in the arrangement has been recognized. For example, a company might offer a large customer some amount of free products simply as a goodwill gesture. ASC 605-50 does not require an overall reduction in revenue due to the offer, but does specify that the free products or services become deliverables. In effect, the offer of free products modifies previous arrangements to include additional deliverables, which are, at the time of the offer, undelivered items. At that point, it may be necessary for the company making the offer to "derecognize" revenue, which would be "rerecognized" when the free products are delivered.

EXAMPLE: VENDOR CLASSIFICATION OF PROMOTIONAL ALLOWANCES

The Boston Beer Company, Inc. Form 10-K—Fiscal Year Ended December 26, 2009

The Company reimburses its wholesalers and retailers for promotional discounts, samples and certain advertising and marketing activities used in the promotion of the Company's products. The reimbursements for discounts to wholesalers are recorded as reductions to net revenue. The Company has sales incentive arrangements with its wholesalers based upon performance of certain marketing and advertising activities by the wholesalers. Depending on applicable state laws and regulations, these activities promoting the Company's products may include, but are not limited to, the following: point-of-sale merchandise placement, product displays and promotional programs at retail locations. The costs incurred for these sales incentive arrangements and advertising and promotional programs are included in advertising, promotional and selling expenses during the period in which they are incurred. Total advertising and sales promotional expenditures of $59.1 million, $63.7 million and $64.2 million were included in advertising, promotional and selling expenses in the accompanying consolidated statements of income for fiscal years 2009, 2008 and 2007, respectively. Of these amounts, $5.7 million, $5.5 million and $5.4 million related to sales incentives, samples and other promotional discounts and $29.4 million, $29.5 million and $29.5 million related to advertising costs for fiscal years 2009, 2008 and 2007, respectively.

The Company conducts certain advertising and promotional activities in its wholesalers' markets and the wholesalers make contributions to the Company for such efforts. Reimbursements from wholesalers for advertising and promotional activities are recorded as reductions to advertising, promotional and selling expenses.

EXHIBIT 11-1: CHARACTERIZATION OF PAYMENTS FROM VENDOR TO CUSTOMER

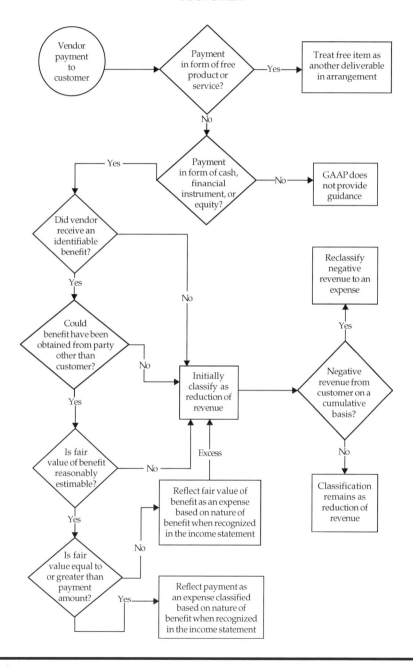

Customer Classification

General Model

Cash or equity consideration received from a vendor is presumed to be a reduction of cost of sales when it is recognized in the income statement (prior to recognition in the income statement, the payment would be recognized as a reduction of inventory or prepayments for services). This presumption can only be overcome if the customer can demonstrate that the payment relates to either (1) assets or services provided by the customer to the vendor (in which case the payment is treated as revenue when recognized in the income statement) or (2) a reimbursement of costs incurred by the customer to sell the vendor's products (in which case the payment is treated as a reduction of the related cost when recognized in the income statement) (ASC 605-50-45-13).

To conclude that the payment relates to the sale of assets or services by the customer to the vendor, the customer must provide the vendor with a separately identifiable benefit (goods or services). To be considered an identifiable benefit, the customer should be able to: (1) illustrate that it would have entered into an exchange transaction with another (nonvendor) party to provide that benefit, and (2) determine the fair value of the benefit. If the amount of the payment from the vendor is greater than the fair value of the identifiable benefit provided to the vendor, the excess should be reflected as a reduction of cost of sales when recognized in the income statement (ASC 605-50-45-14).

To demonstrate that the payment relates to a reimbursement of costs incurred by the customer to sell the vendor's products or services, the customer must incur an incremental, identifiable cost. If the amount of the payment from the vendor is greater than the incremental, identifiable cost incurred by the customer, the excess should be reflected as a reduction of cost of sales when recognized in the income statement (ASC 605-50-45-15).

EXAMPLE: CUSTOMER CLASSIFICATIONS OF PROMOTIONAL ALLOWANCES

Safeway Inc. Form 10-K—Fiscal Year Ended January 1, 2011

Vendor allowances totaled $2.9 billion in 2010 and $2.6 billion in both 2009 and 2008. Vendor allowances can be grouped into the following broad categories: promotional allowances, slotting allowances and contract allowances. All vendor allowances are classified as an element of cost of goods sold.

Promotional allowances make up approximately 90% of all allowances. With promotional allowances, vendors pay Safeway to promote their product. The promotion may be any combination of a temporary price reduction, a feature in print ads, a feature in a Safeway circular or a preferred location in the store. The promotions are typically one to two weeks long.

Slotting allowances are a small portion of total allowances (approximately 5% of all allowances). With slotting allowances, the vendor reimburses Safeway for the cost of placing new product on the shelf. Safeway has no obligation or commitment to keep the product on the shelf for a minimum period.

Contract allowances make up the remainder of all allowances. Under a typical contract allowance, a vendor pays Safeway to keep product on the shelf for a minimum period of time or when volume thresholds are achieved.

Promotional and slotting allowances are accounted for as a reduction in the cost of purchased inventory and recognized when the related inventory is sold. Contract allowances are recognized as a reduction in the cost of goods sold as volume thresholds are achieved or through the passage of time.

Vendor's Sales Incentives Offered Directly to Consumers

A vendor may issue sales incentives that a consumer will present to a reseller for redemption (e.g., manufacturer's coupons redeemed by retailers when presented by consumers). Resellers facilitate the redemption of these incentives by acting as middlemen or agents between the vendor and consumer. If these types of sales incentive arrangements possess the following characteristics, they are not treated as sales incentives by the reseller (ASC 605-50-45-19):

- The incentive can be presented by a consumer to resellers that accept manufacturer's incentives as partial (or full) payment of the price charged by the reseller for the vendor's product.

- The incentive results in the reseller receiving a direct reimbursement from the vendor (or a clearinghouse authorized by the vendor) based on the face amount of the incentive.

- The incentive was not influenced by or negotiated in conjunction with any other incentive arrangements between the vendor and the reseller (i.e., the incentive is between the manufacturer and the consumer).

- The reseller is acting in the capacity of an agent for the vendor (either expressly or implied) in redeeming the incentive presented by the consumer.

These characteristics are intended to identify those sales incentives where a reseller receives a payment from the vendor solely to reimburse it for acting as the vendor's agent in redeeming a sales incentive that is between the vendor and consumer. Requiring a reseller to record this type of sales incentive as a reduction in cost of sales would not properly reflect the reseller's role in the transaction.

If a sales incentive possesses all of the above characteristics, the reseller should account for its involvement in the redemption on the balance sheet. The appropriate balance sheet treatment is to record a receivable, in the amount of the sales incentive (from the vendor at the time of the sale to the consumer), with the full sales price included as revenue. If a sales incentive does not possess all of these characteristics, the reseller should apply the model in ASC 605-50-45-13. Application of this model to a manufacturer's coupon that lacks one or more of the characteristics discussed above would likely result in the recognition of the vendor's payment to the reseller as a reduction in cost of sales on the reseller's income statement. It is highly unlikely that such an incentive would meet the criteria to be treated as revenue or a selling cost reimbursement when recognized in the reseller's income statement.

EXAMPLES: VENDOR'S SALES INCENTIVES

BJ's Wholesale Club Form 10-K—Fiscal Year Ended January 30, 2010

Manufacturers' Incentives Tendered by Consumers

We record consideration from manufacturers' incentives (such as rebates or coupons) in net sales when the incentive is generic and can be tendered by a consumer at any reseller and we receive direct reimbursement from the manufacturer, or clearinghouse authorized by the manufacturer, based on the face value of the incentive. If these conditions are not met, we record such consideration as a decrease in cost of sales.

Application to Certain Common Arrangements

The guidance in ASC 605-50 applies to any situation in which payments are made from a vendor to a customer. Application of these models to several common types of arrangements is discussed below.

Cooperative Advertising Arrangements

In a cooperative advertising arrangement, the vendor makes a payment to a customer for including the vendor's products in the customer's advertising.

Vendor classification. Such arrangements may seem to meet the first criterion of the model in ASC 605-50-45-2. Because the vendor can separately purchase advertising from, for example, a newspaper, magazine, or radio station, a cooperative advertising arrangement would appear to include an identifiable benefit that could have been obtained from a party other than the customer. However, the substance of some cooperative advertising arrangements makes it difficult to ascertain the identifiable benefit. For example, some arrangements do not specify the amount or type of advertising the customer must purchase to qualify for the cooperative payment. In other arrangements, the payment amount is determined by the total purchases made by the customer, which makes the arrangement appear similar to a volume discount or rebate. For a cooperative advertising arrangement to meet the second criterion of the model in ASC 605-50-45-2—reasonable estimate of fair value of the benefit received—it is generally necessary for the arrangement to specify the type and volume of advertising to be provided. Without this information, fair value cannot be determined. If both criteria are met, the vendor's payment should be reflected as a cost incurred, to the extent it does not exceed the estimated fair value of the advertising received. If the amount of the vendor's payment exceeds the estimated fair value of the advertising received, then (a) the estimated fair value of the advertising received should be reflected as a cost incurred and (b) the excess of the vendor's payment over the estimated fair value of the advertising received should be reflected as a reduction of revenue.

EXAMPLE: COOPERATIVE ADVERTISING AND BUYDOWN PROGRAMS

Helen of Troy Limited Form 10-K—Fiscal Year Ended February 28, 2011

We offer our customers certain incentives in the form of cooperative advertising arrangements, volume rebates, product markdown allowances, trade discounts, cash discounts, slotting fees and similar other arrangements. In instances where the customer provides us with proof of performance, reductions in amounts received from customers as a result of cooperative advertising programs are included in our consolidated statements of income in SG&A. Customer incentives included in SG&A were $12.71, $10.40 and $11.81 million for the fiscal years 2011, 2010 and 2009, respectively.

Other reductions in amounts received from customers as a result of cooperative advertising programs are recorded as reductions of net sales revenue. Markdown allowances, slotting fees, trade discounts, cash discounts and volume rebates are all recorded as reductions of net sales revenue.

Customer classification. In cooperative advertising arrangements, the customer may be able to demonstrate that the payment relates to the reimbursement of advertising costs if there is an incremental, identifiable cost related to selling the vendor's products or services. If the customer has documentation to support the incremental and identifiable nature of the cost, the vendor's payment should be reflected as a reduction in that cost. Any amount of the vendor's payment in excess of the reimbursed cost should be reflected as a reduction of cost of sales. The cost reimbursement reduction should be reflected in the sales and marketing expense (or similar) line item on the income statement. If the customer does not have documentation to support the incremental and identifiable nature of the cost, it must recognize the vendor's payment as a reduction of cost of sales.

ILLUSTRATION: COOPERATIVE ADVERTISING ARRANGEMENTS

EXAMPLE 1

Facts: Company D provides satellite television services. It sells the hardware (a satellite dish and receivers) necessary to receive its services through retailers that sell the hardware and arrange installation. The hardware is purchased from Company D and retailers receive an advertising allowance of $100 for each receiver sold and activated. This allowance is shown as a deduction on the related invoice. The retailers are expected to include Company D's products and service in local advertisements. However, retailers are not required and do not provide any documentation to Company D on how the advertising allowance was used.

Vendor Classification Discussion: The first condition of the ASC 650-50 model is not met. Company D cannot identify the benefit that has been received because retailers do not provide documentation of any advertising. Therefore, the allowances should be characterized as a reduction of revenue in Company D's income statement.

Customer Classification Discussion: The retailers do not have documentation to support the incremental, identifiable nature of the costs incurred to sell Company D's products and services required by the model in ASC 605-50-45-15. Therefore, the payments should be characterized as a reduction of cost of sales when recognized in the retailers' income statements.

EXAMPLE 2

Facts: Company E provides satellite television services. It sells the hardware (a satellite dish and receivers) necessary to receive its services through retailers that sell the hardware and arrange installation. The hardware is purchased from Company E and retailers receive an advertising allowance of $100 for each receiver sold and activated. This allowance is shown as a deduction on the related invoice. Retailers are required by their contract with Company E to use the advertising allowance to advertise Company E's products and services and to provide documentation of these expenditures to Company E.

Vendor Classification Discussion: Company E receives an identifiable benefit (advertising) from the retailers that is sufficiently separable from the retailers' purchases of Company E's products. Company E could have purchased advertising from another party that does not purchase Company E's satellite dishes and receivers. Therefore, the first condition in the ASC 605-50-45-2 model is met. Because Company E receives documentation of the advertising expenditures, it can likely estimate the fair value of the benefit received based on the prices charged for similar advertising. Thus, the second condition can likely be met. As a result, the lesser of the fair value of the advertising and the amount of the allowance would be characterized as an expense. If the amount of the allowance exceeds the fair value of the benefit, this excess would be characterized as a reduction of revenue.

Customer Classification Discussion: The retailers have documentation to support the incremental, identifiable nature of the advertising costs incurred to sell Company E's products and services as required by the model in ASC 605-50-45-15. As a result, the lesser of the amount of the payment or the amount of the related advertising costs is recognized as a reduction in advertising expense when recognized in the retailers' income statements. Any amount of the payment in excess of the related advertising costs is recognized as a reduction of cost of sales when recognized in the retailers' income statements.

Slotting Fees and Allowances

The terms "slotting allowances" and "slotting fees" describe a family of practices that involve payments by manufacturers and wholesalers to persuade downstream resellers to stock, display, and support particular products. They are most commonly used by grocery retailers who are asked to stock a new product or to devote a certain amount of shelf space to a product or family of products. Slotting fees are increasingly used for other retail products as well, such as computer software, compact discs, books, magazines, apparel, over-the-counter drugs, and tobacco products.

Vendor classification. Because of the nature of slotting fees and allowances, it is almost impossible for the first criterion in ASC 605-50-45-2 to be met. Although a vendor might argue that a slotting fee gives an identifiable advertising benefit due to greater awareness of the product, this benefit can only be obtained from the customer. In other cases, a slotting fee might provide the vendor with exclusivity in its product category in a particular store. Although exclusivity might be an identifiable benefit, it can only be obtained from the customer. As a result, the first criterion is not met. In addition, the second criterion would be difficult to meet, because of the extreme variation in slotting fee amounts, and the fact that such payments are never made to parties that are not also customers of the payer.

Some argue that slotting fees should be accounted for as a cost incurred by a vendor to lease shelf space from a retailer. Although certain slotting fee arrangements are indeed written in the form of a lease, they generally do not provide the vendor/lessee with the right to access and use the shelves for a specified period of time. Instead, control of the shelf space continues to be retained by the retailer. In addition, a true lease would give the vendor/lessee ownership of the products on the shelf, because the vendor/lessee would control the space and the receipts from the sale of these products would belong to the vendor/lessee. However, in a slotting arrangement, proceeds from the sale of such products are recorded as the retailer's revenues. For these reasons, a slotting fee arrangement does not meet the accounting definition of a lease, even if its legal form appears to be one.

EXAMPLE: TRADE PROMOTION, SLOTTING FEES, AND COUPON PROGRAMS

Spectrum Brands Form 10-K—Fiscal Year Ended September 30, 2009

The Company also enters into various arrangements, primarily with retail customers, which require the Company to make upfront cash, or "slotting" payments, to secure the right to distribute through such customers. The Company capitalizes slotting payments; provided the payments are supported by a time or volume based arrangement with the retailer, and amortizes the associated payment over the appropriate time or volume based term of the arrangement. The amortization of slotting payments is treated as a reduction in Net sales and a corresponding asset is reported in Deferred charges and other in the accompanying Consolidated Statements of Financial Position.

Customer classification. The nature of slotting fees and allowances makes it difficult for a customer to demonstrate that it is either providing an identifiable benefit to the vendor or incurring an incremental, identifiable cost related to selling the vendor's products or services. This is because the customer will most likely be unable to prove that it could enter into an exchange transaction with the same terms as a slotting fee arrangement with parties other than its vendors. Similarly, the cost of the space provided by the customer to the vendor in a slotting fee arrangement would not be considered an incremental, identifiable cost. As a result, slotting fees and allowances should almost always be treated as a reduction in cost of sales in the income statement.

Some argue that slotting fees should be accounted for as a cost incurred by a vendor to lease shelf space from a retailer. Although certain slotting fee arrangements are indeed written in the form of a lease, they generally do not provide the vendor/lessee with the right to access and use the shelves for a specified period of time. Instead, control of the shelf space continues to be retained by the retailer. In addition, a true lease would give the vendor/lessee ownership of the products on the shelf, because the vendor/lessee would control the space and the receipts from the sale of these products would belong to the vendor/lessee. However, in a slotting arrangement, proceeds from the sale of such products are recorded as the retailer's revenues. For these reasons, a slotting fee arrangement does not meet the accounting definition of a lease, even if its legal form appears to be one.

> **OBSERVATION:** Certain retailers lease a portion of the store to a provider of products. However, in these situations, the retailer only receives lease revenue, not the revenue from the sale of products, and the lessee controls the products in the leased portion of the store (see "Leased Departments" earlier in this chapter).

Coupons and Rebates

Coupons and consumer rebates are the most widely used sales incentives. Some coupons and rebates are offered by a retailer directly to the consumer; others are given by product manufacturers to the end consumer, even though the consumer purchases the product through a retail reseller.

Vendor classification. Coupon or rebate offers are promotions instituted and managed by marketing departments and are considered a marketing expense. As a result, in the absence of any accounting guidance, many vendors reported the costs of these discounts as a marketing expense and recorded the normal selling price of the related products or services as revenue. However, based on the model in ASC 605-50-45-2, coupons and rebates must be characterized as a reduction in revenue, because there is no separately identifiable benefit received by the vendor.

Customer classification. The consumer should treat the cash payment received from the vendor or the redemption value provided by the reseller as a reduction of cost of sales based on the model in ASC 605-50-45-13. This is because the consumer does not provide any products or services to the vendor in return for the payment and the payment does not relate to a reimbursement of any particular cost.

Reseller classification. If a reseller is involved in redeeming the coupon, the reseller's treatment of the reimbursement from the vendor depends on whether the coupon or rebate possesses the characteristics discussed earlier under "Vendor's Sales Incentives Offered Directly to Consumers." If the coupon or rebate possesses these characteristics, the retailer would account for the coupon or rebate on its balance sheet rather than on its income statement. If the coupon or rebate does not possess these characteristics, the model in ASC 605-50-45-13 would apply and payment from the vendor would be recorded as a reduction in cost of sales.

In many cases, the retailer receives a "fee" for redeeming coupons. This fee should be analyzed to determine whether it should be recognized as revenue or as a reduction in cost of sales or another cost altogether. Generally, the analysis of this "fee" under ASC 605-50-45-13 would result in a reduction to cost of sales because (a) the related activity does not provide an identifiable benefit to the vendor and (b) the customer has not incurred an incremental, identifiable cost related to that activity.

Buydowns

Buydown programs generally involve a vendor agreeing to compensate a retailer for lower-than-expected per unit revenue from certain products during a specified time period. In return, the retailer agrees to run a promotion for the vendor's product involving a reduced selling price, rebate, or some other discount. In contrast to cooperative advertising, buydown programs generally do not require expenditures by the retailer for advertising or promotion. Buydowns are known by different names in various industries. For example, the "factory to dealer incentives" often mentioned in automobile advertisements are a form of buydown program.

Vendor classification. Much like a coupon or rebate, payments under a buydown program are always considered a reduction in revenue rather than an expense, because there is no separable identifiable benefit received from the customer as required by the model in ASC 605-50-45-2.

Customer classification. Much like a coupon or rebate where only the vendor and consumer are involved, payments under a buydown program are always a cost of sales reduction under the model in ASC 605-50-45-13 because no products or services are provided by the customer to the vendor and because the payment does not relate to reimbursement of any particular cost.

ILLUSTRATION: CLASSIFICATION OF PAYMENTS FROM VENDORS TO CUSTOMERS

EXAMPLE 1

Facts: Company Z markets and sells a popular brand of peanuts. One of Company Z's contracts makes it the exclusive peanut supplier for a major airline. Company Z sells its peanuts to the airline at discounted prices. In addition, Company Z agrees to purchase a minimum amount of airline tickets from the airline to be used for travel by Company Z's personnel. If Company Z does not purchase the minimum amount of travel by the end of any year of the contract, it must make an additional payment for the shortfall. The prices Company Z pays for plane tickets are comparable to those available to the general public.

Vendor Classification Discussion: With respect to the air travel, Company Z receives an identifiable benefit from the airline. This benefit is sufficiently separable from the airline's purchase of Company Z's peanuts because Company Z could have used any other airline for its corporate travel. Therefore, the first condition in ASC 605-50-45-2 is met. The second condition is also met because the fair value of the plane tickets can be determined based on the prices paid by the general public for similar tickets. As Company Z pays these same amounts, as long as Company Z actually uses at least the minimum purchase requirement for corporate travel, all of the payments to the airline may be characterized as expenses. If Company Z is required to make a payment at year-end due to a shortfall in travel purchases, the amount of the shortfall would be characterized as a reduction in revenue, because it would represent a payment that is over and above the fair value of the benefit received.

Company Z may also believe it is obtaining other benefits from the airline, such as exclusivity and visibility to a captive audience, but these benefits are not separable from the sales arrangement, nor could their fair value be determined. As a result, no amount of the shortfall payment could be classified as an expense based on this rationale.

Customer Classification Discussion: With respect to the air travel, the airline is providing a service that it would offer to other, non-vendor customers. In addition, the airline is providing this service to Company Z at prices comparable to those available to the general public. As a result, if Company Z actually uses at least the minimum purchase requirement for corporate travel, all of the payments to the airline may be classified as revenue by the airline based on the model in ASC 605-50-45-13. To the extent that Company Z is required to make a payment at year-end due to a shortfall in travel purchases, the amount of the shortfall payment would be characterized as a reduction in the cost of the peanuts.

EXAMPLE 2

Facts: Company Y makes frozen desserts and sells them through grocery and warehouse stores. As part of an arrangement to sell a large quantity of products to a large grocery store chain, Company Y agrees to reimburse the chain for special display freezers that will display Company Y's products. The freezers will include Company Y's logo on the outside and will have racking and other components specifically designed to highlight Company Y's products. The grocery chain will pay an independent third party to design and build the freezers. Company Y and the grocery store chain believe that the new display freezers will increase sales of Company Y products at the chain's stores. However, the grocery store chain has no obligation to continue purchasing Company Y's products.

Vendor Classification Discussion: The first condition in ASC 605-50-45-2 is not met because Company Y does not receive an identifiable benefit that is sufficiently separable from the arrangement to sell products to the grocery store chain. Company Y could only enter into such an arrangement with a reseller of its products. The consideration therefore should be characterized as a reduction in revenue.

Customer Classification Discussion: If the chain has support for the amount it spends to purchase the freezers from the independent third party such that the cost is identifiable and incremental under the model in ASC 605-50-45-15, it should recognize the payment from Company Y as a reduction in the cost of these freezers when recognized in the income statement.

EXAMPLE 3

Facts: Company Y makes frozen desserts and sells them through grocery and warehouse stores. As part of an arrangement to sell a large quantity of products to a grocery store chain, Company Y agrees to give special display freezers to the chain to display Company Y's products. The freezers include Company Y's logo on the outside and have racking and other components specifically designed to highlight Company Y's products. Company Y currently owns the freezers, as it purchased them from an independent third party and modified them as necessary to effectively display its products. Company Y and the grocery chain believe that the new display freezers will increase sales of Company Y's products at the chain's stores. However, the grocery store chain has no obligation to continue purchasing Company Y's products.

Vendor Classification Discussion: The consideration that Company Y gives to the chain consists of "free" products (the freezers). Consideration in the form of "free" products or services is treated as a deliverable in the arrangement under the model in ASC 605-50-45-3, rather than as a refund of revenue. Therefore, Company Y should record the cost of the freezers as an expense when recognized in its income statement. In addition, a portion of the revenue from the arrangement should be allocated to the freezers.

Customer Classification Discussion: ASC 605-50-15-2 does not address situations where consideration received by the customer is other than cash or equity. Therefore, the customer's accounting treatment of the "free" freezers should be based on all available facts and circumstances.

EXAMPLE 4

Facts: Company G is an auto manufacturer that sells its products to consumers through a network of dealers. Company G plans to run a nationwide promotion in which its dealers will stay open late for a two-week period and purchasers will receive factory rebates on vehicles purchased during the same two-week period. Company G agrees to reimburse its dealers for the extra payroll costs they will incur during the promotion for keeping the dealerships open longer.

Vendor Classification Discussion: The first condition in ASC 605-50-45-2 is not met because Company G does not receive an identifiable benefit that is sufficiently separable from Company G's sale of automobiles to the dealer. The payroll reimbursements should therefore be characterized as a reduction in revenue on Company G's income statement.

Customer Classification Discussion: If the dealers can demonstrate that the additional payroll costs incurred are identifiable and incremental under the model in ASC 605-50-45-15, the payment from Company G should be recognized as a reduction in payroll costs in the income statement. The dealers will need to consider the nature of their payroll costs when determining whether these costs are identifiable and incremental. Hourly wages would be considered incremental; salaries would not. In addition, most benefit-related payroll costs would most likely not be considered incremental. If the amount of the payment from Company G is greater than the amount of identifiable and incremental reimbursed costs, the excess should be reflected as a reduction in cost of sales.

NEGATIVE REVENUE

Because revenue only relates to amounts received from customers, negative revenue should generally not exist. However, negative revenue might exist for a reporting period or a particular transaction under several circumstances. For example, if a company underestimates the amount of returns it will receive on sales with return rights, it will eventually need to reverse some previously recognized revenue when the additional returns occur. Negative revenue can also exist because of payments made by a vendor to the customer that exceed the revenue from that customer but do not provide a separately identifiable benefit, as discussed above. For example, a company may agree to pay an upfront slotting allowance to have its products sold in a store for the first time. If the initial product order is less than the slotting fee, negative revenues would result.

As part of its deliberations on payments from vendors to customers, the EITF considered whether the existence of negative revenue for a reporting period, a transaction, or some other segment of a company's transactions should be recharacterized as an expense. The EITF concluded that negative revenue amounts may only be reclassified as an expense if, at a particular point in time, the company would have recognized negative revenue for a specific customer on a cumulative basis since it began selling to the customer (ASC 605-50-45-7). This is consistent with the model for classifying payments made to customers because it analyzes the vendor-customer relationship as a whole, rather than on a transaction-by-transaction or other basis.

Based on this conclusion, it is clear that a payment at the inception of a customer relationship, and before the customer makes any commitment to purchase products or services from the vendor could be recharacterized as an expense, even if there is no separately identifiable benefit. However, this recharacterization would not be appropriate to the extent that the customer contractually agrees to make future purchases from the vendor as part of the arrangement including the upfront payment, and it is probable that such purchases will be in amounts greater than the upfront payment (ASC 605-50-45-9). In this event, the payment to the customer would result in an asset, rather than an immediate expense. The asset would be amortized (as a reduction of revenue) as the customer makes the related purchases.

The evaluation of whether negative revenue results from cost recognition on a cumulative basis should be made whenever any cost must be recorded in the income statement. Thus, any additional revenues received from the customer at a later date would not result in a "re-reclassification" of the negative revenue that was previously reclassified as an expense.

ILLUSTRATION: NEGATIVE REVENUE

EXAMPLE 1

Facts: Company C provides computer technology support services to large corporations. Company C enters into an arrangement with Customer D to provide information technology troubleshooting and installation support. Company C will charge specified hourly rates for various services that Customer D may ask it to perform. Customer D agrees to publicize its relationship with Company C through the issuance of a press release, to inform all of its personnel of the arrangement with Company C, to allow Company C to meet with its employees to "pitch" its capabilities and to ensure that Company C's dedicated technology support phone number for Customer D is conspicuously placed throughout Customer D's facilities. In part to defray the costs Customer D will incur in these activities, Company C makes a $500,000 payment to Customer D at the inception of the arrangement. However, Customer D also uses other technology support companies and will continue to do so even after the relationship with Company C is put into place. As a result, Customer D does not guarantee any level of purchases from Company C.

Discussion: The $500,000 payment would normally be treated as a reduction of revenue, because Company C gets no separately identifiable benefit in exchange. However, because this payment is made before any revenue is received from Customer D, it results in negative revenue from Customer D on a cumulative basis. Because there is negative cumulative revenue and because Customer D has not contractually agreed to make future purchases from Company C, the entire $500,000 payment may be recharacterized as an expense. Even when revenue is received from Customer D in the future, the $500,000 payment may remain classified as an expense, as the negative revenue model cannot be applied retroactively.

EXAMPLE 2

Facts: Same as Example 1, except that Customer D had previously used Company C as a service provider and has purchased $800,000 in services from Company C over the past two years. The new arrangement raises Company C's profile significantly with Customer D. Company C believes that the additional publicity from Customer D will result in more business for Company C, rather than other technology support providers.

Discussion: As in Example 1, there is no separately identifiable benefit from the $500,000 payment, so it should be initially characterized as a reduction in revenue. In addition, even though Customer D makes no purchases at the time the new contract is signed, it has made $800,000 in purchases from Company C in the past. On a cumulative basis, Company C has positive revenue of $300,000 from Customer D. Therefore, the $500,000 payment should remain classified as a revenue reduction, even if it results in negative revenue for the reporting period.

EXAMPLE 3

Facts: Same as in Example 1, except that Customer D guarantees that it will purchase at least $800,000 in services from Company C over the next two years.

Discussion: There is no separately identifiable benefit from the $500,000 payment, so it should be initially characterized as a reduction in revenue. Because the contract includes a commitment to make purchases, Company C should consider these purchases in its determination of whether it is appropriate to recharacterize the payment as an expense. Because the committed purchases are greater than the upfront payment, the payment should not be recharacterized as an expense. In this case, Company C would likely conclude that the purchase commitment from Customer D represents an asset. The $500,000 would therefore be capitalized and amortized pro rata as a reduction in revenue over the $800,000 in purchases by Customer D.

PAYMENTS BY A SERVICE PROVIDER TO A MANUFACTURER OR A RESELLER

Certain services are provided through equipment that must be purchased by the end-customer. The equipment may be manufactured, distributed, and sold by third parties to end-users without the direct participation of the service providers. A service provider may offer incentives to manufacturers or resellers to reduce the cost of such equipment to the end-customer thereby increasing the demand for and sales of the service.

The financial reporting guidance of ASC 605-50-45-2 and 45-3 must be used to determine whether the consideration given by the service provider to the manufacturer or reseller should be treated as "cash consideration" or "other than cash consideration" when that consideration can be linked contractually to the benefit received by the customer of the service provider (ASC 605-50-25-14).

The Task Force also decided that the characterization of the consideration (as "cash consideration" or "other than cash consideration") should be based on the form of the consideration directed by the service provider to be provided to the service provider's customer (ASC 605-50-25-16).

EXAMPLE: INCENTIVE PAYMENTS BY A SERVICE PROVIDER

Sirius XM Radio, Inc. Form 10-K—Fiscal Year Ended December 31, 2009

Revenue Recognition

At the time of sale, vehicle owners purchasing or leasing a vehicle with a subscription to our service typically receive between a three-month and twelve-month prepaid subscription. Prepaid subscription fees received from certain automakers are recorded as deferred revenue and amortized to revenue ratably over the service period which commences upon retail sale and activation. We reimburse automakers for certain costs associated with the satellite radio installed in the applicable vehicle at the time the vehicle is manufactured. The associated payments to the automakers are included in Subscriber acquisition costs. These payments are included in Subscriber acquisition costs because we are responsible for providing the service to the customers, including being obligated to the customers in the case of an interruption of service.

We record an estimate of rebates that are paid by us to subscribers as a reduction to revenue in the period the subscriber activates service. For certain rebate promotions, a subscriber must remain active for a specified period of time to be considered eligible. In those instances, the estimate is recorded as a reduction to revenue over the required activation period. We estimate the effects of mail-in rebates based on actual take-rates for rebate incentives offered in prior periods, adjusted as deemed necessary based on take-rate data available at the time. In subsequent periods, estimates are adjusted when necessary. For instant rebate promotions, we record the consideration paid to the consumer as a reduction to revenue in the period the customer participates in the promotion.

Subscriber Acquisition Costs

Subscriber acquisition costs consist of costs incurred to acquire new subscribers and include hardware subsidies paid to radio manufacturers, distributors and automakers, including subsidies paid to automakers who include a satellite radio and a prepaid subscription to our service in the sale or lease price of a new vehicle; subsidies paid for chip sets and certain other components used in manufacturing radios; device royalties for certain radios; commissions paid to retailers and automakers as incentives to purchase, install and activate radios; product warranty obligations; and provisions for inventory allowance. Subscriber acquisition costs do not include advertising, loyalty payments to distributors and dealers of radios and revenue share payments to automakers and retailers of radios.

Subsidies paid to radio manufacturers and automakers are expensed upon installation, shipment, receipt of product or activation. Commissions paid to retailers and automakers are expensed upon either the sale or activation of radios. Chip sets that are shipped to radio manufacturers and held on consignment are recorded as inventory and expensed as Subscriber acquisition costs when placed into production by radio manufacturers. Costs for chip sets not held on consignment are expensed as Subscriber acquisition costs when the automaker confirms receipt.

PRESENTATION OF CERTAIN COSTS BILLED TO CUSTOMERS

Shipping and Handling

Many companies sell goods that are shipped directly to customers and charge a separately identified "shipping and handling" fee on the customer invoice. Other companies do not charge a separate fee and instead advertise "free" shipping. When a separate shipping and handling charge is included, the method of determining the amount of the charge varies. Some companies merely pass through third-party shipping charges, while others attempt to recover a portion of their internal costs as well. Other companies charge shipping and handling fees on a basis that bears no relation to the costs incurred.

The EITF concluded that amounts billed to a customer for shipping and handling should be classified as revenue in the income statement. The conclusion is partially based on the fact that a company has the ability to alter its pricing between its product prices and its shipping and handling charge to achieve similar results (ASC 605-45-45-20).

The EITF also concluded that shipping and handling costs should be classified as an expense. Therefore, it is not appropriate to offset shipping and handling costs incurred and shipping and handling revenue received against one another in the income statement. Rather, the two must each be reported separately (ASC 605-50-45-21). This conclusion is consistent with the conclusions reached on reporting revenue gross versus net. The seller acts as a principal in purchasing the shipping from the postal service or private shipping company and in the transaction with the customer. Therefore, shipping and handling costs and revenues should not be reported on a net basis, even if the cost is merely "passed through" to the customer without any markup.

DISCLOSURE ALERT: If shipping and handling costs are classified within cost of sales on the income statement, no separate disclosure of these costs is required. However, if shipping and handling costs are significant and are not classified within cost of sales, the amount must be disclosed and the line item in which they are included must be identified (ASC 605-45-50-2).

EXAMPLE: SHIPPING AND HANDLING COSTS

Colgate-Palmolive, Inc. Form 10-K—Fiscal Year Ended December 31, 2009

Shipping and handling costs may be reported as either a component of cost of sales or selling, general and administrative expenses. The Company reports such costs, primarily related to warehousing and outbound freight, in the Consolidated Statements of Income as a component of Selling, general and administrative expenses. Accordingly, the Company's gross profit margin is not comparable with the gross profit margin of those companies that include shipping and handling charges in cost of sales. If such costs had been included in cost of sales, gross profit margin as a percent of sales would have decreased by 730 bps, from 58.8% to 51.5%, in 2009 and decreased by 780 and 790 bps in 2008 and 2007, respectively, with no impact on reported earnings.

Out-of-Pocket Expenses

Service providers often incur incidental expenses while performing work for their clients. These "out-of-pocket" expenses include travel costs (e.g., hotel charges, airline tickets, car rentals, meals) and costs of supplies, printing and copying. In many cases, the customer reimburses the service provider for these costs, in addition to the agreed-upon service fee. In other cases, the arrangement fee is stated as a single figure that includes both out-of-pocket costs and the service fee.

Prior to 2001, there was no specific accounting guidance on how to characterize out-of-pocket costs and the related reimbursements. Many companies that routinely billed such costs to their customers accounted for the reimbursements as an offset to the related expenses. This was viewed as appropriate because it resulted in gross margins that included the service fee and the related direct costs of providing the service, without a gross-up for out-of-pocket costs. When companies used this accounting policy, some disclosed the amount of out-of-pocket expenses that had been netted against reimbursements; others did not.

The EITF addressed the income statement classification of reimbursements for out-of-pocket expenses in ASC 605-45-45-23 and concluded that these reimbursements should be characterized as revenue, rather than as an offset against the related expenses. This is consistent with the conclusion reached on how to account for shipping and handling costs and is based on the principles underlying gross versus net revenue reporting. The EITF concluded that with respect to the purchase of travel, supplies, and other out-of-pocket costs, the service provider acts as a principal, not as an agent. Furthermore, the EITF decided that the customer does not purchase the travel or supplies, but only the services offered by the service provider. As a result, out-of-pocket costs are like any other cost incurred in providing the service; the fact that the arrangement fee varies based on the amount of such costs should not cause the accounting to be any different.

EXAMPLE: OUT-OF-POCKET EXPENSES

Kforce Inc. Form 10-K—Fiscal Year Ended December 31, 2010

Net service revenues represent services rendered to customers less credits, discounts, rebates and allowances. Revenues include reimbursements of travel and out-of-pocket expenses ("billable expenses") with equivalent amounts of expense recorded in direct costs of services.

Sales and Excise Taxes

Sales and excise taxes are taxes based on sales or purchase activity. Although various names are used, this discussion refers to sales taxes as a tax on the purchaser and excise taxes as a tax on the seller. In most jurisdictions, the selling party remits both sales and excise taxes to the government. For sales taxes, the seller acts as a collection agent when it charges the customer and remits this amount to the government.

Because sales taxes are imposed on the purchaser, the conceptually correct accounting would have the seller not record such amounts on the income statement at all. Any amounts collected would be recorded as a payable to the government that is settled upon payment.

Excise taxes, however, are imposed on the seller of goods or services and therefore could appropriately be classified as an expense in cost of sales. Alternatively, because these taxes are not discretionary and reduce the amount of revenue that is available to cover the company's expenses (unless they can be passed on to the end-customer), it has also been acceptable to report excise taxes as a reduction of revenue.

For companies that do business in a number of jurisdictions that have transaction-based taxes like sales and excise taxes, tracking whether the tax is legally imposed on the seller or the purchaser of the goods and services, in order to get the conceptually correct accounting in each jurisdiction, might be difficult. ASC 605-45-50-3 concludes that, rather than determining how to record each tax in each jurisdiction, the income statement presentation of taxes is an accounting policy decision that should be disclosed as required by ASC 235, *Notes to Financial Statements*.

Disclosure of the amounts of taxes in interim and annual financial statements is required, if significant, for any of these taxes reported gross (ASC 605-45-50-4).

DISCLOSURE ALERT: SEC registrants must disclose the amount of excise taxes included in revenue if the amount exceeds 1% of sales. The classification of excise tax payments should also be disclosed (ASC 225-10-S99-2) (REG S-X, Rule 5-03).

EXAMPLE: SALES TAXES

Staples, Inc. Form 10-K—Fiscal Year Ended January 29, 2011

Revenue is recorded net of taxes collected from customers that are remitted to governmental authorities, with the collected taxes recorded as current liabilities until remitted to the relevant government authority.

UNCOLLECTIBLE AMOUNTS AND BAD DEBTS

As noted throughout this product, one of the criteria for revenue recognition is that collectibility must be reasonably assured. When collectibility is in doubt, it is not acceptable for a company to recognize revenue along with a bad debt expense. Although presenting both amounts would result in a correct calculation of operating income, it would inappropriately overstate revenue by including revenue that has not met the collectibility criterion.

Even when revenue is considered collectible and can be recognized when the other criteria have been met, circumstances may subsequently arise that make payment unlikely. When this occurs, a company may need to recognize bad debt expense. Bad debts can be distinguished from sales that do not meet the collectibility criterion because bad debts result from sales that were considered collectible at the time of delivery but became uncollectible sometime thereafter. The classification of bad debt expenses is not specified in U.S. GAAP, although the SEC requires them to be presented as expenses (generally selling or marketing expenses) rather than as a reduction of revenue (ASC 225-10-S99-2) (REG S-X, Rule 5-03(b)(5)).

Readers also should refer to Chapter 3, "General Principles," and the Covad Communications Form 10-K—Fiscal Year Ended December 31, 2007 example on revenue recognition when collectibility is not reasonably assured.

BALANCE SHEET PRESENTATION

Accounting guidance on the classification of cash received in advance of revenue recognition (deferred revenue) is still somewhat scarce. Although the deferred revenue liability caption is acknowledged in several FASB and EITF pronouncements, no literature actually describes what liabilities qualify as "deferred revenue."

Cash Received Before Revenue Recognition (Deferred Revenue)

Many reasons have been provided throughout this product to explain why, under certain circumstances, revenue recognition should be prohibited even after cash is received. When this occurs, a liability must be recorded for the cash received in excess of whatever revenue can be recognized. For example, when a right of return exists, no revenue is recognized if returns cannot be reliably estimated. As a result, any amounts received must be recognized as a liability. When returns can be estimated, revenue can only be recognized up to the extent of expected returns. Therefore, if full payment is made, a portion will still need to be reflected as a liability.

When these deferred liabilities are recognized, a question arises as to how they should be characterized. Possible characterizations include deferred revenue, a deposit liability, debt, or a contra-receivable account.

In general, amounts classified as deferred revenue should be ultimately expected to result in revenue recognition. Thus, advance payments that are received before services are performed are usually classified as deferred revenue because these amounts will be recognized as revenue upon performance of the service. Similarly, payments received upon delivery of a product, where revenue recognition is prohibited due to a customer acceptance clause, may be characterized as deferred revenue in the balance sheet.

Any amounts that are expected to be refunded to a customer may not be included in deferred revenue. For example, revenue that is not recognized based on expected returns should be classified in a separate monetary liability account, labeled with a caption such as "customer deposits" (ASC 605-10-S99, A4a, ques. 1) (SAB Topic 13A4a, ques. 1). It is also not acceptable to reflect a product return liability as an offset to accounts receivable. This is because the reserve for product returns is an estimate of cash that will be returned to customers—it is not a valuation account related to the accounts receivable balance.

The following chart lists some of the common reasons for revenue to be deferred once cash has been received and identifies whether it is generally appropriate to record the related liability as deferred revenue. When the reason for the deferral is that the revenue has not yet been earned, the liability may be reflected as deferred revenue. However, if the reason for the deferral is related to a concern about whether the fee is fixed or determinable or whether a true sale has occurred, the liability should not be characterized as deferred revenue.

Reason for Deferral	Deferred revenue?
Estimated returns or price protection when estimates can be made	N
Right of return or price protection exists and no estimate can be made	N
Estimated refunds under sales incentives	N
Product not yet delivered	Y
Service not yet performed	Y
Standard warranty when estimate of costs cannot be made	Y
Extended warranty	Y
Product financing arrangement	N
No persuasive evidence of an arrangement	N
Refundable deposit against variable fee	N
Product delivered—awaiting acceptance	Y
Delivered item in a multiple-deliverable arrangement does not have value to the customer on a standalone basis	Y
Lack of vendor-specific objective evidence of fair value to allocate revenue in a multiple-element software arrangement	N
No revenue is allocated to the delivered item in a multiple-deliverable arrangement that meets the criteria to be accounted for separately, or only a portion of the revenue that would otherwise have been allocated to the delivered item is ultimately allocated to that item, due to all or a portion of the payment being contingent upon delivery of an as-yet-undelivered item	Note 1
Note 1: Generally, the liability in this situation should be characterized as deferred revenue. However, classification of the liability may be affected by the approach taken to account for the totality of the arrangement (i.e., it may be affected by the approach taken to account for both the revenue and cost elements of the arrangement). For a discussion of the revenue accounting in this situation, see Chapter 4, "Multiple-Deliverable Revenue Arrangements." For a discussion of how costs associated with the delivered item are treated in this situation, see Chapter 8, "Miscellaneous Issues."	

Accounts Receivable and Deferred Revenue

There are situations when it is unclear whether deferred revenue, or another liability, should be recognized. For example, consider a transaction in which delivery has occurred, there is a right of return, returns cannot be estimated and payment, although due under normal terms, has not yet been received. Because returns cannot be estimated, no revenue may be recognized (see Chapter 5, "Product Deliverables") and the inventory shipped should remain on the seller's books. However, a final sales agreement does exist and, except for the right of return, the fee is fixed or determinable. Therefore, it may not be clear whether a receivable should be recorded, with an offsetting entry to either deferred revenue or another liability account.

The SEC staff believes that it is generally not appropriate to record a receivable in this case. Because the conditions for revenue recognition have not yet been met and payment not made, neither party has fulfilled its obligations under the contract. As a result, SEC registrants should treat the contract as an executory contract under which neither party has performed. This treatment results in neither a receivable nor a liability in the financial statements. This position is consistent with ASC 985-605-55-32 (TPA 5100.58) where the AICPA Task Force on software revenue recognition issues effectively concluded that a receivable does not exist (and therefore cannot be considered transferred for accounting purposes) when revenue cannot be recognized due to extended payment terms.

The SEC staff's position is generally preferable for private companies. However, private companies may recognize these receivables if they meet the definition of an asset in CON-6, which requires the customer to be unconditionally obligated to pay the receivable balance.

PRACTICE POINTER: Although the receivable and related deferred revenue may not be reflected in the financial statements, a company may wish to record these entries in its internal records to ensure that receivables are properly tracked and that obligations related to potential returns are considered. When the receivable and deferred revenue are not reflected in the financial statements, a company using this procedure should ensure that these assets and liabilities are eliminated.

This is particularly important because financial statement users generally assume that amounts shown as deferred revenue have already been paid. As a result, recording deferred revenue when payment has not yet been received may cause a user to misunderstand the company's cash flow position.

Sales of Future Revenue

In certain situations, a company may receive payment from a third party and agree to pay the third party for a defined period a specified percentage or amount of the revenue, or of a measure of income, of a particular product line, business segment, trademark, patent, or contractual right. For example, a sale of future revenue occurs when a company sells its rights to receive payments from a customer to a third party before the revenue related to these payments has been recognized.

ASC 470-10-25 addresses the classification of the amounts received by the company in these situations. The nature of the payment generally precludes immediate recognition in income due to the payments owed to the third-party investor. In most cases, these payments cannot be classified as deferred revenue, but should instead be reflected as debt. Any of the following factors creates a presumption that classification as debt is required (ASC 470-10-25-2):

1. The transaction does not purport to be a sale (that is, the form of the transaction is debt).
2. The enterprise has significant continuing involvement in the generation of the cash flows due the investor (for example, active involvement in the generation of the operating revenues of a product line, subsidiary, or business segment).
3. The transaction is cancelable by either the enterprise or the investor through payment of a lump sum or other transfer of assets by the enterprise.
4. The investor's rate of return is implicitly or explicitly limited by the terms of the transaction.
5. Variations in the enterprise's revenue or income underlying the transaction have only a trifling impact on the investor's rate of return.
6. The investor has any recourse to the enterprise relating to the payments due the investor.

CLASSES OF REVENUE

When a company gets its revenue from different product or service categories, separate presentation of revenue from each category may be appropriate. This is especially true if the various categories of sales transactions are expected to have different gross margins or other economic characteristics. In SEC filings, separate presentation of revenues and related cost of sales is required for each of the following categories of transactions:

1. Tangible product sales;
2. Public utility operations;
3. Rentals;
4. Service transactions; and
5. All other sources (ASC 225-10-S99-2) (REG S-X, Rule 5-03(b)(1)).

DISCLOSURE ALERT: See Chapter 12, "Disclosures," for information about required disclosures.

SEC REGISTRANT ALERT: In a December 2007 speech, the SEC staff discussed whether revenue from product and service deliverables can be displayed separately on the income statement when a vendor is unable to separate a multiple-deliverable arrangement. SEC staff indicated that separate display of product and service revenue may be appropriate when the vendor has a reasonable basis for developing a separation methodology and it can be consistently applied, clearly disclosed and not misleading. However, a systematic allocation with no basis other than consistency or based on contractually stated amounts would likely be insufficient.

EXAMPLE: PRESENTATION OF MULTIPLE CLASSES OF REVENUE

[See the *International Business Machines* example earlier in this chapter.]

CHAPTER 12
DISCLOSURES

CONTENTS

BACKGROUND

The first 11 chapters of this book have focused largely on getting the numbers right. This chapter, instead, focuses on footnote and other disclosures regarding revenue recognition. Despite the fact that this discussion takes up many fewer pages, disclosures regarding revenue recognition are, in many instances, as important to the financial statements as getting the accounting for revenue correct. Revenue-related disclosures provide the user of the financial statements with critical information related to the types and terms of the sales transactions entered into by the company, and how those transactions have been reflected in the financial statements. Without clear and transparent disclosures, the usefulness of financial information is greatly impaired.

The importance of revenue-related disclosures is raised even further when there are multiple potential accounting treatments for a transaction, when transactions are complex and include unusual terms, whenever atypical sales transactions take place, and when significant changes in estimates have occurred.

In addition to disclosures in the footnotes to financial statements that are required or encouraged by GAAP, significant additional revenue-related disclosure for public companies usually appears in the Management's Discussion and Analysis section of annual and quarterly reports. MD&A is intended to provide thoughts about the company's financial position and results of operations through the eyes of management, including explanations of changes in results from period to period, thoughts on near-term liquidity and potential changes in financial position, and analysis of the success or failure of strategic decisions. As such, the MD&A typically explains the reasons for increases or decreases in revenue from period to period, a discussion of any uncertainties regarding the company's ability to continue to generate revenue at similar levels, disaggregated data about revenue from different segments of the business, and other discussion related to revenue.

Disclosures related to sales transactions and revenue recognition policies continue to receive tremendous scrutiny from regulators and users of financial statements. Preparers of financial statements should be focused on providing transparent revenue recognition discussions to provide investors insight. In this regard, preparers should take advantage of the opportunity in footnotes and MD&A to shed light on difficult judgments and estimates that are necessary, in many cases, to determine how to record revenue.

In addition to helping to meet investor needs, clear disclosures also greatly reduce the chances of harsh regulatory or litigation-related actions. The frequency, number, and critical nature of highly publicized revenue restatements, SEC enforcement actions, and legal difficulties for companies accused of manipulating revenue continues to be high. The best defense for a well-intentioned company trying to apply the revenue standards in good faith is a well-drafted set of disclosures. Once the accounting treatments are disclosed and the reasons for those treatments are clearly articulated, claims that the preparer was attempting to deceive users of the financial information are very difficult to uphold, and deviation from the treatment used by others is much easier to accept.

This chapter provides many examples of revenue recognition disclosures. In many instances, the details of the disclosures are not specifically required by GAAP, but rather were included by the company in an attempt to provide a good view into its revenue recognition accounting. This kind of high-level thinking is often necessary to drafting good revenue disclosures because, like accounting guidance related to revenue, no single accounting standard provides comprehensive disclosures guidance and, as a result, disclosure requirements are scattered across the authoritative literature. Consequently, some requirements are very general (i.e., they apply to all types of sales transactions), whereas others are very specific (i.e., they apply to only certain types of sales transactions).

GENERAL DISCLOSURE REQUIREMENTS

LISTING OF APPLICABLE LITERATURE

ASC	ASC Topic/Subtopic	Publication	Subject
235-10	Notes to Financial Statements/Overall	APB-22	Disclosure of Accounting Policies
270-10-50	Interim Reporting/ Overall	APB-28	Interim Financial Reporting
850-10	Related Party Disclosures/Overall	FAS-57	Related Party Disclosures
280-10	Segment Reporting/ Overall	FAS-131	Segments Reporting
205-20-50	Presentation of Financial Statements/ Discontinued Operations	FAS-144	Discontinued Operations
205-10	Presentation of Financial Statements/Overall	FAS-154	Accounting Changes and Error Corrections
605-25-50	Revenue Recognition/ Multiple-element Arrangements	ASU 2009-13	Multiple-Deliverable Revenue Arrangements
275-10	Risks and Uncertainties/ Overall	SOP 94-6	Disclosure of Certain Significant Risks and Uncertainties
605-45-50	Revenue Recognition/ Principal Agent Considerations	EITF 99-19	Reporting Revenue Gross as a Principal versus Net As an Agent

ASC	ASC Topic/Subtopic	Publication	Subject
605-45-50	Revenue Recognition/ Principal Agent Considerations	EITF 00-10	Shipping and Handling Fees and Costs
235-10-S99	Notes to Financial Statements/Overall	REG S-X, Rule 4-08	Financial Statement Requirements, Rules of General Application, General Notes to Financial Statements
225-10-S99-2	Income Statement/ Overall	REG S-X, Rule 5-03	Financial Statement Requirements, Commercial and Industrial Companies, Income Statements
605-10-S99	Revenue Recognition/Overall	SAB Topic 13	Revenue Recognition

Accounting Policies

General

Companies are required to disclose the significant accounting policies used in the preparation of their financial statements (ASC 235-10-50). In determining which policies to disclose, the guidance requires consideration of which accounting principles followed by the entity materially affect the determination of financial position, cash flows and results of operations. The disclosure is intended highlight important judgments made in the application of principles, and should include those policies that involve a selection from acceptable alternatives, industry-specific accounting methods, or unusual applications of GAAP (ASC 235-10-50-12).

Given these parameters, it would appear that disclosure of a revenue recognition accounting policy would almost always be necessary. But in case there was any doubt, ASC 235-10-50-12 specifically mentions "important judgments as to appropriateness of principles related to recognition of revenue" as part of the required accounting policy disclosures. Therefore, just about the only kind of company that might not need to cover revenue recognition in its accounting policy footnote would be a development stage company that has not yet started generating revenue. However, such a company should consider discussing the accounting policy it expects to follow once it commences its revenue-generating activities.

The SEC staff has communicated its observations related to revenue recognition accounting policy disclosures in a variety of ways.

In ASC 605-10-S99 (SAB Topic 13), the SEC staff states that it would always expect a registrant to disclose its revenue recognition accounting policies given the judgment ordinarily exercised in accounting for sales transactions (ASC 605-10-S99, B, ques. 1) (SAB Topic 13B, ques. 1). In speeches given in December 2002, members of the SEC staff observed that revenue recognition accounting policy disclosures should be more complete and precise. Specifically, the staff suggested that revenue recognition accounting policy disclosures:

- Address all material revenue streams;
- Consider whether the sources of revenue described in the notes parallel those discussed in the business section;
- Discuss explicit or implicit acceptance conditions, contingencies, or other circumstances that could affect the timing and amount of revenue recognized;
- Address multiple-deliverable arrangements; and
- Describe the basis for gross or net presentation.

In early 2003 the SEC staff issued the Fortune 500 Report. This report resulted from the SEC's Division of Corporation Finance's (Corp Fin) review of all annual reports filed by Fortune 500 companies. The Fortune 500 Report provides insight into areas commonly questioned by Corp Fin during its reviews of annual reports. One area specifically mentioned in the Fortune 500 Report relates to revenue recognition accounting policy disclosures. A common request from Corp Fin was for companies to expand or clarify their revenue recognition accounting policy disclosures. Corp Fin highlighted certain industries in the Fortune 500 Report as those that require specific improvements in their revenue recognition accounting policy disclosures:

- *Computer software, computer services, computer hardware, and communications equipment*—Expanded disclosure for software and multiple-deliverable arrangements.

- *Capital goods, semiconductors, and electronic instruments and controls*—Improved disclosures for deferred revenue, revenue recognition for products with return or price protection features, requirements for installation of equipment, and other customer acceptance provisions.

- *Energy*—Improved disclosures of the material terms of energy contracts.

- *Pharmaceutical and retail*—Improved disclosures related to accounting for product returns, discounts and rebates, and co-op advertising arrangements with retail companies.

Additional disclosures regarding revenue recognition may be required in the MD&A as a component of the disclosure of critical accounting policies. Pursuant to the December 2001 "Cautionary Advice" release, companies were requested to discuss their critical accounting policies beginning with December 31, 2001, 10-K filings. A Proposed Rule was issued in April 2002 that would formally require this discussion in future filings.

The SEC guidance describes critical accounting policies as policies that are both:

> . . . important to the portrayal of the company's financial condition and results, and they require management's most difficult, subjective or complex judgments, often as a result of the need to make estimates about the effect of matters that are inherently uncertain.

Given this description, revenue recognition would qualify as a critical accounting policy for many public companies.

In December 2003, the SEC issued Release No. 33-8350, Interpretation—Commission Guidance Regarding Management's Discussion and Analysis of Financial Condition and Results of Operations, which incorporated components of the Proposed Rule. While the rest of the Proposed Rule was not finalized by the SEC, SEC registrants still should ensure that they take into consideration the guidance in the SEC's Cautionary Advice when preparing their annual reports.

EXAMPLES: REVENUE-RECOGNITION POLICIES

General Electric Company Form 10-K—Fiscal Year Ended December 31, 2010

Sales of Goods and Services

We record all sales of goods and services only when a firm sales agreement is in place, delivery has occurred or services have been rendered and collectibility of the fixed or determinable sales price is reasonably assured.

Arrangements for the sale of goods and services sometimes include multiple components. Most of our multiple component arrangements involve the sale of goods and services in the Technology Infrastructure segment. Our arrangements with multiple components usually involve future service deliverables such as installation, training or the future delivery of ancillary equipment. In such agreements, the amount assigned to each component is based on the total price and the undelivered component's objectively determined fair value, determined from sources such as the separate selling price for that or a similar component or from competitor prices for similar components. If fair value of an undelivered component cannot be satisfactorily determined, we defer revenue until all components of an arrangement are delivered.

Except for goods sold under long-term agreements, we recognize sales of goods under the provisions of U.S. Securities and Exchange Commission (SEC) Staff Accounting Bulletin (SAB) 104, Revenue Recognition. We often sell consumer products, home videos and computer hardware and software products with a right of return. We use our accumulated experience to estimate and provide for such returns when we record the sale. In situations where arrangements include customer acceptance provisions based on seller or customer-specified objective criteria, we recognize revenue when we have reliably demonstrated that all specified acceptance criteria have been met or when formal acceptance occurs. In arrangements where we provide goods for trial and evaluation purposes, we only recognize revenue after customer acceptance occurs. Unless otherwise noted, we do not provide for anticipated losses before we record sales.

Certain of our sales of goods and services involve inconsequential or perfunctory performance obligations. These obligations can include non-essential installation or training, and in some instances provision of product manuals and limited technical product support. When the only remaining undelivered performance obligation under an arrangement is inconsequential or perfunctory, we recognize revenue on the total contract and provide for the cost of the unperformed obligation.

We recognize revenue on agreements for sales of goods and services under power generation unit and uprate contracts; nuclear fuel assemblies; larger oil drilling equipment projects; aeroderivative unit contracts; military development contracts; and long-term construction projects, using long-term construction and production contract accounting. We estimate total long-term contract revenue net of price concessions as well as total contract costs. For goods sold under power generation unit and uprate contracts, nuclear fuel assemblies, aeroderivative unit contracts and military development contracts, we recognize sales as we complete major contract-specified deliverables, most often when customers receive title to the goods or accept the services as performed. For larger oil drilling equipment projects and long-term construction projects, we recognize sales based on our progress towards contract completion measured by actual costs incurred in relation to our estimate of total expected costs. We measure long-term contract revenues by applying our contract-specific estimated margin rates to incurred costs. We routinely update our estimates of future costs for agreements in process and report any cumulative effects of such adjustments in current operations. We provide for any loss that we expect to incur on these agreements when that loss is probable.

We recognize revenue upon delivery for sales of aircraft engines, military propulsion equipment and related spare parts not sold under long-term product services agreements. Delivery of commercial engines, non-U.S. military equipment and all related spare parts occurs on shipment; delivery of military propulsion equipment sold to the U.S. Government or agencies thereof occurs upon receipt of a Material Inspection and Receiving Report, DD Form 250 or Memorandum of Shipment. Commercial aircraft engines are complex aerospace equipment manufactured to customer order under a variety of sometimes-complex, long-term agreements. We measure sales of commercial aircraft engines by applying our contract-specific estimated margin rates to incurred costs. We routinely update our estimates of future revenues and costs for commercial aircraft engine agreements in process and report any cumulative effects of such adjustments in current operations. Significant components of our revenue and cost estimates include price concessions, performance-related guarantees as well as material, labor and overhead costs. We measure revenue for military propulsion equipment and spare parts not subject to long-term product services agreements based on the specific contract on a specifically-measured output basis. We provide for any loss that we expect to incur on these agreements when that loss is probable; consistent with industry practice, for commercial aircraft engines, we make such provision only if such losses are not recoverable from future highly probable sales of spare parts for those engines.

We sell product services under long-term product maintenance or extended warranty agreements in our Technology Infrastructure and Energy Infrastructure segments, principally in Aviation, Energy and Transportation, where costs of performing services are incurred on other than a straight-line basis. We also sell product services in Healthcare, where such costs generally are expected to be on a straight-line basis. For the Aviation, Energy and Transportation agreements, we recognize related sales based on the extent of our progress towards completion measured by actual costs incurred in relation to total expected costs. We routinely update our estimates of future costs for agreements in process and report any cumulative effects of such adjustments in current operations. For the Healthcare agreements, we recognize revenues on a straight-line basis and expense related costs as incurred. We provide for any loss that we expect to incur on any of these agreements when that loss is probable.

NBC Universal records broadcast and cable television and Internet advertising sales when advertisements are aired, net of provision for any viewer shortfalls (make goods). We record sales from theatrical distribution of films as the films are exhibited; sales of home videos, net of a return provision, when the videos are delivered to and available for sale by retailers; fees from cable/satellite operators when services are provided; and licensing of film and television programming when we make the material available for airing.

GECS Revenues from Services (Earned Income)

We use the interest method to recognize income on loans. Interest on loans includes origination, commitment and other non-refundable fees related to funding (recorded in earned income on the interest method). We stop accruing interest at the earlier of the time at which collection of an account becomes doubtful or the account becomes 90 days past due. Previously recognized interest income that was accrued but not collected from the borrower is evaluated as part of the overall receivable in determining the adequacy of the allowance for losses. Although we stop accruing interest in advance of payments, we recognize interest income as cash is collected when appropriate, provided the amount does not exceed that which would have been earned at the historical effective interest rate; otherwise, payments received are applied to reduce the principal balance of the loan. We resume accruing interest on nonaccrual, non-restructured commercial loans only when (a) payments are brought current according to the loan's original terms and (b) future payments are reasonably assured. When we agree to restructured terms with the borrower, we resume accruing interest only when it is reasonably assured that we will recover full contractual payments, and such loans pass underwriting reviews equivalent to those applied to new loans. We resume accruing interest on nonaccrual consumer loans when the customer's account is less than 90 days past due and collection of such amounts is probable. Interest accruals on modified consumer loans that are not considered to be troubled debt restructurings (TDRs) may return to current status (re-aged) only after receipt of at least three consecutive minimum monthly payments or the equivalent cumulative amount, subject to a re-aging limitation of once a year, or twice in a five-year period.

We recognize financing lease income on the interest method to produce a level yield on funds not yet recovered. Estimated unguaranteed residual values are based upon management's best estimates of the value of the leased asset at the end of the lease term. We use various sources of data in determining this estimate, including information obtained from third parties, which is adjusted for the attributes of the specific asset under lease. Guarantees of residual values by unrelated third parties are considered part of minimum lease payments. Significant assumptions we use in estimating residual values include estimated net cash flows over the remaining lease term, anticipated results of future remarketing, and estimated future component part and scrap metal prices, discounted at an appropriate rate.

We recognize operating lease income on a straight-line basis over the terms of underlying leases.

Fees include commitment fees related to loans that we do not expect to fund and line-of-credit fees. We record these fees in earned income on a straight-line basis over the period to which they relate. We record syndication fees in earned income at the time related services are performed, unless significant contingencies exist.

The following table presents our revenues by revenue source (in millions):

	Year Ended December 31,		
	2008	2009	2010
Advertising revenues:			
Google websites	$14,414	$15,723	$19,444
Google Network websites	6,715	7,166	8,792
Total advertising revenues	21,129	22,889	28,236
Other revenues	667	762	1,085
Revenues	$21,796	$23,651	$29,321

Google AdWords is our auction-based advertising program that enables advertisers to place text-based and display ads on our websites and our Google Network members' websites. Display advertising comprises the videos, text, images, and other interactive ads that run across the web on computers and mobile devices, including smart phones and handheld computers such as netbooks and tablets. Most of our AdWords customers pay us on a cost-per-click basis, which means that an advertiser pays us only when a user clicks on one of its ads. We also offer AdWords on a cost-per-impression basis that enables advertisers to pay us based on the number of times their ads appear on our websites and our Google Network members' websites as specified by the advertiser.

Google AdSense refers to the online programs through which we distribute our advertisers' AdWords ads for display on our Google Network members' websites, as well as programs to deliver ads on television broadcasts.

We recognize as revenues the fees charged advertisers each time a user clicks on one of the text-based ads that are displayed next to the search results pages on our website or on the search results pages or content pages of our Google Network members' websites and, for those advertisers who use our cost-per impression pricing, the fees charged advertisers each time an ad is displayed on our members' websites. We report our Google AdSense revenues on a gross basis principally because we are the primary obligor to our advertisers.

Google ads for televisions enable advertisers, operators, and programmers to buy, schedule, deliver, and measure ads on television. We recognize as revenue the fees charged advertisers each time an ad is displayed on television in accordance with the terms of the related agreements.

We also offer display advertising management services such as media planning, buying, implementation, and measurement tools for advertisers and agencies, and forecasting and reporting tools for publishers. We recognize the related fees as other revenues in the period advertising impressions are delivered.

Google Checkout is our online shopping payment processing system for both consumers and merchants. We recognize as revenues any fees charged to merchants on transactions processed through Google Checkout. Further, cash ultimately paid to merchants under Google Checkout promotions, including cash paid to merchants as a result of discounts provided to consumers on certain transactions processed through Google Checkout, are accounted for as an offset to revenues.

We generate fees from search services on a per-query basis. Our policy is to recognize revenues from per-query search fees in the period we provide the search results.

We also generate fees from the sale and licensing of our Search Appliance products, which include hardware, software, and post-contract support primarily for two years. Prior to 2010, as the deliverables were not sold separately, sufficient vendor-specific objective evidence did not exist for the allocation of revenue. As a result, we recognized the entire fee for the sale and license of these products ratably over the term of the post-contract support arrangement. Beginning the first quarter of 2010, we adopted the new accounting guidance which requires us to allocate the consideration of the arrangement to each of the deliverables based on our best estimate of their standalone selling prices as there is no vendor-specific objective or third-party evidence of the selling prices. As a result, we now recognize revenue allocated to the hardware and software at the time of sale and revenue allocated to post-contract support ratably over the term of the service arrangement. The adoption of this new accounting guidance did not have a material impact on our consolidated financial statements.

In addition, we generate fees through the licensing of our Google Apps products. We recognize as revenue the fees we charge customers for hosting the related enterprise applications and services ratably over the term of the service arrangement.

Revenues realized through display advertising management services, Google ads for televisions, Google Checkout, search services, Search Appliance, and Google Apps were not material in any of the years presented.

We recognize revenues as described above because the services have been provided, the fees we charge are fixed or determinable, we and our advertisers or other customers understand the specific nature and terms of the agreed upon transactions and collectability is reasonably assured.

We record deferred revenue upon invoicing or when cash payments are received in advance of our performance in the underlying agreement on the accompanying Consolidated Balance Sheets.

Salesforce.com, Inc. Form 10-Q—Fiscal Quarter Ended April 30, 2011

Revenue Recognition

The Company derives its revenues from two sources: (1) subscription revenues, which are comprised of subscription fees from customers accessing the Company's enterprise cloud computing application service and from customers purchasing additional support beyond the standard support that is included in the basic subscription fee; and (2) related professional services such as process mapping, project management, implementation services and other revenue. "Other revenue" consists primarily of training fees.

The Company commences revenue recognition when all of the following conditions are satisfied:

- There is persuasive evidence of an arrangement;
- The service has been or is being provided to the customer;
- The collection of the fees is reasonably assured; and
- The amount of fees to be paid by the customer is fixed or determinable.

The Company's subscription service arrangements are non-cancelable and do not contain refund-type provisions.

Subscription and Support Revenues

Subscription and support revenues are recognized ratably over the contract terms beginning on the commencement date of each contract, which is the date the Company's service is made available to customers. Amounts that have been invoiced are recorded in accounts receivable and in deferred revenue or revenue, depending on whether the revenue recognition criteria have been met.

Professional Services and Other Revenues

The majority of the Company's professional services contracts are on a time and material basis. When these services are not combined with subscription revenues as a single unit of accounting, as discussed below, these revenues are recognized as the services are rendered for time and material contracts, and when the milestones are achieved and accepted by the customer for fixed price contracts. Training revenues are recognized as the services are performed.

Multiple-Deliverable Arrangements

The Company enters into arrangements with multiple deliverables that generally include subscription, premium support, and professional services.

Prior to February 1, 2011, the deliverables in multiple-deliverable arrangements were accounted for separately if the delivered items had standalone value and there was objective and reliable evidence of fair value for the undelivered items. If the deliverables in a multiple-deliverable arrangement could not be accounted for separately, the total arrangement fee was recognized ratably as a single unit of accounting over the contracted term of the subscription agreement. A significant portion of the Company's multiple-deliverable arrangements were accounted for as a single unit of accounting because the Company did not have objective and reliable evidence of fair value for certain of its deliverables. Additionally, in these situations, the Company deferred the direct costs of a related professional service arrangement and amortized those costs over the same period as the professional services revenue was recognized.

In October 2009, the Financial Accounting Standards Board ("FASB") issued Accounting Standards Update No. 2009-13, "*Revenue Recognition (Topic 605), Multiple-Deliverable Revenue Arrangements—a consensus of the FASB Emerging Issues Task Force*" ("ASU 2009-13") which amended the previous multiple-deliverable arrangements accounting guidance. Pursuant to the new guidance, objective and reliable evidence of fair value of the deliverables to be delivered is no longer required in order to account for deliverables in a multiple-deliverable arrangement separately. Instead, arrangement consideration is allocated to deliverables based on their relative selling price. The new guidance also eliminates the use of the residual method.

In the first quarter of fiscal 2012, the Company adopted this new accounting guidance on a prospective basis. The Company applied the new accounting guidance to those multiple-deliverable arrangements entered into or materially modified on or after February 1, 2011 which is the beginning of the Company's fiscal year.

The adoption of this new accounting guidance did not have a material impact on the Company's financial condition, results of operations or cash flows. As of April 30, 2011, the deferred professional services revenue and deferred costs under the previous accounting guidance are $58.7 million and $27.5 million respectively which will continue to be recognized over the related remaining subscription period.

Under the new accounting guidance, in order to treat deliverables in a multiple-deliverable arrangement as separate units of accounting, the deliverables must have standalone value upon delivery. If the deliverables have standalone value upon delivery, the Company accounts for each deliverable separately. Subscription services have standalone value as such services are often sold separately. In determining whether professional services have standalone value, the Company considers the following factors for each professional services agreement: availability of the services from other vendors, the nature of the professional services, the timing of when the professional services contract was signed in comparison to the subscription service start date, and the contractual dependence of the subscription service on the customer's satisfaction with the professional services work. To date, the Company has concluded that all of the professional services included in multiple-deliverable arrangements executed have standalone value.

Under the new accounting guidance, when multiple deliverables included in an arrangement are separated into different units of accounting, the arrangement consideration is allocated to the identified separate units based on a relative selling price hierarchy. The Company determines the relative selling price for a deliverable based on its vendor-specific objective evidence of selling price ("VSOE"), if available, or its best estimate of selling price ("BESP"), if VSOE is not available. The Company has determined that third-party evidence of selling price ("TPE") is not a practical alternative due to differences in its service offerings compared to other parties and the availability of relevant third party pricing information. The amount of revenue allocated to delivered items is limited by contingent revenue, if any.

For certain subscription services and professional services, the Company has established VSOE as a consistent number of standalone sales of these deliverables have been priced within a reasonably narrow range. The Company has not established VSOE for a majority of its subscription services due to lack of pricing consistency, the introduction of new services and other factors. Accordingly, the Company uses its BESP to determine the relative selling price.

The Company determined BESP by considering its overall pricing objectives and market conditions. Significant pricing practices taken into consideration include the Company's discounting practices, the size and volume of the Company's transactions, the geographic area where services are sold, price lists, its go to market strategy, historic contractually stated prices and prior relationships and future subscription service sales with certain classes of customers. The determination of BESP is made through consultation with and approval by the Company's management, taking into consideration the go-to market strategy. As the Company's go-to-market strategies evolve, the Company may modify its pricing practices in the future, which could result in changes in selling prices, including both VSOE and BESP.

Deferred Revenue

Deferred revenue primarily consists of billings or payments received in advance of revenue recognition from subscription service described above and is recognized as the revenue recognition criteria are met. The Company generally invoices customers in annual or quarterly installments.

Accordingly, the deferred revenue balance does not represent the total contract value of annual or multi-year, non-cancelable subscription agreements.

Billings against professional services arrangements entered into prior to February 1, 2011 will generally be added to deferred revenue and recognized over the remaining related subscription contract term.

Deferred revenue that will be recognized during the succeeding twelve month period is recorded as current deferred revenue and the remaining portion is recorded as noncurrent.

Deferred Commissions

Deferred commissions are the incremental costs that are directly associated with non-cancelable subscription contracts with customers and consist of sales commissions paid to the Company's direct sales force.

The commissions are deferred and amortized over the non-cancelable terms of the related customer contracts, which are typically 12 to 24 months. The commission payments are paid in full the month after the customer's service commences. The deferred commission amounts are recoverable through the future revenue streams under the non-cancelable customer contracts. The Company believes this is the preferable method of accounting as the commission charges are so closely related to the revenue from the non-cancelable customer contracts that they should be recorded as an asset and charged to expense over the same period that the subscription revenue is recognized. Amortization of deferred commissions is included in marketing and sales expense in the accompanying condensed consolidated statements of operations.

Multiple Revenue Streams

Companies engaging in multiple types of sales transactions should disclose the accounting policies related to each significant type of sales transaction (ASC 605-10-S99, B, ques. 1) (SAB Topic 13B, ques. 1). For example, if a company has one product-selling division and one service-selling division, and each division accounts for a significant percentage of total sales, the company should disclose the revenue recognition accounting policies for both the product-related and service-related revenue streams.

EXAMPLE: MULTIPLE REVENUE STREAMS

Eastman Kodak Company Form 10-K—Fiscal Year Ended December 31, 2009

REVENUE

The Company's revenue transactions include sales of the following: products; equipment; software; services; equipment bundled with products and/or services and/or software; integrated solutions; and intellectual property licensing. The Company recognizes revenue when realized or realizable and earned, which is when the following criteria are met: persuasive evidence of an arrangement exists; delivery has occurred; the sales price is fixed or determinable; and collectibility is reasonably assured. At the time revenue is recognized, the Company provides for the estimated costs of customer incentive programs, warranties and estimated returns and reduces revenue accordingly.

For product sales, the recognition criteria are generally met when title and risk of loss have transferred from the Company to the buyer, which may be upon shipment or upon delivery to the customer site, based on contract terms or legal requirements in certain jurisdictions. Service revenues are recognized as such services are rendered.

For equipment sales, the recognition criteria are generally met when the equipment is delivered and installed at the customer site. Revenue is recognized for equipment upon delivery as opposed to upon installation when there is objective and reliable evidence of fair value for the installation, and the amount of revenue allocable to the equipment is not legally contingent upon the completion of the installation. In instances in which the agreement with the customer contains a customer acceptance clause, revenue is deferred until customer acceptance is obtained, provided the customer acceptance clause is considered to be substantive. For certain agreements, the Company does not consider these customer acceptance clauses to be substantive because the Company can and does replicate the customer acceptance test environment and performs the agreed upon product testing prior to shipment. In these instances, revenue is recognized upon installation of the equipment.

Revenue for the sale of software licenses is recognized when: (1) the Company enters into a legally binding arrangement with a customer for the license of software; (2) the Company delivers the software; (3) customer payment is deemed fixed or determinable and free of contingencies or significant uncertainties; and (4) collection from the customer is reasonably assured. If the Company determines that collection of a fee is not reasonably assured, the fee is deferred and revenue is recognized at the time collection becomes reasonably assured, which is generally upon receipt of payment. Software maintenance and support revenue is recognized ratably over the term of the related maintenance period.

The Company's transactions may involve the sale of equipment, software, and related services under multiple element arrangements. The Company allocates revenue to the various elements based on their fair value. Revenue allocated to an individual element is recognized when all other revenue recognition criteria are met for that element.

The timing and the amount of revenue recognized from the licensing of intellectual property depend upon a variety of factors, including the specific terms of each agreement and the nature of the deliverables and obligations. When the Company has continuing obligations related to a licensing arrangement, revenue related to the ongoing arrangement is recognized over the period of the obligation. Revenue is only recognized after all of the following criteria are met: (1) the Company enters into a legally binding arrangement with a licensee of Kodak's intellectual property, (2) the Company delivers the technology or intellectual property rights, (3) licensee payment is deemed fixed or determinable and free of contingencies or significant uncertainties, and (4) collection from the licensee is reasonably assured.

At the time revenue is recognized, the Company also records reductions to revenue for customer incentive programs. Such incentive programs include cash and volume discounts, price protection, promotional, cooperative and other advertising allowances, and coupons. For those incentives that require the estimation of sales volumes or redemption rates, such as for volume rebates or coupons, the Company uses historical experience and internal and customer data to estimate the sales incentive at the time revenue is recognized.

In instances where the Company provides slotting fees or similar arrangements, this incentive is recognized as a reduction in revenue when payment is made to the customer (or at the time the Company has incurred the obligation, if earlier) unless the Company receives a benefit over a period of time, in which case the incentive is recorded as an asset and is amortized as a reduction of revenue over the term of the arrangement. Arrangements in which the Company receives an identifiable benefit include arrangements that have enforceable exclusivity provisions and those that provide a clawback provision entitling the Company to a pro rata reimbursement if the customer does not fulfill its obligations under the contract.

The Company may offer customer financing to assist customers in their acquisition of Kodak's products. At the time a financing transaction is consummated, which qualifies as a sales-type lease, the Company records equipment revenue equal to the total lease receivable net of unearned income. Unearned income is recognized as finance income using the effective interest method over the term of the lease. Leases not qualifying as sales-type leases are accounted for as operating leases. The Company recognizes revenue from operating leases on an accrual basis as the rental payments become due.

The Company's sales of tangible products are the only class of revenues that exceeds 10% of total consolidated net sales. All other sales classes are individually less than 10%, and therefore, have been combined with the sales of tangible products on the same line in accordance with Regulation S-X.

Incremental direct costs (i.e. costs that vary with and are directly related to the acquisition of a contract which would not have been incurred but for the acquisition of the contract) of a customer contract in a transaction that results in the deferral of revenue are deferred and netted against revenue in proportion to the related revenue recognized in each period if: (1) an enforceable contract for the remaining deliverable items exists; and (2) delivery of the remaining items in the arrangement is expected to generate positive margins allowing realization of the deferred costs. Otherwise, these costs are expensed as incurred and included in cost of goods sold in the accompanying Consolidated Statement of Operations.

Management's Discussion and Analysis of Financial Condition and Results of Operations

For public companies, the discussion of accounting policies is supplemented to a great extent by the narrative disclosures in MD&A, as this discussion gives management the opportunity to explain how its business operations and accounting policies together resulted in the reported financial position and results of operations.

The rule requiring MD&A explains its objective in very broad terms. Revenue is mentioned several times, with rule requiring specific discussion of the following revenue-related points (SEC Regulation S-K, Item 303 (A)(3)):

- Any known trends or uncertainties that have had or are expected to have a material impact on revenues.

- Known events that will cause a material change in the relationship between costs and revenues.

- Discussion of the extent to which material increases in revenues are attributable to increases in prices or to increases in the volume or amount of goods or services being sold or to the introduction of new products or services.

- The impact of inflation and changing prices on the registrant's net sales and revenues and on income from continuing operations.

- Any other significant components of revenues that, in the registrant's judgment, should be described in order to understand the registrant's results of operations.

Of course, the last bullet above leaves the possible breadth and depth of revenue discussion in MD&A wide open. That openness is intentional. The MD&A rule is intended to be very principle-based, and essentially asks the company to discuss any information that would be important to a reader of the financial statements looking to gain an understanding of the company's financial position and results of operations. As such, writing a high-quality MD&A disclosure takes thought and effort.

The MD&A disclosures should not include merely a repetitive explanation of mathematical calculations of how much revenue changed, but instead a discussion that goes behind the numbers to provide management's views on why things changed and whether they will change again in the future. In this regard, highlighting unusual items is key, as is pointing out the longer-term trends in revenue recognition.

EXAMPLE: MANAGEMENT'S DISCUSSION AND ANALYSIS

Orbitz Worldwide, Inc. Form 10-K—Fiscal Year Ended December 31, 2010

Results of Operations

Comparison of the year ended December 31, 2010 to the year ended December 31, 2009

	Years Ended December 31,			
	2010	**2009**	**$ Change**	**% Change**
		(in thousands)		
Net revenue				
Air	$274,568	$269,643	$ 4,925	2%
Hotel	203,821	183,658	20,163	11%
Vacation package	115,161	117,026	(1,865)	(2)%
Advertising and media	49,353	59,534	(10,181)	(17)%
Other	114,584	107,787	6,797	6%
Total net revenue	757,487	737,648	19,839	3%

Net Revenue

Net revenue increased $19.8 million, or 3%, for the year ended December 31, 2010 compared with the year ended December 31, 2009.

Air. Net revenue from air bookings increased $4.9 million, or 2%, for the year ended December 31, 2010 compared with the year ended December 31, 2009. Foreign currency fluctuations had a nominal impact on the increase in air net revenue.

Domestic air net revenue decreased $17.3 million due to lower average net revenue per airline ticket, which was partially offset by an $8.1 million increase in domestic air net revenue due to higher transaction volume. The lower average net revenue per airline ticket was primarily driven by the elimination of most air booking fees on our domestic leisure websites in April 2009. Higher net revenue per airline ticket from merchant air transactions and higher commissions from those airlines with variable commission structures, both of which were the result of higher average air fares, and the reduction to the unfavorable contract liability as a result of the termination of the Charter Associate Agreement between American Airlines and us effective December 2010 (see Note 9—Unfavorable Contracts of the Notes to Consolidated Financial Statements) partially offset the lower net revenue per airline ticket. The higher transaction volume primarily resulted from the removal of most booking fees.

International air net revenue increased $14.1 million (excluding the impact of foreign currency fluctuations) primarily due to higher transaction volume, partially offset by lower average net revenue per airline ticket. The lower average net revenue per airline ticket was primarily driven by lower air override revenue, which represents incentive-based commissions received from certain suppliers when volume thresholds are met, and a shift in air bookings towards markets where average booking values are lower and where we earn lower margins, partially offset by higher credit card fee revenue.

Hotel. Net revenue from hotel bookings increased $20.2 million, or 11%, for the year ended December 31, 2010 compared with the year ended December 31, 2009. Foreign currency fluctuations drove $6.8 million of this increase. The increase in net revenue from hotel bookings, excluding the impact of foreign currency fluctuations, was $13.4 million.

Domestic hotel net revenue increased $14.0 million due to higher transaction volume and $1.3 million due to higher average net revenue per transaction. The higher average net revenue per hotel transaction was driven by higher hotel ADRs, fewer promotional coupons issued by us, more timely receipt of customer refund reimbursements from hotels and higher payment vendor rebates, partially offset by a significant reduction in hotel booking fees charged on our domestic leisure websites and a lower average length of stay.

International hotel net revenue declined $1.9 million (excluding the impact of foreign currency fluctuations) primarily due to a decline in hotel net revenue for HotelClub driven by lower average net revenue per transaction and lower transaction volume for European destinations and, to a lesser extent, in the Pacific. The lower average net revenue per transaction was primarily driven by a shift in the geographic mix of HotelClub's bookings away from European destinations and towards markets where average booking values are lower and where we earn lower margins. A change in our estimate of the redemption rate for points earned under the loyalty program at HotelClub also contributed to the lower net revenue per transaction. The decline at HotelClub was partially offset by an increase in hotel net revenue at ebookers primarily due to higher transaction volume due to improved functionality of our technology platform and improvements to our European hotel supply.

Vacation package. Net revenue from vacation package bookings decreased $1.9 million, or 2%, for the year ended December 31, 2010 compared with the year ended December 31, 2009. Vacation package net revenue decreased by $0.2 million due to foreign currency fluctuations. The decrease in net revenue from vacation package bookings, excluding the impact of foreign currency fluctuations, was $1.7 million.

Lower transaction volume due in part to higher average package prices drove an $8.1 million decrease in domestic vacation package net revenue. This decline was partially offset by a $1.2 million increase in domestic vacation package net revenue due to higher average net revenue per transaction, as a result of higher average air fares, higher ADRs and fewer promotional coupons issued by us, partially offset by lower hotel breakage revenue.

International net revenue from vacation packages (excluding the impact of foreign currency fluctuations) increased $5.2 million primarily due to higher transaction volume.

Advertising and media. Advertising and media net revenue decreased $10.2 million, or 17%, for the year ended December 31, 2010 compared with the year ended December 31, 2009. This decrease is primarily due to a $13.1 million decline in net revenue from membership discount programs which we discontinued on our domestic leisure websites effective March 31, 2010. We do not expect to generate any material net revenue from third party membership discount programs on our websites in the future. This decrease was offset in part by additional advertising and media revenue driven by our ongoing efforts to monetize our websites globally.

Other. Other net revenue is comprised primarily of net revenue from car bookings, cruise bookings, destination services, travel insurance and our hosting business. Other net revenue increased $6.8 million, or 6%, for the year ended December 31, 2010 compared with the year ended December 31, 2009.

The increase in other net revenue was primarily driven by higher global travel insurance revenue and higher car net revenue for our domestic leisure brands. Travel insurance revenue increased primarily due to a change in estimate related to the timing of our recognition of this revenue. Historically, we recorded travel insurance revenue one month in arrears, upon receipt of payment, as we did not have sufficient reporting from our travel insurance supplier to conclude that the price was fixed or determinable prior to that time. However, in the first quarter of 2010, our travel insurance supplier implemented more timely reporting, and as a result, we are now able to recognize travel insurance revenue on an accrual basis rather than one month in arrears. Travel insurance revenue further increased due to a higher attachment rate, higher average air fares and higher air transaction volume. Car net revenue for our domestic leisure brands increased primarily due to higher transaction volume, partially offset by lower average daily rates for car rentals. These increases were partially offset by a $6.3 million decline in hosting revenue due primarily to the termination of one of our airline hosting agreements in 2010.

Changes in Estimates

Revenue recognition and financial reporting require various estimates. Examples include estimates of (1) returns for product sales, (2) revenues, costs to complete, and percentage-of-completion for construction contracts, (3) price protection liabilities for product or service sales, and (4) settlements under cost reimbursement arrangements. Estimates, by their very nature, are subject to change. Disclosure regarding a change in estimate generally is not required for routine estimates. However, to the extent a change in a routine estimate is material, disclosure is required. Disclosure also is required if the change in estimate affects several future periods. These disclosures should consist of the effect on income from continuing operations, net income (or, when appropriate, changes in the applicable net assets or performance indicator), and any related per share amounts of the current period.

Certain changes may not have a material effect in the period of change but are reasonably certain to have a material effect in later periods. These changes in estimate must be described in disclosures whenever the financial statements of the period of the change are presented (ASC 250, *Accounting Changes and Error Corrections*; 250-10-50-1).

SEC REGISTRANT ALERT: SEC registrants must disclose material changes in estimated product returns (ASC 605-10-S99, B, ques. 1) (SAB Topic 13B, ques. 1).

EXAMPLES: CHANGE IN ESTIMATE

Response Genetics, Inc. Form 10-K—Fiscal Year Ended December 31, 2010

Effective April 1, 2010, the Company recognizes all product revenue from its ResponseDX tests on an accrual basis. Through March 31, 2010, the Company recognized revenue from Private Payors on a cash basis as the Company had not, until then, established a collection history. As of April 1, 2010, a pattern of collections had been established and the Company began to record revenues from Private Payors of ResponseDX on an accrual basis.

For accounting purposes, the change from the cash basis to the accrual basis of recording revenue for ResponseDX tests paid by Private Payors, is considered a change in accounting estimate leading to a change in accounting principle. The change in accounting estimate was derived from the establishment of a reasonable basis to estimate the amount to be collected from certain Private Payors. This change in estimate resulted in the change in accounting principle from the cash basis to the accrual basis of revenue recognition for ResponseDX tests paid by Private Payors. Accordingly, the Company has recorded in the second quarter a one-time adjustment to increase revenue by $1,507,187, which represents the amount of ResponseDX tests completed in prior periods for which cash payment under the former revenue recognition method had not been received as of April 1, 2010. Since all sales of Response DX tests are on the accrual basis from April 1, 2010, the Company does not expect any future one-time adjustments to revenue. The revenue recorded from ResponseDX sales to Private Payors for the period from April 1, 2010 to December 31, 2010 was $4,388,270. As a result of the conversion from the cash basis to the accrual basis of recording revenue for ResponseDX tests paid by Private Payors, the Company recognized a total of $1,902,667 more in revenue during the year ended December 31, 2010, respectively, than it would have recognized had the Company continued to recognize such amounts on the cash basis during this same period.

The Company has its Medicare provider number which allows it to invoice and collect from Medicare. Invoicing to Medicare is primarily based on amounts allowed by Medicare for the service provided as defined by Common Procedural Terminology (CPT) codes. ResponseDX revenues related to Medicare billings are recorded at established billing rates net of an estimated billing adjustment, based on reporting models utilizing historical cash collection percentages and updated for current effective reimbursement factors. Response DX revenue related to Private Payors are recorded at established billing rates less an allowance to reflect the revenue at the amounts expected based on historical collections patterns.

Orbitz Worldwide, Inc. Form 10-K—Fiscal Year Ended December 31, 2010

During the first quarter of 2010, we had a change in estimate related to the timing of our recognition of travel insurance revenue. Prior to the first quarter of 2010, we recorded travel insurance revenue one month in arrears, upon receipt of payment, as we did not have sufficient reporting from our travel insurance supplier to conclude that the price was fixed or determinable prior to that time. Our travel insurance supplier implemented timelier reporting, and as a result, beginning with the first quarter of 2010, we were able to recognize travel insurance revenue on an accrual basis rather than one month in arrears. This change in estimate resulted in a $2.5 million increase in net revenue and net income and a $0.02 increase in basic and diluted earnings per share for the year ended December 31, 2010.

Risks and Uncertainties

The two primary types of revenue-related risks and uncertainties that must be disclosed relate to the uncertainties inherent in making estimates and the risks inherent in the concentration of business activities.

Estimates

As discussed earlier in this chapter, accounting for sales transactions often requires the use of estimates. For example, when products are sold with return rights, the company must be able to make reasonable and reliable estimates of expected returns prior to recognizing any revenue. A company must disclose any significant estimates involved in accounting for revenues, including the nature of the related uncertainty and an indication that it is at least reasonably possible that a change in those estimates will occur in the near term (ASC 275-10-50-6 through 50-15). In the case of significant estimates of product returns, a company should disclose the existence and nature of the return right, and the fact that it is at least reasonably possible that a change in product return estimates will occur in the near term. In addition, a company is encouraged, but not required, to disclose (a) the factors that cause its estimates to be sensitive to change and (b) the risk-reduction techniques it uses to mitigate losses or the uncertainties that may result from future events (ASC 275-10-50-10 and 50-11).

EXAMPLES: USE OF SIGNIFICANT ESTIMATES

General Electric Company Form 10-K—Fiscal Year Ended December 31, 2009

Revenue recognition on long-term product services agreements requires estimates of profits over the multiple-year terms of such agreements, considering factors such as the frequency and extent of future monitoring, maintenance and overhaul events; the amount of personnel, spare parts and other resources required to perform the services; and future billing rate and cost changes. We routinely review estimates under product services agreements and regularly revise them to adjust for changes in outlook. We also regularly assess customer credit risk inherent in the carrying amounts of receivables and contract costs and estimated earnings, including the risk that contractual penalties may not be sufficient to offset our accumulated investment in the event of customer termination. We gain insight into future utilization and cost trends, as well as credit risk, through our knowledge of the installed base of equipment and the close interaction with our customers that comes with supplying critical services and parts over extended periods. Revisions that affect a product services agreement's total estimated profitability result in an adjustment of earnings; such adjustments increased earnings by $0.2 billion in 2009, decreased earnings by $0.2 billion in 2008 and increased earnings by $0.4 billion in 2007. We provide for probable losses when they become evident.

Qwest Communications International, Inc. Form 10-K—Fiscal Year Ended December 31, 2009

Revenue Recognition and Related Reserves

We recognize revenue for services when the related services are provided. Recognition of certain payments received in advance of services being provided is deferred until the service is provided. These advance payments received, primarily activation fees and installation charges, as well as the associated customer acquisition costs, are deferred and recognized over the expected customer relationship period, which ranges from one to four years. Customer arrangements that include both equipment and services are evaluated to determine whether the elements are separable based on objective evidence. If the elements are deemed separable and separate earnings processes exist, total consideration is allocated to each element based on the relative fair values of the separate elements and the revenue associated with each element is recognized as earned. If these criteria are not satisfied, the total advance payment is deferred and recognized ratably over the longer of the contractual period or the expected customer relationship period.

We believe that the accounting estimates related to customer relationship periods and to the assessment of whether bundled elements are separable are "critical accounting estimates" because: (i) they require management to make assumptions about how long we will retain customers; (ii) the assessment of whether bundled elements are separable is subjective; (iii) the impact of changes in actual retention periods versus these estimates on the revenue amounts reported in our consolidated statements of operations could be material; and (iv) the assessment of whether bundled elements are separable may result in revenue being reported in different periods than significant portions of the related costs.

As the telecommunications market experiences greater competition and customers shift from traditional land-based telecommunications services to wireless and Internet-based services, our estimated customer relationship period could decrease and we will accelerate the recognition of deferred revenue and related costs over a shorter estimated customer relationship period.

Concentrations

A company may concentrate its revenue-related business activities by (1) selling only to a particular customer or a small group of customers, (2) selling only a limited number of products or services, or (3) limiting the market or geographic area in which it operates (ASC 275-10-50-18 through 50-22). While these types of concentrations may represent prudent business decisions, they ultimately carry with them the acceptance of concentration risk. A company that bears concentration risks may be required to disclose those risks if (1) the concentrations make the company vulnerable to the risk of a near-term severe financial statement impact, and (2) it is at least reasonably possible that the events that could cause the severe impact will occur in the near term (ASC 275-10-50-16).

EXAMPLES: CUSTOMER CONCENTRATION RISK

Mattel, Inc. Form 10-K—Fiscal Year Ended December 31, 2009

A small number of customers account for a large share of Mattel's net sales. In 2009, Mattel's three largest customers, Wal-Mart, Toys "R" Us and Target, in the aggregate, accounted for approximately 40% of net sales, and its ten largest customers, in the aggregate, accounted for approximately 50% of net sales. The concentration of Mattel's business with a relatively small number of customers may expose Mattel to a material adverse effect if one or more of Mattel's large customers were to significantly reduce purchases for any reason, favor competitors or new entrants, or increase their direct competition with Mattel by expanding their private-label business. Customers make no binding long-term commitments to Mattel regarding purchase volumes and make all purchases by delivering one-time purchase orders. Any customer could reduce its overall purchases of Mattel's products, reduce the number and variety of Mattel's products that it carries and the shelf space allotted for Mattel's products, or otherwise seek to materially change the terms of the business relationship at any time. Any such change could significantly harm Mattel's business and operating results.

Major Customers

Sales to Mattel's three largest customers accounted for 40%, 38%, and 41% of worldwide consolidated net sales for 2009, 2008, and 2007, respectively, as follows:

	For the Year		
	2009	2008	2007
	(in billions)		
Wal-Mart	$1.0	$1.1	$1.1
Toys "R" Us	0.7	0.7	0.7
Target	0.5	0.5	0.6

The Mattel Girls & Boys Brands US and Fisher-Price Brands US segments sell products to each of Mattel's three largest customers. The International segment sells products to Wal-Mart and Toys "R" Us. The American Girl Brands segment sells its children's publications to Wal-Mart and Target.

Related Party Transactions

The existence of related party transactions raises many questions. What is the nature of the transactions? How significant are the transactions to the company's business? Do the transactions occur on an arm's-length basis? To help address these and other questions, a company is required to disclose certain information regarding revenue-generating transactions with related parties. This information includes (1) the nature of the company's relationship with the related party, (2) the nature of the sales transaction itself, (3) any other information necessary to gain an understanding of the effects the transaction has on the financial statements, (4) the dollar amount of sales transactions to related parties for each of the income statements presented, and (5) period-over-period changes in sales terms with the related parties. These disclosure requirements do not apply to sales transactions that occur in the ordinary course of business or those that are eliminated in consolidation (ASC 850-10-50-1).

When making related party disclosures, a company should take care not to inappropriately represent that transactions with related parties occurred on an arm's-length basis. Such a representation should only be made if it can be substantiated (ASC 850-10-50-5).

SEC REGISTRANT ALERT: In SEC filings, the amount of related party sales should be disclosed on the face of the income statement and statement of cash flows, and the amount of related party accounts receivable should be disclosed on the face of the balance sheet (ASC 235-10-S99) (REG S-X, Rule 4-08(k)). This disclosure is required even if the sales were in the ordinary course of business.

In addition, in early 2003, the SEC staff issued the Report Pursuant to Section 704 of the Sarbanes-Oxley Act of 2002 (Section 704 Report). In compiling the information in the Section 704 Report, the SEC staff studied enforcement actions filed during the period July 31, 1997, through July 30, 2002. One of the areas of improper accounting where a significant number of enforcement actions were brought by the SEC related to disclosure of related party transactions. The SEC staff noted in the Section 704 Report that "Failure to disclose related party transactions hides material information from shareholders and may be an indicator of weaknesses in internal control and corporate governance procedures." This finding is a strong indication that more attention should be given to identifying and disclosing related party transactions.

EXAMPLE: RELATED PARTY SALES

Acxiom Corporation Form 10-K—Fiscal Year Ended March 31, 2009

The Company leased an aircraft from a business owned by a former officer and director. Rent expense under this lease was approximately $0.9 million for the years ended March 31, 2008 and 2007. The lease has been terminated.

The Company paid $0.6 million in fiscal 2007 in NASCAR sponsorship fees to a company which was partially owned by the son of a former officer of the Company until January 2004. Since January 2004, neither the former officer nor his son has an ownership interest in the sponsored company. However, the sponsored company has other ongoing business relationships with both the officer and his son. In return for the sponsorship, the Company received publicity for the Acxiom brand and hospitality facilities for customers at race events.

The Company has an agreement to sell Acxiom products and services to a company whose majority shareholder is a family member of a former officer and director of the Company. Under the agreement, the Company received revenues of approximately $2.6 million in fiscal 2008 and $2.2 million in fiscal 2007. The accounts receivable balance was approximately $0.9 million at March 31, 2008.

Seasonal Revenue

Certain companies experience seasonality in their revenue streams. For example, if a company sells natural gas to residential customers in Illinois where the climate requires significant usage in winter but not summer (because electricity is primarily used to cool homes), the company would expect to sell significantly higher volumes of natural gas in the winter months. If this fact is not explained in the company's interim results, financial statement users may not gain insight into what annual revenues will look like. Therefore, companies that experience seasonality in their revenue streams must disclose the seasonal nature of their activities and consider providing supplemental information in their interim reports consisting of revenues for the 12-month period ended at the interim date for the current and prior years (ASC 270-10-45-11).

EXAMPLE: SEASONAL REVENUE

Reddy Ice Holdings, Inc. Form 10-K—Fiscal Year Ended December 31, 2009

Seasonality

The packaged ice business is highly seasonal, characterized by peak demand during the warmer months of May through September, with an extended peak selling season in the southern United States. Approximately 69%, 69%, 68%, 70%, and 70% of our annual revenues occurred during the second and third calendar quarters in each of 2009, 2008, 2007, 2006 and 2005. For information on our revenues per quarter for each of 2009 and 2008, see Note 17 to our audited financial statements included under Item 8. As a result of seasonal revenue declines and a less than proportional decline in expenses during the first and fourth quarters, we typically experience lower margins resulting in losses during these periods. In addition, because our operating results depend significantly on sales during our peak season, our quarterly and annual results of operations may fluctuate significantly as a result of adverse weather during this peak selling period if the weather is unusually cool or rainy on a national or regional basis.

Presentation-Related Disclosures

Gross versus Net

As discussed in Chapter 11, "Presentation," a company may be required to report revenues on a net basis. For example, a travel agent that bears minimal or no risks related to the airline tickets it sells, must report as revenue only the commission it receives for selling the airline ticket, not the price of the airline ticket itself. In this and other situations where companies are required to report revenues on a net basis, the company is permitted, but not required, to disclose the gross transaction volume related to these net revenues. If gross amounts are disclosed, care should be taken such that these amounts would not be construed as either revenues or part of the total net income or loss (ASC 605-45-50-1).

Shipping and Handling Costs

As discussed in Chapter 11, "Presentation," a company is required to present shipping and handling fees charged to customers as revenue and the related shipping and handling costs it incurs as expense. If the shipping and handling costs are classified within cost of sales on the income statement, no disclosure of such costs is required. If such costs are significant and are not classified within cost of sales, then the amount of shipping and handling costs must be disclosed and the line item in which they are included must be identified (ASC 605-45-50-2).

Excise Taxes

As discussed in Chapter 11, sales or excise taxes that relate directly to sales may be presented as reductions of revenue instead of as an expense. The classification of payments received for such taxes should be disclosed. If significant, the amount included in revenue on a gross basis must be disclosed (ASC 605-45-50-4). SEC registrants must disclose the amount of excise taxes included in revenue if that amount exceeds 1% of sales (ASC 225-10-S99-2) (REG S-X, Rule 5-03).

Disaggregated Information about Revenue

ASC 280 requires SEC registrants to disclose certain information by segment. Certain revenue-related information is required as part of those disclosures (ASC 280-10-50-21, 22; 280-10-50-30, 32; 280-10-50-40 through 50-42).

ASC 205-20 requires the disclosure of certain information related to discontinued operations. Certain revenue-related information is required as part of those disclosures (ASC 205-20-50-6).

SPECIFIC DISCLOSURE REQUIREMENTS

The authoritative literature requires other disclosures that are intended to provide users of financial statements with incremental information about specific sales transactions and the related revenue accounting issues. Many of these disclosure requirements have been promulgated by SEC staff through ASC 605-10-S99 (SAB Topic 13), announcements at EITF meetings, and in documents published by the SEC's Division of Corporation Finance. Although these disclosure requirements are not mandatory for private companies, private entities should strongly consider applying them for the benefit of financial statement users.

LISTING OF APPLICABLE LITERATURE

ASC	ASC Topic/ Subtopic	Publication	Subject
845-10-50	Nonmonetary Transactions/ Overall	APB-29	Accounting for Nonmonetary Transactions
730-20-50	Research and Development/ Research and Development Arrangements	FAS-68	Research and Development Arrangements
460-10	Guarantees/ Overall	FIN-45	Guarantees

ASC	ASC Topic/ Subtopic	Publication	Subject
605-20-50	Revenue Recognition/ Services	EITF 99-17	Accounting for Advertising Barter Transactions
505-50-50	Equity/Equity-Based Payments to Non-Employees	EITF 00-8	Accounting for an Equity Instrument to Be Received in Conjunction with Providing Goods or Services
605-25-50	Revenue Recognition/ Multiple-element Arrangements	ASU 2009-13	Multiple-Deliverable Revenue Arrangements
605-28-50	Revenue Recognition/ Milestone Method	ASU 2010-17	Milestone Method of Revenue Recognition
N/A	N/A	ITC	FASB Invitation to Comment: Accounting for Certain Service Transactions
605-10-S99	Revenue Recognition/ Overall	SAB Topic 13	Revenue Recognition
N/A	N/A	CIRP-8/01	SEC Division of Corporation Finance—Current Issues and Rulemaking Projects (August 2001)
605-20-S99	Revenue Recognition/ Services	EITF D-96	Accounting for Management Fees Based on a Formula

Multiple-Deliverable Revenue Arrangements

Many sales transactions involve more than one item or deliverable. For example, a company may sell equipment and services to install the equipment. The revenue recognition policy, and the timing of revenue recognition, for each of those deliverables may be different, such that the allocation of revenue between or among items would have a major effect on the amount of revenue that should be recognized in an accounting period. This requires consideration of how to separate the deliverables and allocate the amount of consideration to each item. As it relates to multiple-deliverable arrangements, a vendor should disclose the following (ASC 605-25-50) (ASU 2009-13, par 13 and 14) by similar type of arrangement:

- The accounting policy for recognition of revenue from multiple-deliverable arrangements (e.g., whether deliverables are separable into units of accounting);

- The description and nature of such arrangements, including performance-, cancellation-, termination-, or refund-type provisions;

- The nature of a company's contractual arrangements that result in the performance of multiple revenue-generating activities, including the type of products and services to be delivered, and information about the timing of delivery or performance for the deliverables in the arrangement;

- Whether the arrangements requiring multiple deliverables consist of more than one unit of accounting and the basis for this conclusion, including the reasons that deliverables are not separated, if applicable;

- How revenues are allocated between separate units of accounting when there is more than a single unit, including the general timing of revenue recognition for significant units of accounting;

- Information about the determination of selling price for the significant deliverables, including whether vendor-specific objective evidence of third-party evidence of selling price was used, and, if not, the significant inputs and assumptions used to estimate selling price; and

- When it has a significant effect on the allocation of arrangement consideration, the effect and causes of changes in the selling prices of deliverables.

In addition, the accounting policy followed for each unit-of-accounting should be described in the vendor's accounting policy disclosures discussed earlier in this chapter. For example, if a multiple-deliverable arrangement involves the sale and installation of equipment and the multiple-deliverable arrangement is separated for accounting purposes, the accounting policy disclosures should cover the individual accounting policies for each separate item.

SEC REGISTRANT ALERT: SEC registrants must disclose how multiple-deliverable arrangements are determined and valued (ASC 605-10-S99, B, ques. 1) (SAB Topic 13B, ques. 1).

In addition, in early 2003 the SEC staff issued the Summary by the Division of Corporation Finance of Significant Issues Addressed in the Review of the Periodic Reports of the Fortune 500 Companies (Fortune 500 Report). This report resulted from the SEC's Division of Corporation Finance's (Corp Fin) review of all annual reports filed by Fortune 500 companies. The report provides insight into areas commonly questioned by Corp Fin during its reviews of annual reports. One area specifically mentioned in the Fortune 500 Report relates to accounting for multiple-deliverable arrangements. Corp Fin specifically indicated that companies in the computer software, computer services, computer hardware, and communications equipment industries could improve their disclosures by expanding the discussion related to multiple-deliverable arrangements.

EXAMPLE: SEPARATION OF ITEMS, MULTIPLE-DELIVERABLE ARRANGEMENTS

Apple, Inc. Form 10-K/A—Fiscal Year Ended September 26, 2009

Revenue Recognition for Arrangements with Multiple Deliverables

For multi-element arrangements that include tangible products that contain software that is essential to the tangible product's functionality and undelivered software elements that relate to the tangible product's essential software, the Company allocates revenue to all deliverables based on their relative selling prices. In such circumstances, the new accounting principles establish a hierarchy to determine the selling price to be used for allocating revenue to deliverables as follows: (i) vendor-specific objective evidence of fair value ("VSOE"), (ii) third-party evidence of selling price ("TPE"), and (iii) best estimate of the selling price ("ESP"). VSOE generally exists only when the Company sells the deliverable separately and is the price actually charged by the Company for that deliverable.

For both iPhone and Apple TV, the Company has indicated it may from time-to-time provide future unspecified software upgrades and features free of charge to customers. The Company has identified two deliverables generally contained in arrangements involving the sale of iPhone and Apple TV. The first deliverable is the hardware and software essential to the functionality of the hardware device delivered at the time of sale, and the second deliverable is the right included with the purchase of iPhone and Apple TV to receive on a when-and-if-available basis future unspecified software upgrades and features relating to the product's essential software. The Company has allocated revenue between these two deliverables using the relative selling price method. Because the Company has neither VSOE nor TPE for the two deliverables the allocation of revenue has been based on the Company's ESPs. Amounts allocated to the delivered hardware and the related essential software are recognized at the time of sale provided the other conditions for revenue recognition have been met. Amounts allocated to the unspecified software upgrade rights are deferred and recognized on a straight-line basis over the 24-month estimated life of the related hardware. All product cost of sales, including estimated warranty costs, are generally recognized at the time of sale. Costs for engineering and sales and marketing are expensed as incurred.

For all periods presented, the Company's ESP for the software upgrade right included with each iPhone and Apple TV sold is $25 and $10, respectively. The Company's process for determining its ESP for deliverables without VSOE or TPE considers multiple factors that may vary depending upon the unique facts and circumstances related to each deliverable. The Company believes its customers, particularly consumers, would be reluctant to buy unspecified software upgrade rights related to iPhone and Apple TV. This view is primarily based on the fact that upgrade rights do not obligate the Company to provide upgrades at a particular time or at all, and do not specify to customers which upgrades or features will be delivered in the future. Therefore, the Company has concluded that if it were to sell upgrade rights on a standalone basis, such as those included with iPhone and Apple TV, the selling price would be relatively low. Key factors considered by the Company in developing the ESPs for iPhone and Apple TV upgrade rights include prices charged by the Company for similar offerings, the Company's historical pricing practices, the nature of the upgrade rights (e.g., unspecified and when-and-if-available), and the relative ESP of the upgrade rights as compared to the total selling price of the product. In addition, when developing ESPs for products other than iPhone and Apple TV, the Company may consider other factors as appropriate including the pricing of competitive alternatives if they exist, and product-specific business objectives.

The Company accounts for multiple element arrangements that consist only of software or software-related products, including the sale of upgrades to previously sold software, in accordance with industry specific accounting guidance for software and software-related transactions. For such transactions, revenue on arrangements that include multiple elements is allocated to each element based on the relative fair value of each element, and fair value is generally determined by VSOE. If the Company cannot objectively determine the fair value of any undelivered element included in such multiple-element arrangements, the Company defers revenue until all elements are delivered and services have been performed, or until fair value can objectively be determined for any remaining undelivered elements. When the fair value of a delivered element has not been established, but fair value exists for the undelivered elements, the Company uses the residual method to recognize revenue if the fair value of all undelivered elements is determinable. Under the residual method, the fair value of the undelivered elements is deferred and the remaining portion of the arrangement fee is allocated to the delivered elements and is recognized as revenue.

Except as described for iPhone and Apple TV, the Company generally does not offer specified or unspecified upgrade rights to its customers in connection with software sales or the sale of extended warranty and support contracts. A limited number of the Company's software products are available with maintenance agreements that grant customers rights to unspecified future upgrades over the maintenance term on a when and if available basis. Revenue associated with such maintenance is recognized ratably over the maintenance term.

Nonmonetary Revenue Transactions

In general, a company should disclose both the nature of these transactions and the basis for recognizing revenues (ASC 845-10-50). The EITF has addressed the accounting for two specific types of nonmonetary revenue transactions—those where equity instruments are received and barter transactions involving advertising.

PRACTICE ALERT: Round-trip transactions receive a significant amount of attention by the SEC staff and were an area of focus in the SEC staff's 2003 Report Pursuant to Section 704 of the Sarbanes-Oxley Act of 2002 (Section 704 Report). In compiling the information in the Section 704 Report, the SEC staff studied enforcement actions filed during the period July 31, 1997, through July 30, 2002. In addition, round-trip transactions have also been a focus in SEC staff speeches. The SEC staff characterizes round-trip transactions in the Section 704 Report as transactions that "involve simultaneous pre-arranged sales transactions often of the same product in order to create a false impression of business activity and revenue." The SEC staff cited a number of enforcement actions in the Section 704 Report where registrants inappropriately used round-trip transactions to boost revenue. Essentially, the types of round-trip transactions identified by the SEC staff in the Section 704 Report should be treated as nonmonetary transactions (see Chapter 8, "Miscellaneous Issues," regarding accounting for nonmonetary transactions). To the extent a registrant enters into round-trip transactions, appropriate disclosure is required.

Equity Instruments Received in Conjunction with Providing Goods or Services

When a company receives equity instruments in exchange for providing goods or services, it should disclose the amount of gross operating revenue recognized as a result of such transactions (ASC 505-50-50).

EXAMPLE: EQUITY INSTRUMENTS IN EXCHANGE FOR SERVICES

LoJack Corporation Form 10-K—Fiscal Year Ended December 31, 2009

In June 2005, we entered into a ten year trademark license agreement with Absolute Software, Inc., or Absolute, a Vancouver, British Columbia, Canada based computer theft recovery company to brand its consumer offering LoJack for Laptops®. In addition to an annual per unit royalty, we were granted 1,000,000 (on a post split basis) warrants to purchase Absolute's common stock with vesting on a pro rata basis over a five year period commencing on July 1, 2006. We concluded that a measurement date is not achieved until the warrants become vested and exercisable. Prior to reaching a measurement date, the fair value of unvested warrants is calculated utilizing a Black-Scholes option pricing model and the earned and unearned revenue is adjusted to fair value. Once a measurement date has been reached, the fair value of vested warrants is measured and the revenue related to the vested warrants becomes fixed with revenue recognized over the remaining term of the licensing agreement. Subsequent to reaching a measurement date, the vested warrants are accounted for as derivatives, which requires the warrants to be recorded at fair value at each reporting date with any changes in fair value being recorded in the statement of operations. We classify the gains (losses) on investments in other income (expense). During the years ended December 31, 2009, 2008 and 2007, we recognized $879,000, ($997,000) and $2,342,000 in revenue (contra revenue) and $377,000, ($1,290,000) and $575,000 in other income (expense), respectively, related to the Absolute warrants, and the common shares received upon exercise of the warrants that vested in June 2009 and June 2008. In January 2004, together with an affiliate of Comcast Corporation and other investors, the Company launched TV One, an entity formed to operate a cable television network featuring lifestyle, entertainment and news-related programming targeted primarily towards African-American viewers.

Advertising Barter Transactions

A company that enters into advertising barter transactions should disclose the amount of revenue and expense recognized from these arrangements. If the facts and circumstances did not permit the company to record revenue or expense for some or all of these transactions (e.g., fair values were not determinable in accordance with the literature), the company should disclose information such as the volume and type of advertising surrendered and received (ASC 605-20-50).

Guarantees and Indemnifications

Scope

As discussed in Chapter 4, "Multiple-Deliverable Revenue Arrangements," revenue arrangements may include guarantees or indemnifications from one party to the other. Extensive disclosures are required for guarantees and indemnifications that fall within the scope of ASC 460. Guarantees and indemnifications that possess any of the following characteristics fall within the scope of ASC 460 for disclosure purposes, except as described further below (ASC 460-10-15-4):

- Contracts that contingently require the guarantor to make payments (either in cash, financial instruments, other assets, shares of its stock, or provision of services) to the guaranteed party based on changes in an underlying that is related to an asset, liability, or equity security of the guaranteed party.

- Contracts that contingently require the guarantor to make payments (either in cash, financial instruments, other assets, shares of its stock, or provision of services) to the guaranteed party based on another entity's failure to perform under an obligating agreement (performance guarantees).

- Indemnification agreements (contracts) that contingently require the indemnifying party (the guarantor) to make payments to the indemnified party (guaranteed party) based on changes in an underlying that is related to an asset, liability, or equity security of the indemnified party.

- Indirect guarantees of the indebtedness of others even though the payment to the guaranteed party may not be based on changes in an underlying that is related to an asset, liability, or equity security of the guaranteed party.

ASC 460 (FIN-45) does not apply to certain types of guarantees or indemnifications that have one of the above characteristics, in many cases because the accounting and disclosure for the excluded items is covered in other literature. The guarantees and indemnifications that possess one of the above characteristics that are sometimes included in revenue arrangements and are excluded include (ASC 460-10-15-7):

- Guarantees of the residual value of leased property at the end of a lease term by the lessee if the lessee accounts for the lease as a capital lease.

- Guarantees involved in leases that are accounted for as contingent rent.

- Guarantees (or indemnifications) that are issued by either an insurance company or a reinsurance company and accounted for under the related industry-specific authoritative literature, including guarantees embedded in either insurance contracts or investment contracts.

- Vendor rebates where the contract contingently requires the vendor to make payments to the customer based on the customer's sales revenues, number of units sold, or similar events.

- Guarantees (or indemnifications) whose existence prevents the guarantor from being able to either account for a transaction as the sale of an asset or recognize the profit from that sale transaction. An example of this situation is a software arrangement where the software vendor participates in the customer's financing through either (a) indemnifying the financing party against claims beyond the software vendor's standard indemnifications or (b) guaranteeing the customer's loan with the financing party. In these situations, a presumption exists that the fee in the arrangement is not fixed or determinable. If the presumption cannot be overcome, revenue is not recognized until the fee can be deemed fixed or determinable (see Chapter 10, "Software—A Complete Model"). In this situation, it is the guarantee or indemnification that prohibits the recognition of revenue. As a result, the guarantee or indemnification does not fall within the scope of ASC 460.

Despite these exclusions, many guarantees and indemnifications included in sales arrangements are subject to ASC 460. Examples include product warranties; a manufacturer's guarantee of a loan from a third-party lender to its customer to buy the manufacturer's product; and an indemnification in a software licensing agreement that indemnifies the licensee against liability and damages arising from any claims of patent, copyright, trademark, or trade secret infringement by the software vendor's software. Other guarantees and indemnifications included in sales arrangements are discussed in Chapter 4, "Multiple-Deliverable Revenue Arrangements."

Disclosures

When a guarantee or indemnification is subject to ASC 460, the guarantor is required to disclose the following information about each guarantee, or each group of similar guarantees, even if the likelihood of the guarantor having to make any payments under the guarantee is remote (ASC 460-10-50-4):

- The nature of the guarantee, including the approximate term of the guarantee, how the guarantee arose, and the events or circumstances that would require the guarantor to perform under the guarantee.

- Except for product warranties and similar guarantees (which are discussed below), the maximum potential amount of future payments (undiscounted) the guarantor could be required to make under the guarantee. That maximum potential future payment should not be reduced by the effect of any amounts recoverable under recourse or collateralization provisions in the guarantee (the disclosure of which is addressed below in the fourth bullet point). When the terms of the guarantee provide for no limitation to the maximum potential future payments under the guarantee, that fact must be disclosed. When the guarantor is unable to develop an estimate of the maximum potential amount of future payments under its guarantee, the guarantor must disclose the reasons why it cannot estimate this amount.

- The nature of (1) any recourse provisions that would enable the guarantor to recover from third parties any amount paid under the guarantee and (2) any assets held either as collateral or by third parties that, upon the occurrence of any triggering event or condition under the guarantee, the guarantor can obtain and liquidate to recover all or a portion of the amounts paid under the guarantee. The guarantor must indicate, if estimable, the approximate extent to which the proceeds from liquidation of those assets would be expected to cover the maximum potential amount of future payments under the guarantee.

The disclosure of the maximum potential amount of future payments is not required for product warranties and similar guarantees related to the performance of nonfinancial assets owned by the guaranteed party. Instead, the guarantor is required to disclose the following information (ASC 460-10-50-8):

- The guarantor's accounting policy and methodology used in determining its liability for product warranties (including any liability, for example, deferred revenue, associated with extended warranties), and

- A rollforward of the changes in the aggregate product warranty liability for the reporting period. That rollforward should present the beginning balance of the liability, the reductions in that liability for payments made (in cash or in kind) under the warranty, the changes in the liability for accruals related to product warranties issued during the reporting period, the changes in the liability for accruals related to pre-existing warranties (including adjustments related to changes in estimates), and the ending balance of the liability.

EXAMPLE: PRODUCT WARRANTIES

A.T. Cross Company, Form 10-K—Fiscal Year Ended January 2, 2010

Warranty Costs: The Cross Accessory Division's Cross-branded writing instruments are sold with a full warranty of unlimited duration against mechanical failure. CAD's accessories are sold with a one-year warranty against mechanical failure and defects in workmanship and timepieces are warranted for a period of two years. Costa and Native sunglasses are sold with a lifetime warranty against defects in materials and workmanship. Estimated warranty costs are accrued at the time of sale. The most significant factors in the estimation of warranty cost liabilities include the operating efficiency and related cost of the service department, unit sales and the number of units that are eventually returned for warranty repair. The current portions of accrued warranty costs were $0.5 million at January 2, 2010 and January 3, 2009 and were recorded in accrued expenses and other liabilities. The following chart reflects the activity in aggregate accrued warranty costs:

	Years Ended		
	January 2, 2010	January 3, 2009	December 29, 2007
	(Thousands of Dollars)		
Accrued Warranty Costs—Beginning of Year	$1,823	$1,730	$1,736
Warranty costs paid	(592)	(754)	(534)
Warranty costs accrued	375	568	413
Impact of changes in estimates and assumptions	330	252	115
Warranty liabilities assumed	—	27	—
Accrued Warranty Costs—End of Year	$1,936	$1,823	$1,730

Contingencies Related to Revenue Recognition

Any number of contingencies may be present in a revenue transaction—for example, rights of return or refund, customer acceptance conditions, warranties, and price protection. The resolution of these contingencies may have a material effect on the financial statements of future periods. Companies should strongly consider whether the potential effects of these contingencies are significant enough to warrant disclosure.

SEC REGISTRANT ALERT: When such contingencies exist, SEC registrants are required to disclose the following information: (1) the accounting treatment afforded the contingency, (2) significant assumptions used in accounting for the contingency, (3) material changes in the contingency, and (4) reasonably likely uncertainties that may affect the contingency (CIRP-8/01).

In addition, in early 2003 the SEC staff issued the Summary by the Division of Corporation Finance of Significant Issues Addressed in the Review of the Periodic Reports of the Fortune 500 Companies (Fortune 500 Report). This report resulted from the SEC's Division of Corporation Finance's (Corp Fin) review of all annual reports filed by Fortune 500 companies. The report provides insight into areas commonly questioned by Corp Fin during its reviews of annual reports. One area specifically mentioned in the Fortune 500 Report relates to accounting for certain contingencies. Corp Fin specifically indicated that companies in certain industries could improve their disclosures related to contingencies such as price protection and product returns. Specifically:

- Companies in the capital goods, semiconductor, and electronic instruments and controls industries could improve their disclosures related to revenue recognition for products with return or price protection features and customer acceptance provisions.

- Companies in the pharmaceutical and retail industries could improve their disclosures related to product returns, discounts, rebates, and co-operative advertising arrangements.

Fees for Services

In general, a service provider should disclose information concerning unearned service revenues and deferred costs of services, including an indication of the periods in which the related services will be performed (ITC, par. 26). Depending on the nature of the service provided and the terms of the arrangement, additional disclosures may also be required. These situations are discussed below.

SEC REGISTRANT ALERT: If an SEC registrant recognizes revenues from service fees over the service period based on progress towards completion or based on separate contract items or milestones, the registrant must disclose how revenues from service fees are measured. This should include, but may not be limited to, the following:

1. How progress is measured (cost-to-cost, time-and-materials, units-of-delivery, units-of-work-performed);

2. Types of contract payment milestones and how they relate to substantive performance and revenue recognition events;

3. Whether contracts with a single counterparty are combined or bifurcated;

4. Contract items permitting separate revenue recognition and how they are distinguished;

5. Whether the relative fair value or residual method is used to allocate contract revenue among items; and

6. Whether fair value is determined based on vendor-specific evidence or by other means (CIRP-8/01).

Contingent Fees—Management Fees Based on a Formula

Given that acceptable alternatives may exist to account for management fees based on a formula, a company must disclose the accounting policy it elects to account for such fees.

SEC REGISTRANT ALERT: SEC registrants are also required to disclose whether they have recorded any revenue at risk due to future performance contingencies, the nature of the contracts giving rise to the contingencies, and, if material, the amount of any such revenue recorded (ASC 605-20-S99).

Refundable Service Fees

The accounting for refundable service fees is not discussed in the accounting literature. Therefore, whatever policy is applied to these transactions is a choice among available alternatives. Companies with a significant amount of refundable service transactions should therefore disclose the policy used to account for them, in accordance with ASC 235-10.

SEC REGISTRANT ALERT: To the extent an SEC registrant provides services where the fees are refundable, it must disclose the accounting policy followed to account for those refundable fees. The registrant must also provide a rollforward of the unearned revenue and refund obligations liabilities. Such rollforwards should consist of the balance at the beginning of the period, the amount of cash received from customers, the amount of revenue recognized in earnings, the amount of refunds paid, other adjustments (explained), and the balance at the end of the period (ASC 605-10-S99, A4a, ques. 1) (SAB Topic 13A4a, ques. 1).

EXAMPLE: REFUNDABLE FEES

BlackRock, Inc., Form 10-K—Fiscal Year Ended December 31, 2009

The Company receives carried interest from certain alternative investments upon exceeding performance thresholds. BlackRock may be required to return all, or part, of such carried interest depending upon future performance of these investments. BlackRock records carried interest subject to such claw-back provisions as performance fees on its consolidated statements of income upon the earlier of the termination of the alternative investment fund or when the likelihood of claw-back is mathematically improbable. The Company records a deferred carried interest liability to the extent it receives cash or capital allocations prior to meeting the revenue recognition criteria. At December 31, 2009 and 2008, the Company had $13 million and $21 million, respectively, of deferred carried interest recorded in other liabilities on the consolidated statements of financial condition.

Research and Development Activities

When a company is engaged in performing research and development activities for others, it should disclose the significant terms of these arrangements (including royalty agreements, purchase provisions, license agreements, and commitments to provide additional funding or services). It should also disclose the amount of revenue earned and costs incurred under such contracts. If a company has entered into more than one such arrangement, it may exercise judgment in aggregating the arrangements for disclosure purposes (ASC 730-20-50).

If the company accounts for its research and development activities using the milestone method, that fact must be disclosed, and the company must explain how it determines whether milestones are substantive (ASC 605-28-50-2) (ASU 2010-17).

SEC REGISTRANT ALERT: SEC registrants must also disclose how they apply their revenue recognition policies for each major revenue stream (e.g., research and development services, license agreements, product sales, consulting) and payment form (e.g., upfront fees, milestone fees, royalty payments) in their research and development arrangements. If different revenue recognition policies are followed for a particular major revenue stream or payment form due to varying facts and circumstances, or contractual terms, each policy should be separately described. In many cases, especially for recognition of milestone payments, it will be necessary to discuss the facts and circumstances resulting in the culmination of the earnings process (CIRP-8/01).

EXAMPLE: COLLABORATION AND LICENSE AGREEMENT

Regeneron Pharmaceuticals Form 10-K—Fiscal Year Ended December 31, 2009

The Company earns collaboration revenue in connection with collaboration agreements to develop and commercialize product candidates and utilize the Company's technology platforms. The terms of these agreements typically include non-refundable up-front licensing payments, research progress (milestone) payments, and payments for development activities. Non-refundable up-front license payments, where continuing involvement is required of the Company, are deferred and recognized over the related performance period. The Company estimates its performance period based on the specific terms of each agreement, and adjusts the performance periods, if appropriate, based on the applicable facts and circumstances. Payments which are based on achieving a specific performance milestone, involving a degree of risk, are recognized as revenue when the milestone is achieved and the related payment is due and non-refundable, provided there is no future service obligation associated with that milestone. Substantive performance milestones typically consist of significant achievements in the development life-cycle of the related product candidate, such as completion of clinical trials, filing for approval with regulatory agencies, and receipt of approvals by regulatory agencies. In determining whether a payment is deemed to be a substantive performance milestone, the Company takes into consideration (i) the nature, timing, and value of significant achievements in the development life-cycle of the related development product candidate, (ii) the relative level of effort required to achieve the milestone, and (iii) the relative level of risk in achieving the milestone, taking into account the high degree of uncertainty in successfully advancing product candidates in a drug development program and in ultimately attaining an approved drug product. Payments for achieving milestones which are not considered substantive are accounted for as license payments and recognized over the related performance period.

****

In October 2006, the Company entered into a license and collaboration agreement with Bayer HealthCare LLC to globally develop, and commercialize outside the United States, the Company's VEGF Trap for the treatment of eye disease by local administration ("VEGF Trap-Eye"). Under the terms of the agreement, Bayer HealthCare made a non-refundable up-front payment to the Company of $75.0 million. In August 2007, the Company received a $20.0 million milestone payment from Bayer HealthCare (which, for the purpose of revenue recognition, was not considered substantive) following dosing of the first patient in a Phase 3 study of VEGF Trap-Eye in the neovascular form of age-related macular degeneration ("wet AMD"). In July 2009, the Company received a $20.0 million milestone payment from Bayer HealthCare following dosing of the first patient in a Phase 3 study of VEGF Trap-Eye in Central Retinal Vein Occlusion ("CRVO"). In addition, the Company is eligible to receive up to $70 million in additional development and regulatory milestones related to the VEGF Trap-Eye program. The Company is also eligible to receive up to $135 million in sales milestones when and if total annual sales of VEGF Trap-Eye outside the United States achieve certain specified levels starting at $200 million.

The Company will share equally with Bayer HealthCare in any future profits arising from the commercialization of VEGF Trap-Eye outside the United States. If VEGF Trap-Eye is granted marketing authorization in a major market country outside the United States and the collaboration becomes profitable, the Company will be obligated to reimburse Bayer HealthCare out of its share of the collaboration profits for 50% of the agreed upon development expenses that Bayer HealthCare has incurred (or half of $138.4 million as of December 31, 2009) in accordance with a formula based on the amount of development expenses that Bayer HealthCare has incurred and the Company's share of the collaboration profits, or at a faster rate at the Company's option. Within the United States, the Company is responsible for any future commercialization of VEGF Trap-Eye and retains exclusive rights to any future profits from such commercialization in the United States.

Agreed upon VEGF Trap-Eye development expenses incurred by both companies in 2007 and 2008 under a global development plan, were shared as follows:

—	2007	The first $50.0 million was shared equally and the Company was solely responsible for up to the next $40.0 million.
—	2008	The first $70.0 million was shared equally and the Company was solely responsible for up to the next $30.0 million.

In 2009 and thereafter, all development expenses will be shared equally. Neither party was reimbursed for any development expenses that it incurred prior to 2007. The Company is also obligated to use commercially reasonable efforts to supply clinical and commercial product requirements.

Bayer HealthCare has the right to terminate the Bayer Agreement without cause with at least six months or twelve months advance notice depending on defined circumstances at the time of termination. In the event of termination of the agreement for any reason, the Company retains all rights to VEGF Trap-Eye.

For the period from the collaboration's inception in October 2006 through September 30, 2007, all up-front licensing, milestone, and cost-sharing payments received or receivable from Bayer HealthCare had been fully deferred and included in deferred revenue for financial statement purposes. In the fourth quarter of 2007, Regeneron and Bayer HealthCare approved a global development plan for VEGF Trap-Eye in wet AMD. The plan included estimated development steps, timelines, and costs, as well as the projected responsibilities of and costs to be incurred by each of the companies. In addition, in the fourth quarter of 2007, Regeneron and Bayer HealthCare reaffirmed the companies' commitment to a diabetic macular edema ("DME") development program and had initial estimates of development costs for VEGF Trap-Eye in DME. As a result, effective in the fourth quarter of 2007, the Company determined the appropriate accounting policy for payments from Bayer HealthCare and cost-sharing of the Company's and Bayer HealthCare's VEGF Trap-Eye development expenses. The $75.0 million up-front licensing payment and the $20.0 million milestone payment received in August 2007 from Bayer HealthCare are being recognized as collaboration revenue over the related estimated performance period in accordance with the Company's revenue recognition policy as described in Note 2. In periods when the Company recognizes VEGF Trap-Eye development expenses that the Company incurs under the collaboration, the Company also recognizes, as collaboration revenue, the portion of those VEGF Trap-Eye development expenses that is reimbursable from Bayer HealthCare. In periods when Bayer HealthCare incurs agreed upon VEGF Trap-Eye development expenses that benefit the collaboration and Regeneron, the Company also recognizes, as additional research and development expense, the portion of Bayer HealthCare's VEGF Trap-Eye development expenses that the Company is obligated to reimburse. In the fourth quarter of 2007, the Company commenced recognizing previously deferred payments from Bayer HealthCare and cost-sharing of the Company's and Bayer HealthCare's 2007 VEGF Trap-Eye development expenses through a cumulative catch-up.

The Company recognized $67.3 million, $31.2 million, and $35.9 million of collaboration revenue from Bayer HealthCare in 2009, 2008, and 2007, respectively. In 2009, collaboration revenue from Bayer HealthCare included the $20.0 million milestone payment received in July 2009 which, for the purpose of revenue recognition, was considered substantive. In addition, in 2009, 2008, and 2007, the Company recognized as additional research and development expense $37.7 million, $30.0 million, and $10.6 million, respectively, of VEGF Trap-Eye development expenses that the Company was obligated to reimburse to Bayer HealthCare.

Bill and Hold Sales Transactions

When revenue is recognized before delivery in a product sale, a company is exposed to greater risks than in a transaction where revenue is only recognized after delivery. Therefore, a company that recognizes revenue before delivery in bill and hold transactions should disclose this policy if the amount of revenue recognized in bill and hold transactions is material.

SEC REGISTRANT ALERT: When revenue is recognized on bill and hold sales, registrants should disclose the risks and uncertainties surrounding warehousing arrangements with distributors and their potential effect on the financial statements. This disclosure might include the registrant's relationship with distributors, that fixed commitments to purchase goods are obtained prior to revenue recognition, whether the registrant has modified its normal billing and credit terms, or that the distributor carries the risk of decline in the market value of bill and hold inventory.

INDUSTRY-SPECIFIC DISCLOSURE REQUIREMENTS

All companies, regardless of industry affiliation, are subject to the general and specific disclosure requirements discussed in the previous sections of this chapter. In addition to these requirements, the authoritative literature mandates incremental disclosures for certain industries. The industry-specific disclosure requirements for construction contractors and franchisors are discussed below. In addition, a list of authoritative literature with other industry-specific disclosure requirements is also provided.

LISTING OF APPLICABLE LITERATURE

ASC	ASC Topic/ Subtopic	Publication	Subject
912	Contractors— Federal Government	ARB-43	Government Contractors
605-35-50	Revenue Recognition/ Construction-Type and Production-Type Contracts	ARB-45 and SOP 81-1	Contract Accounting
952-605-50	Franchisors/ Revenue Recognition	FAS-45	Franchise Fee Revenue
932	Extractive Activities—Oil and Gas	FAS-69	Disclosures about Oil and Gas Producing Activities, an amendment of FASB Statements 19, 25, 33, and 39
980	Regulated Operations	FAS-71	The Effects of Certain Types of Regulation
942	Financial Services— Depository and Lending	SOP 01-6	Accounting by Certain Entities (Including Entities with Trade Receivables) That Lend to or Finance the Activities of Others
940	Financial Services— Brokers and Dealers	AAG-BRD	Brokers and Dealers in Securities
910	Contractors— Construction	AAG-CON	Construction Contractors

ASC	ASC Topic/ Subtopic	Publication	Subject
954	Health Care Entities	AAG-HCO	Health Care Organizations
N/A	N/A	ARA-1991	Frequent Flyer Programs
210-10-S99	Balance Sheet/ Overall	REG S-X, Rule 5-02	Financial Statement Requirements, Commercial and Industrial Companies, Balance Sheets
605-15-S99-3	Revenue Recognition/ Products	SAB Topic 8B	Retail Companies Finance Charges

Construction Contractors

In general, a construction contractor should disclose the basic accounting policy it has adopted to account for revenues from construction contracts. This disclosure should include a discussion of the method used to (1) account for construction-related revenues and costs (e.g., percentage-of-completion, completed contract) and (2) segment or combine construction contracts for accounting purposes (ASC 605-35-50-1). To the extent the contractor deviates from its basic accounting policy (because the facts and circumstances and relevant accounting literature support such a deviation), that deviation should be disclosed (ASC 605-35-50-3; 605-35-50-5).

Percentage-of-Completion

Contractors must disclose the method(s) used to measure progress toward completion (e.g., effort expended, units produced) (ASC 605-35-50-2).

Completed Contract

The contractor must disclose the criteria used to determine when a contract is "complete" (ASC 605-35-50-4).

Claims

To the extent a contractor recognizes revenue related to a claim, the amounts recorded should be disclosed (ASC 605-35-50-6). To the extent a contractor does not meet the requirements to record the claim or the amount of the claim exceeds the recorded contract costs, the contractor should consider whether disclosure of the related contingent asset is required (ASC 605-35-50-8). If a contractor adopts a policy of not recognizing revenue related to a claim until the amounts have been received or awarded, that policy should be disclosed (ASC 605-35-50-7). See the Jacobs Engineering disclosure of claims in Chapter 9, "Contract Accounting."

Subsequent Events

Events occurring after the date of the financial statements that are outside the normal exposure and risk aspects of the contract should be disclosed as subsequent events (ASC 605-35-50-10).

Costs

Given the uniqueness of accounting for construction contract costs, there are incremental disclosure requirements related to these costs. These requirements include disclosing total contract costs related to unapproved change orders, claims or other items subject to similar uncertainties surrounding their determination or realizability. In addition to the aggregate amount, the contractor should also disclose (1) the nature and status of the significant items included in the total and (2) the basis on which these amounts are recorded (e.g., cost or realizable value). To the extent progress payments have been netted against contract costs at the balance sheet date, the contractor should disclose those netted amounts as well (ASC 910-20-50).

For precontract costs or other costs deferred as a result of an unapproved change order, the contractor should disclose its deferral policy and the related amounts (ASC 910-20-50).

SEC REGISTRANT ALERT: Registrants are also required to make the following disclosures related to contract costs: (1) when program accounting is applied, the assumptions used, including total units estimated to be sold under the program, units delivered, and units on order, (2) amounts of manufacturing and other costs incurred on long-term contracts carried forward under the "learning curve" concept put forth in ASC 605-35 and the portion of those costs that would not be absorbed in cost of sales on existing firm orders, (3) amounts that are not expected to be recorded under contract, and (4) the elements of deferred costs (ASC 210-10-S99) (REG S-X, Rule 5-02.6).

Receivables

The unique nature of accounting for construction contracts also results in receivable balances with attributes that may not necessarily be found in receivables related to normal product or service sales. This gives rise to incremental disclosure requirements related to construction contract receivables. These requirements include disclosing the following receivable balances as of the balance sheet date (ASC 910-310-50-1 through 50-3):

1. For billed or unbilled amounts subject to uncertainty regarding their determination or realizability (e.g., unapproved change orders, claims) the contractor must disclose, either on the face of the balance sheet or in a note thereto, (a) the amount, (b) a description of the nature and status of the significant items included in the amount, and (c) the portion, if any, expected to be collected after one year.

2. For other unbilled amounts, the contractor must disclose (a) the amounts, (b) a general description of the prerequisites for billing, and (c) the portion, if any, expected to be collected after one year.

3. For retainages billed but not collected, a contractor must disclose, either on the face of the balance sheet or in a note thereto, (a) the amounts included, (b) the portion (if any) expected to be collected after one year,

and, (c) if practicable, the years in which the amounts are expected to be collected.

In addition, to the extent receivables include amounts with maturities beyond one year, the following should be disclosed: (a) the amount that matures after one year, (b) if practicable, the amounts maturing in each year, and (c) either (i) the related interest rates, (ii) an indication of the average interest rate on all receivables, or (iii) the range of rates on all receivables (ASC 910-310-50-4).

SEC REGISTRANT ALERT: The SEC staff requires all registrants (i.e., all commercial and industrial companies, not just those considered long-term contractors) that enter into long-term contracts to make the same disclosures required of a construction contractor. For purposes of this view the SEC staff defines long-term contracts as (1) all contracts accounted for under the percentage-of-completion method and (2) any contracts or programs accounted for on the completed contract basis that involve material amounts of inventories or unbilled receivables and that will be performed over a period in excess of 12 months (ASC 210-10-S99) (REG S-X, Rules 5-02.3 and 5-02.6).

Franchisors

Franchise agreements capture the significant commitments and obligations of the franchisor. The nature of these commitments and obligations should be disclosed by the franchisor (ASC 952-440-50).

Franchise Fees

As it relates specifically to franchise fees, the franchisor must disclose the following:

1. Information about any franchise fee revenue being recognized on the cost recovery or installment basis due to collectibility concerns (ASC 952-605-50-1); and

2. The portion of franchise fees represented by initial rather than continuing franchise fees (ASC 952-605-50-2).

Regarding initial franchise fees, the following disclosures should also be made, if significant:

1. Relative contribution of initial franchise fees to net income; and

2. Likelihood that initial franchise fees will decline in the future due to franchise sales reaching a saturation point (ASC 952-605-50-2).

Franchisor-Owned versus Franchised Outlets

Franchisors must present specific information for both franchisor-owned outlets and franchised outlets. This information includes revenue- and cost-related information for each outlet group. In addition, to the extent there are significant changes in the number of franchisor-owned or franchised outlets during the period, the number of franchises sold and purchased must be disclosed along with the number of franchisor-owned and franchised outlets in operation (ASC 952-605-50-3).

EXAMPLE: FRANCHISE FEES

McDonald's Corporation Form 10-K—Fiscal Year Ended December 31, 2010

Revenue Recognition

The Company's revenues consist of sales by Company-operated restaurants and fees from franchised restaurants operated by conventional franchisees, developmental licensees and foreign affiliates.

Sales by Company-operated restaurants are recognized on a cash basis. The Company presents sales net of sales tax and other sales-related taxes. Revenues from conventional franchised restaurants include rent and royalties based on a percent of sales with minimum rent payments, and initial fees. Revenues from restaurants licensed to foreign affiliates and developmental licensees include a royalty based on a percent of sales, and may include initial fees. Continuing rent and royalties are recognized in the period earned. Initial fees are recognized upon opening of a restaurant or granting of a new franchise term, which is when the Company has performed substantially all initial services required by the franchise arrangement.

Franchise Arrangements

Conventional franchise arrangements generally include a lease and a license and provide for payment of initial fees, as well as continuing rent and royalties to the Company based upon a percent of sales with minimum rent payments that parallel the Company's underlying leases and escalations (on properties that are leased). Under this arrangement, franchisees are granted the right to operate a restaurant using the McDonald's System and, in most cases, the use of a restaurant facility, generally for a period of 20 years. These franchisees pay related occupancy costs including property taxes, insurance and maintenance. Affiliates and developmental licensees operating under license agreements pay a royalty to the Company based upon a percent of sales, and may pay initial fees.

The results of operations of restaurant businesses purchased and sold in transactions with franchisees were not material either individually or in the aggregate to the consolidated financial statements for periods prior to purchase and sale.

Revenues from franchised restaurants consisted of:

In millions	2010	2009	2008
Rents	$5,198.4	$4,841.0	$4,612.8
Royalties	2,579.2	2,379.8	2,275.7
Initial fees	63.7	65.4	73.0
Revenues from franchised restaurants	$7,841.3	$7,286.2	$6,961.5

Future minimum rent payments due to the Company under existing franchise arrangements are:

In millions	Owned sites	Leased sites	Total
2011	$ 1,244.4	$ 1,104.6	$ 2,349.0
2012	1,213.7	1,075.6	2,289.3

In millions	Owned sites	Leased sites	Total
2013	1,177.1	1,038.5	2,215.6
2014	1,132.6	986.9	2,119.5
2015	1,075.3	926.1	2,001.4
Thereafter	8,664.2	6,715.1	15,379.3
Total minimum payments	$14,507.3	$11,846.8	$26,354.1

At December 31, 2010, net property and equipment under franchise arrangements totaled $13.4 billion (including land of $3.9 billion) after deducting accumulated depreciation and amortization of $6.7 billion.

CHAPTER 13
FUTURE EXPECTATIONS

CONTENTS

BACKGROUND

Financial reporting issues in revenue recognition have increasingly occupied the financial reporting community in recent years. As a result, standard-setters around the world have undertaken a wide range of revenue-related projects. Some of these projects have brought changes in accounting for topics such as multiple-deliverable arrangements and research collaborations.

However, a far more significant change to the accounting literature on revenue recognition now appears to be on the horizon, as the FASB and IASB seem to be on track to completing a major project on revenue recognition in 2012.

This project would replace virtually all the guidance that currently exists on revenue recognition with a single model to be applied to all contracts with customers. Guidance would also be provided on accounting for certain costs of revenues. There would be no industry- or transaction-specific revenue recognition guidance. While the accounting for most revenue transactions, such as retail sales to consumers, would likely remain the same, many companies would see significant changes to their revenue recognition policies.

The primary goal of the project is to develop a comprehensive revenue recognition framework that provides broadly applicable guidance. In doing so, the FASB intends to reduce complexity, eliminate inconsistencies in existing revenue recognition standards and practices, and establish clear principles that can be applied in addressing questions or issues as they arise. Further, because the project is a joint project with the IASB and the two Boards are, so far, in agreement on all aspects of the project, it appears likely that the completion of the project will result in convergence between U.S. GAAP and IFRS in this important area. The FASB and IASB issued an exposure draft entitled "Revenue from Contracts with Customers" in late June 2010. After receiving comments, the boards redeliberated the conclusions in the 2010 exposure draft and plan to issue a second exposure draft in the 4th quarter of 2011 (the "ED").

Although the ED had not yet been issued as this book was being written, substantive deliberations had been completed. This chapter should, therefore, be accurate in terms of describing the proposal in the ED. However, additional detail is likely to emerge when the is available. An update of this chapter will be posted to CCH's Accounting Research Manager in early 2013 to reflect any additional insight gleaned from the ED once it is published. This chapter provides an overview of the proposals that are expected to be in the ED. (Although the ED had not yet been issued as this book was being written, substantive deliberations had been completed.) Its organization generally follows the organization of Chapters 3 through 12 of this publication. Of course, this discussion is preliminary based on only several weeks of review and consideration and will likely refine the understanding of the potential effects of the proposals. In addition, of course, the FASB and IASB will redeliberate all of these proposals again before the final standard is issued. The boards plan to issue the new standard, after receiving comment on and redeliberating the proposals in the ED, in the 2nd or 3rd quarter of 2012. It is intended that the new standard would be applied retroactively (i.e., previous reporting periods would be recast to reflect the new guidance), with some concessions to make retroactive application easier. The effective date of the new standard has not yet been determined, but the Boards have indicated that it will not be effective before calendar year 2015.

By definition, anybody reading this book must have some interest in revenue recognition accounting. Given that interest, it is important that readers not only follow the redeliberations of the proposals in this exposure draft as they occur, but also provide their input to those redeliberations. Information on the status of the project and on opportunities to provide input to the FASB can be found, along with the exposure draft itself, at www.fasb.org.

GENERAL PRINCIPLES

Contracts with Customers

The ED would apply to recognition of revenue from all contracts with customers except leases and a few other narrow topics. The guidance in the ED is also not intended to apply to certain arrangements in which companies collaborate with a goal of together producing a product for sale, even if the collaborators make payments to each other as well. In these arrangements, the collaboration partners are not acting as customers of one another. Companies in a few industries, such as agriculture and the production of commodities, traditionally recognize revenue without respect to whether a customer contract exists, but the vast majority of revenue transactions would be within the scope of the new standard.

Contract Existence

The exposure draft would require that, for a contract to exist for the purposes of revenue recognition:

- The contract must have commercial substance (i.e., the entity's future cash flows must be expected to change as a result of the contract);
- The parties to the contract must have approved the contract and be expected to satisfy their respective obligations;
- The entity must be able to identify each party's rights regarding the goods or services to be transferred; and
- The entity must be able to identify the terms and manner of payment for those goods or services.

In addition, the ED specifies that if both parties can terminate the contract before any performance occurs, the contract does not exist for purposes of revenue recognition.

These criteria, in general, are similar to the evaluation required under current GAAP to determine whether there is "persuasive evidence of an arrangement." The exposure draft points out, again consistent with current GAAP, that contracts need not be written. Rather, an entity's practices and processes for establishing a contract would be considered in assessing whether the above criteria are met.

Contract Combination

The exposure draft would require that legally separate contracts be combined for accounting purposes (i.e., they would be treated as one contract) if the contracts were entered into contemporaneously with the same or related counterparties if one or more of the following are true:

- The contracts were negotiated as a package with a common commercial objective;
- The fee in one contract depends upon aspects of the other contract; or
- Some or all of the goods or services in one contract would be combined with some or all of the goods or services in the other contract into a single

performance obligation under the principles in the ED related to identifying separate performance obligations.

If two contracts are combined for revenue recognition purposes, the consideration received by the seller would be aggregated and allocated to individual performance obligations (see subsequent discussion) without regard to the amounts specified in the individual contracts.

In general, this guidance is consistent with current practice under existing standards, as described in Chapter 4, "Multiple-Deliverable Revenue Arrangements." However, as the contract combination guidance in GAAP today is narrowly-scoped, there may be entities that are not considering that guidance at all. The ED's proposals would, of course, be applicable to all entities.

Contract Modifications

U.S. GAAP provides very little guidance on accounting for contract modifications, with the result being that there is diversity in practice as to when modifications are taken into account and how their effects are recognized.

For example, assume a contract to provide three years of services at $100,000 per year is modified half-way through the third year to change the annual price for the third year to $70,000 and add three more years to the contract at $70,000 per year. Under current practice, some might book the cumulative effect of the change, and conclude that the contract is now a six-year contract with a total fee of $480,000, such that revenue for the two and a half years already passed should be adjusted to be $200,000 by "derecognizing" $50,000 in previously recognized revenue, which would be recognized over the remaining four years of the contract.

However, the more common treatment for such a modification would be to recognize the effects prospectively, not adjust previously recognized revenue, and simply recognize only $20,000 in additional revenue during year three, and then $70,000 per year for the remainder of the contract. As there is little guidance in U.S. GAAP on modifications, both methods would generally be considered acceptable.

Under the exposure draft, the effect of contract modifications would be determined when the modification meets the requirements to be considered part of the contract, using an analysis similar to the one described above under "Contract Existence." At that time, a modification that only changes the transaction price would be treated like any other change in the transaction price (see discussion below). The modification would be treated as a separate contract if it results only in the addition of a new performance obligation at a price consistent with the value of that new performance obligation and makes no other significant changes to the contract. When these criteria are met, the modification would not affect the accounting for the original contract.

If, however, the modification changes the contract in any other way, the contract would be re-evaluated at the date of the modification. In substance, the remaining performance obligations in the modified contract would be treated as a new contract. The transaction price to be applied in in evaluating the modified contract would be the modified transaction price less the amounts previously allocated to performance obligations that were satisfied in full prior to the modification. Therefore, the effect of the modification would generally be reflected prospectively.

However, performance obligations that were partially satisfied at the modification date would be included in the new analysis. Therefore, the amounts assigned to those obligations could change, resulting in a need to book a cumulative adjustment to revenue previously recognized on those partially-satisfied obligations.

For the example above, the application of the guidance in the ED would be to consider the remaining performance obligation in the modified contract as a new contract. The remaining performance obligations include the added years 4–6, as well as half of the obligation related to year 3. The consideration for those four performance obligations is $280,000, or $70,000 per year. As the obligation related to year 3 is 50% completed at the modification date, $35,000 in revenue should be recognized related to that obligation. Based on the pre-modification contract, $50,000 would have already been recognized, meaning that $15,000 in revenue would be "de-recognized" in a cumulative catch-up adjustment. The revenue recognized for years 1 and 2 under the original contract would not be affected, however, as those performance obligations were fully satisfied at the modification date.

This guidance would likely change the accounting for modifications for many companies in several ways. First, the prescribed treatment for determining whether to record a cumulative adjustment is likely not consistent with current practice for most companies. In addition, the fact that modifications are only to be considered whether they meet the criteria to be part of the contract will be significant change for many entities that follow contract accounting under ASC 605-35, as modifications are often taken into account before they are formally added to the contract.

Satisfaction of Performance Obligations

The exposure draft would require that revenue be recognized when an entity satisfies a performance obligation identified in the contract by transferring goods or services to the customer. In many instances, a performance obligation is satisfied at a single point in time—for example, when a purchased product is physically delivered to the customer. In other instances, performance occurs continuously over a period of time—for example, a provider of transaction processing services satisfies its obligation to its customer over time as it performs those services.

This requirement is comparable to the "Delivery" requirement under current GAAP, and both the Completed Performance and Proportional Performance models, as discussed throughout this book, would be applicable under the guidance in the exposure draft.

Typically, an obligation that is deemed to be satisfied at a single point in time would result in revenue recognition when work is completed; while an obligation that is satisfied over time would lead to revenue recognition as the work is performed. Therefore, concluding that a performance obligation is satisfied over time would generally result in earlier revenue recognition.

The ED includes guidance to help determine whether an obligation is satisfied over time or not, and provides that this is the case if either:

- *Performance of work creates or enhances an asset that is controlled by the customer as the work is performed.* For example, a construction contract that builds on land owned by the customer would likely conclude that this criterion is met.

- *Performance does not create an asset with alternative use to the vendor, and either:*

  — The customer receives a benefit as the work is performed.

  — A replacement vendor, if brought in to complete the work, would not need to reperform work already done.

  — The vendor has a right to payment for performance to date even if the customer could cancel the contract for convenience.

Given these criteria, it is likely that most contracts that are accounted for under the Proportional Performance model under today's GAAP would continue to be accounted for that way.

For contracts satisfied at a point in time, the ED specifies that satisfaction would be deemed to occur when the customer obtains control of the promised good or service, as evidenced by the customer's ability to direct the use of and receive the benefit from, that good or service. While judgment will be necessary to determine when the customer has control of a good or service, the exposure draft notes that the following factors are all indicators that control has passed:

1. *The customer has an unconditional obligation to pay.* If a customer is unconditionally obliged to pay for a good or service, typically that is because the customer has obtained control of the good or service in exchange. An obligation to pay is unconditional when nothing other than the passage of time is required before the payment is due.

2. *The customer has legal title.* Legal title often indicates which party has the ability to direct the use of, and receive the benefit from, a good. Benefits of legal title include the ability to sell a good, exchange it for another asset, or use it to secure or settle debt. Hence, the transfer of legal title often coincides with the transfer of control. However, in some cases, possession of legal title is a protective right and may not coincide with the transfer of control to a customer.

3. *The customer has physical possession.* In many cases, the customer's physical possession of a good gives the customer the ability to direct the use of that good. In some cases, however, physical possession does not coincide with control of a good. For example, in some consignment and in some sale and repurchase arrangements, an entity may have transferred physical possession but retained control of a good. Conversely, in

some bill-and-hold arrangements, the entity may have physical possession of a good that the customer controls.

4. *Risks and rewards of ownership have passed to the customer.* If the risks and rewards of ownership have passed to the buyer, it is likely that control has passed as well. On the other hand, the more risks and rewards that the seller retains, the more likely it is that the seller retains control.

In most instances, it seems that this guidance would lead to a conclusion on "delivery" under the Completed Performance model that is the same as the conclusion that would be reached under current GAAP.

Transaction Price

Variable Consideration

The exposure draft specifies that revenue recognition is to be based on allocating to the consideration to be received by the seller to the individual performance obligations in the contract. For many contracts, measuring the consideration to be received is simple, as the contract states a fixed price. However, some contracts have prices that vary based on the vendor's performance, the customer's use of the goods or services, or other factors.

The exposure draft indicates that the objective in dealing with uncertain consideration is to estimate the amount that the vendor will be entitled to receive under the contract. Making such an estimate could involve measuring the probability-weighted amount of consideration expected to be owed or predicting the most likely outcome of a contingency. The vendor would use whichever of those methods it expects would be most predictive of the amount to which the entity will actually be entitled.

Consider an arrangement where an entity agrees to provide a service for a fee of $1,000, with the possibility of earning an additional $100 if the service is completed before a particular date. If the entity enters into many similar contracts with these terms with many customers in the same market, it is likely that the entity would have the ability to estimate the likelihood of completing the service before the specified date. For example, historical evidence may suggest that the company meets the target date 70% of the time. In that case, the entity would initially estimate the transaction price at $1,070 for each transaction. If historical experience holds true, the outcome of the large number of transactions would, on average, result in $1,070 of consideration being due, even though some transactions would result in $1,000 and some $1,100.

On the other hand, if the contract with the potential bonus is a unique contract for the entity, applying the "most likely" method would produce a better estimate of the actual amount to be collected, as the lack of a large pool of similar transactions would prevent the entity from, on average, collecting the $1,070 that a probability-weighted estimate would provide. In this situation, if the entity believed there was a 70% chance of meeting the performance target, it would initially measure the transaction price at $1,100.

This guidance on estimating an uncertain transaction price would require an estimate to be made no matter how reliable that estimate would be. That is, a company would be required to make an estimate even if it had no experience with arrangements and even if the factors creating the uncertainty were entirely in the customer's control, such as a transaction price that varies based on customer usage of a piece of equipment. In either case, initial estimates of the transaction price would be adjusted over time through the completion of the contract, with allocation to performance obligations being adjusted as the transaction prices estimates change.

However, in order to ensure that revenue that is subject to excessive uncertainty is not recognized, the ED would limit the amount of revenue to be recognized under a contract at any point in time to the amount that the entity is reasonably assured of being entitled to. Amounts subject to variability would not be considered to be reasonably assured of being due if any of the following were true:

- *The customer could avoid the payment by making choices without breaching the contract.* A sales-based royalty would meet this criterion.

- *The entity has no (or very little) experience with similar contracts in similar circumstances.* Therefore, as an entity moves into a new line of business, a new market, or a new regulatory environment, it would likely be unable to conclude, for some period of time, that any amounts subject to variability were reasonably assured to become due.

This guidance in the proposed exposure draft addresses the issue of the "Fixed or Determinable Fee." Current GAAP generally requires that any amounts that are not initially fixed or determinable be considered part of the transaction fee only when the uncertainty is resolved. However, the exposure draft would loosen that restriction, allowing the contingent payments to be taken into account in revenue recognition as long as the likelihood of earning the payment was at least reasonably assured, and the outcome of the uncertainty was not in the customer's control.

Collectibility

Under the guidance in the exposure draft, collectibility would not be a consideration in terms of recognizing revenue, as it currently is under U.S. GAAP. Instead, revenue would always be recognized based upon the consideration due under the contract, regardless of the likelihood of collection. However, estimates of losses due to non-collectibility would be recorded when revenue is initially recognized and updated subsequently. Those non-collectibility (or "bad debt") losses would be recorded in a contra-revenue account, not as a separate expense.

This would be a very different treatment than provided for under current standards, which provide that no revenue should be recognized if collectibility is not reasonably assured. In addition, the requirement that all losses due to non-collection be reflection as reductions of revenue is also a change from current practice, which typically recognizes such losses as a selling expense.

Time Value of Money

The exposure draft requires that the estimated transaction price be adjusted to reflect the time value of money if there is a significant financing component to the transaction, which may exist if payment to the seller occurs significantly before or after the transfer of goods or services to the customer. The ED provides, however, that if the period between payment and transfer of goods and services is less than one year, no financing component need be recognized.

In the event there is a significant financing component in a transaction, the result will either be interest income or expense to reflect the implicit lending or borrowing. If payment is received significantly in advance, interest expense would be accrued between the time payment is received and revenue is recognized, with the accrued interest being added to the amount of revenue to be recognized. If payment is to be received significantly after the performance obligation is satisfied, revenue would initially be recognized at a discounted amount, with interest income being recognized until payment is received.

Current U.S. GAAP does not require interest expense to be recognized on advance payments, so the requirement to recognize the implicit borrowing on long-term advance payments would be a change for some companies. In practice, interest income is typically recognized under current GAAP if payment is due more than one year after delivery, so there may be little change in this area.

Onerous Performance Obligations

A long-standing question in U.S. GAAP is whether losses on contracts should be recognized when those losses are estimated, or only when the losses are actually incurred. The exposure draft would resolve this question by requiring that a loss be recognized for any performance obligation that is satisfied over a long period of time for which the expected costs of performance exceed the transaction price allocated to that performance obligation.

The limitation of the onerous guidance to obligations satisfied over a long period of time will essentially mean that losses are only recorded under this test for long-term service obligations for which costs are estimated to exceed the allocated revenue. The amount of the loss to be recorded would be the lower of the excess of expected costs over the allocated revenue or a stated termination fee. The estimates of such losses would be updated continuously until the performance obligation has been satisfied.

Losses on sales of goods for less than cost, while generally not within the scope of the onerous performance obligation guidance, would continue to be recognized under inventory accounting guidance by recording the inventory at the lower of cost or market.

Overall, the different between current GAAP and the proposal in the ED is likely to be small, as contract losses are rarely recognized outside of long-term service contracts today. However, the fact that the new guidance would be broadly applicable, and would be applied at the performance obligation level (rather than the contract level) could lead to more onerous contract losses being recorded.

Breakage

As discussed in Chapter 3, "General Principles," GAAP does not currently provide guidance on addressing situations in which customers do not exercise all of their rights to goods or services. As such, there is significant diversity in practice regarding the effect of breakage on revenue recognition.

As this issue has become more significant in recent years, some practitioners have favored a model that allows this "breakage" to be taken into account if sufficient experience exists such that the amount of breakage is reasonable estimable. In those cases, the total revenue from the transaction would be allocated to the performance obligations that are expected to be fulfilled, rather than all of the contractual obligations. In the event breakage cannot be reasonably estimated, practice generally recognizes revenue taking into account all contractual obligations, with the revenue allocated to those obligations that are not fulfilled only when the likelihood of the customer claiming its rights to those goods or services is remote, which may not be until the right expires.

The exposure draft includes guidance with respect to breakage that is largely consistent with the model described in the previous paragraph. For companies following that model, then, the ED's proposals would not result in significant change. However, as practice is diverse, other companies would experience significant change.

Changes in Estimates

Although revenue recognition under current GAAP requires numerous estimates, revenue recognition under the exposure draft would require even more estimates. Whenever estimates are used in accounting, the question arises about how to account for changes in those estimates. Different parts of GAAP treat changes in estimates differently. Sometimes—for example, a change in estimated useful life of a long-lived asset—changes in estimates are accounted for prospectively. In other instances—for example, a change in estimated costs under a contract accounted for under the percentage of completion method—changes are accounted for by recording a cumulative adjustment to reflect the new estimate.

Much like the area of contract modifications, GAAP guidance on recording changes in estimates having to do with revenue recognition is incomplete. For example, consider a contract to provide access to fitness clubs that includes a large initiation payment and monthly dues. So long as monthly dues are paid, no further initiation payments are required. However, once the member ceases paying monthly dues, he or she must pay a new initiation fee to rejoin the clubs. Under current GAAP, the initiation fee would be deferred and recognized as revenue over the expected term of the membership. When that estimate changes, the question arises as to whether the effect of the change should be recognized by a cumulative adjustment to take into account the new life, or simply by taking the remaining unamortized initiation fee and spreading it out over the new estimate of the remaining membership life. Most companies facing this type of issue use the prospective method to account for such changes in estimates.

While the exposure draft is not explicit on all changes in estimates, many examples that include changes in estimates are included. In every instance, the exposure draft requires that the change in an estimate be accounted for using a cumulative adjustment. The logical conclusion to be drawn is that changes in estimates should always be reflected using a cumulative adjustment. This would represent a significant change in the way many changes in estimates are handled.

MULTIPLE-DELIVERABLE ARRANGEMENTS

Identifying Performance Obligations

The exposure draft requires that an entity identify all promised goods or services in a contract, including those that are explicitly provided for and those that arise from the entity's customer business practices. Examples of such promises, which are referred to as performance obligations, include:

1. goods produced by an entity for sale (e.g., inventory of manufacturer) or purchased by an entity for resale (e.g., merchandise of a retailer);
2. arranging for another party to transfer goods or services (e.g., acting as an agent of another party);
3. standing ready to provide goods or services (e.g., when-and-if available software products);
4. constructing or developing an asset on behalf of a customer;
5. granting licenses, rights to use, and options; and
6. performing a contractually agreed task (or tasks).

In most cases, it will be fairly easy to determine whether a term of a contract represents a performance obligation, and it is likely that the same items that would be identified as "deliverables" under current GAAP would be identified as performance obligations under the guidance in the exposure draft.

However, current practice allows deliverables to be treated as inconsequential or perfunctory and therefore excluded from the analysis of revenue recognition, when certain criteria are met. For example, post-contract customer support in software arrangements generally requires deferral of revenue, but when the obligation is considered inconsequential, only the accrual of costs is required. Similarly, installation of certain products is sometimes considered inconsequential, resulting in the recognition of all revenue on product delivery, with accrual of costs of the installation, rather than deferral of some revenue to be recognized upon installation. The exposure draft, however, does not provide for any performance obligations to be excluded from the analysis.

Separating Performance Obligations

Once the performance obligations have been identified, the exposure draft then provides that those obligations be accounted for separately if both of the following are true:

- *The risks the entity assumes in providing the goods and services are separable.* For example, while a construction contractor provides a number of different goods and services to the customer, the risks assumed by the contract are not separable because the contractor integrates those goods and services into the single item (the building) that the customer desires.

- *The good or service is "distinct."* A good or service would be considered to be distinct if either vendor regularly sells the good or service separately, or the customer can use the good service on its own or with other resources that are readily available to the customer.

If a good or service is not considered distinct on its own, it must be combined with other promised goods or services to identify a bundle that is distinct.

The "distinct" requirement appears to be very similar to the evaluation required under current GAAP of whether deliverables have standalone value to the customer, and therefore this part of the exposure draft is unlikely to result in significant changes to the separation of multiple-deliverable arrangements. The requirement that a group of goods or services be considered as a single performance obligation if the vendor integrates them into a single item is not present in current GAAP, but this seems designed to ensure that construction and project management contracts are accounted for as a single unit, which is generally the case today under contract accounting. In that regard, this provision may not result in a significant change in practice either.

Allocating Consideration

Under the guidance in the exposure draft, consideration would be allocated to each distinct good or service (or group of goods or services) based on the relative standalone selling prices of the goods or services at the inception of the contract. Where such standalone prices are not known, they would be estimated. If the standalone selling price of a particular performance obligation is considered highly variable, its standalone price in a particular transaction could be estimated using the residual method. Other methods of allocation, such as reliance on stated prices in the contract, would be prohibited, and revenue would not be re-allocated based upon changes after contract inception in the standalone selling prices of the distinct goods or services. This is generally consistent with the requirements of U.S. GAAP after the changes made by ASU 2009-13, except that ASU 2009-13 did away with the residual method, while the ED would bring that method back in limited situations.

Pursuant to the guidance discussed above on measuring the transaction price, the estimated transaction price could change after some performance obligations are complete due to the resolution of a contingency such as the outcome of a performance target. When this occurs, the amounts allocated to individual performance obligations would, generally, be immediately adjusted to take into account the new estimated transaction price. This could result in increasing or decreasing revenue at the time of the change in estimate, to the extent allocations to already satisfied performance obligations are changed.

However, the exposure draft allows for changes in the estimated transaction price to be allocated entirely to specific performance obligations if (1) the contingent payment terms relate specifically to that performance obligation, and (2) the amount allocated to that particular performance obligation (including amounts relating to the resolution of the contingency) is reasonable relative to the amounts allocated to other performance obligations.

The provisions in the ED regarding the allocation of changes in the transaction price would fill in a gap that exists in current standards, as there is no guidance on this topic. In addition, because of the "fixed or determinable" limitation in current GAAP, the adjustments to estimated transaction price can generally only go up, while the ED's proposals could result in changes going in both directions. Given these points, it is clear that the guidance on changes to transaction price would result in a change in practice if the ED's proposals are finalized.

PRODUCTS

Many aspects of revenue recognition related to the sale of goods (products) would be unchanged by the proposals in the exposure draft. As under current GAAP, revenue related to a sale of goods would generally be recognized under a Completed Performance model at the time the goods are transferred to the customer.

However, because the primary focus is on control of the goods in question rather than risks and rewards of ownership, it is possible that revenue would be recognized under the proposals in the exposure draft in situations when it would not be recognized under current GAAP. This is, however, not entirely clear, as consideration of the risks and rewards of ownership is one of the indicators as to whether control has been transferred.

In addition, the application of the proposals to certain other issues that commonly arise in a sale of products will lead to some changes in the timing of revenue recognition.

Evaluating when Performance Is Completed

As in current GAAP, a performance obligation to provide goods to a customer will often be satisfied upon physical delivery and transfer of title, because these events generally denote the transfer of control of the goods. In some instances, contracts may provide the customer with control even before physical delivery—this may occur in arrangements for customer-designed products. The application of the guidance in the exposure draft to such arrangements is discussed later in this chapter in the "Contract Accounting" section.

Shipping Terms

Shipping terms (FOB shipping point vs. FOB destination) would affect the timing of revenue recognition the same way they do under current GAAP as the party that holds title during transit is also usually the party that controls the goods during transit.

Retention of Title

In some cases, the seller may retain certain rights or a limited form of title even after delivery. Where the effect of these rights is simply to protect the seller's right to payment, their retention by the seller would not affect the conclusion that control of the goods has passed to the buyer. This is similar to today's practice.

Consignments

If rights retained by the seller after delivery allow for the seller to reclaim the goods at will, or to direct the customer's use or disposition of the goods, the seller has retained control of the assets and revenue would not be recognized. Transactions like these are generally termed consignment sales. The requirements of the exposure draft on evaluating post-delivery rights appear to result in similar accounting for consignments to practice today.

However, current GAAP requires certain transactions where control of the goods passes to the customer to be accounted for as consignments, with no revenue recognized until the products are resold. This would occur in situations where the seller retains the risks and rewards of ownership through its agreements with its reseller customer (e.g., through a combination of a right of return, price protection provisions, and delayed payment), even though control of the products rests with the customer. Under the provisions of the exposure draft, it is not clear whether such arrangements would prohibit revenue recognition, because, while retentions of risks and rewards of ownership under current guidance almost invariably prohibits revenue recognition, under the proposals in the ED, retention of risks and rewards would be just one of several things to consider assessing whether control of the goods has transferred.

Clearly, this situation is one that requires a significant amount of judgment today, and would require a significant amount of judgment under the guidance in the exposure draft as well.

Bill and Hold Arrangements

The exposure draft provides guidance on bill and hold arrangements requiring the seller, as in other arrangements, to evaluate when control of the goods passes to the customer. The exposure draft acknowledges that control may pass to the customer even though the goods remain on the seller's premises. In order to reach that conclusion, the exposure draft would provide that:

1. There must be a substantive reason for the bill-and-hold arrangement;
2. The product must be identified separately as the customer's;
3. The product must be currently ready for delivery; and
4. The entity cannot use the product or sell it to another customer.

While these provisions include most of the restrictive criteria in current U.S. GAAP, the requirement for a fixed delivery schedule is not included, which may result in more bill and hold arrangements qualifying for revenue recognition before the goods are physically delivered.

Customer Acceptance Provisions

The exposure draft discusses customer acceptance provisions in similar detail and with similar conclusions as the discussion currently included ASC 605-10-S99 (SAB Topic 13). In substance, the existence of customer acceptance provisions is evaluated as a part of the performance obligation. If the seller can objectively determine that the customer acceptance provisions have been met when control of the goods is transferred to the customer, then those provisions do not raise a question as to whether the performance obligation has been satisfied, and revenue recognition is unaffected.

However, where compliance with the acceptance provisions cannot be objectively measured, the seller would be unable to conclude it has satisfied its performance obligation until acceptance occurs, and revenue recognition would not occur until that point. This would be the case, for example, if the acceptance provisions were wholly subjective, such that the product was essentially sent for evaluation purposes without a commitment to pay.

Warranties

Current accounting standards specify different treatment for product warranties based upon whether they are standard warranties or separately priced extended warranties. Standard warranties do not inhibit or delay revenue recognition so long as the costs of honoring them can be estimated, while separately priced extended warranties are treated as a separate deliverable, with revenue recognized over the warranty period.

The exposure draft would also treat some warranties as separate performance obligations to which revenue would be recognized, and others as simply elements of cost, but the distinction would be different.

The ED notes that while warranties generally are meant to provide assurance that the product delivered meets that agreed-upon standards, some warranties actually include post-delivery services as well. For example, some automobile warranties include oil changes and other preventative maintenance during the term of the warranty. In addition, some warranties (referred to as "assurance" warranties) are meant to implicitly provide a service by virtue of an "insurance" element that covers the owner of the product against expected wear and tear. The inclusion of such services in a warranty would, under the proposals in the ED, require that the warranty be treated as a separate performance obligation, which would result in revenue being allocated to the warranty.

The ED would also provide that if the customer has the option to purchase a warranty separately from the vendor (e.g., from a third party service provider or insurance company, or because the warranty is part of a separate negotiation with the seller, rather than being a standard part of a product sale), then the warranty would be treated as a separate performance obligation. On the other hand, if the warranty were included in the product purchase, with no potential for the customer to purchase the warranty separate from the product, it would be treated as part of the product performance obligation. Revenue would not be deferred, and the estimated costs of fulfilling the warranty would be accrued by the vendor. This distinction is similar to the distinction between standard and separately priced extended warranties that exists in current US GAAP.

The accounting for warranties, then, would be similar to current GAAP, except for warranties that include subsequent services. Those warranties would always be treated as separate performance obligations under the ED, while current GAAP allows such warranties to be treated as part of the product deliverable when they are standard warranties. Therefore, more warranties would be treated as separate performance obligations under the guidance in the exposure draft than under current GAAP.

Rights of Return

The exposure draft reasons that the existence of a right of return does not change the fact that the customer obtained control of the goods when they were transferred, so the mere existence of such a right does not prohibit revenue recognition. Further, the right of return would not be considered to be distinct from the goods, and consequently is not a separate performance obligation. Therefore, the Boards decided that the accounting for a right of return should be based on the looking at the right of return as creating uncertainty as to whether the transaction will be completed.

As a result of this, the exposure draft's guidance on rights of return would result in virtually no change to current practice. So long as the likelihood of the customer exercising its refund right can be reasonably estimated, revenue would be recognized for the portion of products delivered that are not estimated to be returned, and revenue would not be recognized for products expected to be returned. The estimate of the refund liability would be updated continuously, and the company would also record an asset for products expected to be returned, presuming that such products would have value. In the event that the likelihood of the customer exercising its right of return cannot be estimated, no revenue would be recognized until a reasonable estimate is possible or the return period expires.

Product Financing Arrangements

Under current GAAP, if a seller has the obligation to repurchase goods sold (either unconditionally or upon request by the customer) at an amount above the purchase price, the transaction is typically considered a financing arrangement, rather than a sale. As such, no revenue is recognized, and the seller records the proceeds as debt.

The exposure draft looks at such arrangements differently, again adhering to the view that revenue recognition should be prohibited only if the terms of the arrangement indicated that the customer does not have control of the goods.

Thus, if the seller has the right to reclaim the products (a call option), or if there is an unconditional repurchase agreement (a forward), revenue could not be recognized upon transfer of the products because the customer would be constrained in its use of the product. If the exercise price of the call or forward were equal to or greater than original sale price, the transaction would be considered a financing, and if the exercise price were lower than the original sale price, the transaction would be considered a lease, with the difference between the sale price and the repurchase price recognized as lease revenue from the sale date to the repurchase date. This accounting analysis would also be applied in a situation in which the purchaser has the option to require the seller to repurchase the goods, and there is a significant economic incentive to exercise that right.

However, if the customer can require the seller to repurchase the goods, but can also elect not to exercise that right (a put option), the exposure draft reasons that, unless there is a significant economic incentive for the customer to exercise the option, in which case the option would be treated the same as a forward, the customer effectively has a right of return. As such, sales with put options are treated the same as rights of returns. This would result in revenue recognition being acceptable upon transfer of goods to the customer in certain situations where it would not be acceptable under current GAAP. Such a transaction would be considered a financing transaction if the repurchase price were greater than the original sale price.

Price or Value Protection

Some goods are sold with price or value protection clauses that require the seller to return money to the customer in the event the price or value of the product decreases within a certain period of time or before the customer resells the goods. Under the guidance in the exposure draft, such clauses would be treated like any other clause that results in variable consideration. The effect of the variability would be reflected in the estimated transaction price. This would likely allow revenue recognition in certain situations in which current practice does not, because the ED would allow for estimates to be made even when price protection is outside of the vendor's control (e.g., because the vendor agrees to match a competitor's price), whereas current GAAP would generally treat such a situation as causing the price not to be fixed or determinable.

Trade-in Rights and Resale Value Guarantees

While these topics are not covered in the exposure draft, it seems likely that their existence would not prohibit revenue recognition on transferred goods, because neither of them impacts the customer's control of the assets. The accounting for many arrangements with these provisions would therefore change with the new guidance.

A trade-in right would likely be considered a right of return that would be analyzed based on the likelihood of the right being exercised. To the extent a trade-in right was expected to be exercised, a refund liability to the customer for the amount of the trade-in price would be recognized, and the arrangement would likely be treated as a lease, with the difference between the sale price and the trade-in price being recognized as lease revenue from the date of sale to the date the trade-in right is exercisable. For the portion of sales for which the trade-in right is not expected to be exercised, the right would have no effect on revenue recognition under the exposure draft's guidance.

A resale value guarantee would likely result in a conclusion that the transaction price is uncertain or variable. This would be treated just like any other provision that creates uncertainty, with revenue initially being recognized based on the probability-weighted best estimate of the consideration that would not need to be refunded to the customer. Alternatively, some resale value guarantees might be treated as separate performance obligations.

SERVICES

Many aspects of revenue recognition related to the sale of services would also be unchanged by the proposals in the exposure draft. As under current GAAP, revenue related to a sale of services would generally be recognized under a Proportional Performance model as the services are transferred to the customer.

In addition, the ED's guidance on determining whether performance is completed at a single point in time or over a period seems likely to, in general, result in similar conclusions as to when the Completed Performance model should be applied to a service transaction.

The exposure draft includes proposed guidance dealing with costs of revenues, which would include the costs of service contracts. Currently, there is no such guidance for most service contracts, with the result being that there is diversity in practice. The exposure draft's guidance would narrow that diversity, requiring some changes.

Evaluating when Performance Is Completed

The most significant issue that would be faced by service providers under the proposals in the exposure draft is determining whether control of the services passes to the customer continuously throughout the performance period, or whether control is instead transferred only when services are complete, or when a particular event occurs.

The exposure draft provides guidance on this issue, as discussed previously in this chapter. The guidance states that performance is completed over time if either:

- Performance of work creates or enhance an asset that is controlled by the customer as the work is performed.
- Performance does not create an asset with alternative use to the vendor, and either:
  - The customer receives a benefit as the work is performed.
  - A replacement vendor, if brought in to complete the work, would not need to reperform work already done.
  - The vendor has a right to payment for performance to date and the vendor is expected to fulfil the contract as promised.

The concepts in that guidance suggest that in evaluating whether control of services transfers continuously or only upon completion, a service provider should consider, at least, the following factors, many of which would be considered under current GAAP as well:

- *Whether the customer has the ability to direct the provision of services as they are performed.* For example, a contract to design a piece of software for a specific purpose would usually allow the customer to direct the work, change the specifications, evaluate each piece of work as it is done, and otherwise control the services throughout the process. In contrast, a contract for processing of payroll may not allow such control. If the customer can direct the provision of services as they are performed, the service is likely to be one for which the asset created has no alternative use to the service provider.

- *Whether the service is useful to the customer in a partially completed state.* For example, in a contract to clean the windows of a high-rise building, it is clear that the customer benefits from each window as it is cleaned.

- *Whether payment is due (and nonrefundable) throughout the service period or only upon completion.* If payment is due only upon completion of services, that may indicate that the customer does not receive value from (and control of) the services until that point.

- *Whether the contract identifies only the final act in a series of acts.* In this case, the actions before the final act may not comprise performance obligations at all, and therefore their performance could not satisfy a performance obligation. For example, a contract for data conversion services may result in the need for the service provider to study the customer's current data systems, design new interfaces, and purchase and deploy new hardware. As the customer does not benefit from those activities as they are performed, and they do not result in progress that would be useful to a replacement vendor, it would appear that such activities would result in revenue being recognized over a period of time.

Recognizing Revenue under the Proportional Performance Model

When transfer of control of the services occurs throughout the performance period, the exposure draft's guidance on methods of revenue recognition is comparable to current practices. The goal is to find a pattern that reflects the transfer of control of goods or services to the customer.

A method that relies on assessing the outputs of the services provided at a point in time in comparison to the total expected outputs would often be the most representationally faithful method. For example, revenue on a contract to resurface a road might compare lane-miles complete with the total lane-miles in the project.

Methods based on the passage of time might be appropriate if the services are performed repeatedly over a period of time and there is no reason to expect the provisions of services to be concentrated in certain periods. For example a cable television company or a health club would likely be able to recognize its service revenue on a straight-line basis under the provision of the exposure draft.

The exposure draft also acknowledges that input methods, such as costs incurred, would also be appropriate in some circumstances. However, the exposure draft notes that such methods must be used carefully, as costs do not necessarily faithfully depict the transfer of services to the customer. For example, a contract involving the outsourcing of payroll processing to a service provider for a number of years might involve greater expenditures by the processor in early periods as the processor gains familiarity with its new client's procedures and systems. Those higher costs, however, would not be reflective of a higher transfer of service to the customer, and therefore should not be used in determining how much revenue to recognize.

The ED also provides that vendors using a cost-to-cost method should not recognize profit on the transfer of materials transferred to the customer's control in advance of the vendor providing service under the contract. For example, a construction contractor might purchase materials and have them delivered to the customer's location early in a project, so that they are available for us as construction progresses. The ED would allow revenue to be recognized upon delivery of such materials only in an amount equal to the cost of the materials.

In general, the guidance on measuring progress toward completion is consistent with current standards, although the cautions and changes in application of the cost-to-cost model might impact certain companies.

Recognizing Costs of Services

Under current GAAP, there is little guidance on the recognition of costs of providing services. The exposure draft would provide general guidance on accounting for the costs of revenues that would apply to all transactions. See the discussion later in this chapter.

Advance (Up-front, Initiation, Activation) Fees

Under the guidance in the exposure draft, these fees would not affect the timing of revenue recognition, as revenue would only be recognized as services are performed. Therefore, if initial services represent a transfer of control of a distinct good or service to the customer, revenue would be recognized whether an advance payment was received or not, and if initial services do not result in a transfer of control of a distinct good or service, no revenue would be recognized even if an advance payment were received.

Applying the exposure draft's provisions in this context should have little or no effect on practice, as current practice similarly does not regard the receipt of a payment as an indication that revenue has been earned.

The only effect of the exposure draft's provisions on accounting for arrangements with advanced fees is the requirement that the time value of money be taken into account if it is significant. Where a significant fee is received in advance of revenue being recognized, it may be necessary to recognize the time value of money by recording interest expense and increasing the "deferred revenue" obligation between the receipt of the advance fee and the recognition of revenue.

Post-Performance Obligations

When service arrangements include customer acceptance provisions, warranties, rights of return, and other post-performance continuing obligations, the accounting would generally be same as discussed in the "Products" section of this chapter for similar obligations.

Research and Development Arrangements

The guidance in ASC 730-20 on determining whether an R&D arrangement effectively entails an obligation to repay funding would not be affected by the guidance in the exposure draft. However, the exposure draft includes language that appears to indicate that amounts received from collaboration partners would generally not be considered revenue as the partner would generally not be considered a customer. If so, this might result in payments between collaboration partners being excluded from the revenue recognition guidance.

If collaboration arrangements were essentially excluded from the ED, this would likely leave practice to develop over time, or leave the accounting for collaboration arrangements the same as it currently is.

INTELLECTUAL PROPERTY

Current GAAP specifically discusses recognition of revenue for the licensing of some kinds of intellectual property, including software, franchise rights, and motion pictures, but is silent with regard to other intellectual property licenses. However, issues that appear similar are not always addressed consistently in this guidance, and licenses of many other types of intellectual property are not addressed at all. The exposure draft attempts to correct many of these problems by providing guidance that would be broadly applicable to licenses of intellectual property.

Evaluating when Performance Is Completed

The exposure draft provides that a license to intellectual property is a performance obligation that the vendor satisfies at the point in time that the customer obtains control of the license. In general, this would be later of the beginning of the license period and the point at which the customer has been provided whatever know-how, physical media, or other information is necessary to use the intellectual property. The entity's performance obligation is treated similarly to the performance obligation undertaken by a company that distributes products. So long as the licensor need not perform any continuing services to allow the licensee to use the intellectual property, the exposure draft concludes there is no ongoing performance obligation.

However, if the contract includes other performance obligations in addition to the license to intellectual property, the vendor would need to consider whether the license and one or more of those other obligations should be combined for purposes of revenue recognition. If, for example, the license were combined with a service that is performed over time because the license is not "distinct," the license revenue would be recognized over the service period.

The model described in the exposure draft generally would treat all intellectual property licenses consistent with the treatment of non-exclusive licenses described in Chapter 7, "Intellectual Property Deliverables," of this publication.

Continuing Performance Obligations

The evaluation of warranties, rights of return, and customer acceptance provisions with regard to intellectual property deliverables under the exposure draft would mirror the evaluation of similar provisions in respect of obligations to transfer goods. See the discussion previously in this chapter. However, certain other "post-delivery" performance obligations are unique to (or at least far more common in) intellectual property arrangements.

When-and-If-Available Deliverables

These clauses require the seller or licensor to provide the customer with access to enhancements or upgrades made during the license term, but do not require the seller to make or attempt to make such enhancements or upgrades. Under current GAAP, when-and-if-available clauses are often considered to constitute another deliverable in the arrangement. However, such clauses may often be considered to be inconsequential if the seller does not expect to provide any such enhancements or upgrades.

When-and-if-available obligations are specifically identified as an example of a performance obligation in the exposure draft. As performance obligations may not be excluded from the analysis under the exposure draft on the basis of being inconsequential, this may cause a change in practice. However, if the likelihood of creating any upgrades or enhancements is low, the standalone selling price of a right to such items would also likely be quite low, such that the amount of revenue to be allocated to such a when-and-if-available obligation may be immaterial.

Patent Maintenance and Defense

These clauses require the seller or licensor to defend patent or technology rights during a license period. The exposure draft notes that such a clause is not a performance obligation because it does not embody a promise to transfer a good or service to the customer. The fact that customers might be interested in the entity protecting its rights does not mean that such actions involve a transfer of goods or services.

As a result, patent defense clauses would not affect revenue recognition under the exposure draft, consistent with the conclusion under current GAAP.

Industry-Specific Intellectual Property Models

Current U.S. GAAP includes guidance on accounting for provisions of certain intellectual property transactions. For example, franchising, distribution and broadcast of motion pictures, television programming, and music and software licensing all are specifically addressed in U.S. GAAP. While only specific issues are addressed in some of these areas, the accounting models for franchising, motion pictures, and, particularly, software, are very well developed.

All of this historical guidance would be deleted under the proposals in the exposure draft. As software revenue recognition has been treated as a separate chapter in this publication in the past, the effects of the elimination of the software guidance are discussed later in this chapter. Immediately below are discussions of the most significant ways that franchise and motion picture revenue recognition would change under the proposals in the exposure draft.

Franchises

Current GAAP generally allows a substantial portion of initial franchise fees to be recognized as revenue when a franchise outlet opens because, by that point, the franchisor will have provided all of the "initial services." Deferral of an initial franchise fee beyond store opening would only occur if ongoing products or services are sold to the franchisee at less than their typical selling prices. In substance, to the extent any of the initial franchise fee relates to the fee for use of the franchisor's intellectual property, that revenue may be recognized upon store opening.

It appears that the provisions of the ED would largely leave this accounting unchanged. So long as the agreement to provide an ongoing supply of products and services did not include a discount, that ongoing arrangement would not be considered a performance obligation in the contract. As such, all of the typical performance obligations would be fulfilled by the time of store opening.

Motion Pictures

Revenue recognition for motion picture distribution and licensing fees is likely to remain largely the same. As licenses of films generally do not involve ongoing services by the licensor, revenue from the license can be recognized at the beginning of the license period, which is similar to current GAAP. In addition, the restriction on recognizing revenue related to sales-based royalties and similar items until those sales have occurred will result in a pattern of recognition that is consistent with the way such contingent items are handled under current GAAP.

MISCELLANEOUS ISSUES

Costs of Revenue Transactions

Fullfillment Costs

Under current GAAP, there is little guidance on the recognition of costs of providing goods and services. In many cases, the appropriate accounting for costs of revenue is easy to determine. For example, capitalized inventory costs are recorded as costs of sales when revenue is recognized on the related goods.

As noted in Chapter 6, "Service Deliverables," direct costs of providing services are usually capitalized if they are incurred before revenue can be recognized because the contract is accounted for under the Completed Performance model, and expensed as incurred if revenue is recognized under the Proportional Performance model. However, because current GAAP provides no guidance on such costs, there is diversity in practice and the area is ripe for disagreements on the appropriate accounting treatment.

The potential for diversity and disagreement grows when one moves beyond direct costs of providing goods or services. For example, many companies incur set-up or administrative costs related to activities that are necessary to allow fulfillment of their performance obligations, but do not actually transfer any goods or services to the customer. While it is clear that incurrence of such costs does not result in revenue recognition, questions constantly arise about whether such costs can be capitalized.

The exposure draft would resolve a good portion of the uncertainty and diversity, as it provides general guidance on accounting for the costs of revenues. First, the exposure draft notes that costs incurred in fulfilling a customer contract might involve the creation of an asset as defined in other parts of the Codification. For example, if a company purchases computer hardware that will be used in providing management services to a customer, that hardware would be capitalized as fixed assets.

Other costs incurred in fulfilling a contract would be capitalized as an asset if they meet all of the following criteria:

1. *Relate directly to a contract.* For example, direct materials and labor, depreciation of equipment used in fulfilling the contract, costs that are specifically reimbursable under the contract, costs of subcontractors working directly on the project. This would include costs incurred before the contract is finalized if they relate specifically to an anticipated contract. For example, if a service provider starts work before a contract is final as a show of good faith to the customer, the costs could be capitalized.

2. *Generate or enhance resources of the entity that will be used in satisfying performance obligations in the future (i.e., the costs relate to future performance).* Costs of waste or errors, for example, would not meet this criterion, as they do not enhance resources that will be used to fulfill the performance obligation. Similarly, costs of providing service for which revenue has already been recognized may not be capitalized, even if costs of providing similar service are expected to be lower in the future.

3. *Are expected to be recovered.* This would generally involve consideration of the remaining revenue and costs to be incurred on the project. So long as sufficient margin were anticipated, the costs would meet this criterion. This criterion would also serve as the impairment test for any amounts capitalized.

Any asset recognized under these provisions would be amortized as service is provided, consistent with the pattern of revenue recognition.

Applying this guidance would often result in accounting that is similar to current practice, although the particular application might change in some circumstances.

Costs of Obtaining a Contract

While current GAAP provides guidance on contract acquisition costs in respect of certain transactions, the guidance is narrow and scope and the various models are inconsistent with one another, making it difficult to determine appropriate principles to apply to other transactions. As discussed in Chapter 8, "Miscellaneous Issues," many companies do capitalize contract acquisition costs based on a model developed by analogy to the scant guidance in GAAP, but other companies do not, creating significant diversity in practice.

The exposure draft proposes to resolve this diversity by requiring that incremental costs of obtaining of a contract be capitalized so long as they are expected to be recovered, as discussed above. The capitalization would be limited to those costs that would not have been incurred had the contract not been obtained, and would not be required for contracts less than one year in length. Any asset recognized under these provisions would be amortized as service is provided, consistent with the pattern of revenue recognition.

The proposals in the ED would resolve significant diversity in practice by setting forth a consistent model. As the proposal takes something of middle ground in comparison to policies in use today, some companies would find themselves capitalizing costs that they currently expense, while others would need to expense a portion of the costs they currently capitalize. Sales commissions are the most common example that would qualify for capitalization. However, because the model limits capitalization to incremental costs, those companies that capitalize a portion of salespersons' salaries would need to change their policy.

Costs of Sales Incentives

Guidance on sales incentives did not exist in U.S. GAAP until 2000, when the EITF began addressing the topic in a series of issues. The EITF gradually provided guidance on recognition of the costs of coupons and rebates, volume purchase discounts, offers of discounts on additional purchases, and other topics. While the EITF declined to address customer loyalty programs (e.g., airline frequent flyer programs), the IFRS Interpretations Committee did address such programs. The principles underlying the guidance issued by the EITF and IFRIC have, by and large, been incorporated into the exposure draft.

Coupons and Rebates

Coupons and rebates are examples of situations in which the customer can take advantage of a discount by making only a single purchase. In that regard, they, like many other contract terms, cause the amount of consideration to be received (and retained) by the seller to be uncertain. As such, the exposure draft requires that the seller record revenue based upon the probability-weighted expected outcome of coupon and rebate arrangements, so long as reasonable estimates can be made (see discussion under "General Principles" above). Of course, these estimates should be adjusted for changes until the program is complete. If a reasonable estimate cannot be made, the seller would initially assume that all coupons or rebates will be redeemed.

When the coupon, rebate, or other discount offer is made separately from the sale of the related goods or services, the exposure draft provides that the estimated reduction of revenue should be recognized at the later of the point in time that the company promises to pay the consideration (including via a promise implied by the vendor's business practices), and the point in time when the goods or services are transferred to the customer.

This guidance is virtually identical to current U.S. GAAP, and therefore there should be little change in the accounting coupons and rebates.

Volume Rebates and Other Discounts on Future Purchases

There are many different programs in which customers are offered a discount if they make additional purchases from the vendor. Some arrangements offer a customer a coupon on an additional item when they make a purchase. In other situations, companies may offer a volume rebate as an incentive for a customer to purchase larger quantities of goods or services during a particular period of time. These are all examples of arrangements where a customer is offered some form of discount or rebate only if the customer makes additional purchases from the entity.

If the offer of a discount on future purchases provides the customer with a material right that would not otherwise be available to the customer, that option is considered an additional performance obligation under the exposure draft. Revenue would be allocated to the option based on the best of estimate of its standalone selling price. However, because such a standalone selling price is often not directly observable (as companies rarely sell separately rights to discounts), the exposure draft provides that the standalone selling price should be estimated by reference to the amount of the discount, as adjusted for discounts that would otherwise be available to the customer and the likelihood that the option will be exercised.

For example, assume a company offers a 40% discount on future purchases to its customers with a maximum discount of $40 (i.e., the discount is good on up to $100 in additional purchases). Also assume that the company estimates that half of its customers will utilize the discount, and that, when they do, they will purchase an average of $80 of additional products. Finally, assume that customers that have not made previous purchases are generally eligible for a 10% discount on an $80 purchase.

In this situation, the company would estimate the standalone selling price of the option to purchase additional products at a discount at $12 (30% incremental discount x 50% chance of exercise x $80 average purchase). If the company were unable to make reasonable estimates of the amount of the options that would be exercised, it would estimate the standalone value of the option to purchase additional products at a discount at $30 (30% incremental discount x maximum eligible purchase of $100).

In the event the discount on future purchase is offered to customers at some point after their original purchase, the offer would constitute a contract modification, and should be treated as discussed previously, in the "General Principles" section of this chapter.

Although current guidance in U.S. GAAP does not comprehensively address these situations, practice often follows a similar analysis, at least in principle. As such, while the guidance in the exposure draft on this topic would result in a change for some companies, others would see little difference.

Loyalty Programs

U.S. GAAP does not provide guidance on customer loyalty programs, such as frequent flyer programs. As noted in Chapter 8, "Miscellaneous Issues," some companies treat points offered in a loyalty program as an additional deliverable in an arrangement, while others instead simply accrue the expected cost of redeeming the loyalty program points.

The exposure draft would require that offers of points or miles in a loyalty program be treated as a separate performance obligation when such points are offered as part of a sales transaction. The accounting would follow the accounting for discounts on future purchases, as described above, when the points are to be redeemed with the seller. The standalone selling price of the point would be estimated by reference to value of the goods or services that the point could be redeemed for, adjusted for the likelihood of redemption. The estimate of likelihood of redemption would be continuously updated, and revenue reallocated, until the points are redeemed or expire.

This guidance is virtually identical to current IFRS standards, and is also the framework used by many companies following U.S. GAAP. However, those companies using the "accrued cost" method would see a significant change in the accounting for their loyalty programs under the guidance in the exposure draft.

Related Party Sales

The exposure draft would not change any of the guidance or practical concerns in respect of related party sales. Those transactions would still generally be reported like similar sales to unrelated parties, with additional disclosures necessary. Of course, it would still be necessary to consider whether the substance of such transactions is truly reflected in the contractual arrangements.

Nonmonetary Transactions

The exposure draft would not change current guidance regarding nonmonetary transactions. Such transactions would continue to be recognized at fair value so long as they have commercial substance. In the event that the fair value of any noncash consideration cannot be reasonably estimated, the value would be measured indirectly based upon the standalone selling prices of the goods or services in the arrangement.

In the event that the customer contributes goods or services to the vendor to assist in fulfilling the contract, the vendor should recognize those goods or services as revenue under the contract only if it obtains control of them.

The only exception to the principle that noncash consideration should be recognized at fair value continues to be exchanges of inventory between entities in the same line of business to facilitate sales to end customers. Those transactions are not considered revenue-generating transactions and are generally recorded at cost.

CONTRACT ACCOUNTING

Currently, there are special requirements (ASC 605-35) on accounting for certain contracts to provide products or facilities designed and built to customer specifications. As discussed in Chapter 9, "Contract Accounting," these special requirements apply to contracts for the construction of buildings, ships, complex equipment, and similar large projects if the items are built to customer specifications. The contracts to which this special accounting applies are generally large, unique contracts. Contracts for the production of goods using a standard manufacturing process in which large quantities are manufactured and sold are specifically scoped out of the specialized accounting model.

For contracts covered by the contract accounting guidance, revenue is generally recognized under a Proportional Performance model called percentage-of-completion accounting, such that revenue is recognized as work is performed, even before the product is delivered to the customer. The recognition of revenue on the sale of products before delivery is, of course, inconsistent with the model for recognizing revenue on most product sales.

The exposure draft would eliminate the special accounting model that applies to these contracts. Instead, the construction and specialized production contracts that would today be accounted for under ASC 605-35 would be evaluated under the same model that applies to all other customer contracts.

Proportional Performance vs. Completed Performance

In a contract to build or produce goods to customer specifications, the exposure draft would result in accounting under a Proportional Performance model as production or construction occurs only if the customer controls the asset as it is produced, manufactured, or constructed. If the customer gains control of the asset only upon completion, revenue would be recognized under the Proportional Performance model only if performance does not create an asset with alternative use to the vendor, and either:

- The customer receives a benefit as the work is performed.

- A replacement vendor, if brought in to complete the work, would not need to reperform work already done.

- The vendor has a right to payment for performance to date and expects to fulfil the contract.

Building on those criteria, there are a number of factors that should be considered in determining whether revenue could be recognized over time or not, including:

- *Payment terms.* If the customer has an unconditional obligation to make progress payments, which are nonrefundable even if no further work is performed, that would likely result in revenue recognition over time.

- *Legal title.* If the customer holds legal title to the asset as it is created, that would indicate that the customer controls the asset as it is created or enhanced.

- *Physical possession.* If the asset is constructed on the customer's land or in-place at the customer's facility, this should indicate that the customer obtains control of the asset as it is produced.

- *Risks and rewards.* If the customer has substantially all of the risks and rewards of the asset, it is likely that control of the asset has also been transferred.

Combining and Segmenting Contracts and Contract Modifications

The determination of whether to combine multiple contracts into one for accounting purposes, as well as the determination of whether a contract should be segmented and treated as multiple contracts, would be handled as discussed above under "General Principles," as there will no longer be guidance specific to the contracts currently covered by ASC 605-35. Segmentation of contract would generally not occur under the guidance in the ED. However, the situations in which segmentation of contracts would occur under current guidance would likely be situations in which the performance obligations would be considered separate, so the effect on revenue recognition might be minimal.

On the other hand, because the ED would apply the general guidance on modifications to arrangements currently in the scope of ASC 605-35, there could be significant change in this area. Contractors typically take change order into account before they are contractually agreed under current literature, but that would not be permitted under the proposals in the ED.

Applying the Proportional Performance Model

Under the exposure draft, the application of the Proportional Performance model to a contact currently covered by ASC 605-35 would be the same as the application of that model to any other contract to which it applies. There are many similarities between the accounting that would apply under the exposure draft and percentage-of-completion accounting as applied under ASC 605-35. As the discussion above under "Service Deliverables" in this chapter notes, both output and input methods would still be available. However, there would still be several changes to the accounting.

First, of course, is the possibility that those currently applying percentage-of-completion accounting might have to switch to a Completed Performance model under the new exposure draft (see discussion above). But even presuming continued use of a Proportional Performance model, the exposure draft does not provide for an accounting policy that results in a constant gross margin throughout the project, which is almost always the case under ASC 605-35. The exposure draft would require revenue to be measured based on the measure of progress toward completion, while costs, in general, would be recognized as incurred.

In addition, the guidance in the exposure draft might result in less use of the cost-to-cost model of assessing performance, or change that way that model is applied, because of the caution that cost-to-cost models should only be used if they can be applied in a way that accurately depicts the transfer of goods or services to the customer. When the cost-to-cost method is used, the ED's requirements related to recognizing no profit on the delivery of materials to the customer that are not yet consumed in production will change the application of the cost-to-cost model.

Applying the Completed Performance Model

Other than the fact that it may apply more frequently, the application of the Completed Performance model should be virtually identical to the application of the completed contract method under ASC 605-35.

Revenue and Cost Elements

As in other areas, the estimate of contract revenues would, under the exposure draft, be the same for all contracts. Thus, the inclusion of variable pricing in a construction contract, the effects of change orders and other modifications, the estimation of contract costs, and the treatment of loss contracts, for example, would be the same for these contracts as discussed previously in this chapter under "General Principles."

This would result in differences in the way these issues are handled currently for some companies. However, it is difficult to generalize as to the effects of these differences.

SOFTWARE

U.S. GAAP has specially developed guidance for sales of software (ASC 985-605). The exposure draft would eliminate all of it. Instead, contracts for the sale of software would be evaluated using the same guidance that applies to all other arrangements. This would result in many changes to the accounting for software transactions.

Fixed or Determinable Fees and Collectibility

Current GAAP presumes that the fee in a software arrangement with extended payment terms is not fixed or determinable because of the possibility that a software vendor would provide concessions to the customer in order to secure payment. Therefore, ASC 985-605 requires that revenue from an arrangement with extended payment terms be recognized only as collected unless the presumption can be overcome. Under the exposure draft, there would be no such presumption.

The exposure draft does require the time value of money to be considered when payment terms are extended significantly beyond the point at which revenue is recognized. And extended payment terms might very well increase the chances that a customer would not pay all amounts contractually due. Of course, a pattern of granting concessions would need to be considered in identifying the performance obligations under the contract.

While these are all the same issues that cause the presumption that currently exists with respect to extended payment terms in software arrangements, they would merely be items to consider under the exposure draft. The existence of extended payment terms would not presumptively prohibit revenue recognition in software sales as it does now.

Delivery

Under the provisions of the exposure draft, the obligation to transfer software to the customer would generally be considered to be satisfied at the same time that delivery is considered to occur under ASC 985-605, except that the performance obligation could not be satisfied before the beginning of the license term, even if the customer as physical possession of the software before then (see discussion above under "Intellectual Property").

Multiple-Element Arrangements

The exposure draft's provisions regarding arrangements with multiple perform-ance obligations are similar, in many respects, to the requirements of ASC 985-605 with regard to arrangements with multiple software elements. However, there are several differences that could result in significant changes to the way software companies account for multiple-element arrangements.

Separation of Elements

ASC 985-605 prohibits separation of software elements and recognition of reve-nue on delivered elements if there is not vendor-specific objective evidence of the fair value of any undelivered elements. The exposure draft includes no such prohibition. So long as the elements are distinct (or in software terms, so long as the elements are not essential to each other's functionality), they would be separated under the guidance in the exposure draft. Allocation of revenue would be based upon the best estimates of the standalone selling prices of the elements. While VSOE would be the best estimate if it existed, the existence of VSOE would no longer be a condition precedent to allow separation of software elements.

Obviously, this change would allow faster recognition of revenue in many software arrangements.

PCS

ASC 985-605 specifically indicates that post-contract customer support should be treated as single element, even if includes technical support and the right to when-and-if-available upgrades and enhancements. Under the exposure draft, however, performance obligations are treated separately for accounting purposes if they are distinct. Because the when-and-if-available upgrades and the technical support serve separate functions, it is likely that they would considered distinct, and thus, PCS that is now accounted for as a single element would likely be accounted for as two or more performance obligations.

The practical effect of this difference may be small, as it is likely that a vendor would conclude that both the technical support and when-and-if-available upgrades are provided ratably over the term of the PCS arrangement.

However, in certain instances, ASC 985-605 allows a vendor to determine that PCS is inconsequential, in which case no revenue need be allocated to the PCS element. As the exposure draft requires allocation of revenue to all obligations to transfer goods or services to the customer, this would no longer be possible under the guidance in the exposure draft.

PRESENTATION

Gross vs. Net Presentation

When some of the goods or services provided pursuant to a contract with a customer are provided by parties other than the entity, the question arises as to whether the entity should report the transaction on a "gross" basis, recognizing revenue for the full amount paid by the customer, and expenses for the cost of having another party provide the goods or services, or on a "net" basis, reflecting only the difference between the amount paid by the customer and the amount paid to the third party provider of goods or services as revenue. Essentially, the question is whether the entity is acting as a principal or an agent in the transaction.

The exposure draft's guidance on this issue would require the entity to consider whether its performance obligation is to provide the goods or services themselves, or simply to match the buyer and seller. The indicators described in the exposure draft are similar to those that are currently used to distinguish gross vs. net revenue transactions, and therefore it is likely that the same conclusions would be reached under the exposure draft's provisions as are currently reached by entities applying U.S. GAAP.

Payments from a Vendor to Customer

When an entity makes a payment to a customer, it is sometimes difficult to determine whether that payment is for the purchase of a good or service from the customer or is instead effectively an adjustment of the sales price of the goods or services being provided by the entity to the customer. Under the provisions of the exposure draft, that determination would turn on whether the customer provides the entity with a good or service that is distinct, under the same definitions used to determine whether to separately account for performance obligations in a contact with multiple performance obligations (see previous discussion in the "Multiple-Deliverable Arrangements" section of this chapter).

If an entity receives a distinct good or service, at least a portion of the consideration paid to the customer (up to the fair value of the distinct good or service received) would be reported as the cost of that good or service, rather than a reduction of revenue. If an entity does not receive a distinct good or service, the entire payment to the customer would be considered an adjustment of the transaction price in the sale of the entity's goods or service to the customer. Uncertainty about whether the customer will "earn" the payment (e.g., because the payment is conditional on a specified volume of purchases) would be handled just like any other uncertainty in transaction price, as discussed previously under "General Principles."

This guidance is generally similar to current GAAP, and therefore the exposure draft would not significantly change practice in this area.

Uncollectible Amounts

As previously discussed in the "General Principles" section of this chapter, under the guidance in the exposure draft, collectibility would not be taken into account in determining whether to recognize revenue or in estimating the transaction price. However, all bad debt provisions would be recognized in a contra-revenue accounting, which would be a change from current practice.

Balance Sheet Presentation

U.S. GAAP is currently virtually silent on the issue of how assets and liabilities resulting from transactions with a customer should be presented. The exposure draft would clarify this issue considerably, as it provides descriptions of the various balance sheet items that might arise out of customer contracts.

Contract Asset or Liability

The most significant part of the balance sheet presentation guidance surrounds the contract asset or liability. The exposure draft states that any contract under which one of the parties has performed results in the recognition of either a contract asset or liability.

For example, if the customer prepays all or a portion of the transaction price, the entity would record a contract liability. A contract liability would also be created representing the portion of goods that are estimated to not meet customer acceptance criteria, as discussed previously. The contract liability would be settled, and revenue recognized, when the entity satisfies its performance obligation. Conversely, if the entity satisfies a performance obligation (and therefore recognizes revenue) but is not yet entitled to payment, a contract asset would be recorded. Similarly, a contract asset would be recorded if the entity makes a payment to its customer that is considered an adjustment of the transaction price before revenue is recognized.

The contract asset or liability would encompass amounts that might under current GAAP be reflected as deferred revenue or unbilled receivables.

Accounts Receivable

A receivable would be recognized whenever the entity has an unconditional right to payment pursuant to the terms of the contract. This would not exist if the payment obligation would be triggered only once the entity performs under the contract. Note that the existence of a receivable would not necessarily mean that revenue could be recognized. Instead, recording a receivable would adjust the contract asset or liability if the entity's right to payment becomes unconditional other than because of satisfaction of a performance obligation.

This treatment is largely consistent with current practice, but the clear definition will likely improve consistency.

Onerous Performance Obligations

The liability for an onerous performance obligation would be presented separately from contract liabilities because the onerous performance obligation liability would not be settled by satisfying a performance obligation and recording revenue, but instead by incurring costs.

Contract Cost Asset

Any asset recorded for contract costs capitalizable pursuant to the capitalization guidance in the exposure draft (as discussed above under "Costs of Revenue Transactions") would be recognized separate from the contract asset because only transfers between the entity and its customer affect the contract asset.

DISCLOSURES

Because there is no guidance in current GAAP that applies to revenue recognition transactions generally, there are also no generally applicable disclosure requirements. Instead, as discussed in Chapter 12, there are specific disclosures required for certain transactions and certain issues. In other areas, only the general requirements to disclose important accounting policies apply.

The exposure draft would replace virtually all of the disclosures currently required with a single set of requirements meant to "enable users of financial statements to understand the amount, timing, and uncertainty of revenue and cash flows arising from contracts with customers."

The exposure draft specifically describes a number of qualitative and quantitative disclosures that are meant to help achieve that goal. It also puts on the entity making the disclosures the obligation to ensure the objective is met, including a requirement that an entity make disclosures beyond those specifically required if necessary to meet the objective.

The required disclosures include a number of items that are similar to disclosures that would generally be expected to be made under current accounting standards. However, there are also several required rollforwards that go beyond information that is typically provided. As such, it is likely that the information needed to meet the ED's disclosure requirements is more detailed than is currently required. The required disclosures would include the following:

- A disaggregation of revenue into categories (e.g., product lines, geography, type of customer, duration, etc.) that best depict how the amount, timing, and uncertainty of revenue and cash flows are affected by economic factors.
- A rollforward from the opening to the closing aggregate balance of contract assets and contract liabilities, separately showing, if material:
  — revenue from the satisfaction of performance obligations;
  — revenue from allocating changes in the transaction price to performance obligations satisfied in previous periods;

- — cash and other consideration received;
- — amounts transferred to receivables; and
- — any additional items necessary to understand the rollforward.
- Information about performance obligations, including:
  - — the goods or services promised, highlighting any situations in which the company is acting as an agent;
  - — the events that typically satisfy its performance obligations;
  - — the significant payment terms;
  - — obligations for returns, refunds, and other similar obligations; and
  - — types of warranties and related obligations.
- For contracts with original expected durations of more than one year, the amount of the transaction price allocated to the remaining performance obligations along with an explanation of when it expects to recognize revenue for those performance obligations.
- A rollforward of any liability recognized for onerous performance obligations, with a discussion of the nature of the related performance obligations, why those performance obligations have become onerous, and when the obligations will be satisfied.
- When performance obligations are satisfied over a performance period instead of at a single point in time, the methods (e.g., output methods, input methods, and methods based on the passage of time) used to recognize revenue, and an explanation of why such methods are a faithful depiction of the transfer of goods or services.
- Information about the methods, inputs, and assumptions used to determine the transaction price (e.g., how variable consideration was estimated), to estimate standalone selling prices of promised goods or services, to measure obligations for returns, refunds, and other similar obligations, and to measure the liability recognized for onerous performance obligations.
- A rollforward of the carrying of any asset arising from the capitalization of costs to acquire or fulfill a contract, disaggregated by major type of cost, as well as a description of the amortization period.

Cross-Reference

ORIGINAL PRONOUNCEMENTS TO 2012 *REVENUE RECOGNITION GUIDE*

This locator provides instant cross-references between an original pronouncement and the chapter(s) in this publication in which the pronouncement is covered. Original pronouncements are listed chronologically on the left and the chapter(s) in which they appear in the 2012 *Revenue Recognition Guide* on the right. To find where in the 2012 *Revenue Recognition Guide* a topic from the FASB Accounting Standards Codification™ is discussed, please use the topical index that follows this cross-reference index.

ACCOUNTING RESEARCH BULLETINS (ARBs)

(Accounting Research Bulletins 1–42 were revised, restated, or withdrawn at the time ARB No. 43 was issued.)

ORIGINAL PRONOUNCEMENT	2012 *REVENUE RECOGNITION GUIDE* REFERENCE
ARB-43, Ch. 4	
Restatement and Revision of Accounting Research Bulletins, Chapter 4, Inventory Pricing	Miscellaneous Issues, ch. **8**
ARB-43, Ch. 11	
Restatement and Revision of Accounting Research Bulletins, Chapter 11, Government Contracts	Contract Accounting, ch. **9**
ARB-45	
Long-Term Construction-Type Contracts	General Principles, ch. **3** Contract Accounting, ch. **9** Software—A Complete Model, ch. **10** Disclosures, ch. **12**

ACCOUNTING PRINCIPLES BOARD OPINIONS (APBs)

ORIGINAL PRONOUNCEMENT	2012 *REVENUE RECOGNITION GUIDE* REFERENCE
APB-10	
Omnibus Opinion—1966, Installment Method of Accounting	General Principles, ch. **3**
APB-21	
Interest on Receivables and Payables	Product Deliverables, ch. **5** Service Deliverables, ch. **6** Intellectual Property Deliverables, ch. **7**
APB-22	
Disclosure of Accounting Policies	Disclosures, ch. **12**
APB-28	
Interim Financial Reporting	Disclosures, ch. **12**
APB-29	
Accounting for Nonmonetary Transactions	Miscellaneous Issues, ch. **8** Software—A Complete Model, ch. **10** Disclosures, ch. **12**

FINANCIAL ACCOUNTING STANDARDS BOARD STATEMENTS (FASs)

ORIGINAL PRONOUNCEMENT	2012 *REVENUE RECOGNITION GUIDE* REFERENCE
FAS-5	
Accounting for Contingencies	General Principles, ch. **3** Multiple-Deliverable Revenue Arrangements, ch. **4** Product Deliverables, ch. **5** Service Deliverables, ch. **6** Contract Accounting, ch. **9** Software—A Complete Model, ch. **10**
FAS-13	
Accounting for Leases	General Principles, ch. **3** Multiple-Deliverable Revenue Arrangements, ch. **4** Intellectual Property Deliverables, ch. **7** Presentation, ch. **11**

ORIGINAL PRONOUNCEMENT	2012 *REVENUE RECOGNITION GUIDE* REFERENCE
FAS-45	
Accounting for Franchise Fee Revenue	Multiple-Deliverable Revenue Arrangements, ch. **4**
	Intellectual Property Deliverables, ch. **7**
	Presentation, ch. **11**
	Disclosures, ch. **12**
FAS-48	
Revenue Recognition When Right of Return Exists	General Principles, ch. **3**
	Multiple-Deliverable Revenue Arrangements, ch. **4**
	Product Deliverables, ch. **5**
	Service Deliverables, ch. **6**
	Intellectual Property Deliverables, ch. **7**
	Software—A Complete Model, ch. **10**
FAS-49	
Accounting for Product Financing Arrangements	General Principles, ch. **3**
	Product Deliverables, ch. **5**
FAS-57	
Related Party Disclosures	Disclosures, ch. **12**
FAS-60	
Accounting and Reporting by Insurance Enterprises	Miscellaneous Issues, ch. **8**
FAS-66	
Accounting for Sales of Real Estate	General Principles, ch. **3**
	Multiple-Deliverable Revenue Arrangements, ch. **4**
FAS-68	
Research and Development Arrangements	Service Deliverables, ch. **6**
	Disclosures, ch. **12**
	Future Expectations and Projects, ch. **13**
FAS-71	
Accounting for the Effects of Certain Types of Regulation	General Principles, ch. **3**
FAS-86	
Accounting for the Costs of Computer Software to Be Sold, Leased, or Otherwise Marketed	Software—A Complete Model, ch. **10**

ORIGINAL PRONOUNCEMENT	2012 *REVENUE RECOGNITION GUIDE* REFERENCE
FAS-91	
Accounting for Nonrefundable Fees and Costs Associated with Originating or Acquiring Loans and Initial Direct Costs of Leases, an amendment of FASB Statements No. 13, 60 and 65 and a rescission of FASB Statement No. 17	Miscellaneous Issues, ch. **8**
FAS-98	
Accounting for Leases, an amendment of FASB Statements No. 13, 66, and 91 and a rescission of FASB Statement No. 26 and Technical Bulletin No. 79-11	Intellectual Property Deliverables, ch. **7**
FAS-131	
Disclosure about Segments of an Enterprise and Related Information	Disclosures, ch. **12**
FAS-133	
Accounting for Derivative Instruments and Hedging Activities	General Principles, ch. **3** Multiple-Deliverable Revenue Arrangements, ch. **4** Presentation, ch. **11**
FAS-140	
Accounting for Transfers and Servicing of Financial Assets and Extinguishments of Liabilities, a replacement of FASB Statement No. 125	General Principles, ch. **3** Service Deliverables, ch. **6** Miscellaneous Issues, ch. **8** Future Expectations and Projects, ch. **13**
FAS-144	
Accounting for the Impairment or Disposal of Long-Lived Assets	Disclosures, ch. **12**
FAS-153	
Exchanges of Nonmonetary Assets, an amendment of APB Opinion No. 29	Miscellaneous Issues, ch. **8**
FAS-154	
Accounting Changes and Error Corrections, a replacement of APB Opinion No. 20 and FASB Statement No. 3	Disclosures, ch. **12**

FASB INTERPRETATIONS (FINs)

ORIGINAL PRONOUNCEMENT	2012 *REVENUE RECOGNITION GUIDE* REFERENCE

FIN-45

Guarantor's Accounting and Disclosure Requirements for Guarantees, Including Indirect Guarantees of Indebtedness of Others, an interpretation of FASB Statements No. 5, 57, and 107 and rescission of FASB Interpretation No. 34

Multiple-Deliverable Revenue Arrangements, ch. **4**
Product Deliverables, ch. **5**
Service Deliverables, ch. **6**
Intellectual Property Deliverables, ch. **7**
Software—A Complete Model, ch. **10**
Disclosures, ch. **12**

FASB ACCOUNTING STANDARDS UPDATES (ASUs)

ORIGINAL PRONOUNCEMENT	2012 *REVENUE RECOGNITION GUIDE* REFERENCE

ASU 2009-13

Multiple-Deliverable Revenue Arrangements

Multiple-Deliverable Revenue Arrangements, ch. **4**
Service Deliverables, ch. **6**
Intellectual Property Deliverables, ch. **7**
Miscellaneous Issues, ch. **8**
Contract Accounting, ch. **9**
Software—A Complete Model, ch. **10**
Disclosures, ch. **12**

ASU 2009-14

Certain Revenue Arrangements That Include Software Elements

Multiple-Deliverable Revenue Arrangements, ch. **4**
Intellectual Property Deliverables, ch. **7**
Software—A Complete Model, ch. **10**

ASU 2010-17

Milestone Method of Revenue Recongition

Service Deliverables, ch. **6**
Disclosures, ch. **12**

FASB TECHNICAL BULLETINS (FTBs)

ORIGINAL PRONOUNCEMENT	2012 *REVENUE RECOGNITION GUIDE* REFERENCE
FTB 90-1	
Accounting for Separately Priced Extended Warranty and Product Maintenance Contracts	Product Deliverables, ch. **5** Service Deliverables, ch. **6** Miscellaneous Issues, ch. **8**

FASB STAFF POSITIONS (FSPs)

ORIGINAL PRONOUNCEMENT	2012 *REVENUE RECOGNITION GUIDE* REFERENCE
FSP FIN 45-1	
Accounting for Intellectual Property Infringement Indemnifications under FASB Interpretation No. 45, *Guarantor's Accounting and Disclosure Requirements for Guarantees, Including Indirect Guarantees of Indebtedness of Others*	Multiple-Deliverable Revenue Arrangements, ch. **4** Intellectual Property Deliverables, ch. **7** Software—A Complete Model, ch. **10**
FSP FIN 45-2	
Whether FASB Interpretation No. 45, *Guarantor's Accounting and Disclosure Requirements for Guarantees, Including Indirect Guarantees of Indebtedness of Others*, Provides Support for Subsequently Accounting for a Guarantor's Liability at Fair Value	Multiple-Deliverable Revenue Arrangements, ch. **4**

FASB STAFF IMPLEMENTATION GUIDES

ORIGINAL PRONOUNCEMENT	2012 *REVENUE RECOGNITION GUIDE* REFERENCE
FAS-133 Guide	
Guide to Implementation of Statement 133 on Accounting for Derivative Instruments and Hedging Activities	Multiple-Deliverable Revenue Arrangements, ch. **4**

FASB CONCEPTS STATEMENTS (CONs)

ORIGINAL PRONOUNCEMENT	2012 *REVENUE RECOGNITION GUIDE* REFERENCE
CON-5	
Recognition and Measurement in Financial Statements of Business Enterprises	A Brief Survey of Revenue-Related Literature, ch. 2 General Principles, ch. 3 Multiple-Deliverable Revenue Arrangements, ch. 4 Product Deliverables, ch. 5 Service Deliverables, ch. 6 Miscellaneous Issues, ch. 8 Presentation, ch. 11 Future Expectations and Projects, ch. 13
CON-6	
Elements of Financial Statements	A Brief Survey of Revenue-Related Literature, ch. 2 Multiple-Deliverable Revenue Arrangements, ch. 4 Miscellaneous Issues, ch. 8 Presentation, ch. 11 Future Expectations and Projects, ch. 13

FASB INVITATION TO COMMENT (ITC)

ORIGINAL PRONOUNCEMENT	2012 *REVENUE RECOGNITION GUIDE* REFERENCE
ITC	
FASB Invitation to Comment: Accounting for Certain Service Transactions	Service Deliverables, ch. **6** Disclosures, ch. **12**

AICPA STATEMENTS OF POSITION (SOPs)

ORIGINAL PRONOUNCEMENT	2012 *REVENUE RECOGNITION GUIDE* REFERENCE

SOP 81-1

Accounting for Performance of Construction-Type and Certain Production-Type Contracts	General Principles, ch. **3** Multiple-Deliverable Revenue Arrangements, ch. **4** Service Deliverables, ch. **6** Contract Accounting, ch. **9** Software—A Complete Model, ch. **10** Disclosures, ch. **12** Future Expectations and Projects, ch. **13**

SOP 94-6

Disclosure of Certain Significant Risks and Uncertainties	Disclosures, ch. **12**

SOP 97-2

Software Revenue Recognition	General Principles, ch. **3** Multiple-Deliverable Revenue Arrangements, ch. **4** Intellectual Property Deliverables, ch. **7** Contract Accounting, ch. **9** Software—A Complete Model, ch. **10** Future Expectations and Projects, ch. **13**

SOP 00-2

Accounting by Producers or Distributors of Films	General Principles, ch. **3** Multiple-Deliverable Revenue Arrangements, ch. **4** Intellectual Property Deliverables, ch. **7**

SOP 04-2

Accounting for Real Estate Time-Sharing Transactions	Future Expectations and Projects, ch. **13**

AICPA AUDIT AND ACCOUNTING GUIDES (AAGs)

ORIGINAL PRONOUNCEMENT	2012 *REVENUE RECOGNITION GUIDE* REFERENCE
AAG-CAS	
Audits of Casinos	Presentation, ch. **11**
AAG-CON	
Audit and Accounting Guide for Construction Contractors	Contract Accounting, ch. **9** Disclosures, ch. **12**
AAG-FGC	
Audit and Accounting Guide for Audits of Federal Government Contractors	Contract Accounting, ch. **9**

AICPA TECHNICAL PRACTICE AIDS (TPAs)

ORIGINAL PRONOUNCEMENT	2012 *REVENUE RECOGNITION GUIDE* REFERENCE
TPA 5100.38	
Determination of Vendor-Specific Objective Evidence After the Balance Sheet Date	Software—A Complete Model, ch. **10**
TPA 5100.39	
Indicators that Multiple Contracts Should be Viewed as Single Arrangements	Multiple-Deliverable Revenue Arrangements, ch. **4** Software—A Complete Model, ch. **10**
TPA 5100.41	
Effect of Prepayments on Revenue Recognition	Software—A Complete Model, ch. **10**
TPA 5100.43	
Promises to Correct Software Errors (Bug Fixes)	Software—A Complete Model, ch. **10**
TPA 5100.45	
License Mix Arrangements	Software—A Complete Model, ch. **10**
TPA 5100.46 & .47	
Nonmonetary Exchanges Involving Software	Software—A Complete Model, ch. **10**
TPA 5100.49	
Accounting for Post-Contract Customer Support When Contract Accounting Is Applied	Software—A Complete Model, ch. **10**

ORIGINAL PRONOUNCEMENT	2012 *REVENUE RECOGNITION GUIDE* REFERENCE
TPA 5100.50	
Definition of More-Than-Insignificant Discount	Miscellaneous Issues, ch. **8** Software—A Complete Model, ch. **10**
TPA 5100.51	
Accounting for Significant Incremental Discounts	Miscellaneous Issues, ch. **8** Software—A Complete Model, ch. **10**
TPA 5100.55	
Fair Value of PCS with a Consistent Renewal Percentage (But Varying Renewal Dollar Amount)	Software—A Complete Model, ch. **10**
TPA 5100.56	
Concessions	Software—A Complete Model, ch. **10**
TPA 5100.57	
Overcoming Presumption of Concessions in Extended Payment Term Arrangements	Software—A Complete Model, ch. **10**
TPA 5100.58	
Effect of Prepayments on Software Revenue Recognition—Transfer of Receivable Without Recourse	Software—A Complete Model, ch. **10** Presentation, ch. **11**
TPA 5100.59	
Subsequent Cash Receipt in an Extended Payment Term Arrangement	Software—A Complete Model, ch. **10**
TPA 5100.61	
Effect of Prepayments on Software Revenue Recognition When Vendor Participates in Customer Financing	Software—A Complete Model, ch. **10**
TPA 5100.62	
Indicators of Incremental Risk and Their Effect on the Evaluation of Whether a Fee Is Fixed or Determinable	Software—A Complete Model, ch. **10**
TPA 5100.64	
Indicators of Vendor Participation in Customer Financing That Do Not Result in Incremental Risk	Software—A Complete Model, ch. **10**
TPA 5100.68	
Fair Value of PCS in Perpetual and Multi-Year Time-Based Licenses	Software—A Complete Model, ch. **10**

ORIGINAL PRONOUNCEMENT	2012 *REVENUE RECOGNITION GUIDE* REFERENCE
TPA 5100.70	
Effect of Commencement of an Initial License Term	Software—A Complete Model, ch. **10**
TPA 5100.71	
Effect of Commencement of an Extension/ Renewal License Term	Software—A Complete Model, ch. **10**
TPA 5100.72	
Effect of Additional Product(s) in an Extension/Renewal of License Term	Software—A Complete Model, ch. **10**
TPA 5100.73	
Arrangement Containing an Option to Extend a Time-Based License Indefinitely	Software—A Complete Model, ch. **10**
TPA 5100.74	
Effect of Discounts on Future Products on the Residual Method	Software—A Complete Model, ch. **10**
TPA 5100.75	
Fair Value of PCS Renewals Based on Users Deployed	Software—A Complete Model, ch. **10**

CONSENSUS POSITIONS OF THE EMERGING ISSUES TASK FORCE (EITFs)

ORIGINAL PRONOUNCEMENT	2012 *REVENUE RECOGNITION GUIDE* REFERENCE
EITF 85-20	
Recognition of Fees for Guaranteeing a Loan	Multiple-Deliverable Revenue Arrangements, ch. **4**
EITF 88-18	
Sales of Future Revenues	Service Deliverables, ch. **6** Software—A Complete Model, ch. **10** Presentation, ch. **11**
EITF 91-6	
Revenue Recognition of Long-Term Power Sales Contracts	Service Deliverables, ch. **6**
EITF 91-9	
Revenue and Expense Recognition for Freight Services in Process	Service Deliverables, ch. **6**
EITF 93-11	
Accounting for Barter Transactions Involving Barter Credits	Miscellaneous Issues, ch. **8**

ORIGINAL PRONOUNCEMENT	2012 *REVENUE RECOGNITION GUIDE* REFERENCE
EITF 95-1	
Revenue Recognition on Sales with a Guaranteed Minimum Resale Value	Product Deliverables, ch. **5**
EITF 95-4	
Revenue Recognition on Equipment Sold and Subsequently Repurchased Subject to an Operating Lease	Product Deliverables, ch. **5**
EITF 99-5	
Accounting for Pre-Production Costs Related to Long-Term Supply Arrangements	Miscellaneous Issues, ch. **8**
EITF 99-17	
Accounting for Advertising Barter Transactions	Miscellaneous Issues, ch. **8** Disclosures, ch. **12**
EITF 99-19	
Reporting Revenue Gross as a Principal versus Net as an Agent	Presentation, ch. **11** Disclosures, ch. **12**
EITF 00-3	
Application of AICPA Statement of Position 97–2 to Arrangements That Include the Right to Use Software Stored on Another Entity's Hardware	Intellectual Property Deliverables, ch. **7** Software—A Complete Model, ch. **10**
EITF 00-8	
Accounting by a Grantee for an Equity Instrument to Be Received in Conjunction with Providing Goods or Services	Miscellaneous Issues, ch. **8** Disclosures, ch. **12**
EITF 00-10	
Accounting for Shipping and Handling Fees and Costs	Presentation, ch. **11** Disclosures, ch. **12**
EITF 00-21	
Revenue Arrangements with Multiple Deliverables	Multiple-Deliverable Revenue Arrangements, ch. **4** Service Deliverables, ch. **6** Intellectual Property Deliverables, ch. **7** Miscellaneous Issues, ch. **8** Contract Accounting, ch. **9** Software—A Complete Model, ch. **10** Disclosures, ch. **12** Future Expectations and Projects, ch. **13**

ORIGINAL PRONOUNCEMENT	2012 *REVENUE RECOGNITION GUIDE* REFERENCE
EITF 01-2	
Interpretations of APB Opinion No. 29	Miscellaneous Issues, ch. **8**
EITF 01-8	
Determining Whether an Arrangement Contains a Lease	General Principles, ch. **3** Multiple-Deliverable Revenue Arrangements, ch. **4** Product Deliverables, ch. **5** Service Deliverables, ch. **6**
EITF 01-9	
Accounting for Consideration Given by a Vendor to a Customer (Including a Reseller of the Vendor's Products)	General Principles, ch. **3** Miscellaneous Issues, ch. **8** Software—A Complete Model, ch. **10** Presentation, ch. **11**
EITF 01-14	
Income Statement Characterization of Reimbursements Received for "Out-of-Pocket" Expenses Incurred	Presentation, ch. **11**
EITF 02-3	
Issues Involved in Accounting for Derivative Contracts Held for Trading Purposes and Contracts Involved in Energy Trading and Risk Management Activities	Presentation, ch. **11**
EITF 02-16	
Accounting by a Customer (Including a Reseller) for Certain Consideration Received from a Vendor	Miscellaneous Issues, ch. **8** Presentation, ch. **11**
EITF 03-10	
Application of Issue No. 02–16 by Resellers to Sales Incentives Offered to Consumers by Manufacturers	Presentation, ch. **11**
EITF 03-11	
Reporting Realized Gains and Losses on Derivative Instruments That Are Subject to FASB Statement No. 133 and Not "Held for Trading Purposes" as Defined in Issue No. 02–3	Presentation, ch. **11**
EITF 03-12	
Impact of FASB Interpretation No. 45 on Issue No. 95–1	Product Deliverables, ch. **5**

ORIGINAL PRONOUNCEMENT	2012 *REVENUE RECOGNITION GUIDE* REFERENCE
EITF 04-13	
Accounting for Purchases and Sales of Inventory with the Same Counterparty	Miscellaneous Issues, ch. **8**
EITF 06-01	
Accounting for Consideration Given by a Service Provider to Manufacturers or Resellers of Equipment Necessary for an End-Customer to Receive Service from the Service Provider	General Principles, ch. **3** Presentation, ch. **11**
EITF 06-03	
How Taxes Collected from Customers and Remitted to Governmental Authorities Should Be Presented in the Income Statement (That Is, Gross versus Net Presentation)	Presentation, ch. **11**
EITF 07-1	
Accounting for Collaborative Arrangements Related to the Development and Commercialization of Intellectual Property	Intellectual Property Deliverables, ch. **7**

SEC RULES AND REGULATIONS (REGs)

ORIGINAL PRONOUNCEMENT	2012 *REVENUE RECOGNITION GUIDE* REFERENCE
REG S-X, Rule 4-08	
Financial Statement Requirements, Rules of General Application, General Notes to Financial Statements	Disclosures, ch. **12**
REG S-X, Rule 5-02	
Financial Statement Requirements, Commercial and Industrial Companies, Balance Sheets	Contract Accounting, ch. **9** Disclosures, ch. **12**
REG S-X, Rule 5-03	
Financial Statement Requirements, Commercial and Industrial Companies, Income Statements	Presentation, ch. **11** Disclosures, ch. **12**
FRR 23	
The Significance of Oral Guarantees to the Financial Reporting Process	General Principles, ch. **3**

SEC STAFF ACCOUNTING BULLETINS (SABs)

ORIGINAL PRONOUNCEMENT	2012 *REVENUE RECOGNITION GUIDE* REFERENCE
SAB Topic 13	
Revenue Recognition	Introduction, Ch. **1**
	A Brief Survey of Revenue-Related Literature, ch. **2**
	General Principles, ch. **3**
	Multiple-Deliverable Revenue Arrangements, ch. **4**
	Product Deliverables, ch. **5**
	Service Deliverables, ch. **6**
	Intellectual Property Deliverables, ch. **7**
	Miscellaneous Issues, ch. **8**
	Software—A Complete Model, ch. **10**
	Presentation, ch. **11**
	Disclosures, ch. **12**
	Future Expectations and Projects, ch. **13**
SAB Topic 8A	
Retail Companies—Sales of Leased or Licensed Departments	A Brief Survey of Revenue-Related Literature, ch. **2**
	Presentation, ch. **11**

SEC STAFF POSITIONS

ORIGINAL PRONOUNCEMENT	2012 *REVENUE RECOGNITION GUIDE* REFERENCE
EITF D-96	
Accounting for Management Fees Based on a Formula	General Principles, ch. **3**
	Disclosures, ch. **12**

SEC CURRENT ISSUES AND RULEMAKING PROJECTS (CIRPs)

ORIGINAL PRONOUNCEMENT	2012 *REVENUE RECOGNITION GUIDE* REFERENCE
CIRP 8/01	
SEC Division of Corporation Finance— Current Issues and Rulemaking Projects (August 2001)	Disclosures, ch. **12**

SEC STAFF REPORTS

INDEX

(Note: For references to Original Procurements, see the Cross-Reference starting on 14,001)

G

N

O

P

PRO

STO